Survey Research and
Public Attitudes in
Eastern Europe and
the Soviet Union

Pergamon Titles of Related Interest

Desfosses   SOVIET POPULATION POLICY
Foster   COMPARATIVE PUBLIC POLICY AND CITIZEN
        PARTICIPATION
Schulz/Adams   POLITICAL PARTICIPATION IN COMMUNIST
        SYSTEMS

Related Journals*

CHILDREN AND YOUTH SERVICES REVIEW
EVALUATION AND PROGRAM PLANNING
HABITAT INTERNATIONAL
INTERNATIONAL JOURNAL OF INTERCULTURAL RELATIONS
WOMEN'S STUDIES INTERNATIONAL QUARTERLY

*Free specimen copies available upon request.

PERGAMON POLICY STUDIES ON INTERNATIONAL POLITICS

Survey Research and Public Attitudes in Eastern Europe and the Soviet Union

Edited by
William A. Welsh

Pergamon Press
NEW YORK • OXFORD • TORONTO • SYDNEY • PARIS • FRANKFURT

Pergamon Press Offices:

U.S.A.	Pergamon Press Inc., Maxwell House, Fairview Park, Elmsford, New York 10523, U.S.A.
U.K.	Pergamon Press Ltd., Headington Hill Hall, Oxford OX3 0BW, England
CANADA	Pergamon Press Canada Ltd., Suite 104, 150 Consumers Road, Willowdale, Ontario M2J 1P9, Canada
AUSTRALIA	Pergamon Press (Aust.) Pty. Ltd., P.O. Box 544, Potts Point, NSW 2011, Australia
FRANCE	Pergamon Press SARL, 24 rue des Ecoles, 75240 Paris, Cedex 05, France
FEDERAL REPUBLIC OF GERMANY	Pergamon Press GmbH, Hammerweg 6, Postfach 1305, 6242 Kronberg/Taunus, Federal Republic of Germany

Library of Congress Cataloging in Publication Data

Welsh, William A.
  Survey research and public attitudes in Eastern
Europe and the Soviet Union.

  (Pergamon policy studies)
  Includes bibliographies and index.
  1. Public opinion polls—Europe, Eastern.
2. Public opinion polls—Russia. I. United States.
International Communication Agency. II. Title.
HM261.W44 1980   303.3'8   79-27902
ISBN 0-08-025958-8

Printed in the United States of America

This book is dedicated to our colleagues in Eastern Europe and the Soviet Union with the hope and anticipation of welcoming them as collaborators on a revised edition.

Contents

List of Tables ix

Preface
William A. Welsh xxi

Introduction: An Overview of the Status of Survey Research
in Eastern Europe and the Soviet Union
William A. Welsh 1

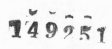

Chapter

1   THE SOVIET UNION
    Linda L. Lubrano, Wesley A. Fisher, Janet Schwartz, and
    Kate Tomlinson 13

2   YUGOSLAVIA
    Susan L. Woodward 80

3   BULGARIA
    William A. Welsh, with *Mark Arabadjief* 136

4   CZECHOSLOVAKIA
    George Klein and *Jaroslav Krejčí* 204

5   GERMAN DEMOCRATIC REPUBLIC
    Peter Christian Ludz 242

6   HUNGARY
    Robert Blumstock 319

7   POLAND
    Barclay Ward 389

8   ROMANIA
    Daniel N. Nelson 436

9   SUMMARY AND CONCLUSIONS
    William A. Welsh 482

Index of Names 507

Subject Index 517

About the Contributors 563

List of Tables

Table

1.1. Education of Soviet Sociologists and Their Current Positions......18

1.2. Opinions about Movies among Young People in Moscow.........22

1.3. Attitudes toward Different Art Media by Visitors to Exhibits
in Estonia (1969-70) (percentages).......................23

1.4. Possession of Cultural Articles by Different Social Groups in
Nizhnii Tagil (percentages) 26

1.5. Opinions on Premarital Sexual Relations among Moscow
Students Aged 14-16 (N=600) (percentages) 26

Table

1.6. Distribution of Married Women in the USSR by Expected
      Number of Children (1972)...........................28

1.7. Reasons for Divorce in Rural Western Belorussia (N=637)
      (percentages) 29

1.8. Plans of Eighth Graders on the Basis of Social Origins
      (percentages) 31

1.9. Plans of Secondary School Graduates in Lithuania
      (percentages) 32

1.10 Youth Adaptation and Their Motives for Selecting a Workplace
      (percentages) 38

1.11 Initial Motives for Working on Fishing Boats................39

1.12. Labor Turnover of Workers at State Farms in the Moscow
      Region (percentages) 39

1.13. Individual Labor Disputes Related to Automation............41

1.14. Education and the Preferred Use of Additional Time among
      Workers in Taganrog 44

1.15. A Rational Time Budget and the Actual Activities of Urban
      Workers at the End of the 1960s 45

1.16. Audience Interest and Knowledge Received in Political
      Education (percentages)..............................47

1.17. Sources of Political Information in Moscow (percentages).......50

1.18. The Attitudes of Propagandists toward Their Work 50

1.19. Party Status and Work Satisfaction among Deputies in
      Local Soviets (percentages)..........................51

1.20. Difficulties Faced by Deputies in Local Soviets according
      to Social Position (percentages) 52

Table

1.21. Party Status and Attitudes of Local Deputies toward the
      Usefulness of Their Work (percentages) 54

1.22. Acquisition of Proficiency in a Second Language in
      Cities of Moldavia (percentages). 57

1.23. Linguistic Behavior of Rural Tatars (percentages) 58

1.24. Influence of Linguistic Characteristics on Ethnic-Cultural
      Orientations (percentages). 60

1.25. Relationships between Age and Cultural-Evaluative
      Orientations (percentages). 61

2.1. Women on the Future (percentages) 90

2.2. Classification of Sociopolitical Activism of Serbian Youth 93

2.3. Weaknesses in the Delegate System: Reasons Most Often
      Cited by Young Delegates to Communal Assemblies
      in Serbia (N=198) 95

2.4. Self-Management Orientation among Serbian Youth, 1974
      (N=1,548) (percentages). 98

2.5. Rankings of Priorities of Students by Income and Parents'
      Occupation 100

2.6. Factory Workers' Knowledge about Their Firm in a Large
      Zagreb Factory, 1973 (N=467) 103

2.7. Attitude Toward Risk Among Employees in Yugoslav
      Industry 105

2.8. Willingness To Bear Risks according to Sociofunctional
      Groups 105

2.9. How Working Women Spend Their Free Time in Yugoslavia
      (N=1,479) (percentages). 114

2.10. Satisfaction of Basic Needs in Slavonija and Baranja
      (N=3,223) (percentages). 114

Table

2.11.   Forms of Participation and the Structure of Interests as
        Identified by Factor Analysis. 117

2.12.   Reasons for Nonparticipation and the Structure of Interests
        as Identified by Factor Analysis 117

2.13.   Understanding of Basic Sociopolitical Concepts (Croatia) 119

3.1.   Patterns of Reading of *Narodna Mladezh* by Education of
        Readers (percentages). 144

3.2.   Perceived Adequacy of Press Treatment of Family Life, by
        Marital Status and Place of Residence (percentages). 148

3.3.   Readership of National Newspapers among Subscribers to
        Regional Newspapers (percentages). 148

3.4.   Cultural Activities and Participation in Housework among
        Bulgarian Working Women (percentages) 151

3.5.   Occupation by Formal Education and Age Group
        (percentages of each occupational group). 156

3.6.   Qualities Valued Most in Colleagues and Friends by
        Komsomol Members, 1973 (percentages). 159

3.7.   Qualities Admired Most in Komsomol Associates by
        Komsomol Members, 1973 (percentages). 159

3.8.   Motives for the Performance of Komsomol Tasks by
        Secondary Students, by School Grade (percentages). 168

3.9.   Sense of Collective Responsibility among Factory Workers
        in Gabrovo (percentages) 168

3.10.   Distribution of Principal Leisure-Time Activities of Workers
        in Enterprises on a 5-Day Week (percentages) 175

3.11.   Reading of Literature by Socio-Occupational Group
        and Level of Qualification (percentages) 175

Table

3.12. Basic Types of Life Plans of Sofia Postsecondary Students,
       by Sex (percentages) 178

3.13. Preferences for Nine Categories of Life Aspirations among Sofia
       Postsecondary Students, by Sex (percentages). 178

3.14. Basic Type of Life Plans of Sofia Postsecondary Students, by
       Father's Education (percentages) 182

3.15. Major Factors Inhibiting Involvement in Criminal Activity
       (N=3,929) (percentages). 182

3.16. Rankings of Negative Influences in Society by General
       Population, Leadership, and Administrative Subsamples
       (N=2,906) 188

3.17. Type of Party Work Preferred by Local Party
       Secretaries (N=570) (percentages). 188

3.18. Bases for Accepting Selection as Party Secretary
       (N=570) (percentages) 190

3.19. Qualities Thought To Be Most Important for Party
       Secretaries (N=570) (percentages). 190

3.20. Party Secretaries' Perceptions of Their Most Important
       Functions (N=570) (percentages) 191

3.21. Bases of Relationships of Party Secretaries with Party
       Rank-and-File (N=570) (percentages) 191

3.22. Bulgarians' Views of "What Country Is the Greatest Supporter
       of Peace and Socialism in the World," by Place of Residence,
       Age, Occupation, and Education (percentages) 194

4.1.   The Structure of Reader Interest among Czech Youth 211

4.2.   Sample Utilized for the Collection of Micro-Census
       Data, 1976. 214

4.3.   Personal Income in Czechoslovakia by Deciles, 1976 215

Table

4.4. An Overview of Youth Leisure-Time Activity 221

4.5. Relative Public Appreciation of Leisure-Time Alternatives
      (percentages) 222

4.6. Political Knowledge of Working Youth (percentages) 225

4.7. Socialism and Capitalism: Securing the Values (percentages) 226

4.8. Views on the Content of Political Education. 230

4.9. An Evaluation of the Importance of the Political Work of the
      SZM (Association of Socialist Youth) among Working People
      and the Socialist Relationship to Work (percentages) 231

5.1. Age Structure of Television Viewers, 1973 (percentages). 257

5.2. Social Structure of Television Viewers, 1973 (percentages) 257

5.3. Structure of Television Programming, 1973 and 1975. 259

5.4. Day-Care Services for Infants and Preschool Children, 1975-77 . . . 262

5.5. Divorces, 1975-77 265

5.6. Legitimate and Illegitimate Births, 1974-76 265

5.7. Youth Population by Age and Sex, 1977 272

5.8. Production Workers Working One, Two, or Three Shifts:
      Percentage Distribution, 1962-67 272

5.9. Semiskilled Workers, Skilled Workers, and the Intelligentsia:
      Their Opinions on Different Issues of the Work Situation
      (percentages) 274

5.10. The Structure of the Time Budget of the GDR Population Aged
      18-65 Years, by Sex and Vocation, 1973 279

5.11. Amount of Leisure Time (Average Minutes per Day) at People's
      Disposal, by Sex, Employment, and the Existence of Children, in
      Hoyerswerda, 1966 280

Table

5.12. Amount of Leisure Time (Average Minutes per Day) at People's
Disposal, by Vocational Groups and Sex, in Hoyerswerda, 1966. . . 281

5.13. Leisure Time Spent in Primary Activities (in Average Minutes per
Day) by the People in Hoyerswerda, 1966 282

6.1. Proportions of Selected Professions Classified as "Heavy Media
Users" (percentages) 326

6.2. Proportions of "Heavy Media Users" by Amount of Education
(percentages) 326

6.3. Distribution of the Adult Readers of Nationwide Daily
Newspapers according to Education, 1972 (percentages). 327

6.4. Distribution of the Adult Readers of Nationwide Daily
Newspapers according to Occupation, 1972 (percentages) 328

6.5. Distribution of High Scorers on Five Types of Information
according to Education (percentages) 329

6.6. Distribution of High Scorers on Five Types of Information
according to Occupation (percentages) 329

6.7. Frequency of Mention of Stimuli Considered Most Important
on the Basis of Three Selections (percentages). 332

6.8. Occupational Plans of Youth (percentages). 337

6.9. Perspectives on Economic Issues among Youth (percentages). 337

6.10. Distribution of Free-time Activities among Apprentice
Skilled Workers (percentages) 338

6.11. Opinions on the Balance of Power between the Two World
Systems (N=922) (percentages) 340

6.12. Evaluations of Working Conditions by Workers (percentages). . . . 343

6.13. Evaluations of Work Characteristics by Workers
(percentages) 344

Table

6.14. Workers' Perceptions of Their Potential Involvement in
      Decision Making (percentages)........................346

6.15. Evaluation by Workers of Party Involvement in Specific
      Activities (percentages)..............................347

6.16. Occurrence of Conversational Themes within the Circles of
      Blue-collar and White-collar Workers (percentages)............348

6.17. Structure of Activities of the Adult Population in 1963
      and 1972 (in hours)..................................350

6.18. Religious Identification of the Adult Population in 1972, 1974,
      and 1975, in Seven Independent Samples (percentages).........355

6.19. Moral Attitudes and Preferences according to Occupation
      (percentages).......................................357

6.20. Human Qualities: Preferred and Perceived (percentages).........358

6.21. Workers' Evaluation of Importance of Social Issues
      (percentages).......................................360

6.22. Suicides according to Age and Sex.....................361

6.23. Perspectives on Income Differences in 1973 and 1974
      (percentages).......................................364

6.24. Perspectives on Income Differences according to
      Amount of Education (percentages)....................365

6.25. Perceived Trends in the International Influence of the
      USSR, the United States, and China....................368

6.26. Perceived Role Played by Five Nations in World Affairs
      (weighted average, by educational level) N=792..............369

6.27. Perceptions concerning Future Development of Relations
      among the Three Countries: USSR, China, and the United
      States (percentages) N=830...........................370

Table

6.28. Perceptions of the Closeness of Neighboring Countries
on Four Dimensions (percentages) 373

6.29. Quality of Household Management according to Per Capita
Income, in Forints (percentages) 376

6.30. The Distribution of Family Financial Decisions
by Location and Occupation (percentages). 378

7.1. Nonreadership by Availability of News Kiosks 395

7.2. Nonreadership by Level of Formal Education 395

7.3. Local Newspaper Readership by Locale of Residence
(percentages) 395

7.4. Readership of Major Urban and Rural Daily Newspapers
by Sex (percentages) 397

7.5. Readership of Weekly Press by Sex (percentages). 397

7.6. Selected Characteristics of *Trybuna Ludu* and *Życie
Warszawy* Readership (percentages) 399

7.7. Motives for Reading Foreign Press by Level of Formal
Education (percentages) 399

7.8. Ownership of Radio and Television Sets by Occupation
and Place of Residence (percentages). 401

7.9. Radio Program Listening Practices by Educational Level
(percentages) 401

7.10. Evaluation of Television Programs (percentages) 405

7.11. Importance of Family and Other Values by Age Group
(percentages) 405

7.12. Ideal Spouse Models by Sex (rank orders) 407

7.13. Belief That Wives Should Not Work Outside the Home
by Category of Respondent (percentages) 407

Table

7.14. Ambitions of Youth (percentages) 409

7.15. Ambitions of Youth by Sex (percentages) 409

7.16. Perceived Importance of Education and Other Factors in the
      Realization of Ambitions (percentages) 411

7.17. Factors Contributing to Prestige (percentages) 411

7.18. Youth Perceptions of Decisive Values for a Happy Life by
      Place of Residence (percentages) 412

7.19. Youth Rankings of Material Desires by Place of Residence
      (percentages) 412

7.20. Frequency of Experienced Forms of Behavior of Others
      (percentages) 414

7.21. Accepted Norms by Age Groups (percentages) 414

7.22. Occupational Prestige 416

7.23. Youth Views of Own Work by Place of Residence
      (percentages) 416

7.24. Youth Perceptions of Most Important Tasks of Government
      by Place of Residence (percentages) 422

7.25. Youth Perceptions of Factors Impeding National Development
      by Place of Residence (percentages) 422

7.26. Perceived Necessity for Social Commitment (percentages). 424

7.27. Perceived Necessity for Social Commitment and
      Citizen Influence (percentages) 424

8.1. Sources of Public Knowledge about 1970 Floods. 444

8.2. Reading after Television Introduced in Home (percentages). 444

8.3. Importance of Current Events in Media to Public
      and Specialists (percentages) 447

Table

8.4.   Television and Radio Penetration in Selected Romanian
       Counties, 1974 449

8.5.   Types of Agricultural Work Units and Their Membership
       in 1971 and 1972 451

8.6.   Social and Moral Values of Youth and Prior Generations
       (percentages) 456

8.7.   Ranking of Values among Romanian Youth 456

8.8.   Career Satisfaction and Desire To Change Jobs among
       Young Workers, by Industry 461

8.9.   Participation in Production Meetings by Young Workers
       according to Factory Type (percentages) 461

8.10. Perceived Effect of Workers' Proposals according to
       Factory Type (percentages) 462

8.11. Participation in General Assemblies of the Enterprise
       by Organizational Identity (percentages) 462

8.12. Leisure-time Preferences of Workers 465

8.13. Leisure-time Preferences (percentages). 466

8.14. Ranking of Values in Câmpeanu Sample 468

Preface

The societies of Eastern Europe are experiencing accelerating changes which, although infrequently of an overtly political nature, are of potentially great political significance. Some of these changes result from economic growth and modernization and the now familiar alterations in occupational and social structure, as well as in private consumption preferences that accompany modernization. Some changes have their origins in the cautious groping of national leaders for a viable balance between domestic and external pressures. Other changes can be traced to the faltering dynamism of imposed or imported value and belief systems. If these sources of change are perhaps more clearly defined today, they nevertheless have been discernible for some time.

There is a new wellspring of changes joining those observed over a longer period. The newcomer is the role of citizen attitudes in governance. The existence of these attitudes is hardly new, nor is their expression. Manifestations of citizen concern have had episodic significance in some East European societies, perhaps especially in Hungary and Poland in 1956, in the events surrounding Gierek's ascendance in Poland, during the Prague Spring of 1968, and during the Polish strikes in 1980. But on a continuing basis, public attitudes have assumed importance for governance only through Yugoslavia's self-management structures, and there only in qualified and limited ways.

What is new, then, is that public attitudes are being investigated more fully and more openly in the Soviet Union and Eastern Europe. The expression of public attitudes is being cautiously encouraged in most of these societies. As a result, the manifestations of mass thinking are more systematic and continuing. In short, surveys of public attitudes are increasingly common and apparently institutionalized practices in most of the European socialist societies. It was this expansion of survey research, and the apparent potential significance of its results, that prompted the research on which this book is based.

It should hardly be necessary to stress that these developments do not necessarily signal "liberalization" or constitute *prima facie* evidence of emergent "pluralism." Some "liberalization" or "pluralism" may well be implied in some East European societies—but by no means in all, and by no means uniformly or irreversibly in any. In the introductory chapter we explore some of the functions performed by the burgeoning use of survey research in Eastern Europe and the Soviet Union. Underlying much of this heightened activity is a desire on the part of existing political authorities to govern more effectively, with a more sensitive understanding of how the articulate and concerned citizenry views its social, economic, and political present and future. A more effective sounding of the public pulse may yield more efficient and comfortable control of mass by elite.

Regardless of whether one is inclined to render this interpretation as "realistic" or as "cynical," however, the fact remains that the institutionaliza-tion of public attitude surveys is likely to have at least two additional effects. First, citizen concerns which are not incontrovertibly inconsistent with the policy preferences of dominant elites are more likely than in the past to receive a reasoned hearing. Second, the public expression, albeit circumscribed, of one's views can be habit-forming. By asking for citizen views—and by printing them for circulation—political authorities in Eastern Europe and the Soviet Union are taking an important step toward legitimizing their expression. The experience of these and other highly structured socialist systems (China, for example) suggests that the legitimation of speaking out can be reversed, but only at significant cost.

It is worth emphasizing that not all citizens of socialist societies have conscious attitudes about social, economic, and political issues of the day, with the possible exception of certain concerns about standard of living and level of remuneration. We know this to be true, of course, of every modern society, to say nothing of less modern ones. Nor are all of the citizens of these socialist societies being asked for their views, even indirectly. Systematic national samples are still rare in survey research in Eastern Europe and the Soviet Union. Thus polls are hardly surrogates for referenda or other modes of political representa-tion. The significance of survey research, and of its results, must therefore be assessed with specific reference to its practice in each socialist country. We attempt to do that in this book.

This research was made possible by a contract with the United States International Communication Agency. We are grateful to James McGregor, Gregory Guroff, and Roy Bisbee of USICA for their support and encouragement. The views expressed in this book, however, are entirely those of the authors and not of the USICA.

The cooperation and assistance of many other persons were critically important. Some of these persons are named subsequently in the book's chapters. Some of our colleagues in Eastern Europe asked that they remain unnamed. We honor this request with regret and at the same time admiration and understanding, and urge their attention to the dedication page of this book.

The Editor owes special thanks to several persons, two in particular. Ellen Haselhuhn served as administrative officer for the project, a task which quickly assumed dimensions that neither she nor I imagined at the outset. Ms. Haselhuhn also typed part of the manuscript. Barbara Gilbert also prepared portions of the manuscript. More than that, she kept the Editor's determination strong, even through a third revision of much of more than 800 pages of typescript. Most of all, she did nearly all of the final composition of the book on an IBM Electronic Composer, preparing more than 500 pages of material in four months of spare-time work. Those familiar with electronic composition will recognize the dimensions of that accomplishment. Darcy Bisenius composed some of the tables. Judy Schroeder and Michelle Haselhuhn provided typing assistance. Helga Hundegger assisted with proof reading. Production of the book was under the capable guidance of Angela Clark, Gwen Bell, Jack Hoffman, and Diane Zeeman, of Pergamon.

My pleasure at seeing the results of this collaborative effort published is diminished by the untimely death of my colleague and friend, Peter Christian Ludz, in September, 1979. The tireless energy, remarkable thoroughness, and thoughtful insight that characterized his work are evident in his chapter on the German Democratic Republic in this volume. His contributions to scholarship, in the United States as well as in the Federal Republic of Germany, and to public policy making in Germany, were significant. We shall miss him.

Introduction:
An Overview of the Status
of Survey Research in
Eastern Europe and
the Soviet Union

William A. Welsh

FOCUS OF THE STUDY

Survey research in the socialist systems of Eastern Europe and the Soviet Union is still in its infancy. Few serious surveys were conducted by academic researchers prior to the late 1950s. There already have been ebbs and flows in the evolution of survey research, but in most of these systems it continues to expand, albeit cautiously. The flavor and roles of this research vary somewhat with specific conditions in the respective countries; broadly, however, survey research has arrived. It could not have done so without official sanction and support. This support has been forthcoming principally because survey research represents an effective mechanism by which governments can better understand the increasingly complex needs and concerns of citizens. There are important, policy-relevant respects in which the societies of Eastern Europe have become dramatically more complex in the past 20 years. Effective governance in the future demands an understanding of this complexity and of its implications for citizen postures toward political authority.

1

In the earlier seminal work on public opinion in socialist systems,[1] Zvi Gitelman commented on the somewhat paradoxical position of survey research in these systems: in one sense, it represents an attempt to measure what most of these regimes have to one extent or another tried to suppress. Without pausing here to unravel the apparent paradox, we would emphasize that, with the probable exception of Czechoslovakia, these regimes are not trying nearly as hard now as they have in the past to suppress expressions of public needs and concerns. This is not to suggest that a desire to mold and guide public opinion is not a principal underlying motivation for better understanding that opinion, or that the suppression of public concerns is no longer in evidence. Indeed, more than 25 percent of Polish respondents in one recent survey felt that "suppression of social criticism" was a major factor impeding social development. Nevertheless, the ground rules for articulation of citizen concerns clearly have changed in nearly all of these societies.

It is worth underscoring at the outset what this volume is—and is not—about. Our task is to examine the development of survey research in the socialist systems of Eastern Europe and the Soviet Union for a three-year period, 1975 through 1977. We do not trace the evolution of survey research in these countries, nor do we attempt to explain the fluctuations which have brought survey research to its current status. Our emphasis is not on survey research as a technique, but rather on what the published or otherwise generally available results of this research tell us about these societies. We summarize these results under ten headings: Media Habits, Family and Women, Education and Youth, Work and Workplace, Leisure Time, Moral and Ethical Preferences and Life Aspirations, Social Problems and Social Policy, Politics and Ideology, Ethnicity and Foreign Cultures, and Market Research. Of necessity, this outline is not followed precisely in every chapter in the volume. Thus Market Research is not dealt with for several countries because it is not a sufficiently well-established area of inquiry to warrant attention. In a few cases, chapter authors have combined some of the topics to reflect more accurately the actual organization and conduct of research in their countries.

We emphasize that no attempt is made in this volume to provide comprehensive pictures of these societies under our ten topical headings. That is, we deal only with the results of survey research, or with studies which are necessary to place survey results in meaningful context. Nevertheless, the now substantial breadth of subject matter dealt with in surveys in many Eastern European countries provides fascinating insights into some of the most important contemporary circumstances in those societies.

Throughout this volume we refer as a matter of convenience to surveys of "attitudes." This focus requires explication, in two respects. First, we actually deal with values, beliefs, and attitudes. A careful distinction among these terms would suggest the *values* are "ought" or "should" statements; *beliefs* are "is" statements, or perceptions of reality; and *attitudes* are mental structures for integrating values and beliefs, e.g., one's extent of open mindedness or dogmatism. Unfortunately, there is little uniformity in the use of these three concepts, even in Western social-psychological and sociological literatures, and even less in the reports of survey research from Eastern Europe and the Soviet Union. We felt that it would serve no useful purpose to impose an artificial conceptual uniformity on this very diverse collection of work.

As will become apparent, we deal not only with "attitudes," broadly defined, but also with self-reports of behavior. Many of the most interesting surveys done in Eastern Europe and the Soviet Union report what people say they do rather than what they say they think. Although we have therefore cast our nets relatively broadly, it is worth emphasizing that we must stop short of characterizing this as a study of "public opinion." Many important dimensions of public opinion are not addressed in the survey research carried out in these societies; similarly, public opinion manifests itself in numerous forms other than responses to survey research questions.

Generally, the authors of the chapters in this volume have covered whatever literature seemed at all likely to contain reports of survey research. In addition, a number of us have benefited from the gracious help of colleagues in Eastern Europe who have provided copies of important unpublished studies. Among the countries studied, there are some modest differences in the information sources that have been covered. Where the volume of available survey research is great, authors have concentrated on the output of academic research institutes and/or major nonacademic institutes having professional staffs of empirically trained sociologists. This is especially characteristic of the chapters on Yugoslavia, Poland, Hungary, and the Soviet Union. For countries where much less is published by such institutes, we have drawn more heavily from the major daily and periodical presses. The importance of doing this was especially clear in the cases of Bulgaria and the German Democratic Republic. The research appearing in the press is often conducted by academic researchers, but not published elsewhere. At the same time, the seriousness and methodological sophistication of the research examined does vary, both among types of sources and among countries, as the chapters of this volume demonstrate.

This volume does not represent an attempt to explore in any depth the political, ideological, and scholarly discussions taking place in the Soviet Union and Eastern Europe concerning appropriate conceptions of public opinion, or the appropriate means of studying it. Gitelman has dealt admirably with the background of these discussions, and with their substance up to the mid 1970s. There have been some subtle but important changes in the last four or five years; what Gitelman calls a "pluralist" (as opposed to monist) view of public opinion is more clearly in ascendance. The appeals of the reflective/propaganda function of surveys are more in evidence and more clearly remarked, but at the same time the importance to effective governance of sensitive, accurate readings of mass concerns is more generally accepted. There is also increased concern for upgrading the theoretical and methodological infrastructure of survey research, a fact which implies a recognition in Eastern Europe and the Soviet Union that the procedural *desiderata* of practical policy-oriented inquiry, on the one hand, and scientifically acceptable research, on the other hand, are not as different as had been thought.

Especially because we think it important to communicate the findings of what has for us been an exciting research undertaking to as broad an audience as possible, we have tried to place reasonable length limitations on the chapters of this volume. For most of the countries represented here, much more could have been written, notwithstanding our reasonably specific parameters of coverage. Some of the chapter authors submitted draft manuscripts nearly twice the length of what appears here. We have tried to pare and refine, while stopping short of oversimplification or distortion.

ROLES AND CONDUCT OF SURVEY RESEARCH IN EASTERN EUROPE AND THE SOVIET UNION

The topical emphases of survey research have been similar across Eastern Europe and the Soviet Union, with some slight variations by country. Various topics having to do with youth represent the single most researched area in recent years, followed by surveys dealing with workers' attitudes toward their work and workplace environments. The subjects of the changing professional and personal roles of women, and the impact of these changes on the family, also are frequently addressed. There are cross-cutting themes identifiable, as well; principal among these are a concern for the antecedents of social activism and political participation and a desire to better understand the personal and social characteristics that define distinctions among subgroups of the population, i.e., the social stratification system. It is worth emphasizing that there is a distinction between emphasis in research done and emphasis in research published. A good deal of survey research now is being done on political and ideological questions and on certain categories of social problems. A considerable part of this research is never published or made generally available.

Our emphasis may appear to some readers to be critical of the societies we are studying. Such an emphasis is not intended. If what we report seems to have a critical flavor, it is because there is an understandable focus in Soviet and East European research on issues which require public attention. It is worth mentioning that, in some respects, the leadership in these societies are their own harshest critics. They tend to judge themselves and their societies against the elusive yet demanding yardsticks of an idealized and mature socialist system. Thus the indifference of East European and Soviet citizens toward crimes of various categories is lamented; yet what comparable evidence we have suggests that this indifference is no greater than exists in other societies at similar levels of social and economic development. Similarly, surveys show what is held to be an unfortunate neglect of literature among Eastern European populations; yet the reading of prose and poetry is no lower in Bulgaria than it is in the United States, for example. Surveys have painfully documented the state of job dissatisfaction among young workers in most socialist systems, yet the phenomenon is widespread in industrialized Western societies, as well.

In this connection, we should recognize that for any society, there are different contexts in which data such as these may be viewed. There has been a strong tendency, not only in the West but in Eastern Europe itself, to assume that the most salient contextual features of these societies have to do with their overt political and ideological characteristics, and their accompanying form of socioeconomic organization. Yet it may be that the systemic characteristics most relevant for understanding contemporary Eastern Europe have relatively little to do with these more visible attributes. There are contexts defined by history, culture, and resource availability that appear to be at least as important. Thus, for example, surveys suggest myriad problems in contemporary Bulgarian and Romanian societies. Viewed against the idealized goals of a mature socialist society, the impressions are not particularly favorable. But viewed in the context of rapidly modernizing Balkan countries, extracting themselves from a legacy of lagging social and economic development, the problems that trouble Bulgarian and Romanian leaders and citizens today are not particularly difficult to understand.

Although survey research continues to grow in most of the countries of Eastern Europe, there are some important variations in the current circumstances affecting the conduct of such research. Leaving Yugoslavia aside, the situation is perhaps most positive in Hungary; it is probably most constrained in Czechoslovakia. Circumstances might be characterized as stable in the Soviet Union, Poland, and Bulgaria, whereas the outlook at the moment is at least somewhat less positive in Romania and the German Democratic Republic.

The circumstances of survey research in Yugoslavia are, of course, special in several respects. There is more survey research done in Yugoslavia than anywhere else among the European socialist countries, and there is less political interference in the selection of topics or the publication of results. At the same time, survey research has entered a new phase in Yugoslavia in the 1970s, one characterized by a) the simultaneous decentralization and tightening of the supply of funding, b) "republicanization" of research, involving a virtual elimination of national surveys, c) reduction in the amount of survey research being published, and d) renewed emphasis on practical applications of surveys done under contract with economic enterprises. This last characteristic has resulted in a proliferation of ad hoc surveys done in specific work locations. Collectively, these new circumstances suggest not a decline in survey research, but a reorientation. We can expect that the methodological quality of this research will continue to improve; it is already among the best done in any of the socialist countries. At the same time, the virtual elimination of national surveys and the increase in narrowly focused studies that may be presumed to be of limited comparability with other work, should make the cumulation of findings on any given subject substantially more difficult. Overall, however, the situation in Yugoslav research remains positive. There is no central (federal or other) planning of research, and the principal influences on topical selection are funding possibilities and the interests of researchers. Sampling is as systematic as anywhere in Eastern Europe, and the quality of data analysis, though inconsistent, is often high.

In Hungary, not only is the use of survey research increasing, but the proportion of studies conducted that ultimately yield published results is growing significantly. In his chapter on Hungary, Robert Blumstock argues that the principal constraint on publication is now shortage of space in journals. The changing situation is illustrated by the fact that the Mass Communications Research Center no longer considers studies it does under contract to the Agitprop Commission of the Party Central Committee to be secret. At the same time, there is a *samizdat* publication which carries articles which have been rejected by the leading sociological outlets. However, this publication, called "Profile," itself may be achieving a quasi-legitimate status. There seems to be little constraint on topics for Hungarian survey research, with the clear exceptions of issues concerning the legitimacy of the regime, the validity or salience of Marxism-Leninism as a guiding doctrine, and Soviet military presence.

In the countries in which the circumstances of survey research appear to be stable—the Soviet Union, Poland, and Bulgaria—the enterprise remains basically decentralized, both regionally and institutionally. In the Soviet Union, there is a very large number of institutions carrying out survey research, and there appears to be relatively little central direction in topic selection or research methodology. At the same time, it is clear that the general directions of research are sensitive to Party-defined priorities; in her chapter, Linda Lubrano notes that some trends may be evident toward a modest centralization of research planning. Significantly, Lubrano notes that about one-half of all survey research done in the Soviet Union appears to be published; this figure is undoubtedly higher than the average for Eastern Europe.

Survey research is similarly decentralized in Poland; there is no central planning or coordination. Each of the numerous institutes conducting survey research seems to have a great deal of latitude in planning and carrying out its research program, subject of course to both financial constraints and the ubiquitous informal political parameters. Since 1976, there is some evidence of a declining proportion of survey results being published—as little as one-quarter of the total research output may now find its way into print—but there is no evidence so far that the vitality of the research enterprise itself has been affected by this decline in publication. In Bulgaria, less is being published than was the case five years ago, but this does not appear to be related to political circumstances. Rather, survey research in Bulgaria seems to be in the inquiry phase of a natural research cycle. There is somewhat greater central planning and coordination of survey research in Bulgaria than is the case with Poland or the Soviet Union, but this planning takes place only in the most general terms; there is not a specific central research plan in the social sciences. The role of enterprises which contract for survey research is naturally important in specifying topics. The informal guidance of Party priorities is strong, as well. Survey research in Bulgaria is enjoying increased financial support, as provided in the 1975 law on the organization and financing of sociological, social-psychological, and survey studies.

Things are rather less positive in Czechoslovakia, the German Democratic Republic, and Romania. The painful Czechoslovak experience in this regard is already widely understood. In the post-1968 period, most sensitive topics have been dropped, and far less is being published than during the middle 1960s. Nevertheless, most of the research institutes that previously conducted surveys are still operating. In almost every case, these institutes are now directly attached to government ministries, and the control over research topics appears to be close. Formally, decisions regarding release of the (few) copies of studies done apparently rests with institute directors, but many of these appear to have been placed in their positions for political reasons. In the German Democratic Republic, survey research is far more centralized than elsewhere in Eastern Europe. There is a specific central plan for social science research, and a hierarchical system of coordination of these studies embracing both government agencies and scientific research institutions. Control is exercised directly over the selection of topics, as well as indirectly through financial allocations from the state.

In Romania, the circumstances of survey research began to cloud in 1973. The conduct of surveys had expanded rapidly in the late 1960s and early 1970s, and there was at that time considerable optimism about the openness and vitality of this and other elements of empirical sociological inquiry. Apparently, however, the practical political antecedents of the growth of survey research were more powerful than had been thought. Daniel Nelson, in his chapter on Romania, suggests that Ceauşescu's needs to consolidate political power and to identify problem areas in Romanian society, constituted a major reason for the support the survey research enterprise had received. Since 1973, the amount of survey research being done has declined, several institutes have been closed or significantly reduced in staff, and the published output has been correspondingly reduced. The selection of research topics now appears to be under reasonably tight control, and reflects a strong emphasis on practical applications of survey results.

There are pockets of methodological excellence in the survey research done in Eastern Europe and the Soviet Union, but casual and even insensitive procedures are more typical. One of the difficulties is that approximately one-half of the persons involved in survey research in most of these countries have no formal training in empirical sociology. Systematic sampling procedures are most consistently used in Yugoslavia, Poland, and Hungary, and there is evidence of reasonably sound sampling in the Soviet Union and Czechoslovakia. Sampling is likely to be casual at best in surveys reported from the German Democratic

Republic, Romania, and Bulgaria. Studies of a single location, with questions apparently asked of whatever respondents are available, are common.

There are similar variations in the quality of data analysis, although the mode is again simplistic. The reporting of simple univariate descriptive statistics is common; there are some studies that contain no tables, and from which the reader must construct quantitative summaries of the findings. The use of multivariate techniques of data analysis is unusual, except in Yugoslavia. More sophisticated modes of analysis also appear with some regularity in Polish, Soviet, Hungarian, Czechoslovak, and East German publications. They are almost wholly absent from the reported results of survey research in Romania and Bulgaria.

The roles, or functions, of survey research are viewed in slightly different ways among the countries studied, but the basic orientations are similar. As Lubrano suggests in her chapter on the Soviet Union, these functions might be divided into three general categories: cognitive (understanding of social processes); practical (providing guidance in the formulation of public policy); and ideological (political and normative education and socialization). There are different ways that this basic distinction might be elaborated; we offer one possible approach here. Survey research may be seen as performing one or more of seven functions. The sequence should not be interpreted as indicating order of importance.

1. *Cognitive.* Survey research provides a basis for mapping citizen thinking on a variety of subjects. More specifically, surveys may identify the perceived relationship between individual values and social objects—the assessed worth of various social objects as filtered through the prisms of individual interests and values. Similarly, such research reveals how people relate their general world views or ideological postures to the specific circumstances in which they live.

2. *As a policy tool.* Survey research is a means toward more effective governance, since it helps identify the social problems and concerns said to be most important by citizens. Relatedly, surveys can identify citizen preferences regarding future societal development. Finally, survey research may be used (although it has only rarely been used for this purpose in the past) to ascertain citizen reactions to specific governmental policies.

3. *As a safety valve.* Surveys provide citizens an opportunity to express their opinions; this process itself may imply to some that these opinions are thereby being given attention.

4. *Demonstration/propaganda effect.* For all of the difficulties that these surveys often reveal about contemporary life in socialist societies, the fact remains that a considerable proportion of the responses given are politically appropriate. There is every reason to believe that the Party leadership has come to understand that many citizens are more impressed by being told that their fellow citizens *do* believe certain things than by hearing from the leadership that they *should* believe.

5. *To train research cadres.* One of the instrumental functions performed

by the conduct of survey research is to nurture a discipline of systematic social inquiry, not only among academic researchers, but also among the functionaries and staffs of mass organizations and economic enterprises. One of the accompaniments of an increasingly vital survey research apparatus is the availability of cadres who are competent in methods of taking accurate measure of the public pulse. An important part of more effective governance is developing the means for sensitive inventorying of the moods and concerns of the population, as well as a capacity for the regime to be accurately introspective about itself.

6. *To strengthen specific organizations.* In some instances, survey research may be used to protect and/or improve important institutions and organizations. The principal examples are survey research designed to improve the functioning of the Komsomol (especially in Bulgaria, where it came under critical scrutiny in the late 1960s and early 1970s), and the entrusting of survey research responsibilities to academic institutes whose leaders or members were under political fire.

7. *Scholarly inquiry.* Lest we overemphasize the applied, instrumental functions of survey research in socialist systems, we should recognize that there exists a scholarly community which shares in considerable part the commitment of scholars everywhere to describing and explaining social reality. The strongly applied character of all social research in Eastern Europe and the Soviet Union to the contrary notwithstanding, one cannot meet and talk with researchers at an institute of sociology at a national academy of sciences in any of these countries without coming away with a reassurance that many of the values of scientific inquiry are, indeed, universally shared.

THE ISSUES OF VALIDITY AND RELIABILITY

Notwithstanding the considerable resources being invested in survey research in Eastern Europe and the Soviet Union, it is not unreasonable to wonder aloud whether our attention to this research is really justified. Validity and reliability problems of survey research are very real in systems which are both highly structured and characterized by a significant ideological overlay. A careful examination of these issues is beyond the scope of this volume, but some brief attention to them seems necessary.

The extent of validity problems in survey research undoubtedly varies among the countries we are studying; we suspect these problems are greatest in East Germany and Czechoslovakia, and smallest in Yugoslavia and Hungary, for reasons suggested by the foregoing discussion of the varying circumstances of survey research. At least four sources of validity problems may be identified. First, there is the distinct likelihood of norm-seeking responses. Some answers are likely to reflect less the respondent's genuine feelings, and more his or her anticipation of the "correct" or expected replies. We assume that anticipatory, norm-seeking responses are motivated in part by a fear of possible sanctions for inappropriate responses, and in part by the same sorts of personality factors which encourage this response syndrome in many respondents in Western societies. It should be noted that, even for the same set of respondents, this tendency may vary depending upon the identity of the interviewer or sponsoring organization. For example, Bulgarian researchers conducted an experiment in which two separate samples of respondents in the same Party organization were asked identical questions concerning the effectiveness of Party political education. In one case, the interviewing was done by a group of sociologists from a local research institute, and in the other, the polling was done by members of the city Party committee. When the Party workers themselves did the interviewing, positive evaluations of Party political education were, on the average, 15 percent higher in every category of respondents.

Second, validity problems may result from created, or artificial responses. It is well known that some respondents will express opinions even when they do not really have them, or at least did not have them until the question was asked. This is a difficulty in survey research everywhere, but especially in systems in which political information levels tend to be low, and in which people are accustomed to cue taking in formulating politically relevant responses.

Third, there is the problem of "leading" questions. There is little doubt that, especially when the survey has a demonstration/propaganda function, questions frequently leave little to chance. When surveys are designed for this purpose, that fact usually is evident. More serious is the case where the purposes of the research appear to be cognitive, but the questions nevertheless provide structured or biased options to the respondents. It is significant that researchers in Eastern Europe and the Soviet Union have themselves recently begun to criticize this aspect of the conduct of surveys. Finally, one could imagine that there could be direct manipulation—that is, alteration—of responses by those conducting the research. The number of circumstances in which this would be useful would seem to be small, indeed; after all, if the results do not seem attractive or appropriate, they can simply be suppressed. Alternatively, it is not difficult to insure the correct responses, if that is one's purpose. We know of no documented example of alteration of survey responses, but the possibility remains.

In addition to these potential problems of validity, there is the issue of reliability. Here we refer to the consistency or stability of survey responses; if the same questions were asked of another sample, similarly selected, would the responses be essentially the same? Sampling is the key to the reliability problem in Eastern European and Soviet surveys. As we have suggested, sampling is often very casual, especially for surveys conducted by newspapers and periodicals but sometimes even in studies done by research institutes attached to the academies of sciences. For the Western scholar, the problem is further complicated by the fact that sampling procedures often are not reported; when they are, only the number of respondents and the geographical locale of the study normally are given. Other characteristics of the sample (e.g., sociodemographic characteristics of respondents) are infrequently described. Thus we usually have inadequate bases for inferring reliability.

As in the case with difficulties of validity and reliability in survey research everywhere, there are no fully satisfactory answers to these problems. To one degree or another, most of these problems plague researchers carrying out such studies anywhere. Unfortunately, shared misery is not necessarily the first step toward cure. But we can offer some points of at least partial, modest reassurance.

First, we accept as a premise that no political administration anywhere consciously chooses to operate on the basis of inaccurate information about the concerns of citizens. We are prepared to assume that accuracy is important, especially in political and social environments where authorities recognize full well that citizen discontent has been, or is, significant. That is, accuracy is most important where it is assumed that citizen views are likely to be critical. For this reason, the chapters in this volume tend to concentrate on surveys dealing with societal problem areas. That is not to overlook the distinction between surveys designed to elicit information and those designed to extract input for propaganda mechanisms. In most cases we believe that reports from the latter category of surveys are easy to identify. Further, even these are useful as indicators of areas in which the regimes feel it important to attempt to reinforce their legitimacy.

Second, and relatedly, many of the results of surveys dealt with in this volume *are* implicitly or explicitly critical of existing social, economic, and even political conditions. Perhaps the extent of criticism reported understates the collective level of citizen concern on some of these issues—although we think it unlikely that a disharmonious score would be played out, changing only the loudness with which it is performed. In our opinion, the survey responses dealt with in this volume tend to have high face validity. They appear to reflect citizen concerns about issues which we know from other sources to be important in these societies. The responses further seem reasonable as descriptions of conditions in modernizing societies, regardless of their forms of political and economical organization or prevailing ideological orientation.

Third, we strongly suspect that there is a direct and close relationship between the amount of confidence a given regime has in its standing with its own population, and the openness with which surveys are carried out, analyzed, and published. Thus on this ground we could anticipate substantial openness—albeit for somewhat different sets of reasons—in Yugoslavia, Hungary, Bulgaria, and the Soviet Union. We would expect great caution and restraint in Czechoslovakia and East Germany. And we might anticipate a mixed, uncertain, perhaps fluctuating posture toward survey research in Poland and Romania, given the corresponding recent uncertainties in their domestic political situations. The evidence very much seems to support these expectations. Overall, the growing self-confidence of most of these regimes is a factor in encouraging at least a modestly relaxed handling of survey research.

Finally, there is the combination of broadly similar findings and modest inter-nation contrasts which generally seem reasonable in the context of cultural and socioeconomic differences among them. This also implies some confidence in the validity of the findings. The likelihood that parallel findings which were merely artifacts of method and/or political circumstances could be generated in several countries is a good deal less than the likelihood of observing artificial results in a single location.

What we have said in the last few paragraphs does not allay all concerns about the validity (and does not really address the problem of reliability) of survey results in the Soviet Union and Eastern Europe. This information—as is the case, we would insist, with information on these societies from any source— must be consumed intelligently. On balance, we believe that these surveys tell us a good deal about what is happening in Eastern Europe and the Soviet Union and often provide fascinating and candid insights into what is becoming an increasingly complex process of socioeconomic and political evolution.

NOTE

1. Walter D. Connor and Zvi Y. Gitelman, *Public Opinion in European Socialist Systems* (New York: Praeger Publishers, 1977).

1 The Soviet Union

Linda Lubrano
with Wesley Fisher
Janet Schwartz
Kate Tomlinson*

AN OVERVIEW OF SURVEY RESEARCH IN THE SOVIET UNION

Political and social changes in the USSR have contributed to the nature and development of sociological research during the last 10 to 15 years. Emerging from a preoccupation with philosophy, Soviet sociology was not formally institutionalized until the late 1960s, a time when survey techniques gained legitimacy and government support.[1] The political constraints on sociological inquiry became more pressing after 1971; but within the parameters of persistent political limitations, the amount of survey research being done has expanded considerably.

There are more than 460 institutions conducting some form of social research in the Soviet Union[2] and many of them use survey techniques in the process of data collection. Research has been decentralized thus far, both institutionally and regionally, although most of the major centers are affiliated with the USSR and Republican Academies of Sciences or are located in Moscow. Universities and industrial establishments often carry out their own surveys outside the academy system and are subordinated to their own ministerial bureaucracies. Some institutes are organized around research plans that define the main themes of work; they may focus on one general area (for example, the all-Union Institute for the Study and Prevention of Crime, under the USSR Supreme Court and USSR Procuracy)[3] or on several areas of social research (for example, the Institute of Sociological Research in Moscow and the Institute of Social and Economic Problems in Leningrad, both under the USSR Academy of Sciences). Other institutions conduct surveys as a subsidiary effort to gather data that will supplement their primary responsibilities in the areas of teaching or production.

Although the Communist Party of the Soviet Union clearly has a hand in determining what types of surveys will be carried out, there does not seem to be a unified plan which all researchers must follow: "We do not intend," said Brezhnev at the jubilee session of the USSR Academy of Sciences, "to dictate to you the details of specific scientific topics or the ways and methods of conducting research—those are the business of scholars themselves. The main directions of the development of science, the main tasks presented by life itself, we will determine together."[4] During the last few years, however, there has been much discussion about the need for central planning of survey research. This may include coordinated efforts to study social problems from a variety of disciplinary perspectives and attempts to increase the effectiveness of survey research for social management.[5]

A number of steps toward the central coordination of survey research is already evident: 1) the increased importance of the Institute of Scientific Information in the Social Sciences (INION) of the USSR Academy of Sciences in the late 1970s as a depository and distributor of published research; 2) the establishment of a network of about fifty research operational points throughout the country under the auspices of the Institute of Sociological Research, USSR Academy of Sciences, and the development of a data archive in the Sector of Information and Coordination of Sociological Research at that institute;[6] 3) the attempt to standardize information maintained by personnel departments and other offices in order to facilitate broader sampling of the population;[7] 4) the consideration of questions of cost in determining sample size, so as to facilitate the planning and financing of research;[8] 5) the actual achievement of a national sample of readers of *Pravda* during the last two years;[9] and 6) the likelihood that Soviet scholars will be able to poll samples of the entire USSR population through use of the above-mentioned research operational points, with the cooperation of the USSR Central Statistical Administration.

Survey research in the USSR today officially has three functions: a *cognitive* function, to understand social processes; a *practical* function, to help in the planning of Soviet society; and an *ideological* function, to educate the masses in communism and to oppose bourgeois ideas.[10] Although the practical, applied aspects of survey research are the ones most frequently noted in Soviet publications, the cognitive aspects should not be overlooked in view of the gradual replacement of other information-gathering techniques (such as informer networks and letters to editors) by public opinion polls and the previous neglect of surveys during the Stalin period. Soviet scholars engaged in social research are often motivated by intellectual curiosity and by a professional commitment to good research. At the same time, their work is usually expected to identify social problems and public concerns. The ideological function of survey research is seen in the direct dissemination of selected results through the mass media.

If the results of the survey research were to be taken seriously by policy makers, they could be used to socialize the population in accordance with a prescribed value structure and to mobilize people to do things that they would not otherwise do. In this sense, survey data could serve as an instrument in the formation of policies that would influence public behavior. Indeed, Soviet sociologists have expressed this notion informally in the following way: Attitudes and motivations are the result of a person's upbringing (*vospitanie*) and existing social conditions; if someone's behavior deviates from acceptable social norms, it is necessary to learn the circumstances under which alternative (i.e., unacceptable) attitudes developed; wherever possible, these data can then be used to improve social conditions so as to guide the individual in the right direction, namely toward a communist orientation to life. While these assumptions may be challenged in principle, they meet even greater difficulties in practice.

The effectiveness of survey research as a policy tool in the USSR has been limited by at least four factors: 1) the limitation of most of the studies in the last ten years to regional samples, often larger than necessary, and not representative of other locations; 2) a potential distortion in the responses to questionnaires, as a result of loaded questions and/or a fear of reprisals;[11] 3) the unevenness in the quality of data analysis, which reduces the continuity and comparability of results; and 4) the politicization of the sociology profession which, in addition to the limitations on choice of research topics and on the dissemination of results (conditions compatible with policy-oriented research), may interfere with the research process itself. Recent efforts toward the centralization of survey research may reflect a conscious decision by political leaders to overcome the first and third limitations. However, if the data are to be valid and reliable (and presumably more useful to policy makers), the research process must be insulated from political pressures as much as possible.

The quality of methodology in Soviet survey research is uneven and seems to vary according to the institute where the work is done, and by whom; data processing ranges from simple tabulations to sophisticated techniques. In research on education, for example, V. V. Ksenofontova uses cross-tabulations, while S. G. Vershlovskii and L. N. Lesokhina use path analysis and M. Kh. Titma uses factor analysis.[12] Other differences may stem from the varied purposes of the research: In some areas, such as in the study of political attitudes, surveys serve as audience inventories, or feedback mechanisms, in which descriptive data predominate; in other areas, such as in research on orientations toward work, surveys are used to test hypotheses that require more statistical analysis and interpretation. An across-the-board assessment of quality is difficult also because the information on research design and methodology is not always reported, nor are all the data and analyses published. Yet, there seems to be a greater effort in recent years to provide more background information than in the 1960s.

One of the main arguments for centralized coordination of Soviet survey research is the extremely varied background of pollsters and the consequently poor quality of much research. The survey research establishment in the USSR is now rather large,[13] but 55 percent of Soviet sociologists have not received an education in sociology proper, nor in the related fields of philosophy, economics, and computer engineering[14] (see table 1.1). The credentials of survey researchers are somewhat better among those located in Moscow and in scholarly organizations; much of the best work is being done by ethnographers and demographers rather than by sociologists. While centralization of research would presumably raise the general quality of surveys, it would probably increase the continuing political pressure on sociological research in general.

THE ORIENTATION OF THIS STUDY

This study examines recent publications of Soviet survey research on media habits, family and women, education and youth, work and workplace, leisure time, politics and ideology, ethnicity and foreign cultures. Issues of moral and ethical preferences are included in the literature on family, youth, and politics; material on life aspirations is covered primarily in the section on education, and secondly under leisure time and work. Social problems and social policies are evident in all sections of this chapter and, therefore, are not treated as a separate topic.   Some social problems, such as crime and juvenile delinquency, are omitted. We looked for surveys on religion (in conjunction with the ethnicity section) and for surveys on *byt* (i.e., attitudes toward daily living conditions), but we did not give these themes extensive treatment. While we did not look for material that is specifically called "market research," many of the Soviet studies on media habits, leisure time, ethnicity, and other topics are, in many ways, studies of consumer attitudes and preferences (see the Bibliography at the end of this chapter).

We systematically reviewed the bibliographical directories of the Institute of Scientific Information in the Social Sciences (INION), namely *Novaia sovetskaia literatura po obshchestvennym naukam* and *Obshchestvennye nauki v S.S.S.R.: referativnyi zhurnal*, for publications of surveys on the above seven topics during the period 1975-77. In addition, we checked the major Soviet journals and newspapers that were likely to have data on these topics. All of the data discussed in this chapter came from surveys conducted by Soviet scholars within the USSR and published there; no other forms of data were used in our analysis.

A substantial portion of Soviet research is considered "closed," and the results of many studies receive limited distribution. While we do not know what portion of the closed research includes survey data, we can estimate (from conversations with Soviet sociologists) that approximately one-half of all Soviet social research is published. A considerable amount of data appears in *Sotsiologicheskie issledovaniia*, other Soviet journals, newspapers, and books.[15] Evidence indicates that the published material is generally of better quality, especially that done by people in scholarly organizations (that is, the USSR Academy of Sciences and higher educational establishments). Sociologists who do good research want recognition from their colleagues, and they therefore have an interest in getting their findings published. Soviet editors of professional journals place quality controls on what is accepted for publication, as do editors elsewhere. Thus, the use of published data in this chapter (mainly from scholarly research institutes, except for some additional materials issued by political and industrial organizations) represents the bulk of the most important recent work on our seven topics.

SURVEYS OF PUBLIC ATTITUDES AND BEHAVIOR IN THE SOVIET UNION

Media Habits

Scholars in the Soviet Union have given considerable attention in recent years to the media habits of the Soviet population. Most of the studies on this topic have focused on the effectiveness of information disseminated through the mass media. Data on the preferences and reactions of the public to certain subject matter and to different types of media provide guidelines for those who package the news and various forms of mass culture. This could be considered a form of consumer research since it deals with the public selection of certain kinds of information and entertainment available in the mass media.

One way to study the effectiveness of information in the news media is to look at the selective reading habits of Soviet citizens. Several studies have shown a public preference for information on foreign affairs. This was illustrated, for example, in a study of the readers of the newspaper *Taganrogskaia pravda* in the Donbass City of Taganrog. Readers of the paper read 60 percent of the articles dealing with the world outside the Soviet Union, 44 percent of the articles on the USSR, and only 30 percent of the articles on Taganrog. The most popular materials on local conditions concerned the population's daily "way of life." Fifty-one percent of such articles were read, compared with only 18 percent of the articles on economic production. These findings were consistent for all

Table 1.1. Education of Soviet Sociologists and Their Current Positions

Position	Total		Education					
		Sociology	Philosophy and Scientific Communism	Economics	Other Humanities	Natural Sciences	Engineering Technical	Unknown
Employed in sociology:								
Teachers	75	2	30	11	21	1	5	5
Scientific workers	443	35	100	60	148	17	28	55
Party and Komsomol workers	6	1	2	1	1	0	0	1
Engineer-sociologists in production	115	10	25	13	33	4	19	11
Administrators	126	13	27	23	32	8	6	17
Editors-publishers	8	1	0	0	5	0	0	2
Research assistants and students	48	8	5	5	26	1	1	2
Percentage	100	8.5	23.0	13.0	33.3	4.0	7.2	11.0
Total	821	70	189	113	266	31	59	93

Table 1.1 Continued

Position	Total	Sociology	Philosophy and Scientific Communism	Economics	Other Humanities	Natural Sciences	Engineering Technical	Unknown
Not employed in sociology:								
Teachers	682	6	267	85	208	31	13	72
Scientific workers	509	7	131	99	187	21	26	38
Party and Komsomol workers	96	0	13	9	32	1	13	28
Engineers in enterprises	40	0	0	5	10	1	22	2
Administrators	158	1	30	28	50	10	16	23
Editors-publishers	38	0	5	2	26	0	1	4
Research assistants and students	68	1	14	10	13	2	5	24
Percentage	100	1	29	15	33	4	6	12
Total	1591	15	460	238	525	66	96	191

Source: A. I. Demidova, "Professional'naia podgotovka sotsiologicheskikh kadrov," *Sotsiologicheskie issledovaniia*, 1978, no. 3, p. 202.

socioeconomic groups. As would be expected, however, those people who claimed to have an interest in Party and trade union work read more than the average on local affairs.[16]

Some studies seek the public's direct evaluation of newspaper coverage. A series of surveys conducted in the Voronezh region of the RSFSR, for example, were devoted to the public's reaction to press coverage of socialist competition in industry.[17] A study of 1,020 workers in factories in the Liskinskii district of Voronezh found that 67.9 percent of the readers of the local paper *Leninskoe znamia* read materials on socialist competition regularly, 60 percent felt that the newspaper covered such questions satisfactorily, and 27.6 percent wanted more coverage, while 8 percent wanted less coverage. Materials which attracted readers' attention the most were those dealing with exemplary achievements in socialist competition and articles about workers as people.[18] Asked what newspaper forms of moral encouragement they considered to be most effective, 30.5 percent of the readers of *Za izobilie* (a newspaper of the Rossoshanskii district of Voronezh *oblast'*) chose photographs of exemplary workers, 26.8 percent said the "honors" section of the newspaper,[19] 15.3 percent mentioned congratulatory telegrams, 13.6 percent cited the symbolic raising of a flag, 11 percent said the presentation of a pennant, and 8.6 percent chose the presentation of a commemorative document.[20]

Another indication of media effectiveness is the attention that people give to the information presented in public lectures. Audiences often ignore the lecture's subject matter and prefer, instead, to discuss nonpolitical and personal issues. A study of public lectures on sociopolitical themes in Taganrog found, for example, that not many questions were asked after the presentations. Six percent of the lectures evoked no questions at all, 54 percent got less than five questions, 30 percent evoked six to ten questions, and only 6 percent got more than ten. Many of the questions from the audience dealt with events that had not been covered in the newspapers. Forty percent of the lecturers said they had frequent discussions with their audiences on the latter's personal problems, which bore no relation to the themes of the formal presentations. Audiences were concerned, instead, with questions of housing (49 percent), relations in the family (38 percent), the upbringing of children (33 percent), and other domestic issues.[21]

Elsewhere, Soviet surveys have revealed the preferences and reactions of different audiences to movies, exhibits, and other forms of mass media. There are an estimated 108 million moviegoers per month in the USSR as a whole. Among these, about 53 million go to the movies only once or twice a month, 33 million go three or four times a month, and 22 million go more than once a week. The more educated tend to go less, while young people between 11 and 24 years old are particularly active moviegoers. An analysis of 1,040 film rentals in the Sverdlovsk *Oblast'* from 1970 to 1974 showed that the most attended films were melodramas (followed by adventure and detective films, cinematic epics, and comedies); they were made by the major Soviet studios, in color, and in several series. The most attended films in Moscow from 1964 to 1973 were those on contemporary themes, those made by the central studios, screen versions of literature, those with a simple chronological plot, lavish productions, and those with an active hero and a good title. Attendance was usually higher for musicals, comedies, and children's films, but popularity and attendance at films were not necessarily consistent with film evaluations. For example, in the Sverdlovsk *Oblast'* the film "The Twelve Chairs" ranked second in box-office receipts in 1970-74, but thirty-second according to the audience's evaluation, while Bulgakov's more serious film, "Flight" was twenty-second at the box office and fourth in audience evaluation.[22]

A questionnaire distributed to the urban scholarly intelligentsia of the Armenian S.S.R. found that published criticism of a film had little effect on a moviegoer's choice of films or reactions to them. A majority knew of the positive reaction of their friends to a film before they themselves went to see it. This reliance on friends was somewhat more true for those in the natural sciences and for those under 50 years of age. Only 23 percent of the respondents were affected by a review in the press. The same was true in the Sverdlovsk *Oblast'*. There the main factors affecting choice of a film were the studio where it was made (especially the popular studios of Mosfilm and Lenfilm) and the film's director. Those under 30 years of age and women paid more attention to the actors in a film. Over half of the Sverdlovsk respondents said that they chose a movie because it was a film version of something they had read. [23] A study of 1,006 moviegoers in Moscow (aged 18-30) showed that the most memorable characteristics of movies were the extent to which the film dealt with ethical issues and was "realistic" in relation to their own lives[24] (see table 1.2).

The preferences of the public were examined also in a study of the reactions that people had to the Exhibition of Economic Achievements in Moscow between 1971 and 1974. The most popular exhibits were those that encircled the spectator and those that provoked the question: "What is it?" The visual appeal of exhibits was particularly important for attracting youngsters, while more mature visitors were interested more in information and in learning something new.[25] A survey of people attending art exhibits in the Estonian S.S.R. found that their general level of information about art depended more on reading than on the frequency of visits to art exhibits or on general educational levels. The type of art preferred by visitors to exhibits was primarily oil painting (73.2 percent), followed by applied art (31.7 percent), graphics (25.6 percent), watercolors (23.4 percent), sculpture (20.5 percent), and artistic photography (14.7 percent). Very few respondents claimed that the type of medium used had no significance for them. In general, the main expectation from the various arts (painting, music, theater, film) was that they should provide an "emotional experience"[26] (see table 1.3).

Public use of the mass media outside the home, especially movies, has generally declined as a result of the increase in television watching and other forms of mass media in the home.[27] In a 1974 Leningrad survey, it was found

Table 1.2. Opinions about Movies among Young People in Moscow

Opinions about the "Most Memorable Film"	Age Groups							
	18-20		21-24		25-30		All Ages	
	Rank Order[a]	Percentage[b]	Rank Order	Percentage	Rank Order	Percentage	Rank Order	Percentage
Corresponds to reality	1	45	1	39	1	39	1	41
Shows important moral problems	2	35	2	38	2	36	2	36
Helps one to know new things	4	30	4	26	8	10	5	22
Reveals social problems in a lifelike manner	3	33	3	30	3	33	3	32
Shows something the viewer lived through	9	9	10	7	8	10	9	29
Helps in the attainment of goals and ideals	8	16	9	15	9	9	8	13
Makes one think about or to change one's opinions	5	22	8	17	6	15	7	18
Is interesting and gripping	4	30	5	25	4	25	4	27
Gives the possibility of rest and enjoyment	7	20	7	19	5	20	6	20
Has a hero with whom it is easy to identify	6	21	6	20	7	14	7	18

[a]Relative importance of each film characteristic in that age group.

[b]Percentage of people in that age group who selected that characteristic as important.

Source: V. N. Gritchin, "Molodezh i kino," *Sotsiologicheskie problemy kul'tury* (Moskva: Institut sotsiologicheskikh issledovanii and Sovetskaia sotsiologicheskaia assotsiatsiia, 1976), p. 68.

Table 1.3. Attitudes toward Different Art Media by Visitors to Exhibits in Estonia (1969-70)
(percentages)

Expressed Attitude	Art Media					
	Music	Cinema	Theater	Literature	Fine Arts	Art in General
Art is primarily entertainment for me	38.7	42.8	19.5	13.0	8.1	25.1
Art helps me get away from the cares met in life or at work	11.9	11.7	5.6	6.8	2.1	5.1
Art brings the enjoyment of artistic virtuoso to me	9.9	7.8	33.7	10.7	34.7	24.0
Art awakes in me various feelings: joy, sadness, et cetera	26.1	9.2	11.8	9.3	4.8	15.2
Art helps me to understand social problems	- -	6.7	5.1	9.0	0.1	2.5
Art helps me to acquire moral and ethical convictions	0.1	5.1	8.1	9.2	2.0	3.3
Art is a joke and a game that is impossible to take seriously	0.1	1.4	1.5	- -	0.4	0.1
Art inspires me to create	1.6	0.6	1.0	1.8	6.0	0.9
Art teaches me to see beauty and to enjoy it	3.1	0.8	2.5	2.1	33.3	3.8
Art broadens my horizons, gives me new knowledge	1.6	7.9	4.7	31.5	3.5	8.4
Art brings to me what I do not find in daily life	3.2	3.0	2.3	3.5	2.1	1.6
Respondent gave own opinion different from those listed in questionnaire	1.2	0.4	0.8	0.8	0.8	0.7
No answer	2.5	2.6	3.4	2.3	2.1	9.3
Total	100.0	100.0	100.0	100.0	100.0	100.0

Source: V. I. Laidmiae, *Izobrazitel'noe isskustvo i ego zritel'* (Tallinn: Eesti Raamst, 1976), pp. 185-86.

that almost 65 percent of the respondents had a television set, a radio, and a loudspeaker.[28] A similar study by L. N. Kogan compared media exposure in different socioeconomic groups in the town of Nizhnii Tagil. Workers, specialists, and white-collar employees did not differ very much in the extent to which they had radios, televisions, et cetera. The only major differences were in the size and content of libraries and record and tape collections, all of which engineering-technical personnel were more likely to have than were workers[29] (see table 1.4). Almost 71 percent of the Leningrad sample said that they looked at television almost every day, 83.2 percent listened to the radio daily, while 74.9 percent read newspapers regularly. These proportions were higher in each category than in the 1960s and they have evidently stabilized in the 1970s.[30]

It is difficult to determine the extent to which the media habits of the Soviet population are reflections of the availability of certain forms of media (for example, television versus movies), since the content and the packaging of films and programs also affect the public's choice of media exposure. Screen versions of literary classics remain more popular than films with propaganda themes; and recent changes in Soviet television programing[31] are directed toward increasing its public appeal—which is important not only in areas of entertainment, but also to retain public interest in the official news media.

Family and Women

Recent studies of the family have concentrated on the formation and dissolution of households. Scholars have pursued this topic largely because of the increasing divorce rate throughout the USSR, the continued low fertility of the population in European Russia, and the need to plan for improvements in housing. Much of this research has been done by demographers, and it differs from the earlier work of sociologists at the Institute of Sociological Research, USSR Academy of Sciences. There was extensive philosophical discussion in the 1960s on the social role and importance of the family, especially after the publication of *Marriage and the Family in the USSR* by A. G. Kharchev[32] and preceding the 1968 changes in family law. However, surveys published between 1975 and 1977 have concentrated on family behavior rather than on public attitudes toward the family as an institution. Another topic not prevalent in recent surveys is the changing role of women in society, mainly because it was covered to a great extent before 1975.

Studies published in 1976 and 1977 continue to demonstrate that the decision to marry in the Soviet Union is viewed primarily as a matter of love. In fact, however, parental presence also plays a major role, due to the shortage of housing and child services. Soviet ideology has emphasized the importance of love in the formation of families, with the assumption that marriages before 1917 were based more on economic pressures. Love is highly propagandized in the mass media, in popular literature, and in the education process. Now not only urban dwellers, but even collective farmers in Western Belorussia have overwhelmingly cited love as their main reason for getting married.[33] At the same time, there is evidence of growing liberalism regarding premarital sexual relations, particularly if love is involved: A survey in Moscow showed that a plurality of students aged 14-16 approved of premarital relations when the couple was in love. Students in general education were more liberal on this point than were students in technical schools (see table 1.5). The same survey found that young people were far more likely to learn about sex from acquaintances their own age or older than from parents or teachers.[34]

Because of residential patterns, parents also play a role in the marital decisions of Soviet youth. Ninety-three percent of the parents of rural Belorussian couples in the above study knew of their children's decision, and 79.6 percent approved of it.[35] This is hardly surprising in view of the fact that most couples plan to live with parents after getting married. Another study revealed that less than half (46.4 percent) of the couples marrying in Kiev in 1970 planned to live separately from their parents,[36] and 64 percent of the couples surveyed in a micro-region of Moscow in 1977 had lived with parents at the beginning of their married lives.[37] The majority of couples in Kiev and in Moscow lived with the husband's parents rather than with the wife's.[38] Data from these studies are potentially useful for government planning of apartment units and other forms of housing.

A survey of 540 Leningrad families found that 25 percent of the couples lived with parents, 16 percent were within a half-hour's ride or walk, and 59 percent were further than a half-hour away. The preference, however, was to live nearby (66 percent wanted to be within a half-hour's walk or ride). Those just married were more likely to want to live separately, while those with children (who needed the childcare services of relatives) were more likely to want to live nearby or together with parents. In answer to the question, "What help from your relatives could not be replaced by the development of social services?" 50 percent said child care, more than 30 percent cited food preparation, and 12 percent said care for the sick.[39] The presence of parents was found in Moscow to act as a form of control and to be a stabilizing factor for children's marriages unless the arguments between husband and wife concerned the parents. Conflicts were more likely to be between a wife and her husband's parents than between a husband and his wife's parents.[40]

Studies of the family include data on the roles of husbands and wives. In a survey by A. I. Antonov and A. N. Krivoruchko, married men and women were asked about their own roles and those of their spouses. Men were more likely to express certainty in identifying themselves as heads of their families. Women were more likely to be sure that they as wives were not, but neither did they think that their husbands were. A majority of the couples surveyed, therefore, had difficulty in agreeing on who was the head of the family. In general, there was more agreement on the content of the wife's role and the wife's desir-

Table 1.4. Possession of Cultural Articles by
Different Social Groups in Nizhnii Tagil
(percentages)

Article	Social Group		
	Workers	Specialists	White-Collar Employees
Radio, loudspeaker	93.4	82.9	90.6
Television	82.8	82.9	91.5
Camera, movie camera	32.9	43.4	27.3
Phonograph	23.8	27.0	31.0
Transistor receiver	21.0	35.6	17.0
Guitar	11.4	15.1	13.2
Accordion	8.6	9.2	10.4
Upright piano	0.9	7.2	4.7

Source: L. N. Kogan, "Sblizhenie sotsial'nykh grupp v sfere sotsialisticheskoi kul'tury,"
Sotsiologicheskie issledovaniia, 1977, no. 2, p. 38.

Table 1.5. Opinions on Premarital Sexual Relations among
Moscow Students Aged 14-16 (N = 600)
(percentages)

"In your opinion, should there be intimate relations between boys and girls before marriage? "	Student Category	
	Students In Vocational Schools	Students In General Education
No, never	24.0	15.6
If they have decided to marry	10.0	12.5
If they love each other	28.6	43.7
It is their own decision, regardless of plans for the future	15.3	15.6
Have not thought about it	21.3	12.5
No answer	0.8	0.1
Total	100.0	100.0
N	300	300

Source: V. G. Alekseeva, "Neformal'nye gruppy podrostkov v usloviiakh goroda," *Sotsiologicheskie issledovaniia,* 1977, no. 3, p. 64.

able traits than on the role and characteristics of the husband.[41] In a survey of 139 families in Dubna, it was found that there were more disagreements and conflicts when husbands helped with the housework than when they did not.[42] Although not specified in the study, these conflicts may be based on the traditional self-image of men as heads of their families, despite the mass media campaign to reduce the double burden on women and to equalize relationships within the family.

As noted above, an important concern of Soviet demographers has been the declining birthrate among European Russians. In accordance with this concern, two major studies of attitudes toward fertility were published between 1975 and 1977.[43] These documented, in particular, the huge gap between the married female Moslem population and the married female non-Moslem population in their expected numbers of children. In a 1972 national survey, Central Asian and Azerbaidzhani women expected an average of 5.76 children, while Russian women expected only an average of 2.00[44] (see table 1.6). While the European population expects to have fewer children than its ideal (preferred) number, the Moslem population expects to have somewhat more children than its ideal number. In fact, there has been an *increase* in both the expected and ideal numbers of children among recent cohorts of uneducated Moslem women. The situation of more educated Moslem women, however, is similar to that of European Russian women since their ideal number exceeds their expected number of children, but their expected number is still twice as many as that of women in European Russia.[45]

Finally, the rising divorce rate has prompted surveys on the reasons given by couples for the termination of marriages. Surveys in the Ukraine and in Belorussia showed that most divorce actions were initiated by wives. The most common reason given by wives was the alcoholism of the husband. Husbands seeking a divorce tended to claim incompatibility of character and interference by parents. In fact, the latter often turned out to be objections by the wife's parents to the husband's drinking (see table 1.7). More men than women had a de facto second family at the time of the divorce. Judges in rural Belorussia found men guilty of causing the family breakup 56.2 percent of the time, women 5.3 percent, and both of them 37.1 percent of the time.[46]

Education and Youth

Soviet surveys on education and youth stress the impact of social background on a person's educational achievements and early career development. They reveal the persistent ways in which the learning orientations of youth and the subsequent choice of professions are affected by the occupations and educational levels of one's parents. In fact, the career aspirations of youth often reflect a social decision rather than an occupational one; that is, young people

Table 1.6. Distribution of Married Women in the USSR
by Expected Number of Children (1972)

Ethnodemographic Groups and Nationalities		Average Expected Number of Children
I	Russians	2.00
II		2.15
including	Ukrainians	2.08
	Belorussians	2.31
	Moldavians	2.62
III		2.14
including	Latvians	1.99
	Lithuanians	2.23
	Estonians	2.18
IV		5.76
including	Uzbeks	6.26
	Tadzhiks	5.97
	Turkmens	5.93
	Kirgizi	6.04
	Kazakhs	5.01
	Azerbaidzhani	4.89
Other nationalities not included in the basic ethnodemographic groups:		
	Georgians	2.83
	Armenians	3.42
	Tatars	2.86
	Jews	1.71

Note: I-IV is a standardized grouping used by the USSR Central Statistical Administration.

Source: *Skol'ko detei budet v sovetskoi sem'e* (Moskva: Statistika, 1977), p. 26.

Table 1.7. Reasons for Divorce in Rural Western Belorussia (N = 637)
(percentages)

Reasons for Divorce	Source of Opinion		
	Court	Wife	Husband
Alcoholism	38.7	44.3	10.6
Incompatibility of character	15.1	6.7	22.2
Adultery of spouse	9.4	12.6	15.3
Thoughtless entrance into marriage	8.5	2.0	4.5
Lengthy period of separation (for objective reasons)	5.4	3.8	3.1
Loss of feelings for unexplained reasons	5.3	8.6	12.3
Cruelty	3.6	5.6	0.6
Sentencing to imprisonment for 3 years or more	3.3	2.6	2.1
Physical and mental diseases	2.1	1.7	2.6
Interference of parents and other relatives	1.5	4.4	11.3
Infertility	0.8	0.7	1.0
Physiological incompatibility	0.3	0.3	0.5
Other reasons	6.0	6.7	6.0
Total	100.0	100.0	100.0

Source: V. T. Kolokol'nikov, "Brachno-semeinye otnosheniia v srede kolkhoznogo krest'-ianstva," *Sotsiologicheskie issledovaniia,* 1976, no. 3, p. 82.

select a career more because of its accompanying social status than because of the quality and nature of work.[47] Also evident is the fact that young people place higher values on personal relationships and on the educational process than they do on their future careers.

Data on the education and career prospects of students show only an incremental upward mobility in the social status of succeeding generations. A typical study on this topic is one by F. R. Filippov, who examined the educational goals and achievements of 47,000 students at four grade levels: eighth and tenth graders, and freshmen and seniors from the higher educational establishments (*vysshie uchebnie zavedeniia*, or *vuz*). The last two samples were representative of the social composition of all students in the USSR, but the tenth-grade sample had a smaller proportion of workers' children (in relation to the total population) because many of them continued their education in vocational schools. Filippov found that a child's preparation for elementary school, his or her preferences for secondary education, and the *vuz* dropout rates depended on the education and social position of the parents. Whereas 70.5 percent of the children whose mothers had less than an elementary education were poorly prepared for school, only 4.9 percent of the children from higher-educated mothers lacked preschool training. Filippov noted that this reflected the different values of the parents regarding the early education of their children.[48]

The impact of family differences persisted at the level of secondary schools, where 35.2 percent of workers' children, 33.7 percent of collective farmers' children, and 60.6 percent of specialists' and employees' children planned to attend ninth grade. Considerably fewer children of specialists and employees expected to go to specialized or technical institutes. This difference continued among tenth graders who planned to enter a *vuz* immediately after graduation (54.6 percent of the children of employees and specialists, 36.7 percent of workers' children, and 7.2 percent of collective farmers' children). Filippov compared these data with tendencies from the 1960s and found that there was a significant drop in the percentage of students planning a higher education (from 80-90 percent in the 1960s to 46 percent in the 1970s), while at the same time a much greater percentage looked forward to attending secondary specialized institutions. According to Filippov, this meant that *vuzy* and secondary specialized institutions were now considered more equally desirable than before, especially among workers' children[49] (see table 1.8). Similar findings were reported by V. Gentvainite in a study of secondary school graduates in Lithuania[50] (see table 1.9).

Family background not only influenced the educational aspirations of youth; it also affected their success in school. Almost 77 percent of the students whose fathers had a higher education planned to attend a *vuz*, compared with only 26.2 percent of those whose fathers had just an elementary education. After enrollment in a *vuz*, the dropout rate was considerably higher among the children of workers. The percentage of students in *vuzy* whose parents were workers dropped from 31.2 percent in the first year to 26.2 percent in the

Table 1.8. Plans of Eighth Graders on the Basis of Social Origin
(percentages)

Life Plans	All Children	Social Origin		
		Children of Workers	Children of Collective Farmers	Children of Employees[a] and Specialists
To Study				
in ninth grade	40.8	35.2	33.7	60.6
in secondary specialized schools	20.5	22.8	22.3	14.5
in secondary vocational schools	11.0	13.6	13.8	3.5
in regular vocation schools	4.6	5.2	7.4	1.4
in other training programs (kursy)	1.9	2.3	3.2	0.3
Subtotal	78.8	79.1	80.4	80.3
Only to work	1.1	1.2	1.8	0.3
To work and to study in secondary educational establishments	3.8	4.4	4.8	1.0
Undecided or no answer	16.3	15.3	12.5	18.3
Subtotal	21.2	20.9	19.1	19.6
To receive a higher education in general	76.1	76.0	74.6	79.6
To receive a higher education in day schools	72.3	71.6	69.8	78.6

[a]White-collar personnel (sluzhashchie)

Source: F. R. Filippov, "Rol' vysshei shkoly v izmenenii sotsial'noi struktury sovetskogo obshchestva (itogi vsesoiuznogo issledovaniia)," Sotssiolo-gicheskie issledovaniia, 1977, no. 2, p. 45.

Table 1.9. Plans of Secondary School Graduates in Lithuania

(percentages)

Type of Family	Place of Residence	Desire to Continue Study			Intend to Work and Study	Intend Only to Work	Other Answers and No Response
		In *Vuzy*	In Technical Schools	In Vocational Schools			
Worker	Village	41.1	41.1	11.0	3.5	2.2	1.1
	Small Town	62.4	30.4	2.0	5.0	--	0.2
	Big City	43.4	14.2	3.2	9.7	0.5	29.0
Collective Farmer	Village	34.3	44.5	10.6	5.7	2.3	2.6
	Small Town	47.9	44.8	2.1	4.2	--	1.0
	Big City	46.0	23.0	7.7	15.4	7.7	0.2
Specialist	Village	72.7	18.2	6.1	--	--	3.0
	Small Town	73.3	20.0	--	2.2	--	4.5
	Big City	94.2	1.5	--	3.1	--	1.2
Employee[a]	Village	50.0	33.3	--	16.7	--	--
	Small Town	59.0	33.3	--	--	7.7	--
	Big City	70.3	17.6	--	--	5.9	6.2
Worker–Collective Farmer	Village	34.5	36.2	17.2	1.7	3.4	6.8
	Small Town	38.3	41.7	20.0	--	--	--
	Big City	33.3	16.7	--	33.3	--	16.7
Worker–Specialist	Village	62.5	31.2	6.3	--	--	--
	Small Town	68.3	16.7	3.3	1.7	--	10.0
	Big City	83.3	3.4	1.9	7.4	1.9	2.1

Table 1.9 Continued

Type of Family	Place of Residence	In *Vuzy*	In Technical Schools	In Vocational Schools	Intend to Work and Study	Intend Only to Work	Other Answers and No Response
Worker-Employee[a]	Village	33.3	26.7	20.0	--	--	20.0
	Small Town	70.0	29.3	--	2.4	--	--
	Big City	69.1	10.3	2.6	7.7	2.6	7.7
Collective Farmer-Employee[a]	Village	45.5	45.5	--	9.0	--	--
	Small Town	71.4	14.3	--	--	--	14.3
Specialist-Collective Farmer	Village	50.0	20.0	--	--	20.0	10.0
	Small Town	71.4	14.3	14.3	--	--	--
Specialist-Employee[a]	Village	66.7	33.3	--	--	--	--
	Small Town	70.0	10.0	5.0	--	--	15.0
	Big City	90.7	3.7	--	5.6	--	--

[a]White-collar personnel (*sluzhashchie*)

Source: V. Gentvainite, A. Matulenis, and M. Tal'iunaite, "Sotsial'naia orientatsiia vypusknikov srednikh shkol," *Sotsiologicheskie issledovaniia*, 1977, no. 2, pp. 74-75.

senior year. The distribution of working class children among institutions of higher learning was 26.7 percent in universities, 34.5 percent in technical *vuzy*, and 38.1 percent in teachers' *vuzy*; by the senior year the percentages had dropped to 19.9 percent, 30.1 percent, and 29.8 percent respectively.[51] Similar findings were reported in a study by V. I. Brudnyi and A. B. Kaganov, who surveyed 9,000 students in the southern Ukraine. Their data showed that children of collective farmers were less likely than children of white-collar workers and specialists to apply to a *vuz* and many of them dropped out by the third year.[52]

Such differences in educational achievements are not unexpected. To the extent that higher education serves as a vehicle for upward social mobility, these data document the incremental nature of changes in social stratification. One factor that may contribute to the more gradual shifts in career aspirations and to the general decline (since the 1960s) in desires for higher education is the growing heterogeneity of family class backgrounds. V. V. Ksenofontova's study of eighth- and tenth-grade students in Sverdlovsk showed that there has been a reorientation of youth in favor of worker occupations and a decline (from 81.8 percent in 1965 to 47.5 percent in 1970) in the number of young people who want to become part of the upper intelligentsia. Ksenofontova felt that this was due to the heterogeneity of the families, where the father was a worker or a specialist and the mother was a white-collar worker (*sluzhashchaia*) or vice-versa. Children from homogeneous families generally wanted to raise their social status, whereas children from heterogeneous families tended to perpetuate a status midway between that of their parents.[53]

A study which emphasizes another factor in early career development is one that was conducted in the Estonian S.S.R. by M. Kh. Titma. It is an examination of the "subjective aspects of professional self-determination," that is, the attitudes of the individual toward occupational choice.[54] Titma did a longitudinal analysis of young students, at the time of their graduation from secondary schools in 1966, as *vuz* students in 1969, and as *vuz* graduates in 1971. He compared these data with surveys of students in technical schools and with surveys of engineering-technical workers in the labor force. The major variable in his analysis was "the attractiveness of certain occupations," as revealed by an interval scale on which students rated various professions at different stages of their educational development. Titma found that, despite the changing evaluations of specific occupations over time, all three groups gave top ranking to professions within the creative intelligentsia.[55] This was consistent with the growing number of applicants in the humanities and with the decline in engineering applications (but it contrasted with the general trends noted above by Filippov and Ksenofontova).

Several characteristics of work were considered as part of a person's assessment of that occupation's attractiveness. When graduating from secondary schools, students considered the opportunities for "personality development" much more important in the selection of a career than they did later on. The possibility of developing one's abilities on the job was rated most highly by students in technical schools. Income was a significant factor in the career evaluations of young workers; status, while less important than income to the workers, was more important to them than to any other group. Creativity was given a relatively low rating by all groups except the young workers, 60.7 percent of whom said it was important. According to Titma, opportunities for creativity are usually greater in occupations that require higher education, and presumably creativity should be even more significant for those who are more educated, but this was not the case.[56]

Titma considered these data to be potentially useful for social planning, that is, for the regulation of occupational choice. He was particularly concerned, however, with an unexpected shift in orientations as students went from secondary day schools through universities. Many of them entered institutions of higher education as bridges to certain occupations, but subsequently they valued learning as an end in itself. Students considered professional preparation for their future social contributions as less important than the humanistic aspects of their education. Titma felt that this was undesirable, because it diverted the attention of youth from occupational development and from a "communist attitude toward work."[57]

The value orientations of youth were explored further in another article by Titma in 1977. Using the above data, he discussed the cognitive, emotional, and behavioral aspects of personality development at different stages of young people's careers. Among those who had just graduated from secondary schools, sports were valued much more highly than any professional interest. Students in their first year of higher education placed greater value on entertainment, mass communication, and interpersonal relations in small groups than they did on a profession. After they reached the third year of higher education, they demonstrated more favorable attitudes toward professional preparation, but love and interpersonal relations were still considered much more important.[58]

After finishing their formal education, young specialists (i.e., *vuz* graduates) and young workers had different orientations toward their work. Workers had a stronger emotional commitment to their jobs, despite the fact that these jobs had less opportunities for self-expression. Young specialists, by contrast, developed stronger personal ties during their experiences in *vuzy*, and their leisure activities distracted them from the realities of everyday life.[59] As a result, they subsequently lacked the dedication and commitment to work that, according to Titma, would be socially desirable. Titma recommended, therefore, that a more positive value be placed on one's future occupation earlier in the careers of young specialists. This could be done, he suggested, by including work experiences (with remuneration) in the education process itself.[60]

Work and the Workplace

Two themes most prevalent in recent Soviet literature on industrial workers are the high degree of labor turnover and problems of automation. Both themes are tied to the issue of worker satisfaction, a topic that has persisted at least since the 1960s.[61] An underlying assumption is that "a satisfied worker is a more productive worker," if not directly in terms of output then indirectly through greater job stability. The first theme focuses primarily on the younger members of the labor force, and the second highlights the changing nature of work relationships within industrial enterprises. Both themes have a very pragmatic orientation, since they deal with the everyday problems of industry.

N. V. Ivanova, A. E. Kotliar, and M. I. Talalai have examined some of the characteristics of, and reasons for, labor turnover. Ivanova's data came from a 1969-72 study of industrial establishments and a 1971-75 study of machine-building enterprises, both in Leningrad.[62] On the basis of questionnaires and personal interviews, she looked at labor turnover that resulted from personal choice and job dissatisfaction rather than from new technology or family pressures. The highest turnover occurred among younger workers and among those in the lower occupational grade levels (*razriad*) with low wages, most likely the same people. Approximately two-thirds of those leaving their jobs were between the ages of 18 and 35; almost 91 percent were in grade levels 1 to 3; and almost 40 percent earned only 69 to 90 rubles per month.[63] Since the data were not reported with constant age cohorts for each year, it is difficult to know whether the higher labor turnover of youth reflected a growing dissatisfaction with working conditions from generation to generation or a typical characteristic of early career development.

The data reported by Kotliar and Talalai suggest that dissatisfaction with the job position and low wages may have been a significant factor in the mobility of young workers for several reasons, such as 1) an incompatibility between personal interests and initial job placement, 2) a lack of symmetry between educational background/training, job expectations, and employment realities, 3) a need to seek better opportunities for the support of young families, and 4) the "restlessness" of youth. Kotliar and Talalai based their findings on two samples of workers, one drawn from 105 enterprises in 73 cities of the RSFSR and the other involving 35,000 young workers in the RSFSR and Belorussia. Their data indicated that the first three years on a job were the most important for adaptation to the work experience. Young workers were generally successful in raising their productivity and in participating in social organizations[64] during this period. Nonetheless, they were still more likely than older workers to change jobs. Almost 80 percent of those between the ages of 25 and 29 already had families to support, but dissatisfaction with living and housing conditions was not cited as frequently as "poor job placement" and "inadequate job training." Poor job placement resulted from the fact that most young workers (three-fourths) entered their new occupations without appropriate skills and were therefore placed in low positions.[65] This was compounded by their lack of prior knowledge about the nature of the enterprise and the work experience, which led to false expectations and disappointments (see table 1.10).

Other factors that contributed to worker dissatisfaction and to high labor turnover were the poor organization of work and the inability to raise one's qualifications through the continuation of formal study programs. Both factors were examined also in the L. I. Lobanova study of over 6,000 workers in construction ministries.[66] Attempts to improve one's skills may have been related to the desire for higher wages and a more interesting job. Such desires were prevalent especially among young workers in one of the machine-building plants of Leningrad.[67] In this case, however, "more interesting work" meant the ability to choose the rate and rhythm of work as part of a team processing an order. While the specific reasons for dissatisfaction may differ, it is important to note that the problem of labor turnover is not limited to any one sector of the economy. N. A. Sviridov obtained similar findings in his study of a fishing fleet,[68] as did Iu. K. Ivanov and V. D. Patrushev in their survey of collective farmers[69] (see tables 1.11 and 1.12).

The second major theme in Soviet literature on work is the impact of automation on the content of work, on the role of trade unions, and on the nature of labor disputes. An evaluation of the content and conditions of work was carried out by V. V. Krevnevich as part of a cross-national study on the social consequences of automation. He compared five automated and five nonautomated car-producing plants according to a combination of objective and subjective indicators. Automation had affected the relationships between mental and physical labor, especially in the role of the machine operator. Many of the operator functions disappeared in the automated plants, so that physical labor (which had occupied 80 percent of the operator's time) was almost entirely replaced by "passive and active observation" of machine processes.[70] Operators were often replaced, therefore, by more highly qualified adjustment and maintenance workers (*naladchiki* and *remontiki*, respectively). Consequently, automation not only changed the content of labor, but also caused an adjustment in occupational composition. In the Krevnevich study, for example, the proportion of operators to *naladchiki* changed, respectively, from 81 percent and 9 percent in nonautomated plants to 38 percent and 26 percent in automated plants.[71]

On the basis of more subjective indicators, automation appeared to shift dissatisfaction from the content of work to general working conditions. On a scale of 1 to 9, workers in the Krevnevich study were asked to evaluate the nature and quality of their work (according to such characteristics as variety, independence, responsibility, professional preparation, and opportunities) and the conditions of their working environment (including the facilities and equipment, wages and insurance, and the social relationships in the collective). In almost all cases, evaluations of the above work characteristics were higher in

Table 1.10. Youth Adaptation and Their Motives for Selecting a Workplace
(percentages)

Motives for the Selection of a Workplace	Specific Proportion of Workers Indicating That Motive[a]	Type of Adaptation		
		Participating in the Rationalization of Work	Satisfied With Work	Tying Their Future with the Present Enterprise
Example of friends	19.6	8.9	58.5	31.3
Nearness of home	15.8	9.6	40.4	29.2
Announcement of the enterprise	15.8	7.0	47.6	23.1
Advice of parents	15.3	8.9	58.5	31.3
Possibility to combine work with study	9.6	11.4	49.0	26.0
Availability of an apartment	7.6	6.9	33.7	20.2
Preliminary practical familiarity with the enterprise	7.5	13.0	55.9	33.8
Closeness to the profile of an educational establishment	6.7	12.4	52.1	35.4
Payment for work	5.6	10.7	51.8	32.4
Educational base of the enterprise	4.1	11.0	51.9	27.9
Advice of a commission on the labor organization of youth	3.3	6.4	53.7	21.3
Recommendation of school	1.7	10.3	61.9	34.5
Other motives	16.2	9.0	43.1	22.9
All motives	----	9.2	51.7	27.3

[a]Each respondent indicated one or several motives for the selection of an enterprise. Therefore, the total number of chosen motives is greater than the number of respondents (i.e., this column is greater than 100 percent).

Source: A. E. Kotliar and M. I. Talalai, *Molodezh' prikhodit na proizvodstvo* (Moskva: Profizdat, 1978), p. 22.

Table 1.11. Initial Motives for Working on Fishing Boats

Motives	Percentage of Each Motive		
	In the Entire Group	Among Men	Among Women
Wanted to earn a little more	28.6	28.0	29.2
The sea attracted me	15.4	13.7	17.2
Went to work in the sea because of family circumstances	14.1	11.7	16.0
There was no apartment on shore (at the place of permanent residence)	12.2	12.1	12.3
Friends or parents advised me	10.1	11.0	9.3
Wanted to see the Far East; wanted to settle in Vladivostok	4.9	0.8	8.6
My profession was tied to work on the sea, on fishing boats (was assigned)	8.1	14.0	2.4
Wanted to acquire a new profession	2.4	3.0	1.7
All other motives	4.2	5.7	3.3
Total	100.0	100.0	100.0

Note: Data taken from a 1970-72 study of fishing fleet employees in Vladivostok. The sample size was 1,957 and consisted of fishermen (25.4 percent), workers without technical preparation (59.1 percent), and skilled workers (15.5 percent).

Source: N. A. Sviridov, "Osobennosti adaptatsii lichnosti k slozhnim proizvodstvennym usloviiam," *Sotsiologicheskie issledovaniia*, 1977, no. 2, p. 87.

Table 1.12. Labor Turnover of Workers at State Farms in the Moscow Region
(percentages)

Professional Group	Percentages		
	The Entire Group	Those Under 30	Those Over 30
Field workers	34.7	49.0	34.7
Stock-raisers	31.2	61.0	31.2
Engineering-technical workers and employees[a]	28.1	41.7	28.1
Machine operators	27.2	34.4	27.2

[a] White-collar personnel (*sluzhashchie*)

Source: Iu. K. Ivanov and V. D. Patrushev, "Vliianie uslovii truda na udovletvorennost' trudom rabotnikov sel'skogo khoziaistva," *Sotsiologicheskie issledovaniia*, 1976, no. 3, p. 66.

the automated plants, where both operators and *naladchiki* felt that the work was more interesting in its novelty, variety and opportunities for the use of their knowledge and creative potential. Yet, as automation increased, the expectations and requirements for support systems became more complex, placed greater demands on management, and made workers more conscious of their working conditions.[72]

The impact of automation on the role of trade unions was examined by M. N. Nochevnik and V. I. Usenin. As part of a cross-national study, they interviewed Soviet workers and trade union officials in two automated and two nonautomated car-producing plants. Approximately three-fourths of the workers in both types of plants (70.3 percent and 75.2 percent, respectively) said that automation did not change the role and significance of trade unions.[73] However, the rest of the workers felt that automation increased the role of trade unions, because new technology created different kinds of problems related to changes in the content and conditions of work. This view was corroborated by other evidence that trade unions actually participated more in decision making at automated plants.[74] Over 40 percent of the workers in automated plants and 34.9 percent in nonautomated plants evaluated the work of trade unions as "significant" in supporting worker advancements; and many in both automated and nonautomated plants were either "fully satisfied" (34.8 percent and 25.6 percent, respectively) or "basically satisfied" (54.3 percent and 61.5 percent, respectively) with trade union activities[75] (see table 1.13).

Trade unions played an increasingly important role in the labor disputes that arose in automated plants. With the introduction of new technology, many skilled workers tried to move to other departments (without automation), where they could continue their traditional work habits. Of those who shifted to the automated lines, some encountered serious difficulties in adaptation to the new job. In both cases, trade unions tried to alleviate the disputes that developed between workers and administrators.[76] Poor relationships between workers and managers were not often discussed in the survey literature, but Soviet scholars have dealt with this problem in the 1970s. For example, V. I. Brudnyi discussed worker dissatisfaction with "coarse" administrators who did not distribute work fairly and who showed a general indifference to workers' needs and opinions (for example, 33 percent of the workers said that "it is not possible to discuss questions with management," 31.2 percent said that "management ignores workers' opinions on the distribution of work," and 27.6 percent said that "management ignores the sensible suggestions of workers").[77] This was unfortunate because, as indicated elsewhere,[78] poor leadership and the lack of communication with workers can reduce the cohesiveness of working groups, thus contributing further to the entire syndrome of dissatisfaction and labor turnover.

While the above studies concentrated on industrial workers, job satisfaction has been explored for other occupational groups as well. In a recent book, for example, V. A. Iadov presented a social-psychological portrait of engineers,

Table 1.13. Individual Labor Disputes Related to Automation

The Possibilities and Character of Individual Labor Disputes	Enterprises (I-IV)[a]
Did the introduction of new equipment involve individual labor disputes between workers and administrators?	
Often	-, - -, - - -, - - [b]
Sometimes	I, II, III, IV
If "yes," did the trade union support the basic position of the worker?	
Yes	I, II, III, IV
No	-, - -, - - -, - -
If there were individual disputes, what kinds of questions were involved?	
Wages	I, II
Work load	-, - -
Technical safety	-, - -
Transfers	III, IV
Dismissals	- - -, - -
Working time and work shifts	I, IV

[a]Enterprises I and II were automated; enterprises III and IV were not automated.
[b]A dash indicates that the option was not selected.

Source: M. N. Nochevnik and V. I. Usenin, "Rabochii klass, avtomatizatsiia i profsoiuzy," *Rabochii klass i sovremennyi mir,* 1977, no. 2, p. 21.

based on their attitudes toward work and their use of leisure time. He found that job satisfaction and feelings of personal fulfillment did not necessarily coincide with a person's contribution to social production.[79]

Leisure Time

Time budget analysis has been the focal point for Soviet surveys of leisure time since the 1920s. The most recent literature generally has the same goal of assist-ing with economic planning that the earlier research had, but Soviet social scientists are now using broader sampling techniques and more elaborate data analysis. For example, a survey conducted by the Institute of Economics of the Latvian Academy of Sciences in 1972 has produced, for the first time, a large set of detailed tables on weekly time budgets for a stratified sample of an entire union republic.[80] Expenditures of time do not necessarily represent mass attitudes and preferences. They often reflect changes in economic and social conditions (such as the availability of consumer services and automation in industry). These studies are useful, however, for comparisons between official views on the ideal use of leisure time and the actual behavior of the population.

There has been an increase in the amount of free time that Soviet citizens (especially women) have available.[81] For example, from 1923-24 to 1967-70 the amount of time spent on housework and on private plots was reduced from 35 hours per week for the typical adult family member to 18.5 hours per week. At the same time, adult cultural pursuits increased from 6.7 hours to 17.3 hours per week.[82] Meanwhile, the introduction of the five-day week has somewhat reduced the time women spend on daily housework in Leningrad, and it has generally increased free time for women more than it has for men. Men now spend more time than do women taking care of children on Saturdays, and evidently there has been an increase in "family togetherness" for leisure activities on weekends.[83] Nonetheless, there continues to be a discrepancy in the amount of leisure time for men and for women; men had one and one-half to two times more free time than did women working outside the home in 1972.[84]

The use of leisure time varies with a person's education, socioeconomic status, and place of residence. Persons with more education and greater wealth tend to have more free time, as do those with better housing and household appliances, and they use their time more for reading and less for television than do those of lower socioeconomic status. In the 1972 Latvian study, for example, it was found that men with higher education had 10 to 12 hours more free time than did men with only an elementary education.[85] The same study showed that although rural residents had less free time than did urbanites, they watched television and listened to the radio more than did the city-dwellers, while urban residents spent more time in study and in events outside the home.[86]

Similar tendencies were evident also in the ways that citizens would prefer to use extra leisure time. When asked in the study by L. A. Gordon, E. V. Klopov, and L. A. Onikov what they would do if they had more leisure time, the less educated members of the sample responded that they would prefer to watch more television, to spend more time on housework, to go to movies, and to take care of their children (in that order). Meanwhile, those with more education responded that they would prefer to read more, to take care of their children, to go to movies, and to watch television (in that order)[87] (see table 1.14).

Soviet social scientists have registered their concern over the ways that citizens use their leisure time. They advocate that this time be used productively, i.e., in a way that will contribute to society or to one's own personal fulfillment. According to the ideal "rational time budget" presented by Gordon and Klopov in 1977, the population was apparently spending too little time on such things as physical culture and sports, civic and political work, visiting theaters, reading, and child care, and too much time on resting, housework, socializing with friends, and watching television[88] (see table 1.15). The latter activities were considered lacking in "content" or too passive to be socially useful.[89] Further comparisons between the officially preferred and actual uses of leisure time may reveal the effectiveness of the Soviet mass media in influencing the attitudes and behavior of Soviet citizens.

Politics and Ideology

Three central themes in Soviet political surveys are 1) the effectiveness of Party propaganda and agitation;[90] 2) social activism for the maintenance of public norms; and 3) the work of Party and government officials. Each of these themes is related to the general role of political officials in mobilizing the public toward active support of the system. The questions are political to the extent that they solicit information on the influence of Party activities on public attitudes and vice versa.

There are obvious methodological difficulties in the observation of propaganda/agitation effectiveness. At the minimum, however, one would have to know precisely what the Party wants to achieve by the dissemination of certain messages.[91] One of the goals of Communist Party propaganda is to raise the level and quality of political education among its members so they can be more effective in dealing with the public, both as agitators and as role models. The purposes of Party agitation are not stated explicitly in Soviet surveys, but at least two goals can be inferred from the kind of questions that have been asked. One is to politicize the public in its *awareness* of Party policies and the other is to induce the public to support the system actively through *participation* in community life. The effectiveness with which the first goal is met can be observed at the level of cognition, whereas the test of the second is in behavior. We shall focus first on the reception and evaluation of information by the public

Table 1.14. Education and the Preferred Use of Additional
Time among Workers in Taganrog

| | Education Achieved | | | |
| | Fourth to Sixth Grade | | Specialized Secondary Education | |
Types of Activity	Percentage	Rank	Percentage	Rank
Work for additional pay	9	11	4	13
Housework	52	2	38	5
Work in the garden or private plot	18	8	18	9
Upbringing and care of children	48	4	61	2
Meeting with friends	28	7	34	7
Activities outside the home: movies, theatre	50	3	54	3
Rest and relaxation at home: television watching	61	1	50	4
Reading	40	5	65	1
Study, self-education	10	10	36	6
Hobbies	12	9	13	11
Sports and physical culture	1	13	15	10
Rest outside the city	33	6	32	8
Civic work	6	12	9	12

Note: The respondent was permitted to indicate not more than five of thirteen possible answers to the question: "If you had more free time at your disposal, what would you do with it? " The table gives the relative proportion of those who indicated a particular type of activity as a percentage of the number in each educational group.

Source: L. A. Gordon, E. V. Klopov, and L. A. Onikov, *Cherty sotsialisticheskogo obraza zhizni: byt gorodskikh rabochikh vchera, segodnia, zavtra* (Moskva: Znanie, 1977), p. 151.

Table 1.15. A Rational Time Budget and the Actual Activities of Urban Workers at the End of the 1960s

Types of Activities	Rational Time Budget for Workers in Large Cities (average hours per week)	Actual Budget of Time for Workers in Industrial Establishments of Dnepropetrovsk, Zaporozh'e, Odessa, Kostroma	
		Hours per week	Percentage of Rational Budget
Sleeping, eating, taking care of one's self and other personal necessities	70.0	64.5	92
Time at work	35.0	41.1	127
Travel to and from work, lunch breaks, changes of shift	10.0	11.4	114
Civic work and sociopolitical activity	2.5	1.0	40
Housework	12.5[a]	19.5	156
Daily cultural life, including reading	6.0	3.7	62
radio and television	5.0	6.2	124
movies, theatres, museums, and other public shows	2.5	1.3	52
studying	3.5[b]	4.0	114[b]
amateur talents, hobbies, and other kinds of creative activity	2.5[c]	0.8	32
Physical culture, sports, hunting, fishing, trips out of town	6.0	0.7	12
Meetings with friends, having guests, and other kinds of socializing	4.0	5.2	130
Activities with children	7.5	5.9	79
Unassigned expenditure of time, rest	1.0	2.8	280

[a]With equal time spent by men and by women.

[b]This includes studying done during working time; the entire magnitude of time spent on study in the rational time budget exceeds by 1.5 - 2 times the expenditure in the actual time budget.

[c]This includes creativity in some of the other activities.

Source: L. A. Gordon and E. V. Klopov, "Ratsional'nyi biudzhet vremeni: podkhod k probleme i opyt nachal'nogo rascheta," *Sotsiologicheskie issledovaniia,* 1977, no. 1, p. 29.

and then on the issue of social activism.

Surveys on the effectiveness of propaganda and agitation have dealt with the following general questions: Who listens to Party propaganda/agitation? What is their level of political awareness? What is the public's attitude toward what it hears? What are some alternative forms of information? Two studies, one in a book by I. T. Levykin and one by M. F. Nenashev, addressed different aspects of the first question. Levykin noted the increase in the percentages of young people on collective and state farms who attended Party lectures regularly (from 60 percent in 1964 to 73 percent in 1971). He attributed this to more free time, to better education, and to improved lecture preparation and organization.[92] A review of Nenashev's book called attention to the high percentage of people (72.2 percent in the Cheliabinsk region of the RSFSR) who said that they visited political information centers "with pleasure," but the reviewer criticized the fact that a majority of the sample (N > 2,000) attended political lectures less than nine times a year and 15.8 percent believed that political information at these lectures was irrelevant, out-of-date, and unconvincing.[93]

A different study showed the effectiveness of propaganda by a comparison of the levels of political awareness among workers who did or did not attend Party lectures. More than 90 percent of those who attended, and 65.7 percent of those who did not attend, understood the "correct" reasons for the relaxation of international tensions. The authors concluded on the basis of responses to several questions that students in the system of political education were two or three times better informed about the practical and theoretical aspects of contemporary problems[94] (see table 1.16). Of course, it is possible that the people who attended Party lectures were already more aware of political issues than those who did not. On the other hand, those who did not attend the lectures may have received their information on politics from other sources, as was the case among industrial workers. P. V. Pozdniakov reported, for example, that 94.1 percent of his sample from industrial enterprises received political information from newspapers, compared with only 25.8 percent from Party lectures[95] (see table 1.17).

At least two studies have dealt with the relationships between political consciousness and personal characteristics. In a survey of students at Moscow State University, E. G. Balagushkin and M. M. Kovaleva found that factors such as age, marital status, and the use of free time directly affected a person's involvement in, and attitudes toward, political education. "Cool" or indifferent (prokladnyi) attitudes toward Party propaganda prevailed among those students who were generally disruptive in the dormitories and less serious about their work.[96] In a more detailed analysis of personality traits, Iu. M. Orlov and B. A. Babin found that the attraction to sociopolitical work was correlated most highly with "the need to acquire authority," with "the desire for social interaction," and with "an achievement orientation" (in that order). Other important personality characteristics were the desires for status, prestige, knowledge, and creativity.[97] This was generally true for students, young work-

Table 1.16. Audience Interest and Knowledge Received in Political Education
(percentages)

Types of Seminars and Education of Audience	Audience Evaluation of Knowledge Received in Studies			Propagandist Evaluation of Audience Interest in Political Studies		
	Knowledge Noticeably Improved	Difficult to Say	Little Change in Knowledge	Deep and Strong	Superficial	Not Discernible
Types of Seminars:						
Beginning Section	56	20	5	56	44	--
Middle Section	47	20	7	40	60	--
Advanced Section	45	23	8	46	52	--
Komsomol Training	37	46	14	9	83	--
Education Level:						
Seventh-ninth grade	54	31	11	38	60	2
Secondary (general)	63	26	11	31	67	2
Secondary (specialized)	62	25	8	48	52	--
Incomplete higher	40	53	7	60	40	--
Higher education	44	41	14	38	53	--

Note: No information on the sample was given in the source (see below), pp. 196-210, but the surveys were probably conducted in city Party organizations of Tomsk, Kolpashev, Mogilev and Bobruisk, as noted in the source, p. 4. Data were drawn from two earlier studies: *Metodika i tekhnika statisticheskoi obrabotki pervichnoi sotsiologicheskoi informatsii* (Moskva and Leningrad: 1968) and *Metodika i tekhnika statisticheskoi obrabotki materialov sotsiologicheskikh issledovanii ideologicheskoi raboty* (Moskva: 1973), as cited in the source, p. 196.

Source: V. G. Baikova et al, *Politicheskoe obrazovanie: sistema, metodika, metodologiia* (Moskva: Mysl', 1976), p. 204.

ers, engineers and technical personnel, and scientists. Women and unmarried people had a slightly stronger need for sociopolitical involvement than did men and married people, regardless of social group. But the impact of Communist Party membership varied according to social groups: the workers who were most strongly motivated toward sociopolitical work tended to be Party members, whereas the engineers and technical personnel who had strong sociopolitical needs tended not to be Party members.[98]

Party propaganda is particularly effective when it is transformed into approved social activism. Such behavior often reflects a person's sense of social obligation and his or her sensitivity to peer pressures. Several studies have dealt with this issue by looking at interpersonal communication and public tolerance of social inactivism. Research in this area can be considered to be attitudinal when the data reveal the extent of a person's commitment to public activity, and his or her degree of tolerance for those who are more apathetic or passive toward violations of social norms.

The impact of peer pressure on social activism was examined by A. A. Tarasenko in his study of 1,005 workers, engineers and service personnel in Minsk. More than 90 percent of his sample (and 94.5 percent of another sample of factory workers) indicated that their behavior was affected by the opinions of the collective, and they believed that each citizen had a social duty to report violations of public order.[99] However, many of them did not actually get involved in reporting public violations, and even fewer people participated in hearings at Comrade's Courts, partly because of indifference and a reluctance to testify in front of officials.[100] Further research showed that social activism varied according to a person's education, occupation, and general cultural background. For example, those who felt that they had fulfilling and socially meaningful jobs and those with higher education and more interest in the arts tended to be more involved in community affairs.[101] A. A. Terent'ev supported these findings in his own survey at Gor'kii State University, where the students with the highest grades (and those who subsequently acquired leadership positions on their jobs) tended to be the most politically active.[102]

Elsewhere sociologists have complained about the low involvement of citizens in political work and the high tolerance of social inactivism. Some people spent as little as 4.3 percent of their spare time on political work,[103] and others (45 percent of a sample surveyed by V. M. Sokolov) failed to condemn people who deviated from the norms of "communist morality."[104] Many young people said that sometimes failure to fulfill one's obligations to society was justified, and Sokolov concluded that these respondents tended toward a more "materialistic" and "self-centered" view of life.[105] Such criticisms are offset by comparisons with earlier periods of Soviet history when social activity was much lower. Calculations by V. G. Mordkovich, for example, indicated that the amount of leisure time spent on organized public work increased from 3.3 percent in 1922-23 to 36.7 percent in 1965-66;[106] L. V. Sokhan' reported that, according to the data of E. A. Kabo, 52.4 percent of the workers in Moscow participated in public meetings in 1926 and 95 percent did so in 1972, partly as the result of an increase in leisure time.[107]

Party members must be well informed and properly trained in their role as agitators if public lectures are to be effective in raising the consciousness and activism of Soviet citizens. However, a survey of Communist Party members in twelve industrial and agricultural organizations revealed that one-third of them did not learn about the date of Party meetings until the night before, and one-third never spoke at such meetings. Many said that Party discussions had little positive results, and only 40 percent of another sample of propagandists (in Belorussia) said that they carried out their work "with pleasure" and satisfaction.[108] One difficulty that propagandists faced was the heterogeneity of the student body and the lack of correspondence between the students' educational backgrounds and the types of political lectures they attended.[109] More serious, however, was the fact that propagandists were often unprepared to lead political classes effectively, and this inhibited the development of student enthusiasm and interest[110] (see table 1.18).

Finally, we should mention that Soviet scholars have also taken inventory of the activities of government officials who, although not involved directly in Party propaganda or agitation, are dealing with the public as deputies to local soviets. A detailed analysis of time spent on regular and deputorial work, in a book by B. K. Alekseev and M. N. Perfil'ev, complements the above studies on Party activities by drawing attention to another politically active segment of Soviet society. Through a combination of demographic and attitudinal data, Alekseev and Perfil'ev did a longitudinal study of 500 deputies at the Vasileostrovskii and Moskovskii local soviets in Leningrad from 1961 to 1971. The authors analyzed their data on time expenditures and on deputy attitudes in terms of social position, social origin, Party affiliation, education, age, and sex. Many of the survey questions were designed to identify the perceptions of deputies toward the electorate, toward social and political organizations, and toward the effectiveness and personal satisfaction of their work[111] (see tables 1.19, 1.20, and 1.21).

Ethnicity and Foreign Cultures

The most important Soviet research on attitudes toward one's own nationality and toward other ethnic groups has been conducted in recent years by the Sociology Section of the Institute of Ethnography, USSR Academy of Sciences. The data discussed below represent the published portions of a continuing project at that institute on "Optimization of the Sociocultural Development and the Coming Together of Nations in the USSR," under the leadership of Iu. V. Arutiunian. Partially standardized surveys have been carried out in Moldavia, the Tatar A.S.S.R., the Karelian A.S.S.R., and Georgia for cross-regional com-

Table 1.17. Sources of Political Information in Moscow
(percentages)

Source	Respondents Using this Source
Newspapers	94.1
Television	74.0
Radio	71.8
Magazines	33.6
Discussions at work	29.0
Lectures	25.8
Literature	22.8
Political reports	18.7
Discussions with friends	17.6
Documentary movies	13.6
Meetings at the collective	12.5
Discussions with relatives	11.1

Note: Based on a sample of more than 1,300 workers, service personnel, engineer-technical and scientific workers at a series of industrial enterprises in Moscow.

Source: P. V. Pozdniakov, *Effektivnost' kommunisticheskoi propagandy* (Moskva: Politizdat, 1975), p. 81.

Table 1.18. The Attitudes of Propagandists toward Their Work

Desire of Propagandists to Conduct Propaganda Work	Audience Satisfaction with the Organization of Political Studies[b]			
	Percentage[a]	Yes	Sometimes	No	No Response
I work with desire and I feel satisfied	45	72	23	1	4
I work with desire, but I do not feel adequately prepared	31	65	23	2	10
I work with desire, but I do not see the results	22	65	25	4	6
I work without desire	1	77	8	8	7
No answer	1	80	15	5	--

Note: Data drawn from surveys of city Party organizations in the Tomsk region of the RSFSR.
[a]Percentage of all propagandists interviewed.
[b]In percentages for each response by propagandists.

Source: V. G. Baikova et al., *Politicheskoe obrazovanie: sistema, metodika, metodologiia* (Moskva: Mysl', 1976), p. 222.

Table 1.19. Party Status and Work Satisfaction among Deputies in Local Soviets
(percentages)

Conditions Necessary for Work Satisfaction	Party Status							
	Party Member		Party Candidate		Komsomol Member		No Party Affiliation	
	1969	1971	1969	1971	1969	1971	1969	1971
Social significance (prestige) of the work	15.8	11.0	17.9	3.2	20.0	5.3	1.6	8.0
Opportunity to develop one's initiative and creativity	14.6	14.8	14.8	16.2	10.0	10.9	11.8	11.5
Independence and responsibility in work fulfillment	17.7	19.9	14.8	22.6	20.0	19.5	19.5	18.8
Participation in organizations administering the work process	7.8	7.3	5.8	3.2	----	1.5	6.3	3.1
Opportunity to raise one's qualifications and professional growth	8.6	8.8	8.8	3.2	20.0	14.8	11.9	13.9
Level of pay	10.0	8.6	11.7	16.2	20.0	13.6	14.7	12.6
Prospects for advancement at work	4.2	3.1	5.8	3.2	----	3.7	4.9	3.9
Absence of overexertion in labor	4.2	4.7	5.8	9.7	----	5.3	6.8	6.3
Presence of a creative collective	8.5	10.1	5.8	3.2	----	8.7	8.3	7.4
Concern of the administration for the creation of necessary conditions of labor	8.6	11.7	8.8	19.3	10.0	16.7	14.2	14.5
Total	100	100	100	100	100	100	100	100
Percentage of 1969 or 1971 sample according to Party status	56.2	50.2	1.2	1.6	0.6	14.2	42.0	34.0

Note: Table is based on answers to the question: "What, in your opinion, is necessary for obtaining satisfaction in work?" Answers to the same question are broken down by social position (in the source below, p. 162), by social origin (in the source, pp. 180 - 81), by education (in the source, pp. 215-17), by age (in the source, pp. 248-49), and by sex (in the source, p. 278). In each case, the authors also provide a percentage breakdown for the entire sample(s).

Source: B. K. Alekseev and M. N. Perfil'ev, *Printsipy i tendentsii razvitiia predstavitel'nogo sostava mestnykh sovetov* (Leningrad: Lenizdat, 1976), pp. 196-97.

Table 1.20. Difficulties Faced by Deputies in Local Soviets According to Social Position
(percentages)

Difficulties Noted by Local Deputies	Social Position					
	Workers		Intelligentsia		Employees[a]	
	1969	1971	1969	1971	1969	1971
Inadequate general education and cultural level	4.8	4.2	----	0.2	1.4	----
Weakness of professional preparation	2.0	5.0	0.2	0.4	----	3.1
Ignorance of the basics in administration and legislation	8.2	9.6	3.4	5.4	11.0	12.5
Little life experience	1.6	7.5	0.8	1.0	----	15.7
Absence of organizational skills	6.0	6.4	0.4	0.4	1.4	6.2
Little experience in deputorial activities	13.4	20.4	5.6	10.6	11.0	15.7
Overload in basic work	15.6	14.0	31.8	36.2	24.6	9.4
Overload of social commissions	7.2	4.6	13.0	14.4	9.6	3.1
Remoteness of election district from residence or from place of work	8.4	8.4	7.2	5.8	8.2	9.4
Limitation of deputy rights	11.6	6.2	17.0	9.8	8.2	9.4
Apathy of voters in the district	5.8	4.0	7.8	6.0	9.6	6.2
Absence of proper information on the status of business in election neighborhoods, in enterprises, and institutions	2.4	2.0	2.0	2.4	1.4	----

Table 1.20 Continued

	1969	1971	1969	1971	1969	1971
Inattentiveness of separate executive organs and officials to questions presented to deputies	5.2	3.4	7.0	5.6	8.2	3.1
Inadequate help in work from the standing commissions and executive committees	0.8	0.1	0.4	0.4	2.6	- - -
Inadequate help in work from local Party, mass and independent social organizations	3.4	2.2	1.8	1.0	1.4	3.1
Constant help from local institutions in organizing the work of deputies	3.6	2.0	1.6	0.4	1.4	3.1
Total	100	100	100	100	100	100
Percentage of 1969 or 1971 sample in each social position	50.0	57.6	45.2	40.2	4.8	2.2

aWhite-collar personnel (*sluzhashchie*)

Note: Table is based on answers to the question: "What kind of difficulties do you find in your work?" Answers to the same question are broken down by Party membership (in the source below, pp. 204-205), by education (in the source, pp. 232-35), by age (in the source, pp. 264-67), and by sex (in the source, pp. 283-84). In each case, the authors also provide a percentage breakdown for the entire sample(s).

Source: B. K. Alekseev and M. N. Perfil'ev, *Printsipy i tendentsii razvitiia predstavitel'nogo sostava mestnykh sovetov* (Leningrad: Lenizdat, 1976), pp. 170-71.

Table 1.21. Party Status and Attitudes of Local Deputies toward the Usefulness of Their Work
(percentages)

	Party Status							
	Party Member		Party Candidate		Komsomol Member		No Party Affiliation	
Useful Aspects of Deputy Work	1969	1971	1969	1971	1969	1971	1969	1971
Work with the mandate of the voters	16.7	16.3	15.8	26.4	33.3	15.1	18.5	18.5
Receiving voters, consideration of complaints and proposals	20.4	23.0	26.3	42.2	----	28.4	23.4	25.7
Preparation of questions for sessions of the Soviet	8.6	7.0	5.3	----	----	3.1	6.3	6.5
Preparation of questions for the Soviet's executive committee	8.4	8.7	5.3	----	----	5.0	6.3	4.6
Work with the standing commissions	22.3	18.1	15.8	15.7	50.0	27.7	26.0	26.4
Implementation in the election district of decisions made by the Soviet and its executive committee	8.4	10.3	10.5	15.7	----	9.4	6.7	8.0
Verification of the fulfillment of government resolutions and decisions made by central and local organs	10.0	10.7	10.5	----	----	6.9	4.4	7.0
Agitation and propaganda work in the election district	5.2	5.9	10.5	----	16.7	4.4	4.0	3.3
Total	100	100	100	100	100	100	100	100
Percentage of 1969 or 1971 sample according to Party status	56.2	50.2	1.2	1.6	0.6	14.2	42.0	34.0

Note: Table is based on answers to the question: "Which area of your activities as a deputy do you consider the most fruitful?" Answers to the same question are broken down by social position (in the source below, pp. 168-69), by education (in the source, pp. 225-27), by age (in the source, pp. 257-59), and by sex (in the source, p. 281). In each case, the authors also provide a percentage breakdown for the entire sample(s).

Source: B. K. Alekseev and M. N. Perfil'ev, *Printsipy i tendentsii razvitiia predstavitel'nogo sostava mestnykh sovetov* (Leningrad: Lenizdat, 1976), p. 202.

parisons of the components of ethnicity, the observance of ethnic rituals, and the causes and consequences of bilingualism.[112]

A survey taken in 1974, and reported in an article by G. V. Starovoitova, tried to identify those factors which people considered to be the main components of ethnicity. People in three towns of the Tatar A.S.S.R. (Kazan', Al'met'-evsk, and Menzelinsk) were asked by Tatar interviewers, "What, in your opinion, should be the main factor in determining a person's nationality?" Responses differed according to a person's education and socioeconomic status. In general, 47 percent of the sample cited the nationality of the father as the most important factor. The more educated and younger Tatars placed greater emphasis on the way a person himself defined his nationality. When asked about the most distinguishing feature of ethnic groups, those with lower socioeconomic status chose external manifestations such as language ability, while the more educated more often chose characteristics of personality. Physical characteristics were not frequently selected because racial mixing has resulted in relatively few distinctions between the physical appearances of Tatars and Russians.[113]

When asked if they recognized members of their own ethnic group on the city streets by their external appearances, 25 percent of the Tatars thought that they recognized members of their own nationality easily (despite racial mixing), 38 percent believed that they sometimes recognized members of their own nationality, 19 percent said they did not recognize them, and 18 percent said they did not pay attention to the nationalities of passersby. People with less education were more likely to respond that they could recognize other Tatars, while those with higher education were more likely to say that they did not pay attention to the nationalities of passersby. Respondents from smaller towns where there had been less of an ethnic mix claimed to notice nationalities more.[114]

With regard to the observance of ethnic rituals, the same study showed that more educated people were less likely to celebrate ethnic holidays, although they still observed funeral rites. There was a generational division in the observance of rituals between those born prior to the collectivization of the Tatar A.S.S.R. in 1930-34 and those born after it. More interesting, perhaps, was the fact that Tatars who had grown up outside the Tatar A.S.S.R. demonstrated stronger ties with Tatar culture than did those who had lived only within the Tatar A.S.S.R. This may be due to the effects of propaganda campaigns in the autonomous republic against Tatar rituals.[115] (From the published analysis it was not clear whether or not the group growing up outside the Tatar A.S.S.R. was controlled for the effects of age and education, cited as variables above.) The implication of the study was that Soviet ethnic administrative units may be sources of ethnic pride and may help to keep nationality self-identification alive; while at the same time the media campaigns within autonomous republics may contribute to the disappearance of specific ethnic customs and rituals.[116]

A third characteristic of ethnic studies in the USSR is the attention given to the origins and consequences of bilingualism. Surveys have revealed aspects of bilingualism not seen previously in Soviet census data. A 1971 study of Moldavia by S. I. Bruk and M. N. Guboglo showed, for example, that the degree of bilingualism was greater than had been reported in the 1970 census. An overwhelming majority of Moldavians were able to hold a conversation in Russian with adequate fluency, especially those who were younger and better educated. More Russians in the Moldavian S.S.R. knew Moldavian than had been reported in the census data, although they spoke Moldavian more poorly than Moldavians spoke Russian. Significant for the retention of ethnic identity was the fact that when Moldavians knew Russian, they used it at work, but they continued to speak Moldavian at home.[117]

Initially, the school system served as the place for Moldavians to learn Russian, as might be expected. But earlier survey data failed to show the importance of informal relationships in this process. The acquisition of the second language occurred also outside the formal workplace, usually among friends. Apparently, contacts with friends were far more significant for learning both languages than was army experience, one's family of origin, or adult classroom instruction (see table 1.22). This was true both for Moldavians learning Russian and for Russians learning Moldavian.[118]

The consequences of language training in Russian schools were seen in a study of the media habits of rural Tatars. Tatars learn Russian both in Tatar-language schools and in Russian-language schools, and they presumably acquire greater Russian fluency in the latter. However, their use of Russian or Tatar after school is largely a cultural choice and may reflect the impact of the school on their cultural identity and on their general way of life. Rural Tatars who graduated from Russian-language schools read more in Russian, listened to the radio more in Russian, and watched television programs in Russian more often than did those who graduated from Tatar-language schools.[119]

With regard to their daily cultural habits, bilingualism among rural Tatars seemed to encourage them to read more in general and to watch more television in general, but in the absence of controls in the Tatar data for education or income, it is difficult to know whether bilingualism per se caused greater media exposure[120] (see table 1.23). A 1971 poll in Moldavia and an additional survey in the city of Kishinev in 1973 did control for such factors, in order to demonstrate that Moldavians speaking Russian were more interested in their studies and in upward mobility. Moldavians who did not speak Russian were more interested in activities around the house and were less likely to give "content" to their leisure time, i.e., to attend movies, concerts and plays, to listen to the radio, to watch television, to read newspapers, and to study.[121]

Bilingualism tended to increase the amount of time a person spent reading newspapers, watching television, listening to the radio, and reading fiction. This was true even when controlling for education levels and for socioeconomic status. The impact of bilingualism was greater, however, for workers than for the intelligentsia, especially with regard to the choice of television programs.

Table 1.22. Acquisition of Proficiency in a Second Language in Cities of Moldavia
(percentages)

| Nationality and Age Groups | "If you know a second language (Russian for Moldavians, Moldavian for Russians) where did you acquire it?" | | | | | |
	School	Army	Family of Origin	Contact with Friends	Higher Educational Institution	N
Moldavians:						
18-19 years	84.5	----	11.9	21.4	10.7	217
20-24 years	75.2	9.9	8.0	24.3	15.9	553
25-29 years	68.9	18.5	11.3	24.4	11.8	321
30-39 years	48.6	15.0	12.3	33.3	7.4	1139
40-49 years	33.0	21.1	10.7	39.9	5.3	350
50-59 years	21.9	14.8	16.3	42.3	4.1	195
60 and older	17.1	10.2	12.2	42.4	----	170
Total	53.0	14.4	11.0	32.7	9.0	2359
Russians:						
18-19 years	41.1	----	13.7	24.7	2.7	60
20-24 years	33.0	----	9.3	20.5	4.2	147
25-29 years	21.7	----	8.3	24.2	3.2	93
30-39 years	18.3	----	9.9	26.3	----	558
40-49 years	15.6	----	8.2	28.8	----	230
50-59 years	11.3	----	8.5	33.1	----	163
60 and older	9.7	----	11.6	24.6	----	227
Total	18.1	----	10.0	26.9	2.0	1057

Note: (1) In every age category some of the respondents indicated more than one place of acquisition of a second language. (2) Among the Moldavians in the older age categories and among Russians in all age categories, some of the respondents were unable to say where they had acquired a second language. In the first instance, the percentages total more than 100 percent; in the second, less than 100 percent. Data are for 1971.

Source: S. I. Bruk and M. N. Guboglo, "Faktory rasprostraneniia dvuiazychiia i narodov SSSR (po materialam etnosotsiologicheskikh issledovanii)," Sovetskaia etnografiia, 1975, no. 5, p. 26.

Table 1.23. Linguistic Behavior of Rural Tatars
(percentages)

Forms of Linguistic Behavior	Type of School	
	Those Who Graduated from a School in which Russian was the Language of Instruction	Those who Graduated from a School in which Tatar was the Language of Instruction
In which language is fiction usually read?		
Tatar	3.3	27.4
Russian	55.7	16.2
Both	41.0	56.4
In which language are radio and television programs listened to or viewed?		
Tatar	- - - -	14.1
Russian	31.1	7.1
Both	68.9	78.8
Which language is most often spoken at work?		
Tatar	11.0	48.1
Russian	47.5	17.3
Both	41.5	34.6
Which language is most often spoken at home?		
Tatar	34.4	77.6
Russian	27.9	2.5
Both	37.7	19.9

Note: N equals 302 (61 who graduated from schools with Russian instruction and 241 from schools with Tatar instruction). The table refers to rural Tatars who have a better command of Russian than they do of Tatar or an equal command of both.

Source: S. I. Bruk and M. N. Guboglo, "Faktory rasprostraneniia dvuiazychiia i narodov SSSR (po materialam etnosotsiologicheskikh issledovanii)," *Sovetskaia etnografiia*, 1975, no. 5, p. 27.

Moldavian workers were five times less likely to watch literary programs if they did not know Russian. On the other hand, bilingualism did not change the program preferences of the intelligentsia, except that intellectuals were twice as likely to watch scientific and technical programs if they knew Russian.[122]

A person's choice of literature, regardless of the language in which it was written, was also affected by his knowledge of two languages. Bilinguals read more in their areas of professional specialization and more political literature than did unilinguals, who were more likely to read fiction concerning World War II, adventure stories, and detective and historical novels. Bilingualism affected a person's preference for Russian and other cultural products other than his own. Bilingual Moldavians, for example, more often chose the Russian classics and such plays as Tennessee Williams' *A Streetcar Named Desire* instead of Moldavian plays, and they preferred Russian films to Moldavian films.[123] A 1972 survey of the urban population of the Karelian A.S.S.R. showed that Karelians who knew Russian had less knowledge of Karelian culture and liked Karelian culture less than they did Soviet culture and less than those who did not know Russian[124] (see table 1.24). A general preference for non-Karelian culture was evident in the older generations as well as among young people, although the older groups showed a preference for traditional Russian folk culture whereas the younger groups liked urban contemporary Soviet cultural forms better[125] (see table 1.25).

In general, these studies show a concern with the impact of Russian language training on the cultural identities and preferences of different ethnic groups. The observance of ethnic rituals and issues of ethnic identity are related directly to bilingualism and suggest that in some ways ethnic differences may be breaking down.

CONCLUSION

Soviet sociologists have continued to expand their research efforts since the 1960s, despite the political restrictions of the early 1970s. Although it remains uneven, the quality of research has gradually improved in recent years, and apparently the best work is still being published. While the most important work is done at the institutes of the USSR Academy of Sciences and at other scholarly organizations, social research is conducted in a variety of institutions geographically dispersed throughout the Soviet Union. It is too soon, thus far, to assess the full impact of greater central coordination on the future content and quality of survey research in the USSR.

The absence of complete information on methodologies and sampling techniques makes it difficult to draw general conclusions from the various studies, but we can make a few observations about them. First, recent survey data reveal the continuing importance of socioeconomic status and educational

Table 1.24. Influence of Linguistic Characteristics on Ethnic-Cultural Orientations
(percentages)

Ethnic-Cultural Orientations	Linguistic Characteristics				
	Speaks Fluently		Speaks Both Fluently	Considered Native	
	Karelian	Russian		Karelian	Russian
a) Those who do not know Karelian folk dances	40.0	69.9	53.8	46.1	72.4
b) Those who like					
Karelian folk dances	14.9	3.5	9.6	10.7	1.7
Russian folk dances	47.5	34.4	42.4	40.3	35.6
Ballet	16.3	25.0	25.8	25.5	23.4
Contemporary dances	17.7	31.5	17.3	19.0	33.5
c) Those who do not know Karelian folk songs	61.8	80.0	64.0	64.9	85.0
d) Those who like					
Karelian folk songs	11.9	2.9	6.2	9.1	1.8
Russian folk songs	56.6	38.2	55.4	51.1	39.6
Contemporary Soviet songs	25.2	48.2	32.9	33.8	48.8
e) Those who prefer to listen to					
Karelian folk music	11.5	2.7	6.3	7.3	1.5
Russian folk music	63.3	37.7	52.8	53.7	36.0
Classical, symphonic music	2.9	9.2	9.9	8.2	11.1
Popular music	20.1	48.2	27.8	28.1	49.9

Source: E. I. Klement'ev, "Natsional'no-kul'turnye orientatsii karel'skogo gorodskogo naseleniia," *Sovetskaia etnografiia*, 1976, no. 4, p. 66.

Table 1.25. Relationships between Age and Cultural-Evaluative Orientations
(percentages)

Cultural-Evaluative Orientations	Age Groups							
	16-19 years N=90	20-24 years N=137	25-29 years N=102	30-34 years N=164	35-39 years N=182	40-49 years N=317	50-59 years N=142	60 or more years N=28
a) Those who do not know Karelian folk dances	76.2	67.8	59.1	46.0	48.8	39.5	25.8	36.7
b) Those who like								
Karelian folk dances	0.9	5.2	6.4	2.5	7.1	9.1	15.0	36.0
Russian folk dances	6.1	14.3	16.6	43.1	47.0	53.1	58.5	48.0
Ballet	21.9	24.0	27.5	30.6	25.7	25.3	17.0	4.0
Contemporary dances	65.8	53.9	38.5	16.9	14.8	7.2	3.4	4.0
c) Those who do not know Karelian folk songs	81.8	82.0	74.0	66.5	69.7	66.3	60.4	62.4
d) Those who like								
Karelian folk songs	1.7	3.2	0.9	6.1	6.3	5.2	11.1	17.2
Russian folk songs	11.1	23.4	33.6	54.7	53.0	61.6	64.7	69.0
Contemporary Soviet songs	76.1	59.5	57.8	34.3	34.3	27.1	19.6	6.9
e) Those who like								
Karelian folk music	0.0	1.5	1.5	17.9	11.9	34.3	22.4	17.9
Russian folk music	11.5	14.5	27.7	46.8	52.8	66.9	68.9	67.9
Classical, symphonic music	3.8	11.8	12.5	10.5	10.6	6.7	6.8	6.0
Popular music	84.6	69.7	57.1	32.7	28.1	16.4	11.5	0.0

Source: E. I. Klement'ev, "Natsional'no-kul'turnye orientatsii karel'skogo gorodskogo naseleniia," *Sovetskaia etnografiia*, 1976, no. 3, p. 61.

levels in the formation of public attitudes and behavior. Second is the attention given by sociologists to the way Soviet citizens conduct their lives. Many survey questions are based on the assumption that each person ought to lead a productive and socially useful life. Answers to these questions show, however, that efforts to instill officially approved patterns of social behavior are counterbalanced by the citizens' more personalized concerns and by informal channels of communication.

The interrelationship of socioeconomic status and educational levels was seen in the studies that dealt with the impact of family backgrounds on the career aspirations of youth. The growing heterogeneity of socioeconomic status within the family has contributed to an incremental pace of upward mobility. Young people seem to be very conscious of the status associated with certain occupations, and this becomes an important motivating factor in their career choices. The leisure time and media habits of people also vary according to their social status and education. The same variables affect the way a person defines ethnic identity, and they interact with bilingualism in influencing the reading habits and cultural preferences of ethnic minorities.

Soviet citizens are encouraged through the mass media to conduct their lives in a manner that is productive, both at work and in their use of leisure time. Surveys on work emphasize the importance of job satisfaction, not only for personal fulfillment, but also for a reduction of labor turnover. Meanwhile, the results of surveys on education show that job satisfaction and labor productivity often depend on the career orientations of youth and on the training which students acquire before they enter the work force. Many of the attitudes toward leisure activities also are formed during the educational process. Officially, the use of leisure time is expected to be "productive" in the sense of fostering a public-mindedness among citizens and a constructive or creative use of one's skills. Yet, the actual behavior of Soviet youth and adults does not coincide with the "rational time budget" prescribed by sociologists.

As in other societies, there seems to be a natural tension between the personal interests of individual citizens and their social obligations. Many respondents in the surveys demonstrated less than a full commitment to social activism and political involvement. This was evident in the reluctance of people to testify at Comrade's Courts and in the selective attention given by the public to local newspapers and to political lectures. Propagandists seem to have some difficulties in the political education and mobilization of their audiences. Instead, people tend to be influenced more by informal channels of communication in a variety of ways, from peer approval or disapproval of their social activities, to their media habits and the learning of a second language.

A third observation is that Soviet survey research serves both as a feedback mechanism and as an inventory of changing social conditions. In many of the surveys, sociologists try to elicit the public's response to official information and to cultural products disseminated through the mass media. Knowledge of the effectiveness of formal communication channels is potentially useful for the packaging of future materials. At the same time, surveys can reveal social trends in such areas as family planning, ethnic relations, and the mores of youth. Many of the social conditions discussed above (for example, automation, changing roles within the family, an increase in leisure time and in media exposure) are not unique to the Soviet Union, but are typical characteristics of modern industrial societies. While the initial enthusiasm of Soviet sociologists and social planners for survey research as a *deus ex machina* in the identification of mass attitudes and in policies of social conditioning has been toned down considerably, these data may still provide a valuable input to the formation of social policies.

APPENDIX: SCIENTIFIC-RESEARCH SECTIONS OF THE
SOVIET SOCIOLOGICAL ASSOCIATION

Sociological Problems of Labor
Sociological Problems of the Family and Style of Life
Sociology of Culture
Sociology of the Problems of the Village
Ethno-Sociological Research
On the Means of Mass Information, the Effectiveness of Ideological Work and
    Public Opinion
Time Budgets of Laborers
Sociology of Education
Social Planning and Forecasting
Sociological Problems of Science
Sociology of Politics and International Relations
Social Structure of Soviet Society
Sociological Problems of City Planning and of Architecture
Sociological Problems of Demography
Sociological Problems of Law and Criminology
On the Problems of Social Psychology
On the Methods and Techniques of Sociological Research
Sociology of Developing Nations
Sociological Problems of Physical Culture and Sports
Sociological Problems of "Automobilization"
Sociolinguistics
On the History of Sociology
Sociology of Regional and Urban Development
Sociological Problems of Youth
Social Problems of Religion

Source: M. N. Topalov, "Sovetskaia sotsiologicheskaia assotsiatsiia AN SSSR,"
Sotsiologicheskie issledovaniia, 1977, no. 4, pp. 174-75.

NOTES

* We want to express our appreciation to Murray Feshbach for his advice in the location of materials and to Bruce Cooper for his research assistance.

1. Although the Soviet Sociological Association was established in 1958, the Institute of Concrete Social Research was not formed until 1968. The latter was reorganized into the Institute of Sociological Research in 1972. For further details, see Dmitri Shalin, "The Development of Soviet Sociology, 1956-1976," *Annual Review of Sociology*, vol. 4 (Palo Alto, California: Annual Reviews, Inc., 1978), pp. 171-91.

2. Institut sotsiologicheskikh issledovanii A.N. S.S.S.R., Sovetskaia sotsiologicheskaia assotsiatsiia, *Sotsiologicheskie tsentry S.S.S.R.* (Moskva: Institut sotsiologicheskikh issledovanii, 1976). A recent report divides the network of sociological research centers into 1) the academies of sciences and universities, 2) Party institutions, and 3) industrial enterprises. See U.S. International Communication Agency, *Soviet Research Institutes Project: Interim Report* (R-31-78), prepared by Blair Ruble, The Kennan Institute, Washington, D.C., November 1978, pp. 627-28. (Typewritten.)

3. Surveys on crime are not included in this chapter. For a discussion of Soviet research on crime, see Peter Solomon, "Specialists in Soviet Policy Making: Criminal Policy, 1938-70," in *Social Scientists and Policy Making in the U.S.S.R.*, edited by Richard Remnek (New York: Praeger Publishers, 1977), esp. pp. 15-18.

4. L. I. Brezhnev, "Rech' na iubileinoi sessii A.N. S.S.S.R.," *Pravda*, October 8, 1977, p. 1. The "main directions and tasks" are set by the Presidium of the USSR Academy of Sciences. See its "Directive" of December 22, 1977, "Concerning the Activity of the Sector of Philosophy and Law of the USSR Academy of Sciences" in "Kompleksnaia programma nauchnykh rabot—osnova dal'-neishego razvitiia sovetskoi sotsiologicheskoi nauki," *Sotsiologicheskie issledovaniia*, 1978, no. 2, pp. 3-11. See also T. V. Riabushkin, "XXV s'ezd KPSS i zadachi dal'neishego razvitiia sotsiologicheskikh issledovanii," *Sotsiologicheskie issledovaniia*, 1977, no. 2, pp. 3-13.

5. "Vysokii dolg sovetskikh filosofov," *Pravda*, September 19, 1975, p. 2; "Sotsiologicheskie issledovaniia—na sluzhbu stroitel'stva kommunizma," *Sotsiologicheskie issledovaniia*, 1976, no. 2, pp. 3-9; V. I. Chuprov and V. P. Shchenev, *Sotsiologicheskaia informatsiia i prakticheskie voprosy koordinatsionnoi raboty v oblasti sotsiologii* (Moskva: Institut sotsiologicheskikh issledovanii, 1977), pp. 9-30.

6. Chuprov and Shchenev, pp. 23-24.

7. V. S. Paniukov and V. M. Golovatiuk, "Sotsial'naia pasportizatsiia trudovikh resursov goroda," *Sotsiologicheskie issledovaniia*, 1978, no. 3, pp. 185-92.

8. V. E. Shliapentokh, "Problemy reprezentativnosti sotsiologicheskoi informatsii," *Sotsiologicheskie issledovaniia*, 1976, no. 2, pp. 3-9.

9. I. V. Muchnik et al., "Problemy postroeniia vsesoiuznoi territorial'noi vyborki dlia sotsiologicheskikh issledovanii," *Sotsiologicheskie issledovaniia*, 1978, no. 1, pp. 162-69.

10. G. V. Osipov et al., eds., *Rabochaia kniga sotsiologa* (Moskva: Nauka, 1976), pp. 34-40.

11. V. Shubkin noted in a recent article, for example, that sociologists had won the trust of the employees of an institute by proclaiming that the goal of their research was the improvement of the institute's "psychological climate." The staff members, believing these assurances, thought that the confidential ratings of their colleagues would be used only for these purposes. But the comments about their colleagues were used as the basis of demotions and dismissals. V. Shubkin, "Granitsy," *Novy mir*, February 1978, pp. 187-217.

12. V. V. Ksenofontova, "Kharakternye cherty sotsial'noi orientatsii podrastaiushchego pokoleniia razvitogo sotsialisticheskogo obshchestva," in *Sotsial'-naia i professional'naia orientatsiia molodezhi i problemy kommunisticheskogo vospitaniia*, edited by M. Kh. Titma (Tallinn: Institut sotsiologicheskikh issledovanii A.N. S.S.S.R. and Institut istorii A.N. E.S.S.R., 1977); S. G. Vershlovskii and L. N. Lesokhina, "Rabochaia molodezh' i obrazovanie," *Sotsiologicheskie issledovaniia*, 1975, no. 2, pp. 90-99; M. Kh. Titma, "Formirovanie zhiznennykh orientatsii uchashcheisia molodezhi (na materialykh Estonskoi S.S.S.R.)," *Sotsiologicheskie issledovaniia*, 1977, no. 3, pp. 52-59.

13. In 1977 there were 2,550 individual members and 460 institutional members of the Soviet Sociological Association. M. N. Topalov, "Sovetskaia sotsiologicheskaia assotsiatsiia A.N. S.S.S.R.," *Sotsiologicheskie issledovaniia*, 1977, no. 4, p. 172.

14. A. I. Demidova, "Professional'naia podgotovka sotsiologicheskikh kadrov," *Sotsiologicheskie issledovaniia*, 1978, no. 3, p. 203.

15. The journal *Sotsiologicheskie issledovaniia* has been issued quarterly since July 1974 by the Institute of Sociological Research, USSR Academy of Sciences.

16. A. V. Zhavoronkov, "Potreblenie materialov gorodskoi gazety," in *Sotsiologicheskie problemy obshchestvennogo mneniia i deiatel'nosti sredstv massovoi informatsii*, edited by V. S. Korobeinikov (Moskva: Institut sotsiologicheskikh issledovanii, 1976), pp. 55, 57, 61.

17. *Chelovek, piatiletka, pressa* (Voronezh: Izdatel'stvo Voronezhskogo universiteta, 1976).

18. L. Vybornov, "Obshchestvennaia tribuna," in *Chelovek, piatiletka, pressa*, pp. 176, 174.

19. The "honors" section of the newspaper is where individuals and groups of citizens are praised for their special achievements or social contributions.

20. I. Sukhochev, "Moral'noe pooshchrenie peredovikov sorevnovaniia," in *Chelovek, piatiletka, pressa*, p. 182.

21. A. A. Vozmitel', "Formirovanie obshchestvennogo mneniia v razvitom sotsialisticheskom obshchestve," in *Sotsiologicheskie problemy obshchest-

vennogo mneniia, pp. 48-49.

22. M. I. Zhabskii, "Sotsiologiia kino: opyt i problemy," *Sotsiologicheskie issledovaniia*, 1977, no. 4, pp. 105-108.

23. S. A. Davtian, "O vliianii predvaritel'noi informatsii na vybor fil'ma," *Sotsiologicheskie issledovaniia*, 1977, no. 1, pp. 105-106.

24. V. N. Gritchin, "Molodezh i kino," in *Sotsiologicheskie problemy kul'tury* (Moskva: Institut sotsiologicheskikh issledovanii, 1976), p. 68.

25. A. N. Dolzhanskaia, "Vystavka i ee posetitel'," in *Sotsiologicheskie problemy kul'tury*, pp. 112-13.

26. V. I. Laidmiae, *Izobrazitel'noe isskustvo i ego zritel'* (Tallinn: Eesti Raamat, 1976), pp. 83, 117, 187-88.

27. Zhabskii, pp. 108-109.

28. B. M. Firsov and K. Muzdybaev, "K postroeniiu sistemy pokazatelei ispol'zovaniia sredstv massovoi kommunikatsii," *Sotsiologicheskie issledovaniia*, 1975, no. 1, p. 177.

29. L. N. Kogan, "Sblizhenie sotsial'nykh grupp v sfere sotsialisticheskoi kul'tury," *Sotsiologicheskie issledovaniia*, 1977, no. 2, p. 38.

30. This figure was comparable in other cities. See Firsov and Muzdybaev, p. 115.

31. Dan Fisher, "Change Is In The Air On Soviet TV," *The Washington Post*, January 21, 1979, p. K2.

32. A. G. Kharchev, *Brak i sem'ia v S.S.S.R.: opyt sotsiologicheskikh issledovanii* (Moskva: Mysl', 1964).

33. V. T. Kolokol'nikov, "Brachno-semeinye otnosheniia v srede kolkhoznogo krest'ianstva," *Sotsiologicheskie issledovaniia*, 1976, no. 3, p. 80. Although it is known, historically, that economic conditions played an important role in the formation of families among peasants and others, without comparable data for the pre-1917 period, it is impossible to know the relative significance of love, economic pressures, and other factors in family life.

34. V. G. Alekseeva, "Neformal'nye gruppy podrostkov v usloviiakh goroda," *Sotsiologicheskie issledovaniia*, 1977, no. 3, pp. 64-65.

35. Kolokol'nikov, p. 81.

36. L. V. Chuiko, *Braki i razvody* (Moskva: Statistika, 1975), p. 90.

37. I. Iu. Rodzinskaia, "Vlianie starshego pokoleniia na stabil'nost' molodoi sem'i," in *Vzaimootnoshenie pokolenii v sem'e*, edited by Z. A. Iankova and V. D. Shapiro (Moskva: Institut sotsiologicheskikh issledovanii, 1977), p. 85.

38. Chuiko, p. 90; Rodzinskaia, p. 89.

39. V. L. Ruzhzhe, I. I. Eliseeva, and T. S. Kadibur, "Opyt issledovaniia semeinykh grupp," *Sotsiologicheskie issledovaniia*, 1976, no. 1, pp. 115-17, 120.

40. Rodzinskaia, pp. 90, 93.

41. A. I. Antonov and A. N. Krivoruchko, "Opyt analiza vzaimootnoshenii suprugov," in *Problemy sotsiologicheskogo izucheniia sem'i*, edited by Z. A. Iankova (Moskva: Institut sotsiologicheskikh issledovanii, 1976), p. 145 and *passim*.

42. Z. A. Iankova and P. A. Protasova, "Sovremennaia struktura vnutrise-meinykh otnoshenii," in *Problemy sotsiologicheskogo izucheniia sem'i*, pp. 38-40.

43. V. A. Belova, *Chislo detei v sem'e* (Moskva: Statistika, 1975); *Skol'ko detei budet v sovetskoi sem'e* (Moskva: Statistika, 1977).

44. *Skol'ko detei budet*, p. 24.

45. Belova, pp. 133-35, 167-68; *Skol'ko detei budet*, p. 72.

46. Kolokol'nikov, pp. 81-85; Chuiko, pp. 139-40.

47. In their study of 9,000 boys and girls completing secondary education in the Lithuanian S.S.R., Gentvainite and others documented a tendency toward the reproduction of the social statum of the intelligentsia. (See table 1.9.) This was evident particularly in homogeneous families of specialists, in which at least 70 percent of the graduates aspired to a specialty requiring higher education. V. Gentvainite, A. Matulenis, and M. Tal'iunaite, "Sotsial'naia orientatsiia vypusknikov srednikh shkol," *Sotsiologicheskie issledovaniia*, 1977, no. 2, pp. 74-75.

48. F. R. Filippov, "Rol' vysshei shkoly v izmenenii sotsial'noi struktury sovet-skogo obshchestva (itogi vsesoiuznogo issledovaniia)," *Sotsiologicheskie issledo-vaniia*, 1977, no. 2, pp. 44, 47. This was part of a study conducted under M. N. Rutkevich at the Institute of Sociological Research between 1973-75, called "Vysshaia shkola kak faktor izmeneniia sotsial'noi struktury razvitogo sotsial-isticheskogo obshchestva."

49. Filippov, pp. 45, 48-49. Data from Sverdlovsk and Nizhnii Tagil showed that only half as many tenth graders planned to attend a *vuz*, whereas the percent-age wanting a secondary specialized education almost tripled.

50. V. Gentvainite, A. Matulenis, and M. Tal'iunaite, "Sotsial'naia orientatsiia vypusknikov srednikh shkol," *Sotsiologicheskie issledovaniia*, 1977, no. 2, pp. 74-75.

51. Filippov, pp. 49-50.

52. V. I. Brudnyi and A. B. Kaganov, "Sotsial'nye istochniki formirovaniia studenchestva," *Sotsiologicheskie issledovaniia*, 1977, no. 2, p. 79.

53. V. V. Ksenofontova, "Kharakternye cherty sotsial'noi orientatsii podrasta-iushchego pokoleniia razvitogo sotsialisticheskogo obshchestva," *Sotsial'naia i professional'naia orientatsiia molodezhi i problemy kommunisticheskogo vos-pitaniia*, ed. M. Kh. Titma (Tallinn: Institut sotsiologicheskikh issledovanii A.N. S.S.S.R. and Institut istorii A.N. E.S.S.R., 1977), p. 56 and *passim*.

54. M. Kh. Titma, *Vybor professii kak sotsial'naia problema* (Moskva: Mysl', 1975), pp. 9-10.

55. Ibid., p. 128.

56. Ibid., pp. 176, 179.

57. Ibid., pp. 164-65, 170.

58. M. Kh. Titma, "Formirovanie zhiznennykh orientatsii uchashcheisia molo-dezhi," *Sotsiologicheskie issledovaniia*, 1977, no. 3, pp. 53, 55-56.

59. V. G. Alekseeva, in a study of informal groups in general secondary and

vocational schools, called attention to the importance of exerting increased social controls over the leisure-time activities of teenagers. Alekseeva, however, was concerned not only with the attitudes toward and the significance of work, but also with the moral state of youth and with the problems that arose from abortions and illegitimate births among teenagers. V. G. Alekseeva, "Neformal'-nye gruppy podrostkov v usloviiakh goroda," *Sotsiologicheskie issledovaniia*, 1977, no. 3, pp. 60-70.

60. Titma, "Formirovanie zhiznennykh orientatsii," p. 57.

61. See, for example, A. G. Zdravomyslov, V. A. Iadov, and V. P. Rozhin, *Chelovek i ego rabota* (Moskva: Mysl', 1967).

62. The 1969-72 study was done under the auspices of the Sociological Laboratory of the Leningrad Finance-Economics Institute; the 1971-75 study was conducted by Ivanova. See N. V. Ivanova, "Stabil'nost' rabochikh kadrov—reserv povysheniia effektivnosti proizvodstva." *Sotsial'nye problemy sokrashcheniia tekychesti kadrov i formirovaniia stabil'nykh proizvodstvennykh kollektivov*, ed. B. Z. Kononiuk (Moskva: Institut sotsiologicheskikh issledovanii A.N. S.S.S.R., 1977), p. 92.

63. Ibid., p. 94.

64. Social organizations refer to the Komsomol, trade unions, and labor brigades.

65. A. E. Kotliar and M. I. Talalai, "How to Keep Young Cadres in Their Jobs," *Ekonomika i organizatsiia promyshlennogo proizvodstva* (July/August, 1977), pp. 26-43, trans. *Current Digest of the Soviet Press* 29, no. 34 (1977): 1-3. See also A. E. Kotliar and M. I. Talalai, *Molodezh' prikhodit na proizvodstvo* (Moskva: Profizdat, 1978).

66. L. I. Lobanova, "Osobennosti issledovaniia tekuchesti rabochikh-stroitelei," in *Sotsial'nye problemy sokrashcheniia tekuchesti kadrov i formirovaniia stabil'-nykh proizvodstvennykh kollektivov*, edited by B. Z. Kononiuk (Moskva: Institut sotsiologicheskikh issledovanii A.N. S.S.S.R., 1977), pp. 82-90.

67. I. Minaeva, "On the Road: A Psycho-Social Portrait of the Worker Collective," *Znanie—Sila*, 1977, no. 10, pp. 57-59, trans. by Joint Publications Research Service, no. 70297.

68. N. A. Sviridov, "Osobennosti adaptatsii lichnosti k slozhnim proizvodstvennym usloviiam," *Sotsiologicheskie issledovaniia*, 1977, no. 2, pp. 85-94.

69. Iu. K. Ivanov and V. D. Patrushev, "Vliianie uslovii truda na udovletvorennost' trudom rabotnikov sel'skogo khoziaistva," *Sotsiologicheskie issledovaniia*, 1976, no. 3, pp. 60-70.

70. Fifty-eight percent of their time was spent on observation of the functioning of machine systems and 12 percent was spent on maintenance and adjustment. V. V. Krevnevich, "Avtomatizatsiia kak uslovie povysheniia soderzhatel'nosti truda i udovletvorennosti trudom," *Sotsiologicheskie issledovaniia*, 1977, no. 1, p. 87.

71. Ibid., p. 90.

72. Ibid., p. 91-92.

73. M. N. Nochevnik and V. I. Usenin, "Rabochii klass, avtomatizatsiia i prof-soiuzy," *Rabochii klass i sovremennyi mir*, 1977, no. 2, p. 12.

74. Participation in trade union activities, committee and commissions, involved 89.1 percent of the workers questioned in the Nochevnik-Usenin study. However, in several earlier publications on worker activities in trade unions (early 1970s), participation averaged about 50 percent, measured by attendance at trade union meetings. Only a very small percentage of workers (approximately 10-12 percent) were directly involved in the activities of public organizations. Worker participation may have increased; however, it is possible that in the Nochevnik-Usenin study, either workers exaggerated their activities during the interviews, or only the most active workers were included in the sample.

75. Nochevnik and Usenin, p. 15.

76. Ibid., pp. 20-21.

77. V. I. Brudnyi, "Psikhologo-pedagogicheskie metody upravleniia proizvodstvennym kollektivom," *Nauchno-tekhnicheskaia revoliutsiia: lichnost', deiatel'-nost', kollektiv*, ed. V. G. Antonenko and B. A. Rutkovskii (Kiev: Naukova dumka, 1975), p. 269. Specific data on sampling not given.

78. A. G. Kovalev, *Kollektiv i sotsial'no-psikhologicheskie problemy rukovodstva* (Moskva: Politizdat, 1975).

79. V. A. Iadov, ed., *Sotsial'no-psikhologicheskii portret inzhenera* (Moskva: Mysl', 1977), p. 156 and *passim*.

80. *Balans vremeni naseleniia Latviiskoi S.S.R.* (Riga: Zinatne, 1976). For a discussion of studies published before 1975, see V. I. Bolgov, *Biudzhet vremeni pri sotsializme* (Moskva: 1973). Also see L. Gordon and E. Klopov, *Chelovek, posle raboty* (Moskva: Nauka, 1972).

81. Soviet publications are not completely clear on the distinction between "free time" and "leisure time." Free time refers usually to *all* disposable, non-working time (including eating and sleeping); leisure time refers usually to non-working time used for relaxation, education, and other activities.

82. L. A. Gordon, E. V. Klopov, and L. A. Onikov, *Cherty sotsialisticheskogo obraza zhizni: byt gorodskikh rabochikh vchera, segodnia, zavtra* (Moskva: Znanie, 1977), p. 149.

83. A. V. Netsenko, *Sotsial'no-ekonomicheskie problemy svobodnogo vremeni pri sotsializme* (Leningrad: Izdatel'stvo Leningradskogo universiteta, 1975), pp. 47-49.

84. *Balans vremeni naseleniia*, pp. 160-72.

85. Ibid., p. 167; Netsenko, p. 47. See also Gordon, Klopov, and Onikov, *passim*.

86. *Balans vremeni naseleniia*, p. 167.

87. Gordon, Klopov, and Onikov, p. 151.

88. L. A. Gordon and E. V. Klopov, "Ratsional'nyi biudzhet vremeni: podkhod k probleme i opyt nachal'nogo rascheta," *Sotsiologicheskie issledovaniia*, 1977, no. 1, p. 29.

89. Despite the interpretation of these activities as relatively "passive," they do in fact provide a useful social function. This is especially true for television,

which serves as an important medium for the transmission of official information and culture.

90. In the Soviet Union, propaganda refers to political education, especially within the Party, and agitation refers to the dissemination of political messages for purposes of mass mobilization.

91. If the intention is to influence public opinion and/or public behavior in a certain way, then one would have to survey a sample of the population both before and after the agitation statement and try to control for the impact of other variables. The studies discussed in this section do not use this approach, however.

92. I. T. Levykin, *Sotsial'no-psikhologicheskie faktory v lektsionnoi propagandy* (Moskva: Znanie, 1975), p. 16.

93. "Glavnoe-effektivnost'", *Agitator*, 1975, no. 1, pp. 51-53, a review of M. F. Nenashev, *Effektivnost' ideino-vospitatel'noi raboty: nekotorye problemy i puti resheniia* (Moskva: Politizdat, 1974).

94. V. G. Baikova et al., *Politicheskoe obrazovanie: sistema, metodika, metodologiia* (Moskva: Mysl', 1976), pp. 30-31. See the study on public awareness of materials from the 25th Party Congress: S. P. Goriunov, "Sotsiologicheskie issledovaniia v partiinoi rabote," *Sotsiologicheskie issledovaniia*, 1976, no. 4, pp. 79-83.

95. P. V. Pozdniakov, *Effektivnost' kommunisticheskoi propagandy* (Moskva: Politizdat, 1975), p. 81.

96. E. G. Balagushkin and M. M. Kovaleva, "Issledovanie deistvennosti ideino-vospitatel'noi raboty v studencheskikh obshchezhitiia," *Vestnik Moskovskogo universiteta*, 1976, no. 6, pp. 76-82. In this study, attendance at Party lectures was higher among unmarried, older students who spent less time on entertainment.

97. Iu. M. Orlov and B. A. Babin, "Sistemnyi analiz potrebnosti molodezhi v obshchestvenno-politicheskoi deiatel'nosti," *Sotsiologicheskie issledovaniia*, 1977, no. 3, pp. 207-211.

98. Ibid., pp. 212-14.

99. A. A. Tarasenko, *Obshchestvennoe mnenie i povedenie lichnosti* (Minsk: Nauka i tekhnika, 1975), p. 66. Only 60.8 percent of another sample in Voronezh reported that the collective and the Komsomol had the greatest influence on their behavior.

100. Ibid., pp. 106-118.

101. Ibid., pp. 122-30.

102. A. A. Terent'ev, "Sotsial'naia aktivnost' studentov i Komsomol," *Molodezh' i sovremennost'*, ed. A. A. Terent'ev (Gor'kii: Volga-Viatskoe knizhnoe izdatel'stvo, 1976), pp. 52, 47.

103. V. A. Selivanova, "O nekotorykh ob"ektivnykh faktorakh razvitiia tvorcheskoi aktivnosti trudiashchikhsia mass," *Sotsial'no-politicheskie problemy sozdaniia i funktsionirovaniia razvitogo sotsialisticheskogo obshchestva* (Riga: Latviiskii gosudarstvennyi universitet, 1976), p. 71.

104. V. M. Sokolov, "Formirovanie kommunisticheskogo mirovozzreniia molodezhi," *Sotsiologicheskie issledovaniia*, 1976, no. 2, p. 35. This was based on a sample of 1,000 young people in the Sverdlovsk district of Moscow in 1972-73.

105. Sokolov, pp. 35-36. The same study depicted the socially inactive citizens as those who had a more negative or pessimistic attitude toward life in general.

106. M. V. Kirillova, "Formirovanie obshchestvenno-politicheskoi aktivnosti kak cherty lichnosti," in *Nauchno-tekhnicheskaia revoliutsiia: lichnost', deiatel'nost', kollektiv*, edited by L. V. Sokhan' and V. A. Tikhonovich (Kiev: Naukova Dumka, 1975), p. 142.

107. L. V. Sokhan', "Vlianie ntr na sotsial'nuiu aktivnost' lichnosti," in *Nauchno-tekhnicheskaia revoliutsiia*, p. 30.

108. A. Samodelov, "Ispol'zovanie konkretnykh sotsiologicheskikh issledovanii v partiinoi rabote," *Partiinaia zhizn'*, 1976, no. 20, p. 30. The Belorussian data are from V. Sikorskii, "Sotsiologicheskie issledovaniia effektivnosti partiinoi propagandy," *Politicheskoe samoobrazovanie*, 1975, no. 1, p. 40.

109. Forty-nine percent said that one-fifth of their students had educations which did not correspond to the type of political lectures they attended; 60 percent said that the student body was also very heterogeneous in its occupational structure. Nonetheless, 58 percent of the Party lecturers said that they were satisfied with the formation of their student groups. Baikova et al., pp. 96-97.

110. From 14 to 52 percent of the propagandists in various cities said that they did not feel prepared well enough to lead political classes effectively; they were not teaching the subjects they learned in training; and 22-60 percent said they were unable to make the students' interests "profound and steadfast." Baikova et al., pp. 116, 212, 121, respectively. Iu. Litvintsev related these problems to cadre stability in "Zabotimsia o stabil'nosti ideologicheskikh kadrov," *Partiinaia zhizn'*, 1975, no. 12, pp. 64-69. For a more positive assessment, see Goriunov, pp. 79-83.

111. B. K. Alekseev and M. N. Perfil'ev, *Printsipy i tendentsii razvitiia predstavitel'nogo sostava mestnykh sovetov* (Leningrad: Lenizdat, 1976).

112. For a discussion of the project as a whole and for the methodology, see Iu. V. Arutiunian, "Sotsial'no-kul'turnye aspekty razvitiia i sblizheniia natsii S.S.S.R. (Programma, metodika i perspektivy issledovaniia)," *Sovetskaia etnografiia*, 1972, no. 3, pp. 3-19.

113. G. V. Starovoitova, "K issledovaniiu etnopsikhologii gorodskikh zhitelei, *Sovetskaia etnografiia*, 1976, no. 3, pp. 46-49.

114. Ibid., pp. 50-51. We have not found publications of surveys on the perception of nationalities outside the USSR, although responses to questions on cultural preferences sometimes referred to foreign cultural products. See Klement'ev, n. 124.

115. Ibid., pp. 53-54, 52.

116. Surveys conducted recently by institutions other than the Institute of Ethnography also are concerned with the issue of ritual observance, but these

studies are not of comparable quality. See, for example, I. B. Usmankhodzhaev, "Under the Impact of a New Way of Life," *Current Digest of the Soviet Press* 27, no. 30 (1975): 21-22.

117. S. I. Bruk and M. N. Guboglo, "Faktory rasprostraneniia dvuiazychiia u narodov S.S.S.R.," *Sovetskaia etnografiia*, 1975, no. 5, pp. 20, 22-23.

118. Ibid., pp. 25-26.

119. Ibid., p. 27. Media habits may also reflect the availability of programs in different languages, but that factor was not considered in this study.

120. Ibid., p. 29.

121. S. L. Nesterova, "Dvuiazychie i kul'tura naseleniia Moldavii," *Sovetskaia etnografiia*, 1975, no. 5, pp. 72-74 and *passim*.

122. Ibid., pp. 73-77.

123. Ibid., pp. 77-80.

124. E. I. Klement'ev, "Natsional'no-kul'turnye orientatsii karel'skogo gorodskogo naseleniia," *Sovetskaia etnografiia*, 1976, no. 3, p. 66.

125. Ibid., pp. 60-64.

BIBLIOGRAPHY

An Overview of Survey Research in the USSR

Akademiia nauk SSSR, Institut sotsiologicheskikh issledovanii, Sovetskaia sotsiologicheskaia assotsiatsiia. *Sotsiologicheskie tsentry SSSR*. Moskva: Institut sotsiologicheskikh issledovanii, 1976.

Brezhnev, L. I. "Rech' na iubileinoi sessii AN SSSR." *Pravda*, 8 October 1975, p. 1.

Chuprov, V. I., and Shchenev, V. P. "Nauchno-metodicheskie i prakticheskie predposylki razvitiia edinoi sistemy upravleniia, planirovaniia i koordinatsii sotsiologicheskikh issledovanii v strane." In *Sotsiologicheskaia informatsiia i prakticheskie voprosy koordinatsionnoi raboty v oblasti sotsiologii*. Edited by V. I. Chuprov and V. P. Shchenev. Moskva: Institut sotsiologicheskikh issledovanii, 1977.

Demidova, A. I. "Professional'naia podgotovka sotsiologicheskikh kadrov." *Sotsiologicheskie issledovaniia*, no. 3 (1978), pp. 201-205.

"Kompleksnaia programma nauchnykh rabot—osnova dal'neishego razvitiia sovetskoi sotsiologicheskoi nauki." *Sotsiologicheskie issledovaniia*, no. 2 (1978), pp. 3-11.

Osipov, G. V. et al., eds. *Rabochaia kniga sotsiologa*. Moskva: Nauka, 1976.

Paniukov, V. S., and Golovatiuk, V. M. "Sotsial'naia pasportizatsiia trudovikh resursov goroda." *Sotsiologicheskie issledovaniia*, no. 3 (1978), pp. 185-92.

Shalin, Dmitri. "The Development of Soviet Sociology, 1956-1976." *Annual Review of Sociology*, volume 4. Palo Alto, California: Annual Reviews, Inc., 1978.

Shliapentokh, V. E. *Problemy reprezentativnosti sotsiologicheskoi informatsii.* Moskva: Statistika, 1976.

Shubkin, V. "Limits." *Novy mir*, February 1978, pp. 187-217. Trans. in *Current Digest of the Soviet Press* 30, no. 9 (1978): 4-7.

"Sotsiologicheskie issledovaniia—na sluzhbu stroitel'stva kommunizma." *Sotsiologicheskie issledovaniia*, no. 2 (1976), pp. 3-9.

"Vysokii dolg sovetskikh filosofov." *Pravda*, 19 September 1975, p. 2.

Media Habits

Chelovek, piatiletka, pressa. Voronezh: Izdatel'stvo Voronezhskogo universiteta, 1976.

Davtian, S. A. "O vliianii predvaritel'noi informatsii na vybor fil'ma." *Sotsiologicheskie issledovaniia*, no. 1 (1977), pp. 105-106.

Firsov, B. M., and Muzdybaev, K. "K postroeniiu sistemy pokazatelei ispol'zovaniia sredstv massovoi kommunikatsii." *Sotsiologicheskie issledovaniia*, no. 1 (1975), pp. 113-20.

Kogan, L. N. "Sblizhenie sotsial'nykh grupp v sfere sotsialisticheskoi kul'tury." *Sotsiologicheskie issledovaniia*, no. 2 (1977), pp. 34-41.

Koitla, Kh. "Mneniia rabochikh i inzhenerov o prirode konflikta mezhdu geroiami literaturnogo proizvedeniia." *Sotsiologicheskie issledovaniia*, no. 2 (1978), pp. 116-17.

Korobeinikov, V. S., ed. *Sotsiologicheskie problemy obshchestvennogo mneniia i deiatel'nosti srestv massovoi informatsii.* Moskva: Institut sotsiologicheskikh issledovanii, 1976.

Laidmiae, V. I. *Izobrazitel'noe isskustvo i ego zritel'.* Tallinn: Eesti Raamat, 1976.

Mansurov, N. S.; Kalaitan, N. E.; and Sdobnov, V. M., eds. *Sotsiologicheskie problemy kul'tury.* Moskva: Institut sotsiologicheskikh issledovanii, 1976.

Zhabskii, M. I. "Sotsiologiia kino: opyt i problemy." *Sotsiologicheskie issledovaniia*, no. 4 (1977), pp. 102-110.

Family and Women

Belova, V. A. *Chislo detei v sem'e.* Moskva: Statistika, 1975.

Bondarskaia, G. A. *Rozhdaemost' v SSSR.* Moskva: Statistika, 1977.

Chuiko, L. V. *Braki i razvody.* Moskva: Statistika, 1975.

Filiukova, L. F. *Sel'skaia sem'ia*. Minsk: Nauka i tekhnika, 1976.

Gerasimova, I. A. *Struktura sem'i*. Moskva: Statistika, 1976.

Iankova, Z. A., ed. *Problemy sotsiologicheskogo izucheniia sem'i*. Moskva: Institut sotsiologicheskikh issledovanii, 1976.

_____, and Shapiro, V. D., eds. *Vzaimootnoshenie pokolenii v sem'e*. Moskva: Institut sotsiologicheskikh issledovanii, 1977.

Inderbiev, M. T. "Sotsial'no-gigienicheskaia kharakteristika abortov v Checheno-Ingushskoi ASSR." *Zdravookhranenie Rossiiskoi Federatsii*, no. 5 (1975), pp. 24-26

Kolokol'nikov, V. T. "Brachno-semeinye otnosheniia v srede kolkhoznogo krest'ianstva." *Sotsiologicheskie issledovaniia*, no. 3 (1976), pp. 78-87.

Perekonna-probleemid II. Tartu: Tartu Riiklik Ulikool, 1975.

Ruzhzhe, V. L.; Eliseeva, I. I.; and Kadibur, T. S. "Opyt issledovaniia semeinykh grupp." *Sotsiologicheskie issledovaniia*, no. 1 (1976), pp. 113-20.

Skol'ko detei budet v sovetskoi sem'e. Moskva: Statistika, 1977.

Solov'ev, N. Ia. *Brak i sem'ia segodnia*. Vilnius: 1977.

Education and Youth

Alekseeva, V. G. "Neformal'nye gruppy podrostkov v usloviiakh goroda." *Sotsiologicheskie issledovaniia*, no. 3 (1977), pp. 60-70.

Aver'ianov, L. Ia. "Vliiania obrazovaniia na izmenenie sotsial'noi orientatsii rabochei molodezhi." In *Sotsial'no-professional'naia orientatsiia molodezhi v usloviiakh razvitogo sotsializma*. Edited by F. R. Filippov. Moskva: Institut sotsiologicheskikh issledovanii AN SSSR, 1977.

Brudnyi, V. I., and Kaganov, A. B. "Sotsial'nye istochniki formirovaniia studenchestva." *Sotsiologicheskie issledovaniia*, no. 2 (1977), pp. 78-81.

Filippov, F. R. "Rol' vysshei shkoly v izmenenii sotsial'noi struktury sovetskogo obshchestva (itogi vsesoiuznogo issledovaniia)." *Sotsiologicheskie issledovaniia*, no. 2 (1977), pp. 42-51.

Gentvainite, V.; Matulenis, A.; and Tal'iunaite, M. "Sotsial'naia orientatsiia vypusknikov srednikh shkol." *Sotsiologicheskie issledovaniia*, no. 2 (1977), pp. 74-75.

Ksenofontova, V. V. "Kharakternye cherty sotsial'noi orientatsii podrastaiushchego pokoleniia razvitogo sotsialisticheskogo obshchestva." In *Sotsial'naia i professional'naia orientatsiia molodezhi i problemy kommunisticheskogo vospitaniia*. Edited by M. Kh. Titma. Tallinn: Institut sotsiologicheskikh issledovanii AN SSSR and Institut istorii AN ESSR, 1977.

Titma, M. Kh. "Formirovanie zhiznennykh orientatsii uchashcheisia molodezhi (na materialykh Estonskoi SSR)." *Sotsiologicheskie issledovaniia*, no. 3 (1977), pp. 52-59.

_____. *Vybor professii kak sotsial'naia problema*. Moskva: Mysl', 1975.

Vershlovskii, S. G., and Lesokhina, L. N. "Rabochaia molodezh' i obrazovanie." *Sotsiologicheskie issledovaniia*, no. 2 (1975), pp. 90-99.

Work and the Workplace

Brudnyi, V. I. "Psikhologo-pedagogicheskie metody upravleniia proizvodstvennym kollektivom." In *Nauchno-tekhnicheskaia revoliutsiia: lichnost', deiatel'nost', kollektiv.* Edited by V. G. Antonenko and B. A. Rutkovskii. Kiev: Naukova dumka, 1975.

Iadov, V. A., ed. *Sotsial'no-psikhologicheskii portret inzhenera.* Moskva: Mysl', 1977.

Ivanov, Iu. K., and Patrushev, V. D. "Vliianie uslovii truda na udovletvorennost' trudom rabotnikov sel'skogo khoziaistva." *Sotsiologicheskie issledovaniia,* no. 3 (1976), pp. 60-70.

Ivanova, N. V. "Stabil'nost' rabochikh kadrov—rezerv povysheniia effektivnosti proizvodstva." In *Sotsial'nye problemy sokrashcheniia tekychesti kadrov i formirovaniia stabil'nykh proizvodstvennykh kollektivov.* Edited by B. Z. Kononiuk. Moskva: Institut sotsiologicheskikh issledovanii AN SSSR, 1977.

Kotliar, A. E., and Talalai, M. I. "How to Keep Young Cadres in Their Jobs." *Ekonomika i organizatsiia promyshlennogo proizvodstva,* July-August 1977, pp. 26-43. Trans. in *Current Digest of the Soviet Press* 29, no. 34 (1977): 1-3.

———, and Talalai, M. I. *Molodezh' prikhodit na proizvodstvo.* Moskva: Profizdat, 1978.

Kovalev, A. G. *Kollektiv i sotsial'no-psikhologicheskie problemy rukovodstva.* Moskva: Politizdat, 1975.

Krevnevich, V. V. "Avtomatizatsiia kak uslovie povysheniia soderzhatel'nosti truda i udovletvorennosti trudom." *Sotsiologicheskie issledovaniia,* no. 1 (1977), pp. 85-92.

Lobanova, L. I. "Osobennosti issledovaniia tekuchesti rabochikh-stroitelei." In *Sotsial'nye problemy sokrashcheniia tekuchesti kadrov i formirovaniia stabil'nykh proizvodstvennykh kollektivov.* Edited by B. Z. Kononiuk. Moskva: Institut sotsiologicheskikh issledovanii AN SSSR, 1977.

Minaeva, I. "On the Road: A Psycho-social Portrait of the Worker Collective." *Znanie—Sila,* no. 10 (1977), pp. 57-59. Trans. in Joint Publications Research Service, no. 70297.

Nochevnik, M. N., and Usenin, V. I. "Rabochii klass, avtomatizatsiia i profsoiuzy." *Rabochii klass i sovremenny mir,* no. 2 (1977), pp. 10-22.

Riazhiskikh, I. A. "Rol' ispol'zovaniia vkliuchennogo nabliudeniia dlia izucheniia zhizn' proizvodstvennogo kollektiva." *Sotsiologicheskie issledovaniia,* no. 3 (1975), pp. 91-99.

Sviridov, N. A. "Osobennosti adaptatsii lichnosti k slozhnim proizvodstvennym usloviiam." *Sotsiologicheskie issledovaniia*, no. 2 (1977), pp. 85-94.

Leisure Time

Balans vremeni naseleniia Latviiskoi SSR. Riga: Zinatne, 1976.
Bolgov, V. I. *Biudzhet vremeni pri sotsializme.* Moskva: 1973.
Gordon, L. A., and Klopov, E. V. "Ratsional'nyi biudzhet vremeni: podkhod k probleme i opyt nachal'nogo rascheta." *Sotsiologicheskie issledovaniia*, no. 1 (1977), pp. 19-30.
_____; Klopov, E. V.; and Onikov, L. A. *Cherty sotsialisticheskogo obraza zhizni: byt gorodskikh rabochikh vchera, segodnia, zavtra.* Moskva: Znanie, 1977.
Netsenko, A. V. *Sotsial'no-ekonomicheskie problemy svobodnogo vremeni pri sotsializme.* Leningrad: Izdatel'stvo Leningradskogo universiteta, 1975.

Politics and Ideology

Alekseev, B. K., and Perfil'ev, M. N. *Printsipy i tendentsii razvitiia predstavitel'- nogo sostava mestnykh sovetov.* Leningrad: Lenizdat, 1976.
Baikova, V. G. et al., *Politicheskoe obrazovanie: sistema, metodika, metodo- logiia.* Moskva: Mysl', 1976.
Balagushkin, E. G., and Kovaleva, M. M. "Issledovanie deistvennosti ideino- vospitatel'noi raboty v studencheskikh obshchezhitiiax." *Vestnik Mos- kovskogo universiteta*, no. 6 (1976), pp. 76-82.
"Glavnoe-effektivnost'," *Agitator*, no. 1 (1975), pp. 51-53.
Goriunov, S. P. "Sotsiologicheskie issledovaniia v partiinoi rabote." *Sotsio- logicheskie issledovaniia*, no. 4 (1976), pp. 79-83.
Levykin, I. T. *Sotsial'no-psikhologicheskie faktory v lektsionnoi propagande.* Moskva: Znanie, 1975.
Litvintsev, Iu. "Zabotimsia o stabil'nosti ideologicheskikh kadrov." *Partiinaia zhizn'*, no. 12 (1975), pp. 64-69.
Orlov, Iu. M., and Babin, B. A. "Sistemnyi analiz potrebnosti molodezhi v obshchestvenno-politicheskoi deiatel'nosti." *Sotsiologicheskie issledo- vaniia*, no. 3 (1977), pp. 204-214.
Pozdniakov, P. V. *Effektivnost' kommunisticheskoi propagandy.* Moskva: Politizdat, 1975.
Safarov, P. A. "Organy gosudarstvennogo upravleniia i obshchestvennoe mnenie naseleniia." *Gosudarstvo i pravo*, no. 1 (1975), pp. 20-27.
Samodelov, A. "Ispol'zovanie konkretnykh sotsiologicheskikh issledovanii v

partiinoi rabote." *Partiinaia zhizn'*, no. 2 (1976), pp. 26-31.
Sikorskii, V. "Sotsiologicheskie issledovaniia effektivnosti partiinoi propagandy." *Politicheskoe samoobrazovanie*, no. 1 (1975), pp. 37-41.
Sokolov, V. M. "Formirovanie kommunisticheskogo mirovozzreniia molodezhi." *Sotsiologicheskie issledovaniia*, no. 2 (1976), pp. 29-36.
Tarasenko, A. A. *Obshchestvennoe mnenie i povedenie lichnosti*. Minsk: Nauka
i tekhnika, 1975.
Terent'ev, A. A. "Sotsial'naia aktivnost' studentov i Komsomol." In *Molodezh'
i sovremennost'*. Edited by A. A. Terent'ev. Gor'kii: Volga-Viatskoe
knizhnoe izdatel'stvo, 1976.

Ethnicity and Foreign Cultures

Arutiunian, Iu. V. "Sotsial'no-kul'turnye aspekty razvitiia i sblizheniia natsii v
SSSR (Programma, metodika i perspektivy issledovaniia)." *Sovetskaia
etnografiia*, no. 3 (1972), pp. 3-19.
Bruk, S. I., and Guboglo, M. N. "Faktory rasprostraneniia dvuiazychiia u narodov SSSR (po materialam etnosotsiologicheskikh issledovanii)." *Sovetskaia
etnografiia*, no. 5 (1975), pp. 17-30.
Klement'ev, E. I. "Natsional'no-kul'turnye orientatsii karel'skogo gorodskogo
naseleniia." *Sovetskaia etnografiia*, no. 3 (1976), pp. 57-67.
Nesterova, S. L. "Dvuiazychie i kul'tura naseleniia Moldavii (po materialam
etnosotsiologicheskogo issledovaniia v Moldavskoi SSR)." *Sovetskaia
etnografiia*, no. 5 (1975), pp. 71-81.
Starovoitova, G. B. "K issledovaniiu etnopsikhologii gorodskikh zhitelei (po
materialam oprosa naseleniia trekh gorodov Tatarskoi ASSR)." *Sovetskaia etnografiia*, no. 3 (1976), pp. 45-56.
Usmankhodzhaev, I. B. "Under the Impact of a New Way of Life." *Current
Digest of the Soviet Press* 27, no. 30 (1975): 21-22.

Bibliographical Directories

Novaia sovetskaia literatura po obshchestvennym naukam: Series on *filosofskie
nauki, ekonomika, gosudarstvo i pravo*, and *istoriia, arkheologiia, etnografiia* (12 issues per year, 1975-77).
Obshchestvennye nauki v SSSR, referativnyi zhurnal: Series on *filosofskie nauki,
problemy nauchnogo kommunizma, ekonomika*, and *gosudarstvo i pravo*
(4-6 issues per year, 1975-77).
Bibliographical listings in *Sotsiologicheskie issledovaniia* (4 issues per year, 1975-
77).

A Compendium of Opinion Polls Conducted in the USSR from 1960 to 1975. Compiled by Sergei Voronitsyn, Radio Liberty Research Division, Munich.
Sotsial'nye problemy truda trudovykh kollektivov. Bibliography of publications, 1966-75.
Valentei, D. C., and Burnazheva, E. Iu. *Bibliografiia po problemam narodo-naseleniia: 1972-1975.* Moskva, 1977.
ABSEES Soviet and East European Abstract Series, volumes 6 and 7. Glasgow: University of Glasgow Press, 1975 and 1976.

Journals and Newspapers (1975-77)

Agitator
Current Digest of the Soviet Press
Kommunist
Komsomol'skaia pravda
Letopis' gazetnykh statei
Letopis' zhurnal'nykh statei
Literaturnaia gazeta
Mirovaia ekonomika i mezhdunarodnye otnosheniia
Molodoi kommunist
Partiinaia zhizn'
Sotsiologicheskie issledovaniia
Sotsialisticheskii trud
Sovetskaia etnografiia
SShA
Vestnik Leningradskogo universiteta (Series on *Ekonomika, filosofiia, pravo*)
Vestnik Moskovskogo universiteta (Series on *Teoriia nauchnogo kommunizma*)
Voprosy filosofii
Voprosy pedagogiki
Zhurnalist

2 Yugoslavia

Susan L. Woodward

AN OVERVIEW OF SURVEY RESEARCH IN
THE SOCIALIST FEDERATED REPUBLIC OF YUGOSLAVIA

Survey research in Yugoslavia entered a new stage in the early 1970s. The financially easy and politically flexible days of the 1960s gave way to tight financial constraints and to declining interest on the part of political bodies in broad surveys of public opinion. Sociological research in its early stages had been dominated by *anketomanija*[1] (survey-mania): piling up survey responses without much attention to the quality of questions and methods or to the theoretical purpose of a survey. A new generation of researchers, together with greater concern for cost effectiveness and financial accountability, aimed at correcting these weaknesses. In addition to encouraging higher quality and greater planning of research, however, this meant that fewer survey studies could now be done. Politicians also withdrew some support from public opinion sampling, for reasons that are not completely clear; the perceived failure of social science research to predict or to help resolve the nationality conflicts of 1967-71 may have played an important part. Instead, politicians turned to their own informal studies of the opinions of political activists, whom they now considered more trustworthy, and they imposed some restrictions on which survey results could be published.

Also in line with political changes after the Croatian crisis and the 1974 Constitution, most survey research has been "republicanized." The national public opinion surveys ceased in 1970. Only the Slovenians and the Macedonians continue the periodic surveys of public opinion—annually in Macedonia, every two years in Slovenia.[2] Nationwide projects may share a general research question, but are composed in fact of six to eight separate and often different republican and provincial studies, and communication among scholars across republican lines appears to be declining. At this point it is difficult to judge whether this is an unexpected consequence of the decentralization of the financing of scientific research to the republic, and sometimes local level, or whether the consequence was intended so as to lower the prospect of cross-republic (ethnic) comparisons and thus of potential conflict.

Outside of the scientific circles, there has been an explosion of the use of survey techniques in ad hoc, relatively unsystematic, small-scale (and usually unpublished) sampling of opinion in enterprises, by trade unions and the mass media, or by door-to-door canvassing for narrowly focused local planning or commercial interests. At the same time, therefore, that less sociological research is being financed, and more of it remains buried in internal documents of a research institute or the contracting association, many more Yugoslavs are being asked to express their opinion to anonymous pollsters on a wide range of subjects.

The practice of survey research in Yugoslavia is guided by three constraints: available funding, the skills and personalities of individual researchers, and the political atmosphere in the country. There is no federal planning of such research, nor is there a federal fund for social science research. Since 1974, funding for scientific research is similar to the financing of all nonprofit and service activities, such as education or health, that is, through a self-managing interest community (SIC). The SIC is an assembly of producers (in this case, research institutes that present their proposal for a year's work) and of users (anyone with funds who wants a piece of research done—usually large economic enterprises, various ministries of government such as the Secretariat for Legislation, the republican central committee of the League of Communists, or urban planning institutes).[3] They negotiate directly over which research is to be funded and who will provide the funds. A research institute does well to find additional outside sources, since the SIC grant is usually insufficient. An institute can contract directly with a user in the course of a year for minor projects, and it often initiates ideas for research, which it persuades users to finance. At all times, however, it must hold public hearings on its research proposals which, although they are rarely attended by any but fellow researchers, are meant to establish public control and scientific accountability over research that is funded.

Five consequences of this new system are identifiable. 1) Wealthier republics and enterprises dominate social science research—far more comes from
Slovenia than Bosnia, for example. 2) Little research can be done by individuals
outside research institutes or university faculties.[4] 3) Such research will be
increasingly guided by practical and socially relevant concerns, and less of it will
be published. 4) Market principles will increasingly determine who does research—the institute with the largest number of Ph.D.s on its staff,[5] or the most
persuasive spokesman, or the most "entrepreneurial" staffs will have the resources to do research. These criteria may not lead to research in areas where it
is needed, but where the skilled researcher and successful institute are.[6]
5) Increasing numbers of social scientists are leaving research for business or
university teaching to avoid the uncertainties of the new system.

Any association, if it hires a sociologist, may conduct surveys. The majority of survey research, however, is still done by sociological institutes in the
capital cities[7] and by faculty and degree candidates at the universities (particularly in the political science and philosophy—under sociology—faculties). A
significant recent addition, however, is from market research companies and the
staffs of radio, TV, and newspapers.[8] Thus, survey research for scholarly inquiry
and as a training ground for new social scientists continues, but at a somewhat
slower pace. The practical side is gaining. Surveys designed by teams of experts
and representatives of political groups (the Socialist Alliance of Working People,
the League of Communists, and the trade unions) to take the social "pulse" as a
guide to the success of political changes, the need for reform, and as a source of
information for public discussion are no longer of interest to leaders, particularly
those in the League of Communists, and its associated organizations. Although it
now appears that these politicians probably never read the results of surveys
they commissioned anyway, they also appear to have been frightened by their
inability to control the consequences of the extensive freedom of speech of the
late 1960s. Now, out of a distrust of the results of broad surveys of public
opinion, an uneasiness about the potential use of surveys done by foreign
researchers, and a belief that such surveys contradict the direct, bottom-to-top
process of democracy consistent with self-management, leaders in the Party have
withdrawn financial support from general polls, and have imposed a three-year
delay on the publication of any survey results that may be politically sensitive.
They would rather send their own staff to towns and factories to "have
conversations." Finally, applied survey research as a policy tool is growing
rapidly out of the new contracting system and the burgeoning fields of urban
and spatial planning.

With the exception of the ad-hoc, small-scale surveys in work organizations
or trade unions (generally recognized to be of low quality in terms of sampling,
questionnaire design, and training of interviewers), the quality of sociological
research in Yugoslavia is very high. It is also based on a careful following of the
American literature, often by sociologists trained in the United States. Research

staffs are now highly specialized, focusing in such areas as urban sociology, rural sociology, political sociology, industrial sociology, communications research, and psychology and politics. Research designs always take serious account of the cultural differences within Yugoslavia: 1) samples are generally randomly chosen from voting lists after regions, towns, and settlements have been selected by proportional stratification from census information, and 2) interviewers must be from the area of their respondents so that they are familiar with their mentality and habits. Samples for most studies average 2,000 respondents. Most sampling bias is handled by statistical calculation of error, although there is a tendency, particularly in Serbia, to depend on urban populations and to doubt the validity of results from rural areas and small towns. Interviewers are almost universally graduate students, usually in sociology, who are chosen by rigorous testing and are then trained. Systematic supervision of interviewers in the field is built into all survey projects. The only exception to this format is in marketing research, which relies more on a permanent staff of trained and supervised retirees and housewives.

The most common method of data analysis until recently was simply description, usually reporting percentages. However, the use of multivariate techniques such as factor analysis is now increasingly common in work published in Croatia and Slovenia. Two new methods that depend on sophisticated computer-based manipulations are receiving much attention recently: 1) the development of a federal, or at least of a number of republican, data banks of social indicators that can be available to policymakers along with instructions on how to obtain ready answers to their practical questions, and 2) the collection of as much information as possible about the socioeconomic changes occurring in the various regions as a result of modernization and an attempt to find patterns among these data to overcome past assumptions about similarities and differences and to provide explanations and predictions of change. This attention to change has not been focused on attitudinal research, however. Both longitudinal surveys and secondary analysis of older data are rare, and the only exploration of trends in attitudes from surveys taken over a number of years has been made by Zvonarević and Spitak on their Croatian public opinion surveys from 1967 to 1973.[9]

The care taken in designing surveys is not always reflected in their reporting: the source of survey respondents and the circumstances influencing their responses are not always given, operational definitions of analytical terms are hard to find, and conclusions are often vague and only partially supported by the data reported. The deliberate attempt by researchers to "mask" questions that may be politically sensitive in order to obtain more accurate responses is not discussed with the results.[10] In addition to the influence of inadequate reporting and of urban-rural differences, interpretation of survey results must be cautious when individual questions of a more directly political nature are at issue, in spite of the increasingly methodological self-consciousness of Yugoslav sociologists.

Any discussion of the substantive results of survey research must also take into account its "republican" nature. Any survey is made within one republic and thus does not represent Yugoslavs but Serbs, Slovenes, or Bosnians. Such research is so decentralized that no comprehensive account is feasible. In addition, however interesting the questions and results of small, ad-hoc surveys by work organizations and newspaper staffs may be, they must be ignored here because of their doubtful reliability and validity and the necessarily unrepresentative nature of any portion of such studies.

THE ORIENTATION OF THIS STUDY

The following discussion is based on a search of Yugoslav social science periodicals published during 1975-77, and on extensive conversations with sociologists at research institutes in Belgrade, Zagreb, and Ljubljana in 1978 about their current work and about unpublished research conducted during 1975-77.[11] With a few exceptions, the results reported here come from published periodical articles, special reports, and books. Material was gathered from attitudinal surveys that related to the ten substantive topics of this project. The report slights material from Bosnia, Montenegro, Macedonia, Kosovo, and the Vojvodina. It excludes all those studies protected for three years (1975-77) under concern for their political sensitivity, a problem of particular importance in Serbia and Slovenia. Evidence of attitudes is also limited to studies considered major and important by myself and Yugoslav sociologists, since the number of actual studies, and the hundreds of research institutes conducting them, is unmanageable. Thus, this report probably represents an accurate survey of the reliable findings during 1975-77 without the supporting evidence and less significant but interesting detail that a larger volume would include.

SURVEYS OF PUBLIC ATTITUDES AND BEHAVIOR IN THE S.F.R. OF YUGOSLAVIA

Media Habits

Media and communications research is one of the fastest growing fields of sociological inquiry in Yugoslavia. During 1975-77, this research tended to focus on five major concerns: 1) the extent to which people inform themselves about domestic politics, 2) the media they rely on as a source of that information, 3) the nature of TV, radio, and newspaper audiences, 4) audience preferences in programming, and 5) the content of the emerging Yugoslav mass culture.

The level of information among ordinary citizens takes on a crucial quality in a society where each should be intimately engaged in societal decision making. This is reflected in the activity of empirical sociologists. Thus, Mladen Zvonarević began the surveys of Croatian public opinion in the 1960s out of concern for adequate information. Pavao Novosel has turned his interest in political culture, youth, and self-management into a specialization in communications research at the workplace and in socio-political organizations. The creator of all-Yugoslav public opinion surveys, Firdus Džinić, left his post in charge of the national poll in 1978 to head audience and programming research at Radio-Television Belgrade. All three sociologists were acting in response to the increasing importance of the media and of the processes of impersonal communication in Yugoslav society.

Yugoslavs now inform themselves predominantly by means of radio and television news programs. In the 1976 survey of Macedonian public opinion (N=1,149), 52.1 percent informed themselves daily by radio, and 62.3 percent by television. Only 24.6 percent used a daily newspaper, 11.9 percent relied on friends, and 2.96 percent cited meetings. If one adds Macedonians who seek information about public events at least once a week, the television audience rises to 75.2 percent, the radio audience to 69.3 percent, and the press to only 44.1 percent. In the case of all three media, the most significant determinant of daily exposure of public information was the respondent's level of formal education. Radio listening grows gradually with education. For newspaper readers, a sharp increase occurs between secondary school and higher education of any form. And the jump in television audience comes between the illiterate and the rest of the population.[12]

Pavao Novosel found in a central Zagreb commune that television was even the source of information for activities of delegates, citizens elected by the smallest self-managing unit in every sector of society as its representative to decision-making assemblies.[13] Asked where they obtained their most complete and useful information, 30 percent of the responding delegates cited television, 24 percent said at meetings of basic organizations of associated labor (the smallest work unit in an enterprise), and 22 percent chose general assemblies of work organizations (the committee of the whole for an enterprise). When asked to name predominant sources of information, however, 61 percent said television, 46 percent cited radio, 35 percent mentioned a newspaper or magazine, and 34 percent said general assemblies of work organizations.[14]

Socioeconomic differentiation in media audiences shows up very clearly in Serbia, and there is some evidence that this pattern, both among social groups and between regions, is found throughout Yugoslavia. One-third of the sampled populations of Kosovo, Montenegro, Macedonia, and Bosnia-Herzegovina—the poorest regions—do not use the mass media as a source of information at all, whereas the Yugoslav average is one-fifth. The Belgrade population that is completely outside the system of mass communication on the other hand is only 8 percent. In the Serbian sample, researchers expressed concern over the unsatisfactory use of the information function of newspapers, radio, and TV among members of the Albanian nationality, among the illiterate and inadequately literate, and among farmers, while housewives and students (age 15 and up) follow closely. Members of the League of Communists use media sources of information most of all the population subcategories, due mainly to their greater readership of daily newspapers. League members are matched in their levels of access to information, however, by urban residents, men, professionals and officials, the retired (especially by radio), and the better educated.[15]

Audience and programming research is done in two ways: Radio-Television Belgrade and Ljubljana each have monthly publications[16] that report their surveys of who is watching what television programs and when (most watch between 7:30 and 9:30 in the evening, and the most popular programs are still news and politically informative ones), and sociologists occasionally report on the results from public opinion surveys.

A survey of 2,500 adults (aged 15 and older) in each of eight regions of Serbia found that Serbs are following Yugoslav, European, and worldwide trends in the standstill of daily newspaper circulations. According to a UNESCO study for 1971-72, Yugoslav daily newspaper readership takes second-to-last place in Europe, above Albania only. At 10 newspaper copies for every 100 people, Serbia is considered to be on the margin of minimally adequate communication by means of the press, whereas Yugoslavia as a whole falls below this minimum. All weekly papers are also in a less favorable situation than they were ten years ago, except *Komunist*, whose readership has increased. *Komunist* readership seems to vary with League membership, although the increase in readership is not only among League members. Even audiences for light entertainment journals have begun to decline after a rapid growth in popularity up to 1972. Researchers conclude that there seems to be little growth for this medium except among "family" magazines.[17]

The radio still has the largest audience, though its expansion has slowed enough to suggest that, except in Kosovo, radio has reached its saturation point. Television, on the other hand, is expanding rapidly and has much room yet to grow. Of the Serbian sample, 28 to 30 percent use one or more media of daily information while 28 percent are informed daily by all three media. Nonetheless, the number of occasional or nonusers of the mass media has remained the same since 1964. Changes have occurred in the doubling of those who now use all three media and in the shift to television. In 1974, there were 13 television sets per 100 people in Serbia. Researchers find further that ownership of a set leads to its regular use as a source of information, and that the use of one medium leads cumulatively to the use of another.[18]

The particularly obvious urban-rural and educational differences in the ownership of television sets have led social scientists to be concerned about the increasing social stratification of cultural activities into old forms of high and low culture. In the Zagreb region in 1972, 78.5 percent of Zagreb residents owned a television set while in the settlement farthest from the center, 25.6

percent owned televisions. If one looks at educational and occupational levels, the range goes from a low of 13 percent to a high of 88 percent. Sociologists also chart a decline in the more personal forms of entertainment once associated with rural populations, and an increase in what they call "urban imperialism." One sociologist refers to this as the "cultural marginalization" of urbanization, that is, the increasing dominance of mass media as forms of entertainment rather than visiting, conversation, theater, or participant cultural activities, and the overwhelming interest in popular and folk music rather than more "serious" music or cultural and information programs.[19]

Yugoslav researchers are paying more attention to the increased importance of mass media among Yugoslavs as the dominant source of information and increasingly as the main source of entertainment as well. Newspapers tend to be used for information, radio for recreation, and television for both. Nonetheless, in Serbia one can be sure only that 30 percent of the population uses some means of information daily. Further, mass media habits are clearly differentiated by socioeconomic categories—occupation, education, income, sex, political activism, age, and urban-rural and regional residence. The television era has arrived in Croatia and Slovenia, but about one-third of the population in the southern areas, especially in Kosovo, are in no contact at all with mass media (including newspapers). When they are, it is still the radio. In addition, researchers argue that the decade shows a regrettable decline in serious cultural tastes in favor of popular music, journals, and television shows, at the same time that most citizens are still far from adequately informed.

Family and Women

Rapid economic development and industrialization and a socialist order committed to equality were bound to bring changes in the family and the role of women. Curiosity among Yugoslav sociologists about the extent of such changes has led in the last decade to many studies, such as of the consequences of the greater employment of women and the decline in patriarchal forms of authority, as well as attempts to gather information necessary for policies to ease women's "double burden" of work and home and for population planning.

Changes in the family are most vivid and most researched in the rural family. This is especially true in Croatia because of the strength of rural sociology in the Croatian intellectual tradition.[20] Rural households are increasingly households of the elderly as the younger generation moves to towns and industrial employment. Nonetheless, a survey of 271 families in Croatia shows that in 58.7 percent of the cases, the grown, emigrated children still help their parents, both financially (30 percent) and in work on the farm (37.2 percent). Sons assist their parents more than do daughters, and children help their parents more than parents help their children.[21] Research among Croatian rural families shows a decline in the high value once placed on land, an increase in the emphasis on personal rather than collective work, greater individualism and independence of family members, and a general weakening in the traditional patterns of authority and sex roles within the family.[22] Women who remain on the farm, however, find that land-consolidation programs and mechanization of farm work, both aspects of recent rural development programs, have made their life worse: the manual labor that they do has only increased as the reforms increase the size of farms.[23] This may be one reason why rural women are significantly less involved in social and political organizations than are women from urban backgrounds.[24]

Although long-term research in Slovenia by Mirjana Ule and Silva Mežnarić on the socio-political activities of women has yet to be published, Yugoslav-wide samples show women to be much less active than men. When women are active, they show an interest in the Red Cross, the Conference for the Social Activity of Women, libraries, and the Society for Yugoslav Children rather than in cultural-artistic activities, sports, or professional associations. Their participation in self-management is only at the lowest levels: voters' meetings and apartment house councils. They hold leadership positions only in so-called "women's organizations," and more than 70 percent of employed women do not spend even one day a month on social activities.

Since most attitudinal surveys in Yugoslavia find little variation by sex, these behavioral differences (as in mass media behavior) are worth noting. They also lend support to the explanation given by a study of 1,479 employed women throughout Yugoslavia:[25] 85.1 percent said their inactivity was because they were overburdened and overworked; 97.8 percent have obligations at work, maintain the house, and often contribute additional earnings to the household. In 69.5 percent of the cases, the women do all the household tasks. While women's employment outside the home (along with their increased education, smaller families, and participation in self-managing organs) has led to a process of democratization and equalization of conjugal relations, so that 60 to 80 percent of the sample showed equality between spouses in family decisions, women do not show an interest in relieving their burdens by dividing household tasks more equally among family members. Instead, they argue that their burdens are due to an insufficient number of child-care centers and household appliances. Solutions, they say, will come from "social intervention," that is, greater provision of services, household appliances, facilities for child care, and a shortening of the work day, larger incomes, and liberation from the third shift for women.

Women work in Yugoslavia primarily to increase the family income and to gain the greater economic freedom that comes with retaining part of their income for their own needs, even though their employment also leads to additional family expenses. At the same time, 50 percent of the sampled working women are convinced that their employment negatively influences their children's upbringing. Nearly as many—47.5 percent—would prefer not to work at all, and 34.4 percent would quit in order to care for their children better. Of those who would remain working, 45.8 percent would prefer to change jobs, and only 35 percent appear satisfied with their current employment. Women do not as a rule participate in strikes and work stoppages—27.7 percent of the sample had done so once and 8.4 percent more than once. This may be explained by the difference between their needs and those of the men with whom they work. Fully 90.6 percent of the women receive no special privileges for their mothering and housewife roles, 30.6 percent want reduced work hours for women, and 26.8 percent want facilities for child care at their place of employment. In contrast, 77.3 percent of the women say their pay is the same as that of men in similar jobs.

The difficulties posed by female employment for the raising of children appears to have lowered fertility rates among working women, although fertility also declines with higher levels of schooling, which raises the age of marriage, of conception, and of giving birth, and encourages family planning. These difficulties do not appear to lead to family disharmony or a greater likelihood of divorce, nor do they lessen the mother's contact with her child's school. Indeed, women's employment appears to increase family harmony, encourage greater involvement of the father in his child's upbringing, and democratize family relations. At the same time, education may be as important an influence on improving women's condition, as suggested by the finding that the least educated women use only natural forms of contraception and have the largest number of abortions.[26] Although nationality rather than religion or parental attitudes (socialization) appears to predict attitudes toward fertility and contraception, sufficient research on women's attitudes toward contraception has been done only in Slovenia in a study commissioned by the World Health Organization. A study of family planning and intermarriage in Croatia will soon be completed. However, the nationalist concern over the decreasing number of "pure" Croatians (due to a declining birth rate and to an increase in inter-ethnic marriages) that seems to have motivated this research may lead to concern among political leaders that misunderstanding of the research might exacerbate ethnic tensions. If so, they could prevent its publication for some time.

The future for women looks fairly optimistic if one examines attitudes alone, as suggested by table 2.1.[27] Behavioral indicators, however, suggest more caution. In Slovenia, where the equalization of men's and women's roles within the family and society is most advanced, there appears to be great internal differentiation. Members of one group—the politically active League of Communists—rarely speak of the values of women's liberation, but act out far greater equality. Another group is of high status in terms of sociopolitical involvement, occupation, education, and residence, and holds the values of women's equality strongly, but does not appear to act these values out. A third group is best defined by their religiosity and their heavily consumer-oriented standard of living. For this group, equality is neither behavior nor value. The slowness with which the second group is moving toward changes in women's

Table 2.1. Women on The Future
(percentages)

| | Perceived Degree of Certainty | | | | | | | |
| Question | The Year 1981 | | | | The Year 2000 | | | |
	Certain	Probably	Improbable	Don't Know	Certain	Probably	Improbable	Don't Know
1. Many people will work 30 hours a week or less, especially women. N=	7.4 (110)	45.6 (675)	32.3 (477)	14.2 (210)	36.9 (546)	39.7 (587)	8.0 (119)	14.9 (220)
2. Our workers will be able to fly to the Adriatic or other Yugoslav regions for the weekend. N=	5.3 (78)	38.1 (564)	44.3 (655)	11.8 (174)	28.9 (427)	43.1 (637)	14.5 (215)	13.0 (193)
3. Medical science will cure cancer and poliomyelitis. N=	9.8 (145)	51.2 (757)	25.7 (380)	12.8 (189)	45.3 (670)	38.9 (576)	5.0 (74)	10.3 (152)
4. Nuclear energy will be the main force in industry. N=	11.7 (173)	42.1 (623)	25.8 (381)	19.9 (295)	40.8 (603)	36.2 (536)	5.5 (82)	17.0 (251)
5. Many of our villages will have a theater, concert hall, gallery and library. N=	13.0 (193)	48.5 (718)	27.8 (411)	10.1 (149)	42.5 (628)	40.5 (599)	7.2 (107)	9.3 (138)
6. The UN will be a world government with a strong army. Wars will disappear. N=	4.6 (68)	24.0 (355)	45.4 (671)	25.6 (378)	15.1 (224)	31.6 (467)	24.9 (368)	27.9 (413)

Table 2.1 Continued

Question	Certain	Probably	Improbable	Don't Know	Certain	Probably	Improbable	Don't Know
7. Divorce will be common and easy to do. N=	22.4 (332)	41.8 (618)	23.5 (347)	11.8 (175)	46.3 (685)	27.4 (405)	12.2 (180)	13.7 (202)
8. All employed mothers will occupy a special place in the family, at work, and in society. N=	6.1 (90)	35.1 (519)	45.7 (676)	12.6 (187)	24.1 (356)	42.5 (629)	19.2 (284)	13.7 (203)
9. Every family will have a comfortable, well-furnished apartment with kitchen appliances. N=	7.1 (105)	28.7 (425)	55.3 (818)	8.4 (124)	24.9 (369)	42.9 (634)	21.6 (320)	10.1 (149)
10. All workers will be able to afford a holiday abroad if they wish to do so. N=	4.7 (70)	19.4 (287)	64.4 (952)	11.0 (163)	15.1 (223)	40.0 (591)	31.1 (460)	13.4 (198)
11. Co-existence among nations will resolve many world economic, social, racial, and ethnic problems. N=	5.2 (77)	37.5 (554)	33.6 (497)	23.3 (344)	21.0 (310)	39.2 (580)	15.3 (227)	23.9 (354)

Source: Miro A. Mihovilović, "Žene o Budućnosti," in Mihovilović et al., *Žena Izmedju Rada i Porodice: Utjecaj zaposlenosti žene na strukturu i funkciju porodice* (Zagreb: Institut za Društvena Istraživanja Sveučilišta u Zagrebu, 1975), p. 198.

roles suggests evolutionary rather than revolutionary changes. At the same time, the third, traditional group is the largest and appears, to some extent, to represent a return to traditional values. As a result of the desire in this group for higher quality services than can be bought, the woman returns to the home and to more household tasks than before in order to provide the higher quality of food, cleaning, and service desired.[28]

Education and Youth

In socialist societies, including Yugoslavia, youth are viewed as the most aware sector of society, as a way of glimpsing the future of these societies, and as a guide to changes yet needed to reach a desired future. It is not surprising, then, that sociologists should direct much of their research toward them. The attitudes of youth, along with the development of workers' self-management, dominate the first decade of sociological research in Yugoslavia. During 1975-77, this research focused on the ideological orientations and the activism of youth, as well as on the plight of rural youth.

In October 1973, after student strikes in 1968 and 1971, 41.5 percent of the Croatian population polled (N=2,000) thought youth had too little influence on Yugoslav social development. Although this view varied with age, only a small minority thought youth had too great an influence on Yugoslav developments.[29] In Serbia, a 1974 survey of 1,600 youth and 198 youth delegates to town assemblies found this influence limited by the small numbers of active youth—only 5 percent were intensely active (see table 2.2 for this classification)—and by the inadequacy of youth's understanding of the "complex mechanism of self-managing decision making."[30] Judging by the 93 percent of the young delegates who said they expected help from older delegates in fulfilling their responsibilities but rarely got it, this inadequacy comes from insufficient instruction and experience for the tasks of representation and decision making.

According to this survey, almost half of Serbian youth (47.8 percent) are politically passive—not involved in any sociopolitical organizations or action. Those who are active are more likely to participate in sociopolitical organizations (especially in the League of Youth) than in self-managing (elective, workplace-based) bodies, and only a small group of youth is active in both spheres. The League of Youth appears to be the "school" for political involvement, predicting almost entirely which youth will remain active, but the core of activism in both politics and self-management is among youth who also are members of the League of Communists. To the investigators' surprise, 50 percent of the youth surveyed wanted to be members of the League of Communists, yet were not; in particular, rural youth expressed an above-average interest in joining both the League of Communists and the League of Youth. Although youth consider the new delegate system (see note 13) as a stimulus to greater

Table 2.2. Classification of Sociopolitical Activism of Serbian Youth

Active youth:

1. Intensely active: positive answers to one or more of questions 1-5 below and to questions 6-7.
2. Moderately active: positive answers either to one question from group 1-5 or to questions 6 and 7.
3. Weakly active: a positive answer to question 7.

Inactive youth:

1. Potential activists: positive answers to any of questions 8, 9, or 10; they need not be formal members of sociopolitical or self-managing organs.
2. Inactive members of an organization: positive answers to any of questions 11 through 15.
3. Totally inactive: do not possess one characteristic of those listed in any of the other categories; completely outside social or political action.

Distribution of Responses
(N = 1,798)

Question	Affirmative Responses (%)
1. Participates in preparing meetings	35
2. Performs concrete duties and tasks for the organization	16
3. Takes part in local work projects	48
4. Takes part in federal work projects	5
5. Takes part in practical projects organized by the League of Youth of Serbia	51
6. Gives suggestions, criticism at meetings	21
7. Seeks explanations, supports suggestions at meetings	17
8. Is familiar with the program and plans of the organ	29
9. Refers to problems in the work environment	53
10. Refers to "youth" problems	51
11. Attends meetings	81
12. Performed a function for the organization or organ	20
13. Membership in self-management organs	26
14. Membership in the League of Communists	24
15. Membership in the League of Youth	67

Source: Srćko Mihailović, "Političko i Samoupravno Angažovanje Omladine," in Vladimir Goati et al., *Društveno-Političko Angažovanje Omladine* (Belgrade: Institut Društvenih Nauka, Beograd, and the RK SSO Srbije, 1977), pp. 36-41.

activism among their peers, their view of the weaknesses of both the delegate system and the League of Youth points clearly to reasons for low levels of both participation and influence: the unsatisfactory flow of information between delegates and their constituencies, and dominance by the top leadership (see table 2.3).

Active youth differentiate along socioeconomic lines. The active core is found among youth employed as highly skilled, industrial workers. Rural youth, high school and university students, and unskilled and semiskilled industrial workers are less active or even passive. It is interesting to note, however, that these weakly involved rural youth and high school students participate most (96 percent) in voluntary labor projects, such as building a road or aiding earth-quake torn cities, especially when they are locally organized. But their responses to attitude surveys suggest that they are not strongly inclined to self-management as an ideal. The 5 percent who are most active (the highly skilled workers) resemble more strictly a traditional political elite—only 20 percent took part in volunteer work projects, and they had applied and been selected for the more desirable, federally organized projects. These   activists hold leading positions in organizations, and demonstrate most attachment on attitude surveys to the ideals of self-management (76 percent).[31]

Although Goati et al. find no strong relationship between a youth's social class and his inclination to be active, Tomanović[32] found an interesting pattern in a study of almost 2,000 Serbian youth in 1969 and 1970. Overall, the higher the socioeconomic background of the youth, the less interest they show in established forms of political participation. But distinct differences could be identified. The higher the income of employed youth, the more they participate. For university students, on the other hand, greater participation is correlated with poorer socioeconomic backgrounds. Socioeconomic status does not differentiate political participation at all, however, among high school students. Further, the poorer university student is more likely to participate in spon-taneous, less-organized activities, such as demonstrations or making speeches at meetings, whereas the wealthier employed youth participates in established forms of political organization, such as positions in the League of Communists.

Interviewing 968 Belgrade university students about the singular student strikes of June, 1968, Tomanović also discovered the highest levels of active participation among students from the poorest and peasant families. Not only were the most disadvantaged the most active, but their protests, he argues persuasively, were also not a "new left" movement but a classical, left-oriented articulation of the social dissatisfaction of the underprivileged.   Although accepting self-management principles, these students were highly critical of Yugoslav practice, in particular of social inequalities. Further, the student demonstrators were not particularly alienated (measured by their agreement or not with the assertion, "City people are cold and impersonal; it is difficult to find new friends in the city."), and they earn better school grades than those who did not participate.

Table 2.3. Weaknesses in the Delegate System: Reasons Most Often Cited
by Young Delegates to Communal Assemblies in Serbia (N = 198)

Reasons Given	Percentage of Respondents
1. Unsatisfactory ties between delegations and delegates and their electoral base	62
2. Unsatisfactorily developed means of gaining information	51
3. Lack of interest on the part of workers and citizens in becoming involved in public life	44
4. Difficulties in finding a consensus among different interests within assembly decision making	32
5. Decisive influence still retained by directors of work organizations over major decisions	24
6. The influence of leadership and executive organs in assemblies is still too great	18

Source: Mijat Damjanović, "Ocene o Delegatskom Sistemu," in Vladimir Goati et al., *Družt-veno-Političko Angažovanje Omladine* (Belgrade: Institut Društvenih Nauka, Beograd, and the RK SSO Srbije, 1977), p. 161.

Findings concerning the ideological orientation of youth in Yugoslavia are extremely sensitive to the research design and instrument. Goati et al. for example, find that 61 percent of their sample is "self-management oriented" (see table 2.4), whereas 24 percent hold a mixture of self-management and other orientations and 15 percent hold an eclectic mixture of non-self-management ideologies. But they also find that positive responses are more frequent if an assertion is phrased positively than if it is stated negatively.[33] Tomanović finds that 55-64 percent of high school students and 37-51 percent of employed youth say they are supporters of socialism when asked, although only 33-35 percent identify self-management as the most important value of socialism (rather than, for example, social equality).[34] Šiber, in a study of 1,588 rural Croatian youth in 1974, finds a serious problem: his respondents simultaneously accept the values of self-managing socialism and of bourgeois democracy (multiparty politics, individual freedoms).[35]

According to Goati et al., opposition to the principles of self-management is found most among unemployed youth and youth temporarily working abroad. Their findings also agree with those of Tomanović, who emphasizes material circumstances: the more satisfied one is with one's material situation and the more hopeful one is about one's future, the more supportive one is of self-managing socialism. Furthermore, although social equality is the prime value of socialism to these youth, the value of self-management and socialist democracy grows in importance with income. Unemployed youth and young engineers are most critical of Yugoslav practice, and the poorer and less secure the youth, the more egalitarian his orientation. Fully one-third of the surveyed Serbian youth believe income differences should be smaller and taxes should be more progressive, but this is less true of employed youth than of student youth and less true of students in the scientific-technical and the economic faculties than of students in the humanities and the social sciences. Once more, as one's material circumstances improve, the range of income differentials one finds acceptable, and even desirable, widens.

According to Tomanović, the emphasis on economic equality is found among poorer youth and declines as employed youth gain in income and education, whereas the wealthier the student youth, the more in favor of economic development, and its implied inequalities, he becomes. Personal freedoms take last place among social values that need realizing, as the data for students illustrates [36] (see table 2.5).

Finally, Tomanović finds what others have found among Yugoslav adults, that socioeconomic background influences essentially every aspect of educational and occupational choice. Such evidence supports the conclusion of Goati et al. that the "struggle for self-managing ideology. . .to the extent that it is fought in isolation from the struggle for an improved social position of youth, will have very little effect."[37] Čalić, in a study of active Serbian youth who nevertheless showed disappointingly low levels of ideological-theoretical knowledge about self-managing socialism, also argues that only successful development of socialist self-managing practice itself and practical experience among youth will raise their theoretical consciousness.[38]

The unexpected findings in the Serbian studies concerning rural youth's aspirations for greater political participation makes the study of 1,588 rural youth in 66 Croatian villages in 1974 by a team from the Center for Rural, Urban, and Spatial Sociology of Zagreb University of particular interest.[39] Differences in attitudes and behavior between rural and urban youth are declining, according to this study. Nonetheless, rural youth still live in less favorable conditions. They have less access to the cultural and educational institutions of cities. Their free time, if any, is used simply to recuperate from work rather than to explore other sides of their personalities. The workload they carry is out of proportion to the rights they receive in family decision making or independence in spending. They are subject to far greater unemployment than are urban youth. Thus rural youth who choose farming as a vocation tend to do so because of a lack of alternatives. The "flight from agriculture" is, for the two-fifths of the sample who do leave, a search for educational and vocational opportunities in the cities. They leave to avoid the burdensome work and family conditions in the countryside, not because of any psychological attraction for cities. Training for farming still comes through apprenticeship and practical experience, even though farmers believe that specialized instruction in schools would be far better.

Although rural youth show little political involvement and are more religious than urban youth, both of these characteristics are declining, and their views of family, marital, and personal life are almost indistinguishable from those of their urban compatriots. Indeed, this change, and the finding that schools and the mass media have greater influence on political socialization than does the family, have increased conflicts between generations in the Croatian countryside.

There nonetheless remains a great difference between the urban and rural population in level of education obtained. According to Petak, the start of formal education begins the process whereby rural children become more like urban youth and less like the rural youth of previous generations.[40] Level of education predicts attitudinal differences far better than do differences in occupation, income, or political activity.

Research on the youth in Yugoslavia has revealed changes in the last ten years, including a closing in the rural-urban gap in attitudes; greater differentiation of attitudes within the population by region, income, and occupation; an increase in "modern" attitudes toward family, leisure, and lifestyle; and different levels of commitment to the Yugoslav method of building socialism. A clear pattern of positive association between an individual's material and status position and his attitude toward self-managing socialism also emerges. Relatively naive views of socialism in the early years give way to a more critical and differentiated range of opinion by the end of schooling and the acceptance of employment. Yet these studies also show that a Yugoslav's ideological view of

Table 2.4. Self-Management Orientation among Serbian Youth, 1974 (N = 1,548)
(percentages)

Assertion:	Response				
	Agree Completely	Agree	Undecided	Disagree	Disagree Completely
1. "It is better that everyone in a Basic Organization of Associated Labor participate in making important decisions, even if those decisions taken are not always the best."	32 (5)	26 (4)	18 (3)	11 (2)	13 (1)[a]
2. "In the interest of maintaining socialist order, it is best that the country be governed by a group of professional politicians."	20 (1)	13 (2)	29 (3)	15 (4)	23 (5)
3. "Direct decision making in enterprises leads to economic chaos."	11 (1)	14 (2)	29 (3)	24 (4)	23 (5)
4. "The belief that workers at this level of education can manage the economy is naive."	12 (1)	12 (2)	25 (3)	28 (4)	23 (5)
5. "The right to decision making in enterprises (BOALs) ought to be given only to expert and politically conscious workers."	16 (1)	16 (2)	20 (3)	26 (4)	22 (5)
6. "Decision making in the BOAL should not be entrusted to only one group of people no matter how expert or politically correct the decision."	36 (5)	23 (4)	17 (3)	11 (2)	12 (1)
7. "Realizing self-managing principles will not improve the material position of workers very much."	8 (1)	9 (2)	30 (3)	28 (4)	26 (5)
8. "Not one suggestion to the collective should be adopted if a majority does not stand behind it."	27 (5)	26 (4)	12 (3)	7 (2)	29 (1)
9. "If the right people to manage the enterprise could be found, direct government by the majority would not be necessary."	9 (1)	12 (2)	22 (3)	33 (4)	24 (5)
10. "Self-management overburdens and imposes responsibility on workers."	10 (5)	13 (2)	22 (3)	30 (4)	26 (5)

Table 2.4 Continued

Assertion:	Agree Completely	Agree	Undecided	Disagree	Disagree Completely
11. "Participation in the governance of the enterprise leads to much greater commitment at work."	44 (5)	29 (4)	15 (3)	6 (2)	7 (1)
12. "Self-management makes a just distribution of personal incomes possible."	41 (5)	28 (4)	17 (3)	7 (2)	6 (1)

[a]Each answer is awarded points on a scale of 1 to 5, according to its orientation in favor of or opposed to self-management. The most favorable response is given a 5, the least favorable, a 1. The following distribution shows the extent of self-managing and non-self-managing orientations among Serbian youth.

Distribution of Responses

Points	Intensity of orientation	Frequency	Percent of Sample
1. 18 or fewer	Extreme non-self-management orientation	12	1
2. 19-23	Strong non-self-management orientation	19	1
3. 24-28	Moderate non-self-management orientation	62	4
4. 29-33	Weak non-self-management orientation	143	9
5. 34-38	"Mixed type"	372	24
6. 39-43	Weak self-management orientation	322	21
7. 44-48	Moderate self-management orientation	288	19
8. 49-53	Strong self-management orientation	184	12
9. 54 or more	Extreme self-management orientation	146	9
Totals		1,548	100

Source: Dragomir Pantić, "Odnos Omladine Prema Samoupravljanju," in Vladimir Goati et al., *Društveno-Političko Angažovanje Omladine* (Belgrade: Institut Društvenih Nauka, Beograd, and the RK SSO Srbije, 1977), pp. 115–16, 121.

Table 2.5. Rankings of Priorities of Students by
Income and Parents' Occupation

Value (according to order in survey)	Student's Material Position (income)							
	Low 1-2	3	4	5	6	7	High 8-9	Overall
1. Socialist democracy	6	7	6	5	6	7	5	7
2. Increase production	7	5	4	3	4	2	1	3
3. Social equality	1	1	2	1	2	3	4	2
4. Social planning	10	10	10	9	9	10	10	10
5. Distribution according to work	6	6	5	6	7	6	6	5-6
6. Personal freedoms for citizens	9	9	9	10	10	9	8	9
7. Reducing social differences	2	2	1	2	1	1	2	1
8. Self-management	3	3	3	4	5	4	3	4
9. Improving the standard of living	4	4	7	7	3	5	7	5-6
10. Solidarity within society	8	8	8	8	8	8	9	8

Value	Occupation of Student's Parents[a]						
	1	2	3	4	5	6	7
1. Socialist democracy	6	5	2	5-6	7	6	3
2. Increase production	2	7	5	2-4	6	1	1
3. Social equality	1	1	7	1	2	4	6
4. Social planning	10	10	10	10	9	10	10
5. Distribution according to work	5	4	6	5-6	5	7	4
6. Personal freedoms for citizens	9	9	9	8	10	9	9
7. Reducing social differences	3	2	1	7	1	2	5
8. Self-management	4	3	3	2-4	3	3	2
9. Improving the standard of living	7	6	4	2-4	4	5	7
10. Solidarity within society	8	8	8	9	8	8	8

[a] 1 = private farmers; 2 = semi- and unskilled workers; 3 = skilled and highly skilled workers; 4 = private craftsmen; 5 = office workers with high school education; 6 = office workers with higher education; 7= managers

Source: Velimir Tomanović, *Omladina i Socijalizam* (Belgrade: Mladost, 1977), pp. 89-90.

the world continues to develop well after entering adulthood.

Although youth are less favorably disposed to socialism the poorer their material circumstances (especially if they are unemployed), participation in sociopolitical organizations and self-managing bodies seems to be found among the poorer youth. Interest in participation also declines as socioeconomic status improves. Consistent differences between youth still in school and those already at work also suggest an early development of the attitudinal cleavage between industrial workers and professional-managerial occupations in Yugoslavia.

Within this wide differentiation and general acceptance (averaging 60 percent) of self-management, however, one finds a strong current of criticism of Yugoslav practice, and especially of social inequality, among youth. The potential for active protest seems small, on the other hand, since youth are not agreed on the definition of equality or their reasons for criticism, and since even those few who do participate differ on whether to use established forums or informal demonstrations and strikes.

Work and the Workplace

Industrial sociology is the oldest and most developed subfield of Yugoslav social science. A fascination with their novel system of workers' self-management led Yugoslavs and others, particularly Americans, to study its effects on the distribution of power, on decision making in the firm, and on workers' alienation from its earliest stages. Such studies predominate in the first decade of social science publishing in Yugoslavia, for example, in the pages of *Sociologija*, the organ of the Yugoslav Sociological Association. Methodologically, these studies reflect the influence of American sociologists (especially of Arnold Tannenbaum) and usually rely on opinion surveys. By 1975, the sophistication of questions and analysis and the accumulation of knowledge were impressive, but the special role of this research in Yugoslav sociology had disappeared as the study of other subjects became more fully developed. Furthermore, the most important research on work in Yugoslavia during the 1970s, the Yugoslav portion of a collaborative European project on industrial democracy done by Veljko Rus and Vesna Pusić, was not yet ready for publication.

By the mid-1970s Yugoslav research on the structures of power, participation, and decision making in the self-managed enterprise began to reveal the dominance of the administrative-executive staffs over all enterprise decisions and the lack of influence of workers, even members of the workers' council.[41] Sociologists admitted that it was difficult to judge whether this was a change away from the conditions of increased but distinctly limited democracy of the 1960s, or a change in the measuring instruments: better surveys and observational methods. Josip Obradović went so far as to identify an "elite" within the enterprise, based on Croatian research, composed of the director, his assistants, the heads of the firm's professional staffs (particularly the administrative staffs), and experts without executive positions but employed in the firm's offices. These individuals were predominantly members of the League of Communists, were the most educated in the firm, and were not members of the workers' council. This elite decides all major issues, regardless of the issue area, and they dominate in all forms of participation. Obradović is only beginning to attempt to explain these results, so contradictory of self-management theory. Thus far he argues that whatever leads a person into top levels of the enterprise hierarchy, usually by way of informal organizations in the firm, determines his influence and participation. In this research, Obradović points to an individual's level of education and to membership in the League of Communists.[42]

A similar pattern is found by Ivan Šiber in his study of the levels of information held by employees in a large machine tool factory on the outskirts of Zagreb (N=464). Employees are badly informed; they answer correctly an average of 17 out of 32 key questions.[43] Their answers suggest that information in the firm is unstructured and that communication processes and content are not suited to the task of self-management. Šiber finds, as does Obradović, that variation in the level of accurate information can best be explained by personal characteristics, especially one's level of education, but also by one's place in the firm hierarchy (executive positions above all), by the extent of social contact at one's job, and by the years of employment at that firm. Less important but contributing factors were participation in self-management organs, membership in the League of Communists, and functions held in socio-political organizations. These attitudes—such as one's perceived influence in the firm and one's sense of identification with it—contributed almost nothing to explaining an employee's lack of knowledge. This throws additional doubt on the validity of conclusions based on survey research in Yugoslavia, at least in the field of industrial sociology. Both Šiber and Obradović find that observation produces better results on participation than do attitude surveys.[44]

Šiber finds that workers have disappointingly low levels of information felt to be necessary for participation in workplace decision making. This finding is the major concern of Novosel's summary volume, *Delegatsko Informiranje*. He reports shocking levels of ignorance in 1973 (see table 2.6). He also cites a study by Vujević, who used a random sample of 760 Croatians to study the degree to which citizens were familiar with concepts such as inflation, investment, and profitability. No more than 29 percent of the unskilled and semiskilled workers knew these concepts; more than 45 percent of the skilled and highly skilled understood the terms. Like Šiber, Novosel points to the inadequacy of communication networks in the firm as a major cause of such ignorance. For example, 78 percent of a large sample of Croatian workers say their opinion is rarely or never sought about enterprise issues, and 59 percent say it is fairly or very difficult to find someone who can inform them about matters which are unclear. A content analysis of newsletters in Croatian factories confirms the poverty of information available to workers.[45]

Table 2.6. Factory Workers' Knowledge about Their Firm
in a Large Zagreb Factory, 1973 (N = 467)

Item of Information	Percentage of Correct Responses
1. The percent of Yugoslav total production produced by their factory	10
2. The average monthly income for a specified skilled worker for the previous month	16
3. What loss (gain) their firm realized in the previous year	7
4. What communal funds the entire firm maintains	12
5. The market on which they get the best price	27
6. The financial position of their firm (more often in debt or in demand)	27
7. The extent of customers' complaints about the firm's products	31
8. The average number of working days lost per BOAL (smallest work unit) due to illness and absence	1
9. The opportunities within the firm to learn other skills and obtain a higher skill qualification	13
10. How large the firm's research staff is in comparison with similar firms in Yugoslavia	6
11. The number of BOALS in the firm	32
12. Who approves the final accounts of the firm	31
13. The approximate number of persons employed in the firm	18

Source: Pavao Novosel, *Delegatsko Informiranje: Modeli samoupravne komunikacijske akcije* (Zagreb: Biblioteka Komunikacijske Znanosti, 1977), pp. 32-33.

This exploration of the less successful side of self-management dominates the research reported in the 1975-77 period on the workplace. Mesić argues that women workers are a "half phase" behind male workers in the political culture of self-management, although his survey of 1,000 Zagreb factory workers reveals little difference in the distribution of responses between men and women, except that the percentage of "don't knows" is far higher among the women than the men. According to Mesić, the lack of knowledge and of interest in participation among women is due to their heavy burden with household and family functions (a conclusion generally accepted by all Yugoslavs who write about women).[46]

Silvano Bolčić finds that, contrary to the self-management principle that the enterprise should be a collective entrepreneur, only a narrow group within the collective actually performs the entrepreneurial function by participating in decisions about the firm's business. What is more serious, in light of the current instability of the economy, is the unwillingness of employed workers to bear the negative consequences of collective decisions (that is, to accept a reduction in their personal incomes as a result of poor business). Only 15.1 percent in an all-Yugoslav sample of 916 workers expressed an unreserved willingness to take risks (accept the consequences of reduced income), and 7.9 percent thought the society ought to cover enterprise losses. Those with the greatest influence and role in decision making in the firm seemed to hold to a "right to irresponsibility." Membership in self-managing bodies did not change this unwillingness, but it did lessen with a respondent's level of education. Nor is there a direct connection between risk-taking attitudes and the profitability of one's enterprise[47] (see tables 2.7 and 2.8). In the face of these unwelcome findings, Bolčić argues that the instability of the Yugoslav economy comes from broader social problems, including unrealistic expectations concerning the behavior of work organizations as economic actors; broader, structural changes in society are the precondition of lasting changes in economic performance.[48]

Finally, Vladimir Arzenšek has sought the causes of strike activity in Yugoslav firms by surveying 14 Slovenian industrial enterprises subject to strikes during 1973-74. Strikers, according to Arzenšek's sample, are male, urban dwelling, downwardly mobile, elementary school educated, and often minority group members, but they are just as likely to be members of workers' councils as not. Arzenšek argues that two factors are most powerful in identifying an inclination to strike: 1) alienation, in the sense of a feeling of powerlessness, of externally caused frustrations, of frequent experiences with injustice, and of an arrogant and unresponsive management; and 2) a rejection of the legitimacy of structures within the enterprise in which management has the dominant position. Workers who strike see the political system as inadequately representing their interests, see relations between the working class and other groups as antagonistic, and consider the trade unions incapable of mediating conflicts between workers and management because members of the trade union organization are under the influence of the enterprise's management.[49]

Table 2.7. Attitude Toward Risk Among Employees in Yugoslav Industry

Response	Number and Percentage of Respondents	
	N	%
1. Personal incomes of all employees should be reduced	138	15.1
2. Personal incomes of only those who did not carry out their obligations should be reduced	242	26.4
3. Personal incomes of managers should be reduced because it is their responsibility that no losses occur	218	23.8
4. Losses should be covered at the expense of enterprise funds, not by reducing personal incomes	157	17.1
5. Society ought to cover the losses rather than reduce personal incomes	72	7.9
6. No answer	89	9.7
Totals	916	100.0

Source: Silvano Bolčić, "Preduzetništvo kao determinanta ekonomskih odnosa (Uvodno izlaganje)," in Josip Obradović et al., *Proizvodne Organizacije i Samoupravljanje,* vol. 2, *Čovjek i Sistem* (Zagreb: Filozofski Fakultet Sveučilišta u Zagrebu—Odsjek za sociologiju, 1975), p. 116.

Table 2.8. Willingness To Bear Risks according to Sociofunctional Groups

Group	Percentage indicating complete willingness
1. Workers	16.3
2. Experts	10.3
3. Administrative staff	15.4
4. Managers	28.6

Source: Silvano Bolčić, "Preduzetništvo kao determinanta ekonomskih odnosa (Uvodno izlaganje)," in Josip Obradović et al., *Proizvodne Organizacije i Samoupravljanje,* vol. 2, *Čovjek i Sistem* (Zagreb: Filozofski Fakultet Sveučilišta u Zagrebu—Odsjek za sociologiju, 1975), p. 117.

Research on work and the workplace continues to show the differentiation of attitudes and the extent of conflicts within the Yugoslav enterprise, factors often ignored by the theory of self-management. During 1975-77, the evidence was stronger than ever that enterprise decision making follows a hierarchical (rather than egalitarian) distribution of influence in which level of education and formal position seem most important. In addition to asking questions about the success of self-management in the firm, researchers are beginning to gather information on why workers strike and why firms experience financial difficulties. These circumstances are being traced to more general attitudes about social relations, a just distribution of burdens, and legitimate influence of different groups within Yugoslav society.

Leisure Time

A complete picture of the way Yugoslavs spend their free time is not available for the period 1975-77 for two reasons. First, with the desuetude of the Yugoslav Sociological Association in the 1970s, its section of free-time research under Miro Mihovilović (recently retired) was relatively inactive. Second, an analysis of Slovenians' free-time activities from a major project on the "Development of Slovenia, 1975-77," is not published. Information on leisure time must now be culled from larger projects designed for other purposes. Some of these studies are discussed under the sections on Education and Youth and on Moral and Ethical Preferences and Life Aspirations.

A dominant theme in this research again is the existence of socioeconomic differentiation in cultural needs, cultural activities, and leisure-time pursuits. Urban-rural differences usually appear in studies made by planners inquiring into the cultural needs of a local population. Thus surveys in smaller towns in Croatia (Gospić, Daruvar, and Karlovac) concerning the dissatisfaction of youth find that no place is provided by the commune where youth could gather for leisure activities.[50] Even though towns and cities appear to have better facilities for youth, a study of 1,946 youth in Maribor, Slovenia, found that secondary school youths felt they did not have proper company, enough freedom in the choice of their activities, nor adequate equipment, resources, or buildings for their free-time enjoyment.[51]

Urban-rural origin[52] also plays an important role in the way employed women spend their time. Women born in rural areas spend a far larger percentage of their day on work and on housework than do women from urban areas. The latter tend to find more time to attend to physiological needs (personal hygiene, eating, and sleeping) and to free-time activities (excursions, walks, visiting, concerts, sport, church, reading, or radio and television watching). The time spent on leisure by employed women and the budget available to them also increase with the level of education and professional qualifications, with the level of family income, and with the share of the woman's income in the family revenue, but decline with an increase in the number of children and of family members.[53]

Data on leisure-time pursuits from the 1976 survey of Macedonian public opinion (N=1,149) reveal the heavily rural component of that republic's population. Aside from the 17 percent who said they had no free time, leisure is spent in passive relaxation: 38.1 percent at home with their family, 12.4 percent visiting neighbors and friends, and 9.5 percent watching television. If they had more free time, 23.4 percent of the Macedonian respondents would spend it visiting friends and neighbors, and 47.2 percent would frequent cafés and clubs— although here the difference is great between men (68.2 percent), traditionally allowed more public recreation, and women (25.2 percent).[54]

A Serbian study in 1974 (N=1,000) suggests that such urban-rural differences in leisure-time pursuits are being transformed into differences among social strata. The traditional lifestyle of the peasant does not distinguish between work and leisure; free time from work is spent resting up to work again, socializing with workmates (family and neighbors) where conversation dwells on work matters, or celebrating popular and religious feasts to excess. Yearly vacations are spent at home by 95 percent of the subsample. Where differences occur, they are carefully defined by custom and differentiate along sex and age lines.

Urban lifestyles in Serbia break down into two major categories, the working-class strata (unskilled, skilled, and white-collar) and the middle-upper-class strata (professionals, intellectuals, and managers). For workers, leisure serves the function of escape from existential problems. Above all, skilled workers attend soccer matches and all the activities associated with soccer; 55 percent of the workers rarely miss a match, which is true of only 35 percent of the intellectuals and 19 percent of the peasants. They watch television more than any other social group, and they frequent the neighborhood café almost every evening to meet with their friends. Yearly vacations are spent at home for lack of means by 92 percent of the peasant workers, 73 percent of the unskilled workers, 41 percent of the skilled workers, and only 30 percent of white-collar workers (62 percent of whom have the means to spend it at a tourist spot on the seacoast, in the mountains, or at a lake).

Leisure takes on identity as a distinct, autonomous form of active, self-fulfillment for the middle and upper strata. Forms of entertainment are more varied; for example, 70 percent of the managerial stratum regularly attend the theater, cinema, concerts, and nightclubs, in contrast to about half of the intellectuals, a third of the white-collar workers, a fourth of the skilled workers, and 8 percent of the unskilled workers. A majority of these strata go on weekend excursions, which 78 percent of the skilled workers rarely or never do. Summer holidays are spent in prestige resorts by 78 percent of the intellectuals and 80 percent of the managerial stratum, and winter free time is spent in exclusive cafés and restaurants.[55]

A survey of hobbies in Belgrade (N=502) found that 42.8 percent had no hobby at all. The youngest (ages 20 to 34) were more likely to have hobbies than the oldest (64.4 percent vs. 58.9 percent); more substantial differences were based on stability of residence, occupation, and income. The respondents born in Belgrade had more hobbies than those who had moved there later. Of those holding the highest occupational qualifications, 66.9 percent had a hobby, compared with 39.2 percent of the lowest occupational group. Most striking is that 75.7 percent of the highest income bracket had a hobby, in contrast to only 33.3 percent of the poorest group.[56] Similarly, in a study of cultural needs and facilities in central Croatia, Ivan Magdalenić argues that there is an increasing gap between the audiences for serious culture and those for light entertainment in the area, with Zagreb as the center of high culture (theater, film, music, and art exhibits). The numbers who attend any cultural events are small—almost one-half of the 2,088 respondents from 145 settlements showed no interest at all in light entertainment such as popular and folk music concerts or humorous shows, and 64 percent expressed very little interest in serious culture. This aside, the high costs of attending performances of serious culture—especially the entrance fee and the distance to Zagreb—have turned this category into a privileged activity available to a small, closed circle of consumers.[57]

Finally, studies of free-time activity among women who work show an increasingly privatized and passive use of leisure as well as an increasing similarity between men and women. Thus, 65.8 percent of an all-Yugoslav sample of 1,493 working women said they prefer to spend their free time with their children and family, 73.3 percent said the purpose of free time was for excursions with one's children and husband, and 90.2 percent of the women spend their yearly vacation with members of their family. According to the researcher, the data show that women emphasize simple recreation rather than creative use of free time, and passive forms of relaxation rather than active educational and enlightening activities (see table 2.9). And, the authors of this study point to the tendency of employed women to try to escape greater professional obligations and participation in social responsibilities in order to find more time for themselves. They also find that 38.6 percent of the respondents are dissatisfied with the way they spend their leisure time.[58]

Moral and Ethical Preferences and Life Aspirations

When one considers the newness of the Yugoslav model of socialism and the sensitivity of all political reformers to evaluation, the research of Yugoslav sociologists in the 1970s is courageous, indeed, for it has turned to an assessment of the extent to which objective changes since the revolution had led to the more profound and difficult but ultimately more important changes of human values and social consciousness. Value orientations were the subject of the conference of Croatian sociologists in 1975, the main project in the mid-1970s of the

Institute of Social Sciences in Belgrade, the goal of the massive project on Slovenian development at the Institute for Sociology and Philosophy in Ljubljana, as well as many smaller studies by the Zagreb Institute for Social Research. Previously unpublished works on values from the 1960s have appeared, and ethnologists and psychologists have been brought into the research staffs of sociological institutes or into their own, reinvigorated institutes.[59] Much of this literature is methodological and philosophical—Marxist social scientists attempting a synthesis of their Western methods and their Marxist view of interests and values—but much of the work also represents some of the most sophisticated data analysis to be found in Yugoslav social science.

What these researchers find is a relatively stable, though transitional society in which the ruling ideology of self-management is relatively well established but internally differentiated by social strata on values, lifestyles, and ideological orientations. In a 1974 study of 1,000 Serbs chosen by quota sample according to their region and social stratum,[60] researchers from the Institute of Social Sciences in Belgrade under the direction of Mihailo Popović found a distribution of attitudes remarkably similar to that found by sociologists in modern Western societies. That is, the more favorable the position an individual holds in the social hierarchy, the more intensely he holds the "ruling ideology" of self-management and the more congruent and defined are the elements of his ideological orientation.[61] The lower the social stratum, conversely, the less the support for the constellation of values identified with self-management (e.g., self-management itself, modernism, collectivism, nonegalitarianism,[62] nonmaterialism, and social ownership of property) and the more weakly structured the ideological system of the individual.

Furthermore, the competing ideology in Serbia is found not to be statism, as many have presumed, although there remains strong mass support for etatistic politics among unskilled workers. Rather, it is traditionalism, which the researchers see as a constellation of the following values: individualism, radical egalitarianism, private ownership of property, materialism, and localism, values that the researchers do not hesitate to suggest include explicitly antisystem orientations. Of nine value pairs, Pantić finds that four significantly distinguish social strata: traditionalism-modernism, egalitarianism-nonegalitarianism, individualism-collectivism, and private vs. socially owned property. In some strata, an absolute majority accepts the latter of each of these pairs, while in other strata, an absolute majority rejects it. The greatest intensity of feeling, furthermore, occurs on the issue of property.

Bolčić also finds that there are basically two lines of cleavage (and thus, sources of social tension) in this Serbian sample. The strongest divides according to views on property ownership, and the second along principles by which the distribution of income should be made. Income should be distributed, according to peasants, artisans, and workers, in terms of the amount, quality, difficulty, and danger of work done. The middle strata think income should be distributed according to educational qualifications. Leaders and managers argue that distribution should be made on the basis of educational qualifications and the "complexity" of work tasks.[63]

These and other findings lead the authors to conclude that an individual's interests, reflected in his social stratum, determine his values, not vice versa. Those with higher incomes, education, and social influence identify more with the social order. There is an inverse relationship between the orientation in favor of self-management and the value of radical egalitarianism. The lower strata value work; the higher strata value knowledge. Leaders and managers value social order in addition to knowledge. Leaders and professionals say their goals have largely been fulfilled, whereas workers and peasants say their goals remain unfulfilled. Weaknesses in Yugoslavia currently, according to workers and peasants, are the enrichment of individuals at the expense of others. Private craftsmen, on the other hand, cite certain forms of poverty. White-collar workers and professionals point to undisciplined workers. And leaders focus on both undisciplined workers and the inadequate political education of the people. Even an individual's view of social stratification is affected. A three-class or strata model (lower, middle, upper) of Yugoslav society is almost always pictured, but the content of the model differs. The middle and upper groups measure these strata by social power and see the working class as the largest stratum, whereas workers and peasants measure the strata by material conditions and educational attainment and see the third class, "those who live off others," as the largest. Significantly, researchers identify a "critical point" for the acceptance of the value elements of the ruling, self-management ideology: the completion of secondary school.[64]

Interests not only determine values, but also influence lifestyle, according to this Serbian study. The researchers identify three basic styles of life, that of the peasant, the worker, and the middle-upper strata. The traditional peasant lifestyle is shaped by the maintenance of property and land ownership and by agricultural production. Patterns of investment, consumption, prestige symbols, and even leisure activities are suited to production and property, while individual personal needs are subordinated. Sociability is based on neighborhood and kin, that is, informal and primary ties. In the sample, 83 percent of full-time farmers followed this lifestyle.

The working-class lifestyle, on the other hand, is dominated by the struggle for existence and for material and social security. Every activity is a choice that involves sacrifice. Sociability is utilitarian, whereby friends and especially neighbors take over the function of kin. According to the sample, 75 percent of the working class and 83 percent of unskilled workers belong to this lifestyle.

The lifestyle of the middle and leadership strata is one based on competition for prestige and social distinction. It is, as Pešić describes it, "a permanent invention of new status symbols, purchasing consumer goods and household appliances abroad, purchasing entire household equipment in a relatively short period after the marriage. . .buying land, and building weekend houses whose architectural style is out of harmony with its natural surroundings because it has to satisfy the claims to status of the owners."[65] Socializing takes place within "friendship groupings" formed through school and work, groups that are socially exclusive, unlike those of other strata. This lifestyle is found among 73 percent of the professionals and 70 percent of the leaders. An additional 24 percent of the leaders live an exclusive lifestyle, and only the remaining six percent live the life of the working class (in contrast to 15 percent of the professionals).[66]

These stereotypes, and the homogeneity as well as exclusiveness of the two extremes—farmers and leaders—should not obscure important findings of this study about transitional groups. Thus, the white-collar worker is found to hold the stereotypically average ideological orientation in Serbia, yet half of them (48 percent) live the working class life of primary consumption and half (52 percent) live the status-consumption life of those above them. This same pattern can be seen among peasant-workers: 60 percent see themselves as workers. They hold self-management, socialist orientations far more than traditional values; this is particularly surprising, given their position at the bottom of the income and social-influence hierarchy. Yet 45 percent live the traditional peasant life and 55 percent live the life of workers. In other words, upwardly mobile groups hold the ideological orientations of those above them, representing their aspirations, but split almost evenly in terms of their lifestyle, half of them resembling the stratum above them and half, the stratum below.[67]

The single shared value among all Serbs, according to this study, is their attitude toward religion: 88 to 90 percent of each stratum claim to be non-religious. This apparent achievement of the revolution has been the subject of inquiry in the Roman Catholic regions (Slovenia, Croatia). Opinion polls in the 1970s in Slovenia found 65 percent of all adults saying they believe in God. Researchers explain this as a means of coping with the anomie and normlessness created by modernity and rapid social change but, more importantly, as in Dalmatia, as an expression of "national identity." In a random, proportional sample of 1,741 elementary and secondary school students from 50 schools in central Croatia in 1969, Bahtijarević also finds substantial religiosity.[68] The source of students' beliefs, reminiscent of the traditional, antisystem orientation found in the Serbian study, is the family. Strong believers come from families of less-educated parents who are not members of the League of Communists. Their fathers are farmers, private craftsmen, or workers, and they are usually in schools for unskilled and semiskilled workers. Atheists among students, on the other hand, are Marxists, and come from families of well-educated parents who belong to the League of Communists. These extreme groups, the atheists and the strong believers, each form between 21 and 31 percent of the student sample, and respectively demonstrate far greater congruence in their various attitudes than do the two middle groups—the nonconformist believers and the a-religious—which represent the center 50 percent. Although Bahtijarević finds only a hard core of 4 percent who are strong, practicing believers by the end of high school, the number of secondary school students who are either wholly or partially Marxist is a relatively small 26.1 percent. Many students appear to remain uncommitted in either direction into adulthood. Still, Bahtijarević does find that there is a critical stage at which Croatians' religious beliefs stabilize, between the end of elementary and the beginning of secondary school (i.e., at ages 15 or 16).

Values in the process of planning, values in urbanism, cultural values, and values influencing industrial development, productivity, and self-management were the subjects of research during 1975-1977. The published results of these studies will add significantly to the material cited here on values held by the Yugoslav population.

Social Problems and Social Policy

There has been remarkably little political restraint on research dealing with social problems and social policy. Indeed, the continuing use of surveys under political conditions that elsewhere might have halted research on social issues is probably due to the increasing reliance of local planners on opinion surveys of local residents on problems, dissatisfactions, and potential solutions. Although most of this research is done by contract, such as with an urban planning institute, and is not published, examples of such studies are plentiful. The very extent of this research and the number of research institutes conducting it, however, makes representative sampling of it impossible.

If one judges by the research publicly available, the main social concerns in 1975-77 were urban and spatial planning (e.g., housing, traffic control, and health care facilities);[69] the unequal distribution of services and housing, both within cities and between urban and rural areas;[70] the practical problems of rural residents, particularly as a result of the aging of the agricultural population;[71] and the complex problems relating to the migration of labor within and out of Yugoslavia.[72]

When Croatians (N=2,000) were asked in surveys from 1968 through 1973 to describe the successes and weaknesses thus far of Yugoslav social development, first place among successes was held each year by "the building of new factories, roads, schools, hospitals, etc." Second place was held every year except 1973, when it dropped to fourth, by "improvement of the living standard."[73] Nonetheless, recent research finds that these successes have not been experienced by all Yugoslavs. For example, interviews with representatives to local community councils and with youth in school centers in Istrian communes in 1977 found depressed living standards and a very high rate of youth emigration. Of those youth who leave, 73 percent blamed the absence of higher education facilities and difficulties in obtaining employment. Their suggestions for local improvement were: good roads, higher educational facilities, and new industrial capacity to provide jobs.[74]

In a study of greater Zagreb, urbanologists found strong evidence of social and spatial segregation. The quality of housing, the development of infrastructure, and the distribution of goods and services were directly related to the social class of the neighborhood, and interviewed citizens were well aware of relative inequalities and injustices. The major cause, according to these researchers, is the rapid immigration, particularly of rural residents with few skills, into the urban centers and the inadequacy of housing construction to meet this influx. Thus, housing segregation reinforces work segregation into underprivileged and elite strata.[75] For that reason, they argue, urban planning must take account of the functional specialization of areas within the metropolitan area of Zagreb. No area represents a community where all services and goods are available, and the quality of goods diminishes with distance from the city center.[76]

A major difference in the use of health care facilities between the wealthy and nonagricultural populations, on the one hand, and the poor and agricultural populations, on the other, was found by Cifrić.[77] Since a major reason for this discrepancy is unequal availability of facilities, he recommends building specialized health centers in rural communes. The need for improved health care facilities is supported by a random sample of 3,223 residents of 14 towns in Slavonija and Baranja, Croatia, in May and June, 1975. Tihomir and Lanc find that citizens who are satisfied with the condition of their health are likely to be most satisfied with the condition of other needs. Yet their assessment of the general satisfaction of basic needs in these communes is very low, and it diminishes with age, distance from the center, lower income, less education, and decreasing size of a town. Fewer than half of the respondents are completely satisfied with any elements of their living standard except for food[78] (see table 2.10).

Researchers are also discovering, such as in a survey of Zagreb residents in 1976 about traffic conditions, that citizens have a pronounced awareness of social problems, but that they remain poorly informed about the ways to resolve them. Further, they seldom participate in the decision-making forums where such problems should be discussed. At the same time, studies of social tensions in housing units designed to integrate social classes, or migrants and long-time residents,[79] show that greater attention before construction to popular opinions by architects and urban planners could have prevented many of those tensions.

Politics and Ideology

Because of the nature of the Yugoslav sociopolitical order, it would be difficult to find survey research that does not in some way involve politics and ideology. Thus other sections in this report also provide politically relevant information. Explicitly political survey research, however, is fairly recent. This is true partly because political science faculties are no longer glorified Party schools but

Table 2.9. How Working Women Spend Their
Free Time in Yugoslavia (N = 1,479)
(percentages)

Activity	Frequency		
	Regularly	Occasionally	Never
Listen to the radio	47.1	46.3	6.0
Read the daily newspaper	40.6	52.2	6.4
Watch television	65.9	30.0	3.7
Attend the theater	3.2	31.4	65.3
Attend the cinema	6.5	52.0	41.4
Go to concerts	1.7	20.2	78.0
Go to art exhibits	1.5	14.9	83.5
Attend public lectures	2.4	17.5	79.9
Attend sports events	1.4	16.0	82.5
Attend variety shows, circus, and reviews	1.4	23.4	74.9

Source: Miro A. Mihovilović, "Radno Vrijeme, Slobodno Vrijeme i Kulturne Potrebe Zaposlene Žene," in Mihovilović et al., *Žena Izmedju Rada i Porodice: Utjecaj zaposlenosti žene na strukturu i funkciju porodice* (Zagreb: Institut za Društvena Istraživanja Sveučilišta u Zagrebu, 1975), pp. 190-96.

Table 2.10. Satisfaction of Basic Needs in Slavonija and Baranja (N = 3,223)
(percentages)

Question: To what extent are you able to satisfy your basic needs?

Need		Extent of ability to satisfy		
	Completely	Partly	Minimally	Not at all
Health	33	39	15	11
Food	58	31	7	3
Housing	48	32	11	8
Transportation	29	37	15	16
Educational opportunities	31	36	14	13
Creative work	28			10

Source: Borzan Tihomir and Ante Lanc, *Analiza Zadovoljenja Osnovnih Potreba Stanovnika Slavonije i Baranje.* Paper presented to a symposium on Contemporary Society and the Problems of Human Needs, Stubičke Toplice, Croatia, November 20-21, 1975 .

serious academic institutions, partly because greater political stability encourages more open investigation of remaining problems, and partly because politicians seem finally to have been persuaded by social scientists that constant institutional reform is only valuable if its consequences are studied as they unfold.

The decline in yearly, general polls of public opinion is disappointing in this regard since, in Croatia for example, polls were beginning to show a downward trend in popular satisfaction with the political situation in the country. In 1968, 92 percent were completely or mainly satisfied, in 1972, only 76 percent. Yet in 1973 satisfaction rises to 79 percent, raising important questions about the direction of the trend. The polls also revealed increasing sophistication and differentiation among popular responses to political matters. For example, it has been shown that the closer the social unit, the more critically it is evaluated; the farther away an arena, the better self-management fares in popular estimation; and the number of respondents without an opinion is on the decline, as in one case, from 49 percent in 1967 to 36 percent in 1972.[80]

Nevertheless, many studies are now being made of the League of Communists, and two major, Yugoslav-wide longitudinal studies are being financed. One, called "Yukomuna," on local government, values, and development, grows out of research by Eugen Pusić on local services and also continues the American study, "Values and the Local Community," by P. Jacob et al.[81] It now has research staffs in all eight capitals, is gathering data on self-management and development, including data for complex analyses of socioeconomic patterns in the developmental process, and will begin to publish results soon. The other, on "The Functioning and Realization of the Delegate System in Yugoslavia," is the first serious attempt by Yugoslav social scientists to follow a political decision from its introduction. The delegate system was promulgated in 1974, the theoretical basis and the first round of interviewing for the study began in 1976, and the first data were reported in 1977. In the fall of 1978 researchers went into work organizations and in 1979 the survey of 1977 will be repeated. Sponsored by the Socialist Alliance of Working People, this project is an example of the difficulties of decentralized research: Bosnia-Herzegovina and Montenegro have already dropped out for lack of funds, the Serbian study will be based in Belgrade, and the Slovenes substantially altered their version of the common questionnaire. Nonetheless, the final publication should be a significant, perhaps the first, contribution to an understanding of the differences in decision making and political influence among and within republics.

Preliminary reports from the first stage of testing, replete with warnings as to their premature nature, reveal a pattern reminiscent of early studies on workers' self-management. The characteristics of delegates after the first rounds of elections are similar to the characteristics of those who were first elected to workers' councils. They are male, and increase in age the higher the function. Skilled workers, or farmers in local communities, are chosen at lower levels. At higher levels, the elected are white-collar workers and professionals in the fields of culture-education-science-arts, communications, social services and administration, and local government; members of the League of Communists and to some extent of the Socialist Alliance; those of middle and higher professional education; and those resident in the locality or employed in the work organization more than ten years.

Very few of the respondents want to be elected as delegates, although few say they would refuse if drafted. In Serbia, 4 to 5 percent of the sample say that nothing would prevent their participation, whereas three-fourths say their work at home prevents it. More than half say work on their land or with their children interferes, 24 percent say that supplementary education interferes, and one-fourth say supplemental work and second jobs prevent participation. This may account for the duplication recorded in two-thirds of the cases in persons elected to a self-managing body (workers' councils and local associations) and those elected to a delegate body. At the same time, 44 percent of those interviewed said disagreements often arise between the two bodies. This view may be supported by the fact that 48 percent of Party members denied the presence of such disagreement, while only 14 percent of non-Party workers denied it, and that half of the sample pleaded ignorance.

One researcher does suggest, however, although without elaboration, that on the basis of delegate characteristics and activities, this new system has created a structure for opposition. At the same time, the surveys show above all, especially in the very large number of "don't know" responses, that the new system of delegates is still at the early stages of institutionalization where formalities and rule making dominate over the substance of actual representation and decision making. Indeed, in the Croatian data, only 14 to 33 percent of the delegations had yet adopted written rules of procedure and only 18 to 27 percent had formulated a program of activities. Influence over decision making, furthermore, remains in interest groups outside the sphere of immediate practical decisions and especially, at every stage, with executive boards.[82]

Researchers in Croatia are finding greater variety than these generalizations might suggest, however. As is the case with self-management, patterns of decision making and authority differ greatly by development level (less, partly, highly) of the commune. Major differences also exist among types of economic activity and work organization. An inverse relation appears to exist between "technical" efficiency (speed of decision process, for example) and "interest" efficiency (the extent of discussion and of representation, for example). Interest efficiency improves with the level of development of the community even though this also means a lengthier decision-making process. On the basis of factor analysis, Šiber finds interesting relationships between the form of a delegate's participation and his interests and reasons for participating, whether in the local community or at the workplace[83] (see tables 2.11 and 2.12).

Finally, Županov argues that "while the distribution of influence in work organizations before the constitutional reforms was distinctly oligarchical, the distribution of influence in work organizations now tends toward a polyarchic distribution during the initiative phase and toward a democratic distribution in

Table 2.11. Forms of Participation and the Structure of Interests
as Identified by Factor Analysis

Form of Participation		Interest
Local community		
Factor I	passive	housing problems
	active	finances
Factor II	critical	telephone, post office, the work of sociopolitical organizations
	engaged	daycare centers, playgrounds, finances
Workplace organization		
Factor I	conformist	standard of living, housing, sickness compensation, absence from work
	critical	underdevelopment of self-management, the activities of sociopolitical organizations
Factor II	engaged	the role of their activities within society, finances, illiquidity
	critical	the responsibilities of managers, the techno-bureaucratic structure, interpersonal relations

Source: Ivan Šiber, "Struktura Potreba i Angažiranost u Delegatskim Procesima," in *Izvještaji, Projekt: Funkcioniranje i Ostvarivanje, Delegatskog Sistema,* vol. 5 (Zagreb: Institut za Političke Znanosti i Novinarstvo, Fakulteta Političkih Nauka u Zagrebu, 1977), pp. 64-65, 80-81.

Table 2.12. Reasons for Nonparticipation and the Structure of Interests
as Identified by Factor Analysis

Reasons for Nonparticipation		Interest
Local community		
Factor I	active	finances, public spaces
	uninterested	environmental conservation, housing problems
Factor II	conformist	local problems generally, work organization, bureaucratic relations
	nonconformist	roads, parking problems, traffic, sewers, water-supply, electrical energy
Workplace organization		
Factor I	engaged individuals	finances, illiquidity, the role of their activities within society
Factor II	conformist individuals	the responsibilities of managers, the techno-managerial structure, interpersonal relations, individual incomes

Source: Ivan Šiber, "Struktura Potreba i Angažiranost u Delegatskim Procesima," in *Izvještaji, Projekt: Funkcioniranje i Ostvarivanje, Delegatskog Sistema,* vol. 5 (Zagreb: Institut za Političke Znanosti i Novinarstvo, Fakulteta Političkih Nauka u Zagrebu, 1977), pp. 64-65, 80-81.

the phase of final decisions." Whether this impression is only a change in perceptions or in the real distribution of influence, Županov considers this change positive.[84] And each researcher pointed to small improvements already in the measures available for 1976 and 1977.

Nonetheless, the inadequacies cited in the delegate system are familiar: unsatisfactory ties between delegates and their constituency, a general apathy toward getting involved, and the still great influence of directors and political forums on decision making. The lack of communication between delegates and constituents is the subject of most of the studies. In Belgrade, 37 percent said information was insufficient about the work of the local assembly, 60 percent said they wanted to be informed at the initial stages of a discussion rather than just at the final acclamation, and more than 50 percent said their self-managing bodies are better connected with constituents than the delegates. Only 14 percent said the opposite. Only one-third of the delegates had held meetings for their constituents. Delegates, too, complain that the information they receive from their assemblies is incomplete, irregular, and too general and difficult to understand to be of much use. These problems lead 43 percent to say that they are excluded from the early phases of preparation for decisions.

Finally, Pavao Novosel is concerned that the process by which public opinion is formed may itself be dying out. Daily, informal discussion of communal problems hardly exists at all in the family, or among friends or acquaintances. The nonprovocative nature of information in the mass media does not lead to the development of other forms of communication and the content of information given participants in decision-making bodies is totally unsatisfactory for the decisions being taken.[85] Despite all this, the surveys also reveal strong, positive evaluations of the new system—especially, that it encourages more participation. That this popular evaluation is far more positive than practice would suggest, however, is an important finding with which to judge other surveys requiring popular evaluation of politics and ideology in Yugoslavia.

Despite the extensive opportunities, indeed requirements, for political participation and decision making embodied in the self-management and delegate systems, popular engagement, knowledge, and even awareness are extremely low. A Yugoslav-wide poll in 1970-1971 found that 45.8 percent did not know about even one significant event in politics or the economy during the previous several months. Vujević found in a Croatian sample of 760 that between 40 percent and 85 percent were unable to identify correctly terms in common political usage[86] (see table 2.13).

In a 1977 Serbian sample, citizens' self-evaluations of their knowledge about the work of their local assembly were 33 percent satisfactory, 38 percent poor, and 28 percent not informed at all. Only 28 percent said their knowledge of the city assembly was good, 37 percent had little knowledge, and 35 percent, none at all. Only 23 percent of all those interviewed, including delegates, knew that the delegate system extended to the federal level. Although 63 percent of this sample positively evaluated the new system, 46 percent did not know the

Table 2.13. Understanding of Basic Sociopolitical Concepts (Croatia)

Concept	Percent incorrect answers
Directed (secondary) education	85
Social obligations	79
Irredentism	70
Interest community	71
Underdeveloped country	83
Opportunism	67
Memorandum	68
Sovereignty	71
Etatism (Statism)	48
Quorum	57
Amortization	47
Techno-managerial structure	47
Referendum	50
Fund for collective consumption	47
Gross personal (individual) income	40

Source: Pavao Novosel, *Delegatsko Informiranje: Modeli samoupravne komunikacijske akcije* (Zagreb: Biblioteka Komunikacijske Znanosti, 1977), p. 99.

name of their delegate to the communal assembly, 75 percent did not know their city assembly delegate, only 15 percent knew their delegate from their local association or work organization to the city assembly, and 50 percent did not know of a single decision made by their delegates.[87] And in a sample of 532 "activists" (62 percent held at least one self-managing or delegate function) in a central Zagreb commune, 21 percent knew the number of chambers in their commune assembly, 20 percent knew the first and last names of the president of their commune assembly, 28 percent knew the first and last names of at least one representative to their commune assembly, and 6 percent knew the first and last names of their deputy to the Croatian Parliament. Further, only 20 percent knew the content of at least one agenda item discussed during the previous two months in their commune assembly, 20 percent knew the approximate amount of their commune's budget, and only 15 percent knew the amount of funds set aside for education.[88]

Ethnicity and Foreign Cultures

Yugoslav sociologists have long been more concerned with domestic affairs, internal developments, and—occasionally—Yugoslavia's role in the world, than with the outside. Recent interest in the nearly one million Yugoslavs temporarily working in other European countries since the 1960s, however, is changing this. Yugoslav social scientists, especially at the Center for Migration Research in Zagreb, are providing some of the best and most thorough research on human migration and on foreign workers to be found anywhere. Unfortunately, much of this is recent and unpublished. Such research also focuses on internal labor migrations, such as Albanians and Bosnians in Slovenia. One such inquiry, into living conditions of Albanians from Kosovo working in Slovenia, has found that levels of discrimination and prejudice against the Albanians decline as the respondent's occupational status and education rise, but that many social problems have also been exacerbated by the lack of consultation with consumers—for example, concerning housing—by planners.[89]

Research into interethnic (international, in Yugoslav terms) relations has declined with the decentralization of sociological research and the political reaction to the nationalist events of 1967-71. Nonetheless, it may be interesting to note that public opinion surveys taken in Croatia between 1968 and 1972 consistently found that the youngest groups were the least sympathetic to ethnic nationalism and that the claims made by Croatian nationalists of the widespread popular support for their cause were wildly exaggerated.[90] Even the research on mass media audiences which finds Kosovo to be the most exposed of all Yugoslav regions to foreign "radio-propaganda" also finds that only 1 percent of the radio audience in Serbia as a whole listens to foreign radio programs.[91]

The annual surveys of Croatian public opinion conducted until 1972 by the Institute for Social Research in Zagreb contained the question, "What do you think of Yugoslavia's foreign policy? " Zvonarević and Spitak report that the response always indicated high popular support, but that it did oscillate. Greater support could be found in unsure times, relatively less in peaceful times. They also found pro-Western and pro-Eastern sentiments about equal. Emotional ties of the Croatian public were greatest to Czechoslovakia (51 percent) and to the USSR (19 percent), then to Italy (8 percent) and to the United States (6.5 percent). Croatians were best informed about the United States, France, the USSR, and Egypt, in that order.[92]

The only surveys available between 1975 and 1978 examining public opinion on foreign affairs come from the Macedonian opinion poll of 1976. The Macedonians were asked what events of that year were most important for world peace. The largest group, 40.6 percent, chose the Conference of Nonaligned Nations in Colombo, 12 percent chose Brezhnev's visit to Yugoslavia, 31.3 percent did not know, and the remaining 16 percent spread over six other possibilities. When asked what factors were most significant in maintaining the instability of world peace, 27.8 percent chose the continuing arms race, 14 percent chose the aggressive politics followed by capitalist countries, 11.5 percent chose existing bloc politics, and 9 percent chose the differences of interests between the great powers and the continuing insecurity of detente. A plurality, 31.8 percent, said they were uninformed or gave no answer. Opinions about the unsatisfactory relations between Balkan states focused on the "territorial pretensions and denial of rights to national self-determination as practiced, for example, by Austria and Bulgaria toward Yugoslavia." However, this response declined from 66.6 percent in 1975 to 58.1 percent in 1976, at the same time that the uninformed or no answer response had risen from 12.4 to 25.4 percent.[93]

Market Research

Finally, the picture of recent survey research in Yugoslavia would be noticeably incomplete if the substantial quarterly gathering of information on the buying habits and intentions of 4,000 Yugoslav households were ignored. Market research has been practiced on an all-Yugoslav sample by the Bureau for Market Research since 1962. Although their findings are legally protected as business secrets for three years, this source of information on consumer habits, standard and cost of living, evaluation of housing, food, clothing, cultural, entertainment, and other living conditions, those seeking employment, and responsiveness to advertising should be invaluable—especially since it is analyzed by republic, size of town, and size of household income. What this research says about Yugoslavia is revealing. Unlike most sociological and political research, such "economic" research can easily be done on an all-Yugoslav sample and without interruption over a long period of time. And, whatever the balance between market and plan in macroeconomic decision making in Yugoslavia, individual producers' decisions are made on market criteria and on direct information from attitudinal surveys of consumers' buying habits and plans each quarter.[94]

CONCLUDING COMMENT

The survey results summarized here cover only a portion of such research done in Yugoslavia during 1975-77. Major projects conducted during 1975-77 on mixed industrial-agricultural households; returning foreign workers; Slovenian development and values of planning; differences among elite, expert, and popular opinion on local community planning in Slovenia; the delegate system; and local government all remain to be published. Nonetheless, some patterns are clear.

Yugoslav public opinion and behavior is becoming highly differentiated. A portion of this judgment may be due to the improvement of analytical techniques for the survey data collected by Yugoslav sociologists and to an increasing interest among Yugoslavs in the extent of social stratification emerging as Yugoslav socialism matures. Nonetheless, the evidence seems strong that Yugoslavs do divide into a number of groups when they respond to surveys. A respondent's level of education remains the strongest differentiator. The formerly more powerful rural-urban split is diminishing in importance partly because of education, partly because of the increase in nonagricultural occupations among the rural population.

Income divides Yugoslavs in matters that are personally significant to them, such as in leisure-time pursuits, the ownership of a television set in addition to a radio, and cultural interests. Men and women are almost indistinguishable in attitudes, but they remain very different in their inclination to participate in sociopolitical activities, in their levels of knowledge about social affairs, and in their opportunities for occupational and political advancement. Women and men probably also differ in the demands they would place on funds for collective consumption, since women seem more interested in improved communal services to relieve their heavy household burdens. Although questions asking for a general level of satisfaction with Yugoslav conditions produce a highly stable 60 to 65 percent of apparent support for the regime, when a sample is broken into subgroups such satisfaction turns out to have a highly positive correlation with the respondent's material circumstances. Critical or oppositional attitudes reside in two sets of groups, however: those of very poor material circumstances and especially the unemployed; and those who still hold traditional attitudes, particularly full-time farmers and people in private employment. Finally, both lifestyles and ideological orientations significantly distinguish four or five groups within Yugoslav society.

Self-management also is beginning to look more varied. Although the distribution of influence at the workplace remains oligarchical, and strikes show no sign of abating, there is no longer a single picture that can be drawn of self-managing practice. Differences in forms of participation among individuals, in patterns of decision making among different kinds of economic activity and between communes of different levels of development, and in levels of participation and of knowledge among skill levels are apparent. Research is beginning to reveal a number of conflicts within the previously harmonious view of the self-managed firm. The general enthusiasm shown in attitude surveys for self-management and now for the delegate system is not matched by levels of participation, knowledge, or interest. Sociologists in particular bemoan the poor communications in the various settings of direct democracy basic to the Yugoslav system. Although membership in the League of Communists does not distinguish one's attitudes sharply from nonmembers, it does single out, from a young age, those who will be the most active participants.

Yugoslav society also seems in these studies to be becoming less explicitly political. Leisure is increasingly private. Families are strong, though less traditional. Surveys are being used increasingly to obtain consumer attitudes on products, urban planning, and communal problems such as housing and traffic. Furthermore, there is a strongly pragmatic direction to survey research in the late 1970s, partly because of reforms of the financing of scientific research forcing more contractual arrangements, and partly because of a stage of economic development that seems to be encouraging greater attention to the imbalances of rapid industrialization in social services and to consumer preferences in social planning. The increasing importance of television, among other things, seems to be leading to a more homogeneous, less discriminating taste in culture.

If the survey data reported here are a guide at all—and one of the results of the 1975-77 period was to show their inadequacy in comparison to direct observational techniques in studying workplace participation—then Yugoslav society is showing the signs of industrialization, economic development, and the changes in social relations that are frequently associated with modernization. Self-management has taken on the character of a ruling ideology. Groups are differentiating along socioeconomic lines of education, occupation, and residence. Decision making at the workplace and in the local community increasingly confronts attitudinal conflicts along functional lines. At the same time, the content of popular attitudes retains a more socialist tone, such as in attitudes toward private ownership and collectivism, than is the case in those Western Europe societies in which patterns of social stratification are similar.

NOTES

1. The term was used by sociologist Antun Petak to describe the first generation of postwar Yugoslav sociology. The use of surveys to do sociological research in Yugoslavia, in fact, goes back to the late nineteenth century and the surveys of rural life and legal customs by A. Radić and by B. Bogišić; see Maja Štambuk and Milan Zupančić, "Yugoslavia: National Contribution for the Book: *Rural Communities in Europe; current trends, bibliographies and survey analysis*" (working document, June 1976, Institute for Social Research of the University of Zagreb, Zagreb). In the postwar period, survey research develops coterminously with the discipline of sociology itself. The first issue of the journal of the Yugoslav Sociological Association, *Sociologija*, in 1959, published articles on workers' attitudes toward self-management and part of Rudi Supek's early study of youth's attitudes toward their participation on the work brigade that built the Ljubljana-Belgrade highway. In the same year the sociological institute in Ljubljana did the first of many surveys. In 1961, Supek's *Ispitivanje Javnog Mnjenja* (Zagreb: Naprijed) was published, introducing Yugoslav sociologists to the American literature on survey research. By the mid-1960s, there were sociological institutes in Belgrade, Zagreb, and Ljubljana doing surveys, and methodological disputes raged at sociological conferences.

2. In Skopje, by the Institute for Sociological and Political-Legal Research of the "Cyril and Methodius" University under the direction of Vlado Popovski and Dimitar Mirčev; in Ljubljana, by the Center for Public Opinion Research of the Sociology, Political Science, and Journalism Faculty of the University of Ljubljana, directed by Niko Toš and assisted by Drago Zajc.

3. The Slovenes publish a monthly journal, *Raziskovalec*, which records all projects in all fields of scientific research that have been proposed and the funding granted each.

4. A new federal law during this period also requires foreigners who wish to do research in Yugoslavia to attach themselves formally to a Yugoslav research institute.

5. According to a new law in Croatia, funds are distributed to research institutes on the basis of the formal degrees held by its staff, and a certain proportion of the staff are required to have advanced degrees. Sociologists argue that the value of a project has little to do with the professional qualifications of its staff, but the new methods of financing through self-managing interest communities seem to be leading to harder, more objectifiable measures for decision making than before.

6. A particularly blatant example of this is in the research on contract with the World Health Organization on women's attitudes toward contraception that was done in Slovenia, because the researcher—Katja Boh—was well regarded. There are other areas, such as Kosovo, where the need for such information would seem to be more pressing.

7. Particularly, the Institute of Social Sciences in Belgrade, the Institute for Sociological Research under the University of Zagreb in Zagreb, the Institute for Sociology and Philosophy in Ljubljana, the Institute for Sociological and Political-Legal Research in Skopje, the Economic Institutes in Zagreb, Osijek, and Belgrade, the Institute for Social Research under the Faculty of Political Science in Sarajevo, the Institute of Political Studies in Belgrade, the Institute for Journalism in Belgrade, the Center for Public Opinion Research under the Faculty of Sociology, Political Science, and Journalism in Ljubljana, the Bureaus for Urban Planning in Belgrade, Zagreb, Split, and Ljubljana, the Institute for Social Policy in Belgrade, the Croatian Institute for the Care of Mother and Child.

8. The Bureau for Market Research, with offices in Belgrade, Zagreb, and Ljubljana, Radio-TV Belgrade (especially Firdus Džinić), Radio-TV Zagreb (especially Neda Ostojić), Radio-TV Ljubljana, and the newspapers *Politika, NIN, Večernji Novosti, Delo,* and *Borba.*

9. Mladen Zvonarević and Vlasta Spitak, *Javno Mnijenje Stanovništva S.R. Hrvatske u periodu 1967-1973 god.*(Zagreb: Institut za Društvena Istraživanja, 1976).

10. Ibid. This also is discussed in the writings of Ivan Šiber.

11. In Belgrade, with Vladimir Goati, Firdus Džinić, Ljiljana Bačević, Ljuba Stojić; in Zagreb, with Antun Petak, Ruža First-Dilić, Edhem Dilić, Ivan Šiber, Pavao Novosel, Rudi Supek, Dušica Seferagić, Josip Županov, Slobodan Lazić (from Belgrade), Ljerka Čaldarović, Miroslav Vujević; in Ljubljana, Stane Saksida, Niko Toš, Drago Zajc, Silva Mežnarić, and Andrej Caserman.

12. *Javnoto Mislenje vo S.R. Makedonija 1976: rezultati od anketnoto ispituvanje* (Skopje: Institut za Sociološki i Političko-Pravni Istražuvanja pri Univerzitetot "Kiril i Metodij," 1977), pp. 24-52.

13. Branko Horvat describes this "replacement of traditional elections and parliaments by a system of delegations" with the 1974 Constitution, as follows: "The idea is a very old one in the socialist movement and has now been implemented for the first time nationwide. The 'substance of the delegation system,' according to Edvard Kardelj, one of its architects,

"lies in the fact that the interests of the working people in the assemblies should be directly expressed and defended by their delegates, who retain their regular jobs and so cannot turn into one or another kind of professional political representative. . . . The basic organizations of associated labor as well as each local community would have a delegation—just as they have various committees and commissions—which would be a standing organ of the workers' collective and the workers' council, on the one hand, and the local community on the other." Members of a delegation are elected by direct secret ballot. Delegates representing their respective delegations in the assemblies are elected from among the members of the delegation as a kind of collective deputy. They make up chambers of self-managed communities in the Assembly. A self-managed work organization or community gives instructions to its delegation, and the latter instructs its representative delegate in the Assembly how to act, but does not specify how he is to vote on each individual issue. As the system has been in operation for only a short time, it is too early to comment on its efficiency.

Branko Horvat, *The Yugoslav Economic System: The First Labor-Managed Economy in the Making* (White Plains, N. Y.: International Arts and Sciences Press, Inc., 1976), p. 40.

14. Pavao Novosel, *Delegatsko Informiranje: Modeli samoupravne komunikacijske akcije* (Zagreb: Biblioteka Komunikacijske Znanosti, 1977), pp. 140-41.

15. Firdus Džinić and Ljiljana Bačević, *Masovno Komuniciranje u S. R. Srbiji* (Belgrade: Beogradski Izdavačko-Grafički Zavod Radio-Televizija Beograd, 1977), pp. 130-209.

16. *RTV—Teorija i Praksa*, issued by RTV Belgrade; *Informisanje u praksi*, issued by the Institute for Journalism in Belgrade; and *Študij programa, rtv Ljubljana*.

17. Džinić and Bačević, *Masovno Komuniciranje*, pp. 96-102, 131-53.

18. Ibid., pp. 102-108, 153-81.

19. Antun Petak, "Marginalizacija—jedna tendencija suvremene gradske kulture: Moguči Pristup," *Revija za sociologiju* 5, no. 4 (1975): 36-57. According to Džinić and Bačević, *Masovno Komuniciranje*, radio and television audiences are constantly pressuring for a change in programs in an "undesirable" direction, that is, for more music, especially light and folk music, humor, and entertainment programs; as for the press, they suggest that popular taste has completely conquered the newspapers and magazines in the period of their expansion, leading to an extensive widening of "kič" [trashy art] and "šunda" [trashy literature].

20. See the excellent discussion of this tradition, continued now by the Institute for Rural, Urban, and Spatial Sociology under the Institute for Social Research of the University of Zagreb, and its journal *Sociologija Sela*, in Joel M. Halpern and E. A. Hammel, "Observations on the Intellectual History of Ethnology and other Social Sciences in Yugoslavia," *Comparative Studies in Society and History* 11, no. 1 (1969): 17-26.

21. Ruža First-Dilić, "Medjugeneracijsko ispomaganje u seoskoj porodici," *Sociologija Sela*, nos. 55-56 (May-June 1977).

22. Ruža First-Dilić, *Promjene u Strukturi Primarnih Grupa u Našem Selu* (Zagreb: Centar za Sociologiju Sela, Grada i Prostora Instituta za Društvena Istraživanja Sveučilišta u Zagrebu, 1976).

23. Personal communication from Ruža First-Dilić, based on a project for the World Bank.

24. Miro A. Mihovilović et al., *Žena Izmedju Rada i Porodice: Utjecaj zaposlenosti žene na strukturu i funkciju porodice* (Zagreb: Institut za Društvena Istraživanja Sveučilišta u Zagrebu, 1975).

25. Ibid.

26. Jagoda Klauzer, "Biološko-Reproduktivna Funkcija Zaposlene Žene," in Mihovilović et al., *Žena Izmedju Rada i Porodice*, pp. 43-61.

27. Miro A. Mihovilović, "Žene o Budućnosti," in Mihovilović et al., *Žena Izmedju Rada i Porodice*, p. 198.

28. Mirjana Ule, Silva Mežnarić, and Anuška Ferligoj, "Raspodjela Svakodnevnih Uloga u Porodici Izmedju Želja (Drustva) i Stvarnosti (Porodice)," unpublished manuscript, 1977.

29. Zvonarević and Spitak, *Javno Mnijenje Stanovništva S. R. Hrvatske.*

30. Vladimir Goati et al., *Društveno-Političko Angažovanje Omladine* (Belgrade: Institut Društvenih Nauka, Beograd, and the RK SSO Srbije, 1977), p. 166.

31. Edhem Dilić et al., *Seoska Omladina Danas* (Zagreb: Centar za Sociologiju Sela, Grada i Prostora Instituta za Društvena Istraživanja Sveučilišta u Zagrebu, 1977).

32. Velimir Tomanović, *Omladina i Socijalizam* (Belgrade: Mladost, 1977).

33. Dragomir Pantić, "Odnos Omladine Prema Samoupravljanju," in Goati et al., *Društveno-Političko Angažovanje Omladine*, pp. 105-135.

34. Tomanović, *Omladina i Socijalizam*, pp. 73-100.

35. Ivan Šiber, "Politička socijalizacija seoske omladine," *Sociologija Sela*, nos. 49-50 (July-December 1975), pp. 117-38.

36. Tomanović, *Omladina i Socijalizam*, pp. 89-90.

37. Goati et al., *Društveno-Političko Angažovanje Omladine*, p. 180.

38. Dušan Čalić, "Motiviranost omladine za socijalističko samoupravljanje," *Socijalizam* 20, nos. 7-8 (1977): 1380-91.

39. Dilić et al., *Seoska Omladina Danas.*

40. Antun Petak, "Obrazovanje i profesionalizacija poljoprivrednog zanimanja te socijalistička transformacija sela," *Revija za Sociologiju* 6, nos. 2-3 (August-September 1976).

41. Zvonarević and Spitak, *Javno Mnijenje Stanovništva S. R. Hrvatske*; Vladimir Arzenšek, "Legitimnost Managementa: Pokušaj Institucionalne i Konsensualne Analize" and Josip Obradović, "Participacija—rezultati istraživanja i teoretski modeli," in Josip Obradović et al., *Proizvodne Organizacije i Samoupravljanje*, vols. 2 and 3, *Čovjek i Sistem* (Zagreb: Filozofski Fakultet Sveučilišta u Zagrebu—Odsjek za sociologiju, 1975).

42. Obradović, *Proizvodne Organizacije i Samoupravljanje.*

43. Ivan Šiber, *Radni i Samoupravni Položaj i Informiranost Proizvodjača* (Zagreb: Institut za Političke Znanosti i Novinarstvo, 1976).

44. Šiber, *Radni i Samoupravni Položaj*; and Obradović, "Participacija—rezultati istraživanja."

45. Novosel, *Delegatsko Informiranje*, pp. 70-71.

46. Milan Mesić, "Politička kultura samoupravljanja zagrebačkih radnica," *Žena*, no. 2 (1978), pp. 47-61.

47. Silvano Bolčić, "Preduzetništvo kao determinanta ekonomskih odnosa (Uvodno izlaganje)," in Josip Obradović et al., *Proizvodne Organizacije i Samoupravljanje*, pp. 105-120.

48. Ibid., p. 120.

49. Vladimir Arzenšek, "Otudjenje i štrajk," *Revija za sociologiju* 6, nos. 2-3 (August-September 1976).

50. Miroslav Jilek, "Kreativnost Urbanizirane Mladosti," paper presented to the Seventh Colloquium on the Social and Spatial Creation of a Living Environment and the Free Time of Youth, Dubrovnik, February 2-5,1976.

51. Rudi Lešnik, "Obstacles to Secondary School Youth's Free Time," paper presented to the Seventh Colloquium on the Social and Spatial Creation of a Living Environment and the Free Time of Youth, Dubrovnik, February 2-5, 1976.

52. In Yugoslav literature the difference between origins in an urban environment or a rural one is identified as one's "social origin."

53. Miro A. Mihovilović, "Budžet Vremena Zaposlene Žene"; and Mihovilović, "Radno Vrijeme, Slobodno Vrijeme i Kulturne Potrebe Zaposlene Žene," in Mihovilović et al., *Žena Izmedju Rada i Porodice*, pp. 144-96.

54. *Javnoto Mislenje*, pp. 247-49.

55. Mihailo V. Popović et al., *Društveni Slojevi i Društvena Svest* (Belgrade: Centar za Sociološka Istraživanja, Instituta društvenih nauka, 1977), pp. 143-47, 160-67, 180-84.

56. Ljubinka Bročić, "Survey of Hobbies in Belgrade," paper presented to the Seventh Colloquium on the Social and Spatial Creation of a Living Environment and the Free Time of Youth, Dubrovnik, February 2-5, 1976.

57. Ivan Magdalenić, "Dvije vrste kulturnih potreba stanovnika središnje Hrvatske i mogučnosti zadovoljavanja tih potreba," *Sociologija Sela*, nos. 51-52 (May-June 1976), pp. 97-102.

58. Mihovilović et al., *Žena Izmedju Rada i Porodice*, pp. 144-96.

59. Such as the revived ethnographic institute under the extremely able directorship in Zagreb of Dunja Avguštin-Rihtman or the numerous urban planning and spatial planning institutes, such as in Belgrade, which have recently engaged many psychologists.

60. Popović et al., *Društveni Slojevi*.

61. Dragomir Pantić, "Vrednosti i Ideološke Orijentacije Društvenih Slojeva," in Popović et al., *Društveni Slojevi*, pp. 269-406.

62. Strict egalitarianism, particularly in the sense of leveling, is associated in Yugoslavia with a peasant mentality, one which is neither conducive to economic development nor consistent with Marxist ideology. The more "modern," the more willing one is to consider wage differentials according to skill and not to see this as contrary to socialism. These ideas are best explicated in writings by Josip Županov, but even those are only one part of the very complicated notion of "socialist equality."

63. Silvano Bolčić, "Interesi Društvenih Slojeva i Determinante Njihovog Formiranja," in Popović et al., *Društveni Slojevi*, pp. 65-120.

64. Pantić, "Vrednosti i Ideološke Orijentacije," pp. 269-406.

65. Vesna Pešić, "Društvena Slojevitost i Stil Života," in Popović et al., *Družt-*

veni Slojevi, pp. 137-42.
66. Ibid., pp. 189-90.
67. Popović et al., *Društveni Slojevi, passim*.
68. Štefica Bahtijarević, *Religijsko Pripadanje u Uvjetima Sekularizacije Društva* (Zagreb: Centar za Aktualni Politički Studij Narodno Sveučilište Grada Zagreba, 1975).
69. For example, *Društveni Aspekti Odnosa Prema Prometnom Kompleksu: Sociološka Studija o Prometu u Zagrebu* (Zagreb: 1976), a study made by the Center for Rural, Urban, and Spatial Sociology in Zagreb for the Urbanistic Bureau of the City of Zagreb; *Društveni Aspekti Individualne Stambene Izgradnje u Zagrebu: Sociološka Studija* (Zagreb: September 1975).
70. Projects conducted by urbanologists such as Dušica Seferagić, Vladimir Lay, Ognjen Čaldarović in Zagreb; see, for example, Dušica Seferagić, "Socijalna Segregacija u Rezidencijalnom Prostoru Zagreba," *Pitanja* 9, nos. 11-12 (1977): 38-45, and references within.
71. The work of sociologists at the Center for Rural, Urban, and Spatial Sociology in Zagreb, particularly that of Svetozar Livada; *Sociologija Sela*, nos. 55, 56, and 57.
72. The work of researchers at the Center for Migration Research in Zagreb, under the direction of Ivo Baučić, and the large project on Yugoslav migrants under the direction of Niko Toš at the Center for Public Opinion and Mass Communication in Ljubljana.
73. Zvonarević and Spitak, *Javno Mnijenje Stanovništva S. R. Hrvatske*.
74. Vladimir Lay, *Sociološka Studija za Prostorne Planove Općine Istra* (Zagreb: Centar za sociologiju sela, grada i prostora, 1977).
75. Dušica Seferagić, "Stanovanje kao pokazatelj socijalne segregacije u Zagrebačkom prostoru," *Sociologija Sela*, nos. 47-48 (May-June 1975), pp. 73-81.
76. Ibid.; and Ivan Cifrić, "Učestalosti mjesto zadovoljavanja zdravstvenih potreba nekih kategorija seoskih i gradskih stanovnika," *Sociologija Sela*, nos. 47-48 (May-June 1975), pp. 82-92; Dušica Seferagić, "Gradjani o razvojnim problemima mjesnih zajednica u gradu Zagreba," *Sociologija Sela*, nos. 51-52 (May-June 1976).
77. Cifrić, "Učestalosti mjesto zadovoljavanja zdravstvenih," pp. 82-92.
78. Borzan Tihomir and Ante Lanc, *Analiza Zadovoljenja Osnovnih Potreba Stanovnika Slavonije i Baranje*, paper presented to a symposium on Contemporary Society and the Problems of Human Needs, Stubičke Toplice, Croatia, November 20-21, 1975.
79. Personal communication from Stane Saksida, director, Institute for Sociology and Philosophy, Ljubljana, on research done by his institute in Slovenia.
80. Zvonarević and Spitak, *Javno Mnijenje Stanovništva S. R. Hrvatske*.
81. Eugen Pusić, "Komunalni sistem," in *Teritorijalno-Politički Sistemi: Prilozi Izučavanju Društvenog Sistema*, vol. 1, ed. Eugen Pusić (Zagreb: Filozofski Fakultet Sveučilišta u Zagrebu, Odsjek za sociologiju, 1975), pp. 117-27; Stanko Petković, "Vrijednosne orijentacije prema društvenim promjenama i

metodologija njihova mjerenja," *Revija za Sociologiju* 6, no. 1 (January-March 1976).

82. *Izvještaji, Projekt: Funkcioniranje i Ostvarivanje Delegatskog Sistema*, 5 vols. (Zagreb: Institut za Političke Znanosti i Novinarstvo, Fakulteta Političkih Nauka u Zagrebu, 1977); Vladimir Goati et al., "Funkcionisanje Delegatskog Sistema u Beogradu," *Samoupravno Pravo* 3, no. 1 (January-March 1976): 75-83; Marjan Šetinc, "Delegatski Sistem i Samoupravljanje," *Samoupravno Pravo* 3, no. 2 (April-June 1976): 68-74; Ivan Cifrić, "O Nekim Iskustvima i Pretpostavkama Rada Delegata u Delegacijama OOUR-a," *Naše Teme* 20, no. 5 (May 1976): 684-709.

83. Ivan Šiber, "Struktura Potreba i Angažiranost u Delegatskim Procesima," in *Izvještaji, Projekt: Funkcioniranje i Ostvarivanje*, vol. 5, pp. 35-81.

84. Josip Županov, "Struktura Utjecaja u Delegatskom Sistemu u Općini Prema Podacima Ankete," in *Izvještaji, Projekt: Funkcioniranje i Ostvarivanje*, vol. 5, pp. 82-116.

85. Pavao Novosel, "Neke Značajke Komuniciranja u Delegatskom Sistemu," in *Izvještaji, Projekt: Funkcioniranje i Ostvarivanje*, vol. 2, pp. 68-127.

86. Quoted in Novosel, *Delegatsko Informiranje*, p. 99.

87. Goati et al., "Funkcionisanje."

88. Novosel, *Delegatsko Informiranje*, p. 33.

89. Personal communication from Stane Saksida, Institute for Sociology and Philosophy, Ljubljana.

90. Zvonarević and Spitak, *Javno Mnijenje Stanovništva S. R. Hrvatske*.

91. Džinić and Bačević, *Masovno Komuniciranje*.

92. Zvonarević and Spitak, *Javno Mnijenje Stanovništva S. R. Hrvatske*.

93. *Javnoto Mislenje*, pp. 230-43.

94. *Tržišne Informacije* (Zagreb: Zavod za Tržišne Istraživanja, quarterly).

BIBLIOGRAPHY

Books and Articles

Ahtik, M. "Slobodno Vreme Mladih." *Gledišta*, no. 6 (1976): 593-745.

Arzenšek, Vladimir. "Otudjenje i Štrajk." *Revija za Sociologiju* 6, nos. 2-3 (August-September 1976).

Babović, Dušan. "Zašto Radni Ljudi Izostaju sa Zborova." *Socijalizam* 18, nos. 7-8 (1975): 953-60.

Bahtijarević, Štefica. *Religijsko Pripadanje u Uvjetima Sekularizacije Društva.* Zagreb: Centar za Aktualni Politički Studij Narodno Sveucilište Grada Zagreba, 1975.

_____. "Seoska Omladina i Religija." *Sociologija Sela* 13, nos. 3-4 (July-December 1975).

Beluhan, Aleksandra; Benc, Milan; Štampar, Dubravka; and Trenc, Pavle. "Mišljenje Nastavnika o Nekim Pitanjima Spolnog Života." *Žena* 1 (1976).

Bročić, Ljubinka. "Survey of Hobbies in Belgrade." Paper read at the Seventh Colloquium on the Social and Spatial Creation of a Living Environment and the Free Time of Youth, 2-5 February, 1976, at Dubrovnik.

Čalić, Dušan. "Motiviranost Omladina za Socijalističko Samoupravljanje." *Socijalizam* 20, nos. 7-8 (1977): 1380-91.

Cifrić, Ivan. "O Nekim Iskustvima i Pretpostavkama Rada Delegata u Delegacijama OOUR-a." *Naše Teme* 20, no. 5 (May 1976): 684-709.

_____. "Učestalosti Mjesto Zadovoljavanja Zdravstvenih Potreba Nekih Kategorija Seoskih i Gradskih Stanovnika." *Sociologija Sela* 13, nos. 1-2 (May-June 1975): 82-92.

_____. "Uloga Centralnosti Naselja u Bližoj i Daljnjoj Okolici Grada Zagreba." *Sociologija Sela* 14, nos. 1-2.

Dilić, Edhem. "Migracijske Tendencije Seoske Omladine." *Sociologija Sela* 13, nos. 3-4 (July-December 1975).

_____, et al. *Seoska Omladina Danas.* Zagreb: Centar za Sociologija Sela, Grada i Prostora, Instituta za Društvena Istraživanja Sveučilišta u Zagrebu, 1977.

Djordjević, Toma. *Političko Javno Mnjenje.* Novi Sad: Radnički Univerzitet "Radivoj Cirpanov," 1975.

Društvena Zaštita i Novi Oblici Kriminaliteta. Zagreb: Institut za Društvena Istraživanja Sveučilišta u Zagrebu, 1976.

Društveni Aspekti Individualne Stambene Izgradnje u Zagrebu: Sociološka Studija. Zagreb, September 1975.

Društveni Aspekti Odnosa Prema Prometnom Kompleksu: Sociološka Studija o Prometu u Zagrebu. Zagreb, 1976.

"Društveno-Političko Angažovanje Omladine: Diskusija." *Gledišta*, nos. 1-2

(1977).
Džinić, Firdus, and Bačević, Ljiljana. *Masovno Komuniciranje u S. R. Srbiji.*
Belgrade: Beogradski Izdavačko-Grafički Zavod Radio-Televizija Beograd,
1977.
First-Dilić, Ruža. "Kakav Brak Želimo: Stavovi Seoske Omladine o Idealnom
Bračnom Modelu." *Žena*, no. 6 (1976).
_____. "Medjugeneracijsko Ispomaganje u Seoskoj Porodici." *Sociologija
Sela*, nos. 55-56 (May-June 1977).
_____. *Promjene u Strukturi Primarnih Grupa u Našem Selu.* Zagreb: Centar
za Sociologija Sela, Grada, Prostora Instituta za Društvena Istraživanja
Sveučilišta u Zagrebu, 1976.
_____. "Seoska Omladina i Porodica." *Sociologija Sela* 13, nos. 3-4 (July-
December 1976).
_____. "Seoska Omladina Izmedju Rada i Zadovoljstva." *Naše Teme*, no. 21
(June 1977): 1322-32.
Goati, Vladimir, et al. *Društveno-Političko Angažovanje Omladine.* Belgrade:
Institut Društvenih Nauka, Beograd, and the R.K.S.S.O. Srbije, 1977.
_____. "Funkcionisanje Delegatskog Sistema u Beogradu." *Samoupravno
Pravo*, no. 1 (January-March 1976): 75-83.
Halpern, Joel, and Hammel, E. A. "Observations on the Intellectual History of
Ethnology and Other Social Sciences in Yugoslavia." *Comparative Studies
in Society and History* 11, no. 1 (1969): 17-26.
Horvat, Branko. *The Yugoslav Economic System: The First Labor-Managed
Economy in the Making.* White Plains, N. Y.: International Arts and
Sciences Press, Inc., 1976.
"Istraživanja u Društvenim Naukama: Diskusija." *Gledišta*, no. 5 (1977).
Izvještaji-Projekt: Funkcioniranje i Ostvarivanje Delegatskog Sistema. 5 vols.
Zagreb: Institut za Političke Znanosti i Novinarstvo, Fakulteta Političkih
Nauka u Zagrebu, 1977.
"Javno Mnjenje u Samoupravnom Društvu: Diskusija." *Gledišta* 16, no. 4 (April
1976): 337-414.
Javnoto Mislenje vo S. R. Makedonija 1976: Rezultati od Anketnog Ispituvanja.
Skopje: Institut za Sociološki i Političko-Pravni Istražuvanja pri Univer-
zitetot "Kiril i Metodij," 1976.
Jilek, Miroslav. "Kreativnost Urbanizirane Mladosti." Paper read at the Seventh
Colloquium on the Social and Spatial Creation of a Living Environment
and the Free Time of Youth, 2-5 February, 1976, at Dubrovnik.
Kirinčić, Miroslav. "Odluke Radnih Ljudi i Gradjana u Mjesnim Zajednicama."
Naše Teme 20, no. 6 (June 1976): 895-919.
Kolarić, Vesna, and Supek, Rudi. "Ispitivanje Socijalne Ekspanzije u Seoske
Omladine." *Sociologija Sela* 13, nos. 3-4 (July-December 1975).
Kornhauser, Aleksandra. "Istraživačka Delatnost-Ukrasni Dodatak ili Potreba i
Sastojak Udruženog Rada." *Socijalizam* 18, no. 11 (1975): 1364-72.
Lay, Vladimir. *Sociološka Studija za Prostorne Planove Općine Istra.* Zagreb:

Centar za Sociologiju Sela, Grada i Prostora, 1977.

Lešnik, Rudi. "Srednjoškolci i Slobodno Vreme." *Teorija in Prakse*, nos. 1-2 (1976).

Letić, Franjo. *Informiranje i Informiranost Vanjskih Migranata iz S. R. Hrvatske o Zbivanjima u Domovini*. Zagreb: Centar za Istraživanje Migracije, 1977.

Magdalenić, Ivan. "Dvije Vrste Kulturnih Potreba Stanovništva Središnje Hrvatske i Mogućnosti Zadovoljavanja Tih Potreba." *Sociologija Sela*, nos. 51-52 (January-June 1976): 97-102.

Marangunić, Davor; Maršić, Ivan; and Vidaković, Sunca. "Ocjenjivanja Učenika u Osnovnoj Školi Prema Mišljenja Nastavnika Roditelja i Učenika." *Školski Vjesnik* 27, no. 1 (1975): 29-34.

Mešić, Milan. "Politička Kultura Samoupravljanja Zagrebačkih Radnica." *Žena*, no. 2 (1978): 47-61.

Mihovilović, Miro A. "Slobodno Vrijeme Seoske Omladine." *Sociologija Sela* 18, nos. 3-4 (July-December 1975): 102-116.

_____ , et al. *Žena Izmedju Rada i Porodice: Utjecaj Zaposlenosti Žene na Strukturu i Funkciju Porodice*. Zagreb: Institut za Društvena Istraživanja Sveučilišta u Zagrebu, 1975.

Milovanović, Darinka. *Javno Mnenje u Socijalizmu*. Belgrade: Diplomski Rad Filozofskog Fakulteta, 1977.

Mitov, Cvetan. "Rezultati Nekih Istraživanja o Učenicima čiji su Roditelji u Inostranstvu." *Pedagoški Rad*, nos. 1-2 (1978): 9-17.

Novosel, Pavao. *Delegatsko Informiranje: Modeli Samoupravne Komunikacijske Akcije*. Zagreb: Biblioteka Komunikacijske Znanosti, 1977.

Obradović, Josip, et al. *Proizvodne Organizacije i Samoupravljanje*. Volumes 2 and 3 of *Čovjek i Sistem*. Zagreb: Filozofski Fakultet Sveučilišta u Zagrebu Odsjek za Sociologija, 1975.

Petak, Antun. "Marginalizacija—Jedna Tendencija Suvremene Gradske Kulture: Mogući Pristup." *Revija za Sociologija* 5, no. 4 (1975): 36-57.

_____ . "Obrazovanje i Profesionalizacija Poljoprivrednog Zanimanja te Socijalistička Transformacija Sela." *Revija za Sociologija* 6, nos. 2-3 (August-September 1976).

_____ . "Profesionalne Obrazovanje Poljoprivredne Omladine." *Sociologija Sela* 13, nos. 3-4 (July-December 1975).

_____ . "Zabavna Štampa—Činilac Masovne Kulture." *Naše Teme* 19, nos. 10-11 (October-November 1975): 1501-1604.

Petković, Stanko. "Vrijednosne Orijentacije Prema Društvenim Promjenama i Metodologija Njihova Mjerena." *Revija za Sociologija* 6, no. 1 (January-March 1976).

Planiranje Prostora u Suradnji na Ljudima—Korisnicima Prostora. Zagreb.

Podunavac, Milan. "Politička Socijalizacija i Orijentacija Mladih." *Gledišta*, no. 5 (May 1977): 451-60.

Popović, Mihailo V.; Bolčic, Silvano; Pešić, Vesna; Janićijević, Milosav; and Pantić, Dragomir. *Društveni Slojevi i Društvena Svest*. Belgrade: Centar za

Sociološka Istraživanja, Instituta Društvenih Nauka, 1977.

Puljiz, Vlado, and First, Ruža. "Stavovi Poljoprivrednika o Načinu Osiguranja u Starosti." *Sociologija Sela*, no. 57 (July-September 1977).

Pusić, Eugen, ed. *Teritorijalno-Politički Sistemi: Prilozi Izučavanju Društvenog Sistema*. Volume 1 of *Čovjek i Sistem*. Zagreb: Filozofski Fakultet Sveučilišta u Zagrebu, Odsjek za Sociologija, 1975.

Seferagić, Dušica. "Gradjani o Razvojnim Problemima Mjesnih Zajednica u Grada Zagreba." *Sociologija Sela* 14, nos. 1-2 (May-June 1976): 74-89.

_____. "Socijalna Segregacija u Rezidencijalnom Prostoru Zagreba." *Pitanja* 9, nos. 11-12 (1977):38-45.

_____. "Stanovanje kao Pokazatelj Socijalne Segregacije u Zagrebačkom Prostora." *Sociologija Sela*, nos. 47-48 (May-June 1978): 73-81.

Sekulić, Duško. "Vrijednosne Orijentacije kao Faktori Organizacionog Ponašanja." *Sociologija* 18, nos. 3-4 (1976).

Serdar, Vladimir. *Studij uz Rad na Visokoškolskim Ustanovama u S. R. Hrvatskoj*. Zagreb: Institut za Društvena Istraživanja Sveučilišta u Zagrebu, 1976.

"Starost u Selu." *Sociologija Sela*, nos. 55-56 (May-June 1977).

Supek, Rudi. "Društveni Determinizam i Istraživanje Vrednote." Volume 4 of *Čovjek i Sistem: Vrijednosti i Društveni Sistem*. Zagreb: Filozofski Fakultet Sveučilišta u Zagrebu, Odsjek za Sociologija, 1975.

Suvremeno Društvo i Problemi Ljudskih Potreba i Vrijednosti. Simpozij Sociološkog Društva Hrvatske, 11-12 December, 1975, at Stubičke Toplice.

Šetinc, Marjan. "Delegatski Sistem i Samoupravljanje." *Samoupravno Pravo* 3, no. 2 (April-June 1976): 68-74.

Šiber, Ivan. "Politička Socijalizacija Seoske Omladine." *Sociologija Sela* 13, nos. 3-4 (July-December 1975).

_____. *Radni i Samoupravni Položaj i Informiranost Proizvodjača*. Zagreb: Institut za Političke Znanosti i Novinarstvo, 1976.

Štambuk, Maja, and Zupančić, Milan. "Yugoslavia: National Contribution for the Book: Rural Communities in Europe:Current Trends, Bibliographies, and Survey Analysis." Working document. Zagreb: Institute for Social Research of the University of Zagreb, June 1976.

Tanić, Živan. "Masovne Seoske Emigracije iz Razvijenih Područja Srbije." *Samoupravno Pravo* 2: 63-69.

Tihomir, Borzan, and Lanc, Ante. "Analiza Zadovoljenja Osnovnih Potreba Stanovnika Slavonije i Baranje." Paper read at a Symposium on Contemporary Society and the Problems of Human Needs, 20-21 November, 1975, at Stubičke Toplice, Croatia.

Tomanović, Velimir. *Omladina i Socijalizam*. Belgrade: Mladost, 1977.

Tomić, Stojan. "Institucionalni Sistemi, Participacija i Samoupravljanje." *Socijalizam* 18, no. 4 (1975): 452-567.

_____. "Politička Kultura Samoupravnog Socijalizam." *Sociologija* 18, nos. 1-2 (1976).

Ule, Mirjana, et al. "Raspodjela Svakodnevnih Uloga u Porodica Izmedju Želja (Društva) i Stvarnosti (Porodice)." Unpublished manuscript. Ljubljana, 1977.

Vrcan, Srdjan. "Vezanost Ljudi za Religiju i Crkvu u Nas." *Naše Teme* 19, nos. 7-8, 9 (July-August, September 1975): 1418-41.

Vujević, Miroslav. *Razumijevanje Društveno-Političkih Izraza.* Zagreb, 1976.

Zvonarević, Mladen, and Spitak, Vlasta. *Javno Mnijenje Stanovništva S. R. Hrvatske u Periodu 1967-73.* Zagreb: Institut Društvena Istraživanja Sveučilišta u Zagrebu, 1976.

Journals Consulted

Čovjek i prostor
Gledišta
Informisanje u praksi
Komuna
Kulturni Radnik
Kulturni Život
Migracija
Naše Teme
Nedeljne Informativne Novine (NIN)
Pedagoški Rad
Pitanja
Pogledi
Politička Misao
Pregled
Psihologija
RTV—Teorija i Praksa
Raziskovalec
Revija za Sociologiju
Samoupravno Pravo
Savremenost
Školski Vjesnik
Socijalna Politika
Socijalizam
Sociologija
Sociologija Sela
Sociološki Pregled
Študij program—rtv Ljubljana
Žena

3 Bulgaria
William A. Welsh
with Mark Arabadjief*

AN OVERVIEW OF SURVEY RESEARCH IN BULGARIA

Survey research, as with empirical sociological research more generally, is still in its infancy in Bulgaria. Although some informal surveys appeared in daily newspapers during the 1950s, the first evidence of serious survey studies occurs in 1962. And some of the most important projects undertaken in that year—for example, a study by the Institute of Philosophy at the Bulgarian Academy of Sciences (BAN) of the religious preferences of the population—did not yield published results until five years later.

In 1968, apparently as a result of new directions announced at the Party Plenum in December, 1967, and at the 11th Congress of the Komsomol in January, 1968, several institutional moves were made which improved the opportunities for systematic survey research. The Institute of Sociology at the Academy of Sciences received an independent identity, separate from the Institute of Philosophy. The Center for Scientific Study of Youth was established, attached to the Central Committee of the Komsomol.[1] Sociological laboratories were established in some higher educational institutions, such as the Institute of National Economy in Varna.

It was also in 1968 that field research began on the most ambitious empirical sociological study yet conducted in Bulgaria, the "Sociological Study of Town and Village," under the direction of Zhivko Oshavkov. This study was based on interviews with a national random sample of 18,994 persons aged 15 years or older. The interview process was intensive; each of more than 3,400 interviewers talked with an average of five or six persons over a three-month period. Although the survey method was the basis of the research, a majority of the questions did not deal with attitudinal or opinion items, but rather with descriptions of behaviors and life circumstances of the respondents. The analysis of data for the study required a number of years; isolated results were reported in periodicals beginning in 1974, but the major work summarizing the bulk of the findings appeared only in 1976, under the title, *Sociological Structure of Contemporary Bulgarian Society.*[2] Two other important pieces of survey research were undertaken at the end of the 1960s. Both dealt with leisure time, one done under the direction of Zahari Staikov,[3] and the other under the direction of Misho Tsanov.[4]

Building on the precedent and experience of these large studies, an increasing number of systematic surveys were done in Bulgaria during the first half of the 1970s. One might be tempted, from a simple count of articles appearing in the period 1976-78, to conclude that the amount of survey research being done in Bulgaria is now declining. From everything we have been able to learn, however, this is not the case. Rather, Bulgarian survey research seems to be in an inquiry phase of a natural research cycle. The years 1974-76 saw the publication of the results of a number of studies that had been initiated several years earlier. Since 1976, the efforts of the modest-in-size sociological establishment in Bulgaria have been directed largely toward research, rather than the writing up of results of studies.

Perhaps the most consistently evident characteristic of Bulgarian survey research is its policy relevance, which is not always explicitly remarked, but is nonetheless clear. Survey research, like all aspects of scientific inquiry, is expected to make direct contributions to the building of socialist society. Authors who report survey results without evaluative commentary are chided in published reviews; by contrast, those who both evaluate and link their findings to ideological tenets and/or social issues are applauded.

The pragmatic orientation of survey research in Bulgaria notwithstanding, there has been a noticeable increase since 1974 in the number of thoughtful books and articles urging attention to theoretical and methodological issues. Theoretically, much of this writing has been directed toward clarifying the concept of public opinion and developing a taxonomy of its societal functions. The existence of differences of opinion on these questions among Bulgarian sociologists is real, if subdued. A brief characterization of how the concept of public opinion is treated in the handful of books most frequently cited suggests that the orientations of the writers are neither shallow nor excessively colored by predetermined ideology. We discover that public opinion is viewed in some of the following ways:

1. It performs a *self-regulative function* for society, both by alerting others to the prevailing points of view of their countrymen and by making available to governing bodies evidence about the predispositions of citizens.
2. It represents an expression of the *relationship between individual values and social objects*, the assessed worth of various social objects as filtered through the prisms of individual interest and values. In this connection, there is some disagreement among Bulgarian sociologists as to whether the individual or collective dimensions of judgment implied by this approach should be emphasized.
3. It is an expression of the *relationship between general worldviews* or ideological postures held by the citizenry, on the one hand, and the *specific circumstances* in which people live, on the other hand.
4. It may be viewed as an *expression of the interests of various subgroups* in society.

The methodology of Bulgarian survey research remains somewhat primitive by Western standards, and indeed by the standards of such research in Yugoslavia, Poland, or Hungary. Sampling has been demonstrably casual, apparently largely determined by convenience: studies are done of students at one school, workers at one plant, Party secretaries in a single region. Even within these geographic or institutional settings, random or stratified procedures are not often used. Few national surveys have been done, and with a handful of exceptions those that have been done did not make use of systematic samples.

Data analysis has been correspondingly weak. In more than half of the surveys examined in connection with this project, most or all of the findings were reported without the mention of percentages or frequency distributions. Where tables are presented in research reports, they almost always consist only of univariate descriptive statistics, often percentages only. Sometimes one can find implicit two-way and three-way cross tabulations, especially when researchers are concerned about the overlapping effects of education, place of residence, and nature of occupation as causal factors. Multivariate procedures are almost never used. It is worth noting that the library of the Institute of Sociology at the Bulgarian Academy of Sciences, presumably the strongest specialized library collection in the country for persons interested in systematic sociological research, is very limited in its holdings. Further, much of the methodologically relevant material in its card catalog is dramatically outdated, and little of it comes from Western sources which are generally acknowledged to provide methodological leadership in this field.

There is every reason to believe, however, that this is not a permanent state of affairs. Since 1976, Bulgarian sociologists have issued strident calls for methodological improvement, both in terms of the theoretical and conceptual underpinnings of research and the techniques used in sampling and data analysis.

On theoretical and conceptual questions, both Boris Chakalov[5] and Nano Stefanov[6] have urged two kinds of changes. First, they argue that simple description is not particularly helpful, either for understanding public opinion in the abstract, or for making use of such research for policy purposes. Explanation is required, and this has implications for the design of the research. Second, Chakalov in particular has urged that research move away from an almost exclusive concern with "situational" dimensions of opinion (by which he means opinions focused on, and often determined by, circumstances of the moment) and instead concentrate more on what he terms "current and constant," or more lasting, aspects of public opinion.

On the technical side, an article in *Sotsiologicheski Problemi* in 1976[7] reported important progress toward the development of representative national samples and also proposed improved procedures for doing more meaningful things with survey techniques. The need to move away from territorially particularistic samples toward representative (random and/or stratified) sampling was emphasized. In December, 1975, 30,000 census districts were created in Bulgaria, providing units much smaller than had previously existed. The average population of a census district is between 250 and 300 persons. It has been proposed that 10 to 15 percent of these census units (3,000-4,500 units) should be polled for future national samples. There would be serial use of subsamples, and some systematic panel studies are contemplated.

The same article emphasizes the importance of employing professional interviewers. It is also urged that it is no longer reasonable to consider analyzing the data from national samples without the use of computers. This and other articles also document the increased interest in proper phrasing of survey questions. The recognition that "leading" questions have been common in the past, and that the practical usefulness of responses to such questions is limited, is apparent.[8]

Four types of institutions carry out survey research in Bulgaria. Undoubtedly and deservedly, the most prestigious one is the Institute of Sociology at BAN. Second, there are sociological research units attached to large enterprises and to national or subnational government organs. For example, regional sociological associations formally attached to the local councils have been organized in nearly all of the districts of Bulgaria. Some national government agencies and enterprises maintain their own polling organizations; an example would be the State Cinematography Enterprise. Third, there are survey units attached to professional organizations, such as the Union of Bulgarian Journalists. Finally, the plurality of the surveys conducted in Bulgaria is carried out by polling units attached to various Party organizations and to the Komsomol. Party organizations in the larger cities have their own sociological units, as does the Academy of Social Science and Social Administration.

The most active survey research unit in Bulgaria during the past 10 years has been the Center for the Scientific Study of Youth. The great Bulgarian concern for the values and motivations of young people has been an important stimulus to the activity of this center. The center has carried out numerous studies since its inception in 1968 and reported that it had more than 30 studies underway in early 1978, most under the general theme of "youth in the developed socialist society." Its five major projects in 1978 were "Potential Migration of Peasant Youth," "Youth and Books," "The Scientific-Technological Revolution and Youth," "Young Specialists and their Place in Industry," and "The Young about Themselves." If past practice is future prologue, we can expect that few results from these studies will be published or made generally available. The center publishes one periodical, *Problemi na Mladezhta*, and works with the staffs of two other publications, *Narodna Mladezh* and *Mladezh*. It has been involved in several collaborative projects with similar institutes in other socialist countries.[9]

One of the most important testimonials to the growing significance of survey research in Bulgaria is provided by the Law of June 1, 1975, on the financing of sociological, social-psychological, and survey research.[10] (It is worth emphasizing that, for the first time, the title of the law refers to survey research.) The law dealt with more than merely the substantially increased financial means for carrying out such research. It also outlined a more formal structure for the coordination of these studies. The law provides monitoring roles for the Institute of Sociology at BAN and the Bulgarian Sociological Association. Regional sociological groups also are recognized as part of the planning and monitoring network. The law encourages the creation of polling-research units within organizations and notes that enterprises can enter into contractual agreements with scientific organizations to carry out research, if they do not choose or cannot afford to maintain their own polling unit.

The 1975 law affirms the embedding of survey research in the context of social policy. Significantly, however, it does not stress planning and coordination of the subject matter of studies or of the methods used. That is, the monitoring and coordinating roles assigned to the Bulgarian Sociological Association and the Institute of Sociology at BAN are referred to only in the most general terms, and no hierarchical structure for approving research topics, or for allocating or approving funding for such work, is either acknowledged or urged.

The number of published surveys is substantial and growing—if one counts informal polls conducted by daily and periodical publications, considerably more than 60 appeared between 1975 and 1978. However, it remains the case that a substantial number of surveys, including some of the potentially most interesting, are neither published nor made available for general use. The reader of *Problemi na Mladezhta* is likely to feel much like a penniless child in an ice cream parlor: he knows that there are tasty delights to be had, but he is not permitted to indulge. The disinclination of the center to publish anything other than terse, cursory descriptions of its studies is shared by the various Party organizations that conduct surveys. The only difference is that we usually do not know how much or what kind of research is being done by sociological groups attached to the Party structure.

It is easy for Western social scientists, operating in an environment in which information access is remarkably open, to be frustrated by and ultimately critical of these constraints on the publication of social data. However, two facts remain. First, restrained, conservative publication practices are wholly consistent with the policy-sensitive context in which much of this research is done in Bulgaria. Second, notwithstanding these constraints, there is a substantial amount of survey material being published in Bulgaria today, and it provides us with some fascinating insights into the evolution of this socialist society. It is difficult to say if the results of the surveys covered in this chapter are "representative" of what has been done. We can say that the coverage of what has been published was thorough. But more important, the face validity of many of the results of the studies cited here seems high.

The chapter Bibliography reports the materials covered in the preparation of this essay. Generally, we were able to examine all 1975 through 1977 issues of the relevant sociological publications, primarily *Sotsiologicheski Problemi* and *Problemi na Mladezhta*, as well as the most important publications of the Party and its research arms, including *Politicheska Agitatsia, Novo Vreme, Politicheska Prosveta*, and the publications of the Academy of Social Science and Social Administration. Some publications of professional organizations were covered, especially including *Bulgarski Profsuuzi* and *Bulgarski Zhurnalist.*

The research especially benefited from the help of colleagues at the Institute of Sociology at BAN, who graciously provided access to the Institute's card catalog, collection of bibliographies, and journal and book collections. University libraries and archives in the United States and in Western Europe were used to effect thorough searches of a number of major national daily and periodical publications, such as *Rabotnichesko Delo, Narodna Mladezh, Narodna Kultura, Mladezh, Literaturen Front, Anteni, Pogled, Plamuk,* and others. Occasional references to surveys were located in the Bulgarian Telegraph Agency *News Bulletin.*

This chapter reports the results of surveys conducted or published in Bulgaria during the period 1975-1977. In a few exceptional cases, we include important pieces of research which were published in the last half of 1974 or at the beginning of 1978. It should be emphasized that some of this research was conducted as early as 1968, and in many cases in the early 1970s. The lag between the conduct of research and the publication of results, when such publication takes place, seems extraordinarily long in Bulgaria. It also bears emphasizing that, although the research medium dealt with is surveys, some of the findings deal not with "attitudes" or "opinions," but with self-reports of behavior. Similarly, we occasionally include some data from nonsurvey sources when this seems appropriate to provide context within which survey responses may more appropriately be interpreted.

SURVEYS OF PUBLIC ATTITUDES AND BEHAVIOR IN BULGARIA

Media Habits

Research on media audiences has shared importantly in the expansion of survey research in Bulgaria in the last half of the 1970s. Two factors are especially important in explaining the growing attention to media habits. First, it is widely acknowledged both within and without Eastern Europe that the structured communication of ideas—systematic propagandizing—is critically important in the reweaving of the social fabric in those countries. The existence of a near monopoly in mass communications is an important policy lever for the Bulgarian regime. It is especially important in transmitting the norms and ethics of a socialist society to new generations. Difficulties in the socialist education of young people in Bulgaria have been freely admitted for more than ten years, and problems in the effectiveness of the mass media are thought to be a contributing factor. Thus it is not surprising that the media audience most researched in recent years has been the readership of *Narodna Mladezh*, the Komsomol newspaper.

A second factor has been the dramatic expansion of media coverage, especially television, in Bulgaria during the 1970s. During the period of the sixth five-year plan (1971-1975), the daily circulation of Bulgarian newspapers increased by 30 percent.[11] The largest circulation is that of the Party daily, *Rabotnichesko Delo*; its printing of 750,000 copies is nearly three times that of the next most widely distributed daily.[12]

There are now more than 1.6 million television sets in Bulgaria. More than 67 percent of the Bulgarians above the age of seven years watch television regularly, whereas the popularity of radio is now somewhat lower: 55 percent of the population count themselves as regular radio listeners.[13] During peak telecasting hours, television is watched by nearly six million persons, or approximately three-fourths of the population of the country.[14] Forty-four percent of telecasting time is given over to programs described as "news, sociopolitical, and propaganda broadcasts."

Two general themes may be identified in the recent research on media habits. The first involves identifying the nature of various media audiences, especially the characteristics that distinguish those who only marginally attend the media from those who are more consistent readers, listeners, or viewers. A second theme concerns the effectiveness of various media. This has been examined in terms of general impact on attitudes, thoroughness of transmitting specific pieces of factual information and motivating readers, especially youth, toward "social activism."

The nature of media audiences

The relationship between social background and attention to media varies distinctly between the printed and the electronic media. There is a direct and strong relationship between education and the amount and nature of newspaper reading. However, there are no significant differences in television watching among persons of different educational backgrounds. The principal factor distinguishing persons who do and do not watch television is place of residence; predictably, persons living in the countryside and in small villages are less likely to have access to television sets.[15]

As of 1973, the average Bulgarian viewer watched television 127 minutes in each 24-hour period. Males and city residents used television somewhat more than females and villagers, respectively. There are differences in television viewing by education level; 37.8 percent of persons with only primary education watch television, as compared with 63.4 percent of persons with graduate degrees. However, when place of residence is controlled for, the differences among education levels essentially disappear.

Since there are now more homes with television sets than with radios in Bulgaria, it is not surprising that television watching has cut significantly into previous radio audiences.[16] Nevertheless, approximately one-fourth of the population listens to the radio without any contact with television on an average weekday; on weekends, the percentage increases to 32. Approximately an equal percentage (in this case 26 percent) views television broadcasts without listening to the radio.[17]

A study of young urban readers has been done in an attempt to define more precisely the readership of the newspaper *Narodna Mladezh*.[18] From table 3.1 we discover that persons with only primary or junior high school education are much more likely to be nonreaders than are those with more education. Persons with higher education also are somewhat more likely to read the newspaper in its entirety, whereas persons with less education are characterized by a more selective focus on items of personal interest. However, it is worth noting that the degree of selectivity in the reading of *Narodna Mladezh* among all educational levels was remarked as a source of concern.[19]

Effectiveness of the media

A study by Hristo Bonev attempted to provide a basis for inferences about the effectiveness of the printed media in encouraging social activism among readers of *Narodna Mladezh* and other newspapers with explicit political content.[20] In fact, the data reported are almost entirely descriptive and relational and do not

Table 3.1. Patterns of Reading of *Narodna Mladezh* by Education of Readers
(percentages)

Pattern of Reading	Educational Level						
	Primary	Junior High	Technical	Secondary	Specialized Secondary	College	Doctorate
1. Do not read *Narodna Mladezh*	15.79	5.68	3.80	3.20	1.83	1.83	4.33
2. Usually read everything	15.79	13.26	21.52	15.10	16.44	20.24	22.12
3. Read what catches my eye on the page	31.58	46.53	40.51	47.83	48.25	47.62	47.12
4. Usually read about things which are most often talked and written about (popular subjects)	10.53	10.74	16.46	10.98	11.57	8.53	9.62
5. Read that which is of continuing interest to me	21.05	23.37	17.72	21.97	21.46	17.86	16.83

Source: Zdravko Raikov, "Faktori za povishavane na ideinoto vuzdeistvie na pechata vurhu chitatelskata auditoriya," *Sotsiologicheski Problemi* 8, no. 6 (1978): 68.

provide an adequate basis for causal inference. Nevertheless, inferences are made.

Bonev begins by documenting the extent of readership of the printed media among Komsomol members. He discovers that only 3.5 percent do not read any newspapers and only 8.9 percent do not read magazines on a regular basis. The most commonly read daily newspaper among Komsomol members is *Narodna Mladezh*, which is read by 58.7 percent of the young people surveyed. *Rabotnichesko Delo* is read by 52.1 percent. The most commonly read magazine is *Zhenata Dnes* (45.7 percent); *Mladezh* is read by 30.1 percent.

Notwithstanding this relatively high and consistent exposure of young people to the printed media, Bonev expresses concern that intense exposure does not necessarily lead to social activism. Nonetheless, there is a relationship between social activism and more intense readership. For example, those who read more are more likely to hold positions in the leadership of mass organizations for young people. Those who report satisfaction with the nature of their participation in youth organizations read newspapers more often than those who are less satisfied. Bonev's research suggests, however, that this relationship between newspaper reading and organizational involvement may actually be a function of a third factor, attitudes toward work and work achievement. For example, he discovers that those who are committed to proving themselves professionally read more often than those who do not have such a commitment. Of those who think their knowledge and professional preparation are generally insufficient, readership is identifiably higher than among those who do not recognize such insufficiencies.

Bonev's research also attempted to determine whether young people feel that the printed media are effective mechanisms for correcting social ills. The responses showed considerable skepticism about the effectiveness of newspapers and magazines in this role. For example, 70.8 percent of the young people surveyed feel that the social-criticism role of the printed media should be expanded. Young people believe that social criticism contained in *Rabotnichesko Delo* usually brings results, but this feeling does not hold for other newspapers and magazines. There especially is skepticism about the effectiveness of social criticism appearing in *Narodna Mladezh*. More than 44 percent of the young people surveyed feel that criticisms voiced in *Narodna Mladezh* "only occasionally help," and 12.3 percent think that such criticisms do not help at all. According to those surveyed, the sources of ineffectiveness are two: first, criticisms frequently do not attempt to uncover the actual reasons behind the problems (33.4 percent voiced this view). Second, 12.5 percent believe that the issues on which criticism is made are frequently side or peripheral issues. Only one-third of the young people surveyed believe that the most fundamental weaknesses in Bulgarian society are effectively criticized in *Narodna Mladezh*.

A slightly different approach to examining the effectiveness of *Narodna Mladezh* was reported in 1976.[21] A quasi-experimental study was conducted with a "small group" of young people in connection with a series of newspaper feature articles dealing with aesthetic education that appeared during 1975.

Observations were made of the views of the young people both before and after the discussions appeared in the newspaper. Initially, the studies showed that 70.8 percent of the young people observed were "in whole or in part" familiar with the materials included in the newspaper discussion. Of the 70 percent who were familiar with the content of these feature articles, the research concluded that only about one-half accurately and fully understood the themes presented.

The research ultimately showed that nearly one-half of those polled felt that the newspaper articles had changed their views at least somewhat. The author concludes that the results "point to the great degree of effectiveness of the newspaper" in altering reader attitudes. Less positive interpretations would be equally plausible, especially since less than one-half of the young people polled had both followed the articles, and showed identifiable understanding of the points of view presented by *Narodna Mladezh.*

Doubts about the effectiveness of *Narodna Mladezh* are suggested in another way by Bonev, who found that only slightly more than one-half of its readers feel that the paper "satisfies their expectations."[22] Bonev concludes that greater concern should be shown for the attitudes and expectations of readers, and not merely for the abstract thoroughness or coherence of the presentation of materials in the newspaper.

The effectiveness of means of mass communication in the preparation of young people for family life also has been examined. This was a study conducted in 1975 by the State Committee on Sports.[23] The research was conducted in Vratsa and in Pleven among 6,842 young people aged 15-30. The concept of preparation for family life included sexual, social-psychological, family organizational, and children and family planning dimensions.

Table 3.2 reports responses to a question concerning whether newspapers and magazines print enough about family and married life. Only about 12 percent of the respondents felt that media content in these areas was adequate. When asked what subjects should be treated in more detail, the three most frequently named themes were etiquette of conduct in male-female relationships, developing mutual understanding between young and older persons, and sex education.

One study was found which addressed the informational adequacy of the mass media.[24] This was a study among members of local work collectives as to whether they were aware of the time and place of important meetings of the collective, meetings which were publicized only through the mass media. The percentages of those saying they were informed varied somewhat among locations, but generally between 80 percent and 90 percent of those polled knew when and where such meetings were to be held. The study apparently did not control for the impact of word-of-mouth communication; it is therefore difficult to know whether the media effects were primarily direct or indirect.

Another approach to ascertaining the effectiveness of the press was taken in a study by the Center for Journalism Research in Sofia, which examined the relationship between readership of national publications and readership of regional newspapers.[25] The study proceeded from the premise that regional newspapers play a critical role in communicating certain categories of information: "There is no other method that can surpass the dissemination of mass information through the regional newspaper." A major aspect of this study concerned the overlapping of readership between national and regional newspapers and the related question of whether the regional newspapers unnecessarily duplicated the content of the national publications. Table 3.3 reports the proportion of regional newspaper readers who also subscribe to each of several national daily and weekly publications. Except for subscribers to *Rabotnichesko Delo*, only about one-fourth or fewer of regional newspaper readers subscribe to any given national publication. However, nearly 90 percent of all regional newspaper subscribers also subscribe to at least one national publication.

Local readers view the extent of duplication of news between national and regional newspapers unfavorably. Only 20 percent of these readers felt that there was not excessive duplication. This duplication is seen as unfortunate because it limits the amount of space that regional newspapers can devote to local news. Fully 50 percent of the readers surveyed feel that the regional newspaper is the only systematic source of local news. One-third of the readers indicate that they receive their local news from central newspapers, or from radio and television. Personal communication is identified as the most important channel by 7 percent of the readers.

When asked about the effectiveness of regional newspapers in addressing social problems, these readers showed considerable skepticism. Approximately half believe that the regional newspaper "sometimes but not all the time" can help overcome or alleviate the critical problem of shortages. The other 50 percent of the readers feel that the newspaper cannot help them if they turn to it for a solution to a local problem. One-third of the readers believe that the regional newspapers do not deal with the most important problems of the region. Significantly, those with this concern are primarily economic specialists, political leaders, and readers with advanced degrees.

Recent Bulgarian research on the nature of media audiences has arrived at predictable conclusions: attention to the printed media varies primarily with extent of formal education, whereas contact with the electronic media is primarily distinguished by the difference between the cities, on the one hand, and the villages and rural areas, on the other. The research also demonstrates that television has overtaken radio as the principal electronic medium, except for some rural areas, and for certain periods of time on weekends.

The Bulgarian concern for the effectiveness of the communications media has been reflected in a number of important research projects. Broadly, these studies suggest reasons for some skepticism about the impact of the press, notwithstanding the high level of citizen attention to printed media, as well as the near monopoly of communications held by the regime. Some segments of the population doubt the effectiveness of the press in attacking social problems. Nevertheless, it is significant that such a role for the press could be contem-

Table 3.2. Perceived Adequacy of Press Treatment of Family Life,
by Marital Status and Place of Residence
(percentages)

	Respondent Subsample			
Perceived Adequacy of Press Treatment	Pleven Married Men	Vratsa Unmarried Women	Pleven Married Women	Vratsa Unmarried Men
1. Inadequate	45.5	43.8	46.4	48.8
2. Adequate only on some problems	33.2	32.9	30.8	25.5
3. Adequate	10.9	11.7	12.5	12.8
4. Don't care about such things	8.0	9.4	2.0	9.7
5. No answer	0.2	2.0	8.2	2.9

Source: "Means of Mass Information and Preparation of Young People for Family Life"
[in Bulgarian], *Bulgarski Zhurnalist* (May 1977), pp. 21-29.

Table 3.3. Readership of National Newspapers among
Subscribers to Regional Newspapers
(percentages)

National Newspapers Read	Percent of Regional Newspaper Subscribers Who Read Each Publication
Dailies:	
Rabotnichesko Delo	54.8
Kooperativno Selo	25.4
Narodna Mladezh	25.0
Trud	23.9
Otechestven Front	21.6
Zemedelsko Zname	10.9
Vecherni Novini	8.4
Narodna Armiya	5.7
Weeklies:	
Pogled	33.0
Sturshel	29.1
Anteni	17.1
Literaturen Front	5.9

Source: Center for Journalism Research (Sofia), "Certain Problems of Regional Newspapers
Identified by Sociological Research" [in Bulgarian], *Bulgarski Zhurnalist* (August 1975),
p. 27.

plated, and that the issue is being raised as openly as it is.

Family and Women

Research on the related topics of family life and the role of women has been concentrated on issues having to do with the emancipation of women, especially with efforts to create genuine equality for women at home as well as on the job. A major theme has been the unequal distribution of housework in families where both husbands and wives work outside the home. The persistence of traditional attitudes toward the division of labor within the family has been shown to affect profoundly the lifestyles of women, especially their use of leisure time and their attitudes toward family size.

Differences of opinion concerning the work done by women both outside and in the home also have been examined as a major source of conflicts within young families. There have been studies on the causes of divorce and on attitudes toward abortion. Some of these studies, as well as research on attitudes toward alcoholism, are dealt with in later sections.

The emancipation of Bulgarian women in the 1970s

In Bulgaria in the mid-1970s, women accounted for 48.2 percent of the population of working age, and 46.2 percent of those actually employed.[26] Of the specialists with a high school education in Bulgaria, 55.8 percent are women; 39.8 percent of university graduates are women. Nineteen thousand women delegates constitute 37 percent of the membership of local People's Councils. The commitment of Bulgarian women to their employment seems strong. In a study on "Women in Social Production, Society, and the Family,"[27] 80 percent of the women polled indicated that they intended to work until they reached the age of retirement, which would be 50 or 55 years of age.

In spite of the already significant professional and industrial employment of women in Bulgaria, traditional attitudes toward the division of labor within the family persist, and result in dramatic inequalities in the time available to men and women for relaxation and personal growth. According to a survey study published in the newspaper *Narodna Kultura* in 1977,[28] "The biggest problem facing the Bulgarian woman today is the inequality in housework at home." Data supportive of this conclusion were reported in *Sotsiologicheski Problemi* in 1975.[29] A study done by the Scientific Institute for the Study of Work shows that, on the average, men spend 120 minutes doing housework during the average 24-hour period, whereas the average woman who also holds a job outside the home spends 244 minutes, or slightly more than four hours, on housework. An earlier study had discovered that 39.4 percent of Bulgarian women do the housework alone, 39.2 percent do most of it but with the help of some other members of the family, and 14.5 percent work equally with other members of the household. In the case of fewer than 7 percent of Bulgarian women is the housework primarily or entirely done by someone else. The household work load is shown to be heavier, particularly on weekends, for women who have three or more children under 16 years of age. On the average, women with large families spend more than six hours per weekend day on housework, and an average of more than seven hours per day during their "vacation" periods.

The birth rate has been affected by the heavy burden placed on Bulgarian women in the home. More than 20 percent of the women polled[30] indicated that they did not want to have more children primarily because their workload was excessive. Workloads in the home also affect efforts at professional betterment; 10.2 percent of the respondents indicated that they desire to improve their employment qualifications to obtain better jobs, but are unable to do so because of demands in the home.

The uses of leisure time, particularly for cultural enrichment, by Bulgarian women clearly are constrained by the nature of their housework obligations. Table 3.4 reports the relationship between degree of participation in housework and the reading and cultural interests of Bulgarian women. There are sharp contrasts between women who do most or all of the housework and women who live in households where other members regularly help. Cultural and reading activities are identifiably higher in every category for the latter group. The household workload also was shown to affect sports and other health-related activities of women; for example, women who regularly have help with housework are twice as likely to do morning exercises as are those who have no help.

That the values of Bulgarian women are now identifiably at odds with actual practice seems clear: A 1975 survey conducted by the magazine *Zhenata Dnes*[31] sampled 809 working women. Only 1.9 percent believed that they alone should do the housework; this compares with approximately 30 percent of Bulgarian women who report that they solely have this responsibility. Nearly 30 percent of the respondents believed that the marriage partners should equally divide household duties. In fact, such responsibilities are equally shared in only 11 percent of Bulgarian households. The women who believe in equal division of housework responsibilities are primarily persons with higher status occupations, especially administrative jobs. A significantly smaller proportion of women in the village agricultural cooperatives share this view.

One of the accompaniments of a more independent and assertive outlook on the part of Bulgarian women is a greater concern for how they dress. A poll "conducted in many areas and among different groups of women between 20 and 50 years of age" and appearing in *Narodna Kultura* in 1977[32] concluded that Bulgarian women are increasingly concerned about being able to dress "fashionably," but that they frequently feel they do not succeed. The newspaper reported that this conclusion was not unexpected, but noted that the reasons given for the inability to dress fashionable "were surprising." These

Table 3.4. Cultural Activities and Participation in Housework among Bulgarian Working Women
(percentages)

Cultural Activity	Extent of Housework Participation		
	Do all housework	Do most of the housework	Other household members help regularly
A. Reading			
1. Newspapers	68.1	69.9	77.6
2. Magazines	41.4	44.0	58.9
3. Belles-lettres	40.1	42.1	64.6
4. Scientific literature	12.4	10.9	26.6
B. Events			
1. Art exhibits and galleries	21.5	19.9	29.7
2. Concerts	16.6	13.7	18.8
3. Folk music programs	51.4	53.7	63.5
4. Jazz concerts	30.2	29.2	50.4
5. Theater and literary recitals	51.9	55.8	66.7

Source: Liliyana Spasovska, "Rabotnichkata v Domakinstvoto," *Sotsiologicheski Problemi* 7, no. 2 (1975): 75.

reasons were: 1) women indicate they cannot find modern clothing in the shops, 2) television does not carry adequate programming which would either illustrate new styles of women's clothing, or help women know how or where to obtain such styles, and 3) newspapers and magazines do not print enough in this area, and the quality of the photographs and illustrations in publications that do carry such material is poor.

The changing Bulgarian family

The principal changes that have impacted on the Bulgarian family in the last decade are those which commonly affect modernizing societies: There has been a substantial increase in the number of women working outside the home, and the size of the average family has declined. Further, an ever-larger proportion of Bulgarian families lives in towns and cities. This redistribution of the population brings some people into unfamiliar environments in terms of values and life-styles.

Bulgarian sociologists have been particularly concerned about the impacts of these changes on the young family. One illustrative survey study, for example, deals with the concepts of equality and conflict in the young Bulgarian family.[33] This study, which was conducted in the city of Gabrovo and published in the newspaper *Anteni*, focused on three types of questions: Should wives work outside the home, and if so, under what circumstances? Who should care for the children in working families? How can relationships with the parents of husband and wife be managed so as to minimize familial conflict? These issues were explored in intensive interviews in 100 Gabrovo families; the husband and wife were interviewed independently.

Husbands and wives differed significantly in their feelings about the employment of the woman outside the home. When asked if the woman should stay at home if there were no economic necessity for her to work, 72 percent of the husbands answered in the affirmative, whereas 67 percent of the wives indicated they would not leave their jobs even if material conditions were favorable. Conflicts within the interviewed families over this issue apparently were significant; *Anteni* reported that, for 53 percent of the families interviewed, "The conflicts are not minimal."

The care of the small children of working families also is a source of concern and, in some cases, familial conflict. Sixty percent of the young Gabrovo mothers polled have not entrusted their children to day-care centers, and 14 percent of those who have indicate they would readily leave their jobs in order to care for their children if economic circumstances permitted. The authors of the study report a general "uneasiness" about leaving children in the day-care centers. Conflicts between a woman's desire to care for her child and her desire for professional advancement are most vivid for women who work in highly skilled jobs. Nearly two-thirds of the women who believe that a child should be taken care of until the age of five years by the mother, at the same time do not feel that they should have to leave their jobs for this purpose.

Even more dissonance accompanies the distinction between preference and practice in child care arrangements. Ninety-eight percent of the women and 97 percent of the men surveyed in Gabrovo do not believe that their parents (i.e., the child's grandparents) should take care of the child. But in practice, children in 46 percent of these families were cared for by grandparents. Differences of opinion between husbands and wives on the question of child care are distinct. Of the husbands polled, 86 percent believe that children up to five years of age should be cared for by the mother in the home. The corresponding percentage for the wives interviewed was 72 percent.

Predictably, these concerns about the role of women, the nature of the family, and the impact of having children on professional and personal life-styles affect women's attitudes about appropriate family size. Another study[34] reported in *Anteni* explores women's attitudes on this subject, and examines the effects of factors such as education, age, urban or rural residence, profession, housing conditions, and day-care facilities on these attitudes.

Overall, it is clear that Bulgarian women increasingly prefer smaller families. Among women more than 25 years of age, a preference for three or more children is common. But among younger women, few prefer more than two children, and for some, one child is considered ideal. It is noteworthy that more than 25 percent of the married Bulgarian women between the ages of 20 and 24 years have no children.[35] Education also influences attitudes toward fertility; the higher the degree of formal education, the smaller the preferred family size. More than half of the married Bulgarian women with doctorates, and nearly 45 percent of those with high school diplomas and specialized job training, have only one child. The number of childless married women is two-and-one-half times higher in the cities than in the countryside.

Especially among urban women, housing conditions have a significant effect on preferred family size, although the *Anteni* study does not report specific statistics on the number who felt that housing conditions were a constraint on having children. The limited availability or acceptability of day-care facilities also affects women's perceptions of ideal family size; again, the specific figures are not provided.

If family size is an important consideration for young Bulgarian families, we can expect that the subject of abortion might frequently be an issue of contention for these families. One study[36] suggests that 11 percent of all first pregnancies among married town and city women were aborted; the actual figure is probably higher. The *Anteni* study of equality and conflict in the young family[37] showed that one-third of the arguments in young families in Gabrovo focused on questions concerning the appropriate number of children, including arguments about abortion. The article notes that in many cases such disputes led to "irretrievable damage" to the marriage relationship, and sometimes to divorce.

According to a study mentioned by the Bulgarian Telegraph Agency in 1976,[38] surveys show that unfaithfulness is the most frequent cause of divorce. More than 31 percent of the marriages dissolved in Bulgaria in 1974 were ended for that reason. The rate of unfaithfulness is more than twice as high among men as among women. The survey also showed that families without children are the most vulnerable. More than 36 percent of the persons divorced in 1974 had no children, and another 28 percent had only one child. Divorce is much more frequent among the more highly educated and among residents of Sofia and other major towns. The survey also showed that "in recent years married people have shown a decreasing inclination to adjust themselves to their partners." Whereas in 1965 "incompatibility of temperament" was the cause of only 3 percent of divorces, nine years later it was the reason given for more than 7 percent of the marriages dissolved.

A study done in Vratsa and Pleven on the preparation of young people for family life[39] was mentioned above under Media Habits. The study generally showed that young married couples felt that there were inadequate sources of information to prepare them for the sexual and social-psychological aspects of family life, including child rearing. Especially interesting was the finding that friends, and specialized and general literature and art, were more frequently mentioned as sources of information in preparation for family life than were parents, other close relatives, and teachers. On the average, about 10 percent of the respondents mentioned the latter category of persons close to them, whereas more than 25 percent mentioned friends and literature.

Survey research on family life and women in Bulgaria has emphasized the changing role of women, and the social and psychological accompaniments of that changing role. Women have become important in the work force and are increasingly important in many professions. Their changing professional roles affect their outlooks. But the realization of some of the things they have come to value more highly remains difficult, in part because of the persistence of traditional attitudes about the division of labor within the home, and in part because of economic and related constraints that give them less flexibility in their personal lives and that affect their attitudes toward children and family more generally. Two of the results of these changes have been the emergence of new dimensions of conflict within the Bulgarian family, especially young families, and a sense of inadequacy among young Bulgarians about their preparation for family life. Such developments are wholly consistent with the results of social-psychological research conducted on other modernizing societies.

Education and Youth

Education and youth are the most frequently addressed subjects in Bulgarian survey research in the 1970s. The reasons for this intense interest are not difficult to identify. In any society in which there is a strong commitment to value change, careful attention to the socialization of young people is called for. In the Bulgarian case, the importance of this research is underscored by the difficulties the regime has encountered in this area. The "Zhivkov Theses" on youth, published on December 1, 1967, explicitly acknowledged the serious concern held by the political leadership for the values of young people, their inadequate commitment to social activism, and the ineffectiveness of the Komsomol organization.

There are other reasons for the careful attention paid to education and youth in Bulgarian surveys. Bulgaria is typical of modernizing societies in that education is unambiguously the most important social predictor of citizen values. Further, it is obvious that education is closely related to the existence of class differentials in Bulgarian society. In a society genuinely committed to the minimization of socioeconomic inequalities, a careful understanding of the effects of the educational system is critically important. Table 3.5 demonstrates the substantial differences among basic occupational groups in level of formal education achieved and the differences between older and younger Bulgarians in extent of formal education.

Perhaps it is because of the sensitivity of these problems that a substantial proportion of the research done is not published or otherwise given wide circulation. For the most part, what is published probably is representative of what is done, but it remains the case that there is frustratingly little flesh to put on the skeletal outlines of our understanding of education and youth in Bulgaria, especially given the impressive research apparatus which exists for the purpose of generating information.

Because the concern with youth is pervasive, research relevant to a characterization of Bulgarian youth is reported in several sections of this chapter. As indicated earlier, the readership of *Narodna Mladezh* has been studied with some care. In the following section on Work and the Workplace, we discover that special attention is being given to the concerns of young workers, especially to their job satisfaction. The leisure time of young people receives individual attention. Much of the research on life aspirations naturally focuses on young people. "Hooliganism" and other antisocial manifestations among youth receive attention in the section on social problems.

In the present section we limit our attention to a handful of studies which illustrate the concern of Bulgarian researchers for three general themes: 1) the basic values and social concerns of youth, 2) youth attitudes toward the educational process, and 3) motivations of Komsomol members and the perceived effectiveness of the Komsomol.

Basic values and concerns of youth

The published Bulgarian survey research in this area is focused narrowly on per-

Table 3.5. Occupation by Formal Education[a] and Age Group
(percentages of each occupational group)

Occupation	Did not finish basic education		Did not finish secondary school		Finished secondary school	
	over 28 years	28 or less	over 28 years	28 or less	over 28 years	28 or less
1. Industrial workers	54.5	18.3	4.1	15.0	4.8	12.7
2. Agricultural workers	82.2	30.6	0.6	11.9	0.5	5.7
3. Service and administrative employees	11.6	1.1	5.7	16.0	36.5	45.6

[a] Percentages apparently do not include persons with postsecondary education or persons still enrolled in educational programs.

Source: Veska Kozhuharova, "Sotsialnata Obuslovenost na Interesa kum Hudozhestvenata Literatura," *Novo Vreme* 50 (November 1974): 58.

sonal, as opposed to social, matters. Thus surveys inquire about personal qualities that young Bulgarians find objectionable in others, but do not ask about their concerns with regard to social organizations, the economy, or the polity. Illustrative of surveys on personal matters is a 1977 study of the characteristics that young men and young women dislike in one another.[40] Excessive use of alcohol was identified as the most undesirable quality by both young men and young women; 47 percent of the males do not like females who drink, and 45 percent of the females do not like young men who drink. Forty percent of the young men did not want their future wives to smoke, although many of the men themselves did smoke. Most of the young women, by contrast, have a tolerant attitude toward the use of tobacco by males; only 19 percent of the women were critical of smoking by men. The males also identified other traits they do not like in young women: frivolity in sexual relations (40 percent of the young men named this characteristic); superficiality (34 percent); excessive aggressiveness (29 percent); overweight (27 percent); imitating men (20 percent); and vanity (15 percent).

Responses from the young women were similar, although the modest existence of a double standard with respect to sexual activity is implied; 31 percent of the women objected to frivolity in sexual relations on the part of men. The study showed that young people in rural areas are substantially more critical of most of these "modern" habits than were residents of the cities.

These stated values and preferences of Bulgarian young people appear at least somewhat inconsistent with evidence on actual practice, particularly with regard to smoking cigarettes and the consumption of alcohol. Lyuben Dimitrov[41] reports the results of a survey conducted in 1970 among 1,430 high school students throughout Bulgaria. The data show that 45.5 percent of the students 16 years of age drink alcoholic beverages and 40.7 percent smoke. Above age 17, more than half drink and smoke. Young people from the villages constitute an exception to the rule.

Some change in values in the countryside is suggested by a recent study of rural youth. Bulgarian sociologists surveyed a sample of young men and women in rural villages on the subject, "What is the most important thing in life for you?"[42] Twenty-two percent said that a meaningful occupation was the most important. Approximately 13 percent named each of the factors of friendship, love, and knowledge. Only 4.8 percent of those interviewed regarded material goods as the most important thing. The authors of the study find it especially interesting that knowledge is valued as highly as are love and friendship. The argument is made that young people in the villages have come to recognize that education and knowledge are critical mechanisms for personal advancement.

Two studies reported in *Problemi na Mladezhta* in 1977 provide some information about the values of Komsomol members, and about how these values compare with general population samples. The first was carried out in 1972-1973, and involved surveys of a national sample of Komsomol members[43] focused on personal qualities—the kinds of qualities valued most in good friends, and the qualities most appreciated about associates in the Komsomol. Table 3.6 reports responses to the question, "Which qualities do you value most in your colleagues?" Perhaps most significant is that a Marxist-Leninist world view and ideological orientation was mentioned by only 6.8 percent of the respondents; active participation in the Komsomol was even less frequently mentioned. Helpfulness and a broad educational background are thought to be far more significant than are ideological or political characteristics. When the question was phrased more specifically to refer to qualities admired in participants in Komsomol group activities, the tenor of the responses was only marginally different. The results reported in *Problemi na Mladezhta* (see table 3.7) inexplicably grouped together three factors, including exemplary ideological conviction. But even when ideological conviction is grouped with "broad educational background" and "excellent specialized training," the qualities of "high principles and honesty" are still felt to be more important. Organizationally relevant qualities such as defending the interests of the group and demonstrating organizational skills also were somewhat less important. The authors of the study complain that the fact that the ethic of socialism is not placed first "scandalizes the socialist model."[44]

The second study deals with a survey of 199 workers, soldiers, intelligentsia, and students.[45] The geographical locale of these samples is not given. A number of questions dealing with the nature of authority and social prestige were asked. On some questions, there was little or no difference among the subsets of respondents. For example, all sampled groups agreed that personal qualities are more important than the kind of work one does in determining one's social prestige.

On other questions, however, there were differences between the student sample and the others. The respondents were asked, "What sort of person is the most authoritative individual in our country?" A plurality of the nonstudent samples (34.2 percent) believed that, for most people in Bulgaria, the most authoritative person is one who has "solid connections." An additional 14.1 percent of the nonstudents believed that the most authoritative person is the one who has the greatest social status. In sharp contrast, only 1.5 percent of the students interviewed equated authority with "solid connections," and only 3 percent felt that authority was an accompaniment of social status. A plurality of the student sample (31.8 percent) said that the principal quality of an authoritative person was knowledge; this view was shared by 57.1 percent of the sample of intelligentsia, but by only 17.4 percent of the workers. Approximately one-third of the workers believed that a sense of justice and fair play was the most important quality of authoritative persons; only 13.6 percent of the students, and not a single member of the intelligentsia, agreed.

The authors of the studies were concerned that political-ideological and social ethics considerations were not emphasized by most of the respondents, especially young people. By contrast, the values that seem dominant are ones having to do with personality characteristics and knowledge. To be sure, there

Table 3.6. Qualities Valued Most in Colleagues and
Friends by Komsomol Members, 1973
(percentages)

Quality Valued	Percent of Respondents
1. Friendliness, helpfulness	34.6
2. Broad educational background	30.8
3. Marxist-Leninist world view and ideological conviction	6.8
4. Active Komsomol participation	4.7
5. No answer	2.3
Total	79.2[a]

[a] Apparently 20.8 percent of the respondents named qualities other than those listed.

Source: Kiril Vasilev, "Sotsialniyat Prestizh na Lichnostta," *Problemi na Mladezhta* 7, no. 4 (1977): 10.

Table 3.7. Qualities Admired Most in Komsomol Associates
by Komsomol Members, 1973
(percentages)

Quality Admired	Percent of Respondents
1. Principles and honesty	26
2. Broad educational background; excellent preparation in a specialty; ideological conviction	20
3. Friendliness, sociability	14
4. Defends interests of the group	13
5. Organizational abilities	11
6. Oriented toward sports	2
Total	86[a]

[a] Apparently 14 percent named qualities other than those listed.

Source: Kiril Vasilev, "Sotsialniyat Prestizh na Lichnostta," *Problemi na Mladezhta* 7, no. 4 (1977): 10.

is nothing wrong with being easy to work with, or having knowledge. But the relatively poor showing of the socially prescribed virtues seems to have been a source of some apprehension.

Attitudes toward the educational process

Two studies were identified that deal with the attitudes of students toward educational institutions and the educational process. The first,[46] which involved interviews with 100 students from the technical institute V. I. Lenin in Sofia, focused on student reactions to certain aspects of educational reform. The reforms, instituted in the early 1970s, were designed to increase students' flexibility in choosing specializations and courses of instruction, to make the instructional process more sensitive to the concerns of students, and to ensure that the information dispensed as part of the learning process was concrete and of practical utility, rather than too abstract.

Unfortunately, the only published results from this study that we have been able to identify appeared in the newspaper *Anteni*, and include mostly descriptive and anecdotal results, rather than aggregate tabulations of responses. Nevertheless, in the case of most questions asked, there seems to have been general consensus among the respondents.

For example, nearly all of the students indicated that they chose their area of specialization essentially by chance, or because of idiosyncratic considerations. These responses presumably were not the ones hoped for, since one of the premises on which choice of specialization had been relaxed was that students would choose with a sense of collective and professional rationality. There was similar unanimity in student responses to questions about the factors that were most important in ensuring success in their studies. Nearly all mentioned some aspect of personal motivation and discipline; only a few referred to the structural features of the educational system that were the targets of the reforms. As the author of the *Anteni* article says, "If we judge by the poll, some of the instructors still do not have the necessary psychological make-up."

The second study dealing with student attitudes toward the educational process was carried out by students in the sociological laboratory at the Higher Institute of National Economy in Varna. Established in 1968, the laboratory was initially placed under the Department of Marxism-Leninism at the Institute, but was moved in 1975 to be under the administration of the vice-rector of learned studies. The laboratory does some topical studies, and annually carries out larger studies on the social characteristics of incoming students and of graduating students.

The study of interest to us here is on, "The Ideal Educational Process"; the results were published in *Studentska Tribuna* in 1975.[47] Most of the questions focused on political and ideological training within the Institute. For example, respondents were asked to identify the obstacles that make the struggle against bourgeois influence more difficult. The majority responded that the principal problem was the existence of material shortages in Bulgarian society; only secondarily did they identify problems in ideological work and training. The third and fourth obstacles were bourgeois propaganda and ideological diversions, and the growing contact of Bulgarians with foreigners. Nearly two-thirds of the students polled felt that on meeting a foreigner (presumably from a non-socialist country), a graduate of the Varna Institute could adequately defend the principles of socialism. At the same time, the fact that 36 percent of the students had some doubt about this is considered significant by the authors of the study.

Students were then asked to evaluate the various courses of study at the Institute in terms of the contribution they made to the ability of students to defend socialist principles. The highest scores were given to the Department of Scientific Marxism-Leninism, and the lowest to the Department of Philosophy. Students also said they had the highest regard for instructors in the "ideological disciplines" at the Institute. These latter responses seem socially appropriate. More surprising was the fact that material shortages were thought to represent the most important obstacle preventing effective struggle against bourgeois influence.

The Komsomol: motivations and perceived effectiveness

Zhivkov's great concern with problems in the functioning of the Komsomol, evident in his theses on youth, has been manifested in recent years in a number of interesting studies on that organization. One of the most fascinating was based on a survey of Komsomol members at 21 higher polytechnic schools in the Sofia area.[48] The purpose of this study was to identify the nature of the motives underlying the performance of Komsomol tasks. Samples of students in the eighth through eleventh grades were used. Thus the study provides a basis for inferences about how motivations change as young Komsomol members mature.

Table 3.8 summarizes the major findings of this study. What is especially interesting is that motives focusing on the intrinsic worth of Komsomol membership are predominant for eighth graders, but decline sharply as the students grow older. By contrast, motives which refer to social or personal instrumentalities are relatively unimportant for eighth graders, but become clearly predominant by the time a student is in the eleventh grade. Thus, for example, the response "in order to help fulfill the purposes of the Komsomol" declines from 57.5 percent of the eighth-grade respondents to 28.1 percent of those in the eleventh grade. Similarly, the motive "in order to justify the trust placed in me as a Komsomol member" declines from 61.5 percent to 46.9 percent. By contrast, the motivation of "giving something to society" increases from 38.5 percent to 71.9 percent, and a stated interest in "verifying my own capabilities" increases dramatically from 15.4 percent to 56.2 percent.

These results evidently were not entirely satisfying to the researchers doing the study, for their initial "concrete practical conclusion" stressed the importance of developing greater "emotional attachments" among Komsomol members:

> During the formation of public opinion at school and in the Komsomol particular attention must be given to *emotional factors*. [Emphasis in original] We must strive to awaken more feelings and emotional experiences and to control and direct such experiences . . ..[49]

As we noted above, a study published in *Problemi na Mladezhta* in 1977[50] revealed that Komsomol members value personal characteristics, especially friendly helpfulness and a broad educational background, more highly than an appropriate ideological posture. Even when assessing the qualities thought to be most important for persons actively participating in Komsomol organizational work, "principles and honesty" turn out to be the most important considerations. Taken together, the findings from these several studies suggest that the hoped-for level of emotive and ideological commitment on the part of Komsomol members still has not been obtained.

A study cited by Dimitrov,[51] which involved interviews with 11,430 high school students, also included questions concerning the perceived effectiveness of the Komsomol in certain areas of the school's functioning. For example, students were asked whether the teachers' councils take into account the opinion of the Komsomol in making decisions that affect the nature of schooling. The results report only responses from Komsomol activists, who presumably are inclined to respond affirmatively. Two-thirds of the respondents did indeed respond "yes," but 17 percent answered "only sometimes," and 15.5 percent indicated that the opinion of the Komsomol was never taken into account. Of those who indicated that Komsomol opinions were taken into consideration, the majority stated that this generally occurred when the conduct of Komsomol members was being evaluated. Dimitrov reports that the authors of the study believed that this relatively high level of perceived disregard for the Komsomol was "an expression of inadequate respect for them, and for their capabilities." The authors concluded that, on many questions, no matter what position the Komsomol took the decisive opinion came from the administration and the faculty of the school.

Broadly, the results of the research reported here on education and youth suggest that the desired level and direction of political socialization of youth have not yet been achieved in Bulgaria. Youth are socially conscious, but their level of *socialist* consciousness seems to lag. Bulgarian young people seem to be more pragmatic and instrumental than ideological.

Work and the Workplace

Both the ideological importance of workers and the rapid pace of industrialization in Bulgaria call for systematic attention to characteristics of the workplace and to attitudes of workers toward their work. In Bulgaria, recent surveys recently have addressed four aspects of these topics: basic values concerning work and the workplace, job satisfaction and labor turnover, worker attitudes toward automation, and worker evaluations of organizational and leadership elements in the workplace.

Work and workplace values

The topic of work incentives has been an important one in Bulgaria. Illustrative is a project on "The Role of Moral and Material Incentives in Socialist Work," conducted in a textile factory in Gabrovo.[52] This research addressed various aspects of job satisfaction, feelings of responsibility toward work and colleagues, worker attitudes toward incentive competitions held in the factory, and more general aspects of socialist activism among workers.

When workers were asked what attracted them to their work, a plurality said "love for my profession"; only about 12 percent mentioned material rewards. When asked whether work incentive competitions in their factory were evaluated justly, one-third felt that they were; another 21 percent said that evaluations were just "in part." Seventeen percent felt that the evaluations were not just; 12.7 percent felt that they could not say. These results suggest some skepticism about the work-incentive competitions.

Workers also were asked which nonmaterial incentives they felt were most desirable. There was a preference for rewards focused within the factory setting itself, rather than more broadly in the local community. Thus the two preferred forms of nonmaterial incentives were praise in general meetings of workers and having one's portrait placed on the wall in the factory. Praise in the press, or on the radio, was considered less attractive. The *Rabotnicesko Delo* article does not report worker attitudes toward material incentives.

Problems in the area of work incentives are suggested by a study on worker attitudes in the machine building industry mentioned in *Bulgarski Profsuuzi* in 1978.[53] Three-fourths of the workers polled indicated that they were very willing to attempt to help the work collective fulfill its production quotas, but only 13 percent indicated that they in fact achieved the stipulated norms. When asked to identify the source of inadequate performance, 52 percent mentioned poor working conditions, but the incentive structure also was viewed with concern.

In 1975 and 1976, the Institute of Propaganda and Marxism-Leninism of the Sofia City Party Committee commissioned surveys at two plants in the Sofia area.[54] The focus was on moral and ethical dimensions of relationships among workers, and the effects that these characteristics had on attitudes toward the workplace. Questions also were included about relative preferences for material and nonmaterial incentives.

These studies especially sought to identify workers' sense of responsibility toward one another and toward the enterprise. Generally, the level of responsibility voiced was significantly lower than what had been expected and hoped for. For example, slightly fewer than 50 percent of the workers in each location agreed that an "objectively existing" sense of collective responsibility could be identified. Only about 30 percent in each location indicated that this collective feeling of responsibility was "subjectively" (actually) achieved. Approximately 20 percent of the workers felt that feelings of responsibility existed only in isolated members of the brigade, or not at all.

Workers were asked if "an atmosphere of impatience" exists toward manifestations of irresponsibility on the job. That is, are there overt negative reactions from members of the work collective when co-workers act irresponsibly? With respect to irresponsibility in fulfilling work obligations, about 26 percent in each location indicated that "an atmosphere of impatience" existed. About 15 percent felt that the waste of public property was met with informal negative sanctions; somewhat lower percentages of respondents perceived "impatience" toward those who would not take criticism, or those who exhibited "malice" in their relations with others.

Another section of the survey dealt with worker attitudes toward incentives and sanctions. More than 60 percent of the workers in each location felt that the existing system of incentives and sanctions was just; fewer than 10 percent felt that these were applied unjustly. Significantly, approximately 20 percent of the workers claimed that they were not aware of any incentives or sanctions being applied in their workplace. The survey also attempted to determine whether moral or material incentives were more effective. Results were reported only for the Kremikovtsi metallurgical plant, where 36.5 percent of those polled preferred material incentives alone, and only 12.8 percent preferred moral stimuli alone. The joint use of material and moral incentives was preferred by 46.4 percent of the workers.

Job satisfaction and labor turnover

Industrialization and the increasing use of automated procedures have been accompanied by substantial increases in labor turnover in Bulgaria. For example, in 1973, 56 percent of the workers in the machine building industry in Bulgaria changed jobs. The implications of such a high rate of turnover for production efficiency, as well as for the psychological character of the work environment, are clear. A major study[55] was done during 1974 in ten machine building enterprises throughout Bulgaria in an attempt to identify problems of job satisfaction and reasons for labor migration.

The study divides job terminations into two categories, subjective and objective. The distinction between the two is not completely clear; subjective terminations appear to be ones which were not motivated by specific problems in one's existing job, or specific appeals of an alternative employment possibility. Objective terminations had reference to some specific problem or enticement. This study refers to comparable data gathered in 1970 and notes that the proportion of objective terminations increased from 18 percent in 1970 to 40 percent in 1974, whereas job terminations for subjective reasons declined from 44 to 38 percent. Job terminations for other reasons, principally including dismissals, decreased from 38 percent in 1970 to 22 percent in 1974.

Forty percent of the subjectively motivated job terminations in 1974 were associated with a general dissatisfaction with one's work (specific employment situation) and/or with one's profession (type of work done). Although no figures are given, the article contends that the rapid pace of automation in the machine building industry has a good deal to do with this general level of dissatisfaction. Older workers apparently are dissatisfied because of the introduction of automation, whereas many younger workers find highly mechanized production methods attractive, and are prepared to change jobs to place themselves into an automated work environment.

Dissatisfaction with the level of compensation was a reason for slightly more than 6 percent of the terminations both in 1970 and in 1974. The authors assert, without citing specific evidence in support of this, that worker concerns are frequently with how wages are determined as much as with the absolute level of compensation.

A factor which increased substantially in importance in job terminations between 1970 and 1974 was workers' attitudes toward administrators and managers in the factory. In 1970, slightly more than 1 percent of the job terminations were attributed to improper conduct toward workers by managers; by 1974, this figure was nearly 10 percent. There also was an approximate doubling of the rate of leaving because of poor relationships within the work collective; the percentage went from 1.2 to 2.7.

Not surprisingly, both age and amount of formal education are closely related to the probability of job termination. Nearly 70 percent of the labor turnover in the machine building industry is represented by workers who have been in the work force five years or less, and by workers 30 years of age or younger. A considerable majority of those who changed jobs in 1974 had not finished primary school.

A somewhat different focus on job satisfaction was taken in a study of agricultural specialists done in 1972-1973, and published in *Sotsiologicheski Problemi* in 1977.[56] A representative sample of agricultural specialists throughout Bulgaria was taken; 1.4 percent of all agricultural specialists in the country were included. The study identified attitudes toward job and toward profession more generally. Respondents also were asked what they did to keep themselves current and to improve their professional competence.

The majority of agricultural specialists like their jobs, although job satisfaction varies somewhat among subspecialties. Significantly, the least satisfied are those who hold administrative or other leadership positions.

The commitment to continuing professional training also varies among subspecialties. Among the agricultural accountants, only 40 percent engage in continuing training, whereas 80 percent of the agricultural engineers do so. Continuing professional training is engaged in more by men than by women, and to a greater extent by those older than 36 years of age than by younger agricultural specialists.

Independent of their general affect toward the kind of work they do, the respondents were asked if they would like to change jobs. Overall, 29.1 percent indicated that they would. Of these, most would not like to leave agriculture. Reasons for wanting to change jobs vary. The challenge of more creative work is significantly more important for women than for men. Creativity is also more important for younger workers than for more senior agricultural specialists. Specific characteristics of the profession become less important as workers grow older; personal factors increase in significance with age.

The authors of this study refer to other sociological research in the Soviet Union, Poland, and Bulgaria which demonstrates that agricultural professions are not generally appealing to young people. They conclude that efforts need to be made to make agricultural professions more attractive, and to deepen the commitment of agricultural specialists toward continuing their professional training.

Inferences about job satisfaction also may be made from surveys of problems with work discipline. A 1975 article in *Politicheska Agitatsia*[57] refers to a study done in the Varna, Pleven, and Plovdiv districts concerning the application of sanctions for violations of work discipline. This research showed that the application of sanctions (usually fines) was inconsistent among enterprises, since during a six-month period in 1974 one enterprise recorded only one example of a sanction for work discipline, whereas another enterprise recorded 85 sanctions, and a third had applied 100. During 1973, 2 percent of all cases adjudicated by People's Courts in Bulgaria involved the imposition of penalties for breaches of work discipline. Another study done during a two-month period in 1977, reported in *Bulgarski Profsuuzi*,[58] notes that there were 6,161 violations of work discipline documented in the transport industries, but that only 151 persons had been formally held to account for these violations. The article charged that some enterprise managers and other administrators "closed their eyes" toward such infractions, and that this was demonstrably hurting worker morale.

The study on workplace values that appeared in *Rabotnichesko Delo* in 1977,[59] mentioned above, also asked about the willingness of workers to "make note of" violations of work discipline on the part of their colleagues. In general, approximately 70 percent of the workers indicated they did make notes (mental or actual) but about 27 percent did not. Table 3.9 reports responses to a question concerning co-workers who do not take care of machines and who waste materials. Slightly more than one-third of the workers indicated that they noted such practices because "the interests of society are offended," whereas about 32 percent referred to their responsibilities to the enterprise itself. The authors of the study would prefer to see a reduction in the more than 25 percent who decline to become involved in collective work discipline.

Worker attitudes toward automation

We have noted that industrial automation may induce labor turnover. Danov and Lukanov[60] have reported the results of a study on reactions to automation in a plant in Ruse between 1971 and 1975. The plant has been the site of implementation of both automated management systems and automated production processes, beginning in 1968. The study attempted to identify the reactions of different segments of the enterprise work force to the introduction of these two automated systems. The study included interviews with all 564 persons employed in the plant. These consisted of 385 workers, 56 leadership cadres (primarily department supervisors), 26 automation specialists, and 97 service employees.

Overall, nearly 92 percent of the employees in the plant were said to be initially favorable toward the introduction of the two automated systems. It was discovered, however, that 50 percent of the supporters of these innovations had "confused, speculative and unclear pictures" of what the innovations would involve. It was concluded that they supported these changes by "intuition or inertia." The most ardent supporters of the new systems often were specialists who held doctoral degrees, or high school graduates with advanced technical training. Among the most vigorous opponents were some 20 percent of the managerial and other leadership cadres, primarily at the middle and lower levels of supervision. The authors of the study considered it noteworthy that 35 percent of the opponents were excellently informed about the nature of the innovations, whereas 41 percent of the active supporters were poorly informed. In short, opposition was not necessarily unthinking, nor was support necessarily well founded.

Some of the breakdowns of support and opposition among subgroups of employees in the factory are fascinating. The study discovered that more than 50 percent of the workers were essentially indifferent about the introduction of either automated system. Only 45 percent of the leaders of functional departments (e.g., shop superintendents, heads of planning departments, heads of departments for norm and standard setting) were among the supporters. Nearly 60 percent of the leadership cadres were found to be indifferent toward introduction of the innovations. The authors of the study conclude that "there is a serious problem in the plant with the passive indifference" of many employees.

Table 3.8. Motives for the Performance of Komsomol Tasks
by Secondary Students, by School Grade
(percentages)

Motive[a]	School Grade				
	8th grade	9th grade	10th grade	11th grade	all students
1. In order to fulfill the duties of the Komsomol	57.7	54.3	37.1	28.1	43.7
2. In order to justify the trust placed in me as a Komsomol member	61.5	48.6	42.9	46.9	49.2
3. My love for the Komsomol	53.8	71.4	62.9	50.0	60.2
4. The moral satisfaction of doing public work	34.6	62.9	68.6	31.2	50.8
5. In order to give something to society	38.5	20.0	40.0	71.9	42.2
6. In order to verify my own capabilities	15.4	34.3	31.4	56.2	35.2
7. Others	11.5	5.7	8.6	12.5	9.4

[a]Each respondent could select as many as three motives.

Source: Lyuben Dimitrov, *Obshtestvenoto Mnenie i Vuzpitanieto na Mladata Lichnost. Sotsialno-Pedagogichesko Izsledvane* (Sofia: Narodna Mladezh, 1975), p. 77.

Table 3.9. Sense of Collective Responsibility[a] among
Factory Workers in Gabrovo
(percentages)

Response and Motive	Percent of Respondents
1. Yes, because the interests of society are offended	36.55
2. Yes, because it affects the work collective	31.99
3. Yes, because my personal interests are affected	4.65
4. No, I don't consider this my responsibility	11.08
5. No (no reason given)	15.55

[a]Question: "Do you make notes on the members of your collective who do not take care of machines and waste material?"

Source: "Results of Sociological Research," *Rabotnichesko Delo,* 7 October 1977, p. 3.

And in terms of assessing the impact of the aspects of automation that had already been implemented at the time of the study, the researchers discovered that nearly 50 percent of the personnel of the plant were indifferent about the initial results. Examining the specific breakdowns of support and opposition, one can only puzzle at the assertion that, in general, 92 percent of the employees were supportive.

Evaluation of organizational and leadership elements

The Danov and Lukanov study raised important questions about the role of leadership cadres in industrial enterprises. The authors argued that the "basic reasons" for widespread indifference toward automation included shortcomings based on the personality of leadership cadres, the absence of positive personal examples from the top, and an absence of close, personal relationships between leaders and workers.

An important study was mentioned in *Politicheska Agitatsia*[61] in 1974 concerning the evaluation of leadership cadres in the transportation industry, where the incidence of work-discipline problems has been high. A survey was conducted through district Party organizations in several locations in Bulgaria, and involved interviews with 1,684 persons in the transportation industry. The sample included 1,567 workers; 71 respondents were lower-level officials and supervisors, 32 were heads of departments, and 14 were directors and assistant directors. The poll also included an unspecified number of Party secretaries, heads of professional organizations, and Komsomol secretaries.

The 1974 *Politicheska Agitatsia* report indicates that a number of papers were prepared for a conference which brought together representatives of district Party organizations throughout the country. No specific statistics have been published; the article is self-described as "typological, not quantitative" in character. The surveys emphasized political and ideological indoctrination activities of the leadership cadres, and questions about how they spend their time and how effectively they interact with one another and with subordinates. A premise underlying the study was that effective political and ideological leadership would contribute to more effective work performance on the part of both leaders and subordinates.

Overall, the leadership cadres in the transportation industry were said to have performed well. They interact with subordinates in reasoned and effective ways and apparently spend their time in ways appropriate to their responsibilities. One problem area can be inferred from the vague results reported. Leadership cadres spend, on the average, only about 15 percent of their time on "social and general political questions"; even less time was spent on these matters by the lowest leadership level, which has the most direct contact with workers. The article concludes that the Party needs to take "appropriate measures to correct" this situation.

Finally, a study previously mentioned[62] which was published in *Bulgarski Profsuuzi* in 1978 and which dealt with problems of incentives in a machine factory also sheds some light on worker evaluation of leadership cadres in industry. In this study, 52 percent of the workers felt that working conditions were "poor." Significantly, more than half of the workers indicated that they were not satisfied with the support they received from their labor organization in attempting to correct these problems. The article suggests that this indicates low effectiveness of worker organizations within the enterprise.

Research on work and the workplace in Bulgaria reflects the significant change being experienced in the economy. Rapid industrialization, accompanied by significant efforts at managerial and production automation, have effected important and rapid changes in the work environment for many Bulgarian workers. That there would be identifiable levels of job dissatisfaction, unacceptably high levels of labor turnover in some industries, difficulties in the area of work discipline, and some confusion and indifference toward automated procedures, is not surprising. What is perhaps most noteworthy is the substantial amount of research that is being directed toward these problems, and the relative openness with which the results of much of this research is treated. From a sociological and methodological point of view, research on work and the workplace is among the most interesting and important survey research being done in Bulgaria today.

Leisure Time

The major 1968 research, "Sociological Study of Town and Village," included some questions on leisure time activity.[63] At about the same time, Zahari Staikov and Misho Tsanov began the research for their studies on leisure-time budgets which were eventually published in 1973.[64] Staikov and his colleagues have carried out several studies in the intervening years.

The results of these three major studies are excluded from this chapter.[65] Our effort here is to bring together more recent leisure time research, especially that which is fragmented and less accessible.

This section concentrates on examples of three types of leisure time studies: 1) general studies of the use of leisure time by the general population; 2) attitudes and behavior concerning cinema attendance, including studies of how attendance at movies has changed, and how it compares with competing diversions, especially watching television; and 3) attitudes and behavior regarding the reading of books, especially literary prose and poetry.

It bears emphasizing that the use of free time is thought by the Bulgarian regime to have considerable political significance. This is best illustrated by the concern shown by the Party for the leisure time implications of changing from a six-day to a five-day work week. For example, an article in *Politicheska Agitatsia* in 1975[66] pointed out that this change would increase the annual number of nonworking days for the average worker to 120 per year. Concern was expressed that, on the basis of past experience, workers might not be expected to spend their free time wisely. The article referred to research done by Party sociologists at enterprises that had gone on a five-day week on an experimental basis. The results suggest that a good part of the free time of these workers was not well spent. Table 3.10 summarizes their use of leisure time. Of greatest concern to the author of the article was the fact that very little time was spent in efforts to increase professional qualifications, and that engaging in political or ideological education or Party work was not even mentioned among the activities which primarily consume workers' time.

Another article in the same publication in 1976[67] referred to, but did not report specific data from, a study done in the Stara Zagora area, where 73 percent of the industrial workers were on a five-day work week by mid-1976. The article suggested that the Party was deeply concerned about how workers were spending their free time. A similar concern is voiced in an article in *Sotsiologicheski Problemi* in 1976.[68] Thus the study of the use of leisure time assumes political and ideological importance in Bulgaria.

General studies of the use of leisure time

A study mentioned in *Literaturen Front* in 1975[69] provides a representative overview of the use of leisure time by Bulgarians. The study was carried out by the Institute of Sociology of BAN and was based on a national random sample. The study showed that the average Bulgarian spends approximately 2.5 hours watching television or listening to the radio each day, and spends slightly more than two hours at personal relaxation (including visits with friends), and walks. These two categories of activity constitute 87 percent of the average person's leisure time. This article also stresses reasons for concern about unproductive use of leisure time, and especially emphasizes the importance of educational efforts by the Party.

Similar conclusions are suggested by Nano Stefanov,[70] who cites the results of unspecified studies done of Bulgarian workers. Stefanov reports that 69 percent of the free time of Bulgarian workers is spent on "unproductive" amusements such as listening to the radio, watching television, visiting relatives, playing cards, going for walks, and visiting cafés and restaurants. Sport and tourism activities consume another 7 percent of their time. This leaves a maximum of 24 percent of the worker's free time for activities that could be considered educational. This includes reading, efforts at professional improvement, cultural activities, or attending adult education classes. It is considered especially unfortunate that only 3 percent of Bulgarian workers take evening courses; further, 44.8 percent of the workers polled indicated that they would not be inclined to take classes in the evening even if courses were offered which were of direct interest to them.

Cinema attendance

Movies are a potentially effective form of political and ideological communication, since they can package normative messages in relatively entertaining forms. Although movie attendance is comparatively high in Bulgaria, it has been identifiably affected by the rapid increase in access to television sets. Thus movie attendance in 1970 was at the same level that it had been in 1960, and substantially lower than it was in the years 1965-1968.[71] The decline in movie attendance is particularly noticeable in the villages and small towns, notwithstanding the fact that access to movie theaters has been steadily increased for the rural population; 97 percent of the rural population now has ready access to at least one movie theater. In spite of this, movie attendance in the villages declined from 47.5 million in 1960 to 30.3 million in 1969, a rate of decline clearly exceeding population shifts. We infer that the figure was still lower in the mid-1970s.[72]

A study by the Center for the Scientific Study of Youth, published in 1976,[73] reports the origins and characteristics of films found most interesting by young Bulgarians. Respondents apparently were permitted to volunteer titles of films without suggestion. A total of 278 films was named, 169 of which were made in the socialist countries. Respondents were asked to indicate the films which had "left the deepest impression" on them. Seventy-two of the films so described came from the Soviet Union and 32 from Bulgaria. Next most frequently mentioned were films from the United States (26) and France (25).

The study also attempted to determine the relative preference of young Bulgarian cinemagoers for three distinct types of films. These types were: films that treat problems (preferred by 42.4 percent of the respondents); entertaining-spectacular films (preferred by 41.0 percent); and films combining entertaining and problem-treating approaches (preferred by 16.6 percent).

Bulgaria is second only to the Soviet Union among European countries in cinema attendance per capita; each Bulgarian sees an average of 14 films per year.[74] A 1975 poll done by the Sociological Research Center of the State Cinematography Enterprise[75] revealed that 22 percent of Bulgarians go to the cinema every week, 19.6 percent go two or three times per month, 34 percent seldom go, and only 24 percent never attend films. Men go to movies substantially more often than do women. Not surprisingly, young people, especially up to age 17, are the most active filmgoers. Persons between the ages of 59 and 68 show a nonattendance ratio of 51 percent, and more than three-quarters of the Bulgarians aged 68 or above never attend movies.

Cinema attendance is relatively higher among workers, according to a BTA *News Bulletin* story published in 1975.[76] This study looked at particularly avid moviegoers, those who attend two or more films per week. It was discovered that 14 percent of the workers fall into this category, as compared with 8.9 percent of white-collar employees and 6.4 percent of agricultural workers.

Movie attendance, as with the use of leisure time more generally, is not an innocuous issue from the point of view of the regime. In his 1976 book, *Art and Communication in the Cinema*,[77] Ivan Stefanov notes that the movies not only provide a medium for communicating appropriate values, but also lessen the likelihood that young people will spend time in other activities where they might be subject to bourgeois influence, specifically, modern dancing that has Western origins.

Does an interest in movie attendance reduce the inclination of young Bulgarians to read literature? One informal study done in a single school in Sofia[78] indicates that students still collectively prefer reading a good book to going to a movie. Two more systematic efforts to determine the relationship between the reading of literature and attendance at movies are reported by Stefanov.[79] One study demonstrated a statistical interdependence between reading of literary prose and attendance at movies. The research shows that of those who read literary books, only 2.02 percent do not also attend movies. For those who never read literary materials, the percentage of those who never go to movies jumps to 41. Needless to say, the possibility of third factors being relevant to the relationship between movie attendance and literary reading is very real, but apparently was not examined in this study. Another study was done in 1973 of the cultural interests of young people in Silistra. The findings were similar; of those who attend movies more than twice a week, only 4.5 percent do not read literature. However, of those who do not attend movies at all, 33.3 percent did not read at all. Again, there is no evidence that the influence of other variables (e.g., measures of intelligence or social class) was looked at.

Literature and leisure time

Book publishing has expanded significantly in Bulgaria in the last twenty years. By the mid-1970s, more than 4,000 titles were being published each year, with a total printing of more than 42 million copies. During this same period, there were more than 10,500 libraries in Bulgaria, housing a total of more than 59 million books. In 1975, Bulgarian libraries recorded 3.4 million users, who checked out an average of 13 books per reader. In 1975, Bulgaria had 4,267 reading clubs. All of these figures rank Bulgaria highly among European nations.

These impressive figures notwithstanding, there is evidence that the reading of literature may be declining in some parts of Bulgaria, especially in the towns and larger cities. An article in *Narodna Kultura* in 1977[80] provides some examples of declining readership and library usage and blames these difficulties on three factors: inadequate performance by local librarians, inadequate socialization of the population concerning the importance of reading, and the competition of television. A similar concern was reflected in an article in *Bulgar-*

ski Profsuuzi in 1976,[81] which discussed efforts made in the Gabrovo area to increase reading among workers. New library programs there substantially stimulated worker interest in reading; during the first year of the project, each member of the workers' collectives around Gabrovo read 9 books, on the average, and per person readership was 13 books in areas where branch libraries existed. These figures were substantially higher than for workers in the rest of Bulgaria.

A study appearing in *Novo Vreme* at the end of 1974[82] provides survey evidence helpful in identifying the social factors that define interest in literature. More than 30 percent of the respondents read prose either occasionally or regularly, but 48.6 percent have never read this form of literature. The lack of interest in poetry is even greater; approximately 13 percent read poetry occasionally or regularly, whereas nearly 72 percent have never read poetry. To place these figures in context, the *Novo Vreme* article cites a United States study indicating that between 20 percent (in the United States) and 54 percent (in the Scandinavian countries) of citizens read prose. In this comparison, the level of neglect of literary prose in Bulgaria is modest. Nevertheless, the matter is a source of concern to Bulgarian authorities.

Although there are distinct differences between the cities and the countryside in extent of reading activity, the data demonstrate that education and nature of occupation are the critical social factors. It is because agricultural workers tend to have much less formal education, and are engaged in occupations which allow them substantially less leisure time, that they do not read prose and poetry. Table 3.11 contrasts those who read literature at least once each week with those who never read. Among the respondents classified as "highly qualified" (primarily, this refers to level of formal education), fewer than one-half in every occupational category are in the "never read" category. By contrast, even among administrators and managers, 30 percent of those with low qualifications were found never to read prose.

Research on leisure time usage in Bulgaria reflects a genuine concern on the part of the political authorities for the ways in which citizens, especially workers, spend their free time. There is little inclination to pursue professional improvement, ideological training, or social activism on evenings or weekends. The popularity of television is seen as a mixed blessing: it guarantees exposure of the population to a controlled medium, but nevertheless represents a passive and essentially nonintellectual use of time. The popularity of films is great, though apparently declining. Perhaps of greater concern than the decline in absolute number of moviegoers is the fact only about one-half of young cinema goers in Bulgaria exhibit a preference for films which are partially or largely characterized by socially relevant or "problem treating" themes and approaches. Attention to literature does not seem to have been materially affected by the growing popularity of television, although some areas seem to have experienced a decline in library usage, particularly among workers. Education is again seen as the critical factor in determining the extent and nature of interest of Bulgarians

Table 3.10. Distribution of Principal Leisure-Time Activities of
Workers in Enterprises on a 5-Day Week
(percentages)

Activity	Percent of Leisure Time
1. Physical work	35.40
2. Relaxing outside the city, or with family and friends	27.40
3. Cultural activities (movies, concerts)	16.40
4. Passive relaxation	9.35
5. Sports	6.20
6. Intellectual development	5.25

Source: *Politicheska Agitatsia,* 1975, no. 7, p. 42.

Table 3.11. Reading of Literature by Socio-Occupational Group
and Level of Qualification
(percentages)

	Socio-Occupational Group						
	Agricultural Workers		Industrial Workers		Officials		Scientific and Cultural Workers
	Level of Qualification						
Frequency of Reading Literature	Low	High	Low	High	Low	High	High
1. Once per week	2.8	16.0	8.1	27.8	21.1	58.8	71.62
2. Never	76.3	40.0	60.1	22.9	29.9	3.0	- - - -

Source: Veska Kozhuharova, "Sotsialnata Obuslovenost na Interesa kum Hudozhestvenata Literatura,"*Novo Vreme* 50 (November 1974): 60.

in reading and other uses of leisure time.

Moral and Ethical Preferences and Life Aspirations

Much of the Bulgarian survey research on the subject of values and life aspirations has been summarized in the section on education and youth. There is a handful of studies, however, which deal more specifically with life aspirations of Bulgarian students and with young Bulgarians' evaluations of various occupations.

The results of a major study of the life plans of Bulgarian students were published in *Sotsiologicheski Problemi* in 1977.[83] Interviews were conducted with a random sample of all postsecondary students in Sofia. The article reporting the results of this research represents one of the most conceptually and theoretically thoughtful reports of survey research that has appeared in a Bulgarian publication. The study proceeds on the basis of a detailed typology of life plans. These plans eventually are grouped into three basic types: those with predominantly personal interests and orientations, those with predominantly public or social orientations, and those which are societally oriented, but abstract (and, in the opinion of the authors of the study, usually impractical).

The research reveals that nonmaterial values are far more important to Sofia students than are material ones; the average score for nonmaterial values, especially those referring in some way to achieving happiness in life, is nearly three times higher than is the average value given to achieving material well-being. The study also shows that approximately 43 percent of those polled have publicly oriented life plans, 41 percent have personally oriented plans, and 16 percent have abstract plans. An attempt also was made to assess the "adequacy" (coherence and thoughtfulness) of the students' aspirations. The authors conclude that 65 percent of the students had adequate, well-formulated life plans, whereas 35 percent (including the 16 percent who had abstract plans) did not.

The differences between the life aspirations of men and women students were small. Women were somewhat more concerned about getting the appropriate kind of job, and somewhat less concerned about opportunities for creativity and self expression. And, as shown in table 3.12, men were somewhat more likely to have abstract plans; thus, both publicly oriented and personally oriented life plans were more characteristic of women than of men. But the differences were slight.

The social class of students is the strongest predictor of their life plans. Students from the families of officials (60 percent of the sample) are substantially more likely to have clearly formulated ("adequate") life plans; 93 percent of the students in this category were so classified. Indeed, they were proportionately more likely to specify seven of the nine dimensions of life aspirations presented in table 3.13. The two life goals not more strongly associated with children from officials' families were a desire to be of service to society, and a desire to have well-educated, well-mannered children. These two categories are proportionately more likely to be valued by students from rural backgrounds.

Social class, measured by father's occupation, is a strong predictor of life goals, but the education of the father turns out to have surprisingly little effect. Table 3.14 shows that the distribution between personally oriented and societally oriented life plans of students is virtually identical for students whose fathers have a junior high education or better. Only for students whose father is classified as illiterate was there some variation; here, students were somewhat more likely to have life plans which are societally oriented.

A survey conducted by the Center for the Scientific Study of Youth[84] sheds some light on the evaluation by Bulgarian youth of various occupations. Nearly 8,000 students in grades eight through eleven of both regular secondary and technical schools were interviewed. The geographical locale of the study is not indicated.

The profession of engineer is the one most favored overall by young Bulgarians. It received a score of 4.4 on a five-point scale. The occupation of steel worker was ranked next-to-last (68th). The profession of waiter was last. Most occupations were uniformly valued by students in all grades. In the case of journalism, however, its significance increased at the higher grade levels. There were predictable differences between the opinions of regular secondary school students and those of students in the technical schools. The former showed a preference for the professions of doctor, journalist, and scientific researcher; those in technical schools leaned toward airline pilot, ship master, and electronic technician.

Students were asked why they preferred given professions. Nearly one-fourth said that their rankings were based on the possibilities for creative work. Thirteen percent indicated that one's profession should correspond to one's own personal qualities. Only 3 percent of the young people polled considered material rewards the most important factor in choosing a profession. Slightly more than 2 percent said that they valued jobs that would eventually lead to high administrative positions.

The published summary of this research notes that those who conducted the study were concerned about an apparent "contradiction" between the necessary occupational structure of society and the subjective wishes of young people. In particular, certain (unnamed) professions "which are not of a particularly creative nature, but are important for the economic life of the country," are not highly regarded by young people. It was suggested that this contradiction must be overcome by enlightening young people about the attractive prospects in some professions which did not find favor with them.

An informal, anecdotal, but nonetheless interesting poll was conducted in 1977 by the newspaper *Narodna Mladezh* on the subject of why some men wear beards.[85] The number of men interviewed was not indicated, nor was the

Table 3.12. Basic Types of Life Plans of Sofia Postsecondary Students, by Sex
(percentages)

	Sex		
Type of Life Plan	Men	Women	All Respondents
1. Concrete societally oriented	40.82	43.07	42.65
2. Personally oriented	40.71	42.51	41.47
3. Abstract societally oriented	18.47	14.42	15.88

Source: Hristo Petrov, "Zhiznenite Planove na Bulgarskite Studenti," *Sotsiologicheski Problemi* 9, no. 3 (1977): 85.

Table 3.13. Preferences for Nine Categories of Life Aspirations
among Sofia Postsecondary Students, by Sex
(percentages)

	Sex		
Aspiration	Men	Women	All Respondents
Type I: Concrete societally oriented			
1. Getting preferred employment	18.24	20.15	19.17
2. Success in learning and work	14.15	16.81	15.46
3. Striving to create and express	8.43	6.11	8.03
Type II: Personally oriented			
4. Successful marriage	13.20	14.98	14.09
5. Interesting travels and experiences	10.52	11.61	10.94
6. Well-educated, well-mannered children	10.19	11.40	10.77
7. Material well-being	7.17	4.02	5.66
Type III. Abstract societally oriented			
8. Make others happy	9.98	9.15	9.60
9. Serve society	8.12	5.77	7.28

Source: Hristo Petrov, "Zhiznenite Planove na Bulgarskite Studenti," *Sotsiologicheski Problemi* 9, no. 3 (1977): 84.

geographic locale of the sampling. The answers themselves are sometimes of interest. Equally interesting are the explanations sought by the *Narodna Mladezh* writer for responses received.

There can be little doubt that the image of a bearded male with long hair is in official disfavor in Bulgaria. It is attacked as a slavish imitation of decadent bourgeois practices, and is associated with idlers and ne'er-do-wells. The *Narodna Mladezh* article refers to three kinds of motivations for wearing a beard: tradition, a desire for change, and imitation. The last is said to be illusory and shallow: "Whatever one's outward appearance, it cannot hide his true personal spirit." Yet it is not difficult to read between the lines of the responses given to find not only a desire to be different, but also a rebelliousness against the notion that personal styles should be attributed political significance. If nothing else, this article is remarkable simply because it appeared, and because the subject matter was treated with relative seriousness.

We should recall briefly two other studies which provide important clues to the ethical values and life aspirations of Bulgarians. These two studies were of moral perspectives and socialist consciousness in work brigades,[86] and of the values of rural and village youth.[87] A third relevant study dealt with the views of eleventh graders in the cities on "the meaning of life."[88] These studies yield three general conclusions. First, job satisfaction—the nature of one's work—is very important to most Bulgarians, especially young people. Second, education is attributed great importance, both intrinsically and as an instrument for social advancement. Third, social activism and socialist consciousness are not being adequately inculcated in Bulgarian youth, from the point of view of the regime. These surveys do not suggest that Bulgarian young people are materially oriented or that they are more self-centered in their values and aspirations than are young people of any other modern society. But there is evidence that their commitment to an activist posture in support of prevailing political and ideological norms is modest.

Social Problems and Social Policy

Several of the studies already discussed have highlighted some of the social problems thought by Bulgarians to be most serious. Some of these have to do with family-related problems—for example, divorce, abortion, and familial conflicts surrounding the changing role of women in society. A related problem is that of alcoholism which, although not as serious as in the Soviet Union, is nevertheless a matter of genuine concern. We have noted that young people find excessive drinking to be an undesirable characteristic in members of the opposite sex, and yet that a majority of Bulgarian teenagers beyond the age of 16 do use alcohol. There is a widespread feeling that alcoholism is an important contributing factor to crime. Indirect evidence in support of this belief was presented in *Politicheska Agitatsia* in October, 1975.[89] An effort had been made to close many of the bars in the town of Dimitrovgrad; some have been converted into restaurants that do not serve alcoholic beverages. In the four years of this program (1971-1975), the crime rate in the Dimitrovgrad region had declined by 30 percent. A causal relationship is inferred. The article also refers to similar successful efforts in the Yambol and Blagoevgrad regions.

These social problems aside—and their existence surely is not confined to Bulgaria—recent survey research in Bulgaria has concentrated on two aspects of social problems: attitudes toward crime, the law, and justice; and perceptions of the most critical "negative influences" in Bulgarian society.

Attitudes toward crime, the law, and justice

Some of the results from a major study of the attitudes of Bulgarians toward crime, law, and justice were published in *Sotsiologicheski Problemi* in 1975[90] and 1976.[91] The study is based on a survey instrument of 31 questions administered to 3,929 Bulgarians 14 years of age and older. The representativeness of the sample was achieved through the use of a two-stage nested sampling procedure, which involved obtaining interviews in each of 260 sampling "nests" located in all counties in Bulgaria. The research was carried out by sociologists attached to the county committees of the Bulgarian Communist Party. The questionnaire had been pretested in Sofia and Pernik counties and in the city of Sofia. The validity of questionnaire responses was assessed in part by comparing these results with the findings of other criminological research carried out in three counties (Sliven, Vrasta, and Ruse). This study thus represents one of the most methodologically sophisticated surveys so far done in Bulgaria. The study attempted to determine such things as the extent of awareness of the law, the feelings and values of Bulgarians toward the law and toward certain categories of crime, citizens' assessment of their own conduct, and the willingness of citizens to cooperate actively in the struggle against crime.

Initially, the study asked respondents about the nature of their concern about crime. The vast majority (81.4 percent) said they were concerned about crime because it was "a negative social phenomenon." Only 7.6 percent indicated that they were concerned about crime only insofar as it personally affected them. In the case of 4.2 percent of the respondents, their interest was based on curiosity about the individual incidents of crime. The remaining 6.8 percent either were indifferent, or did not respond to the question. The authors of the study assume that any response other than the first is less than fully desirable, and they analyze the backgrounds of the 18.6 percent who gave other answers. They discover that these predominantly are nonparty persons with low levels of formal education, who have lower-status occupations (agricultural workers, domestics, part-time laborers), and who include a disproportionate number of persons from minority ethnic groups.

The research determined that radio, television, the daily and periodical press, and films are all important in familiarizing citizens with the problems of crime. However, the authors feel that social propaganda designed to intensify public concern about crime has not produced "an optimal reaction." One of the asserted reasons for a relative lack of awareness of crime problems is the fact that most Bulgarian citizens do not have contact with law enforcement organs; 71.2 percent have had no such contact in the last ten years. Persons who have had these contacts show a higher awareness of the seriousness of crime.

A major part of the study sought to determine the extent of Bulgarians' knowledge of the criminal code. The survey discovered that only 4.2 percent of the respondents are aware of the full contents of the code. Partial knowledge is shown by 38.7 percent; this means that 57 percent of the respondents had minimal or no knowledge of the code. Only 18.5 percent of the respondents could properly identify the relative levels of severity of seven types of criminal activity. One-third of those polled could not rank the crimes by severity and were aware that they did not have such information. The remaining 49.2 percent provided answers which were incorrect. The study also showed that about 37 percent of the respondents were not aware of the rights of defense counsel in criminal proceedings, and that 30 percent could identify only punitive functions performed by criminal sentencing, i.e., they were unable to articulate any social roles performed by the sentencing of criminals. The authors of the study characterize this unawareness of the social functions of sentencing as "a deplorable state of affairs."

The study follows a tradition of research in a number of other countries which attempts to determine the likelihood that citizens would call authorities if they witnessed a crime occurring. Comparatively, Bulgarian citizens seem strongly disposed to contact authorities: 78.3 percent said they would do so. Those who definitely would not call authorities constituted 7.7 percent of the respondents, whereas 11.7 percent said they were not sure and that their response would depend on the situation.

What are the factors which inhibit crime in Bulgarian society? Table 3.15 summarizes these data. Personal values were thought to be most important, and respect for law and order and anticipated loss of self-respect also were named by many of the respondents. The study attempted to determine the principal sources of personal values concerning crime, especially among juveniles aged 14 to 18. It was discovered that the family and the school were the most influential factors, being predominant for approximately three-fourths of the young people interviewed. The study lamented the generally weak and sometimes negative effect of close friends and other informal groups. The influence of friends and colleagues was minimal outside the large cities, and in the cities such influences did not necessarily reinforce a concern about crime. The authors also note, without providing percentages of respondents who expressed this thought, that "the negative personal example of some leading personalities in society seriously harms the respect for justice held by other citizens."

Table 3.14. Basic Type of Life Plans of Sofia Postsecondary Students,
by Father's Education
(percentages)

| | Type of Life Plan | |
Father's Education	Personally oriented	Societally oriented
1. Illiterate	43.0	57.0
2. Elementary	47.0	53.0
3. Secondary	47.1	52.9
4. Higher	47.2	52.8

Source: Hristo Petrov, "Zhiznenite Planove na Bulgarskite Studenti," *Sotsiologicheski Problemi* 9, no. 3 (1977): 86.

Table 3.15. Major Factors Inhibiting Involvement
in Criminal Activity (N = 3,929)
(percentages)

Inhibiting Factor	Percent of Respondents
1. Personal values	29.5
2. Respect for law and order	22.9
3. Fear loss of self-respect	22.5
4. Desire not to harm other individuals or society	7.6
5. Fear of punishment	6.1
6. Indecisiveness, risk	1.4
7. Religious values	0.7
Total	90.7[a]

[a] Apparently 9.3 percent of the respondents gave other answers, or no answer.

Source: Baicho Panev, "Nyakoi Problemi na Pravosuznanieto na Bulgarskite Grazhdani," *Sotsiologicheski Problemi* 8, no. 4 (1976): 86.

The research differentiates among occupational groups in terms of "active participation in the struggle against crime." The concept of "active participation" is not defined specifically. Approximately one-half of the managers and other white collar workers interviewed were found to be "active"; the figure drops to 33.3 percent among industrial workers, and 28.9 percent among agricultural workers. The report indicates that Party members and Komsomol members participate more actively than do those without such affiliations; interestingly, no figures are given for these comparisons.

An important part of this study involved identifying those societal factors which encourage criminal acts. More than 50 percent of the respondents indicated that the existence of crime was due in part to shortcomings in government organs, including the negative personal examples of some prominent leaders. Another 43.2 percent of the respondents attributed crime to alcoholism. We can presume that the kinds of crime precipitated by these two factors are different. Problems related to material shortages also were frequently remarked: 21.5 percent of the respondents mentioned inadequately satisfied material needs, and nearly 30 percent referred to theft, greed, and private profiteering. At the other end of the scale, only 5.8 percent of the respondents attributed crime to "remnants of the bourgeois ideology and way of life" in Bulgaria.

Respondents also were asked if they felt that the principle of equality before the law was upheld in the treatment of violations of the law in Bulgaria. One-fourth of those polled felt that this principle was uniformly achieved; 35.8 percent felt that the principle was upheld "in most cases." Thus nearly 40 percent felt that the principle of equality before the law was not upheld in most cases. Relatedly, more than 50 percent of the respondents felt that the sentences given to criminals generally are too light.

The authors of the study felt that a great deal of work remained to be done in developing better information and more appropriate values among Bulgarian citizens in the area of crime, law, and justice. They note that many Bulgarians are essentially unaware of the activities of law enforcement agencies. And they were especially concerned about the unsatisfactory informational and value responses of persons with less than secondary education. At the same time, the article does emphasize that the majority of Bulgarians have well-developed and appropriate value systems with regard to crime and justice.

An article by Dimitur Fidanov in *Sotsiologicheski Problemi* in 1975[92] refers to the preceding study, and describes other research dealing with citizen awareness of crime and the law. Fidanov notes that there is a substantial and distressing distinction between citizens' attitudes toward crimes against personal property, on the one hand, and crimes against socialist property, on the other hand. He cites one survey showing that those who react strongly against crimes against socialist property are only one-half as numerous as those who are deeply concerned about crimes against personal property. That study apparently did not attempt to determine the reasons for this value differential.

Fidanov himself has studied the attitudes of convicted criminals toward crime. He interviewed 38 convicts sentenced for murder or attempted murder, 47 sentenced for rape or attempted rape, and 52 serving time for embezzlement. Fidanov was interested in two kinds of questions. First, he wanted to know to what extent his respondents had felt at the time of committing a crime that they were doing something wrong—i.e., their awareness of legal and moral constraints on their behavior. Second, Fidanov was interested in the importance they attributed to any awareness of the impropriety of their behavior.

The survey reveals that the more serious the nature of the crime, the greater the level of awareness of its impropriety at the time of commission. More than 86 percent of those convicted for murder were aware that what they were doing was wrong. Of those convicted for rape, 71 percent were aware that their behavior was socially unacceptable. Among those convicted of embezzlement, only 44 percent were aware that they were specifically violating a legal norm. Significantly, of course, embezzlement in Bulgaria is a crime against socialist property, whereas murder and rape are crimes against the person of private individuals.

Fidanov discovers that awareness of the law on the part of the persons convicted of "natural crimes" (murder, rape) tends to have minimal effect. This is explained by their low level of education and social awareness. In the case of persons convicted of embezzlement, the problem is not so much awareness of legal or ethical constraints, but rather a subjective ability to define one's own behavior as somehow not being inconsistent with the law. Thus, although we might expect the achievement of a higher level of formal education among the population to eliminate some of the "natural crimes," crimes against socialist property have more subtle cultural and sociopsychological origins and may take longer to eliminate.

Negative influences in society

The national study of citizen attitudes toward crime, law, and justice yielded some information about the social problems that citizens were most concerned about. Two other surveys, one of which has been reported systematically, the other, only anecdotally, provide additional evidence. A study published in *Nauchni Trudove (Filosofiya)*[93] in 1975 asked citizens what negative influences in society are most widespread. A battery of 121 questions was put to a sample of 2,906 persons working in 190 organizations throughout Bulgaria. The research effort required 315 interviewers. Responses are distinguished among a general population sample (N=2,046), leadership cadres (N=561), and administrators and other government personnel (N=109). Table 3.16 reports the rankings given to the 12 negative influences most frequently mentioned by the general population subsample. In most cases the rankings are dramatically different among the three subsamples. Thus the general population sample felt that divorce was the number one negative influence in Bulgarian life, whereas the leadership cadres placed divorce 25th, and the sample of administrators and other government personnel did not rank it in the top 30. Alcoholism was listed third in the general population sample, but 29th by the leadership cadres, and 27th by administrators. The two elite samples attributed more importance to factors such as lack of principles in interpersonal relations and family life and the use of official positions for personal gain. The most obvious case of agreement among the three subsamples was in their rankings of the tendency to interfere in the affairs of others; this was listed first by the leadership cadres, second by the general population sample, and third by the administrators.

This study also involved a comparison between the views of leadership cadres and workers in several work collectives concerning which unsocialist postures toward public property are most common. In general orientation, the responses were quite similar between the two subsamples. However, there was one dramatic difference; the plurality of the workers (41.5 percent) felt that they could not say what sorts of problems existed, whereas only 11 percent of the leadership cadre was similarly undecided.

Broadly, two conclusions emerge from this study. First, the general population is primarily concerned about problems in private morality and in interpersonal relationships, whereas societal elites are more concerned about public morality and practices which make government less efficient. Second, workers are substantially less sensitive to the misuse of socialist property than are leadership cadres in work collectives. The authors of the study attribute this low awareness of and concern about such problems among workers to the poor examples of some leadership cadres, poor accounting and control methods, and administrative negligence, as well as to inadequately developed value systems on the part of the workers.

The other relevant study was an informal poll conducted by the magazine *Zhenata Dnes* in 1978.[94] Young people between the ages of 16 and 26 were asked, "What features in contemporary life do you like or dislike?" The presentation in *Zhenata Dnes* is wholly anecdotal. The responses were varied; in general, however, the concern with public (as opposed to private) morality was greater among this youth sample than was the case for the general population sample in the *Nauchni Trudove (Filosofiya)* study.

Broadly, recent surveys identify four social problem areas: 1) the lack of stability in various dimensions of interpersonal relationships, especially including the family; 2) alcoholism; 3) an inadequate level of socialist consciousness, especially with regard to crimes against socialist property; and 4) abuses and insensitivities in the use of public positions and trust. From what we know comparatively, there is little reason to believe that these problems are more serious in Bulgaria than in other modernizing (or modern) societies. At the same time, the concern of the Bulgarian regime for these difficulties is genuine. One of the impediments to finding solutions to these problems is that the problems are attributed dramatically different significance by persons with different educational levels, and holding different positions in society.

Politics and Ideology

There has been a significant increase in Bulgaria in recent years in the use of empirical research methods, especially surveys, in connection with political and ideological matters. Dimitur Ganchev[95] reports that studies have been done by Party committees at all levels and by government agencies in an effort to better understand citizen views on important policy questions. For example, surveys frequently have been done in preparation for Party conferences. Ganchev cites projects done under rubrics such as "The Vanguard Role of Communists in Bulgarian Society," "The Economic Policies of the Party," "Social and Political Aspects of Party Work," "The Party Convention," "Party Attendance and Discipline," and "Providing Information at Party Meetings." Unfortunately, none of this work has been published or made generally available.

A 1977 article in *Problemi na Mladezhta*[96] mentions methods used to study decision making within the Komsomol. Surveys frequently are used, as is the procedure of placing confederates (i.e., persons with sociological training whose involvement in the research is not known to other participants) in decision-making groups. Again, we found no published results from such studies.

Another topic on which survey research is being done in Bulgaria, but on which no published results are available, is the effectiveness of political and ideological propaganda. A conference of researchers from several socialist states was held in Sofia in October, 1976, to discuss theory, methodology, and some results in propaganda research.[97] One hundred twenty scientific researchers and Party workers participated, including representatives from the Soviet Union and six other socialist countries.

A report on the conference published in *Sotsiologicheski Problemi* notes that "reports were given on a practical experiment in the use of empirical sociological research for increasing the effectiveness of propaganda." No details were provided. In another session of the conference "eight reports and four scientific studies" are mentioned, dealing with important subjects such as 1) the authenticity of the source as a factor affecting the impact of propaganda communications; 2) social stereotyping in the propaganda process; 3) possibilities and limitations on the manipulation of human awareness; and 4) practical problems in the organization and implementation of political and ideological propaganda efforts. Another conference session saw 14 papers presented reviewing results of empirical studies on the effectiveness of media propaganda in socialist systems.

The conference also included some discussion of the limitations (their nature was unspecified in the article) on the usefulness of empirical research in answering important questions about the effectiveness of propaganda. Concern was voiced that social researchers do not always keep propaganda needs in mind when they do studies on public opinion. On the other hand, propaganda cadres do not always make effective use of the sociological research that has been conducted.

Some studies also are being done on the characteristics of persons elected to the National Assembly and to local People's Councils. Initially, these studies dealt only with the social backgrounds and related personal characteristics of elected officials.[98] More recently, studies apparently have been done on attitudes of persons elected to representative positions. As far as we could determine, no results from such studies are yet available.

Several politically relevant studies already have been discussed in earlier sections of this chapter. For instance, studies have been done of the values, motivations, and reading habits of Komsomol members. The perceived effectiveness of Komsomol organizations within the schools also has been examined. We discovered that Komsomol members place more emphasis on agreeable personal qualities and on knowledge than on ideological or political correctness in their friends and organizational associates. Komsomol members also believe that the principal quality of an authoritative person is knowledge. Generally, the hoped-for level of emotive and ideological commitment on the part of Komsomol members does not appear to have been obtained. We also learned that many Komsomol members felt that their organization was not adequately respected in affairs concerning the management of schools.

Two studies of the relationship between reading—especially reading of *Narodna Mladezh*—and social activism have been reported.[99] The studies show that there is statistical interdependence between more intense readership and social activism among young people, but that the relationship is considerably less than perfect. One study suggests that both factors may be products of a third, the level of professional and personal motivation for achievement.

Finally, we previously looked at a study of evaluations of the work of political activists in the transportation industry. In general, these activists received high marks, except for the finding that they spend an inadequate amount of time dealing with "social and general political questions." This shortcoming was especially characteristic of lower-level leadership cadres, those who have the most direct contact with workers.

The most important recent piece of political research using surveys was a study of local Party secretaries and their attitudes toward their work.[100] The study was published in the 1974 volume of *Nauchni Trudove* of the Academy of Social Science and Social Administration, which is attached to the Central Committee of the Party. Structured, lengthy interviews were conducted with 570 Party secretaries. The sample was national, although some of the analyses reported focused on the Gabrovo district. The respondents were asked about the type of Party work they preferred, their motivations for serving, how they organized tasks, what personal qualities they felt were most important for Party secretaries, what sorts of issues people most often brought to them, and the sorts of topics on which they were most frequently asked to lecture or provide formal guidance.

Table 3.17 reports responses to a question about the preferred type of

Table 3.16. Rankings of Negative Influences in Society by General Population,
Leadership, and Administrative Subsamples (N = 2,906)

	Ranking by Subsample		
Negative Influences	General Population (N=2,046)	Leadership Cadres (N=561)	Administrators and Government Personnel (N=109)
1. Divorce	1	25	- -
2. Interference in others' affairs	2	1	3
3. Alcoholism	3	29	27
4. Being "pleasing and toady"	4	3	6
5. Unprincipled interpersonal and family relations	5	2	1
6. Moral looseness and corruption	6	18	23
7. Theft	7	17	18
8. Hooliganism	8	23	24
9. Bureaucratism	9	5	4
10. Smoking among youth	10	- -	- -
11. Using public position for personal gain	11	6	2
12. Avoiding responsibility	12	4	7

Source: Nikolai Danchev, "Sotsialisticheskata Psihika," *Nauchni Trudove (Filosofiya)* 61
(1974), p. 322.

Table 3.17. Type of Party Work Preferred by Local Party Secretaries (N = 570)
(percentages)

Preferred Work	Percent of Respondents
1. Local contacts	27.7
2. Organizational	18.9
3. Administrative	16.5
4. Ideological	6.0
5. No preference	29.5
6. No answer	1.4

Source: Akademiya za Obshtestveni Nauki i Sotsialno Upravlenie pri TsK na BKP. *Nauchni
Trudove* 61 (1974): 341.

Party work. Most interesting are the facts that a plurality (nearly 30 percent) did not have a preference among four categories of Party tasks, and that only 6 percent indicated a preference for ideological work. Relatedly, the Party secretaries were asked if they performed their Party responsibilities "willingly." Nearly two-thirds (65.4 percent) said they did so with great pleasure, or willingly. But 34.6 percent said they did so to some degree unwillingly. Half of those who did some things unwillingly reported that the reason was overwork. But a lack of general acceptance, and the absence of good discipline within the Party organization, also were mentioned.

The article in *Nauchni Trudove* laments the disinclination of many Party secretaries to delegate work responsibilities. When asked how they organize the carrying out of tasks, 46.5 percent of the respondents indicated that they simply do it themselves. Delegating the work to other members of the Party bureau was a strategy used by 31.3 percent; 22.2 percent delegated the task further among active Party members.

How did these Party secretaries come to be selected to that position? Table 3.18 suggests that barely more than one-third genuinely desired the post. Pressure from one or another element of the Party organizations was said to be responsible for their acceptance of the position by 54.7 percent of the Party secretaries. A question also was asked concerning the quality most important for a Party secretary to have. "Will and firmness" was the most important quality (mentioned by 33.9 percent), followed by being demanding and exacting (27.7 percent). Responses to this question are summarized in table 3.19. An essentially hierarchical view of their roles is suggested by the fact that substantially fewer of the Party secretaries mentioned "openness" or "self-initiative" as most important. At the same time, when they were asked to identify the most important responsibility they performed, the majority did not opt for the response which would have suggested a "transmission belt" self-role definition. As indicated in table 3.20, nearly one-half of the Party secretaries indicated that their most important function was to bring together members of the local Party organization and to effectively organize their work. Organizing and fulfilling the decisions of the Party bureau and other components of the Party organization—presumably, the hierarchical, or "transmission belt," response—was considered most important by 29.1 percent.

When asked to define their roles in relation to Party rank-and-file and local citizens—i.e., why people came to see them—they gave responses suggesting a picture of the local Party secretary as a person with adjudicative roles, primarily with respect to economic issues. Thus questions having to do with appropriate payment for work performed, or with the delivery and pricing of various commodities, were the most common to come before them. This information is presented in table 3.21.

Finally, the Party secretaries were asked if they were requested to give lectures on any of four important political topics: 1) Leninist teachings of the Party, 2) instruction in teaching the organization and carrying out of Party work

Table 3.18. Bases for Accepting Selection as Party Secretary (N = 570)
(percentages)

Basis for Acceptance	Percent of Respondents	
1. Own desire and conviction	37.9	
		45.3
2. No particular desire to accept	7.4	
3. Because of insistence of members of the Party bureau	24.7	
		54.7
4. Because of insistence of the Party hierarchy	30.0	

Source: Akademiya za Obshtestveni Nauki i Sotsialno Upravlenie pri Tsk na BKP. *Nauchni Trudove* 61 (1974): 342.

Table 3.19. Qualities Thought To Be Most Important
for Party Secretaries (N = 570)
(percentages)

Most Important Quality	Percent of Respondents
1. Will and firmness	33.9
2. Demanding and exacting	27.7
3. Self-initiative	19.8
4. Openness	13.7
5. Motivation, energy	2.8
6. Others	1.4
7. No answer	0.7

Source: Akademiya za Obshtestveni Nauki i Sotsialno Upravlenie pri Tsk na BKP. *Nauchni Trudove* 61 (1974): 343.

Table 3.20. Party Secretaries' Perceptions of Their
Most Important Functions (N = 570)
(percentages)

Most Important Function	Percent of Respondents
1. Uniting the Party members and organizing our tasks	48.9
2. Organizing and fulfilling the decisions of the Party bureau and the Party organization	29.1
3. Concern for the needs of the people; helping the citizenry with various tasks	16.0
4. Learning the mentality of the collective and the mood of the people	4.9
5. Others	1.1

Source: Akademiya za Obshtestveni Nauki i Sotsialno Upravlenie pri Tsk na BKP. *Nauchni Trudove* 61 (1974): 343.

Table 3.21. Bases of Relationships of Party Secretaries with Party
Rank-and-File[a] (N=570)
(percentages)

Basis of Relationships	Percent of Respondents
1. Determining appropriate payment for work performed	24.0
2. Delivery and pricing of various commodities	23.2
3. Smooth bad relationships	17.9
4. Housing problems, debts	8.8
5. Problems in working conditions, security of jobs	5.6
6. Family problems, parent-child relationships	1.7
Total	81.2[b]

[a] Question: "Why do people come to you most often?"

[b] Apparently, 18.8 percent of the respondents gave other answers, or no answer.

Source: Akademiya za Obshtestveni Nauki i Sotsialno Upravlenie pri Tsk na BKP. *Nauchni Trudove* 61 (1974): 343.

3) economic conditions and policies in Bulgaria, and 4) contemporary international relations, including the foreign relations of Bulgaria. One might have supposed, given the fact that these are local Party officials, that requests would most frequently have dealt with topics two and three, which are subjects presumably closer to the interests of local citizens. In fact, however, the opposite was true. Slightly more than one-third (35.3 percent) said they were asked to lecture on economic conditions, and 45.5 percent were asked to talk about Party work. The percentage rises to 57.6 for Leninist teachings of the Party. However, by far the most popular subject was international relations. Notwithstanding the relatively high level of education these persons collectively represent (about half have doctorates), one must assume that their qualifications for addressing this subject were relatively less impressive.

In his book on *Public Opinion*, Dimitur Ganchev[101] mentions one other politically relevant poll, done on the effectiveness of Party political education. The study is mentioned in the context of a methodological discussion of the influence of interviewers on responses given. Interviews were conducted with Party secretaries, propagandists, and other Party members in one unnamed city. Two separate surveys were conducted, one in which the interviewing was done by members of the city Party committee. When the sociologists did the interviewing, 80 percent of the Party secretaries had a positive view of Party educational activities; 62.5 percent of the Party propagandists were favorable, but only 48.7 percent of the other Party members described Party political education as being successful. When a similar sample was polled by members of the city Party committee, positive evaluations of Party political education were given, on the average, by 15 percent more respondents in each category. Besides being of considerable methodological interest, the findings of this study suggest substantial differences between Party leadership and rank-and-file in the evaluation of the Party's efforts at political education.

It would be not only difficult but presumptuous to attempt to summarize survey research on political and ideological questions in Bulgaria. It is certain that the vast majority of the work done is not made generally available. What is published usually deals in some way with the evaluation of political activism among various leadership cadres or the nature of organizational and political work done within local Party committees. If we were to summarize the results of these narrow sets of studies, we might focus on two points. First, there is substantial variation among leadership cadres in Bulgaria in the way they perceive what they are doing, and in the apparent effectiveness with which they do it. Second, there is a much greater appreciation today than was the case a few years ago of the importance of confronting these kinds of issues through systematic, empirical research. That the research which is published seems quite candid by past standards can be attributed largely to the quantitative precision of the data, and to the now-acknowledged significance that this kind of research has in the evaluation of the political direction of Bulgarian society.

Ethnicity and Foreign Cultures

Little evidence was uncovered of the use of surveys to address either questions of ethnic identification within Bulgaria or attitudes toward foreign countries and cultures. Four studies of some relevance to these topics merit comment.

First, the previously discussed study of attitudes of Bulgarians toward crime, law, and justice[102] did distinguish responses by ethnic group. Unfortunately, very few of the findings reported in *Sotsiologicheski Problemi* were broken down by ethnicity of respondent. We do know that minority ethnic groups, especially Gypsies and Turks, were less likely to correctly see crime as "a negative social phenomenon." These two groups, especially the Gypsies, also differed from the full population sample in identifying factors which inhibit criminal activity. Of the full sample, 6.1 percent mentioned fear of sanctions; for the Gypsies, the percentage was 16.8, and for the Turks, 7.1. Finally, among these two groups the threat of loss of self-respect was a substantially less significant deterrent. This factor was mentioned by 22.5 percent of the full sample, but by only 11 percent of the Gypsies and Turks.

One other recent empirical study directed toward the problems of minority ethnic groups in Bulgaria was found. This is a book by Vladimir Ardenski[103] dealing with the assimilation of the Pomaks, the approximately 280,000 Bulgarian Mohammedans who live primarily in the Rhodope Mountains. Although quantitative results are not reported, Ardenski does cite evidence of tendencies toward assimilation—especially, the increasing practice of Pomaks discarding their Mohammedan names—from interviews with Pomaks in several towns. Bulgarian Moslems dispute Ardenski's assertion that this practice is widespread and growing.

In 1977, *Narodna Kultura* reported the results of a nationwide poll taken nine years earlier under the auspices of the Institute of Sociology of BAN concerning what country in the world was thought to be the greatest supporter of peace and socialism.[104] The collective response was wholly predictable, but there were some modest variations among age, residential, occupational, and educational groups. Table 3.22 summarizes these intergroup differences. Overall, 88.76 percent of the Bulgarians polled named the Soviet Union as the greatest supporter of peace and socialism. The percentages were higher in the cities than in the villages and rural areas; they were higher among younger people, lower among those age 28 or older. Workers were somewhat less likely to name the Soviet Union than were members of the intelligentsia; relatedly, persons with only primary education were less likely to name the Soviet Union than were those who had completed secondary school or who had post-secondary education.

Finally, one of the most fascinating, if apparently unsystematic, studies examined as part of this project was referred to in the course of an article written by Elena Panova, "Amerikanski Vpechatleniya" ("American Impres-

Table 3.22. Bulgarians' Views of "What Country Is the Greatest Supporter of Peace and Socialism in the World," by Place of Residence, Age, Occupation, and Education

(percentages)

Respondent Group	Percent of Respondents Naming the Soviet Union
All respondents	88.76
Cities and towns	
Ages 16 to 28 years	92.85
Older than 28 years	90.17
Villages and countryside	
Ages 16 to 28 years	85.36
Older than 28 years	74.18
Workers	85.91
Intelligentsia	97.12
Primary education	81.26
Secondary education	
	97.22
Post-Secondary education	

Source: *Narodna Kultura,* 4 November 1977, p. 8.

sions"), published in the magazine *Plamuk* in 1974.[105] In the course of relating her frequently positive impressions from a visit to the United States, Panova mentions that a sociologist colleague of hers had conducted an informal survey among students at a high school in Sofia. The question was asked, *"V koya strana iskash da zhiveesh?"* ("In what country would you like to live?"). Panova says that "many" (*mnozina*) of the students responded "America," and when asked to be more concrete, most said "the state of Florida." This was a small study, undoubtedly conducted as casually as it was referred to. But at a minimum what it implies about the internationalization of the perspectives of young people in Bulgaria is significant.

Market Research

The field of market research is very new in Bulgaria. The work being done is narrowly focused— usually commissioned by a particular enterprise— and almost always unsystematic. Results from one market survey of more general relevance were reported in a 1976 issue of *Sotsiologicheski Problemi*.[106] However, no serious effort to uncover other market research studies was made.

CONCLUDING NOTE

Survey research in Bulgaria is new, its number of practitioners small, and its technical and methodological infrastructure weak. It also is constrained by the tentativeness enforced by the political context in which it operates. The nature of this tentativeness has changed. Ten years ago early survey research efforts were undertaken haltingly because political constraints were known to be severe. At the end of the 1970s the tentativeness results from the cautious and sometimes ill-defined loosening of those constraints. Bulgaria may be an "orthodox" (read: expressly Soviet-oriented) system, but the nature of orthodoxy has changed, with identifiable effects on the conduct of concrete social research.

And so the use of surveys—some reasonably systematic, many demonstrably casual yet with policy (if not scientific) worth—continues to grow rapidly. Survey research in Bulgaria is distinguished from its counterpart activity in Poland or Hungary as much by how much is published as by how much is done. Indeed, the evidence we have suggests that surveys concerning politics and youth by units attached to Party organs in Bulgaria are as forthright in the selection of subjects and the formulation of questions as are comparable surveys being done anywhere in Eastern Europe. The bare trickle of published output is frustrating (presumably, for many Bulgarian scholars as well as for those in the West who would better understand contemporary Bulgaria), but it is perhaps understandable in the policy-sensitive context in which it is done and evaluated.

Surveys are seen as instrumentalities for more effective governance, in part because they permit the identification of citizen concerns as well as the mapping of inadequacies in citizen values. These and other roles performed by surveys are of sufficient importance to lead to the expectation that the use of surveys will continue to grow. One other important function is the demonstration/propaganda effect. For all of the difficulties that these surveys reveal about contemporary Bulgarian life, the fact remains that a considerable proportion of the responses given are politically appropriate. One suspects that the Party leadership has come to understand that many citizens are more impressed by being told that their fellow citizens *do* believe certain things than by hearing from the leadership that they *should* believe. And a further function of an increasingly vital survey research apparatus is the training of cadres who are competent in methods of taking accurate measure of the public pulse.

One should not assume from this rendering of the current status of survey research in Bulgaria that the principal regime motivation for nurturing such studies is a desire to consolidate political dominance. There is every evidence that the Bulgarian leadership believes that this is no longer an issue. Further, there are equally persuasive reasons for accepting the sincerity of the leadership's commitment to effecting an efficient and at the same time humanitarian socialism. It cannot do this without developing the means for sensitive inventorying of the moods and concerns of the population, as well as a capacity to be accurately introspective about itself.

This concluding summary emphasizes apparent problems in Bulgarian society. We might hope to be forgiven for this emphasis for two reasons. First, many of the surveys being done focus—understandably—on social problems. Second, there is the legacy of the past: the Bulgarian regime has been vigorous in extolling its own virtues, and energetic in calling its protagonists to task for their shortcomings. Remarking only once that Bulgaria has achieved remarkable socioeconomic development in the past 15 years, in particular, cannot lessen the significance of that observation.

Several generalizations characterizing Bulgarian society and polity are suggested by the studies mentioned in this chapter. Perhaps most striking is the signal importance that formal education continues to have in delineating social, economic, and political distinctions. Almost without exception, where there is value dissensus, education is an accompaniment, whether it has to do with attitudes toward crime, values concerning work, the protection of socialist property, the consumption of printed media, or the use of leisure time. Only the electronic media seem to have transcended the educational watershed: both television viewing and movie attendance are associated primarily with place of residence (urban-rural). Even here the educational factor is relevant, since village and rural residents are substantially less educated.

The critical role of education should not be difficult for leadership elements in Bulgaria to understand; education and socialization are closely linked, after all. What may be encouraging to them is that some of the desired values are found with greater frequency among young people who are both more and more recently educated.

At the same time, all definitely is not well with youth, which accounts for the great and growing attention given by survey researchers to youth questions. Bulgarian youth are socially conscious, nonmaterialistic, idealistic in some respects—but there is evidence that their level of socialist consciousness leaves a good deal to be desired. Few surveys of youth views on current political, social and economic issues are circulated, but what is available suggests a surprising degree of normative insulation of young people from many of the stimuli they receive on a day-to-day basis. Thus they value knowledge and congenial personal qualities in friends and colleagues much more than ideological correctness. Fewer than half prefer films with a normative message. With advancing age in secondary school, even Komsomol members find themselves more motivated by societally and personally oriented considerations, and much less motivated by the intrinsic political character of the organization itself.

But whatever the problems with youth, the difficulties with workers, young and old, are more serious. Their level of social (and socialist) consciousness is lower. They read less and steadfastly refuse to use their leisure time in "productive" ways, such as continuing professional development, political-ideological training or activity, or evening classes. They are not adequately concerned about crimes against socialist property and are less concerned about crime in general. Job satisfaction among them is relatively low and labor turnover high, especially for a society which places constraints on occupational choice and changes of residence.

Survey research identifies other problems, as well. Traditional values concerning the division of labor within families are dramatically affecting the efforts of Bulgarian women to achieve professional equality with men. Their use of leisure time and their attitudes toward family and children also are distinctly affected. In part because of these tensions in the evolution of female roles, conflicts in young families are more evident, as is a general destabilization of interpersonal relationships. Material shortages persist, and apparently contribute both to the crime rate and to overall citizen evaluations of the quality of life. In concert, these problems apparently generate some uneasiness about societal leadership. Thus, more than half of one sample believed that shortcomings in public organs, including the negative examples of prominent persons, contributed to crime. Further, there is evidence of dramatic differences between leadership and citizen assessments of the most significant problems which demand attention.

Not incidentally, however, although these characteristics may be inconsistent with the elusive image of a developed socialist society, they are not unusual for modernizing societies at similar levels of social and economic development. In short, what the results of surveys in Bulgaria may show in part is that the systemic characteristics most relevant for understanding contemporary Bulgaria have nothing to do with its overt ideological and political features. Viewed as a rapidly modernizing Balkan country extracting itself from a legacy of lagging social and economic development, the problems which trouble Bulgarian leaders and citizens today are not difficult to understand. This is not to say that 35 years of communist rule have made no difference; both the pace of improvement and some of the problems can be attributed to the specific political history of the postwar period. But to view the evidence from empirical research solely against the backdrop of recent political experience would do both the research and the experience an injustice.

NOTES

* Among the many people whose cooperation and help were critical to this research, we especially want to thank Lyuben and Krasi Glavanakov.
1. For the name of this center we use here the English translation commonly used by Bulgarian sources. The official name is Tsentur za Sotsiologicheski Izsledvaniya na Mladezhta (Center for Sociological Research on Youth). When created in 1968, it was called Tsentur za Mladezhki Prouchvaniya (Center for Youth Studies).
2. Zhivko Oshavkov, ed., *Sotsiologicheskata Struktura na Suvremennoto Bulgarsko Obshtestvo* (Sofia: BAN, 1976).
3. Zahari Staikov, *Byudzhet na Svobodnoto Vreme* (Sofia: Partizdat, 1973); *idem, Svobodno Vreme i Zhizneno Ravnishte* (Sofia, 1973).
4. Misho Tsanov, ed., *Byudzhet Vremeni Naseleniya NRB v 1970/71 g.* (Sofia: Izdatelstvo Ts SU, 1973).
5. Boris Chakalov, "Nyakoi Problemi na Izuchavaneto na Nastroenniyata i Obshtestvenoto Mnenie," *Sotsiologicheski Problemi* 9, no. 1 (1977): 51-55.
6. Nano Stefanov, *Obshtestvenoto Nastroenie. Sushtnost i Formirane* (Sofia: Partizdat, 1975).
7. Mariya Dineva, "Edna Realna Vuzmozhnost za Povishavane Efektivnostta na Sotsiologicheskite Anketi u Nas chrez Suzdavane na Izbadka-Maika," *Sotsiologicheski Problemi* 8, no. 4 (1976): 91-97.
8. See Valentin Manolov, "Nyakoi Osnovni Metodologicheski Printsipi i Resheniya pri Sustavyaneto na Vuprosnika za Provezhdane na Standartizirano Intervyu," *Statistika* 23, no. 5 (1976): 40-52.
9. For example, see the Center's Russian-language monograph summarizing the proceedings of a 1976 conference of researchers from eight socialist countries, "Standartizatsiya po Sotsiologicheskikh Promenniikh v Izssledovaniyakh Molodezhi," in *Problemii Molodezhi* 10, (1977).
10. *Durzhaven Vestnik*, 1975, no. 41, p. 2.
11. *Bulgarski Zhurnalist*, September 1976, p. 32.

12. *Bulgarski Zhurnalist*, May 1974, p. 30.

13. Bulgarian Telegraph Agency, *News Bulletin*, 1976, p. 11. We had access only to photocopies of the BTA *News Bulletin*. These copies sometimes were incomplete: in particular, dates (other than the year) usually were not identifiable. Further, the *News Bulletin* does not use volume numbers. As a result, notes referring to items in the *News Bulletin* generally will be incomplete. The author has retained photocopies of all *News Bulletin* items used.

14. BTA *News Bulletin*, 1977, pp. 11-12.

15. Elit Nikolov, *Televizionnoto Obshtuvane* (Sofia: Nauka i Izkustvo, 1975), pp. 67-70.

16. Ibid., pp. 70-84.

17. Ibid., p. 75.

18. "Results of Sociological Research on Readership in Bulgaria" [in Bulgarian], *Bulgarski Zhurnalist*, May 1976, pp. 20-22.

19. Zdravko Raikov, "Faktori za Povishavane na Ideinoto Vuzdeistvie na Pechata Vurhu Chitatelskata Auditoriya," *Sotsiologicheski Problemi* 8, no. 6 (1976): 62-73.

20. Hristo Bonev, "Chitatelska i Sotsialna Aktivnost na Auditoriyata," *Sotsiologicheski Problemi* 8, no. 6 (1976): 49-61. See also *Bulgarski Zhurnalist*, March 1977, pp. 14-17, for a summary of this research.

21. "Results of Sociological Research on Readership in Bulgaria" [in Bulgarian], *Bulgarski Zhurnalist*, May 1976, pp. 20-22.

22. Bonev, "Chitatelska i Sotsialna Aktivnost," p. 55.

23. "Means of Mass Information and Preparation of Young People for Family Life" [in Bulgarian], *Bulgarski Zhurnalist*, May 1977, pp. 21-29.

24. *Politicheska Agitatsia*, July 1974, no. 14, p. 46.

25. "Certain Problems of Regional Newspapers Identified by Sociological Research" [in Bulgarian], *Bulgarski Zhurnalist*, August 1975, pp. 27-29.

26. *Bulgaria Today*, 1975, no. 11, p. 13.

27. *Bulgaria Today*, 1975, no. 3, p. 9.

28. *Narodna Kultura*, 16 December 1977, p. 7.

29. Liliyana Spasovska, "Rabotnichkata v Domakinstvoto," *Sotsiologicheski Problemi* 7, no. 2 (1975): 69-81.

30. Ibid., pp. 73-74.

31. Reported in Spasovska, "Rabotnichkata v Domakinstvoto," p. 77.

32. *Narodna Kultura*, 16 September 1977, p. 3.

33. "Mladoto Semeistvo 1969-1973: Ravnovesie i Konflikti," *Anteni*, 14 June 1974, pp. 1, 8-9.

34. Minko Minkov, "Sotsialno-Ikonomicheskite Faktori i Razvitieto na Razhdaemostta," *Anteni*, 20 December 1974, p. 3.

35. Ibid.

36. Cited in BTA *News Bulletin*, 1976, p. 12.

37. "Mladoto Semeistvo" (see note 33).

38. BTA *News Bulletin*, 1975, p. 8.

39. "Means of Mass Information" (see note 23).

40. BTA *News Bulletin*, 1977, p. 10.

41. Lyuben Dimitrov, *Obshtestvenoto Mnenie i Vuzpitanieto na Mladata Lichnost. Sotsialno-Pedagogichesko Izsledvane* (Sofia: Narodna Prosveta, 1975), p. 64.

42. Referred to in a BTA wire transmission, Sofia, 15 July 1977.

43. Kiril Vasilev, "Sotsialniyat Prestizh na Lichnostta," *Problemi na Mladezhta* 7, no. 4 (1977): 3-14.

44. Ibid., p. 11.

45. Reported in Vasilev, "Sotsialniyat Prestizh," pp. 12-13.

46. "Bulgarskiyat Student—s Iziskvaniyat i Budesht," *Anteni*, 28 June 1974, pp. 4-5.

47. "Traditsii i Zadachi," *Studentska Tribuna*, 14 January 1975, p. 3.

48. See Dimitrov, *Obshtestvenoto Mnenie*, pp. 76-81.

49. Ibid., p. 80.

50. Vasilev, "Sotsialniyat Prestizh."

51. Dimitrov, *Obshtestvenoto Mnenie*, p. 69.

52. "Rezultati ot Sotsiologicheski Izsledvaniya," *Rabotnichesko Delo*, 7 October 1977, p. 3.

53. *Bulgarski Profsuuzi*, 1978, no. 2, p. 22.

54. "Moral Practice in the Workers' Collectives" [in Bulgarian], *Bulgarski Profsuuzi*, 1977, no. 5, pp. 22-24.

55. "Problems of Migration of Workers in the Machine-Building Industry" [in Bulgarian], *Bulgarski Profsuuzi*, 1975, no. 2, pp. 11-14.

56. Iordan Kapitanski, "Otnoshtenieto na Selskostopanskite Spetsialisti kum Profesionalniya im Trud," *Sotsiologicheski Problemi* 9, no. 4 (1977): 50-60.

57. *Politicheska Agitatsia*, 1975, no. 8, p. 32.

58. *Bulgarski Profsuuzi*, 1978, no. 2, pp. 23-24.

59. "Rezultati" (see note 52).

60. Vasil Danov and Dimitur Lukanov, "Otnosno Vuzmozhnostite sa Izuchavane na Povedenieto i Otnoshenieto na Razlichnite Kategorii Personal kum Vnedryavaneto na ASU i KAP v Predpriyatiyata," *Sotsiologicheski Problemi* 9, no. 5 (1977): 135-41.

61. *Politicheska Agitatsia*, 1974, no. 1, pp. 47-52.

62. *Bulgarski Profsuuzi*, 1978, no. 2, p. 22.

63. Oshavkov, *Sotsiologicheskata Struktura*.

64. Staikov, *Svobodno Vreme*, and *Byudzhet na Svobodnoto Vreme*; Tsanov, *Byudzhet Vremeni*.

65. We exclude them in part because our purpose is to concentrate on research published during 1975-77. These studies are available, each in a single volume, and thus are relatively accessible to readers with Bulgarian language skills. Further, these studies contain a large quantity of data, not reasonably summarized in a document the length of the present report.

66. *Politicheska Agitatsia*, 1975, no. 7, pp. 42-44.

67. Ibid., 1976, no. 20, p. 78.
68. St. Tsonev, "Bulgarski Opit v Prognozirane na Svobodnoto Vreme," *Sotsiologicheski Problemi* 8, no. 4 (1976): 129-30.
69. *Literaturen Front*, 16 January 1975, p. 1.
70. N. Stefanov, *Obshtestvenoto Nastroenie*, pp. 162-63.
71. Ivan Stefanov, *Izkustvo i Komunikatsiya v Kinoto* (Sofia: Izdatelstvo Nauka i Izkustvo, 1976), p. 100.
72. Ibid., p. 116.
73. Mentioned in BTA *News Bulletin*, 1976, p. 5.
74. BTA *News Bulletin*, 1976, p. 6.
75. Mentioned in BTA *News Bulletin*, 1975, p. 6.
76. BTA *News Bulletin*, 1975, p. 10.
77. I. Stefanov, *Izkustvo i Komunikatsiya*, p. 112.
78. Erika Lazarova, "Knigata—Vsekidnevna Neobhodimost," *Literaturen Front*, 27 April 1978, p. 6.
79. I. Stefanov, *Izkustvo i Komunikatsiya*.
80. *Narodna Kultura*, 8 July 1977, p. 2.
81. *Bulgarski Profsuuzi*, 1976, no. 8, p. 18.
82. Veska Kozhuharova, "Sotsialnata Obuslovenost na Interesa kum Hudozhestvenata Literatura," *Novo Vreme*, 1974, no. 11, pp. 55-66.
83. Hristo Petrov, "Zhiznenite Planove na Bulgarskite Studenti," *Sotsiologicheski Problemi* 9, no. 3 (1977): 77-87.
84. Reported in BTA *News Bulletin*, 1975, pp. 12-13.
85. "Zashto Nosite Brada?" *Narodna Mladezh*, 9 October 1977, p. 4.
86. "Moral Practice" (see note 54).
87. See note 42.
88. *Anteni*, 7 February 1975, p. 8.
89. *Politicheska Agitatsia*, 1975, no. 20, p. 52.
90. Dimitur Fidanov, "Pravosuznanie i Prestuplenie," *Sotsiologicheski Problemi* 7, no. 4 (1975): 48-59.
91. Baicho Panev, "Nyakoi Problemi na Pravosuznanieto na Bulgarskite Grazhdani," *Sotsiologicheski Problemi* 8, no. 4 (1976): 80-89.
92. Fidanov, "Pravosuznanie i Prestuplenie."
93. Nikolai Danchev, "Sotsialisticheskata Psihika," *Nauchni Trudove (Filosofiya)* 61 (1974):320-24.
94. "Time Is Within Us and We Are Within Time" [in Bulgarian] , *Zhenata Dnes*, 1978, no. 1, pp. 18-19. Translated in Joint Publications Research Service no. 70852, 28 March 1978, pp. 13-18.
95. Dimitur Ganchev, *Izuchavane i Formirane na Obshtestvenoto Mnenie* (Sofia: Partizdat, 1974), *passim*, especially pp. 48-52.
96. Angel Kutev and Sasho Savov, "Predi da Trugnat Anketuorite na Put," *Problemi na Mladezhta* 7, no. 4 (1977): 38-44.
97. The conference is described by Todor Petev, "Sotsiologicheski Problemi na Efektivnostta na Propagandata," *Sotsiologicheski Problemi* 9, no. 1 (1977):

161-63.
98. For example, see the brief references in *Bulgaria Today*, 1975, no. 2, p. 3; and 1975, no. 10, p. 13.
99. Bonev, "Chitatelska i Sotsialna Aktivnost"; "Results of Sociological Research" (see note 21).
100. Akademiya za Obshtestveni Nauki i Sotsialno Upravlenie, *Nauchni Trudove* 61 (1974): 341-45.
101. Ganchev, *Izuchavane i Formirane*, p. 66.
102. Panev, "Nyakoi Problemi na Pravosuznanieto."
103. Vladimir Ardenski, *Svoi a ne Chuzhdi* (Sofia: Partizdat, 1975); see especially pp. 167 ff.
104. *Narodna Kultura*, 4 November 1977, p. 8.
105. Elena Panova, "Amerikanski Vpechatleniya," *Plamuk*, 1974, no. 22, pp. 89-98; especially see p. 97.
106. Velko Avramov, "Sotsialno-Psihologicheski Problemi na Stopanskata Reklama," *Sotsiologicheski Problemi* 8, no. 5 (1976): 114-21.

BIBLIOGRAPHY

Daily and Periodical Publications

Mass circulation publications

Covered by direct examination

Anteni
Literaturen Front
Mladezh
Narodna Kultura
Narodna Mladezh
Otechestven Front
Plamuk
Pogled
Rabotnichesko Delo

Covered through indexes

Kooperativno Selo
Puls *

*Not all issues for 1975-77 covered

Studentska Tribuna *
Trud
Vecherni Novini *
Zhenata Dnes *

Specialized publications

Covered by direct examination

BTA *News Bulletin*
Bulgarski Zhurnalist
Filosofska Misul
Istoricheski Pregled
Nauchni Trudove (Filosofiya) *
Novo Vreme
Politicheska Agitatsia
Politicheska Prosveta
Problemi na Mladezhta
Sotsialistichesko Pravo
Sotsialno Upravlenie
Sotsiologicheski Problemi
Statistika

Covered through indexes

Bulgarski Profsuuzi
Izvestiya na Instituta po Filosofiya pri BAN
Nauchni Trudove (Ekonomika) *
Problemi na Vissheto Obrazovanie

*Not all issues for 1975-77 covered

4 Czechoslovakia

George Klein and
Jaroslav Krejči

AN OVERVIEW OF SURVEY RESEARCH
IN CZECHOSLOVAKIA

All intellectual establishments within the country were affected by the mass
removal of more than 300,000 Party members, some of whom had been "the
leading cadres" of the most productive institutes within the country. Under such
circumstances it is not surprising that the quality and quantity of research
suffered.

A casual perusal of Czechoslovak scholarly literature could lead to the conclusion that most survey research had ceased.[1] This did not prove to be the case
on the basis of an in-country investigation. Many research institutes are still
operational and conducting their customary work. It is the information from
their studies which has become restricted. The scope and breadth of authorized
research has declined, and most of it is focused on topics of relatively low
sensitivity.

Survey research in Czechoslovakia is usually carried out by institutes

204

attached to various ministries. Each ministry has an in-house research arm which is financed as a branch of the ministry itself. The primary mission of these institutes is to supply the ministry with data on topics of interest to its policy-making personnel. They also turn out some studies for public release. Since 1970 the published studies have been few, and the research output of the institutes has been highly restricted in circulation. Some studies are circulated in only five or ten copies. Even those studies that are published seldom appear in editions greater than several hundred copies. A few of the studies we have obtained have been printed in editions of 2,000 to 2,500 copies; this seems to be the upper limit. The most visibly active of the institutes is the Institute for Research on Cultural Questions of Prague and Bratislava. This institute conducts, on the average, about ten surveys each year. Only a few of these are published; the rest are for the internal use of its parent Ministry of Culture, and other government agencies.

The problematic status of survey research in the society is reflected in the personnel makeup of the active institutes. The directors of the institutes are generally reliable Party members with a Doctorate or Candidate of Sciences degree in a field appropriate to the work of the institute. In the natural sciences and technology, a few are holdovers from the pre-Dubček era. The greatest personnel changes took place in the social sciences. Institute directors are apparently trusted to decide what materials can be released and which are purely for internal circulation. Frequently, the directors seem to have little technical understanding or interest in research methodology. Their roles are those of business and public relations managers for the institutes. Politically strong directors can shield their staffs from unwelcome criticism. The directors tend to regard their tenure in the institutes as transitional posts until such a time as they are transferred to politically more important functions.

As in other communist societies, the institutes sometimes serve as refuges for a variety of politically compromised individuals. In Czechoslovakia the number of intellectuals with high academic credentials who have been expelled from Party ranks runs into the tens of thousands. Many of these have found employment in the institutes as researchers and are there on the condition that they not persist in oppositional political activity. While their marginal status makes them vulnerable, they suffer the mildest form of "political exile" of all expelled Party members. Such individuals may serve in the role of chief investigator in various studies but that seems to be the permissible limit of their visibility.

The topics researched by the various institutes are dictated by the area of competence of their parent ministries. The methodology of survey research in Czechoslovakia seems generally uniform and of good quality, judging from the methodological descriptions and degree of standardization of the published studies. These contain complete data on the methodology of research, including copies of the research instruments. It seems to be standard procedure to run a pretest of the survey instrument, and the samples appear to be drawn appropriately for the scope of the study. Computers are used extensively in data analysis. These seem to be principally of two types. The Czechoslovak Academy of Sciences uses an IBM 360; other institutions have the Minsk or other Soviet computers at their disposal.[2] The published studies are usually printed by the offset method. The format is clearly standardized; this is evident even in reports which have been published in different centers—Prague, Bratislava, or Brno.

Most of the published studies are subjected to what is called an "opponents' procedure," which resembles the defense of a doctoral dissertation. An Opponents' Commission has the power to recommend modifications, deletions, or even the setting aside of a study. On the basis of the statements attached to most studies, the Opponents' Commission typically consists of two members from within the institute and three members from without. The commission's certification appears at the end of each study with the statement that the opinions written by commission members are on file at the institute.[3] The powers of the commissions must be substantial because the authors have heard discussions of the personalities involved, both from the points of view of their politics and their social science orientation. Outright suppression of studies is rare because none of them originate from the private sector; almost all are products of institute collectives. Their disposition would be ultimately in the hands of the sponsors. Any discourse on the respective powers of the sponsoring institutes and the commissions would be purely speculative because they seem to be nebulous even to individuals within the system.

If one were to venture a guess, most researchers take a turn at being chief investigators or members of opponents' commissions. All participants are well versed in the rules of the game and follow a policy of mutual accommodation in a context that has little tolerance for political missteps. There is little "private" research, in the American sense of the word; even faculty research is largely sponsored. Under the circumstances, questions of publication or nonpublication rarely arise as a matter of individual choice for the authors.

The extent of communication among social science researchers appears to be low. According to some researchers, communications are not the best even within given institutes. This results in part from the philosophy that most data are confidential unless otherwise specified, the opposite of what one might normally expect within a scholarly community.

Most of the studies that are undertaken are released only to a restricted clientele, that is, for the most part the ministries and institutions that have commissioned such work, and it is very difficult for the researchers to judge the impact of their contributions. The data frequently are released piecemeal to the press by the public information officers of the various ministries. Researchers frequently complain about the lack of feedback from their studies.

It would be safe to assume that survey research provides decision-making personnel with data upon which to make and evaluate policy decisions. However, it is doubtful that the present regime will want to risk collecting politically sensitive data because of the role such research played in reinforcing reform tendencies during the Prague Spring. If such studies are made, they are not released into the public domain, and their circulation is restricted to the highest policy-making levels. Published studies concentrate on essentially "safe" topics, ranging from public preferences in the cultural field to satisfactions with employment and housing, but do not approach the really difficult issues of political preferences or fundamental social disaffections.

The institutes provide employment for a range of individuals who are not in political favor, but who are permitted to maintain occupations in line with their previous training, and who might be far more troublesome if they were not provided employment and had no stake in maintaining quiescence vis-a-vis the regime. The institutes and their activities also serve the useful function of maintaining the art of survey research. We have examined hundreds of diploma theses and dissertations from a Czechoslovak university. Only a handful of these relied on original data. Even those diploma theses and dissertations that were data-oriented derived their information from various studies conducted by several institutes.

Compared to research conducted elsewhere in Eastern Europe, the general quality of the studies seems to be high. The technical competence of the researchers and their use of statistics is superior to much of that found even in Yugoslavia, where more research on a wider range of topics is possible. We are aware of no Yugoslav study which would replicate the technical quality of Pavel Machonin et al., *Československá společnost* (The Czechoslovak Society).[4] This massive study, published in 1969, constituted the apex of social science achievement in the reform era. The Machonin study resulted from a charge from Party and state authorities to identify and analyze the condition of Czechoslovak society in the pre-reform era and to pinpoint the sources of Czechoslovak problems. This study is impressive in both its breadth and depth of coverage as well as in its methodology.

Czechoslovak researchers seem very familiar with Western literature and do not hesitate to give full credit to Western sources. These may be balanced by an appropriate number of references to Soviet sources, but there is no apparent effort to disguise the debt to Western scholarship. Citations are precise and comprehensive, which is in marked contrast to studies appearing in some countries in Eastern Europe.

SURVEY RESEARCH ON PUBLIC ATTITUDES AND BEHAVIOR IN CZECHOSLOVAKIA

Media Habits

The main sources of information about the utilization of the media are the researches of the Institute for the Research on Cultural Questions. A great many surveys have not been published, and it is apparent that the institute publishes only a few of the ten or more studies they undertake each year. This proportion is documented by the list of their publications, and the list of future research topics as published in other studies.[5] The official list of publications confirms that we were able to secure the most important published studies in the field. For this topic, media, there are three studies which in effect span the horizon of Czech cultural preferences, from literature and music to the plastic arts.

Significantly, none of these deal primarily with public attention to, or attitudes toward, radio, television, or mass circulation newspapers. The first of the three studies was *Průzkum postojů České veřejnosti ke knize a k jejímu šíření* (Research into the Attitudes of the Czech Public Toward Books and Their Distribution).[6] This study appeared in 500 copies, a surprisingly small edition in view of the substantial investment in research. The sample consisted of 1,372 respondents and the projects utilized 192 trained interviewers who conducted in-depth interviews. The sample was said to be representative; it was stratified by sex, age, and social occupation categories. The age groups were 18-24, 25-39, and 40-54. The social occupational groups were workers, peasants, and other types of employees. The study is subdivided into three major topics: the choice of books, the extent of distribution of books, and the basis on which readers selected the subject matter of the books. It analyzes the position of book-reading in contemporary culture. Concerning the general evaluation of the relevance of books to society, 12 percent of the sample state that the book has lost significance in contemporary society whereas 61 percent report that the book has preserved its significance. For 21 percent, the book has increased in significance; 6 percent had no opinion. In preference for individual genres, books dealing with comic, historical, or travel themes, and books on animals ranked the highest. Utopian literature ranked last.

In comparison with other media, the book did quite well. The study examined intensity of interest in various leisure-time diversions; books were most preferred, followed by television, and then the cinema.

The study concludes that no "trash" literature, such as mass-produced Westerns and detective stories, has been published in Czechoslovakia in the last 25 years, even though there is apparently a great demand for reading matter of this particular nature. The authors of the study venture the hypothesis that it is not also possible to conclude that "bad" books lead to negative attitudes while "good" literature promotes positive ones. This is an implied criticism of the government's restrictive publication policies.

The other extensive study conducted with similar methodology by the same institute is *Průzkum postojů České veřejnosti k populárním zpěvákům* (Research into the Attitudes of the Czech Public Toward Popular Singers).[7] This study attempted to assess the popularity of various singers within different educational and social strata of the population. It tries to discern the reasons for individual singers' popularity and to differentiate among their followings. The study also reveals the hierarchy of preferences in musical tastes among the diverse publics. The research was conducted on a territorially determined sample of respondents by standardized interviews conducted by 150 trained interviewers. The 1,052 respondents were selected in a manner demographically representative for the Czech lands. The sample was divided by sex, age, education, class, and the size of community of residence. Of the interviewers, 91 percent reported satisfaction with the respondents while 9 percent reported difficulties, mainly due to the older respondents' ignorance of popular singers. The data were run on a Minsk-32 computer.[8]

The respondents were queried about their own favorites among popular singers. The singers were then placed into three categories, based on the frequency of favorable response, those who have received more than 30 percent of the preferential statements, the second, more than 10 percent, and the third, all others below 10 percent. The study also states that domestic singers are more popular than foreign singers. Only the British pop singer Tom Jones made it into the second category. The remainder fall under 10 percent. The study notes that contrary to the popular stereotype that only singers from Western capitalist countries are popular, a Polish woman singer ranked third.[9] The study presents extensive data for all preferences relating to styles of music in relation to age, education, and sex.

The third important media study is *Postoje Mládeže k Výtvarnému umění* (The Attitudes of Youth toward the Visual Arts).[10] The study was based on structured interviews with 457 respondents aged 15-24. The apparent inappropriateness of some of the questions for certain categories of respondents raises doubts about the validity of the study, e.g., querying agricultural workers as to their relative preferences for Michaelangelo, Rembrandt, or noted Czech painters. The validity of the questions seem doubtful because 75 percent of the respondents disclaim ever having attended an art exhibition. Nevertheless, the study presents very interesting data about preferred leisure-time activities. Sixty percent of the young people reported that they had no interest in the visual arts;[11] by contrast, 78 percent watched television.[12] The conclusions present a series of suggested policy guidelines to the Ministry of Education for the broadening of opportunities for participation in cultural education. The purpose of the study is to increase the level of cultural appreciation, principally among working class youth who, it is admitted frankly, frequently lack such appreciation. The recommendations call for special attention to young apprentices, workers, and farm youth. In order to achieve this, it would be necessary to sensitize the management of productive enterprises to these concerns.

The recommendations are aimed at the Ministry of Education of the Czech Republic, which would be charged with working out special curricula in art appreciation at nine-year schools and at the special schools for the continuing education of apprentices. The report calls for special attention to youth who live in population centers of fewer than 10,000 inhabitants, who usually seek exposure to culture outside the community, and recommends traveling exhibitions and regionally oriented programs.[13]

The monograph (*Kulturní život mládeže ČSR*) (The Cultural Life of Czech Youth) does not constitute a study.[14] Rather, it is a compilation of masses of data that are at the disposal of the Institute for Research on Cultural Questions. The data resulting from these studies are presented in this monograph in usable form and provide a comprehensive picture of the many aspects of current Czechoslovak cultural life. Yet, the monograph does not throw any light on the sources of the data or on the methodologies by which they were obtained. Some of the studies, as the one previously cited, have been published, while others have not been released. The study provides an index of reader preference for various types of literature (see table 4.1).

Family and Women

The social role of women has been a high priority focus for Czechoslovak researchers. There are at least three reasons for this. First, women in Czechoslovakia represent one of the highest proportions in the work force of any nation. Second, Czechoslovak women participate in society at a relatively high level of educational attainment. Third, there is concern about the relatively low fertility rates among the urban population, especially in Prague, which may be conditioned in part by the relatively low satisfaction among Czechoslovaks with housing conditions. Some of the researches do not deal with women per se but as a part of a broader regional or urban study that may pinpoint the special problems of women. Survey research is only one of several approaches used in research on the role of women.

One important book, which refers to women but unfortunately provides no specific data from surveys, is a collection of studies entitled, *Pracovní podmínky žen* (The Work Conditions of Women).[15] The papers range from analyses of the weights women must lift on the job to public health aspects for the protection of maternal functions. It is a series of seminar papers, obviously prepared for a brief meeting convened for this purpose for people who work in the field. The emphasis is on legal and medical aspects, and the papers are broadly concerned with public policy.[16]

The report "Zpráva o sociologických průzkumech životního prostředí obyvatel hlavního města Prahy" (A Report on the Sociological Research of the Environment of the Inhabitants of the Capital City of Prague) was authored by Helena Janišová.[17] The language of the study is stilted because it creates its own terminology to describe the family and neighborhood aspects of urban life, with such terms as "micro-environment" and "the mezo-urban environment."

The Prague environment is marked by the restriction of urban growth and a resultant low immigration. The city has enjoyed unusual population stability for an urban area of 1,176,000. The city's demographic structure can be further

Table 4.1. The Structure of Reader Interest among Czech Youth

Type of Material	Respondents	
	Number	Percentage
Poetry	154	11.4
Psychological novels	251	18.1
Adventure books	471	34.0
Detective stories	646	46.7
Humor	275	19.8
Socially relevant novels	186	13.5
Travel	159	11.5
Sports	99	7.1
War novels	116	8.4
Historical novels	325	23.4
Biography, memoirs	131	9.5
Books about art	39	2.8
Science fiction	138	9.9
Technical literature	74	5.4
Popular scientific	33	2.4
Girls' novels (adolescent)	119	13.9
Fairy tales	121	8.8
Nature books	87	6.3
All others	4	.03

Source: Anna Randlíková and Iva Maříková, *Kulturní život mládeže ČSR* (Prague: Vydal ústav pro výzkum kultury v Praze, 1976), pp. 38-39; citing Vladimír Hepner et al., *Průzkum postojů České veřejnosti ke knize a k jejímu šíření* (Prague: Institute for Research on Cultural Questions, 1975).

explained by the widespread practice of birth control and small family size, coupled with a high average population age. The proportion of women in the population is higher than in the rest of the country. The proportion of economically active population is declining due to the low birthrate and increasing age structure of the population. The general decline in birthrate in Czechoslovakia has been a source of concern to the authorities for some time. In 1947, the birthrate was 26.3 live births per 1,000 in the Czech Socialist Republic. In 1960, the rate had fallen to 13.3.[18] In comparison with other cities, Prague has the greatest number of families which lack their own apartments. Sometimes three generations must occupy the same living space.[19] The housing pattern of Prague is characterized by a fairly homogeneous distribution of population on a class basis. In the newly developed suburbs, the percentage of worker residents fluctuates between 20 and 36 percent, while in the center city and renewal areas, they comprise between 44 and 53 percent of the population. On the outskirts of the city, workers occupying individual houses represent about 57 percent of the total population. This latter figure is conditioned on the specific traditions of the Czech working class, which frequently combines gardening and mini-agriculture with an urban job.

In 1976, *Sociologický časopis* published the results of research undertaken by the Department of Applied Sociology at the Philosophy Faculty of the University of Olomounc, on the quality of marriage. The sample contained 175 married men and 301 married women.[20] The study revealed that the quality of marriage of the children reflected the quality of marriage of their parents. The reasons for the survival of marriages, ranked in order of importance, were: 1) children, 2) love, 3) dedication, and 4) sexual harmony. Yet, the study also demonstrated that the marriages which were maintained only because of the presence of children were the worst. A happy partnership was reported in 59.7 percent of the cases. The less intense level, harmoniousness, was attained by 82.1 percent of the sample. However, only 47.1 percent registered full sexual satisfaction derived from the marriage relationship. The percentage of dissatisfaction was greater among the men than among the women.

The Slovak journal, *Sociológia*, refers in general terms to a research survey about the conflict between the interests of women as mothers and as "technically" active persons.[21] There is further reference to a study about the experience with computers in marriage bureaus in Czechoslovakia. The research was undertaken on the basis of a selected sample of 27,017 questionnaires, which the respondents had filled out when they registered with the service. The researcher, A. Vanek, came to the conclusion that computers represent a new form for acquainting and selecting marriage partners; they free the individual from traditional methods of choice. Vaněk indicates that 70,000 persons have used this form of mate selection since the service was introduced in 1967.[22]

It is interesting to note that the intelligentsia active in the humanities did not participate in this form of mate selection. In 1974, every second male participant was a worker, and every fifth belonged to the technical intelligentsia.[23]

One of the main stated motivations for contracting marriage was the desire for children, 78 percent among men and 68 percent among women.[24]

The Federal Statistical Office keeps its finger on the pulse of family living standards through "micro-censi" of households carried out in noncensus years. The household is defined as a collective of persons living together and having a common economy. The social group to which each household belongs is defined by its head. Investigations have been carried out among three groups of workers: manual, white collar, and agricultural. The researchers utilized quota sampling, based on the national economic structure and its regional components. The micro-census investigates one percent of the stratified sample of households for income differentials. (For a more complete presentation of the sample, see table 4.2.)

Sociologický časopis of 1976 presents a research report based on a study by Jiří Večerník of the Institute of Philosophy and Sociology of the Czechoslovak Academy of Sciences.[25] The data are based on the micro-census rather than on original survey research. This study presents the range of income distribution among households after taxes by deciles (see table 4.3).

Sociologický časopis of 1977 reports on a study of the differences in the socialization attitudes of parents towards boys and girls.[26] The instrument used in the study was American in origin, namely "The Parental Research Instrument" developed by Schaefer and Bell.   The authors conclude that the Czech family is fairly democratic, with little differentiation in the parental treatment of girls and boys; in the United States data gathered by the same instrument manifested greater differentials. The Czech authors believe that this is based on a higher level of democratization in Czechoslovak marital and family interrelationships. The general conclusions about parental behavior revealed only two statistically significant differences: a) mothers behave toward their sons in a more democratic way than toward their daughters, and b) mothers suppress more sexual expression in their sons than in daughters. The fathers similarly reveal two statistically significant differences: a) fathers suppressed aggressiveness of daughters more than that of sons, and b) fathers prefer the patriarchial type of family interrelationship vis-a-vis the boys rather than vis-a-vis the girls. [27]

Education and Youth

The socialization of youth is a high priority topic. The regime openly acknowledges its problems pertaining to the socialization of a new generation in the precepts of socialism. This concern is reflected in a number of published studies cited in this chapter. Their selection is entirely based on availability, and is not representative. Some of the studies contain a section specifically devoted to youth or are entirely devoted to youth, who are usually defined as those between the ages of 16 and 24. This age span seems to be the operational defini-

Table 4.2. Sample Utilized for the Collection of Micro-Census Data, 1976

| | Households | | | | | | | | |
| | Czechoslovak Socialist Republic | | | Czech Socialist Republic | | | Slovak Socialist Republic | | |
Indicator	Blue-Collar Workers	White-Collar Workers	Cooperative Farmers	Blue-Collar Workers	White-Collar Workers	Cooperative Farmers	Blue-Collar Workers	White-Collar Workers	Cooperative Farmers
Number of households	2113	2030	1091	1489	1500	700	624	530	39
Average number of household members	3.59	3.36	3.70	3.50	3.31	3.61	3.79	3.51	3.8
Average number of earning household members	1.80	1.78	1.81	1.79	1.79	1.81	1.84	1.76	1.8

Source: *Statistická ročenka ČSSR* (Prague: Státní nakladatelství technické literatury, 1977), p. 508.

Table 4.3. Personal Income in Czechoslovakia by Deciles, 1976

Decile Groups	Percentage of Total Personal Income		
	1958	1965	1973
Lowest	3.1	4.2	4.7
2.	5.3	6.1	6.3
3.	6.6	7.0	7.3
4.	7.7	8.0	8.2
5.	8.5	9.1	9.0
6.	10.0	9.9	9.9
7.	11.0	10.9	10.8
8.	12.6	12.3	12.0
9.	14.9	14.2	13.7
Highest	20.3	18.3	18.1
Total	100.0	100.0	100.0

Source: Jiří Večerník, "Dynamika příjmové diferenciace v Československu," *Sociologický časopis*, 1976, no. 5, p. 476.

tion of youth of the Institute for the Study of Cultural Questions. The study *Průzkum postojů České veřejnosti k populárním zpěvákům* (The Attitudes of the Czech Public Toward Popular Singers) attempts to delineate age parameters for the popularity of various types of music.[28] The study concludes that the interest in rock music ("big beat") and country-and-western music declines markedly when the respondents reach their thirties.

The Institute for Research on Cultural Questions published a study *K některým problémům estetické výchovy pracujících* (A Contribution to the Problems of the Esthetic Education of Workers) based on other research conducted by the institute, such as the survey undertaken in connection with the research into the popularity of various pop singers.[29] It is a collection of essays apparently meant to serve as a manual for the youth and cultural centers throughout the Czech lands. It was compiled to provide policy guidance for the cadres active in cultural matters, and it is an example of how survey studies are used to provide guidance for people in the field. The work is a follow-up to a volume published in 1971 under the same title. It concerns itself with the sensitization of workers who already have passed through the formal educational process to the aesthetics of various art forms. One of the interesting facts cited is that only 7 percent of the youth between the ages of 6 and 19 years receive any instruction in the fine arts. The study stresses that the levels of fine-arts appreciation among adults must be even lower. At the same time the study criticizes efforts to "force" high culture down the throats of the masses. It concludes that people must find their own levels of association with creative activity—and that this may be wood or metal working activities which may be as meritorious as listening to symphonies.[30] This series of essays is the best example the authors have of how survey research may be translated into operational policy guidance.

Another such work, previously cited, is based on data collected by the same institute, *Kulturní život mládeže ČSR* (The Cultural Life of Youth in the Czech Lands).[31] This study presents data from various surveys on how Czech youth discriminate among various leisure-time activities and how they rank their preferences for thematic subjects within categories of activity such as motion picture attendance and book reading.

The most important published study in this category based on the collection of original data is Ladislav Macháček's *The Social Activity of Working Youth* issued by the Ideological Department of the Association of Socialist Youth in Bratislava in 1975.[32] This study defined youth as those under 30 years of age and the sample was stratified according to the level of qualification in one's occupation, ranging from apprentice to engineer. The sample was drawn from 14 enterprises with work forces under 30 years, ranging from 46 to 2,701, all in the field of machine building. The sample was further divided between members and nonmembers of the Association of Socialist Youth. It is interesting to note that the membership fluctuated widely between various enterprises, ranging from 63.4 percent to 7.5 percent.[33] This study presents perhaps the largest range of politically relevant data, since it presents various levels of satisfaction of the youth in their relationship to their place of work, ranging from the employment of their skills to attitudes toward supervisory personnel. The study is obviously geared toward providing decision-making personnel of the Youth Association with hard data on youth attitudes, and is designed to guide the organization in its educational and recreational functions. These guidelines cover a range from cultural guidance to personal hygiene.

Josef Alan's *Spolecnost, vzdelani, jedinec* (Society, Education, and the Individual) is the most comprehensive treatment of the Czechoslovak educational system that the authors could discover.[34] The study utilizes statistical data apparently gleaned from other studies and does not rely on any original data. It presents a comprehensive image of the Czechoslovak educational system from an organizational point of view and elucidates how the official ideologies shape current practice. They emphasize the proportion of students of working class origin who reach the university level in comparison with West European countries. The ratio of youth of working class origin in the universities is 46.2 percent, while comparable figures for most West European countries are less than 20 percent of the Czechoslovak percentage.[35] The study does not mention the processes of placement selection in Czechoslovak universities, which are openly political and give preference to those who are of "working-class origin" with the proper "cadre reports" (*kadrovy posudek*). One of the more surprising findings is that among the socialist states Czechoslovakia ranks last in the relative number of university students in the fields of humanities and natural sciences.[36] No explanations are offered beyond the statement that the authors consider this to be an anomalous situation, an obvious reference to the effects of the post-Soviet "normalization." The study also draws attention to the low levels of investment in education relative to other socialist states. This is of course partially because Czechoslovakia started with a far more formidable educational establishment than that of the other socialist states. Sixty percent of the physical plant is more than 60 years old, and Czechoslovakia lags behind Hungary, Poland, Italy, and Denmark in capital investment.[37]

The Czechoslovak educational system suffers from the problem of declining school population due to the drastic drop in the birthrate. The authorities hope to counteract this by a planned slow increase in the total enrollment within each eligible generation above the primary level. The study contains an excellent summary of cross-national and comparative data that detail the position of education in contemporary Czechoslovak society. Despite some apparent shortcomings, education is still highly valued as a source of prestige and social mobility.

The study entitled *Kulturny a spolocensky profil dedinskeho obyvatelstva na Slovensku* (Cultural and Societal Profile of the Rural Population in Slovakia) undertaken by the Department of Theory and Sociology of Culture in Bratislava in 1971 queried a sample of 982 respondents in Slovak villages.[38] Fully 75.5 percent of the respondents affirmed that continuing education ought to be a requirement after the students conclude their full-time schooling and enter full-time employment. Only 5.4 percent disagreed with this position, and 24.1 percent remained undecided. At the time the research was undertaken, only 9 percent of the sample of adult population were taking part in some form of educational activity. Of these, one-third were studying on their own, 11 percent in schools, 6 percent in enterprises, and 2 percent in other educational institutions.[39] It is necessary to take note that these figures concern a rural population in the less-developed portion of the country, namely Slovakia. The authors of the report do not give comparative figures for the Czech Socialist Republic.

Work and the Workplace

One of the most important studies dealing with the sociology of the workplace was undertaken in 1969 by the Czechoslovak Institute for Labor Research in Bratislava.[40] The author, Anton Jurovský, utilized both structured interviews and questionnaires filled out by respondents at home. The instrument was of Western origin and well tested by previous use in Czechoslovakia. The sample was not designed to be representative, but rather to identify attitudes prevailing in a number of enterprises. One sample included 184 professionally trained men and 74 women. In a second sample, the respondents were employed in machine-building enterprises and consisted of 556 men and 372 women.

The author finds a high correlation between employment stability and job satisfaction (r=.45). Further subjective perception of satisfaction with employment was (0.23); proper utilization of individual qualifications (0.41); the opportunity for professional growth and advancement (0.25 and 0.28 respectively); attitude toward work (0.35); and personal values, positive and negative toward work (0.38) and (-0.42).[41] This study presents a rich fund of source materials for those seeking an understanding of work attitudes in a socialist state, which is why it is reviewed even though it is dated.

Research on the social aspects of life in enterprises has been undertaken by a collective of researchers of the Czech Scientific Technical Association in the Department for the Rationalization of Work of the Technical Center of Pardubice.[42] The study consists of essays prepared for a seminar and cites a variety of studies undertaken by the center over a period of years.[43] It illuminates such matters as social interaction in the place of work, the efficiency of the role of socialist organizations within the enterprise as agents of political socialization, problems of leadership in small work groups, and the use of leisure time.

A companion work to this study is another work published by the same group *Pracovní podmínky žen* (Work Conditions for Women) prepared in 1976.[44] The collected essays deal with a variety of topics, ranging from safety in the workplace to legal regulations governing work of women, and the attitudes of workers toward supervisors. The work presents some comparative data with other countries but does not appear to present any original material derived from surveys.

A study, undertaken in southern Slovakia and reported in *Sociológia*, details the Results of the Monographic Research in the "Village D."[45] The research established that 54.4 percent of blue-collar workers preferred to work within a group while 28 percent preferred to work independently. Among white-collar workers the ratio was 50 percent to 36.8 percent. An overwhelming 97.5 percent of cooperative farmers answered in the affirmative the question of "whether cooperation in agricultural production succeeded in solving the future of independent farmers in a satisfactory way."

This is, of course, a politically loaded question, and it would lead the respondents to the belief that the questioners are trying to ascertain their attitude toward collectivized agriculture, the *Jednotné zemědělské družstvo* (The United Agricultural Cooperatives). The 97.5 percent positive response by the agricultural workers speaks for itself. In the same group, 68.7 percent answered that they preferred to work within a group, while 20 percent preferred to work independently. They perceived the economic situation of their own family as good or comparatively good; 93.3 percent of the blue-collar workers responded positively to this question, as did 97.4 percent of the white-collar workers and 95.7 percent of the cooperative farmers. Such unanimity of response raises doubts about the validity of the responses, particularly since questions that were politically less sensitive elicited far greater differentiation. The level of satisfaction with the collectivization of agriculture is not just a casual question on the state of an individual's preferences; it is from the point of view of the respondent a request for a pledge of loyalty. It is within recent memory when tens of thousands of individuals faced reprisals of varying degrees of severity for the expression of open or covert opposition toward collectivization.

One of the more interesting studies concerns the mobility of scientific workers between branches of science.[46] One-fourth of all scientific workers surveyed began their careers in branches of science other than those for which they had been trained. This study was carried out by the Institute of Philosophy and Sociology at the Czechoslovak Academy of Sciences by Eva Křížová.

Some of the work-related studies deal with income distribution and differentials (see table 4.3). The Federal Statistical Office keeps a careful check on income changes by the utilization of a micro-census procedure which investigates a stratified sample of 1 percent of households. The sample is selected according to the number of household members average net per capita income and the branch of industry from which the household derives its main income. The statistical samples are chosen in such a way that they compare with the global data classified by the branch of industry or activity.

Another study, "The City of Prague," concerns income in Prague, where the wage levels are stated to be 108 percent of the national average.[47] This is true despite a relatively high proportion of pensioners. The level of employment of the work force is particularly high in Prague because of the relatively low number of dependent children and an all-pervasive labor shortage. A great number of high-income recipients (top state and Party officials) also are concentrated in Prague. This is the source of the higher per capita income enjoyed by Prague residents. The general orientation of consumption is in the direction of durable goods, such as washing machines, stereos, and television sets. The Prague households occupy a leading position in the country in items associated with cultural consumption and leisure, such as cars or weekend houses.

Leisure Time

The authors have few leisure-time studies at their disposal. Some of the studies previously cited illuminate this facet as a part of an exploration of specific activities, i.e., the studies dealing with the popularity of various singers or preferences for art forms in the plastic arts. The most important concrete data is derived from *The Cultural Life of Czechoslovak Youth* by Anna Randliková and Iva Maříková, where there is a presentation of data that specifies the preferences of youth for recreational forms (see table 4.4). The data for adults are somewhat different and can be found in Hepner's study about the attitudes of the Czech public toward books (see table 4.5). Motion picture viewing, reading, and television viewing were by far the most popular leisure-time activities among youth, followed by sports and dating. It is interesting to note that the theater and concerts fell on the lower end of the continuum.

The studies dealing with the population of Prague throw a very interesting light on recreational conditions as perceived by the respondents.[48] In many countries the capital city is a favorite place of residence because it affords more opportunity for leisure-time activities than does provincial life. Czechoslovakia boasts an extensive network of cultural facilities throughout the country which are visited with some regularity by performers from Prague. Most inhabitants live within commuting distance of recreational facilities. The studies dealing with the population of Prague cite the availability of recreational facilities in the fourth place of preferences as to why people wish to reside in the capital city, behind a healthful environment and accessibility to the workplace and the availability of shopping facilities. The citizens of Prague regard residence in the garden suburbs, which offer both relative freedom from traffic and adequate recreational opportunities, as the ideal life style.[49]

Studies of the rural population of Slovakia offer substantial insight into the utilization of leisure time in a rural setting. While the villages under study are rural, many of their inhabitants hold urban jobs, a frequent pattern in Czechoslovakia. The study of "Village D" in Slovakia, as reported in *Sociológia*, gives some insight into the leisure time of the village population. Cooperative farmers, on the average, have 24 hours of free time every week; blue-collar workers, 27.2 hours; white-collar workers, 27.8 hours; housewives, 26.6 hours, and

Table 4.4. An Overview of Youth Leisure-Time Activity

Activity	Respondents	
	Number	Percentage
Motion pictures	576	41.6
Theater	96	7.0
Reading	516	37.4
Dancing	214	15.5
Listening to records or tapes	190	13.7
Playing musical instruments or singing	83	6.0
Visits to restaurants or coffeehouses	84	6.0
Listening to radio	130	9.4
Television viewing	368	25.5
Meeting with friends	175	12.6
Dating a girl/dating a boy	197	14.2
Attending concerts	12	.8
Attending art exhibits	10	.7
Sports activity	273	19.7
Driving car/motorcycle	92	6.6
Visit to a club	14	1.1
Spectator sports	64	4.6
Going for a walk	72	5.2
Excursions; visits to weekend houses	71	5.1
Volunteer projects (brigades)	4	.3
Helping at home	140	10.1
Public life functions	19	1.4
Handicrafts	136	9.1
Social games	32	2.3
Hobby	110	7.9
Amateur artistic activity	40	2.9
Self-improvement study	97	6.9
Rest; doing nothing	103	7.5
Others	9	.6

Source: Anna Randlíková and Iva Maříková, *Kulturní život mládeže ČSR* (Prague: Vydal ústav pro výzkum kultúry v Praze, 1976), pp. 30-31.

Table 4.5. Relative Public Appreciation of Leisure-Time Alternatives
(percentages)

Activity	Level of Intensity of Appreciation							
	1	2	3	4	5	6	7	No Response
Records, tapes	34	14	13	12	11	7	8	1
Cinema	16	14	17	17	17	12	7	1
Books	3	6	12	15	19	18	27	0
Radio	10	16	23	18	16	11	5	0
Television	5	5	9	13	20	23	24	1

Note: (1) represents the lowest level of intensity
         (7) the highest

Source: Vladimir Hepner et al., *Průzkum postojů České veřejnosti ke knize a k jejímu šíření* (Prague: Institute for Research on Cultural Questions, 1975), p. 113.

students and apprentices, 32.3 hours.[50]

The major portion of free time was utilized primarily for housework, i.e., the improvement and maintenance of family dwelling space. Gardening and work around the home consumed up to 70 percent of the farmers' free time; 65 percent of that of the blue-collar workers, and 60 percent of that of the white-collar workers. The second-ranked activity was radio listening and television viewing, for 60 percent of all respondents. The third-ranked activity was reading. The data did not distinguish between types of reading matter. Of the sample, 60 percent of the white-collar workers reported reading as a leisure activity; 30 percent of the blue-collar workers, and only 23 percent of the cooperative farmers.[51]

Another village study, "Cultural and Societal Profiles of the Village Population in Slovakia," discloses that 90.6 percent of respondents own a refrigerator, 97.1 percent a radio, 76.2 percent a television, 64.4 percent sewing machines, 42.6 percent vacuum cleaners, 10.5 percent tape recorders, 5.3 percent record players, and 17 percent a camera. The report stated that 46.7 percent disposed over their own cultural center, 66.6 percent had a cinema, and 96.7 percent had libraries. Conditions for culture and social life were evaluated by the respondents as good, 17.4 percent; satisfactory, 57.1 percent; bad, 18.1 percent; and almost none, 7.4 percent.[52]

Moral and Ethical Preferences and Life Aspirations

Research on the subjects of moral and ethical preferences of the populace and life aspirations are almost absent from any list of publications available for purchase. These most sensitive topics are frequently approached tangentially in specialized studies dealing with rural populations, attitudes toward the environment, or cultural topics. During the period of 1966 to 1969, the social scientists of the ČSSR enjoyed the greatest latitude to conduct such inquiries and to publish their data. Under the present circumstances it is not the social scientists who dispose over the publication of their data but rather the public relations personnel of the various ministries, and they tend to be very conservative in authorizing the release of any such information, whether it be favorable, unfavorable, or indifferent. They simply do not wish to take the responsibility for providing a forum for individuals who might have been discredited in the previous era but continue as active researchers. The data are frequently released in mass media without reference to the specific study from which they originate.

The working class youth studied by Macháček displayed the unanimity previously discussed when queried about sensitive topics, as reported in *Spoločenská aktivita pracujúcej mládeže* (The Social Activity of Working Youth). This study, undertaken for the Association of Socialist Youth, *Socialistický zväz mládeže* (SZM), comes closest to illuminating some questions of value.[53] It develops comparisons between the levels of political awareness among three categories of respondents: members of SZM, functionaries of SZM, and nonmembers (see table 4.6).

The data elicited are of questionable reliability, despite the apparent efforts by the researchers to administer the questionnaires objectively. On issues concerned with the relative values of capitalism versus socialism, socialism was strongly preferred by up to 97 percent of the respondents; 97.5 percent replied that socialism was superior to capitalism in guaranteeing peace. Only 1 percent thought that socialism was equal to capitalism. Only 0.7 percent of the respondents expressed uncertainty on the question, and no responses stated that capitalism was superior. Similarly, a high percentage, 90.2 percent, affirmed that socialism removed inequalities among individuals while only 0.8 percent maintained the contrary. Interestingly, the most negative responses were elicited by the question if socialism utilizes ideas, thinking, and education better than capitalism. A relatively lower 82.6 percent replied positively; 1.2 percent replied negatively, and the rest of the responses divided between those who did not know or those who felt that perhaps socialism did so (see table 4.7).

By contrast, it is interesting to note the comparatively wider range of responses to questions that are not as ideologically sensitive. Almost 60 percent of the respondents stated that they were dissatisfied with the hygienic conditions prevalent in their respective enterprises.[54]

In the previously cited study of the Slovak "Village D," 96 percent of the respondents expressed at least partial satisfaction with "their life up 'til now." The study comments "that, according to our opinion, [the data] attest to the profound positive influence of socialist changes as well as to the basic conditions of personal and family life, and a high degree of identification with the social evolution experienced by the traditionally oriented countryside toward the present social realities."[55] However, more specific questions about working conditions elicited less unanimous responses. While 25 percent of the respondents indicated dissatisfaction with working conditions, 73.4 percent expressed that they had no fears about the future.[56] It was reported in the same study without the presentation of any percentages that the majority of the villagers could not imagine their existence without religious rituals, such as baptism, confessions, and marriages. This view was shared by people who do not profess a religion. Almost two-thirds reported that religion strengthens morality and that children should have religious instruction. This view was held by 82.4 percent of cooperative farmers and almost three-quarters of the women. Among young parents between the ages of 25-29, 46.4 percent were in favor of religious education and 30.9 percent preferred not to express an opinion on this question. It is interesting to note that the regime apparently has succeeded in inculcating its antireligious position best to those with a secondary or higher education, or that those people having better paid jobs were more reluctant to say what they really felt. Only 39.1 percent of those with secondary education and 25.7 percent with a higher education shared the belief in the need for religious education. It is

Table 4.6. Political Knowledge of Working Youth
(percentages)

Question	Correct Responses			
	Functionaries of SZM	Members SZM	Non-Members	Total
Do you know the title of the military organization which protects ČSSR?	88.8	84.5	78.6	82.1
Could you give an example of a great economic project through which you can surmise the cooperation between the CSSR and the USSR?	88.1	80.8	74.0	78.3
Do you know of any recent measure by the party or government which had a positive effect on living standards?	80.0	72.7	72.8	73.6
Do you know the names of the state organs which represent the equal position of the Slovak people in the CSSR?	76.2	69.2	62.5	66.8
Do you know the name of a contemporary youth construction project?	74.6	59.1	51.9	57.4
Do you know the name of a great action for the securing of peace and security in Europe and in what city?	58.5	44.3	38.3	43.0
Do you know the contents of the program of the SZM?	80.7	48.8	16.8	37.2
Could you name an important personality outside the ČSSR in the realm of politics?	97.7	95.9	95.5	95.9

Key: SZM = Association of Socialist Youth

Source: Ladislav Macháček, *Spoločenská aktivita pracujúcej mládeže* (Bratislava: Vydalo ideologické oddelenie SUV SZM v SMENE, 1975), p. 55.

Table 4.7. Socialism and Capitalism: Securing the Values
(percentages)

Proposition: Socialism has secured under contemporary conditions for mankind the following values better than has capitalism.	Responses			
	Yes	About Equally	No	Don't Know
A guarantee of peace	97.5	1.0	0	.7
Social security (work)	96.0	2.1	.1	1.1
Removes social inequalities between people	90.2	5.4	.8	2.9
Opens great prospects for youth from the broadest strata	93.1	4.3	.1	1.9
Supports the expansion of science, technology, and education	87.9	9.4	.2	1.8
Social security and security in old age	96.8	1.2	.2	1.2
Participation of the working citizens in the solution of social problems (democracy)	80.4	6.9	.6	7.6
Utilizes the thought and ideas and specializes training of individuals	82.6	12.6	1.2	3.0
Reconciles nations and nationalities	93.5	4.6	.2	1.2

Source: Ladislav Macháček, *Spoločenská aktivita pracujúcej mládeže* (Bratislava: Vydalo ideologické oddelenie SUV SZM v SMENE, 1975), p. 65.

reported that even Party members did not have "clear views on the matter." Three-quarters of all respondents stated that co-existence of people with different or nonreligious views was possible. Two-thirds of them expressed no opposition to the marriage of their children to such a person.[57]

These appear to be the only reliable statements as to the ethical value preferences of the population at the present time. They have to be extrapolated from studies on unrelated subjects because there appears to be no major study directly devoted to this issue.

Social Problems and Social Policy

The studies devoted to issues of social policy and problems are most limited. Again, the period of 1966 to 1969 provided the students of Czechoslovak affairs with a formidable array of data which ranged from studies of political participation to views on the activities of the security organs. The pre-1969 regime was in effect a response to perceived social problems that had been ignored and which the Dubček regime raised to the level of mass public consciousness. Much of this public focus upon the accumulation of social problems was mobilized by the published data which were made available on the results of survey research. There are no repetitions of such studies at present. Social problems are at best sometimes illuminated tangentially. Therefore, the authors are forced to rely on the few studies that present some data in this category.

Social deviance is a concept defined both by law and by the mores of a given society, and as Otto Ulč points out in an essay, "Social Deviance in Czechoslovakia," the legal and moral norms do not necessarily coincide.[58] Ulč hypothesizes that the value of deviance depends not only on its actual occurrence but also on the interpretation of a given phenomenon by the state.[59] He estimates the rank order of importance of various forms of social deviance in the post-1969 period to be, in order of declining magnitude: pilferage of socialist property, corruption (the most rapidly increasing nonpolitical deviance), use of drugs as a novelty (mildly rising), and violent crimes, including murder. The last category is in decline, as is repeatedly stressed in the mass media.[60]

There are two studies that have bearing on the major problems of contemporary Czechoslovakia. One was published by the Institute for Research on Cultural Questions in Prague and is entitled *Postoje České veřejnosti k ochraně přírodního prostředí* (The Attitudes of the Czech Public Toward the Protection of the Natural Environment).[61] The second is *Postoje České veřejnosti ke kulturním památkám a památkové péči* (Attitudes of the Czech Public Toward Cultural Monuments and Their Care) published in 1976 by the same institute.[62]

Anyone familiar with the environmental pollution in major cities of Eastern Europe wrought by the precipitous industrialization, Prague not excluded, will appreciate the gravity of these problems. Despite strong legislation, socialist enterprises continue to evade their responsibilities, apparently because of politically strong directors and politically weak enforcement authorities. The studies are based on data collected by the institute during two periods, 1945 to 1950 and 1967 to 1972. The researchers utilized a pretest of 43 questionnaires. The sample consisted of 1,015 adult citizens of the Czech lands and was selected by quota procedure for five characteristics: region, size of community, sex, age, and social composition. In the aggregate, the sample has the same basic characteristics as the total population.[63]

The study led to three major conclusions. First, that the majority of respondents are psychically attached to the countryside and to nature and that this is particularly true of those who live in small communities and feel that they can get along without cities. Second, 75 percent of the respondents report that they are satisfied with the environment around their immediate dwelling; 25 percent report dissatisfaction, while two-thirds consider the stream closest to their home polluted. Third, a slight majority expected a general deterioration in the environment and expected improvements only from institutional intervention rather than from appeals to citizens or popular action programs dependent upon voluntary citizen participation.

Popular criticism is principally aimed at the management of industrial enterprises and their attitudes toward the protection of nature and the environment. These are invariably perceived in a largely negative light by the respondents. The framers of the study conclude that these pessimistic trends ought to be countered by education and propaganda rather than by a planned change of conditions which led to dissatisfactions to begin with.

The major differences in perception between residents of countryside and cities as to the degree of the danger to the environment depended on their respective levels of industrialization. There were also major differences among the respondents by dependent level of education.[64] The negative responses as to the adequacy of the provisions for the protection of the environment correlated with the level of industrialization in a given area. The study concludes with a chapter on the application of the results[65] for the purpose of policy making. Since the study was undertaken by the Ministry of Culture, it is principally aimed at public relations efforts rather than with the root causes of the dissatisfaction.

The other major study deals with the attitudes of the public toward the preservation of cultural monuments. This is an important issue because the Czech lands contain a great number of historically significant sites. Czechoslovakia is one of the few countries which has been spared the ravages of war in the twentieth century. The government is now devoting vast funds for the reconstruction of historical monuments in all parts of the country.

This study contains open-ended questions concerning the respondents' perceptions of the significance of cultural monuments and the need for their protection.

The public attitudes toward the preservation of monuments can be summed up in several categories. Of the respondents, 42 percent view historical monuments as vehicles of education about the life and culture of their ancestors, while 12 percent believed that they reinforce national pride and documented the high cultural standards of the nation. Another 11 percent believe that their presence beautified and enriched life, while 6 percent thought that they documented the sophistication of artists and architects. Only 4 percent thought them to contribute to general education, while 3.5 percent cited their significance for future generations. A scant 5 percent viewed them as tourist attractions or as recreation. Interestingly enough, the question as to whether restoration was ultimately financially profitable did not receive a statistically significant response. Yet, the generally positive attitudes toward the preservation of historical monuments contributed to the feasibility and support for major expenditures.[66]

In summary, these two studies hardly illuminate social problems or cultural policy in contemporary Czechoslovakia. However, they do illustrate the type of study which is released.

Politics and Ideology

The authors have discovered no survey studies which deal primarily with political-ideological questions. The potential sensitivity of this topic is obvious, particularly since such studies undertaken in the late 1960s helped to catalyze the events of the Prague Spring. At the same time, at least some politically and ideologically relevant information is published in studies which do not deal with this topic as a primary focus. Macháček's previously cited *Spoločenská aktivita pracujúcej mládeže* sheds some light on this area. The three main emphases stress the impact of communist education and social activities of the working youth, the impact of sociopolitical activity on the development of the personality, and participation in the Association of Socialist Youth (SZM) in the planning of the social evolution of working collectives.

In one of the studies, the respondents were asked to rank order their priorities for the educational mission of the SZM. The responses presented in table 4.8 would signify a high measure of identification with the goal orientation of the system. The socialization of individuals into a Marxist-Leninist world view, question number four, was ranked first and the explanation of Party policy second. It is interesting to note that the promotion of the significance and mission of the SZM in the society ranked last. This would lead to the conclusion that the global goals of the system are viewed as a priority item over the microlevel.

The data presented in table 4.9 addresses itself to the role of the SZM and exhibits a substantial gap in commitment between those who could be described as "socialist shock workers" (BSP) and those who are not organized in officially sponsored organizations. The responses show a high level of commitment to all

Table 4.8. Views on the Content of Political Education

Question: Do you think the political education of the SZM should
stress the clarification of these questions?

Order	Rank Order of Response
1. to clarify the significance and missions of the SZM in our society and its mission in the building of socialism and the socialist education of youth	11
2. to clarify the politics of the Czechoslovak Communist Party (KSČ) and especially the conclusions of the 14th Congress and its deliberations which affect the youth and SZM	2
3. the deepening of friendship between the nations and nationalities in our republic and the building of socialist patriotism	4
4. the systematic reinforcement of a world view and the formation of a Marxist-Leninist orientation	1
5. the improvement of relations between the peoples and states of the Socialist bloc, especially the USSR	6
6. the promotion of pride of belonging to our socialist country	5
7. the clarification of the revolutionary tradition of the working class, the Communist Party, and the progressive youth movement and of military patriotic education	3
8. to reinforce communist and moral values	9
9. to fight against ideologies and stress the consciousness that imperialism is the main enemy of socialism, progress, and peace	8
10. the explanation of the reasons and consequences of the activities of right wing, opportunistic and antisocialist forces in the party, society and in the organization of youth	10
11. the deepening of a feeling of proletariat internationalism	7

Source: Ladislav Macháček, *Spoločenská aktivita pracujúcej mládeže* (Bratislava: Vydalo ideologické oddelenie SUV SZM v SMENE, 1975), p. 59.

Table 4.9. An Evaluation of the Importance of the Political Work of the SZM (Association of Socialist Youth) among Working People and the Socialist Relationship to Work

(percentages)

The Tasks of Political Work of the SZM	Type of Respondent		
	Nonparticipant in any form of socialist work initiative	Competitors for the Title of BSP	Members in BSP Collectives
An orientation toward working with the newest and youngest employees	78.6	92.6	90.9
Care for the social, cultural, and athletic life of the employees	77.2	88.0	88.2
The evaluation and use of employee suggestions	75.7	88.9	84.7
Care about the development of improvements and inventions	71.3	82.6	85.3
Care in the documentation and information of the workers about the tasks and perspectives of their enterprise	71.4	88.0	88.1
The utilization of various forms of moral evaluation of the workers	69.9	83.5	83.1
The encouragement and organization of socialist competition among the workers	67.8	84.4	87.5
N =	897	108	177

Source: Ladislav Macháček. *Spoločenská aktivita pracujúcej mládeže* (Bratislava: Vydalo ideologické oddelenie SUV SZM v SMENE, 1975), p. 85.

questions dealing with ideological matters, but the elements organized in BSP and SZM manifested statistically higher commitment.

In the study of "Village D" undertaken in southern Slovakia several ideologically relevant questions are included, such as what is more important for man, science or religion. The responses must be viewed in the context of the age structure of the population, in which 36.4 percent of the inhabitants were over sixty. Thus, 42.7 percent of the men responded that they considered science more important than religion; only 26.8 percent of the women gave a similar response. Among the blue-collar workers of the village, 44.8 percent considered science more important than religion, and 28.3 percent of the cooperative farmers ranked science higher. Of the white-collar workers, 59.7 percent considered science more important than religion. Religion was preferred by 12.1 percent of the blue-collar workers, 3.9 percent of white-collar workers, and 25.7 percent of the cooperative farmers. The opinions that science and religion are of equal significance was held by 35 percent of the respondents. Predictably, the preference for science decreased with increasing age. Of those over sixty, only 14.5 percent indicated a preference for science. In the age group between 19 and 24, 62.2 percent preferred science, and in the age group between 16 and 18, 84.6 percent agreed.[67]

In the previously cited study, dealing with the cultural profile of the village population in Slovakia, the villagers' evaluation of the capitalist past was reported to accord with the expectations of the researchers; significantly, however, no supporting data are cited. The authors also indicated that those questioned were not sufficiently aware of the significance of the abolition of classes and of social injustice under socialism.[68] Most of the respondents viewed the improvement of health services as the most important achievement of socialism. The younger generation expressed appreciation for the expanded access to educational opportunities.[69] These assertions are not supported by specific data or footnotes, but the researcher implies that his conclusions are drawn from surveys. According to the report, the respondents who were not members of any officially sponsored political organization, such as the Communist Party, appreciated socialism's concrete results, i.e., material achievements. The functionaries and those who were politically engaged stressed the ideological aspects by proclaiming that nationalization and industrialization were just a precondition for further achievements.[70] In the judgment of the author, this latter position is the "correct" response. The leading position of the Communist Party was viewed "correctly" by the authors, which means that the views of the respondents coincided with the current interpretation of the Party line.

The respondents were asked to state their reasons for the leading position of the Communist Party in Czechoslovak society. The respondents ranked the given reasons as follows:[71]

1. the achievements of the KSČ
2. the Party best expresses the interests of the working people

3. the KSČ program of building a classless society and encouraging the the general development of the individual
4. the surmounting of the social crisis of the year 1968 and etc.

The report continues:

> The negative answers represent 8.7 percent of the total responses. Research into the popularity of the personalities of Czechoslovak presidents went clearly in favor of the representatives of the Communist Party, the KSČ. [More than 80 percent with Gottwald at the head, with 65.8 percent.] The majority of the respondents evaluated their relationship with the USSR positively. In the matter of contemporary questions, the respondents manifested a unanimously positive attitude toward the solution of the Vietnam problem.
>
> On the other hand, the respondents expressed a poor understanding of the significance of the postwar changes in the international situation of Czechoslovakia, such as the increased possibilities for citizen participation in the administration of public affairs. On the other hand, one may assert that the research showed that the relatively high niveau [level] of political perspective of the respondents, as well as the social prestige of the Czechoslovak Communist Party and its political line in the eyes of the participants in the research.

This quotation has been included in full in order to demonstrate the vagueness and opacity with which the data are frequently presented. Those who have long experience in interpreting official pronouncements can assume that the author was making a reference to the less than enthusiastic appreciation of the Czechoslovak alliance with the USSR when he stated that the respondents exhibit a poor understanding of the significance of postwar international changes. It is such hints which say a lot without the actual presentation of data. The very omission of a more comprehensive presentation, such as charts, tables, or references to the sample, speaks for itself.

The report further indicates an unsatisfactory level of appreciation for the opportunities for citizen participation in public matters. More than one-third of the respondents took part in public life through membership in various organizations during the previous 25 years. The younger generation was more willing to take on public responsibilities than the older. The report states that the levels of participation were as follows:[72]

> ROH [trade union movement] — 43.5 percent; the Czechoslovak Red Cross — 18.5 percent; ZCSSP — 17.6 percent; SZM [Association of Socialist Youth] — 12.5 percent; SZZ [Association of Socialist Women] — 10.4 percent, etc. It is necessary to notice for example the strong dispropor-

tionality of both sexes in the *Svazarm* [the army association] and sports organizations, (17.4 percent to 1.1 percent). Similarly, women represented 47.8 percent of the sample; but in the Association of Socialist Women (SZZ) there was only a membership of 10.4 percent. The respondents between the ages of fifteen to twenty-nine were 32 percent but in the SZM they were only 12.5 percent; in the army association, *Svazarm* , and in physical culture organizations they were only 9.6 percent, while 50 percent of the respondents expressed an interest in sports. This shows certain disproportionalities in regard to individual groupings of inhabitants which also point to opportunities for increased organizational activity on the part of village populations in interest groupings.

The studies dealing with ideology and politics are a faithful reflection of the prevailing political situation, in which great stress is placed on the maintenance of tranquility. The studies which are commissioned   try to project this preferred image.

Ethnicity and Foreign Cultures

Czechoslovakia is a multinational state with a population of 15 million, of which roughly 4,600,000 are Slovaks. Expressed in percentages, 65 percent of the population are Czechs, 29 percent Slovaks, and the remaining 6 percent are divided among Hungarians, Germans, and other nationalities. Until October of 1968, Czechoslovakia was a unitary state in which most of the political and economic initiatives flowed from the capital city of Prague and many Slovaks perceived themselves as staffing branch institutions of a national ship of state dominated by the Czech majority. This formed the backdrop of the resistance of many Slovak communist leaders to Antonín Novotný, the former President of Czechoslovakia, who was seen as particularly set in his Czech nationalist orientation. This united such philosophically disparate elements as Alexander Dubček and the current President, Gustáv Husák, in a common front against Czech centralism. The October 1968 Constitution is said to be the only surviving reform of the Dubček era.

The federalization affected all institutions within the state. In the executive branch of government, every ministry in which a Slovak is minister has a state secretary who is Czech and vice versa. The country has two seats of government, Prague and Bratislava. There is a Czech National Council consisting of 200 members and a Slovak National Council of 150 members. The Presidium of the National Assembly has 40 members, 20 Czechs and 20 Slovaks. Gustáv Husák is also the first president of the Czechoslovak Republic who is of Slovak ethnic origin. Since 1968, more Slovaks have gained high government office than in any previous period, and most institutions have been separated into autonomous organizations with separate directorates in Prague and in Bratislava. This has had its effect in the fields of social science. Practically none of the studies in the possession of the authors were conducted on a national basis. Every one of them either covers the Czech lands or Slovakia without any effort at cross-national comparisons. It also seems that the federal ministries do not encourage cross-national studies because they apparently consider the topic too sensitive. The Slovak nationality which has historically lagged behind the Czechs in economic and political development has made significant strides in the communist era in its progress to full economic and cultural parity. This progress was accelerated in 1968 after Slovak leaders gained major positions of influence within the state. Under present circumstances institutes under the jurisdiction of Slovak ministries appear to research purely Slovak questions.

The authors also discovered no study dealing with Czechoslovak attitudes towards societies and cultures outside of Czechoslovakia. The only reference to this area comes in the mention of the positive attitudes of the Slovak village population toward the alliance with fraternal socialist countries, as previously cited. The only hint of this topic comes in studies which refer to attitudes toward "capitalism," usually broadly and vaguely defined. Capitalism is always general rather than specific and appears to embrace all states not governed by Communist Parties. This image does not include any relativistic evaluations of various stages of development in capitalism and the states ruled by social democratic parties or the most rabid conservatives appear under that collective rubric. The use of this broad brush to describe a complex outside world must strike a measure of skepticism in a well educated and sophisticated population. The evidence of a socialization effort to appreciate fraternal socialist countries are everywhere in the form of slogans and displays which extoll the virtues of the Soviet Union and other bloc states and the repetitively negative image presented about the rest of the world.

There are some studies which cite data for other societies on issues which clearly are not ideologically sensitive. Such comparative data tend to be used for illustrative purposes rather than throwing light on the relative performance of other societies. There are no studies available to the authors on Czechoslovak attitudes towards specific foreign policies of other states, friendly or otherwise, and we have concluded that it is doubtful that such studies have been recently undertaken.

CONCLUSION

Social science research in Czechoslovakia is conditioned at present by the situation that existed within the country during the period of the Prague Spring when Czechoslovakia was the most surveyed and openly studied state in the history of the Soviet bloc. The "normalization" in the aftermath of the Soviet intervention of August of 1968 saw the gradual removal of the thousands of intellectuals who had contributed to the Prague Spring from their customary places of activity, and the abolition of some of the institutes responsible for the research. A cursory examination of Czechoslovak sociological journals would lead one to believe that little or no survey research is being done at present and even less published. The authors do not lay claim to knowledge as to how widely survey research is utilized because the sample at our disposal is at best limited. It permits us the generalization that survey research is far from dead, and that a variety of institutes are utilizing survey techniques to produce reports, most of which are restricted in circulation, either by the size of the editions or by overt classification.

The university libraries provide their clientele with essentially three categories of access: a general library card for the student body and general public, which does not permit access to confidential materials; a second, higher category which gives graduate students access to materials in their general areas of interest, and a third level, issued largely to the faculty, which permits free perusal of all foreign journals and confidential materials located in special rooms. Foreign journals from the noncommunist world do not appear on open shelves in periodical rooms which are entirely reserved for periodical literature from the Soviet bloc states, and for some of the Communist press from the West. Most recently, the issues of L'Humanité and Unita, the French and Italian Communist Party organs, have followed capitalist journals onto the restricted list. The most important and most widely read foreign paper, particularly in Bratislava, is the Volksstimme, the Austrian Communist Party organ, which has a vast market, particularly on Fridays when it carries the weekly television schedule in those areas which are within the range of Austrian or German television.

To be meaningful, survey research presupposes both freedom of investigation and the freedom of the respondents to give answers without fear of reprisal. In Czechoslovakia the data consistently illustrate that ideologically sensitive questions produce distributions predictably skewed to favor the current Party line. On a wide variety of issues that do not contain ideological or political content which the respondents view as threatening, the distributions exhibit much greater differentiations of opinion.

Published survey research is confined to the most innocuous fields of inquiry. Typical subject matter is the popularity of books versus the other media, differential attitudes toward popular singers, or public attitudes toward the preservation of historical monuments. The most risque studies explore the attitudes of youth toward work and try to provide guidance for the decision makers in charge of education-propaganda activities. The authors did not discover any studies establishing orders of preference even between various types of television and radio programs. No doubt, the decision makers in the appropriate institutions have such data at their disposal, but it is not available in publishing houses, university libraries, and other usual channels of dissemination. The most important political study is the profile of the village population of

Slovakia, and that was published in only 75 copies, earmarked for internal distribution.

If one assumes that studies are conducted on those areas where the regime's need of information is most critical, the published evidence would indicate that the achievement of higher levels of political and social consciousness among the youth must be one of the most critical areas for the regime. Yet, even there, study after study recommends changes in educational policy as a means of coping with discontent rather than suggesting policy changes.

It is amazing to note that the policy guidance which emerges out of the study dealing with the attitudes of the Czech public toward the natural environment is almost entirely directed toward the improvement of the attitudes of the populace and efforts to guide it along more positive lines toward the authorities charged with protection. This concentration on educational policy is not only a reflection of the attitudes of the researchers but flows out of the entire system of research. Many of the studies cited here emerge from the Institute for Research on Cultural Questions and they are what would be described in the United States as contract research, in this case commissioned by the Ministry of Culture, to guide it into more rational policy decisions. Logically, the conclusions of the studies are usually narrowly gauged to address themselves to the specific interests of the bureaucracy which commissioned the study. In other words, the researchers feel that they are doing a specific piece of work for a special institution with a limited jurisdictional competence and do not address themselves to broader academic questions.

It is significant to note the types of materials which did not come to our attention in the examination of the available materials.

1. We discovered no studies which dealt with the broadest aspects of public policy, i.e., even in the study on the environment there was no mention of the nuclear power controversy in a nation which has made significant investments in this form of energy production.

2. We discovered no public opinion research dealing with foreign policy related issues, or even any mention of such in other studies.

3. Despite the federalization of Czechoslovakia and the crucial nature of the Czech-Slovak relationship, there are no published studies bearing on this key question or on personal attitudes of Czechs or Slovaks toward each other.

4. A major issue of discussion in 1968 was the reformers' wish to introduce a measure of workers' self-management into productive enterprises. Impartial discussion of this topic disappeared from the press and the only reference which now appears is condemnation.

5. We have not been able to discover any significant studies on industrial sociology, a branch of investigation which thrives in other socialist societies, including the USSR.

The topics which appear to be safe for investigation deal largely with the microcosms of the society rather than with its macro problems. The aspects of society which seem to receive the most frequent attention can be categorized under the headings cited below.

1. Studies directed at nonpolitical youth attitudes
2. The use of leisure time
3. Women's studies
4. Investigations into specific problems of social psychology
5. Studies of specific geographic areas

All of these studies carefully avoid the major issues within the society, such as generalized investigations into the legitimacy of personalities and institutions. Occasionally there is some evidence that such studies have been undertaken but the data cited in the publications is both sparse and without special reference to the methodology or scope. For example, when figures are cited for the popularity of Czechoslovak communist presidents, neither the type of questionnaire, the questions, nor definite citations are included.

The state of survey research reflects faithfully the political climate of the country. During the 1960s, the leadership of the state tried to diagnose the ills of the society. Since 1968, the Soviet presence has imposed a return to the principal verity that the leading position of the Communist Party and its policies are not subject to public debate. This has put the mass media, the cultural scene, and survey research into a state of suspended animation. The controversial study rarely surfaces in Czechoslovakia at present, and studies that might provide hard data for dissident elements are kept under tight control. The Party and government are determined to keep its major policies beyond the reach of popular criticism, and the role which survey research played in the preceding era is far from forgotten.

NOTES

1. On Czechoslovak public opinion polling during the Prague Spring, see Jaroslav Piekalkiewicz, *Public Opinion Polling in Czechoslovakia, 1968-1969* (New York: Praeger Publishers, 1972); Zvi Y. Gitelman, "Public Opinion in Czechoslovakia," in *Public Opinion in European Socialist Systems*, ed. Walter D. Connor and Zvi Gitelman (New York & London: Praeger Publishers, 1977), pp. 83-101.
2. Some of the studies specify the type of computer utilized in the methodology chapter, which is part of all studies.
3. A typical opponents' procedure statement can be found at the conclusion of most studies. It is usually worded uniformly at the conclusion of the work.
4. Pavel Machonin, ed., *Československá společnost* (Bratislava: 1969).
5. Anna Randlíková and Iva Maříková, *Kulturní život mládeže ČSR* (Prague: Ústav pro výzkum kultúry, 1976). The prospectus lists a study about the position of television in culture compared to local cultural activity. The authors could not locate a copy.
6. Dr. Vladimir Hepner et al., *Průzkum postojů České veřejnosti ke knize a k*

jejímu šíření (Prague: Institute for Research on Cultural Questions, 1975).

7. Dr. Vladimir Hepner and Iva Maříková, *Průzkum postojů České veřejnosti k populárním zpěvákům* (Prague: Institute for Research on Cultural Questions, 1975).

8. Ibid., p. 22.

9. Ibid., p. 13.

10. M. Šimek and A. Kortunsová-Randlíková, *Postoje mládeže k výtvarnému umění* (Prague: Institute for Research on Cultural Questions, 1972).

11. Ibid., p. 51.

12. Ibid., p. 52.

13. Ibid., pp. 53-54.

14. Randlíková and Maříková, *Kulturní život mládeže ČSR*.

15. *Pracovní podmínky žen* (Pardubice: ČVTS Dům techniky Pardubice, 1977).

16. Ibid. Of the eleven articles, three are in the field of human biology, five are legal-political, and three are technical, dealing with technology which lightens the burden of women's work.

17. Helena Janišová, "Zpráva o sociologických průzkumech životního prostředí obyvatel hlavního města Prahy," *Sociologický časopis*, no. 2 (1976), pp. 224-28.

18. Josef Alan, *Společnost, vzdělání, jedinec* (Prague: Nakladatelství svoboda, 1974), p. 198.

19. Petr Matějů, "Sociologické aspekty vývoje bydlení v Praze," *Sociologický časopis*, no. 1 (1977), pp. 5-7.

20. Karel Vítek and Věra Vítková, "Několik poznatků z výzkumu 476 manželství," *Sociologický časopis*, no. 3 (1976), pp. 348-52.

21. Ladislav Pisca, "K problemom kolizii medzi hospodárskymi a materskymi funkciami žien," *Sociológia*, no. 1 (1975), pp. 55-64.

22. Jiří Prokopec, "Socialní služba KONTAKT—zkušenosti a problémy," *Sociológia*, no. 1 (1976), pp. 79-84.

23. The term "technical intelligentsia" refers to individuals who have had technical training, either in engineering or in a technical school. It does not include those active in the social sciences.

24. Prokopec, pp. 80-81.

25. Jiří Večerník, "Dynamika příjmové diferenciace v Československu," *Sociologický časopis*, no. 5 (1976), pp. 472-83.

26. Anna Koudelková, "Odlišnosti v socializačních výchovných postupech rodičů vůči chlapcům a dívkám," *Sociologický časopis*, no. 3 (1977), pp. 327-33.

27. Ibid.

28. Vladimir Hepner, *Průzkum postojů České veřejnosti k populárním zpěvákům* (Prague: Ústav pro výzkum kultúry, 1975).

29. *K některým problemům estetické výchový pracujících* (Prague: Ústav pro výzkum kultúry, 1976).

30. Ibid., p. 188.

31. Randlíková and Maříková, *Kulturní život mládeže ČSR*.

32. Ladislav Macháček, *Spoločenská aktivita pracujúcej mládeže* (Bratislava: Vydalo ideologické oddelenie SUV SZM v SMENE, 1975).

33. Ibid., p. 8.

34. Alan, *Společnost, vzdělání, jedinec.*

35. Ibid., p. 41.

36. Ibid., p. 34.

37. Ibid., p. 215.

38. Teodor Ollík and Collective, eds., *Kultúrný a spoločenský profil dedinského obyvatelstva na Slovensku* (Prague: Nakladatelství svoboda, 1974).

39. Stefan Sipovský, "Postoje, spósoby a podmienky vo vzdělavaní dedinskeho obyvatelstva," in *Kultúrný a spoločenský profil dedinského obyvatelstva na Slovensku*, eds. Teodor Ollík and Collective (Prague: Nakladatelství svoboda, 1974), p. 59.

40. Anton Jurovský, *Spokojenost s prácou a jej činitelia* (Bratislava: ALFA, 1971).

41. Ibid., p. 179.

42. A collective of researchers is a group of professionals associated in the framework of an institute or some other research organization. While a research team is usually bound together by a single project, the association of a collective is more permanent.

43. Authors collective, *Soužití pracovníků v závodech* (Pardubice: Dům techniky ČVTS Pardubice, 1975).

44. *Pracovní podmínky žen* (Hradec Králové: Federální ministerstvo práce a sociálních věcí, komise pro práci žen ve vědě a technice US ČSTS ČVTS dům techniky Pardubice, 1976).

45. Martin Katriak, "Z výsledkov monografického výskumu v obci D," *Sociológia*, no. 4 (1975), pp. 354-60.

46. Eva Křížová, "K otázce intenzity profesionální mobility ve vědě," *Sociologický časopis*, no. 2 (1975), pp. 170-75.

47. Janišová, "Zpráva o sociologických průzkumech," pp. 224-28.

48. Jiří Linhart, Vladimír Rak, and Jiří Voženílek, "Sociální aspekty ekologické zónace hlavního města Prahy," *Sociologický časopis*, no. 1 (1977), pp. 94-115.

49. Ibid., p. 113.

50. Katriak, "Z výsledkov monografického výskumu," pp. 354-60.

51. Ibid.

52. Viliam Fabry, "Volný čas obyvateľov dediny," in *Kultúrný a spoločenský profil dedinského obyvatelstva na Slovensku*, eds. Teodor Ollík and Collective (Prague: Nakladatelství svoboda, 1974), pp. 49-55.

53. Macháček, *Spoločenská aktivita pracujúcej mládeže.*

54. Ibid., p. 65.

55. P. Prusák, "Politické a morálné postoje dedinského obyvatelstva," in *Kultúrný a spoločenský profil dedinského obyvatelstva na Slovensku*, eds. Teodor Ollík and Collective (Prague: Nakladatelství svoboda, 1974), p. 41.

56. Ibid.

57. Ibid.

58. Otto Ulč, "Social Deviance in Czechoslovakia," in *Social Deviance in Eastern Europe*, ed. Ivan Volgyes (Boulder, Colorado: Westview Press, 1978), p. 24.

59. Ibid., p. 56.

60. Ibid., p. 27.

61. Vladimir Hepner, *Postoje České veřejnosti k ochraně přírodního prostředí* (Prague: Ústav pro výzkum kultúry, 1975).

62. Vladimir Hepner, *Postoje České veřejnosti ke kulturním památkám a památkove péči* (Prague: Ústav pro výzkum kultúry, 1976).

63. Hepner, *Postoje České veřejnosti k ochraně přírodního prostředí*, pp. 18-21.

64. Ibid., pp. 100-101.

65. Ibid., pp. 108-10.

66. Hepner, *Postoje České veřejnosti ke kulturním památkám a památkove péči*, pp. 94-95.

67. Katriak, "Z výsledkov monografického výskumu," pp. 354-60.

68. Prusák, "Politické a morálné postoje dedinského obyvatelstva," p. 40.

69. Ibid., p. 37.

70. Ibid., p. 39.

71. Ibid.

72. Ibid., p. 40.

5 The German Democratic Republic

Peter Christian Ludz

AN OVERVIEW OF SURVEY RESEARCH IN THE GERMAN DEMOCRATIC REPUBLIC (GDR)

Preliminary Remarks

The term "survey research" has no exact equivalent in the German language. The English "survey," as used in the social sciences, can be translated by *Erhebung*; but the term *Erhebungsforschung* is not common usage among German-speaking social scientists. From their point of view, "survey research" includes *bevölkerungsstatistische Erhebungen* (for example, various kinds of censuses), *Umfrageforschung*, a general category including *Markt- und Meinungsforschung* ("market and opinion research"), and *Wahlforschung* ("voting studies"). "Survey research" overlaps with the German *empirische Sozialforschung* ("empirical social science research") or, according to GDR usage, *soziologische Untersuchungen* ("sociological investigations"), as far as the method of *Befragung* (i.e., interviews, questionnaires) is applied and a large number of respondents is involved.

An overview of survey research in the GDR cuts across institutional and disciplinary lines. One has to include research by various university departments and by different party, party-related, and governmental institutions. Sociologists, psychologists, economists, statisticians, demographers, and members of the medical profession are involved in survey research as are various party and government functionaries. In short, survey methods are used by persons among whom hardly any institutional relationships exist. The subject matter of survey research also is disparate and includes topics such as the social position of women, time budgets and leisure time preferences, demographic problems, health matters, and traffic conditions.

In terms of methodology, social scientists in the GDR tend to be rather skeptical about surveys of opinion and about strictly quantitative methods.[1] In stressing what they call "structural questions" and "basic social processes,"[2] they reject quantitative research as such and maintain that quantitative and qualitative research cannot be separated from each other. Likewise, "empirical" surveys are regarded as forming a "unity" with "theoretical" analysis.[3] The notions of qualitative research and theoretical analysis are grounded in *Parteilichkeit* ("party-mindedness" or, in Russian "partiinost") and signal an understanding that all quantitative and/or empirical research entails a political-historical dimension. Thus, a rather strong bias against quantitative methods alone (in the Western understanding of the word) is typical. On this point, German traditions in the social sciences are consistent with the epistemological thrust of Marxism-Leninism.

Most institutions engaged in survey research belong to the realm of the *gesellschaftswissenschaftliche Forschung* ("social science research"), which is a separate, centrally steered branch of science in the GDR. The *Zentraler Forschungsplan der marxistisch-leninistischen Gesellschaftswissenschaften der DDR* ("central research plan of the Marxist-Leninist social sciences in the GDR") lists the principles and tasks of social science research and specifies areas of research.[4]

The main social science institutions involved in survey research can be grouped as they are referred to in the *Zentraler Forschungsplan* for 1976-1980.[5] The *Institut für Meinungsforschung beim Zentralkomitee der SED* (Central Committee Institute for Opinion Research of the Socialist Unity Party of Germany), headed by Helene Berg and located in East Berlin, seems to conduct surveys on a regular basis. As do the departments of the central SED apparatus, this Institute works behind closed doors. The Institute apparently conducts polls, based on representative samples of the GDR population, designed to explore various dimensions of public opinion.[6]

The *Institut für marxistisch-leninistische Soziologie* (Institute for Marxist-Leninist Sociology) at the *Akademie für Gesellschaftswissenschaften* (Academy for the Social Sciences, or AfG, formerly the Institute for the Social Sciences) at the Central Committee of the SED, located in East Berlin, concentrates on "social structure research," i.e., research on classes, strata, and other societal groups, including research in the areas of industrial, urban and rural sociology.[7] The *Akademie der Wissenschaften der DDR* (GDR Academy of Sciences or AdW) houses a number of institutes and committees which conduct surveys, among which the *Wissenschaftlicher Beirat "Die Frau in der sozialistischen Gesellschaft"* (Scientific Committee "The Woman in Socialist Society") seems to be the most active.[8] At the institutions controlled by the *Ministerium für Hoch- und Fachschulwesen* (Ministry for University and Higher Education)—the seven universities, the five technical and five other higher schools, and the three medical academies—institutes (or committees) of sociology, social psychology, demography, or social policy are engaged in survey research of one kind or another.[9]

The *Zentralinstitut für Jugendforschung* (Central Institute for Youth Research or ZfJ) in Leipzig is one of the centers of survey research and social science methodology in the GDR. It is affiliated with the *Amt für Jugendfragen beim Ministerrat der DDR* (Office for Youth at the GDR Council of Ministers), and has close ties with the *Karl-Marx-Universität Leipzig*. Its director, Walter Friedrich, together with Werner Hennig, a prominent staff member, edited the GDR's most comprehensive and sophisticated textbook on sociological methods.[10]

The organizations which direct and coordinate social science research at the above institutions are the *Wissenschaftliche Räte der gesellschaftswissenschaftlichen Forschung der DDR* ("scientific councils of social science research in the GDR"). Within the realm of social science survey research the following *Wissenschaftliche Räte* are important: the *Wissenschaftlicher Rat für soziologische Forschung* (Scientific Council for Sociological Research), located at the AfG and headed by Rudi Weidig; the *Wissenschaftlicher Rat für wirtschaftswissenschaftliche Forschung* (Scientific Council for Economic Research), located at the AdW and headed by Helmut Koziolek; the *Wissenschaftlicher Beirat "Die Frau in der sozialistischen Gesellschaft,"* located at the AdW and headed by Herta Kuhrig; the *Wissenschaftlicher Rat für Jugendforschung* (Scientific Council for Youth Research), located at the ZfJ and headed by Walter Friedrich; and the *Wissenschaftlicher Rat für Sozialpolitik und Demographie* (Scientific Council for Social Policy and Demography), located at the *Gewerkschaftshochschule "Fritz Heckert" Bernau* (Trade Union's Higher School "Fritz Heckert" in Bernau) near East Berlin.[11]

The *Wissenschaftliche Räte* were established beginning in 1968; their functions are legally codified in the resolution of the SED's Central Committee Secretariat of December 13, 1972.[12] Paralleling the *Forschungsrat* (Scientific Council), which covers the natural and technical sciences, the *Wissenschaftliche Räte* for the social sciences have consultative functions. Such consultation extends to research conceptions and submitted proposals, basic theoretical and politico-ideological questions, as well as to the results of research projects.[13] Further, the *Wissenschaftliche Räte*, numbering between 25 and 40 members and composed of scientists from all major institutions of the relevant disciplines (e.g., from sociology departments in the case of the *Wissenschaftlicher Rat für soziologische Forschung*) and representatives of the state and/or the Party, are supposed to coordinate research. They appear to play a major role in shaping the various research plans which guide the work of all research institutions. The *Wissenschaftliche Räte* also evaluate major research proposals. They prepare the decisions on planning and financing which ultimately are taken up by the SED Secretariat or Politbureau, or by the *Abteilung "Wissenschaften"* (Science Department) in the central SED apparatus. It can further be assumed that the *Wissenschaftliche Räte*, perhaps through formal but certainly through informal channels, influence the publication of research data.

Some illustration of the coordinating functions of the *Wissenschaftliche Räte* can be found in a recent GDR publication, which was edited by the *Wissenschaftlicher Beirat "Die Frau in der sozialistischen Gesellschaft"*.[14] This book makes apparent that survey data which had been gathered by different research teams at different institutions are collected at the *Wissenschaftlicher Beirat* and put together into a body of commonly available knowledge. Characteristically, the names of the actual researchers, research teams, or institutions are dropped in this process.

Other institutions engaged in survey research apparently are not directly part of the field of social science as defined by the *Zentraler Forschungsplan*,[15] although they contribute significantly to this research. The *Institut für Marktforschung* (Institute for Market Research) in Leipzig, headed by Herbert Koch, is responsible to the *Ministerium für Handel und Versorgung* (Ministry for Trade and Supply).[16] The *Zentrales Forschungsinstitut für Arbeit* (Central Research Institute for Labor), headed by Kurt Walter and located in Dresden, which contributes to research on work and the workplace,[17] is a branch of the *Staatssekretariat für Arbeit und Löhne* (State Secretariat for Labor and Wages). The *Zentrales Forschungsinstitut des Verkehrswesens der DDR* (Central Research Institute for Traffic Systems of the GDR or ZFdV) in Dresden, headed by Werner Lindner, is affiliated with the *Ministerium für Verkehrswesen* (Ministry of Transportation). It has organized several surveys, beginning in 1965.[18] In 1972, a survey involving 16 East German cities and about 6,000 respondents investigated whether (and why) East Germans use public transportation. The design for these representative surveys on transportation was worked out by the Technical University of Dresden, which also organized the field work, under the guidance of the ZFdV.[19] In 1974, it was decided that the same survey would be conducted every five years.[20]

As is the case in the Soviet Union, other ministries have organized their own "in-house" survey research in a more or less institutionalized form. Other institutes and commissions—for example, at the television and radio broadcasting stations[21]—have been set up to conduct survey research. And sociological work groups in factories use surveys to study and improve the situation of the working people.[22]

The Planning and Financing of Survey Research

Ultimately, the planning and financing of survey research in the GDR are controlled by the SED. In one way or another, the SED is involved at all stages of this research. Researchers must design their projects in accordance with the SED-authorized five-year plans which guide all research activities in the social sciences. The SED, the FDJ (Free German Youth), the FDGB (Free German Trade Union Federation) and other mass organizations keep an eye on all researchers through various channels during the periods of field work, data processing, and evaluation. Finally, the findings are checked by SED-controlled institutions.

Most survey research seems to be *Vertragsforschung* ("contractual research"). The initiating agency and a research institute sign a contract,[23] which will include, among other things, restrictions on publication or other circulation of information from the project.[24] Thus, survey research is likely to be carried out only if a need has been defined by party or state authorities. Usually these authorities finance the surveys, as far as expenses are not otherwise covered (e.g., by free use of state-owned computing centers). Individuals are not allowed to carry out surveys.[25]

The textbook on social research edited by Friedrich and Hennig highlights some specifics of the planning of social science research.[26] Although the *Verordnung über das Berichtswesen* (Decree on [Statistical] Reporting), which the textbook cites as the legal basis for social research, has been replaced by the *Verordnung über Rechnungsführung und Statistik* (Decree on Accounting and Statistics) of June 2, 1975,[27] the formal procedure has presumably remained similar. Proposals for survey research must be submitted to the *Staatliche Zentralverwaltung für Statistik* (State Central Office for Statistics or SZS) for approval.[28] The director of the research institution must notify the SZS of the project and submit a number of documents, such as 1) an outline precisely describing the project in terms of its scientific significance, the application of the findings, the nature of the sample, and the duration and the location of the investigation (accompanied by a statement declaring that the information to be gathered by the project cannot be obtained from other sources); 2) questionnaire instruments (interview schedules); 3) plans for statistical data analysis, including information on data processing methods; 4) the written consent of the state authorities to whose administrative district the respondents belong; and 5) evidence that the work plan has been coordinated with institutions potentially having interest in the project (e.g., in the case of youth problems, the *Amt für Jugendfragen beim Ministerrat der DDR*, the *Zentralrat der FDJ* [Central Board of the FDJ] and some ministries).[29]

According to another new decree, the *Anordnung über die Genehmigung und Registrierung von Berichterstattungen und über Bevölkerungsbefragungen* (Instructions on the Approval and Registration of [Statistical] Reports and on Population Surveys) of November 27, 1975, the directors of research institutes cannot send their applications directly to the SZS. Research applications rather have to be submitted either by the ministers or the heads of other governmental institutions (e.g., the director of the *Amt für Jugendfragen*), by the chairmen of the *Bezirksräte* ("district councils"), or by the President of the AdW.[30]

Since most institutions engaged in survey research have to follow this procedure,[31] the SZS is probably the most important organizational center of survey research in the GDR. Its headquarters in East Berlin and its *Bezirk* ("district") and *Kreis* ("county") branches have at their disposal complete information about the planning of past and current survey research. Moreover, if computers are being used by a research team, the SZS can exercise control over data processing through the local *Rechenzentren* (computing centers), which also store the data tapes.

The potential control by the SZS extends to the final stages of surveys.[32] However, we do not know what this potential control means in terms of actual influence on a research group's report. It does seem as if the SZS has the right to rearrange survey research findings in terms of established *Nomenklaturen* (nomenclatures) and to include them in so called *Formblätter* (printed forms)[33] to increase comparability with other studies. The director of the SZS also must see to it that the distribution of these survey findings conforms to specific, codified (but unpublished) rules of secrecy.

Individual researchers are similarly subjected to severe constraints concerning the discussion and publication of survey results. As detailed later in this chapter, all published data are filtered in various ways. For example, reports often provide only percentages, not absolute figures; or, the sampling procedure is not described. The SED apparently fears the possible effects of allowing a free flow of information to internal would-be critics or to the external "class enemy."

The Roles and Significance of Survey Research

Survey research in the GDR is a policy tool. The *Wörterbuch der marxistisch-leninistischen Soziologie* (Dictionary of Marxist-Leninist Sociology) makes this clear in treating the term *Meinungsforschung*:[34]

> Opinion research in socialism becomes a valuable tool for all *Leitungs-tätigkeit* [leadership activity]. It serves the purpose of bringing the party, the state and the people into closer contact with each other and thus improves their relationships. It facilitates the making of decisions and the preparation of resolutions and policy measures on all levels of socialist society. Opinion research helps to evaluate policy measures.

As a policy tool, survey research has three major functions: to inform the policy makers; to control, manipulate and mobilize the people; and to help the ruling party govern more effectively.

First, through its informative function, survey research supplements information gathered by the various agencies and individuals working within the network of the *Staatssicherheitsdienst* (State Security Police) and, to a certain degree, replaces crude spying techniques which were used in earlier times. Such information may be used in decision making, but it may also serve as an instrument of control, i.e., control of a policy program already implemented. For the Western analyst, it is nearly impossible to determine to what extent results from surveys have influenced decisions or policy evaluations by SED leaders. The following section attempts to provide a basis for understanding the complex processes of information gathering, decision making and policy evaluation in an authoritarian political system. But we must acknowledge that our understanding of how information is actually used is imperfect.

Second, survey research serves the purposes of political and psychological mobilization in that it involves a large number of people and impels them to respond to carefully selected questions. Usually respondents have no choice; they must answer the questions posed by an interviewer, or fill out a questionnaire given to them. Also, it can be assumed that anonymity, although formally granted, is not guaranteed—or, at least, that respondents are not convinced of their anonymity. Anticipatory responses thus seem likely; answers may not reflect actual opinions or attitudes as much as perceptions of the "correct" position.[35] This is one form of mobilization: people are expected to become conscious of the Party line and to adjust to it, while at the same time expressing their own "opinions." Mobilization through survey research has another, more explicit policy-oriented aspect. Results from surveys are used to mobilize the population for specific policy goals. For example, the published results of surveys on the circumstances of working women play down existing problems and seem intended to keep women as employees or to encourage nonworking women to join the work force.

The informative and mobilizing functions of survey research can be regarded as affecting the governmental process. Information gathered by surveys and the mobilization of the people through survey research may help the SED to rule more effectively. Further, however, there are at least a few cases in which public views gathered by surveys seem to have had a direct impact on policies; changes in television programming would be a prominent example. These cases may be of sufficient importance for us to regard this form of policy input as a third policy function of survey research.

Besides being a policy tool, survey research in the GDR may also be viewed as an area of scholarly inquiry. Although more or less party controlled, survey research offers "hiding places" for individual scholars to pursue some of their own intellectual interests. Relatedly, survey research is a field in which Western research techniques may be experimented with in relative safety. Survey research may also provide a reasonably convenient vehicle for training younger scientists and cadres in the techniques of systematic social research. On the whole, however, the policy functions of survey research clearly predominate.

In recent years, social scientists in the GDR seem increasingly to have oriented their work toward the Soviet Union. Soviet studies are being quoted and recommended as examples more often than in earlier years. At the same time, close contacts with Soviet and East European institutions and social scientists seem not to have been particularly effective in the sense of having provided empirically based explanations of common sociopolitical problems. The main reason for this shortcoming lies in the fact that meetings of Soviet and East European social scientists seem to have inner dynamics of their own. Participants tend to concentrate on problems of how to coordinate domestic and international propaganda measures or how to develop new strategies of ideological immunization. But these meetings do not appear to encourage open exchanges among experts. Staff members of empirically oriented Soviet institutes, for instance the Novosibirsk Institute of Sociology, generally are not invited to these meetings.

The Methodology of Survey Research

An assessment of the methodological quality of survey research in the GDR encounters a number of difficulties. First, as noted, survey research is not a clearly delineated field within the social sciences. At least three types of survey research, for which different methodological standards exist, can be distinguished from one another: a) market research, b) demographic, and c) sociological-psychological. A second difficulty is that East German publications often do not reveal research methods, or do so in an incomplete way. Third, especially in sociological-psychological survey research, the ideologically based mistrust by East German social scientists militates against highly quantitative research methods. Finally, the *Praxisverbundenheit* ("practice relatedness") of all East German social science research places real constraints on the use and on the reporting of more sophisticated methods.

Nevertheless, it is possible to provide an overview of the methodology of what, according to the Western understanding, can be called survey research in the GDR by describing foci, sampling approaches and techniques, methods of data analysis, and the mode of presentation of results.

Foci

The foci of all social science research are determined by the *Zentraler Forschungsplan* (see p. 243), which sets a general framework for social research and assigns major themes of research to the *Wissenschaftliche Räte* or to the research institutes. The themes are arranged in a catalogue with major categories and many subcategories. For example, in the 1976-1980 plan, the AfG and the *Wissenschaftlicher Rat für soziologische Forschung* have to treat among other topics subtheme 05.02, defined as "the development of the working class, its character and its structure." This includes, for instance, investigations on the "problems of how to gradually overcome the major differences between blue-collar and white-collar work or between urban and rural structures."[36] This clearly is a major theme of research. Rudi Weidig et al., in an article summarizing East German sociological research efforts, identify two areas of concentration: the "dialectical relationship between the working class and the class of cooperative farmers," and "the development of socialist personalities."[37]

This statement illustrates the focus of East German social research on "structural questions," which in Marxist-Leninist terms refer to "society as a whole." Such a conception apparently requires the researcher to include the current sociopolitical situations, historical conditions, and future (utopian) developments in the research design. The methodological problems thereby raised are complicated because this posture implies a need to combine quantitative and qualitative methods of data gathering and analysis. Friedrich and Hennig refer to this methodological position in stressing the "dialectical conception of the transitions from the quantitative to the qualitative."[38] On the one hand, such formulations are critical of strictly positivist Western social scientists, such as George A. Lundberg and Paul F. Lazarsfeld. On the other hand, this position opens the way for Marxist-Leninist social scientists to use quantitative methods. For example, Friedrich and Hennig define "index" as a "combination of the quantitative properties of a quality which expresses itself in different ways."[39] They apparently would agree with the statement that "there are no appearances which cannot be translated into quantitative terms"[40]—and, we might add, re-translated into qualitative terms. The difficulty with this otherwise reasonable methodological position is that it is entangled with Marxist-Leninist ideology which imposes certain value-laden concepts and severely restricts the logic by which one can move between quantitative and qualitative realms.

Another implication of the emphasis on "structural questions" is *Praxis-verbundenheit*. Research is to be relevant or "concrete" in terms of sociopolitical practice; it is applied research in a rather strict sense. One of its major tasks is to provide *Kennziffern* ("indicators") for social planning by the Party and the state. Notwithstanding the methodological problems of developing social indicators,[41] their applicability in bringing about sociopolitical changes (including changes, for instance, in the behavior of school teachers or in the management of a people's-owned enterprise) occupies a prominent place in survey research in East Germany.[42] The importance of this aspect of research also is indicated by the frequent use of such terms as *Praxisanalyse* (analysis of practice)[43] and *Wirkungsanalyse* (analysis of effects).[44]

Apparently for ideological reasons, East German survey research focuses on workers and cooperative farmers and declares them to be representative of society as a whole. A comprehensive view of social class structure is not attempted. Indeed, East German social scientists argue that class distinctions no longer exist in the GDR, but admit that "social differentiations" do.[45] This rendering is helpful when, for instance, the existence of the intelligentsia under socialism has to be explained, or when the living conditions of such disadvantaged social groups as shift workers or working mothers are investigated.

Sampling Approaches and Techniques

It is sometimes difficult to distinguish between social science surveys and statistical surveys, since both may use questionnaires to gather data and both presume large numbers of respondents selected in some reasonably systematic way. A possible criterion of distinction is that statistical surveys do not collect attitudinal ("subjective") data. However, this distinction is not clean, since social science surveys may well collect "objective" data, for example in leisure time or media habits research. The close relationship between survey research and statistics is acknowledged by East German social scientists.[46] The statistical methods of sampling are treated by referring to established West German authors, especially Oskar Anderson and Hans Kellerer.[47] However, we do not know to what extent or how carefully this theoretical knowledge is applied in actual research work.[48] For example, authors usually maintain that their samples fulfill the requirements of (statistical) representativeness, but no survey reviewed in this report provides enough information for the reader to judge whether or not this is true.

In the GDR, survey research encompasses a) *wissenschaftliche Befragung* (scientific questioning),[49] i.e., interviewer questioning and mailed (or otherwise distributed) questionnaires, and b) *Dokumenten- und Aktenstudium* (evaluation of documents and files). All these techniques receive comprehensive treatment in Friedrich and Hennig's textbook on survey research; the last-named, however, is outside usual Western notions of survey research, and is not represented among the studies reported in this chapter.

East German survey research often focuses on rather small samples of respondents. Within the realm of sociological-psychological survey research, we have found no study which claims representativeness for GDR society as a whole. Representative studies of larger parts of the population may be more difficult because of the bureaucratic procedures set up by the SED for the planning, financing, and conduct of surveys.

Methods of Data Analysis

Judging from studies published during 1975-1977, the most commonly used method of data analysis is the counting of frequencies (including percentage calculations). In most cases it remains unclear whether these simple numerical findings have been subjected to statistical test procedures.[50] More sophisticated statistical methods are known,[51] but apparently applied only in rare cases. Examples of correlation, regression, and factor analysis can be found.[52] Scaling methods also are used with some frequency. They are extensively discussed in theory,[53] and have been used often in youth research.[54]

The demands of *Praxisverbundenheit* can be met only if comparability of the data across studies is achieved. In market research and in youth research, East German social scientists seem to work with an established set of questions which they use repeatedly in order to establish trends. On the whole, however, efforts to obtain an increasing amount of comparable data seem to run counter to the instincts of some Party officials who fear that such systematic accumulation of evidence could make socioeconomic and political problems in society too transparent.

Mode of Presentation

Frequency data and scaling data, if published at all, usually appear in the form of tables or charts, or may simply be mentioned in the text. Over the years, East German social scientists (or the political functionaries who check all manuscripts before publication) have achieved considerable skill in publishing data without saying too much. Subsequent sections of this chapter provide examples which illustrate and attempt to explain this characteristic feature of survey research in the GDR.

THE ORIENTATION OF THIS STUDY

In the GDR, survey research is a widely acknowledged tool of data collection, data evaluation and social planning, although it is not a formally established branch of the social sciences. Hence, surveys cover all of the ten topics targeted in this study, albeit in different ways.

On the topic of politics and ideology as well as on ethnicity and foreign culture, survey data are classified. They are unavailable to the Western scholar and can be treated only briefly here. The subjects of moral preferences and life aspirations, and social problems and social policy have not been the direct object of survey research during the period of this report, but they have been investigated within the range of studies on the media, women, youth, working people, and leisure time. In addition, particularly for social problems and social policy, a rich literature (based partly on statistical evidence) is available. Thus, whereas scarcity of information is responsible for the brief treatment of politics and ethnicity, coverage of the other two topics has to be based on a selective handling of the abundant available materials.

This chapter tries to cover the remaining topics as comprehensively as possible, given limitations of space. Through the footnotes and tables, the reader interested in more detail on specific topics may find guidance to pursue these questions further.

Our report on survey research in the German Democratic Republic is based on a variety of sources. The relevant GDR periodicals treating social issues have been examined systematically. They are:

Berufsbildung
Deutsche Zeitschrift für Philosophie
Einheit
Für Dich
Marktforschung
Neue Deutsche Presse
Neue Justiz
Staat und Recht
Statistische Praxis
Wirtschaftswissenschaft

In addition, the various scientific journals issued regularly (usually quarterly) by East German universities have been consulted. For individual topics more specific journals have been included, such as the *Zeitschrift für die gesamte Hygiene und ihre Grenzgebiete*. Coverage of newspapers and periodicals has been effected through a topical search of the systematic catalogue at the *DDR-Archiv und Bibliothek* (GDR Archives and Library) of the *Zentralinstitut für sozialwissenschaftliche Forschung* (Central Institute for Social Science Research or ZSF) at the Free University of Berlin. Concerning the monograph literature, the library services of the ZSF and of the *Archiv und Bibliothek* of the *Gesamtdeutsches Institut/Bundesanstalt für gesamtdeutsche Aufgaben* (All-German Institute/ Federal Agency for All-German Tasks) in Bonn have been utilized. Both libraries have a systematic catalogue. All publications of the *Schriftenreihe "Soziologie"* have been considered in this study. The series is edited by the *Wissenschaftlicher Rat für soziologische Forschung*. Unfortunately, only a few of the unpublished doctoral dissertations ordered through inter-German library services could be obtained.

In addition to sources from the GDR, relevant West German reference books, monograph literature, and periodicals were consulted.

Limitations on the availability of survey studies, together with the substantive and methodological vagueness of much of what is published, influence the nature of this chapter. Often it has been necessary to combine survey data with information from other, nonsurvey sources in order to provide even reasonably adequate treatment of our targeted topics. More than is the case with most chapters in this volume, this summary must rely in part on the researcher's inferences and judgments. The results of this process are findings which may strike some readers as being indeterminate, especially methodologically. These limitations notwithstanding, the available evidence seems at least marginally adequate to attempt evaluations of the state of the art in survey research, the significance of survey research, and what survey research tells us about certain aspects of societal change in East Germany.

SURVEYS OF PUBLIC ATTITUDES AND BEHAVIOR IN THE GDR

Media Habits

The media situation in East Germany is different from that in other East European countries because the East German media must compete with the two West German television stations and a number of Western radio stations, such as *Deutschlandfunk, RIAS Berlin, Sender Freies Berlin, Norddeutscher Rundfunk, Westdeutscher Rundfunk, Hessischer Rundfunk, Bayerischer Rundfunk, Radio Luxemburg, Europawelle Saar, Südfunk Stuttgart,* and the BBC (which, at specific hours, broadcasts in the German language). It is estimated in the West that West German television and radio broadcasts reach about 90 percent of the GDR population and that up to 40 percent turn on West German stations every day or every night. On the other hand, GDR citizens have almost no access to West German newspapers, magazines, and journals.

Competition between East and West German electronic media makes the situation in the GDR more complex than in other East European countries. The SED propagandists have to confront the "class enemy" on a much more practical basis. After SED General Secretary Erich Honecker stated in 1973 that East Germans were free to turn on West German stations,[55] and after the SED permitted West German color television sets to be purchased by GDR citizens or acquired as gifts,[56] the producers of television and radio programs in the GDR and the Party officials who control their activities have made refined efforts to win over GDR audiences to their own productions and to denigrate West German broadcasts.

The *Staatliches Rundfunkkomitee* (State Radio Committee) supervises five radio programs (*Radio DDR I, Radio DDR II, Stimme der DDR, Berliner Rundfunk, Radio Berlin International*), and the *Staatliches Komitee für Fernsehen* (State Committee for Televised Broadcasting) is responsible for two television stations. These stations are called upon to give attention to "contact with the masses" through audience research. Such research is carried out not only to evaluate media habits and preferences, but also to contribute to what might be called audience mobilization. By questioning people about their reactions to specific programs, or by inviting them to write to the stations, the SED intends to mobilize the people in the sense of stimulating them to attend specific programs, and more generally, to view or listen to GDR stations rather than those in West Germany. Thus, audience research in the GDR extends beyond survey research in the strict sense; it includes the evaluation of listeners' letters, of discussion panels organized by the stations, and of responses by listeners to questions that have been broadcast.

In the 1960s, the *Staatliches Rundfunkkomitee* and the *Staatliches Komitee für Fernsehen* seem to have established their own social research divisions that were responsible for surveys and for the evaluation of listeners' responses. It is known that the work of these departments was influential in the major changes made in January, 1972, in GDR television programming. A survey of 10,000 listeners conducted in 1971 apparently provided data about media habits and preferences of the GDR population.[57]

During the period 1975-1977, sources available in the West provide no evidence of any surveys of television habits comparable to the 1971 study. However, a broad spectrum of measures is used to explore the habits and preferences of GDR audiences. Concerning television broadcasting and its impact, a number of survey-like research techniques are employed. First, approximately 1,000 persons are questioned on a weekly basis about their reactions to television programs.[58] For each survey, a new sample is selected from files kept by the GDR Postmaster-General.[59] Second, *Foren* (roundtable talks) are held regularly (once or twice a month) at which representatives of the television stations discuss questions raised by viewers, mainly Party officials, union representatives, or delegates from various other institutions (e.g., industrial firms or universities). Similar roundtables are organized by the staff of specific programs, e.g., the program *"Umschau,"*[60] or the news program *"Aktuelle Kamera."* In 1976, an average of 50 roundtables per month were held; this compares with only 10 such discussions each month in 1972.[61]

Third, GDR television broadcasts so-called pilot or model programs which afterwards are discussed with the audiences addressed. Fourth, polls sometimes are taken immediately after a program has been broadcast. In 1975, 33 of these *Sofortumfragen* ("on-the-spot polls") were conducted.[62] Fifth, comments mailed or telephoned by television listeners serve television authorities as a source of information about media habits and preferences. Finally, in a live studio feature, the chairman of the *Staatliches Komitee für Fernsehen* sometimes answers questions submitted by viewers.

According to official statistics of 1975, GDR television stations conducted 240 roundtables with members of radio and television audiences (in which 24,167 citizens took part), took 8,374 polls in workshops, and received

1,093,144 contributions (by mail) from audience members.[63]

Radio audience research seems to be less developed, but it serves the same purposes as research on television habits. Here mailed and telephoned comments are the major source of information.[64] The chairman of the *Staatliches Rundfunkkomitee*, Rudolf Singer, has reported that East German radio stations received mailed or telephoned comments from approximately 480,000 listeners in 1971, 850,000 in 1973, and 2 million in 1975. These figures suggest that GDR audiences are responsive to media stimuli, and that responsiveness has increased. This is in line with other findings indicating that over the years, and particularly after the signing of the Final CSCE Act, the population has played a more active part in the public life of the GDR. However, the quality of this responsiveness is hard to evaluate. We do not know what sorts of listeners write to radio stations, and we are not told what opinions they expressed.

This vagueness results from the fact that the social research units of the media and other institutions have published almost none of their results.[65] Further, Western research on the GDR has more or less neglected this area. For example, no study has so far been designed to investigate systematically the letters-to-the-editor in various East German publications. Although it can safely be assumed that many of these letters are written (or ghostwritten, or checked) by Party functionaries or mass organization officials, they nevertheless constitute a considerable quantity of materials from which information about attitudes and preferences of the GDR population could be gathered.

Although detailed data are lacking,[66] some general facts concerning the media habits of the East German population seem to be fairly well established. Media habits in the GDR correspond to a specific pattern of leisure-time activities. We know from many sources that East Germans tend to spend a great deal of their leisure time at home.[67] It can be assumed that many turn on their televisions every evening. There is at least one mass medium—television, radio or the press—which reaches nearly every adult citizen in the GDR every day. Singer asserts that "people of all age groups spend an average of 118 minutes per day, or 26 more minutes than eight years ago, listening to radio alone. On the whole, [an individual's] involvement with press publications and radio and television programs takes about 27 hours per week."[68] In other words, the average GDR citizen is occupied almost four hours per day with reading the papers and listening to radio and television broadcasts. Younger and older people tend to devote less time to the electronic media than do middle-aged people (see table 5.1).

Another factor determining television habits is the rhythm of working and leisure-time hours. Work life in the GDR seems to be more demanding and extends to longer hours than in the West. Thus, East Germans are known to go to bed in the early evening hours. According to the 1971 survey, only 7 percent of the population are still watching television by 10 p.m.

Furthermore, the social stratum to which an individual belongs, as well as his or her political orientation, are pertinent to television habits (see table 5.2). There are two more or less clear-cut groups of GDR audiences: those who hear

Table 5.1. Age Structure of Television Viewers, 1973
(percentages)

Age Group	Television Viewers
14-17 years old	9.6
18-25 years old	10.0
26-35 years old	20.5
36-45 years old	21.5
46-55 years old	15.9
56-65 years old	16.2
66-75 years old	5.2
Older than 75 years	1.1

Source: *Informationen über das Fernsehen der DDR.* Quoted in Heide Riedel, *Hörfunk und Fernsehen in der DDR: Funktion, Struktur und Programm des Rundfunks in der DDR,* ed. Deutsches Rundfunk-Museum (Cologne: Literarischer Verlag Helmut Braun, 1977), p. 131.

Table 5.2. Social Structure of Television Viewers, 1973
(percentages)

Social Class /Stratum	Television Viewers
Workers	33
Employees	27
Intelligentsia	4
Other social strata	2
Pupils, trainees, students	11
Agricultural vocations	4
Nonemployed people (housewives, pensioners)	19

Source: *Informationen über das Fernsehen der DDR.* Quoted in Heide Riedel, *Hörfunk und Fernsehen in der DDR: Funktion, Struktur und Programm des Rundfunks in der DDR,* ed. Deutsches Rundfunk-Museum (Cologne: Literarischer Verlag Helmut Braun, 1977), pp. 130 ff.

and/or watch Western broadcasts and those who don't. Among those who tune to West German television and radio stations more or less regularly, two groups may again be distinguished: a rather small group of those who are looking for additional, particularly political information, and another much more numerous group of those who are interested in learning the details of Western living standards or in receiving entertainment that is not designed to serve SED purposes.[69]

It seems clear that East German audiences want to be entertained in the evening, and not educated. In this respect East German programs compare unfavorably with those transmitted by West German stations. As one television official put it: "We need more looseness, hilarity, and amusement."[70] In addition, GDR audiences seem to like broadcasts that provide everyday information, e.g., on new records and new books,[71] or on household machines and products.[72] To a certain extent, the SED seems to comply with these wishes. The changes of the program structure in 1975, as compared with the situation in 1973, may be interpreted as reflecting some SED adaptation to citizens' preferences (see table 5.3).

Family and Women

The SED's attitude toward the family is ambivalent. On the one hand, the family is praised as the nucleus—"the smallest cell"—of society and thus acknowledged as a factor for societal stability. On the other hand, the family is partially deprived of its stabilizing functions through a complex of labor market, family, and educational policies.

Neither the actual situation of families in the GDR nor the influence of policy measures on the family structure are investigated as such. However, they are indirect objects of all empirical research on the role of women in society and on attitudes and behavior of children and youth.

Women are one of the most researched social groups in East German society. This is initially the result of ideological motivations. East German sources repeatedly cite Karl Marx to the effect that social progress can be evaluated in part by looking at the degree of emancipation of women.[73] But interest in women as a subject of empirical research also has pragmatic grounds: Women are urgently needed as members of the work force.[74] Further, women are regarded as being more gullible than men and more spontaneous in their reactions and thus more susceptible to empirically derived propaganda measures.

All empirical research on women deals in some way with the dual role of women, those who work full or part time and are also housewives and/or mothers. Of the total work force in the GDR, which numbered 8,550,900 in 1977, approximately half (4,032,700) were women who worked full or part time.[75] Compared with other countries, this is a rather high percentage. For in-

Table 5.3. Structure of Television Programming, 1973 and 1975

Program Content	Percent of total broadcast time	
	1973[a]	1975[b]
Information on current events	13.0	12.3
Communication (reports, documentaries, features, investigations)	9.5	16.0
Drama (television movies/plays, motion picture films)	34.5	28.5
Entertainment (music, dance, etc.)	10.5	14.0
Sports	13.5	10.0
Broadcasts for children and youth	9.0	6.5
Education	8.0	4.7
Others (advertisement, miscellaneous)	2.0	8.0

[a]Total broadcast time was 126 hours per week (first program) and 31 hours per week (second program).

[b]Total broadcast time was 133 hours per week (first program) and 73 hours per week (second program).

Source: Fernsehen der DDR, ed., *Informationen über das Fernsehen der DDR* (Potsdam, 1974); *30 Jahre Film- und Fernsehkunst der DDR: Katalog der Ausstellung im Museum für deutsche Geschichte vom 26.3. bis 23.5.1976.* Quoted in Heide Riedel, *Hörfunk und Fernsehen in der DDR: Funktion, Struktur und Programm des Rundfunks in der DDR,* ed. Deutsches Rundfunk-Museum (Cologne: Literarischer Verlag Helmut Braun, 1977), p. 85.

stance, in the Federal Republic of Germany fewer than 40 percent of the total work force are women. In the GDR, almost 80 percent of all women aged 15 to 60 (considered working age) were employed in 1977.[76] This has obvious consequences for family structure: In most East German families the mother or housewife leaves the house to work. The percentage of working women seems to be higher for the 20- to 50-year-old age group than for those over 50 years, even though a relatively high percentage of women who have reached retirement age are still working.[77]

GDR statisticians have not provided figures about family size for some time. From earlier sources[78] we know that the small family—composed of father, mother, and one or two children—dominates in the GDR. Family sociologists in the GDR perceive a general tendency towards a one-child family at present.[79] The GDR clearly has a population-growth problem. It is the only Comecon country with a declining population.[80]

Survey research on the working woman has covered a wide range of family-related topics. For the period 1975-77, the following topics can be identified: 1) the working woman's time budget, 2) women's motives for taking a job, 3) their motives for interrupting a career, 4) the development of children raised in day-care institutions, 5) the school performance of children of working mothers, and 6) the physical well-being of the working woman. There is also one study (results published in 1978) which focuses on the family life of shift workers.[81]

Time-budget studies undertaken by the *Institut für Marktforschung* in 1965 and 1970[82] have discovered that, on the average, women spend 37.1 hours per week with housekeeping. Full-time working women spend 30.8 hours, whereas part-time working women use 40.2 hours. Predictably, nonworking women spend more time on housekeeping: 51.5 hours on the average. This information was confirmed by Eva-Maria Elsner in separate research.[83] Few additional details on how women spend their time are provided. It does appear that there are fewer members in the households of full-time working women, especially fewer small children, than in the households of nonworking women. No doubt working women have less leisure time than do men (and, of course, than do nonworking women), although men contribute their part in housekeeping. The average family of four persons requires 47.1 hours of housekeeping work per week, approximately 79 percent of which is done by the woman.[84] In general, East German research wholly neglects nonworking women; they seem to be regarded as a relic of bourgeois times. The main concern is how to improve the conditions of working women. Although social scientists in the GDR have been studying the problem of how social-policy measures can reduce the time for housekeeping work (e.g., more, better and cheaper household appliances; communal feeding; laundry and cleaning services), they have not been able to suggest satisfactory solutions.[85]

Why do women leave the household to work? The sociology subdivision of the Section for Economics at the *Martin-Luther-Universität Halle-Wittenberg* took a poll on this topic.[86] The majority (51.9 percent) of the respondents answered that, in the first place, they wanted to contribute to the economic development of the country. At the same time, they indicated that they needed the money. The fact that working establishes new social contacts was mentioned by 35.1 percent of the respondents. GDR sociologists view these findings from the perspective of whether idealistic or materialistic motives prevail. Ingrid Hölzler, who provided the data above, holds that idealistic and materialistic motives are of equal priority. By contrast, Anneliese Sälzler and Liselotte Hinze maintain that, according to their investigations, the majority of women aged 20 to 35 years "pursue an occupational career mainly out of idealistic motives."[87]

Whatever the motivation, it seems clear that about 50 percent of the women of working age (15 to 60 years) do not want to be only housewives.[88] It should be noted that such data have ideological connotations. Women of working age who would prefer to work only part time or to look after their households full time are regarded as still adhering to traditional, antisocialist values.

The main problem for working mothers is how to get appropriate day care for their children. This problem exists in the East and West alike. In the GDR, an increasing number of state-owned *Kinderkrippen* (literally, "child's cradles," or "crèches") for infants through three years of age have been established, most of which are day-care institutions (see table 5.4). In 1975, 45 percent of all infants through three years of age were in crèches. In 1975, 82 percent of preschool children were in kindergartens, whereas 70 percent of school children in the first through fourth grades attended *Schulhorte* (school nurseries).[89] Although the number of these institutions is relatively large, there is still a deficiency of appropriate day care for infants and preschool and school children. This can be gathered from research reported by Herta Kuhrig, the chairwoman of the *Forschungsgruppe "Die Frau in der sozialistischen Gesellschaft"* at the AdW. Asked why they have interrupted or would interrupt a career, the women replied that the main reason was or would be the lack of appropriate day care for their children.[90]

Further themes of major concern for GDR social scientists are the mental and emotional development of infants raised in day-time crèches and the school performance of children whose mothers are working outside the home. Members of the *Institut für Hygiene des Kindes- und Jugendalters* (Institute for the Hygiene of Children and Youth), which is controlled by the *Ministerium für Gesundheitswesen* (Ministry for Health Affairs), carried out a comprehensive study in 1971-1974 involving 70 crèches (of a total of more than 5,000) and roughly 6,000 infants. They also questioned approximately 1,500 parents whose infants were in crèches under investigation.[91] The principal finding of the study was that the influence from the family, on the one hand, and the nurses working in the crèches, on the other, cannot be separated from one another. It was also discovered that family social background, especially the parents' educational and vocational level, largely determines a child's development. Thus, according to Zwiener and others, "the higher the mother's educational level, the better the

Table 5.4. Day-Care Services for Infants and Preschool Children, 1975–77

	Infants[a] receiving care				Preschool children[b] receiving care		
Year	in (day-time) crèches	in permanent infant homes	in seasonal homes	per 1,000 infants	in (day-time) kindergartens and weekly homes	in seasonal institutions	per 1,000 children
	(in Kinderkrippen)	*(in Dauerheimen)*	*(in Saisonkrippen)*		*(in Kindergärten und Wochenheimen)*	*(in Saison-einrichtungen)*	
1975	234,941	5,743	1,869	508	693,163	8,238	845
1976	243,775	5,529	1,195	570	671,281	5,279	874
1977	251,856	5,237	897	601	638,767	3,424	892

[a]Infants, 0-2 years old.
[b]Children, 3-6 years old.

Source: *Statistisches Jahrbuch 1978*, pp. 334, 284.

child's development."[92] Whether or not a child belongs to a complete family, i.e., a mother and father living together, has less influence. The book edited by Eva Schmidt-Kolmer seems to conclude that crèche infants are disadvantaged compared to infants reared entirely at home. However, the authors maintain that appropriate policy measures can solve the existing problems.

Concerning the school performance of children of working mothers, Anneliese Sälzler has studied 1,200 fifth-grade children from 15 *Polytechnische Oberschulen* (Polytechnical high schools) in "a large city."[93] The survey reportedly demonstrates that the employment of mothers has no significant influence on the performance of children in school.

Finally, the physical well-being of working women has been a topic of survey research during 1975-77. The *Institut für Sozialhygiene der Medizinischen Akademie Magdeburg* (Institute for Social Hygiene of the Medical Academy in Magdeburg) organized a survey in which the work and family circumstances of about 3,600 women were investigated. The project began in 1969 with interviews on the basis of standardized questionnaires.[94] In another study, health attitudes of women living in the cities were compared with those of a rural female population.[95] Questions concerning birth control were the focus of another survey-like study.[96] The most interesting result from the Magdeburg studies is that women working in the *Landwirtschaftliche Produktionsgenossenschaften* (agricultural cooperatives) and living in the countryside are in better health than the city women, although the workload of the rural women is usually higher.[97] In addition, a relationship between personal health and the amount of leisure time of women living in cities seems to have been established; less leisure time means more health problems.[98]

Taken together, these bits of information yield some valuable conclusions. In the GDR, the family typically does not mirror the traditional pattern of the German family. Traditionally, the mother stays at home, keeps the house, nurses the children, and cares for the well-being of her husband who, as a rule, earns the money outside of the house. By contrast, the family structure in the GDR is substantially influenced by the fact that both the woman and the man usually work outside the home. This change reflects a general tendency in all industrialized countries. But there are some particular features of the East German situation. The proportion of women employed is higher than in other industrial countries in Western or Eastern Europe. The extensive daytime care of infants, preschool children, and early-grade pupils by state-run institutions is a specific feature of GDR society. More than in the West, each family member in the GDR is put into different social reference groups.[99] Thus, the family as a group needs more cohesive strength to survive.

The overall pattern does vary with the income of the father, the education of the parents, and other social factors.[100] For example, families in which one or both parents are shift workers (or employees) constitute a specific group within the overall pattern.[101]

If the mother's inclusion in the work force causes a destabilizing effect on the family, this should be observable in the GDR. The surveys reviewed for this report provide at least indirect hints that the new family is a less stable social unit than the traditional family. One indicator of this is the sheer number of studies that concentrate on working women and children reared by families with both parents employed. Another measure may be the demands made by all researchers that the situation of working women be improved. To these indirect indicators, statistical evidence may be added. The divorce rate in the GDR is very high (see table 5.5), and the number of babies born to unmarried mothers continues to increase over the years (see table 5.6).

The new family propagated by the SED has not yet fully emerged.[102] Now as before, men and women alike are thinking and acting in accordance with some traditional patterns of family life (e.g., housekeeping is considered a woman's affair). Thus, women who work and have a family carry a double burden, and they have less opportunity than do men to develop their personal faculties.

Nevertheless, the structure of the family is in flux. Even the role of the father in the family may be changing. According to Rosemarie Walther, who works at the Section Pedagogics at *Humboldt-Universität*, the father is becoming more involved in the education of his children and spends more of his leisure time with them.[103] This holds for families with small children. Older children, although living together with their fathers and mothers, become increasingly involved in a variety of youth activities and tend to be increasingly integrated into a distinct social stratum of youth.

The various disintegrative and integrative forces that work on the East German family have not been the focus of survey research. Rather, the surveys reviewed here are designed to serve a distinct policy purpose—to improve circumstances for working women so as to help them carry their double burden and to keep them (or win them over) as members of the work force.[104]

Education and Youth

The situation of young people in the GDR has long been a field of study for GDR *Jugendforscher* (youth researchers) and for West German social scientists doing comparative East-West German research.[105] There are two principal reasons for the prominence of youth research in the GDR. First, in terms of both Marxist-Leninist ideology and the SED's social strategy, the young people regarded as the future generation deserve special attention. The reshaping of socialist society depends fundamentally on the values adopted by youth. Young people must receive special consideration from the Party and its mass organizations so as to counterbalance assumed bourgeois or reactionary influences from the family and other sources. The SED policy toward the young shows itself in both extensive support and encompassing control. Youth research is an instru-

Table 5.5. Divorces, 1975–77

| Year | Divorces | |
	Number	Rate per 10,000 population
1975	41,632	24.7
1976	44,803	26.7
1977	43,034	25.7

Source: *Statistisches Jahrbuch 1978*, p. 363.

Table 5.6. Legitimate and Illegitimate Births, 1974–76

| Year | Live and dead infants, born to | |
	married mothers	unmarried mothers
1974	151,108	29,480
1975	153,639	29,590
1976	164,952	31,969

Source: *Statistisches Jahrbuch 1978*, p. 366.

ment used by the SED in pursuing this policy goal. Second, as a practical matter of field research, young people, especially those who are still in school, are more accessible than is the rest of the population.

Youth researchers in the GDR define youth in accordance with the *Jugendgesetz der DDR* (Youth Law) of 1974. "Youth" comprises all GDR citizens aged 14 through 25 years.[106] In 1977 this group numbered 3,253,419 individuals, or 19.4 percent of the population (see table 5.7). In the early 1960s, the students who attended the *Allgemeine polytechnische Oberschulen* (general polytechnical high schools), the *Erweiterte Oberschulen* ("extended" high schools), and the *Berufsschulen* (vocational schools) were prominent objects of research.[107] Since the middle of the 1960s, the emphasis has shifted to include two additional groups, university and higher school students and young workers.[108] However, survey research on youth continues to concentrate on younger (prehigher school or preuniversity) students.[109]

Since 1966, the institutional center of youth research in the GDR has been the *Zentralinstitut für Jugendforschung* (ZfJ) in Leipzig. Its director, Professor Walter Friedrich, and most staff members are psychologists by training. Consequently, publications by members of the institute display a basically psychological orientation. However, youth research in the GDR is conceived to be interdisciplinary. Besides psychology, it includes pedagogy, sociology, economics, and demography.

The ZfJ is required by law[110] to investigate "the conditions and regularities of the development of young people and of socialist youth education" for the specific purposes of providing assistance to all those who implement socialist youth policy measures, and of supporting the FDJ in its work. This official task defines the institute as a policy-oriented institution under direct political control of the FDJ (and thus the SED). Since youth research is viewed as one *Forschungsrichtung* (research approach) within the broad field of Marxist-Leninist social sciences, youth researchers in the GDR must accept certain ideological preconceptions, e.g., the notions that social classes in socialist societies are disappearing and that a gradual rapprochement of classes and strata is already typical of East German society. Moreover, the research plans of youth researchers must be brought into line with the SED's or FDJ's policy intentions. Thus in a sense they are enmeshed in a frustrating mix of wishful thinking and reality-based constraints. This ideologically-based entanglement may make the understanding of certain aspects of reality more difficult; it also affects one's methodological approach.

Nevertheless, Walter Friedrich and his staff have established acceptable scientific standards for the work of the institute. Friedrich has implied that there are difficulties in maintaining a balance between scientific and political acceptability, as when he notes that, "Like all scientific research, youth research does not aim directly, but indirectly, towards providing an orientation for practical politics. . .."[111]

From literature published in 1975-77, we gather that empirical youth research at the ZfJ covers the following subject areas: 1) youth and socialist ideology; 2) youth and work, or the personality development of the working youth; 3) youth and (academic) education, or the personality development of students; 4) youth and (nonacademic) education, or the personality development of *Schüler* and *Lehrlinge*; 5) youth, mass communication, and leisure time; and 6) youth and the family.[112] It appears as if all of these subject areas have been investigated through survey methods (as well as other empirical methods), although only a few studies are treated in the literature available to us.

We have found reports about surveys or survey-like studies on two main topics: the attitude of young people towards marriage and the family, and leisure-time activities of youth. Other specific research topics included the political and ideological attitudes of apprentices,[113] the sports activities of the younger generation,[114] the moral consciousness of selected youth groups,[115] and the attitude of young people toward health matters.[116] However, we should emphasize that surveys are only one research tool among others used by the staff of the ZfJ and by other teams of individuals who engage in youth research. Experiments as well as other methods of personality and small group research are used as well.[117]

Studies on youth attitudes concerning marriage and the family have yielded some interesting results. First, the attitudes of young people on marriage and the family still conform closely to those of their parents. Parental influences are greater than those of mass organizations, for example. Asked whether their parents provided the *Leitbilder* (examples) for their own relationships to their (imagined) husbands and children, more than 84 percent of the young people questioned in a study by Rolf Borrmann and Joachim Schille[118] indicated that their views corresponded fully or in part to those of their parents.

Second, most young people have a positive attitude towards marriage as a social institution and feel that it is the most appropriate basis for men and women to live together. This finding is reported by Erika Sommer in an interview given to the magazine *Für Dich*. It is one of the results of a survey carried out by the Law Section of the *Humboldt-Universität zu Berlin*[119] of 3,200 unmarried men and women aged 16-17 and 19-20 years. Among other questions, the respondents were asked whether or not they regarded marriage as the appropriate institution for living together with the opposite sex; 86 percent responded positively. Approximately 90 percent said that living together without being married was not a possible alternative to marriage for them. Similarly, 90 percent of the respondents said they intended to marry. At the same time, this high level of support for the institution of marriage was not accompanied by a wholly negative attitude toward divorce. Nearly 25 percent of the respondents said they would not regard divorce as a disaster.[120]

Third, nearly all (in this study, 98 percent) young East German men and women apparently believe that a married couple should have children. Sommer informs us that 74 percent of the respondents wanted two children of their own and 13 percent desired three children.[121] These findings have to be viewed against the background of the SED's concerted efforts to increase population growth. Thus, "correct" responses were easy to anticipate; this may have influenced the results. However, attitudes expressed at this rather early age may have questionable relevance to behavior at an older age.

Fourth, most of the sampled groups felt that women should not have to stop working after a reasonable standard of living had been established for the family. However, in East Germany—as elsewhere in Eastern Europe—there are modest differences of opinion between male and female respondents on this issue. Although 88 percent of the young women felt that a woman should be able to continue working outside the home, only 78 percent of the young men agreed.[122]

These four general findings, reported by Sommer, match the results of a survey carried out by the ZfJ involving 1,109 married women and men aged 18 to 28.[123] For example, the young couples definitely have not cut their ties with their parents. Eighty-four percent acknowledge the help of their parents (and 73 percent, of their parents-in-law) in handling daily chores. Concerning attitudes towards divorce, Pinther and his associates confirm that early marriages are particularly endangered during the second to fourth year.[124] The most frequently mentioned reasons for marital conflicts were bad housing conditions, addiction to alcohol or other drugs, disturbed relations to parents or parents-in-law, sexual incompatibility, lack of thriftiness, and insufficient sense of order.[125]

With regard to the number of children desired by young men and women, Pinther's results differ to some extent from those reported by Sommer. While the percentage of those who want no children is equally low (3 percent in Pinther's, 2 percent in Sommer's study), the percentages of those who want one or two children are substantially different. In Pinther's survey, approximately one-third of the respondents who want children at all intend to have only one child, approximately two-thirds want two children, and only 3 percent plan to have three children. Pinther concludes that, "as a rule, the one- or two-child family has emerged."[126]

A mainly positive attitude toward continued women's employment is typical of Pinther's respondents; again, women are a bit more positive than are men.[127] There is also a strongly positive attitude toward what in the GDR is called *Qualifizierung*, i.e., efforts to qualify oneself in evening courses (or other adult education programs) for a higher job position. Eighty-seven percent of the young women (and 88 percent of the young men) agreed to their partner's educational intentions or activities.[128]

In addition to the attitudes of youth toward marriage and the family, young people's leisure-time activities are a major topic of youth research. These latter studies are discussed in a subsequent section of this chapter.

In general, attitudes and behavior of young people constitute a heavily researched field in the GDR. Theoretical and ideological reflection on the situation of youth and on youth research also is highly developed. Walter Friedrich in his speech at the 1975 International Conference held at the ZfJ,[129] mentioned four factors that are critically important in determining the "social position" of young people in the GDR: 1) the fact that in 1976 the first generation of GDR youth educated under the principles set by the *Einheitliches sozialistisches Bildungssystem*[130] will graduate from high school; 2) the growing amount of leisure time and the longer vacation time (three to four weeks) for working youth; 3) the increasing role of the mass media in the ideological education of the youth, where, as Friedrich put it, the "ideological class struggle becomes visible;" and 4) the changing role of the family in socialist society.

Youth research in the GDR sees its major tasks as studying the development of young men's and women's personalities through education, and evaluating the influences on the personality from both the outside and from within, i.e., with reference to both socialpsychological and psychological conditions.

Friedrich maintains that "much progress" in the development of the socialist personality can be observed since 1971.[131] In his view, the attitudes of young people toward the basic goals and values of socialist society have become more firmly positive. However, Friedrich provides little evidence for this position. Also, the empirical results reported by staff members of the ZfJ and the findings of youth research carried out by other institutions do not necessarily lead to Friedrich's conclusions. Rather, they confirm our view that some major influences distract young people from socialist ideals, especially the presently uncontrolled (and perhaps uncontrollable) leisure-time activities, influences from Western mass media, and the impact of family background, including the sometimes traditional personal and social values reinforced within the typical family.

Some skepticism about the circumstances of youth is suggested by the fact that so little youth research is published and that several relevant topics are totally neglected in published studies. Here we might especially mention the topics of job aspirations and preferences concerning field of academic study. Since we know from previously published research that empirical findings in this area have not been particularly encouraging to the SED,[132] we can assume that the lack of published data is not accidental.

Work and the Workplace

Survey research on work and the workplace is part of *Industrie- und Betriebssoziologie* (industrial and workshop sociology), of *Arbeitssoziologie* (labor sociology), or of *Arbeitspsychologie* (psychology of work). Research within the realm of industrial and workshop sociology blossomed in the 1960s and early 1970s.[133] It has been incorporated into what is now called labor sociology, in line with developments in the Soviet Union. Publications from the 1975-77 period give few hints about new research. Often the data come from investigations done in earlier years.

Empirical research on work and the workplace usually focuses on industrial workers. Some research deals with work in agriculture. However, we know of no study that concentrates on other economic sectors, e.g., bureaucracies. Similarly, there appear to be no studies that attempt comparisons among major economic sectors.

A major source of information for empirical research on work and the workplace is the files of industrial firms. For example, studies of labor turnover appear to obtain data not only from surveys conducted by research teams, but also through evaluations of workplace records. If an employee in the GDR wants to change his or her place of work, he or she must submit a letter of resignation indicating the exact reasons for the decision. In most cases, a personal interview with superiors will follow and a *Protokoll* (record of interview) will be written, or a form filled out. We presume that some research institutions have access to these materials.[134]

A prominent institution for research on work and the workplace is the *Zentrales Forschungsinstitut für Arbeit* in Dresden. The Institute appears to cooperate with the Economic Section at the University of Halle-Wittenberg. In 1976, these two units jointly organized the "Third Conference in Labor Sociology" in Halle.[135] This conference and a colloquium held in 1975 at the University[136] provide some hints about research foci in labor sociology. Topics discussed at the conference included: 1) the work situation, work satisfaction and work motivation of employees, including the development of "socialist motivation";[137] 2) influence of work conditions on behavior and aspirations of employees; 3) the evaluation of violations of work discipline; and 4) the role of managers in industry, especially including their influence on the work motivation of employees. Another source[138] mentions three additional topics: 1) the development of social structure within the working class; 2) the development of intellectual and cultural aspirations through the *Betriebskollektiv* (work collective); and 3) the state of collective work and socialist human relationships. Sociological studies on these topics have been carried out in at least four large enterprises. This list of topics attests to the strong influence of Soviet research on East German studies, since these topics are frequently stressed in Soviet research on work and the workplace.

All of these topics probably have been the subject of survey research or of survey-like studies,[139] but little evidence of such surveys is published. Some relevant work has been done by Rudhard Stollberg (professor at the University of Halle-Wittenberg and one of the authorities on industrial sociology in the GDR) and at the AfG, especially its institutes on Marxist-Leninist philosophy and sociology.

Stollberg has conducted several studies on work satisfaction and work motivation,[140] and on shift work and the life conditions of shift workers.[141] The 1978 booklet on shift work represents the only detailed account of a survey on work and the workplace available for the period 1975-77. The respondents were 832 production workers, including 371 working in a three-shift system and 461 working regular day hours. The appendix of the book contains basic demographic information about the sample, but does not provide data on the population from which the sample was drawn. Data were collected mainly by structured interviews, and the field work was carried out in nine (unnamed) industrial enterprises over a period of four months (dates unspecified). The study compared the modes of living of shift and nonshift workers. Questions are included on marital and family relationships, allocation of housekeeping chores, use of leisure time, and health matters. The results reported by the authors are rather frankly stated. However, the authors take care not to overestimate the negative conditions of shift work. They acknowledge that shift work creates problems for family life and for children's education, but they maintain that these problems can be solved.[142] Moreover, they stress the positive consequences of shift work, such as an overall gain in nonworking time and better conditions for housekeeping. Shopping can be done during the day when the shops are not as crowded as during the morning prework or evening afterwork hours.

Thus survey research is again used for mobilization. Shift work is more of a *conditio sine qua non* for the East German economy than for Western countries because of the lack of capital, insufficient inventory of "highly productive machinery," and labor shortages.[143] In 1977, 42.5 percent of GDR production workers were working in shifts (see table 5.8). There is a felt need to increase this percentage in order to better utilize existing production facilities.[144] Social scientists may be able to help the SED motivate workers to accept shift work.

Research done at the *Institut für Gesellschaftswissenschaften beim ZK der SED* is mentioned in a footnote in a booklet by Gerda Nolepa and Lilo Steitz.[145] Little detail on the methods of research is reported, but the focus and the reported results are interesting enough to justify comment. Nolepa and Steitz conducted a type of "social structure research," namely, attitudinal differences within the working class, e.g., among *angelernte Arbeiter* (semiskilled workers), *Facharbeiter* (skilled workers), and members of the scientific-technical intelligentsia. These three groups apparently differ considerably in their opinions and attitudes (see table 5.9). The authors are reluctant, however, to infer the existence of "social differentiation." Thus in interpreting Part B of table 5.9, Nolepa and Steitz state that a high percentage of all three groups responded affirmatively to the statement, "Workers should participate in elaborating new scientific-technical solutions for production,"[146] but fail to point out that considerable differences are apparent in the profiles of the three groups. Furthermore, they maintain that manual and intellectual work are conditioned by technological processes,[147] and that routine manual work will be taken over increasingly by technological devices. This will lead to an increase in intellectual work and a decrease in manual work. "Social differentiations" within the working class, however, are said to disappear in any case because under socialism, both manual and intellectual work become "creative." This conclusion seems

Table 5.7. Youth Population by Age and Sex, 1977

Age	Male	Female	Total
14 years	148,747	142,079	290,826
15 years	146,688	140,118	286,806
16 years	148,100	141,088	289,188
17 years	142,909	136,755	279,664
18 years	141,061	134,205	275,266
19 years	132,467	125,045	257,512
20 years	132,018	124,727	256,745
21 years	133,607	127,090	260,697
22 years	136,672	128,986	265,658
23 years	136,178	128,853	265,031
24 years	135,733	128,474	264,207
25 years	134,493	127,326	261,819

Source: *Statistisches Jahrbuch 1978*, p. 341.

Table 5.8. Production Workers Working One, Two, or Three Shifts:
Percentage Distribution, 1962–77

	Production Workers		
Year	Working One Shift	Working Two Shifts	Working Three Shifts
1962	62.0	18.8	19.1
1964	61.2	17.4	21.4
1966	61.4	17.0	21.6
1970	61.3	14.6	24.0
1972	59.1	14.8	26.1
1974	58.8	14.4	26.7
1976	57.6	14.8	27.5

Source: *Statistische Jahrbücher*, quoted from Martina Jugel, Barbara Spangenberg, and Rudhard Stollberg, *Schichtarbeit und Lebensweise*, Schriftenreihe Soziologie (East Berlin: Dietz, 1978), p. 10.

clearly to overlook some of the empirical findings of the author's own study. Further studies on work and the workplace in industry have been referred to in the literature examined for this report. Because of the lack of access to the studies themselves, they will only be enumerated here. First, Georg Schmelzer, the director of the Subsection *Betriebspädagogik* (industrial pedagogics) of the *Humboldt-Universität zu Berlin* mentions that he has been responsible for surveys on the "pedagogical processes of strengthening and deepening Marxist-Leninist convictions." The surveys carried out in the period 1970-75 involved approximately 3,000 employees. Data in most cases were gathered by questionnaires. This research yielded more than 40 theses, dissertations, and other reports. Second, Schmelzer also mentions a research subgroup headed by G. Schwarz, which produced nearly 90 reports.[148] Third, a research group called "Socialist Social Consciousness," affiliated with the Section on Marxism-Leninism at the Technical University in Magdeburg, developed its own method for an evaluation of the behavior and consciousness of work collectives in people's-owned enterprises. This method, elaborated in 1973, was evaluated through studies, the results of which have been published only in very general terms.[149] Fourth, staff members of the Sociology Chair at the University of Leipzig observed job changes among workers at the *VEB Kombinatsbetrieb "Otto Grotewohl" Böhlen* from 1969 on. Employees were questioned before, during, and after their change of workplace.[150] Finally, some research has been done on work and the workplace in the agricultural sector. Kurt Krambach and Jörg Müller, both affiliated with the AfG, refer to sociological research on the attitudes of collective farm peasants and the conditions of rural life in the GDR.[151] However, the data apparently were not gathered through systematic survey research. Krambach and Müller, who also contributed to the book *Genossenschaftsbauern—gestern, heute, morgen*,[152] used instead statistical materials obtained from institutions such as the *Zentralverwaltung für Statistik*, the *Institut für Ausbildung und Qualifizierung* at the Ministry for Agriculture, and the *Fachgruppe Agrarökonomik* at the University of Leipzig.

Although most results of survey research on work and the workplace are not available, we still are able to draw some conclusions from what is published. At a minimum, incomplete or disguised data may indicate the perspectives and perceptions of SED functionaries and social scientists, including what trends and problems they see in East German society. In this regard, three basic trends in the structure of employment (which, as we know, can be observed in all industrial societies) are perceived: 1) the number of employees in productive sectors of the economy is declining, whereas the number in nonproductive sectors is increasing;[153] 2) the white-collar professions are increasing more rapidly than are the blue-collar professions;[154] 3) the number of qualified personnel (cadres with degrees from the universities, technical colleges, or professional schools) is growing, whereas the number of semiskilled and unskilled workers is declining.[155]

Research on work and the workplace has a distinctly practical, applied

Table 5.9. Semiskilled Workers, Skilled Workers, and the Intelligentsia: Their Opinions on Different Issues of the Work Situation
(percentages)

Work Situation Issues	Occupational Category		
	Semiskilled workers	Skilled workers	Intelligentsia
A. QUESTION: In your place of work, what do you think are the advantages of close cooperation between workers and members of the scientific-technical intelligentsia?			
1. Interest in improving one's qualification increases.	17	16	20
2. Such cooperation provides better opportunities to elaborate and apply new technical solutions to production problems.	22	40	72
3. Mutual understanding, solidarity and teamwork will improve.	25	29	66
4. Such cooperation yields personal material benefits.	16	13	10
5. Through this cooperation we achieve better results in socialist competition.	28	32	51
6. Such cooperation stimulates the initiative of our colleagues who join the innovators' movement.	12	16	33
B. QUESTION: What could encourage the workers and members of the scientific-technical intelligentsia in your company to improve their cooperative work?			
1. The management should provide better information about the substance and the goals of cooperative work.	15	22	25
2. The personal relationships between the workers and the members of the scientific-technical intelligentsia could be much closer.	49	50	51
3. The management should be more resolute in assigning scientific tasks to workers' collectives.	11	18	38
4. Soviet experiences concerning the realization of scientific-technical progress should be better utilized.	17	16	14

	Semiskilled workers	Skilled workers	Intelligentsia
5. Cooperative performance should receive more effective acknowledgment in terms of material and moral rewards.	24	26	35
6. Workers should be included in the development of new scientific-technical solutions for production processes.	30	41	42

C. QUESTION: What do you think is your personal responsibility for the implementation of socialist rationalization?

	Semiskilled workers	Skilled workers	Intelligentsia
1. I have to qualify myself continuously.	23	27	45
2. I have to take part in the innovators' movement.	16	26	45
3. Not only must I do a good job, but I also have to make efforts that my collective performs well.	45	45	49
4. By making my own proposals, I have to participate in the development and implementation of rationalization projects.	15	22	48
5. Since I am informed insufficiently about the rationalization tasks in my place of work, I cannot identify my responsibilities.	11	13	4
6. I have to be actively engaged in the correct fulfillment of the plans concerning my place of work.	37	40	54
7. I do not feel responsible for socialist rationalization.	8	9	1
8. I have never thought about that.	15	10	3

Source: Tables 4,5,6 from Gerda Nolepa and Lilo Steitz, *Wissenschaftlich-technischer Fortschritt — Arbeiterklasse — Schöpfertum*, Schriftenreihe "Soziologie" (East Berlin: Dietz, 1975), pp. 100, 102, 105.

275

flavor. And, although there are some proscribed areas of research, most research teams seem to be quite free in conceptualizing their studies.[156] At the same time, flexibility in interpreting data may be lacking, as the Nolepa and Steitz study seems to illustrate.

Among the problems encountered at the workplace level, the following seem to be the most researched (although not necessarily by surveys) in the 1970s:

1. The importance of various work stimuli: How important are material incentives? What are the real interests and aspirations of working people? How can these be investigated and by what measures can they be met?
2. The various (objective and subjective) reasons for labor turnover; especially, how much influence does the housing situation have?[157] What is the role of the work situation?[158]
3. The complex phenomenon called "work motivation," e.g.: What is the role of the political-ideological consciousness? Do employees with high political-ideological consciousness display more stable work attitudes?[159]
4. The improvement of work productivity: Here the so-called *Leitungstätigkeit* (management activity), i.e., the process of decision making and communication in industrial firms, is the focus of attention.[160]

Leisure Time

The concept of "leisure time" (Marx: "disposable time") used in the GDR is ideologically preconceived. In capitalist societies there is said to exist a contradiction between working time and leisure time, whereas the two form a unity in socialist or communist social orders. In the latter, the individual uses leisure time in a meaningful way, whereas for the individual in capitalist societies leisure time is nothing more than "nonworking time," or time for the regeneration of the capacity for work. The "unity" of leisure time and working time is established in Marxism-Leninism through the concept of "creativity." Both leisure time and working time provide opportunities for creativity. Since under socialist economic conditions, work assumes a new quality, man can develop his creativity in working; he is no longer a tool of the capitalist entrepreneur.[161]

As a practical matter, this ideological preconception has two elements. Leisure time is first seen as a basis for enhancing the quality of human existence; it is also viewed as a stimulus to work efficiency and hence productivity. Both postures imply that leisure time should be increased. The progressiveness of a social system is measured by the amount of available leisure time. However, these two conceptions may differ considerably in their implications for the use of leisure time. The former implies a rather individualistic concept of leisure-time activity: Man, as Marx said, may fish, hunt, or do whatever he likes. The latter entails a goal-oriented concept linked to the needs of the socioeconomic system at large. According to Marxist-Leninist economic theorists, leisure-time activities have the character of resources for greater work efficiency. Hence the question: What is the difference between this view and the view which, according to Marxism-Leninism, is typical of the capitalist entrepreneur?

In East German usage, the concept of leisure time has considerable ambiguity. On the one hand, leisure-time research seeks to determine what individuals actually do during their leisure time. On the other hand, this research is guided by a "pedagogical" impetus; it intends to prove that the leisure time of the individual is not idle or "empty time"[162] but rather useful in an economically, socially, and politically "meaningful" way. The first approach is that of time-budget research; the second encompasses all other empirical research on leisure time. Both approaches, it should be noted, seem to have been stimulated by the clear interest of the SED in keeping close watch on the nonworking activities of the population.

Survey research in the sense of time-budget studies was carried out during the 1960s and early 1970s in the GDR. It was initiated partly through the UNESCO project on the daily activities of urban and suburban populations.[163] The three most important studies were 1) a survey done in 1965, based on a representative national sample consisting of 804 households (1,538 married men and women; hereafter: the GDR Survey I); 2) a 1966 survey of a sample of 1,650 inhabitants of Hoyerswerda, aged 18 to 65 years (hereafter: the Hoyerswerda Survey); and 3) a survey in 1970 involving 1,900 households (hereafter: the GDR Survey II). The GDR Survey I was organized by the Leipzig *Institut für Bedarfsforschung*, which in 1967 was renamed the *Institut für Marktforschung*. For one week (in autumn), the time that each individual spent on different activities was carefully noted. Some results were published.[164] The Hoyerswerda Survey was directed by the *Institut für Planung der Konsumtion und des Lebensstandards* (Institute for the Planning of Consumption and Living Standard) at the *Hochschule für Ökonomie Berlin-Karlshorst* (Higher School for Economics in Berlin-Karlshorst). Results are available in UNESCO publications and in separate publications by GDR authors.[165] In 1973 the just-named institute at the *Hochschule für Ökonomie* seems to have organized a repeat survey of a national sample.[166] The GDR Survey II was carried out by the *Institut für Marktforschung*. Contrary to the 1965 survey, which was based on data gathered for the respondents' activities during one week, the 1970 data result from daily reporting.[167]

A word of caution is necessary in extrapolating findings from the 1960s and early 1970s to present circumstances. When the GDR Survey I was taken, the legally prescribed working time was 45 or more hours per week. On April 1, 1966, it was reduced to 45 hours for normal-schedule workers and 44 hours for shift workers. Thus, the new regulation was in effect when the Hoyerswerda Survey was taken. In 1970 at the time of the GDR Survey II, the normal working time was 43 hours and 45 minutes (42 hours for three-shift workers), and the five-day workweek was in effect. Since May 1, 1977, the regular working time has been 42 hours per week, with the exception of three-shift workers and working mothers with two children, who work only 40 hours. Consequently, leisure time extends to more hours in 1975-77 than in earlier years. A 1975 source states that, if one adds up all weekends and holidays, 125-135 days per year are nonworking days for working people in the GDR.[168]

With this reservation, the data collected in 1965, 1966, 1970, and 1973 illustrate certain tendencies still relevant in 1975-77. It is not so much the absolute figures reported that are relevant, but rather the relationships established among certain variables. First, it is clear that men have more leisure time than do women. The difference is 10.5 hours per week in the GDR Survey I and in the 1973 repeat survey (for the latter see table 5.10), or 13.5 hours in the GDR Survey II; regarding working men and women, it is about 1.4 hours per day in the Hoyerswerda Survey (see table 5.11). Interestingly, married men seem to have much less leisure time at their disposal than do unmarried men (the difference is 1.5 hours per day in the Hoyerswerda Survey[169]), whereas the amount of leisure time for married and unmarried women is nearly equal.

Second, among the social strata in Hoyerswerda, members of the intelligentsia have the most leisure time. Intelligentsia here refers to upper-level white-collar employees, executives and business managers, as well as professionals (see table 5.12). There may be some reason to be skeptical about this finding.[170]

Third, leisure time is filled to a great extent by the mass media. The single activity that consumes the greatest amount of time is watching television (see table 5.13). On the average day, an inhabitant of Hoyerswerda watches 81 minutes of television. Leisure time spent in such passive ways is said to be proportionately too great.[171] In Hoyerswerda, 89 minutes (if *Ausruhen* ("resting") is counted, 99 minutes) out of a daily total of 233 minutes is occupied by "passive" leisure time.

This finding has to be juxtaposed with another. Relatively little time is spent in Hoyerswerda for sociopolitical activities and advanced education (12 minutes and 11 minutes per day, respectively). At the same time, this statistical average may be misleading. From other sources, we know that some population groups in East Germany use their leisure time extensively for education. Understandably, these usually are individuals whose jobs demand high intellectual capacities.[172] And as far as sociopolitical activities are concerned, some time spent on them is probably considered part of working time. However, information on this is lacking.

Other empirical research in the GDR has dealt with leisure time, especially including studies in the fields of literary and cultural sociology and in youth research.[173] "Cultural activities" of the working people were the focus of a project carried out in the years 1972, 1973, and 1975. The project involved representative samples from a department of the VEB "Otto Grotewohl" Böhlen (N=74), from nine work collectives at the VEB GISAG Leipzig (N=130), from the total plant of the VEB "Otto Grotewohl" Böhlen (N=693),[174] and

Table 5.10. The Structure of the Time Budget of the GDR Population Aged 18-65 Years, by Sex and Vocation, 1973

Use of Time	Amount of time (hours and tenths of hours), average per person and per week							
	Population total	Men	Women	Employed workers	Employees	Cooperative farmers	Cooperative craftsmen	Others
Working time	37.1	44.8	29.2	42.0	40.6	42.7	44.1	46.9
Work-related time	6.3	8.4	4.9	7.7	7.0	5.6	7.0	4.9
Time for housekeeping activities etc.	30.8	18.2	42.7	27.3	28.0	32.9	24.5	25.9
Nursing, care, and education of children etc.	3.5	2.1	5.6	2.8	3.5	2.8	3.5	2.1
Satisfaction of (primarily) physiological needs	65.8	64.4	65.8	64.4	65.1	64.4	65.1	66.5
Leisure time	24.5	30.1	19.6	23.8	23.8	19.6	23.8	21.7
Total	168	168	167.8	168	168	168	168	168

Source: *Autorenkollektiv* under the directorship of Günter Schmunk, Gerhard Tietze, and Gunnar Winkler, *Marxistisch-leninistische Sozialpolitik* (East Berlin: Verlag Tribüne, 1975), p. 271.

Table 5.11. Amount of Leisure Time (Average Minutes per Day)
at People's Disposal, by Sex, Employment, and the Existence
of Children, in Hoyerswerda, 1966

Personal Characteristics	Day of Week		
	Workday/weekday	Day off/Sunday	All days
Employed men, total	184 (3.1 hours)	463 (7.7)	267 (4.5)
single	306[a](5.1)	492[b](8.2)	356 (5.9)
married, no child	209 (3.5)	490[b](8.2)	263 (4.4)
married, children	172 (2.9)	457 (7.6)	
Employed women, total	126 (2.1)	284 (4.7)	188 (3.1)
single	118 (2.0)	315 (5.3)	198 (3.3)
married, no child	133 (2.2)	325 (5.4)	186 (3.1)
married, children	127 (2.1)	263 (4.4)	
Housewives, total married	225 (3.8)	329[a](5.5)	241 (4.0)
no child	263[a](4.4)	269[b](4.5)	241 (4.0)
children	218 (3.6)	340[a](5.7)	
Single female heads of household (no child)			295 (4.9)

[a]Sample size between 10 and 29.
[b]Sample size between 4 and 9.

Source: Alexander Szalai, ed., *The Use of Time: Daily Activities of Urban and Suburban Populations in Twelve Countries*, Publication of the European Coordination Centre for Research and Documentation in the Social Sciences, 5 (The Hague and Paris: Mouton, 1973), p. 664.

Table 5.12. Amount of Leisure Time (Average Minutes per Day) at People's Disposal, by Vocational Groups and Sex, in Hoyerswerda, 1966

	Day of Week													All days
	Workday						Day off							
	Vocational Group						Vocational Group							
Sex	Total	High white collar	Low white collar	Craftsman	Skilled	Unskilled	Total	High white collar	Low white collar	Craftsman	Skilled	Unskilled		
Employed men	184	204	175	105[a]	179	172[b]	463	478	460	-	462	443[a]		267
	(3.1)[c]	(3.4)	(2.9)	(1.8)	(3.0)	(2.8)	(7.7)	(7.9)	(7.7)		(7.7)	(7.4)		(4.5)
Employed women	126	123	144	138[a]	128	115	284	318	315[b]	-	266	276		188
	(2.1)	(2.1)	(2.4)	(2.3)	(2.1)	(1.9)	(4.7)	(5.3)	(5.3)		(4.4)	(4.6)		(3.1)

[a]Sample size between 4 and 9.
[b]Sample size between 10 and 29.
[c]Numbers in parentheses refer to hours.

Source: Alexander Szalai, ed., The Use of Time: Daily Activities of Urban and Suburban Populations in Twelve Countries, Publication of the European Coordination Centre for Research and Documentation in the Social Sciences, 5 (The Hague and Paris: Mouton, 1973), p. 664.

Table 5.13. Leisure Time Spent in Primary Activities (in Average Minutes per Day) by the People in Hoyerswerda, 1966

Activities	Minutes per day	Percent of leisure time	Leisure Time Participation	
			Percent participating	Minutes per participant
1. Mass media	108	46.4	82.8	131
among them: television	81		65.2	
read newspaper	13		37.0	
read book	7		11.4	
radio	4		9.2	
read magazine	2		3.9	
movies	1		0.9	
2. Social life and entertaining	38	16.3		
among them: social life outside one's home	17		14.5	113
visiting with friends	11		25.3	45
social life in one's home	10		10.8	93
3. Remaining leisure-time activities	21	9.0	25.6	80
among them: ladies' hobbies	10.9		11.3	
write letters	5.5		12.4	
hobbies	2.4		2.1	
play records	0.4		0.7	
making music	0.3		0.4	
art work	0.1		0.1	
others	0.9		1.3	

Table 5.13 Continued

Activities	Minutes per day	Percent of leisure time	Percent participating	Minutes per participant
4. Sports and other open-air activities	19	8.2	17.3	105
among them: taking a walk, hiking	18		2.5	53
active sports	1			
5. Societal/political activities	12	5.2	9.9	118
6. Adult education	11	4.7	7.2	155
7. Travel to and from leisure-time activities	11	4.7	20.5	54
8. Resting	10	4.3	25.5	41
9. Attendances	3	1.3		
among them: mass culture	1.3		1.4	
sports	0.6		0.6	
theater	0.3		0.2	
museum	0.2		0.1	
Total	233.0	100.1	95.7	243

Source: Compiled from Alexander Szalai, ed., *The Use of Time: Daily Activities of Urban and Suburban Populations in Twelve Countries*, Publication of the European Coordination Centre for Research and Documentation in the Social Sciences, 5 (The Hague and Paris: Mouton, 1973), 576-82; by Bernhard H. Ziegler, *Frei verfügbare Zeit: Theorie, Politik und Realität der Freizeit in der DDR*, Soziologische Arbeitshefte, no. 16 (West Berlin: Technische Universität, 1976), p. 88.

from "a plant in the machine tool industry." The research teams were associated with the University of Jena (D. Strützel, W. Geidel), the University of Leipzig (E. John, G. Baum), and the *Institut für Gesellschaftswissenschaften beim ZK der SED* (F. Staufenbiel). Many analyses of the data were done, but few have been published.[175]

Strützel et al. summarize some of their findings.[176] First, cultural *activities* differ among social strata. Second, cultural *aspirations* display fewer inter-strata differences. Third, the amount of white-collar activity at the workplace as well as one's position in the social hierarchy of the workplace are factors decisively influencing the individual's cultural activity. Finally, the ideological atmosphere of the work collective and the workplace has a great impact on individual cultural activities.

Such findings evoke mixed reactions. As far as can be gathered from the published results, the Berlin-Leipzig-Jena project was carried out at the specific behest of the SED. The study was meant to reinforce the family-like functions which the work collective is supposed to have for the individual.[177] In view of this goal, observed differences in cultural activities among social groups presumably have been understated. The authors' statement that all social strata have nearly the same cultural aspirations is probably in part the product of wishful thinking.[178]

The leisure-time activities and aspirations of the young people have been researched by the staff on the ZfJ for some time. In addition, market researchers have an interest in these topics because youth constitute a significant consumer group. In both of these areas, survey techniques have been used to obtain information about the leisure-time activities and aspirations of young people. The material that has been published—although incomplete—suggests a few interesting conclusions.

First, according to Lothar Bisky,[179] leisure-time activities of young people differ from those of adults. In Bisky's 1971 surveys, he discovered that young people are frequent moviegoers—in contrast to adults, who clearly prefer television to cinema. When they watch television, young people are most interested in movie features. Furthermore, young people listen to radio much more often than do adults.

However, these findings must be viewed with caution, since we know very little about the research methods used. To some extent, we can verify these results by comparing the results of the Hoyerswerda Survey (see table 5.13) with the results of a 1966 survey of 495 seventh-grade children (i.e., girls and boys with an average age of 13 years).[180] The leisure-time habits of the 13-year-old pupils differ from those of the Hoyerswerda population (aged 18 to 65 years) in some respects. Although on the whole the 13-year-olds have nearly twice as much leisure time at their disposal, they spend only a few more minutes per day (about two minutes in the case of girls, and about 16 minutes for boys) watching television. On the other hand, the youth group uses more leisure time going to the movies and to other out-of-the-house events. There also are major differences between the two groups in radio listening.

Second, GDR youth researchers emphasize that youth activities during leisure time vary with age, sex, ideological orientation, and vocational factors, and that they are strongly influenced by social setting and personality variables. However, social-class standing is asserted to be less relevant.[181]

Third, there are essentially no comprehensive studies of young people's time budgets. A few bits of information may be gleaned from sundry studies. Representative surveys carried out by the *Institut für Marktforschung* in 1976 provide some relevant evidence. Ninety-five percent of the respondents said that they go to discothèques regularly, 87 percent go to movies and "other events" regularly, and "a great number" use some of their leisure time for sporting activities.[182] Unfortunately, the meaning of "regularly" is unspecified. Still other surveys reinforce these findings. Bisky states that three out of four moviegoers are young people.[183] The popularity of discothèques and disco music (or "beat," as the East Germans would say) is confirmed by numerous other sources. In 1973, 83 percent of a representative sample of young people said that they had a "very strong" or "strong" interest in "beat"; in 1976, the percentage was 86.[184] In July, 1976, the *Ministerium für Kultur* announced that more than 5,000 discothèques existed in the GDR.

Young people spend an average of two hours per day obtaining information and/or entertainment from the mass media (not counting times when radio music is turned on as background).[185] The reading habits of the young people also have been studied. A representative sample of 34,000 youths who used the facilities of the more than 10,000 *Staatliche Allgemeinbibliotheken* (state public libraries) was questioned.[186] Respondents were grouped according to age and vocational activities. Young people under the age of 18 or those who were still involved in formal learning used the libraries far more often than did other age or vocational groups. In the above-mentioned *Institut für Marktforschung* survey, 26 percent of the respondents (39 percent of the boys and 13 percent of the girls) named reading as their hobby. Reading was also the hobby most often mentioned.[187] It hardly needs to be stressed that the interest of youth researchers in reading habits goes beyond simple fact-finding. An important goal is to analyze and ultimately influence the effects which reading has on attitudes of young people. For example, the Bisky volume refers to a survey which investigated *ideologische Zeitungswirkung* (ideological effects from newspaper reading).[188] Unfortunately, no concrete data on this study are provided.

Other Topics

The preceding five topics are the ones on which surveys have most frequently been done in the GDR during the period 1975-77, and on which at least a few publications are available. On the other topics targeted in this volume, few if any surveys have been conducted, and even indirect evidence is meager. These research areas must, therefore, be treated less extensively here.

Moral and Ethical Preferences and Life Aspirations

The topic "moral and ethical preferences and life aspirations" implies a wide range of issues, including a number of broad questions. Has the GDR population developed a "socialist consciousness"? Can we observe some features of a "national consciousness" in the GDR? Do men and women in the GDR have attitudes which differ from those of citizens in the West, especially in the Federal Republic of Germany? Issues such as these have been addressed in studies done in and about East Germany, but only in a piecemeal, often indirect, fashion. No survey has been attempted which would cover the range of important moral and ethical preferences and life aspirations.

Marxist theory postulates that the individual's moral and ethical preferences and life aspirations will change in accordance with the socialist concept of ownership. Three indicators of these changes are most often cited. First, the socialist personality severs all religious ties, both institutional and cognitive. Second, the socialist personality does not act solely on the basis of personal interests, but also considers social interests—the collective good. If these two sets of interest conflict, the socialist personality will consider personal interests to be less important. Third, the socialist personality develops collectivist attitudes and behavior patterns and overcomes both individualistic and materialistic aspirations associated with the bourgeois personality.

There is at least indirect evidence which permits us to assess the extent to which the socialist personality has been nurtured in East Germany. The moral and ethical preferences and life aspirations of the GDR population may be different from those of people living under bourgeois-capitalist conditions, but they clearly do not seem to meet the standards set for the socialist personality.

Religious ties can be measured in part by church membership. Although official figures on church membership are very difficult to obtain, estimates by church authorities indicate that the majority of the East German population belongs to one of the Christian churches. In 1977, approximately 7.9 million GDR citizens were members of one of the eight *evangelische Landeskirchen* (protestant regional churches), approximately 1.2 million were Roman Catholics, and approximately 100,000 belonged to one of the eight *Freikirchen* (free churches).[189] At the same time, it should be emphasized that active involvement in church activities seems to be rare among all age groups and social strata in East Germany. That most East Germans do not consider themselves atheists seems beyond challenge, but the significance of their largely symbolic attachment to organized churches is frankly difficult to assess.

Whether East Germans are inclined to place collective before personal interests is extraordinarily difficult to say. Even if empirical research were to document such a tendency, it is unlikely that we could determine the extent to which the tendency was voluntary for any given individual. Thus when we learn that "to a great extent" cooperative farmers realize the necessity of industrial production methods and no longer pursue individual interests,[190] we must still puzzle over the origins and implications of this point of view.

What we do know—and this is acknowledged by SED officials[191]—is that the personal (especially, material) aspirations of the people are "growing continuously." This is not typical merely of socialist societies, but it is nonetheless significant that East German political leaders realize that the GDR is on the way to becoming a consumer society. For example, now as before, East Germans sacrifice a good deal of money in order to purchase their own car.[192] East Germans want to live in family homes; a privately owned house ranks high among East German life aspirations.[193] A private home and car are among the top items in a "wish-list" found in a recent publication.[194]

Although the preferences and aspirations of the majority of people in the GDR hardly conform to the principles of Marxist-Leninist morality, there may be certain structural differences in behavior patterns of East Germans as compared to West Germans. To a certain extent, the propagated morals of socialism or communism relieve the individual of the burden of having to choose between different, even antagonistic, patterns of behavior. The lack of pluralism, which is characteristic of GDR society as a whole, has a certain impact on the psychological structure of the individual. For instance, people in the GDR are generally thought to be less flexible in their attitudes. Moreover, we know from refugees' reports how difficult it is for them to adjust to Western modes of life. They are not brought up to cope with a plurality of offerings, material and ideological, in society. They miss binding, authoritative principles, and they display a certain helplessness when confronted with the commercial lifestyle of Western industrial societies.[195]

Social Problems and Social Policy

In the GDR, social policy (formally, *marxistisch-leninistische Sozialpolitik*) is seen as the major political tool for shaping and improving the *sozialistische Lebensweise* (socialist mode of life). The *sozialpolitisches Programm* (program of social policies) adopted at the VIIIth SED Congress in 1971 is said to "influence the step-by-step formation of the socialist mode of life."[196] Social policy includes price policy (for example, the subsidization of consumer goods so as to keep prices stable), housing policy, policies concerning work and the workplace, the distribution of consumer goods and services (including, for example, transportation), health care, social security regulations, programs and services for leisure time and vacation, environmental policies, and programs for the benefit of specific social groups (i.e., youth, working women, the elderly, shift workers, and the rehabilitated).[197]

Citizen reactions to social policy in general and to individual social policy measures in particular are not known to have been the focus of survey research in the GDR. Nevertheless, Western observers have gathered enough evidence[198] to provide a reasonably realistic picture of the population's general attitudes on these matters. East Germans take the social services offered by the government for granted, and they expect continuous improvements. They claim these services as benefits for their hard work—thus taking SED leaders at their word. In addition, since the early 1970s GDR citizens have expressed expectations concerning working and living conditions more openly. In one instance, they may even have elicited a specific response from the SED leadership.[199]

Some specific problem areas of social policy have been mentioned in previous sections of this chapter, for example, the lack of appropriate day care for infants, poor housing conditions and their influence on marital problems, and the disadvantages of shift work compared with regular daytime work. Other problem areas have been identified through market research, which is treated later in this chapter.

In addition, social problems such as crime, juvenile delinquency, and poverty (especially among the elderly) exist in the GDR, as elsewhere. Hard data occasionally are available on these matters,[200] although no surveys have been turned up. Finally, there is evidence of a range of everyday problems, the familiarity of which does not decrease their significance. These include irregularities in supplies and quality of consumer goods (for example, of furniture and textiles), the lack of repair services and spare parts, high prices for imported goods (such as coffee), and cramped living quarters.[201] These everyday problems seem to have a strong impact on population attitudes toward the SED. If the regime is given full responsibility for failure and shortcomings, it also receives credit for improvements that are, in fact, observable. In East Germany, as elsewhere, citizens' aspirations are likely to remain some steps ahead of social policy achievements. This is not only due to a general human condition, but also to the close proximity and constant influence of the other Germany, which, in terms of the fulfillment of consumer wishes, is by far the more advanced system.

Politics and Ideology

The opinions of East German citizens and their attitudes in the realm of politics and ideology are the focus of research carried out by the *Institut für Meinungsforschung beim Zentralkomitee der SED*, presumably on a regular basis.[202] Unfortunately, the Institute published no such data during the period 1975-77. Some information, however, exists for the early 1970s. For example, in 1970-71 a sample of young people (16 to 25 years of age) was questioned about their opinions on the division of Germany, the two German states, and related issues. Among the questions posed was the following: "Do you regard yourself as a German or as a GDR citizen?" Seventy-five percent of the respondents were reported to have said that they were Germans rather than GDR citizens.[203] Jörg R. Mettke, the *Spiegel* correspondent in East Berlin, who was forced to leave the GDR in 1975, reports on a 1972 survey designed to ascertain the opinions of a representative sample of GDR citizens on inter-German matters. Respondents were asked if they preferred the socioeconomic conditions in the GDR to those in the FRG. In addition, respondents were asked to indicate which of the following opinions they most agreed with.[204]

Opinion A: East and West Germany have nothing in common; inter-German relations do not exist.

Opinion B: Many kinship relations exist. This gives a special character to the relationship between the GDR and the FRG. For this reason, one cannot speak of an extreme *Abgrenzung* ("delimitation," or separate identity).

Opinion C: I am against any form of *Abgrenzung*. The notion of separate identity is just designed to impede a process of growing communication between the GDR and the FRG.

The results of this study are unknown. However, the structured responses themselves point to an interesting phenomenon. Responses A and C (note that C was the first-person singular) express the extreme positions: a wholly separate identity vs. no distinction at all. Opinion B is the only moderate position, and it is an almost exact reproduction of the West German Social Democratic Party's point of view on inter-German relations. Thus, it can be assumed that this question was designed to check the appeal which the SPD's view has for GDR citizens. A similar intention can be deduced from accompanying questions on the popularity of Willy Brandt.

Thus, one purpose of SED-controlled opinion polls is to test the attractiveness of West German politicians and their views for the GDR population. As outlined above,[205] East Germans are rather well informed about West German inter-German policies, mainly through television. Most Western analysts assume that the majority of East Germans would support the SPD line (specifically, the middle or right wing of that party) on inter-German politics. This supposition is supported by the fact that the SED rejects publication of the results of surveys such as the one mentioned by Mettke.

In addition to surveys, indirect indicators of citizen attitudes towards politics and ideology include *Eingaben der Bürger* (petitions by citizens)[206] and the *Anträge auf Entlassung aus der Staatsbürgerschaft* (applications to be discharged from citizenship). Another indirect indicator may be the extent of "honorary work" in institutions and committees in the state and mass organizations.[207]

Some estimates have been made of the number of petitions for emigration from the GDR. Robert Havemann, a well known critic of the East German system who lives in the GDR, said in an interview in 1976 that 120,000 East Germans had applied to be discharged from GDR citizenship. After the Havemann interview, East German authorities published a denial concerning 200,000 petitions. The increasing of Havemann's figure in the dementi led Western observers to believe that his estimate was reasonably accurate.[208] The figures on persons leaving the GDR legally published by the West German *Bundesministerium für Innerdeutsche Beziehungen* (Federal Ministry for Inner-German Relations) are also of interest: 7,928 in 1974, 10,274 in 1975, 10,058 in 1976, and 8,041 in 1977. Approximately 50 percent of the emigrants were persons of retirement age, i.e., women older than 60 and men older than 65.

Ethnicity and Foreign Cultures

Ethnic and minority problems hardly exist in the GDR. There is only one minority group, the Sorbs (Wends) who live in the Bautzen-Hoyerswerda area and the Spree Forest. Western observers estimate their number at 35,000 to 70,000. Migrant workers also present no identifiable problems. There are Hungarians, Yugoslavs, Poles, and Turks working in the GDR as *Gastarbeiter*, but their number has not been higher than 100,000 in recent years.[209]

No surveys investigating the attitudes of East German citizens towards countries other than the Federal Republic appear to have been taken. The surveys conducted by the *Institut für Meinungsforschung* may include questions on attitudes towards foreign cultures, but this is only speculation. Attitudes of East Germans toward many foreign countries are prescribed by the official ideology. How faithfully people in the GDR accept these official images is difficult to determine. For the purpose at hand, we can offer a few tessera of the mosaic.

It is reasonable to assume that the effect of the SED propaganda on the people's consciousness and attitudes declines when personal contacts with foreigners and (independent) information about foreign countries increase.[210] Thus, an evaluation of the attitudes towards foreigners and foreign countries must first ascertain what possibilities for contact and information exchange exist and how those possibilities are used. Some data on personal contacts are published in the *Statistische Jahrbücher der DDR*. Precise figures are available on travel both ways between other socialist countries and the GDR, and between the FRG and West Berlin and the GDR. These figures show that contacts with foreigners have increased consistently over the years. Since 1972, the number of instances of foreign travel to the GDR (including travel from the FRG and West Berlin) has been higher or almost as high as the population of the GDR.[211]

Hard data concerning the flow of information from foreign countries to the GDR cannot be obtained. Some particulars are known, however. East Germans have more possibilities than other Eastern Europeans to obtain information from non-Party sources.[212] However, the average East German has virtually no access to printed materials from the FRG, and thus has difficulty evaluating Western information transmitted by television and radio. Further, information from Western electronic media circulates alongside official SED propaganda.

There is reason to believe that internal political propaganda is particularly effective with regard to more distant societies, such as the United States. The genuine provincialism of the average East German, his lack of personal contacts with United States citizens, and language barriers may add to this situation. The most critical factor, however, is that the information about the United States which reaches the average GDR citizen is meager and heavily biased.[213] For example, in the 1975-77 volumes of the weekly magazine *Für Dich*, there was no report on the United States that provided substantial information. *Für Dich* appears to deal with the United States solely for propaganda purposes: unemployment, poverty, crime, and prostitution are the preferred topics, but even these are not treated in a systematic or informative way. The policy seems to be to single out specific events, e.g., the seizure of a 13-year-old prostitute by the Washington police,[214] or selected statistics, e.g., financial cutbacks and dismissals in New York City.[215] Such reports are intended to support the SED's stereotype of the United States as prototypical of capitalist decadence. This treatment in mass circulation publications is ideologically supported by more serious publications, which, although in a different style and with additional arguments, propagate a similarly stereotyped image of the United States.[216] This image includes an emphasis on recurrent and deepening domestic crises,[217] the aggressiveness of a CIA-dominated foreign policy,[218] and the decline of human feelings and cultural values in American society.[219]

Party propaganda is almost surely less effective with regard to images of the Soviet Union and the other East European countries. Information obtained by GDR citizens through travel and other personal contacts undermines the official stereotype of the Soviet Union. Not surprisingly, data on this issue are not available, and we suspect that such data are not collected at all. From other sources we know that anti-Russian feelings and skeptical or arrogant attitudes towards East European neighbors are not uncommon among East Germans.[220] But to the extent to which such attitudes exist, they are not acknowledged by the East German political leadership. To do so would be inconsistent with the concept of socialist or communist brotherhood; it also would fly in the face of political necessities.

Market Research

Markt- und Bedarfsforschung (market and consumer article research) has existed in the GDR since the early 1960s and is an instrument of central planning in the consumer goods industries. The field may be divided into domestic market research and research on foreign markets. The latter will not be treated here. In addition, we limit our attention to those aspects of market research relevant for understanding consumer opinions and attitudes.

The *Institut für Marktforschung* in Leipzig is the most important research institution in this field. In carrying out its role as the coordinating unit for all market research in the GDR, the Institute performs three specific tasks: 1) to supply data which the *Staatliche Plankommission* and the *Ministerium für Handel und Versorgung* (Ministry of Trade and Supplies) use to set up the five-year plans, the annual economic plans, and the supplies plans; 2) to conduct surveys (contracted for by industrial or commercial enterprises) in order to provide data on population demands for specific goods, or data on leisure habits; and 3) to elaborate basic principles for the organization, planning, and methodology of consumer-article and market research with regard to domestic markets.[221]

The second and the third tasks of the Institute warrant further comment here. The Institute seems to be very active in survey research on a wide variety of consumer goods. During the period 1975-77, the journal *Marktforschung*, which the Institute publishes quarterly, reported on surveys of the people's demands for, or consumer habits concerning more than a dozen major categories of consumer goods. *Marktforschung* also published articles about a range of living habits of the GDR population, e.g., the effects of raising pensions on the consumption habits of pensioners, the spending of housekeeping money, travel plans, eating away from home, and the leisure-time activities of school children.

In the area of methodology, members of the Institute published a *Handbuch der Konsumentenbefragung* (Handbook of Consumer Interviewing) in 1972 that covers all stages of consumer surveying, including data analysis. It describes scaling methods and simple and more advanced statistical techniques, and discusses issues concerning the objectivity, reliability, and validity of data. A 1976 handbook-like publication, *Markt- und Bedarfsforschung* (Market and Consumer Article Research), also devotes one chapter to the methodology and techniques of market research. It stresses the importance of interviewing for market research and juxtaposes *Expertenbefragung* (interviews of experts) and *Konsumentenbefragung* (interviews of consumers).[222] *Expertenbefragungen*, however, seems to be a relatively new instrument of GDR market research. Although in theory East German market researchers may have adopted the "delphi method," they appear not to have applied it in practice.[223] Consumer interviewing usually involves representative samples of the population, but it may also be *Kundenbefragung* (interviews of customers).[224] Another research approach that the *Institut für Marktforschung* seems to have tested recently is

Gruppendiskussionen (group discussions). Discussion groups composed of members of a specific social stratum (e.g., students, workers, or employees) are set up, and the same questions (for example, on fashion) are discussed in each group.[225]

Two major methodological problems of market research in both East and West are how to classify individual consumer needs and how to define consumer groups. These problems are discussed in East German literature,[226] but integrative and systematizing efforts seem to remain undeveloped. Market research in the GDR has adopted some Western techniques of survey research; systematic panel surveys are not uncommon, for example.[227] However, as Western specialists state, Western standards have not so far been attained.[228] One reason for this is the shortage of trained personnel.[229] Another factor is the rather low standard of electronic data processing in market research.[230] Both of these deficiencies are acknowledged by East German market researchers.[231]

What information can we draw from the materials published by the *Institut für Marktforschung*? The articles in the journal *Marktforschung* provide few absolute figures; they supply either percentages or index numbers that are difficult to interpret meaningfully. On the other hand, *Marktforschung* for the period 1975-77 does communicate some usable information on subjects such as the distribution of consumer goods in relation to household income, targeted areas of planning, attitudes of specific groups toward specific goods (e.g., youth on fashion), people's shopping habits, consumption patterns differentiated by social groups, approaches to household budgeting, and the influence of social policy measures on consumption (e.g., after a pay raise, how much money is available? On what will it presumably be spent?).

CONCLUSIONS

In the GDR, surveys are widely used for both policy-making and research purposes. They cover a variety of topics and fulfill two major political functions, one primarily technical, the other largely ideological. Survey data, along with other data from social research, may be inputs to social planning, in that they are used as *Kennziffern* (indicators) in the various economic and social plans. Hence, they contribute to the governmental process in a technical way. Survey research also supplies the SED leadership with information that is used by them to apply ideological precepts more effectively in governing. These technical and ideological elements interpenetrate; in many cases they cannot be disentangled.

Viewed from a Western perspective, survey research in East Germany has some peculiarities. It is guided principally by the axiom of *Praxisverbundenheit*. Thus nearly all surveys are oriented toward a specific policy goal, or at least represent preliminary groundwork for allocating or implementing decisions. This practical mission of survey research is constrained by ideological parameters. In audience research, for example, survey researchers are more concerned with mobilizing the listeners than with identifying actual listening preferences. Or, in survey research on working women the emphasis is not so much on describing the actual situation of families in which both parents leave the house to work, but rather on propagating the integration of more women into the work force. Research on social structure has as its major task the empirical confirmation of the growth of the working class (including collectivized farmers) and the decline of all remnant classes or strata of bourgeois society. Thus ideology may limit what questions are asked, what data are published, and what inferences are drawn.

Because of its policy functions and ideological relevance, all stages of survey research are closely supervised by the SED. In principle, the SED leadership is distrustful of survey research. Thus much survey data is treated as classified material. Other data might be published, but only selectively, or in manipulated form. Moreover, one cannot escape the impression that the SED would like to prevent social scientists from developing too much insight into concrete circumstances in the GDR. Hence samples must be kept small, or at least cannot be taken from the East German population as a whole.

The security zone that all governments establish around their power centers is perhaps more spacious in East Germany than in any other European communist system, with the possible exception of the Soviet Union. This presumably is due to the relatively severe legitimacy problems faced by the SED. The external origins of the regime, the broken national identity of the country, and the everpresent influence of developments in the Federal Republic of Germany contribute to these legitimacy problems.[232] The perceived disparities in living standards and political circumstances have nourished the competitive atmosphere between the two German states. Even in the area of survey research, feelings of competition are rather strong because the SED is aware that West German scholars have published more sophisticated and illuminating analyses of social structures and conditions in the GDR than East German scholars themselves have done.

Although its political functions are predominant, survey research must also be evaluated as a branch of social science research. It is part of the theoretical and methodological discussions in the social sciences, particularly in sociology and psychology. These discussions suggest that survey research in the GDR may be in a "transitional" stage. It must be stressed that Marxism-Leninism itself is increasingly subject to internal revisions, with rather remarkable implications for methodology. Further, basic categories of Marxist-Leninist ideology may be losing their rigidity in part through the influence of the Western social sciences. Thus the concept of "class" is increasingly replaced by the concept of "social differentiations," not only because of ideological erosion, but also because East German social scientists have taken an increasing interest in Western theories of social stratification and the methods they imply. At the same time, a specific German tradition in the social sciences that merges easily with Marxism is still alive. This is the emphasis of macro-sociological conceptualization, as represented by Marx himself and later by Max Weber, Georg Simmel, Ferdinand Tönnies, Theodor Geiger, and Karl Mannheim.

The social scientists who actually carry out survey research are influenced by this combination of methodologies, and by the tensions among them. Deeply rooted in Marxism and, to some extent, in the German macro-analytical tradition, many East German social scientists are aware of the shortcomings of what they consider purely quantitative research. They emphasize the importance of considering "qualitative" elements in empirical research, as well. By "qualitative," East German philosophers mean those characteristics of an object which determine its uniqueness and delineate its boundaries with other objects. The peculiar Hegelian and Marxist-Leninist elements of this position notwithstanding, East German social scientists, contribute their part to Western discussions in the social sciences on the face-value distinction. Their efforts in this area deserve the attention of the Western scholar.

Ideological constraints aside, the academic motivations of persons engaged in survey research at the universities and the state- or party-controlled institutions in the GDR should not be overlooked. We recognize this from their contributions to international conferences, such as the ISA and IPSA world congresses. In the GDR as elsewhere, scholars seek to improve their status at home through activities outside their own country. Having one's work known and discussed abroad generally enhances one's prestige at home. Personal ambitions, in turn, affect the state of survey research; the state of the art may be improved through the efforts of scholars whose motivations are solely personal and professional.

To maintain a social science establishment, the SED must encourage some professionalism; this seems to imply some relaxation of political controls. It also means that the SED must permit the publication of at least some data collected by survey research. It is worth emphasizing that the SED leadership would like East German social scientists to act and feel like scholars. They are interested in demonstrating to the international community that the GDR is a modern, open society with high standards of science and technology. This attitude, of course, must be balanced against the SED's concerns about the implications of too many concessions to strictly scientific standards.

The SED's ambivalence toward survey research has resulted in a specific publication policy. It can be taken for granted that different reports are written up for each survey. One may go to the Party secretary in the institution which did the study, another to the institution which ordered it, a third may be circulated at international conferences, and a fourth published. In any case, publication is the stage of reporting that communicates data which have passed through the greatest number of filters. Nevertheless, it may not be the stage that contains the least information.

Without respondents there can be no survey research. What are the general attitudes of East Germans towards being interviewed? How responsive are they to surveys? We can only speculate. It is interesting, for example, that in the materials examined for this report there were very few instances in which a relatively great number of respondents gave no answer. The reasons for this low nonresponse rate are unknown to us. We also do not know how candid people are in their responses to interviews and questionnaires. As a result, it is difficult to say whether published results reflect actual opinions and attitudes. We do know that since the early 1970s, as a result of developments in international politics (detente, the Berlin Accords, the Basic Treaty, CSCE, Eurocommunism) and in national politics (Honecker's social policy program), GDR citizens have become more active in public life and more frank, for example, when interviewed on television. Thus, to an increasing extent recent survey data may reflect the people's actual opinions and attitudes.

Given the policy intentions of and publication restrictions on survey research in the GDR, we have to ask ourselves whether the examination of East German survey research is really worth the effort. I believe the answer is positive, for a number of reasons. First, the topics of survey research are indicative of the problems that the SED must tackle. For the period investigated in this report, these are the problems of specific groups in the work force (working women, shift workers, white-collar professions in industry, and agriculture) and problems associated with the leisure-time activities of youth.

Second, careful attention over time to the relationship between what is published and what is not can provide important evidence about the changing sensitivity of different topics. A kind of sensitivity continuum could be constructed for any given point in time. For the period 1975-77, some topics apparently were so sensitive that they are not covered by survey research at all, e.g., the popularity of leading politicians, or attitudes toward the Soviet Union. Among the topics which were surveyed but seemingly too sensitive to see publication are political attitudes concerning nationality problems and inter-German relations. Next on the continuum would be results from audience research which provide hints concerning the influence of Western media, or audience preferences which are not in line with socialist morality. Market research may be regarded as a similarly sensitive area. Its sensitivity results from the fact that for the SED all social (and market) policies are designed to compete in one way or another with the sociopolitical system in the FRG. Less sensitive areas of survey research are work and the workplace and leisure-time habits, as well as women and youth. On these latter topics, a good deal of data can be obtained.

Third, the balance between unpublished and published results of survey research not only helps chart changing political sensitivities. It also provides a basis for evaluating the current state of Marxist-Leninist ideology in practice. Where can we observe erosive processes? To what extent have Western social sciences contributed to changes in Marxist-Leninist ideology? These and other questions can be answered with greater competence after a careful review of published survey research. In this chapter we have pointed especially to two such ideological modifications: changes in Marxist-Leninist class theory, and ambiguities in the conceptualization of research on leisure time. Finally, our observations may provide a more realistic view of problems of survey research in East Germany. Beyond political sensitivity and ideological constraints, a number of factors influence the state of survey research in the GDR. One of them certainly is the lack of appropriately trained personnel; another is the axiom of *Praxisverbundenheit* that precludes scientific efforts for which no immediate practical goal can be identified. A third factor is the stultifying bureaucratization of survey research, which leaves little room for the individual researcher to develop innovative or creative faculties, and which prevents competent researchers who have become managers of science from continuing to engage in field research. Finally, the persisting relative isolation of East German scholars from international communication in the social sciences does not have a positive effect on survey research in the GDR.

NOTES

1. Walter Friedrich and Werner Hennig state: "Research that concentrates solely on surveying opinions can rarely be encountered in the GDR. If at all, it may be found in market research." See Friedrich and Hennig, eds., *Der sozialwissenschaftliche Forschungsprozess: Zur Methodologie, Methodik und Organisation der marxistisch-leninistischen Sozialforschung* (East Berlin: VEB Deutscher Verlag der Wissenschaften, 1975), p. 407. Concerning "quantitative" versus "qualitative" aspects of social science research, see pp. 281 ff.
2. See the "Zentraler Forschungsplan der marxistisch-leninistischen Gesellschaftswissenschaften der DDR 1976-1980," *Einheit*, 1975, no. 9, pp. 1042-1061; also Rudi Weidig in an interview given to *Tribüne*, 17 May 1974.
3. See the article "Empirische Sozialforschung" in *Wörterbuch der marxistisch-leninistischen Soziologie*, ed. Georg Assmann et al. (East Berlin: Dietz, 1977), pp. 157 ff.
4. Abridged version for the period 1976-80 is published in *Einheit*, 1975, no. 9, pp. 1042-1061. For the period until 1975 see *Einheit*, 1972, no. 2, pp. 169-84.
5. More detailed information about the survey research institutions and their activities is provided in subsequent sections of this chapter.
6. According to recent information, the *Institut für Meinungsforschung* no longer exists. See Michael Naumann, Joachim Nawrocki and Josef Joffe, "Schere im Kopf: Ein Bericht über die Öffentlichkeit in der DDR," *Die Zeit*, 25 May 1979, p. 12.
7. See section of this chapter dealing with work and the workplace.
8. See section of this chapter dealing with family and women.
9. For the period investigated in this report, we have found surveys carried out by the following institutions of this category: *Humboldt-Universität zu Berlin*, University of Halle-Wittenberg, University of Jena, University of Leipzig, Univer-

sity of Rostock, *Hochschule für Ökonomie Berlin-Karlshorst*, Medical Academy of Magdeburg.

10. Friedrich and Hennig, *Der sozialwissenschaftliche Forschungsprozess*. Hennig supplemented this compendium with a reader that provides an overview of methods used in personality research and discusses methodological and substantive problems inherent in personality research. See Hennig, ed., *Zur Erforschung der Persönlichkeit* (East Berlin: VEB Deutscher Verlag der Wissenschaften, 1978).

11. The *Wissenschaftlicher Rat für Sozialpolitik und Demographie* is subordinate to the *Wissenschaftlicher Rat für die wirtschaftswissenschaftliche Forschung*. After the establishment in January, 1978, of an *Institut für Soziologie und Sozialpolitik*, headed by Gunnar Winkler, at the GDR Academy of Sciences, it can be assumed that the *Wissenschaftlicher Rat für Sozialpolitik und Demographie* is no longer affiliated with the *Gewerkschaftshochschule* in Bernau.

12. The resolution (which was never published) is entitled *Grundsätze für die Tätigkeit der Wissenschaftlichen Räte der gesellschaftswissenschaftlichen Forschung der DDR*; see *Einheit*, 1975, no. 9, p. 1052. For some details about the *Wissenschaftliche Räte* and their activities, see Günter Lauterbach and Rudolf Schwarzenbach, "Neue Aspekte der Forschungspolitik: Der Rat für wirtschaftswissenschaftliche und der Rat für staats- und rechtswissenschaftliche Forschung in der DDR," (Erlangen: Institut für Gesellschaft und Wissenschaft an der Universität Erlangen-Nürnberg, Analysen und Berichte, February 1979), esp. pp. 17 ff.

13. "Zentraler Forschungsplan, 1976-1980" (see note 2), p. 1052.

14. *Autorenkollektiv* (Petra Dunskus et al.), *Zur gesellschaftlichen Stellung der Frau in der DDR: Sammelband* (Leipzig: Verlag für die Frau, 1978).

15. All research institutes in this group are directly affiliated with a state agency or a ministry. The *Zentralinstitut für Jugendforschung*, however, which is subordinate to the state *Amt für Jugendfragen*, was not included in this group because its work is explicitly guided by the *Zentraler Forschungsplan* through the *Wissenschaftlicher Rat für Jugendforschung*.

16. For details see market research section of this chapter.

17. See work and the workplace section of this chapter.

18. See W. Christfreund and G. Förschner, "DDR-Verkehrsbefragungen des Personen-, Güter- und Dienstverkehrs 1976 in ausgewählten Städten," *Die Strasse*, 1975, no. 12, pp. 488 ff. See also Ulrich Rabe, "Resümée der Begutachtung von Generalverkehrsplänen ausgewählter Bezirksstädte der DDR," *DDR-Verkehr*, 1976, no. 12, pp. 505 ff.; Renate Fuchs, "Ergebnisse der Begutachtung von Generalverkehrsplänen ausgewählter Bezirksstädte der DDR zum Problem des Fussgänger- und der Radverkehrs," *DDR-Verkehr*, 1977, no. 9, pp. 374 ff. Cf. Käthe Wild, "Personennahverkehr: Ein Schwerpunktprogramm der Verkehrsentwicklung in der DDR," (West Berlin: Forschungsstelle für gesamtdeutsche wirtschaftliche und soziale Fragen, *Analysen*, no. 5, 1977), pp. 35 ff.

19. Ulrich Böhme, "Ausgewählte Ergebnisse zum ersten Durchgang des Systems

repräsentativer Verkehrsbefragungen," *Die Strasse*, 1975, no. 8, pp. 318 ff.
20. Christfréund and Förschner, "DDR-Verkehrsbefragungen," p. 489. Several reports have been written for internal circulation at the Technical University of Dresden and the *Zentrales Forschungsinstitut des Verkehrswesens der DDR*. Some have been quoted in the literature which we have cited in notes 18 and 19.
21. Another example is the *Abteilung Buchmarktforschung* at the *Leipziger Kommissions- und Grossbuchhandel*.
22. Cf. Rudhard Stollberg, *Arbeitssoziologie* (East Berlin: Dietz, 1978), pp. 234 ff.; also Gerd Pietrzynski, "Die Ergebnisse soziologischer Analysen zur wirksamen Entfaltung der Masseninitiative nutzen," in *Initiative und ihre Leitung in der Wirtschaft*, Schriften zur sozialistischen Wirtschaftsführung (East Berlin: Dietz, 1975), pp. 187-200, esp. p. 199.
23. It has a standardized form. See Friedrich and Hennig, *Der sozialwissenschaftliche Forschungsprozess*, p. 198.
24. Ibid., p. 199.
25. See *Verordnung über Rechnungsführung und Statistik* of June 2, 1975, *Gesetzblatt der DDR*, part I, no. 31, pp. 585-92, § 20(5).
26. Friedrich and Hennig, *Der sozialwissenschaftliche Forschungsprozess*, pp. 188 ff.
27. See note 25.
28. Paragraph 18(6) of the *Verordnung über Rechnungsführung und Statistik* (see note 25).
29. Friedrich and Hennig, *Der sozialwissenschaftliche Forschungsprozess*, pp. 202 ff.
30. *Anordnung über die Genehmigung und Registrierung von Berichterstattungen und über Bevölkerungsbefragungen* of November 27, 1975, *Gesetzblatt der DDR*, 1976, part I, no. 1, pp. 13-14, § 6.
31. Exempt from this procedure are market research and media research, the latter insofar as it is carried out by the *Staatliches Komitee für Rundfunk*, the *Staatliches Komitee für Fernsehen*, the *Allgemeine Deutsche Nachrichtendienst* or by press organs (controlled by the *Presseamt des Ministerrates*). See ibid., § 8.
32. Paragraph 23(6) of the *Verordnung über Rechnungsführung und Statistik* (see note 25). See also the *Statut der Staatlichen Zentralverwaltung für Statistik* of July 24, 1975, *Gesetzblatt der DDR*, part I, no. 36, pp. 639-42, § 3.
33. *Statut*, ibid., § 3, § 4.
34. *Wörterbuch Soziologie* (see note 3), p. 426.
35. This assumption gets support from the results of a survey about which Peter Voss, a staff member of the ZfJ, reports: "Über den Einfluss unterschiedlicher Befragungssituationen auf die Untersuchungsergebnisse," in Friedrich and Hennig, *Der sozialwissenschaftliche Forschungsprozess*, pp. 142-45.
36. "Zentraler Forschungsplan, 1976-1980" (see note 2), p. 1058.
37. Rudi Weidig, Kurt Krambach and Joachim Rittershaus, "Bilanz und Aufgaben soziologischer Forschung," *Deutsche Zeitschrift für Philosophie*, 1976, no. 4, pp. 468-84.

38. Friedrich and Hennig, *Der sozialwissenschaftliche Forschungsprozess*, p. 70.

39. Ibid., p. 71.

40. This statement was made in an article on "Sozialforschung und quantitative Methoden," which the Soviet social scientists A. G. Aganbegian and W. N. Shubkin wrote for the GDR publication *Quantitative Methoden in der Soziologie* (East Berlin: Dietz, 1970), p. 23. Cf. St. Wilsdorf, "Marxistisch-leninistische Soziologie und Statistik," *Wissenschaftliche Zeitschrift der Karl-Marx-Universität Leipzig. Gesellschafts- und Sprachwissenschaftliche Reihe*, 1976, no. 3, pp. 263-66, esp. p. 265.

41. For a statement to this effect, which refers to questions as "indicators" in evaluating data collected by interviewing, see Friedrich and Hennig, *Der sozialwissenschaftliche Forschungsprozess*, pp. 393 ff.

42. See for an overview, Peter Förster, "Forschungsergebnisse und gesellschaftliche Praxis," in ibid., pp. 770-90. For more specific information, see the "Zentraler Forschungsplan, 1976-1980," p. 1042; also Joachim Rittershaus in an interview in *Die Wirtschaft*, 1974, no. 19, p. 11.

43. See the reports about *Praxisanalysen* by Rudolf Hundt, "Zur Methodologie in der Unterrichtsmittelforschung unter besonderer Berücksichtigung empirischer Untersuchungen," *Wissenschaftliche Zeitschrift der Martin-Luther-Universität Halle-Wittenberg. Gesellschafts- und Sprachwissenschaftliche Reihe*, 1975, no. 4, pp. 77-99; and by Ingeburg Zeidler, "Der Anteil der Spartakiadebewegung an der Vorbereitung des Kinder- und Jugendsports der DDR," *Wissenschaftliche Zeitschrift der Wilhelm-Pieck-Universität Rostock. Gesellschafts- und Sprachwissenschaftliche Reihe*, 1977, no. 4, pp. 423-27.

44. The term *Wirkungsanalyse* is used by sociologists of literature and the arts. See Dietrich Sommer et al., eds., *Funktion und Wirkung: Soziologische Untersuchungen zur Literatur und Kunst* (Berlin and Weimar: Aufbau-Verlag, 1978). See also Wolfgang Sielaff, "Weiter um die wirkungsanalytische Arbeit bemühen," *Börsenblatt für den Deutschen Buchhandel (Leipzig)*, 1975, no. 3, pp. 33 ff. The term *Wirkungsanalyse* is also applied in media research. See Lothar Bisky, "Wirkungsforschung," in Friedrich and Hennig, *Der sozialwissenschaftliche Forschungsprozess*, pp. 571-85. See also Dieter Wiedemann, "Jugendliche vor der Leinwand: Probleme und Ergebnisse der Filmwirkungsforschung," *Film und Fernsehen*, 1976, no. 11, pp. 29-32.

45. Rudi Weidig, "Die Arbeiterklasse und der Prozess der sozialen Annäherung der Klassen und Schichten," *Einheit*, 1977, no. 2, pp. 229-34. See also Fritz-Helmut Schröder and Rudolf Welskopf, "Aspekte der Dialektik von sozialer Einheitlichkeit und Differenziertheit in der sozialistischen Gesellschaft," *Deutsche Zeitschrift für Philosophie*, 1976, no. 9, pp. 1069-1078.

46. See, for instance, Wilsdorf, "Marxistisch-leninistische Soziologie und Statistik."

47. See Kurt Starke and Rolf Ludwig, "Auswahlverfahren," in Friedrich and Hennig, *Der sozialwissenschaftliche Forschungsprozess*, pp. 226-51.

48. The spectrum extends from well-conceived research (which sometimes

critically reviews the use of "crude" statistical techniques in social science survey research) to studies of little or no sophistication. As an example of the former, see Joachim Freitag, "Einige Probleme des Auswahlplanes sozialstruktureller Untersuchungen," in Manfred Lötsch and Hansgünter Meyer, directors of study, *Zur Sozialstruktur der sozialistischen Gesellschaft*, Schriftenreihe "Soziologie" (East Berlin: Dietz, 1974), pp. 188-98. As an example of the latter, see Gerda Nolepa and Lilo Steitz, *Wissenschaftlich-technischer Fortschritt—Arbeiterklasse—Schöpfertum*, Schriftenreihe "Soziologie" (East Berlin: Dietz, 1975). The Nolepa/Steitz book is discussed subsequently in this chapter.

49. Friedrich and Hennig, *Der sozialwissenschaftliche Forschungsprozess*, pp. 369 ff.

50. An exception to the rule is the study by Martina Jugel, Barbara Spangenberg and Rudhard Stollberg, *Schichtarbeit und Lebensweise*, Schriftenreihe Soziologie (East Berlin: Dietz, 1978). The authors indicate (p. 136) that their results have been subjected to chi-square and other statistical tests.

51. Cf., for example, Arndt Ullmann and Steffen H. Wilsdorf, *Bewertung und Vergleich: Methodologische und methodische Probleme in der soziologischen Forschung*, Schriftenreihe "Soziologie" (East Berlin: Dietz, 1977); also Rolf Ludwig, "Statistische Auswertungsverfahren," in Friedrich and Hennig, *Der sozialwissenschaftliche Forschungsprozess*, pp. 706-49.

52. See, for *Korrelations- und Regressionsanalyse*, Emil Magyas, "Einige Aspekte der Abhängigkeit der Geburtenhäufigkeit von sozial-ökonomischen Faktoren," in Parviz Khalatbari, ed., *Zu Problemen der Demographie: Materialien des Internationalen Demographischen Symposiums Berlin 16. bis 18. Dezember 1974* (East Berlin: Akademie-Verlag, 1975), pp. 149-56; or Gudrun Ranft, "Anwendung der Korrelations- und Regressionsanalyse bei der Planung der Hochschul- und Fachschulkader eines Industriebetriebs," *Sozialistische Arbeitswissenschaft*, 1976, no. 1, pp. 38-46. Correlation and regression analyses seem to be widely applied in market research. See *Autorenkollektiv* under the directorship of Gernot Schneider, *Bedarfs- und Marktforschung* (East Berlin: Verlag Die Wirtschaft, 1976), pp. 181-236. *Faktorenanalyse* has presumably been used in a project on family and day-care center influences on infants. See Eva Schmidt-Kolmer, ed., *Zum Einfluss von Familie und Krippe auf die Entwicklung von Kindern in der frühen Kindheit*, Hygiene in Kinderkollektiven, no. 2 (East Berlin: Volk und Gesundheit, 1977). In general, however, factor analysis is rarely used. Even in theory it is neglected. It receives only a two-page treatment in the reader *Der sozialwissenschaftliche Forschungsprozess*, and the handbook-like publication on market and consumer articles research by the *Autorenkollektiv* under the directorship of G. Schneider (see above) does not mention factor analysis at all.

53. Dieter Schreiber, "Skalierungsprobleme," in *Der sozialwissenschaftliche Forschungsprozess*, pp. 227-334. See also H. Fabiunke et al., *Handbuch der Konsumentenbefragung* (East Berlin: Verlag Die Wirtschaft, 1972), pp. 204-25.

54. See, for example, Hennig, *Zur Erforschung der Persönlichkeit*, pp. 170 ff.;

Gustav-Wilhelm Bathke, "Zu einigen qualitativen und quantitativen Problemen der Einstellungsanalyse," *Wissenschaftliche Zeitschrift der Friedrich-Schiller-Universität Jena. Gesellschafts- und Sprachwissenschaftliche Reihe*, 1977, no. 2, pp. 249-57; Hermann Kaffenberger and Walter Wennrich, "Methodologische und methodische Probleme der pädagogisch-psychologischen Forschung bei Einstellungsuntersuchungen," *Wissenschaftliche Zeitschrift der Friedrich-Schiller-Universität Jena. Gesellschafts- und Sprachwissenschaftliche Reihe*, 1977, no. 2, pp. 227-47.

55. At the Ninth Plenary Session of the Central Committee of the SED (28-29 May 1973), Honecker referred to "the Western mass media, in particular the radio and television stations of the FRG" and in a hitherto famous phrase he remarked that in the GDR "everybody can turn (these stations) on or off whenever they want" (*Neues Deutschland*, 29 May 1973). He made a similar statement in the interview which he gave to the Associated Press (*Neue Deutsche Presse*, 1976, no. 1).

56. West German TV sets are built for the PAL color system, whereas the GDR (along with all other East European countries) has introduced the SECAM color broadcasting system. For this and other facts about television in the GDR, see the article "Fernsehen" in Peter C. Ludz, director of studies, assisted by Johannes Kuppe, *DDR Handbuch*, ed. Bundesministerium für innerdeutsche Beziehungen, 2nd ed. rev. (Cologne: Verlag Wissenschaft und Politik, 1979), pp. 372-75 (hereafter cited as *DDR Handbuch*). It should also be mentioned that adaptors have been developed which make it possible for SECAM television sets to receive PAL color programs.

57. Some results were published in *National-Zeitung*, 12 August 1971. Heide Riedel reprinted and discussed them in her book *Hörfunk und Fernsehen in der DDR: Funktion, Struktur und Programm des Rundfunks in der DDR*, ed. Deutsches Rundfunk-Museum (Cologne: Literarischer Verlag Helmut Braun, 1977), pp. 79 ff.

58. This information was given by Gerd Kaiser, Vice Program Director of the *Fernsehen der DDR*, in an interview for the journal *Neue Deutsche Presse*. See *Informationen*, ed. Bundesministerium für innerdeutsche Beziehungen, 1977, no. 25, p. 8 (hereafter cited as *BMB-Informationen*).

59. In the GDR (as well as in the FRG), the postal authorities charge a fee for TV viewing. For this purpose all TV viewers in the GDR have to register with the *Deutsche Post*.

60. Otto Dienelt, "Ein wissenschaftspolitisches Magazin und seine Zuschauer," *Neue Deutsche Presse*, 1976, no. 19, pp. 24 ff.

61. See Gerd Geissenhöhner, "Das Fernsehen und seine Zuschauer," *Neue Deutsche Presse*, 1976, no. 23, p. 23.

62. Ibid.

63. See *30 Jahre Film- und Fernsehkunst der DDR: Katalog der Ausstellung im Museum für deutsche Geschichte vom 26.3. bis 23.5.1976*, quoted in Riedel, *Hörfunk und Fernsehen*, p. 131.

64. See R. Singer, "Massenverbundene Rundfunkarbeit: Ein Beitrag zur Lösung der Hauptaufgabe," *Neue Deutsche Presse*, 1976, no. 3, pp. 2-3.

65. If results are published, it is the less important data that are available, or the data are incomplete or vaguely defined. For example, a table grouping television viewers according to social structure categories (see table 5.2) is of little worth if definitions for "worker," "employee," etc. are not provided.

66. To some extent, research on media habits of the young people constitutes an exception to this rule.

67. For example, the survey taken in Hoyerswerda in 1966 (as part of the UNESCO time budget study) testifies to this fact. See the table that Bernhard H. Ziegler compiled from A. Szalai, ed., *The Use of Time* (The Hague and Paris: Mouton, 1973), for the GDR in his book *Frei verfügbare Zeit: Theorie, Politik und Realität der Freizeit in der DDR*, Soziologische Arbeitshefte, no. 16 (West Berlin: Technische Universität, 1976), p. 88. The table is reprinted as table 5.13.

68. Singer, "Massenverbundene Rundfunkarbeit," p. 2.

69. Since sufficient data are lacking, we cannot judge to what extent West German radio and television broadcasts have a "stabilizing" or "destabilizing" effect on the East German population. For a discussion of this problem, see Jean-Paul Picaper, *Kommunikation und Propaganda in der DDR*, Bonn aktuell, no. 26 (Stuttgart, 1976), pp. 119 ff.

70. Klaus Hilbig, "Erfahrungen mit dem Kulturmagazin des DDR-Fernsehens," *Neue Deutsche Presse*, 1976, no. 2, p. 21.

71. Ibid., p. 20.

72. Dienelt, "Wissenschaftspolitisches Magazin," p. 25.

73. Karl Marx wrote in a letter to Ludwig Kugelmann, dated December 12, 1868: "Social progress can exactly be measured by the social position of the fair sex (including the ugly specimens)." Karl Marx and Friedrich Engels, *Werke*, vol. 32 (East Berlin: Dietz, 1965), p. 583.

74. In 1977 the female work force was composed of (proportion of total work force in parentheses):

3,649,500 (51.2 percent) workers and employees

  312,400 (41.7 percent) members of agricultural cooperatives and law collective offices

   70,700 (38.9 percent) self-employed and assisting family members.

75. Female apprentices numbered 212,300 (43.1 percent). See *Statistisches Jahrbuch der Deutschen Demokratischen Republik*, ed. Staatliche Zentralverwaltung für Statistik, vols. 1-23 to date (East Berlin: Staatsverlag der Deutschen Demokratischen Republik, 1955-1978), 1978, pp. 90 ff. (hereafter cited as *Statistisches Jahrbuch* with the year of publication).

76. If one adds those women who work as trainees or are students at the various schools, higher schools, and universities, the percentage is 87. See Rolf Bormann and Erna Scharnhorst, "Familie, Familienerziehung und Aufgaben des Klassenleiters," *Pädagogik*, 1978, no. 2, p. 140.

77. For 1971, the percentages of women employed were as follows: 74.5 per-

cent aged 20-25 years; 79.2 percent aged 25-30; 79.6 percent aged 30-40; 79.8 percent aged 40-50; and 69.9 percent aged 50-60. These are data from the 1971 *Volks-, Berufs-, Wohnraum- und Gebäudezählung,* published in the *Statistisches Jahrbuch 1974* (pp. 426 ff.). They are quoted here from *Familienpolitik und Familienplanung in beiden deutschen Staaten,* ed. Friedrich-Ebert-Stiftung, 2nd ed. rev. (Bonn-Bad Godesberg: Verlag Neue Gesellschaft, 1977), p. 11.

For 1972, Heinz Vortmann reports that of women aged 60 to 65, every third was working. See Vortmann, "Beschäftigtenstruktur und Arbeitskräftepolitik in der DDR," *Vierteljahreshefte zur Wirtschaftsforschung,* 1976, no. 1, pp. 35-49.

78. See the appendix "Die Lage der Familien in Mitteldeutschland," in *Bericht über die Lage der Familien in der Bundesrepublik Deutschland,* Deutscher Bundestag, 5. Wahlperiode, Drucksache no. V/2532 (Bonn: Bundesministerium für Familie und Jugend, January 1968), pp. 237-56, esp. pp. 243 ff.

79. Herta Kuhrig, "Die Familie in unserer Gesellschaft," *Einheit,* 1975, no. 5, p. 978.

80. See *Statistisches Jahrbuch* 1978, p. 350.

81. Jugel et al., *Schichtarbeit und Lebensweise.*

82. See the report in *Neue Zeit,* 5 July 1975. See also Eva-Maria Elsner, "Probleme der weiteren Entwicklung der Gleichberechtigung der Frau: Ein Beitrag zur Entwicklung der sozialistischen Lebensweise," *Wissenschaftliche Zeitschrift der Wilhelm-Pieck-Universität Rostock. Gesellschafts- und Sprachwissenschaftliche Reihe,* 1977, no. 2, pp. 109-113, esp. p. 111. See also table 5.4.

83. Elsner (see note 82) wrote her Ph.D. dissertation on "Zu Problemen der Entwicklung der sozialistischen Lebensweise in Neubaugebieten unter besonderer Berücksichtigung des Einflusses des Handels mit Waren des täglichen Bedarfs" (University of Rostock, 1976).

84. These data stem from the above-mentioned 1970 survey by the *Institut für Marktforschung* (see note 82). Cf. W. Speigner, "Zur Stellung der Frau in der sozialistischen Gesellschaft der DDR," *Zeitschrift für die gesamte Hygiene und ihre Grenzgebiete,* 1975, no. 11, pp. 802-809, esp. p. 807. Cf. also *Die Wirtschaft,* 1974, no. 22, pp. 12-13.

85. See Marianne Kayser, Martin Zobel and Bernhard Metzner, "Zu einigen Aspekten der Reduzierung der Hausarbeit," in *Stellung der Frau* (see note 14), pp. 309-34.

86. Reported by Ingrid Hölzler, "Motive der Frauen zur Berufstätigkeit," *Arbeit und Arbeitsrecht,* 1976, no. 20, pp. 620-22. Information given in this article refers to "sociological investigations of *Martin-Luther-Universität Halle-Wittenberg* carried out in some big plants of our Republic." Source material could not be obtained. Rudhard Stollberg, in his article "Was führt zu Arbeitszufriedenheit und Leistungsbereitschaft?" (*Arbeit und Arbeitrecht,* 1976, no. 19, pp. 587-90), apparently bases his argument on the same survey(s).

87. "Beziehungen zwischen beruflicher Belastung, Mutterschaft und Gesundheit der werktätigen Frau in der DDR," in Khalatbari, *Zu Problemen der Demo-*

graphie (see note 52), pp. 126-29, esp. p. 128.

88. Elsner, "Weitere Entwicklung der Gleichberechtigung der Frau" (see note 82), p. 112. I. Hölzler writes that almost 60 percent of working women accept their dual roles as working woman and housewife. See "Motive der Frauen" (note 86), p. 622. H. Scholz, "Die Beziehungen zwischen Umfang und Struktur der Freizeit der Frauen und dem Verbrauch an Waren sowie Dienstleistungen" (Ph.D. dissertation, East Berlin, 1966), is quoted by Elsner as a source documenting the same facts.

89. *Für Dich*, 1976, no. 20, p. 6. For statistical details about the *Kinderkrippen*, see Schmidt-Kolmer, *Einfluss von Familie und Krippe* (see note 52), pp. 22 ff. The figures in the *Statistisches Jahrbuch 1978* for crèches and kindergartens (see table 5.4) differ slightly from those reported by Schmidt-Kolmer.

The *Statistische Jahrbücher* do not publish figures for *Schulhorte*; but Margot Krecker, Gerda Niebsch and Walter Günther, "Gesellschaftliche Kindereinrichtungen—eine Voraussetzung für die Vereinbarkeit von Berufstätigkeit und Mutterschaft" (in *Stellung der Frau* [see note 14], pp. 154-308) reprint the following table as "unpublished statistical data":

Places in School Nurseries for Pupils of Grades One through Four, 1955-1975

Year	Number of Places	Percentage of Children Who Are in School Nurseries
1955	101,844	13.0
1960	278,900	25.9
1965	464,700	44.0
1970	581,600	48.6
1975	715,500	69.8

90. "Forschungsfragen zum Thema Frau," interview with Professor Herta Kuhrig, *Für Dich*, 1976, no. 23, pp. 20-21.

91. Schmidt-Kolmer, *Einfluss von Familie und Krippe* (see note 52). Cf. K. Zwiener, L. Schoder and M. Peschke, "Die Entwicklung von Krippenkindern in Abhängigkeit von der Qualifikation ihrer Mütter," *Zeitschrift für die gesamte Hygiene und ihre Grenzgebiete*, 1975, no. 11, pp. 853-55. Related topics were discussed at three conferences: 1) the "Symposion zu dem Thema 'Berufstätige Frau und ihre Kinder'," organized by the *Institut für Hygiene des Kindes- und Jugendalters* and the *Institut für Sozialhygiene der Medizinischen Akademie Magdeburg* (see the report in *Neue Zeit*, 5 July 1975); 2) the "Wissenschaftliches Kolloquium 'Die Frau in der Familienerziehung'," organized by the *Sektion Pädagogik der Humboldt-Universität zu Berlin* (see the report in *Pädagogik*, 1976, no. 1, pp. 86-90); 3) the "Wissenschaftliches Kolloquium 'Familienerziehung und Familienerziehungsforschung in der DDR'," held in Dresden (see the report in *Pädagogik*, 1976, no. 8, pp. 768-92).

92. Zwiener et al., "Die Entwicklung von Krippenkindern," p. 854.

93. Anneliese Sälzler, "Der Einfluss der Berufstätigkeit der Mütter auf die Schulleistung ihrer Kinder," *Zeitschrift für die gesamte Hygiene und ihre Grenz-*

gebiete, 1975, no. 11, pp. 848-52.

94. See " 'Die Gesundheit der berufstätigen Frau,' Gespräch mit Prof. Dr. Anneliese Sälzler über soziologische Untersuchungen," *Neue Zeit*, 27 February 1975. Also Sälzler and Hinze, "Berufliche Belastung," (see note 87); Liselotte Hinze, Annemarie Rauer, and Werner Büttner, "Zum Gesundheitszustand und Gesundheitsschutz der berufstätigen Frau im Gesundheits- und Sozialwesen," *Die Heilberufe*, 1977, no. 3, pp. 85-86.

95. H. Hüttner and V. Koppisch, "Soziale Differenzen im Gesundheitsverhalten von Frauen in der Stadt und auf dem Lande," *Zeitschrift für die gesamte Hygiene und ihre Grenzgebiete*, 1975, no. 11, pp. 831-37.

96. Ute Fritsche and Renate Sudau, "Geburtenregelung und soziale Umwelt," *Zeitschrift für die gesamte Hygiene und ihre Grenzgebiete*, 1975, no. 11, pp. 838-43.

97. Sälzler, "Gesundheit der berufstätigen Frau." To a certain extent, these results are inconsistent with those presented by Hüttner and Koppisch, "Soziale Differenzen" (see note 95), pp. 831 ff.

98. Sälzler and Hinze, "Berufliche Belastung," p. 129.

99. See below the sections on youth and leisure time.

100. Unfortunately no data on this have been published in the period 1975-77. For some hints, see Rosemarie Walther, "Zur inneren Differenzierung der für den Erziehungsprozess in der Familie bedeutsamen Bedingungen," *Wissenschaftliche Zeitschrift der Humboldt-Universität zu Berlin. Gesellschafts- und Sprachwissenschaftliche Reihe*, 1975, no. 1, pp. 76-81, esp. p. 78.

101. Jugel et al., *Schichtarbeit und Lebensweise*.

102. This is the overall result of talks by reporters of the magazine *Für Dich* with family sociologists from the GDR and other socialist countries. See the article "Revolution in der Familie?" *Für Dich*, 1975, pp. 2, 5-6, and 8.

103. "Zur inneren Differenzierung" (see note 100), p. 77. Walther's remarks are based on results from a Ph.D. dissertation and a Diplomarbeit: K. Hauser, "Die politisch-moralische Erziehung in der Familie unter besonderer Berücksichtigung des Anteils von Mutter und Vater" (Ph.D. dissertation, Humboldt University of Berlin, 1973); W. Forst, "Die Väter im Erleben von Jugendlichen" (Diplomarbeit, Humboldt University of Berlin, 1968).

104. This is bluntly stated by Herta Kuhrig in an interview published in the magazine *Elternhaus und Schule*, 1975, no. 9, p. 5.

105. For the latter see the works published by the *Forschungsstelle für Jugendfragen Hannover*, e.g., Walter Jaide and Barbara Hille, eds., *Jugend im doppelten Deutschland* (Opladen: Westdeutscher Verlag, 1977).

106. Walter Friedrich, *Jugend und Jugendforschung: Zur Kritik der bürgerlichen Jugendpsychologie und Jugendsoziologie* (East Berlin: Deutscher Verlag der Wissenschaften, 1976), p. 162.

107. See table 1, column 5, ("An overview of empirical investigations of Marxist youth research") in Peter C. Ludz, "Soziologie und empirische Sozialforschung in der DDR," in Ludz, ed., *Studien und Materialien zur Soziologie der DDR*,

Kölner Zeitschrift für Soziologie und Sozialpsychologie (Cologne and Opladen: Westdeutscher Verlag, 1964), special issue no. 8, pp. 378-79. *Schüler* were the respondents in about three-quarters of the 48 investigations listed in that table.
108. Friedrich, *Jugend und Jugendforschung*, pp. 174 and 178 ff.
109. Unfortunately, the *Statistische Jahrbücher* do not provide a breakdown of youth by vocational activities. Only the numbers of *Schüler* (2,594,400 in 1977), *Lehrlinge* (492,600 in 1977), *Fachschüler* (162,500 in 1975) and *Hochschüler* (129,600 in 1977) are given. We do not know how many persons in each group are youth, i.e., are not younger than 14 years and not older than 25 years. The most recent breakdown of youth by vocation is based on the already mentioned (see note 77) census of 1971, which unfortunately reports data on the age group 15-24 years (instead of 14-25). Jaide and Hille, *Jugend im doppelten Deutschland*, p. 317, summarize these results. Karl-Heinz Dalichow provides a rather different breakdown for East German youth, without naming his sources: *Schüler*, 33 percent; *Lehrlinge*, 14 percent; *Studenten*, 7 percent; *Berufstätige*, 44 percent; *Hausfrauen*, 2 percent. See Dalichow, "Einige grundlegende Aspekte des Konsumverhaltens der Verbrauchergruppen der Jugendlichen," *Marktforschung*, 1978, no. 2, pp. 16-19.
110. "Statut des Zentralinstituts für Jugendforschung" of July 4, 1973, *Gesetzblatt der DDR*, part I, no. 35, p. 372.
111. Friedrich, *Jugend und Jugendforschung*, p. 161.
112. All these areas of research were treated at the "Wissenschaftliche Konferenz über 'Grundfragen der sozialistischen Persönlichkeitsentwicklung junger Arbeiter und Studenten'," held at the *Zentralinstitut für Jugendforschung*, October 8-10, 1975. See *Forschungen der sozialistischen Berufsbildung*, 1976, no. 1, pp. 42-46; also *Pädagogik*, 1976, no. 4, pp. 377-80. Friedrich lists these areas in his *Jugend und Jugendforschung* (pp. 178 ff.), as well. In addition, he provides some more detailed information about topics of youth research.
113. Werner Gerth, "Politisch-ideologische Einstellungen der Lehrlinge—Voraussetzung und Ergebnis ihres Denkens und Verhaltens," *Berufsbildung*, 1975, no. 9, pp. 373-76.
114. This is a widely researched field; it is impossible to cover it within this report. For an overview of materials, approaches, and results to the beginning of the 1970s, see Dieter Voigt, *Soziologie in der DDR: Eine exemplarische Untersuchung* (Cologne: Verlag Wissenschaft und Politik, 1975), chapter 2: "Sportsoziologie," pp. 22-116. Some results of a 1972 survey were published by Friedrich-Wilhelm Gras in "Theoretische und praktische Fragen zur Ausprägung von Körperkultur und Sport in der sozialistischen Lebensweise unter sozialstruktureller Sicht," *Wissenschaftliche Zeitschrift der Hochschule für Körperkultur Leipzig*, 1977, no. 3, pp. 57-66.
115. As mentioned, for example, in the report by Rolf-W. Bauer and Roswitha Svensson on a "Symposium zu methodologischen Problemen und neueren empirischen Ergebnissen der Erforschung des Rechtsbewusstseins der Persönlichkeit," *Neue Justiz*, 1976, no. 7, p. 207.

116. Under the heading "Survey on Youth and Health," the *BMB-Informationen*, 1977, no. 14, p. 9, report figures published by the *PRISMA* editorial office of the *Fernsehen der DDR*.

117. See, for example, Hennig, *Zur Erforschung der Persönlichkeit*; Wolfgang Kessel, Klaus Knauer and Harry Schröder, eds., *Sozialpsychologische Probleme der Schulklasse: Konferenzbericht* (East Berlin: Volk und Wissen, 1975); Werner Ehrlich, "Zum Verhältnis von Anregungen zu aktiver Tätigkeit und Einstellungs-bildung im pädagogischen Prozess," *Wissenschaftliche Zeitschrift der Friedrich-Schiller-Universität Jena. Gesellschafts- und Sprachwissenschaftliche Reihe*, 1978, no. 1, pp. 89-100; Otmar Schütze, "Pädagogisch-psychologische Probleme der Einstellungsstruktur sozial fehlentwickelter Jugendlicher und ihre Veränderung durch Umerziehung," *Wissenschaftliche Zeitschrift der Friedrich-Schiller-Universität Jena. Gesellschafts- und Sprachwissenschaftliche Reihe*, 1977, no. 1, pp. 161-67. (Schütze reports about his unpublished Ph.D. thesis.) Ruth Fröhlich, "Pädagogisch-psychologische Aspekte der Herausbildung der sozialistischen Einstellung zur Arbeit in der Familie," *Wissenschaftliche Zeitschrift der Friedrich-Schiller-Universität Jena. Gesellschafts- und Sprachwissenschaftliche Reihe*, 1978, no. 1, pp. 53-63. (Fröhlich bases her arguments on *Explorationen*, i.e., in-depth interviews, with parents, which she conducted for her Ph.D. dissertation.)

118. Borrmann and Schille, working with the ZfJ, conducted this survey in 1974. A total of 1,450 youth aged 16 to 20 years was involved. See Rolf Borrmann and Joachim Schille, "Zwitschern die Jungen, wie die Alten sungen?" *Elternhaus und Schule*, 1976, no. 9, pp. 4-5; and *idem*, "Wie wird meine Familie sein?" *Elternhaus und Schule*, 1976, no. 11, pp. 12-13.

119. "Junge Leute: wie stell'n sie sich die Ehe vor?" interview with Erika Sommer, *Für Dich*, 1976, no. 44, pp. 26-27.

120. Also see Borrmann and Schille, "Zwitschern die Jungen."

121. See note 119. These results are confirmed by information given at the *9. Fortbildungstage der Sektion Ehe und Familie der Gesellschaft für Sozialhygiene der DDR*, held at Rostock in November, 1977. The report (*Junge Welt*, November 9, 1977) states: 'Ninety-nine percent of the pupils of the ninth and tenth grades (i.e., those aged 14-15 years, P.L.) want children of their own . . . . It could further be observed that the desire to have children becomes more stable between ages 15 and 17."

122. Sommer (note 119), p. 26. See also *BMB-Informationen*, 1977, no. 13, p. 8, for a note on a survey involving 1,100 married couples and carried out by Dr. Arnold Pinther of the Leipzig ZfJ. The major result of this study seems to have been that both young married women and men do not object to their partner's wish to improve his or her education in evening courses. It may well be that the note in the *BMB-Informationen* refers to data also used by Pinther and Siglinde Rentzsch in their book *Junge Ehe heute* (Leipzig: Verlag für die Frau, 1976).

123. See Pinther and Rentzsch, *Junge Ehe heute*, p. 16. The following additional

information about this survey is provided: Respondents were living in four districts of the GDR; all of them were working (namely, in a machine shop, a textile factory, an electrical industry, or in transportation and public health). At the time of the investigation, 28 percent of the respondents had no children; 50 percent had one child, approximately 20 percent, two children, and 3 percent, three children. The questionnaires consisted of 199 items with multiple choice answers; respondents had to fill them out at their place of work.

124. Ibid., pp. 144 ff.

125. Ibid., p. 131.

126. Ibid., p. 111.

127. Ibid., p. 92.

128. Ibid., p. 96.

129. See *Pädagogik*, 1976, no. 4, p. 378.

130. For details about this system, see "Einheitliches sozialistisches Bildungssystem," in *DDR Handbuch*, pp. 292-316.

131. See Friedrich, *Jugend und Jugendforschung*, p. 156.

132. See Walter Jaide, "Arbeitszufriedenheit bei Jugendlichen in der DDR und der Bundesrepublik Deutschland," in Jaide and Hille, *Jugend im doppelten Deutschland*, pp. 50-68, esp. p. 57.

133. For an overview see Harro Ohlenburg, "Industrie- und Betriebssoziologie in der DDR" (Ph.D. dissertation, Free University of Berlin, 1974).

134. See Heinz Vortmann, "Beschäftigtenstruktur," p. 45; see also Stollberg, *Arbeitssoziologie*, pp. 250-51; and Klaus Ladensack, "Auch bei der Fluktuation: Vorbeugen ist besser als heilen," *Arbeit und Arbeitsrecht*, 1976, no. 21, pp. 647-49.

135. See the report in *Sozialistische Arbeitswissenschaft*, 1976, no. 2, pp. 294-310.

136. See the report in *Sozialistische Arbeitswissenschaft*, 1975, no. 1, pp. 148-51.

137. See Rudi Weidig's speech "Soziologische Probleme der Motivierung und Stimulierung des sozialistischen Arbeitsverhaltens der Werktätigen," printed in *Sozialistische Arbeitswissenschaft*, 1976, no. 2, pp. 261-68.

138. Pietrzynski, "Entfaltung der Masseninitiative," pp. 190-91.

139. Cf. Kurt Ducke, Ingrid Hölzler, and Otto Voigt, "Einige soziologische Probleme der Teilnahme der Werktätigen an der Leitung und Planung im sozialistischen Industriebetrieb," *Wissenschaftliche Zeitschrift der Martin-Luther-Universität Halle-Wittenberg. Gesellschafts- und Sprachwissenschaftliche Reihe*, 1975, no. 6, pp. 111-12.

140. See Rudhard Stollberg, "Arbeitsmotivation und Stimulierung," *Die Wirtschaft*, 1975, no. 12, p. 15; *idem*, "Arbeitszufriedenheit und Leistungsbereitschaft" (see note 86).

141. Jugel et al., *Schichtarbeit und Lebensweise*.

142. Ibid., p. 113. The authors include a catalogue of solutions which they propose for discussion.

143. Cf. Jürgen Strassburger, "Ökonomische und soziale Probleme der Schichtarbeit," *Deutschland Archiv*, special issue 1978, pp. 71-86.

144. See *BMB-Informationen*, 1977, no. 25, p. 8.

145. Nolepa and Steitz, *Wissenschaftlich-technischer Fortschritt.*

146. Ibid., p. 103.

147. Ibid., pp. 167 ff.

148. Georg Schmelzer, "Zu einigen allgemeintheoretischen Grundlagen der sozialistischen Betriebspädagogik," *Wissenschaftliche Zeitschrift der Humboldt-Universität zu Berlin. Gesellschafts- und Sprachwissenschaftliche Reihe*, 1977, no. 3, pp. 349-53, esp. p. 353.

149. See P. Hinze and E. Weckesser, "Einige Probleme und Ergebnisse von Analysen des Verhaltens und Bewusstseins von Arbeitskollektiven," *Wissenschaftliche Zeitschrift der Technischen Hochschule Otto von Guericke Magdeburg*, 1975, no. 6, pp. 561-65.

150. See G. Bernard, "Der Beitrag soziologischer Forschung für die effektive Nutzung des gesellschaftlichen Arbeitsvermögens in der DDR," *Wissenschaftliche Zeitschrift der Karl-Marx-Universität Leipzig. Gesellschafts- und Sprachwissenschaftliche Reihe*, 1976, no. 3, pp. 233-41, esp. pp. 238-41. Also see D. Herter, "Die Einstellung zur Veränderung der Arbeit und zur innerbetrieblichen Umsetzung bei Produktionsarbeitern: Vergleich zweier Untersuchungen im Druckgaswerk des Kombinatsbetriebes VEB 'Otto Grotewohl' Böhlen" (Diplomarbeit, Karl Marx University of Leipzig, 1973).

151. Kurt Krambach and Jörg Müller, "Bauern hier und heute: Bündnispartner der Arbeiterklasse," *Urania*, 1976, no. 10, pp. 30-34.

152. *Autorenkollektiv* under the directorship of Kurt Krambach, *Genossenschaftsbauern—gestern, heute, morgen: Die Klasse der Genossenschaftsbauern im Prozess der Gestaltung der industriemässig produzierenden Landwirtschaft in der DDR* (East Berlin: Dietz, 1977). Cf. the papers by Krambach and his team submitted at the IXth ISA World Congress (Uppsala, August 14-19, 1978): Krambach, "Social Development Processes of Achieving Industry-Like Production in Socialist Agriculture"; Krambach and Müller, "Interrelations between Settlement Structure, Development of Agriculture and Social Development of Peasants in the GDR"; and Krambach and Sonja Voge, "Changes in the Social Functions of Rural Communities in the GDR."

153. See Bernard, "Effektive Nutzung des gesellschaftlichen Arbeitsvermögens" (see note 150), p. 236.

154. Cf. Siegfried Grundmann, Manfred Lötsch, and Rudi Weidig, *Zur Entwicklung der Arbeiterklasse und ihrer Struktur in der DDR*, Schriftenreihe "Soziologie" (East Berlin: Dietz, 1976), p. 163.

155. See Bernard, "Effektive Nutzung des gesellschaftlichen Arbeitsvermögens," p. 236.

156. See, as an example, Horst Nietz, "Wissenschaftliche Arbeitsorganisation und rationeller Einsatz des Arbeitsvermögens," *Wissenschaftliche Zeitschrift der Hochschule für Ökonomie "Bruno Leuschner"*, 1976, no. 2, pp. 52 ff. Another

example of realistic conceptualization is a catalogue which lists the reasons why employees change their place of work. It contains an inclusive list of eight main categories and several subcategories. The catalogue is reprinted in full in Ladensack, "Fluktuation" (see note 134), p. 648.

157. Regina Wunsch, using data from a 1976 publication, stated that prospects for a new and better home make employees accept cutbacks in their wages and deterioration in their conditions of work. They may even accept a position below their level of qualification. See "Betrachtungen zur Motivation der Binnenwanderung in der DDR," *Jahrbuch für Wirtschaftsgeschichte*, 1976, part I, pp. 225-29.

158. In contrast to Wunsch, Stollberg maintains that sociological research provides clear evidence that employees change their places of work only when their assigned work falls short of their capabilities (*Die Wirtschaft*, 1975, no. 12, p. 15). Cf. Stollberg, *Arbeitssoziologie*, pp. 188 ff.

159. The answer is, of course, "yes." See Hinze and Weckesser, "Verhalten und Bewusstsein von Arbeitskollektiven, p. 565. However, the deliberations preceding this answer are quite sophisticated. Hinze and Weckesser, for example, distinguish among different kinds of good or excellent work behavior by pointing to differing motivations: a socialist attitude towards work, an egoistic attitude, an attitude guided by religious principles, or an "inborn inability to do bad work" (p. 561).

160. Cf. the report on a sociological investigation in the *VEB Uhrenwerk Glashütte* in Pietrzynski, "Entfaltung der Masseninitiative" (see note 22), pp. 197 ff.

161. Helga Pätz, "Zu einigen theoretischen Fragen der harmonischen Einheit von Arbeit und Nichtarbeit als Merkmal der sozialistischen Lebensweise," *Wissenschaftliche Zeitschrift der Wilhelm-Pieck-Universität Rostock. Gesellschafts- und Sprachwissenschaftliche Reihe*, 1977, no. 10, pp. 917-22, esp. p. 920. Also see Ursula Enders and Erdmann Harke, "Dialektische Aspekte der Aus- und Weiterbildung der Werktätigen in betriebspädagogischer Sicht," *Wissenschaftliche Zeitschrift der Humboldt-Universität zu Berlin. Gesellschafts- und Sprachwissenschaftliche Reihe*, 1977, no. 3, pp. 371-74.

162. "Empty time," in German *leere Zeit*, is sometimes replaced by the word *Restzeit* ("the remaining time"). See P. Förster, "Überlegungen zu einem marxistischen Freizeitbegriff," in *Lebensweise—Kultur—Persönlichkeit: Materialien vom II. Kongress der marxistisch-leninistischen Soziologie in der DDR, 15.-17. Mai 1974* (East Berlin: Dietz, 1975), p. 84.

163. See Szalai, *Use of Time*.

164. See Gerhard Lippold, "Querschnittanalyse von Zeitbudgets aus elf Ländern: Hauptgesichtspunkte und erste Ergebnisse der Untersuchungen," *Wissenschaftliche Zeitschrift der Hochschule für Ökonomie Berlin-Karlshorst*, 1967, no. 4, pp. 439-47.

165. See, for instance, *Autorenkollektiv* under the directorship of Gerhard Lippold, *Das Zeitbudget der Bevölkerung* (East Berlin: Die Wirtschaft, 1971); M. Quaas, W. Naumann, and G. Lippold, "Einige gegenwärtige und künftige

Probleme der Gestaltung von Arbeitszeit und Erholung," *Zeitschrift für die gesamte Hygiene und ihre Grenzgebiete*, 1969, no. 6, pp. 412-17.

166. The only information we could get about this survey is the table which is reprinted here as table 5.10.

167. See Joachim Braungart and Herbert Fischer, "Zu einigen methodischen Problemen von Zeitbudgeterhebungen für die Marktforschung," *Marktforschung*, 1973, no. 4, pp. 25-29. Cf. Peter Stöckmann, "Mehr Freizeit für berufstätige Mütter," *Marktforschung*, 1973, no. 1, pp. 13-17.

168. Günther Hellfeldt, "Klassenleiter und Freizeiterziehung," *Wissenschaftliche Zeitschrift der Universität Rostock. Gesellschafts- und Sprachwissenschaftliche Reihe*, 1975, no. 10, pp. 793-98, esp. p. 793.

169. This result suggests that a large number of unmarried men live with their parents' families or in some kind of student home so that they do not have to bother with maintaining a household.

170. Table 5.10 strengthens our skepticism, although there the intelligentsia are not named explicitly as a social or vocational group.

171. Cf. Horst Friedrich, "Probleme der Herausbildung der sozialistischen Lebensweise," *Deutsche Zeitschrift für Philosophie*, 1976, no. 2, pp. 135-47, esp. p. 140.

172. Cf. Pätz, "Einheit von Arbeit und Nichtarbeit," p. 920. See also the reports on the "2. Arbeitstagung unter dem Thema 'Pädagogische Erkenntnisse und Probleme der Persönlichkeitsentwicklung im volkseigenen Betrieb'," *Wissenschaftliche Zeitschrift der Humboldt-Universität zu Berlin. Gesellschafts- und Sprachwissenschaftliche Reihe*, 1977, no. 3.

173. A relatively new field of research is tourism, coverage of which is omitted because of lack of space. Major data can be collected relatively easily from the *Statistische Jahrbücher* and from the article "Touristik" in the *DDR Handbuch*. Some more specific data are published in *Marktforschung*; for example, see the articles by Wolfgang Stompler in *Marktforschung*, 1975, no. 4, pp. 19-22; 1976, no. 4, pp. 12-15; and 1978, no. 1, pp. 28-31.

174. We could not discover whether this questionnaire is based on, or coordinated with, the aforementioned.

175. Most reports that might contain hard data on this project were done in the form of theses (for diploma and doctoral degrees) or of papers for internal use. These materials are not available in the West. Some details about the project are given by D. Strützel, W. Geidel, and G. Baum, "Soziologische Untersuchungen zur Kulturentwicklung im Sozialismus," *Wissenschaftliche Zeitschrift der Karl-Marx-Universität Leipzig. Gesellschafts- und Sprachwissenschaftliche Reihe*, 1976, no. 3, pp. 243-47. See also another version of this article in *Weimarer Beiträge*, 1976, no. 7, pp. 176-85. Cf. also the following two books which are outputs of this project: *Autorenkollektiv* under the directorship of Erhard John, *Beiträge zur Entwicklung sozialistischer Kulturbedürfnisse* (East Berlin: Dietz, 1975); *Autorenkollektiv* under the directorship of Fred Staufenbiel, *Kulturelle Bedürfnisse der Arbeiterklasse: Die Entwicklung kultureller Bedürfnisse und ihre*

Wirkung im ökonomischen Reproduktionsprozess (East Berlin: Dietz, 1975). 176. *Weimarer Beiträge*, 1976, no. 7, pp. 181 ff. (see note 175).

177. Cf. in addition to the materials on this project which we have cited in note 175, Wolfgang Sielaff, "Rund 300 Arbeiter wurden befragt," *Börsenblatt für den Deutschen Buchhandel (Leipzig)*, 1975, no. 20, pp. 338-40; also *idem*, "Wirkungsanalytische Arbeit" (see note 44).

178. It should be mentioned that studies on literary and cultural activities and aspirations in the GDR are done by social scientists who are generally thought to be less SED-controlled. For instance, in 1978 a volume was published which contained relatively encompassing information about a survey on literary interests. See Sommer, *Funktion und Wirkung* (see note 44). A representative sample of 1,791 respondents was taken in 1970 from the adult population (14 years and older) of the districts of Leipzig and Halle. The study exemplifies how carefully researchers may work in the GDR. In general, scholars working in the subfield of *Wirkungsanalyse* within literary sociology seem to have initiated quite a number of interesting surveys. See, for summary information, Helma Göhler, "Soziologische Aspekte der Beziehung Persönlichkeit und Literatur," *Wissenschaftliche Zeitschrift der Humboldt-Universität zu Berlin. Gesellschafts- und Sprachwissenschaftliche Reihe*, 1977, no. 1, pp. 131-39.

179. See Lothar Bisky in cooperation with Walter Friedrich et al., *Massenmedien und ideologische Erziehung der Jugend* (East Berlin: VEB Deutscher Verlag der Wissenschaften, 1976), pp. 44 ff. See also Bisky, "Zur kulturvollen Freizeitgestaltung der Jugend," *Einheit*, 1975, no. 3, pp. 319-26.

180. See the report about this survey: H. Philipp, "Analyse des Wochen-Zeitbudgets von 13-jährigen Schulkindern unter besonderer Berücksichtigung der Freizeit," *Ärztliche Jugendkunde*, 1976, nos. 7-8.

181. Bisky, *Massenmedien*, pp. 53 ff.

182. Dalichow, "Konsumverhalten der Jugendlichen," p. 18.

183. Bisky, *Massenmedien*, p. 49.

184. Data are quoted from a survey of 4,000 respondents aged 14-25 years. See Joachim Hahn, "Warum hören Jugendliche Musik in ihrer Freizeit?" *Musik und Gesellschaft*, 1977, no. 9, pp. 513-21. The *Rezeptionsmotive* (i.e., motivations for listening to the various genres of music) also were researched in this survey. In a footnote to his article Hahn informs the reader that these survey results are part of a "comprehensive (and representative) cultural study" of the ZfJ, in which questionnaires were used to obtain the data. It is likely that an article by Dieter Wiedemann relates to the same "cultural study"; see "Ergebnisse einer Untersuchung des Zentralinstituts für Jugendforschung zu kulturellkünstlerischen Interessen und Verhaltensweisen der Jugendlichen," *Junge Generation*, 1975, no. 7, pp. 63-66.

185. See Lothar Bisky and Harald Gehrisch, "Massenmedien und sozialistische Jugenderziehung," *Neue Deutsche Presse*, 1975, no. 12; *Beilage "Theorie und Praxis"*, p. 2.

186. See Rotraud Proll, "Zur Struktur der jugendlichen Benutzerschaft in den

StAB (Staatlichen Allgemeinbibliotheken)," *Der Bibliothekar*, 1976, no. 2, pp. 75-78.

187. Hobbies and leisure-time activities named by the young people (presumably aged 14-25 years) in the 1976 representative sample(s) included:

Hobbies	Named by All Respondents (percentages)	Named by Male Respondents (percentages)	Named by Female Respondents (percentages)
Reading	26	13	39
Sports	24	26	21
Listening to music	21	20	21
Needlework	16	0	32
Handicraft	7	12	2

See Dalichow, "Konsumverhalten der Jugendlichen," p. 18.

188. Cf. chapter 5.1.: "Erfahrungsbericht über Forschungsergebnisse des Zentral-organs der FDJ" by Dieter Langguth, in Bisky, *Massenmedien*, pp. 117-28. The ideological efficacy of the *Junge Welt* was investigated by the *Zentralrat der FDJ* in cooperation with the ZfJ. Langguth mentions that surveys involved 16 classes (ninth and tenth grades, i.e., 14-15 year olds) of *polytechnische Oberschulen der DDR* and that 12 different questionnaires had been submitted to the respondents who had to fill them out themselves, but under supervision of a FDJ official and the class teacher. No hard data are reported by Langguth.

189. These figures are quoted from the article "Kirchen" in *DDR Handbuch*, pp. 586-96.

190. See Krambach, *Genossenschaftsbauern*, p. 188.

191. See "Thesen 'Grundfragen der Bedürfnisentwicklung, der Art und Weise ihrer Befriedigung sowie der Wechselbeziehungen zwischen Produktion und Bedürfnissen—die in der Hauptaufgabe des VIII. Parteitages zusammengefassten Konsequenzen aus dem ökonomischen Grundgesetz des Sozialismus'," in Helmut Koziolek, ed., *Grundfragen der Entwicklung und Befriedigung der Bedürfnisse unter dem Aspekt der untrennbaren Einheit von Ziel und Mittel der Hauptauf-gabe*, Sitzungsberichte des Plenums und der Klassen der Akademie der Wissen-schaften der DDR, vol. 1973, no. 8 (East Berlin: 1973), pp. 1-48, esp. p. 23.

192. For details see Thomas Weymar, "Das Auto: Statussymbol auch im Sozia-lismus," *Deutschland Archiv*, 1977, no. 3, pp. 271-88, esp. p. 284. The effects of the car on the budget of private households have been investigated by the *Institut für Marktforschung*; see Klaus Tauermann, in *Marktforschung*, 1976, no. 3, pp. 31-33. The *Institut für Marktforschung* also surveyed the use of private travelling; see Wolfgang Stompler, in *Marktforschung*, 1976, no. 4, pp. 12-15.

193. To a certain extent the SED complies with these wishes. A GDR source of 1976 reports that 70 percent of all *Wohnungssubstanz* (i.e., apartments, houses, etc.) was privately owned, with 28 percent as rented houses and 42

percent as individual homes. See Jürgen Becker and Horst Lünser, "Zu einigen sozialökonomischen Aspekten der Wohnungsfrage," *Staat und Recht*, 1976, no. 5, pp. 485-504. For an overview of housing conditions and policies in the GDR, see Manfred Melzer, "Wohnungsversorgung und Wohnungsqualität in der DDR" (West Berlin: Deutsches Institut für Wirtschaftsforschung, Wochenbericht 30/78), pp. 291-97; abridged version in *Deutschland Archiv*, 1978, no. 9, pp. 963-68. Cf. Helmut W. Jenkis, *Wohnungswirtschaft und Wohnungspolitik in beiden deutschen Staaten* (Hamburg: Hammonia-Verlag, 1976).

194. See *Sonntag*, 9 July 1978, pp. 8-9. This is a presentation by Gerda Wippold and Dieter Gerold who use materials from a survey stimulated by the *Berliner Rundfunk*. The listeners to the program called *Professorenkollegium* were encouraged to record those things which have a high priority in their lives. The letters received (a "great number") were given to the *Institut für Philosophie* at the AfG for evaluation. The *Sonntag* publication reprinted approximately 30 letters or excerpts. It is interesting to note that one of the presuppositions of market research is that "personal property is playing an increasing role" in the so-called *System der Befriedigung der Bedürfnisse*. See Hans Dietrich, "Einige Probleme der langfristigen Entwicklung der Bedürfnisse," *Marktforschung*, 1977, no. 3, pp. 4-10, esp. p. 9.

195. For a theoretical contribution to these problems, see Waltraud Pälicke, "Über weltanschauliche und politische Parteilichkeit von Leitbildern in der Auseinandersetzung zwischen Sozialismus und Imperialismus," *Wissenschaftliche Zeitschrift der Martin-Luther-Universität Halle-Wittenberg. Gesellschafts- und Sprachwissenschaftliche Reihe*, 1975, no. 3. For reports by refugees about their difficulties in adjusting to Western lifestyles and behavioral patterns, see, for instance, Barbara Grunert-Bronnen, ed., *Ich bin Bürger der DDR und lebe in der Bundesrepublik: 12 Interviews* (Munich: Piper, 1970).

196. *Autorenkollektiv* under the directorship of Günter Schmunk, Gerhard Tietze, and Gunnar Winkler, *Marxistisch-leninistische Sozialpolitik*, ed. Gewerkschaftshochschule "Fritz Heckert" beim Bundesvorstand des FDGB (East Berlin: Verlag Tribüne, 1975), p. 108. For an analysis of the concepts and policy measures of social policy in the GDR, see Wolf-Rainer Leenen, *Zur Frage der Wachstumsorientierung der marxistisch-leninistischen Sozialpolitik in der DDR*, Volkswirtschaftliche Schriften, no. 261 (West Berlin: Duncker & Humblot, 1977).

197. All these areas of social policy are covered in the handbook *Marxistisch-leninistische Sozialpolitik*.

198. See, for example, Leenen, *Wachstumsorientierung*, pp. 155 ff.

199. When the SED did not announce any social policy improvements at the 9th Party Congress, the people seemed to have been extremely disappointed. Consequently, the SED leaders apparently felt that some response was necessary. Just one week after the Party Congress a resolution of further improvements in the working and living conditions in the GDR was published. See the comment on these events by Hans-Dieter Schulz, "Warum eine Woche nach Parteitags-

schluss?" *Deutschland Archiv*, 1976, no. 7, pp. 678-80.

200. The *Statistische Jahrbücher* list the number of criminals convicted and provide a breakdown according to offenses. Additional information is available from the journal *Neue Justiz*. For a detailed analysis, see the *Bericht der Bundesregierung und Materialien zur Lage der Nation 1972*, ed. Bundesministerium für innerdeutsche Beziehungen (Bonn, 1972), chap. 5. This chapter is based on sources up to 1970. However, it still provides the best and most balanced account of crime and juvenile delinquency in the GDR. With regard to poverty of specific groups of the elderly, see Wolf-Rainer Leenen, "Sozialpolitik in der DDR II: Ziele und Massnahmen," *Deutschland Archiv*, 1975, no. 5, pp. 512-23, esp. pp. 516 ff.

201. From time to time such problems are acknowledged by Party officials and by social scientists. For the latter, for example, see Schneider, *Bedarfs- und Marktforschung*, pp. 63 ff.

202. For some organizational details about the *Institut für Meinungsforschung*, see the introductory section of this chapter.

203. Data were reported by a refugee from the GDR.

204. See Jörg R. Mettke, " 'Versuch mal, aus einem Schweizer Käse die Löcher rauszunehmen!' Anmerkungen zur DDR zwischen Entspannung und Abgrenzung," in Jiří Pelikán and Manfred Wilke, eds., *Menschenrechte: Ein Jahrbuch zu Osteuropa*, rororo aktuell, no. 4192 (Reinbek: Rowohlt Taschenbuchverlag, 1977), pp. 346-55, esp. pp. 348-55.

205. See section of this chapter dealing with media habits.

206. See W. Klemm and M. Naumann, *Zur Arbeit mit den Eingaben der Bürger*, Schriftenreihe "Der sozialistische Staat: Theorie–Leitung–Planung" (East Berlin: Staatsverlag der Deutschen Demokratischen Republik, 1977).

207. See, for instance, *Autorenkollektiv, Ehrenamtliche Arbeit: Wie Organisieren?* Schriftenreihe "Der sozialistische Staat: Theorie–Leitung–Planung" (East Berlin: Staatsverlag der Deutschen Demokratischen Republik, 1977).

208. See Karl Wilhelm Fricke, "Zwischen Resignation und Selbstbehauptung: DDR-Bürger fordern Recht auf Freizügigkeit," *Deutschland Archiv*, 1976, no. 11, pp. 1135-39.

209. According to an estimate by Vortmann, foreign workers in the GDR numbered 40,000 to 50,000 in 1976. See Vortmann, "Beschäftigtenstruktur" (see note 77), p. 40.

210. For example, we know some East German scientists who, after having visited the United States for a few months, have changed some of their opinions.

211. See the article "Touristik," in *DDR Handbuch*, pp. 1085-86. See also Schneider, *Bedarfs- und Marktforschung*, p. 71.

212. See the section dealing with media habits earlier in this chapter.

213. So far hardly any systematic study of the image of the United States or the Federal Republic of Germany among the GDR population has been done by Western scholars. A recent publication elaborates "news profiles" of different

socialist and nonsocialist countries by means of a content analysis of *Neues Deutschland*. See Elmar Dieter Otto, *Nachrichten in der DDR: Eine empirische Untersuchung über "Neues Deutschland"*, Bibliothek Wissenschaft und Politik, no. 11 (Cologne: Verlag Wissenschaft und Politik, 1979).

214. See *Für Dich*, 1976, no. 46, p. 17.

215. Under the heading "Miseren wohin man schaut," *Für Dich*, 1976, no. 35, p. 17. See also "Kein Geld für Kranke," *Für Dich*, 1976, no. 24, p. 22.

216. There exist, of course, some rare exceptions to the rule. See Manfred Uesseler, "Sprachliche Widerspiegelung gesellschaftlicher Erscheinungen im Kaptialismus, dargestellt am modernen Englisch," *Deutsche Zeitschrift für Philosophie*, 1977, no. 6, pp. 690-96; Rüdiger Horn, "Die 'New-Left History' in den USA über den kalten Krieg," *Zeitschrift für Geschichtswissenschaft*, 1977, no. 7, pp. 803-15.

217. See Klaus Bollinger, "Die USA 1976–imperialistische Führungsmacht in der Krise," *Deutsche Aussenpolitik*, 1976, no. 6, pp. 867-79, esp. p. 875.

218. See Albrecht Charisius and Eberhard Heidmann, "Militär-Industrie-Komplex der USA kontra friedliche Koexistenz," *Einheit*, 1975, no. 6, pp. 652-59; Christoph Hübner, "Aussenpolitische Konzeptionsvarianten einflussreicher Politiker und Politologen der USA zur Durchsetzung der Ziele des Imperialismus der USA gegenüber Europa in den 70er Jahren," *Wissenschaftliche Zeitschrift der Martin-Luther-Universität Halle-Wittenberg. Gesellschafts- und Sprachwissenschaftliche Reihe*, 1977, no. 1, pp. 55-61; Julius Mader, "Die CIA in den Massenmedien," *Neue Deutsche Presse*, 1976, no. 11, pp. 25-27; John Pittmann, "Hinter der Fassade der amerikanischen Demokratie," *Probleme des Friedens und des Sozialismus*, 1976, pp. 164-71.

219. See, for example, Heinz Förster, "Trivialliteratur in den USA heute," *Weimarer Beiträge*, 1976, no. 8, pp. 96-108.

220. Cf. the *Manifest* of an alleged opposition in the GDR which was published in *Der Spiegel*, 1978, nos. 1 and 2, and reprinted in *Deutschland Archiv*, 1978, no. 2, pp. 199-213. Cf. also Peter Bender, "Die Deutschen werden wieder deutscher," *Deutschland Archiv*, 1978, no. 5, pp. 449-52.

221. *Bedarfs- und Marktforschung* (see note 52), p. 289. Also see Dorothea Hilgenberg, *Bedarfs- und Marktforschung in der DDR: Anspruch und Wirklichkeit* (Cologne: Verlag Wissenschaft und Politik, 1979), pp. 50 ff.; and the article "Markt und Marktforschung," in *DDR Handbuch*, pp. 699-703.

222. Concerning *Expertenbefragung*, which seems to be a rather recently introduced method, see also Herbert Fischer, "Expertenbefragungen vervollständigen das Instrumentarium der Marktforschung," *Marktforschung*, 1978, no. 1, pp. 11-14.

223. Ibid., p. 13. Also see Olaf Schmutzler, "Umfragen in der Wirtschaft: Ein Mittel zur Erhöhung der Effektivität der Marktbeobachtung," *Marktforschung*, 1977, no. 3, pp. 25-29.

224. See Evelin Voss, "Die Kundenbefragung: Ein Instrument der operativen Marktbeobachtung im Warenhaus," *Marktforschung*, 1978, no. 2, pp. 12-16;

idem, "Erste Erfahrungen mit Kundenbefragungen im Einzelhandel am Institut für Marktforschung Leipzig," *Marktforschung*, 1977, no. 1, pp. 4-9. Also see Herbert Fischer, "Kundenbefragungen des Einzelhandels und ihre Probleme," *Marktforschung*, 1976, no. 3, pp. 13-17.

225. See Brigitte Sauer, in *Marktforschung*, 1976, no. 1, pp. 26-29.

226. Consumer needs are grouped into *Bedürfniskomplexe*. See Hilgenberg, *Bedarfs- und Marktforschung in der DDR*, pp. 55 ff. Also so-called *Verbrauchergruppen* are defined. See Olaf Schmutzler, "Zur Analyse des Bedarfs nach Verbrauchergruppen," *Marktforschung*, 1978, no. 2, pp. 9-11; Karl-Heinz Dalichow, "Zum Konsumverhalten wichtiger Verbrauchergruppen," *Marktforschung*, 1977, no. 3, pp. 30-35. Young people, for example, are regarded as a consumer group; see Dalichow, "Konsumverhalten der Jugendlichen."

227. See Herbert Fischer, in *Marktforschung*, 1976, no. 2, pp. 8-12.

228. See "Markt- und Bedarfsforschung in der DDR" (West Berlin: Deutsches Institut für Wirtschaftsforschung, Wochenbericht, no. 23-24/1977), pp. 201-207.

229. Hilgenberg, *Bedarfs- und Marktforschung in der DDR*, p. 55.

230. Cf. the respective discussions, for example, by Marieluise Bischoff and Henning Krieger, "Erfahrungen bei der Speicherung von Befragungsergebnissen," *Marktforschung*, 1976, no. 1, pp. 31-34; Dieter Onken and Uta Müller, "Zur Speicherung von Informationen für die Bedarfs- und Marktforschung," *Marktforschung*, 1976, no. 4, pp. 34-35; Olaf Dobierzin, "Die Auswertung von Befragungen zur Marktbeobachtung über den Kleinrechner C 8205," *Marktforschung*, 1978, no. 1, pp. 24-26.

231. For personnel problems, see Gernot Schneider, *Bedarf—Erzeugnisentwicklung—Markteinführung* (East Berlin: 1974), p. 153. See also Horst Model, *Der Absatz in der sozialistischen Industrie: Aufgaben, Methoden, Organisation* (East Berlin: 1973), p. 128. Cf. Hilgenberg, *Bedarfs- und Marktforschung in der DDR*, pp. 53 ff. Concerning the low standard of electronic data processing, see Schneider, *Bedarfs- und Marktforschung*, pp. 237 ff.

232. For a detailed discussion, see Peter C. Ludz, "Legitimacy in a Divided Nation: The Case of the German Democratic Republic," in Bogdan Denitch, ed., *Legitimation of Regimes: International Frameworks for Analysis*, Sage Studies in International Sociology, no. 17 (Beverly Hills: Sage, 1979), pp. 161-75.

6 Hungary
Robert Blumstock

AN OVERVIEW OF SURVEY RESEARCH IN HUNGARY

While the best of times may never come, it is certainly not the worst of times for Hungarians. For most, potential revolutionary fervor has been replaced by an acceptance of the present which is neither euphoric nor sullen; a recognition of the past which displays neither enchantment nor mournfulness; and a venturesomeness, which at its best, expresses hope, while at its worst exudes a crude cynicism about the future.

Practicality, profit, and productivity are the central issues of public concern. The shift from abstract ideological debates to pragmatic issues has favored the nation's social scientists, who are no longer defined as potential subversive critics of the regime, but as necessary helpmates in the realization of socialism. The benefits of cooptation proffered to social scientists have left them little time or inclination to focus on issues which do not have an immediate relevance. An authoritative recent statement leaves little doubt as to the primary concerns of social research.[1]

The guidance and planning of society, the questions relating to social policy, which goes hand in hand with planning, and the questions connected with its realization as well as the means utilized for its realization, are all becoming the subjects for sociological researches in the Hungarian society of the 1970's.

The result has been marked efforts to generate an informative and useful social science. This in turn has resulted in a plethora of surveys on a wide range of topics, many of which focus on discovering, encouraging, and enhancing the state of "socialist consciousness." This emphasis recently was forcefully underscored by the general secretary of the Hungarian Academy of Sciences, Béla Köpeczi.[2]

On the national level, there is a relatively clear-cut division of labor among research tasks,[3] with surveys conducted under the auspices of one or another of the following research centers: The Institute of Sociology, the Mass Communications Research Center, the Central Statistical Office, the Departments of Sociology at Loránd Eötvös University and Karl Marx University, the Research Center of the Hungarian Trade Unions, the Market Research Institute, and the Department of Market Research at Karl Marx University. However, surveys also are commissioned by local Party Councils, and other organizations such as KISZ (the Communist Youth League). Various provincial university departments of sociology also conduct studies.

Most of the individuals directly involved in research have not been trained specifically as survey researchers, but have acquired these skills through experience or through study in Western Europe or North America. This shortage of trained sociologists has not gone unnoticed. In a brief presented in 1977 to the Agitation and Propaganda Committee of the Party's Central Committee, several proposals concerning the teaching and training of sociologists were made which would further upgrade skills and encourage research.[4] In line with this emphasis is the general encouragement to publish research findings:[5]

> The Party views with a consistent perspective, the importance of making information on public affairs available—this can be seen in the April [1978] decisions of the Central Committee. . . . Political public opinion research shows that publicly available information is more easily communicated, observed and responded to than the simple availability of legal possibilities. This openness of public affairs presupposes that individuals will be able to delineate relationships, sense the movements, and note the constituent changes and the direction of the influences.[6]

What this emphasis has meant is that the results of survey research are quite openly available, with only the shortage of journals delaying the publication of results.

These results suggest a high level of research competence. Although most studies to date have been published only in Hungarian, two new summary works have appeared in English.[7] Some material also was translated for the International Sociological Conference in 1978.[8] The material presented in published works occasionally lacks information on the size or geographical locale of the sample, and the mode of presentation is often simple tables. However, there are signs of increasing methodological sophistication, and future published surveys should show greater analytic detail.[9]

The importance of publication is underlined by the fact that, for example, the Mass Communications Research Center no longer considers the studies it does under contract to the Party Agitation-Propaganda Committee to be secret. For other research centers, everything is publishable depending on the directors of the research institutes or chairmen of departments. This emphasis on publication and making information available is also linked to a concern about the nature, sources, and direction of criticism.[10] Although there are cautions about what can or ought to be published, the emphasis is on publishing as much as possible. As we shall see, many of the studies published are quite forthright in presenting evaluations and criticisms of the current scene.

Notwithstanding this manifest readiness to expose public sentiments, some manuscripts apparently are rejected for political reasons. A *samizdat* type publication called "Profile" has been in circulation for the last few years in which unpublished material is distributed within the confines of the Budapest intelligentsia.[11] The name "Profile" is drawn from the fact that rejected manuscripts are often accompanied by a terse note in which it is stated that the material does not fit the "profile" of the journal to which it was submitted. "Profile" is an open secret, and few penalties have been meted out to those whose work has appeared in it, although some have been punished by loss of their jobs. The existence of this quasi-underground publication implies that censorship does exist in Hungary. Yet this circulation of materials is not impeded and no one has been jailed for writing in it.[12]

The issues discussed in "Profile" highlight the shortcomings in organization and the disjunction in values and public pronouncements in Hungary. This insight, however, is not exclusive to "Profile" authors. Those in politically accountable positions want to address these issues by amassing information, and by identifying appropriate remedial techniques. They recognize that a return to moral directives without adequate information is fruitless.[13]

Thus social research functions as a generator of issues and problems which otherwise would not be discussed. In this sense, research results as well as the researchers themselves operate as a quasi-political "opposition" in which the strengths and weaknesses, successes and failures of policy are made public. Thus, rather than presenting an imposed uniformity, social research is one of the means by which a latent political, social and cultural pluralism is being effected. Research in this context is seen as a means of discovering issues before they have had a chance to crystallize in public awareness, and proponents of one or another interpretation are encouraged to air their views.[14] Similarly, larger dailies have seen a significant increase in the number of letters to the editor.[15] While this does not necessarily signal a pluralistic conception of Marxism, it does suggest that a range of interpretations of policy directives is tolerable.

None of this should imply that surveys have led directly to policy change. What has happened is that many committees at all levels of governance now have a significant input of social science expertise, and have come to see the value of research in forestalling precipitous or ill-advised decisions.

An alternative interpretation, perhaps less charitable to the Hungarian regime, is that this emphasis on social research is simply a device for maintaining power. If this is so, however, the Hungarian regime is hardly alone. Still it is clear that the role and conditions of social research must be altered to conform to the requirements of a one-party system.

Within research centers and institutes there is a pervasive optimism. There seems to be little direct interference in the kinds of topics that can be researched as long as they can be fitted into the guidelines for the respective institutes. One well-placed and well-published researcher at the Mass Communications Research Center argued that the limitations imposed on topics at the center are no different from those imposed at any research institute or university in the West.[16] The fact that some taboo topics do exist, such as questions concerning the legitimacy of the Communit Party, the salience or validity of Marxism-Leninism, and the Soviet occupation of the country, is not surprising. Furthermore, the fact that not every aspect of social existence is researched is more a result of resource limitations and research priorities than of political constraints. Topic selection in survey research may be constrained by the need for random samples; many people, particularly the elderly, cannot or will not answer questions. But even this problem, which has a variety of sources, is being tackled.[17]

Orientation of This Study

Although there were no particular difficulties in gathering data on the ten topics around which this volume is organized, there are problems in selecting material from what is available. Several years ago it was manageable to read and digest practically everything written on public attitudes in Hungary. Now this is a much more formidable task. Without constant monitoring, important material may be overlooked.

Given these problems of coverage, I concentrated on the publications and researchers at the Tömegkommunikációs Kutatóközpont (Mass Communications Research Center) and the Szociológiai Kutató Intézet (Research Institute of Sociology). The Mass Communications Research Center is a constituent part of the Hungarian Radio, whereas the Research Institute of Sociology is linked to the Magyar Tudományos Akadémia (Hungarian Academy of Sciences, or MTA). Several people at each of these institutions work parttime at the universities in

Budapest, have been involved in contract studies for the Agitation-Propaganda department of the Central Committee, and have done work for other research centers such as the Trade Union's Research Institute, the Cooperatives Research Institute, the Central Statistical Office, and the Youth Publishing House.

There are two major sources of published studies: *Szociológia* (Sociology) and *Rádió és Televizió Szemle* (Radio and TV Journal). The former is edited and published by the Sociology Committee of the Hungarian Academy of Sciences. The latter concentrates on material dealing with the media and related topics. In addition, the Mass Communications Research Center published until recently (1978) a series called *Tanulmányok* (Studies) which presents draft material that often is published in edited form in the Radio and TV Journal. I also was provided with available issues of *Módszertan* (Methodology) and *Közlemény* (Reports) where selected substantive and methodological problems are analyzed.[18] There is also a monograph series, in which selected foreign works are translated into Hungarian, and where larger studies or communication efforts can be found.

I was given copies of two preliminary reports. One describes an intensive quality of life project under the supervision of Elemér Hankiss, Róbert Manchin, and László Füstös. The other, *Az Automatizáció és a Munkástudat* (Automation and Workers Self-Consciousness) is part of a long-range study on automation and industrial workers directed by Lajos Héthy and Csaba Makó of the Research Institute of Sociology.

The Joint Publications Research Service (JPRS) translation files for the years 1975-1977 were checked as were the journals, *Statisztikai Szemle* (Statistical Journal), *Demográfia* (Demography), *Társadalmi Szemle* (Social Science Journal), *Marketing és Piackutatás* (Marketing and Market Research), and the *New Hungarian Quarterly*.

In focusing on public attitudes I have largely restricted myself to survey data and have mentioned nonsurvey material only when I thought it necessary to place the surveys in context. To set my mind at ease in terms of the completeness and representativeness of the material studied, I discussed the nature of survey research and my tentative impressions with a number of researchers. More often than not, I was offered new insights, information, and introduced to yet other knowledgeable individuals who accepted me with kindness, patience and forbearance.[19]

SURVEYS OF PUBLIC ATTITUDES AND BEHAVIOR IN HUNGARY

Media Habits

The Mass Communications Research Center in Budapest employs more than 100 people, making it somewhat larger than the comparable research center in the Soviet Union. There are four departments within the center: public opinion, mass communications, social psychology and planning. Two of the core topics for this center are patterns of media usage, and media impact. One of the disquieting generalizations coming out of this research is that frequent media usage does not necessarily lead to higher information levels, particularly among the lower socioeconomic groups.[20]

Radio, television, newspapers

Radio sets are owned by approximately three-quarters of the population, whereas television sets are registered in two-thirds of all Hungarian households.[21] However, the ownership of receivers is not evenly distributed among the population. Both access to, and informational impact of, the media are skewed in favor of those with more education and those in white-collar positions. Unskilled workers, agricultural laborers, and pensioners account for approximately 75 percent of all those without radios. Persons who have not completed eight grades of school account for 69 percent of those without radios.[22]

A closer examination shows a consistent lack of basic cultural and informational instruments among the lower social strata. For example, among those without a radio 57 percent do not have any books at home, 48 percent do not read a daily newspaper and 34 percent do not read any newspapers or magazines. Half of those without a radio of their own never listen to a radio anywhere, whereas only 25 percent of this group never watch television. This finding underscores the entertainment appeal of television.[23]

Several studies show low general awareness of media-transmitted information. One such study focused on the impact of a 1975 radio program reform.[24] One-half of the adult radio listeners did not know about the new program schedule when it was introduced[25] despite considerable publicity in all the media during the several weeks prior to its introduction. The study determined that "for some, the mass media do not represent any source of information."[26]

Similarly, a 1978 study asked whether listeners and viewers had noted changes in the content and informational character of television, radio and newspapers.[27] The results were compared with a similar study done in 1976. The emphasis was on identifying areas of satisfaction with programming and awareness of changes in entertainment as well as informational programs. Fully 28 percent of the respondents indicated that they did not listen to radio, watch television, or read newspapers.[28] No significant differences between the responses to radio and to television programs were noted in either study.[29] Few respondents noticed improvements in informational programs on national and international issues since 1976, but there was reasonable satisfaction with the quality of informational broadcasts. Respondents also were asked which medium provides more exact and reliable information. Thirty-six percent said all three forms were essentially equal, 17 percent said television, 10 percent said radio, and 5 percent did not know.

The relationship among the three media has received attention in several studies designed primarily to define newspaper audiences. One summary study which was published in 1976 brings together two studies initiated in 1972 and in 1974.[30] Thirty-one percent of the respondents are daily users of all three media. Eighty-eight percent of adults are daily newspaper readers; 85 percent of these are also daily radio listeners, but only 56 percent of those who read newspapers are daily television viewers.[31] Thus although radio and television play important roles, the majority of the population still rely primarily on newspapers.

Among those who use all three media daily, there are close ties among usage, occupational stratum and educational level (see tables 6.1 and 6.2). Persons with secondary school education are slightly more frequent media users than are those who have higher education. The difference is attributed to the use of specialized media (e.g., journals, official documents) by university graduates.[32] This finding might also suggest a higher degree of skepticism on the part of the more highly educated who seek other sources to confirm or question information received through the mass media.

Newspapers and magazine preferences vary among social strata. Among those with only primary education, the most popular daily is *Népsport* (People's Sport), whereas among those with secondary school and university education, *Magyar Hirlap* (Hungarian Journal), the semi-official government paper, is most popular (see table 6.3). Similarly, white-collar workers favor *Magyar Hirlap*, whereas industrial skilled workers prefer *Népsport*. Agricultural laborers and housewives read regional dailies more than Budapest newspapers (see table 6.4).

Broadly, we infer that industrial workers and agricultural laborers are uninterested in those papers which stress current affairs, Party information and political analysis. The informational isolation of these two groups, especially the rural inhabitants, has been examined by Ferenc Békés.[33] While Békés' study does not focus solely on the media, but on five specific measures of information—history, politics, economics, geography, and natural sciences—it does confirm in broad terms the general paucity of information among the rural and less-educated population, which is implied in studies directly associated with the media.[34] The work covered in the dissertation is the result of research begun in 1966 when Békés first focused on politics. In 1968 he added more questions on economics and in 1971, questions aimed at assessing historical awareness. In 1972 he began to organize the material. His research documents the close relationships among education, occupation and general knowledge in several subject areas[35] (see tables 6.5 and 6.6).

Table 6.1. Proportions of Selected Professions Classified
as "Heavy Media Users"[a]
(percentages)

Profession		Heavy media users as proportion of total
Leaders, intellectuals	(N=477)	44
Other intellectuals	(N=998)	42
Skilled and trained workers	(N=2,218)	37
Unskilled workers	(N=898)	26
Agricultural manual workers	(N=765)	20
Housewives	(N=1,561)	23
Pensioners	(N=1,653)	26

[a]Heavy media users are those who use all three forms of media (radio, television, and newspapers) daily.

Source: András Szekfű, "A Magyar sajtó olvasói," *Tanulmányok* 8, no. 2 (Budapest: Mass Communications Research Center, 1976), p. 219.

Table 6.2. Proportions of "Heavy Media Users" by Amount of Education
(percentages)

Amount of Education		Heavy media users as proportion of total
No education	(N=175)	3
1 to 2 years	(N=220)	12
3 to 4 years	(N=843)	14
5 to 6 years	(N=3,188)	25
8 years	(N=2,873)	38
Secondary school	(N=1,079)	43
College, university	(N=427)	39

Source: András Szekfű, "A Magyar sajtó olvasói," *Tanulmányok* 8, no. 2 (Budapest: Mass Communications Research Center, 1976), p. 219.

Table 6.3. Distribution of Adult Readers of Nationwide Daily Newspapers according to Education, 1972
(percentages)

Education	Esti Hirlap[a]	Magyar Hirlap	Magyar Nemzet	Népsport	Népszabadság	Népszava	Total sample	County daily total
Fewer than 4 years	6	2	5	3	7	7	14	8
5 to 7 years	23	13	15	18	29	28	36	35
8 years	44	28	32	50	35	36	32	38
Secondary school	19	31	26	20	19	21	12	14
College, university	7	24	22	9	9	6	5	4
No data	1	2	0	0	1	2	1	1
N	806	105	377	404	2,745	873	8,828	3,009

[a]The types of newspapers and their total circulation figures are as follows:

Esti Hirlap (Evening News) = a popular evening tabloid, published and circulated mostly in Budapest, 290,000 copies

Magyar Hirlap (Hungarian News) = semiofficial government daily, 50,000 copies

Magyar Nemzet (Hungarian Nation) = the Patriotic People's Front Daily, 120,000 copies

No circulation figures are given for *Népsport*, the sports news.

Népszabadság (People's Freedom) = the central daily of the Hungarian Socialist Workers Party, 750,000 copies

Népszava (People's Voice) = the trade union's daily, 280,000 copies

Local Dailies: There are 19 county and 2 city dailies in Hungary. All but one are morning papers; their combined edition is 930,000.

Source: András Szekfű, "A Magyar sajtó olvasói," *Tanulmányok* 8, no. 2 (Budapest: Mass Communications Research Center, 1976), p. 224.

Table 6.4. Distribution of Adult Readers of Nationwide Daily Newspapers according to Occupation, 1972[a]

(percentages)

Occupation	Newspaper						Total sample	County dailies
	Esti Hírlap	Magyar Hírlap	Magyar Nemzet	Népsport	Népszabadság	Népszava		
Leaders, intellectuals	9	23	21	9	12	9	5	5
Other intellectuals I	13	23	18	10	12	13	10	8
Other intellectuals II	4	6	4	3	4	4	4	3
Industrial, skilled, and trained workers	23	8	10	34	19	19	17	15
Unskilled workers	11	6	7	12	12	12	12	11
Agricultural manual workers	0	2	0	2	2	2	9	18
Housewives	5	8	7	5	9	9	14	19
Pensioners	18	16	22	9	22	22	14	2
Other	2	5	3	3	0	0	1	1
N	492	62	239	238	568	568	1,942	5,363

[a]The categories of leaders, intellectuals and other intellectuals I and II are difficult to translate into meaningful English terms. In a translation of this table in "Recent Studies–1976-1977," p. 150, intellectuals I are defined as "uncertificated white-collar workers having no direct contact with manual work," while intellectuals II are "uncertificated blue-collar workers directly controlling production."

Source: András Szekfű, "A Magyar sajtó olvasói," *Tanulmányok* 8, no. 2 (Budapest: Mass Communications Research Center, 1976).

Table 6.5. Distribution of High Scorers[a] on Five Types of Information
according to Education
(percentages)

Education	N	Area of Knowledge				
		History	Politics	Economics	Geography	Natural Sciences
Fewer than 8 years	433	26	25	27	25	23
8 years	313	40	41	41	42	41
Secondary school	126	67	62	61	66	64
University	58	73	70	73	73	73
All respondents	930	39	38	40	39	38

[a]Each of the subject areas had 25 factual questions, scaled according to their difficulty. The high scorers were those who were able to answer all of the questions accurately.

Source: Ferenc Békés, "Adalékok az ismeretek méréséhez, struktúrájához és tipológiájához" (Candidate's dissertation, Budapest, 1977), p. 77.

Table 6.6. Distribution of High Scorers on Five Types of Information
according to Occupation
(percentages)

Occupation	N	Area of Knowledge				
		History	Politics	Economics	Geography	Natural Sciences
Intellectuals, managers	62	73	71	74	72	71
Other white collar	100	58	55	55	57	57
Industrial, construction, skilled, and trained workers	112	46	47	47	47	44
Other skilled and trained workers	128	42	43	43	45	43
Pensioners	191	35	33	33	35	30
Unskilled workers	95	30	32	34	29	29
Agricultural laborers	91	29	27	31	27	28
Housewives	151	21	19	23	21	22

Source: Ferenc Békés, "Adalékok az ismeretek méréséhez, struktúrájához és tipológiájához" (Candidate's dissertation, Budapest, 1977), p. 77.

Family and Women

There are several features of Hungarian family and personal life which on super-ficial examination suggest a confused picture of inconstancy and instability coupled with an enthusiastic maintenance of the form, if not the substance, of connubial life. Hungarian surveys suggest a series of antinomies around which family life struggles to maintain continuity. This contrary pattern is evidenced first by the dramatic increase in the incidence of divorce; Hungary's rate of marital dissolution follows closely behind that of the United States and the USSR.[36] At the same time, marriage seems to be more popular now than ever. In 1930, for example, 23.7 percent of the male and 16.8 percent of the female population 20 years of age and older were unmarried, whereas the comparable figures for 1975 are 15.2 percent for men, and 9.1 percent for women.[37] Not-withstanding the survival chances of marriage, few seek to avoid it; as of Jan-uary 1, 1975, 77 percent of the male and 69 percent of the adult female popu-lation were married.[38]

Linked to this increase in both divorce and marriage is the apparently greater tolerance given to premarital sexual experience. In one survey, 80 per-cent of the boys and 71 percent of the girls approved of premarital sex, and 66 percent of the boys and 37 percent of the girls acknowledged having had sexual relations.[39] Correspondingly, there has been an increase during the last several years in common-law relationships, particularly among those under the age of 19, where permission of parents is required for marriage.[40] In this situa-tion, cohabitation avoids the necessity of seeking parental approval, and also indicates the independent posture assumed by young people in important life decisions.

The increases in both marriage and common-law relationships have not offset the decline in births; Hungary has one of the lowest birth rates in Eur-ope.[41] For each year from 1959 to 1973, there were more abortions than live births,[42] and between 1949 and 1970 the number of married couples without children increased by 50 percent.[43] The relative ease with which abortions could be obtained changed in 1974 as a result of a stronger pro-natalist policy, which also increased both maternity and family allowances to encourage the birth rate.[44] These have made full participation in the labor force less attractive, especially for those women who occupy less remunerative positions.[45]

Despite these measures taken to stem the decline in the birth rate, indi-cations are that, with the increased availability of birth control pills and family planning counselling for newly married couples, the increase in fertility will not be altered significantly.[46] Additional evidence collected in a survey at about the same time that this new legislation was introduced, suggests that other factors, particularly the shortage of housing, act to control the number of children a couple contemplate having.[47]

This survey, conducted by the Central Statistical Office, sought to identify the crucial factors affecting family size. For 53 percent of those questioned, three children was considered ideal, whereas 28.1 percent thought two desirable, and 12.8 percent favored four. Less than 1 percent preferred no children, or only one.[48] But these figures contrast markedly with reality, since in 1970 one-third of all nuclear families consisted of couples without children.[49]

The same survey sought to discover the factors which might affect an increase in births. The two most frequently mentioned issues were the availability of apartments for couples and the assurance of places in nursery schools and kindergartens (see table 6.7). A far smaller number mentioned family allowances as an effective stimulant. This disjunction between the hopes of planners, actual conditions, and the plans of the population, is underscored by the respondents' feeling that children should be born early in the marriage.[50]

Access to appropriate housing is an important factor in family planning.[51] The scarcity of housing is a well-known fact.[52] Increasingly, housing construction has fallen to the private or cooperative sector and the costs for these units are escalating. Especially for a young couple with limited means, the shortage of housing is a major deterrent to starting a family.[53] Further, the necessity for couples to accumulate funds for housing and other newly available consumer items, such as automobiles and travel, also helps explain the high proportion of females in the labor force. Women work in Hungary not only out of a concern for self-expression but also out of financial necessity.[54] For many women the pull of tradition and the push of participation in the work force conflict. One indicator of this tension is the fact that the average number of children in an ideal family was not significantly different for men and women. If career interests predominated, it might be expected that women would prefer fewer children,[55] but this is not the case. Although hardly conclusive, these data do suggest a general acceptance on the part of Hungarian women of the duality of their roles as workers and homemakers.

This duality aside, a reversion to traditional roles is not likely. Women now constitute 44 percent of the active wage earners, and 65 percent of all working age women are employed outside the home.[56] Still, there are inequities in access to some jobs. This has consequences for the kinds of work that women perform, which frequently is neither as well paid nor as responsible as that of men with comparable qualifications.[57]

In a study done in Békés County, data show that a larger proportion of women than men are employed as unskilled workers and that their earnings are considerably less than those of their male counterparts. Only at the lowest salary levels is there anything that approaches equal reward for comparable work. To be sure, in a relatively backward, agricultural area such as Békés, women possess little in the way of marketable skills, and have somewhat less schooling than do men. However, the pattern of wage discrimination on the basis of sex appears to hold for the country as a whole.[58]

The traditional division of labor between men and women still seems to exist. The added burden of working outside the home has not altered the notion

Table 6.7. Frequency of Mention of Stimuli Considered Most Important on the Basis of Three Selections
(percentages)

Serial number of selection	Stimuli				
	Flats for young couples getting married	Assurance of places in nursery schools, kindergartens	Flats for families having many children	Reduction in price of children's wear	Part-time work for mothers with young children
I	36.1	16.2	17.2	9.0	7.4
II	17.7	21.8	16.8	12.1	14.0
III	11.6	15.6	10.3	23.9	19.1

Table 6.7 Continued

Serial number of selection	Advantages given to pregnant women at their place of work	Family allowance	Child care allowance	Provision of regular holidays for families with children	Total
I	4.1	6.1	2.9	1.0	100
II	8.7	3.0	3.8	2.1	100
III	9.4	3.8	2.9	3.4	100

Source: Marietta Pongrácz and Edit Molnár, "A népesedési kérdésekkel kapcsolatos közvéleménykutatás néhány előzetes eredménye," *Demográfia* 18, no. 4 (1975), p. 444.

that housework is the woman's domain.[59] These traditional role stereotypes are strongly entrenched; in Békés County, for example, 91 percent of those sampled do not wish to change this division of labor.[60] Challenges to tradition are confined largely to persons with higher socioeconomic status. One study, involving an examination of children's essays, documents the strengths of traditional images of the roles of men and women.[61]

The strain of fulfilling work demands, as well as complying with traditional roles, appears to place Hungarian women under considerable stress. The difficulties in this situation are pinpointed by a study of five women graduating from Semmelweiss University in Budapest.[62] These young female physicians were apprehensive about leaving school before they marry, since they felt that once employed, particularly in the more traditional villages, their chances of marriage would decrease.

The picture of family life, and of the role of women in Hungary, is not simple. In 1964, the dean of Hungarian labor force analysts argued that the benefits of full female labor force participation significantly outweighed the costs for a country intent on increasing productivity.[63] The costs and benefits he had in mind were solely economic. However, there are costs which do not appear on economic balance sheets. For women and the family unit in Hungary, as elsewhere, economic progress is tempered by the manifold social and personal problems generated by this fervid concentration on raising the level of living.

Education and Youth

The educational system in Hungary is one in which chance elements in the channeling of students into career avenues are under continual scrutiny. This "sponsorship"[64] sorting system is directly tied to the manpower needs of the country. It also has the consequence of restricting the outlets for social mobility.

Although postwar mobility in Hungary has not exhibited the dynamism of mobility in the West, the shift from manual to nonmanual occupations and particularly the movement from agriculture to industrial work has had a profound impact on the structure of Hungarian society.[65] The intensity of this shift has been modified by the very success of the metamorphosis of the country from a semi-feudal backwater to a nation in which all of the basic elements of modern life, even if not functioning as well as hoped, are visible. This maturation of the economy has involved a departure from a stress on "revolutionary transformation" to an emphasis on a more structured, if less enthusiastic, basis for coherent organizational patterns. It also involves acceptance and understanding of the necessary disappointments that follow from grappling with economic and political realities.

There is no question that the occupational structure of the country now is less able to absorb and reward all those who seek mobility. This strikes most directly at those at the bottom of the occupational ladder. Similarly, there is an overabundance of certain skills, and there are indications that corrective measures to control this imbalance are already underway.[66] The consequence of these circumstances is to institutionalize the advantages of those who come from privileged backgrounds. That this is already the case is shown by one study which focuses on the social backgrounds of students in different types of schools. The results suggest that social class backgrounds are a crucial determinant of the type of educational stream into which students will be placed.[67]

> In the first forms of the secondary schools (vocational and academic) the share of the children of manual workers is still 54.7 percent in 1966-67. By 1969-70, this share had dropped to 49 percent. In the institutions of tertiary education (colleges and universities) in 1964-65, 54.7 percent of the first year students were the children of manual workers, while in the 1969-70 academic year, it was only 39 percent.

Even within the broad category of secondary schools, where the above figures point to roughly an even split between middle- and working-class students, there are differences based on class divisions. In Budapest, most academic secondary school students come from nonmanual backgrounds. However, although there does appear to be a somewhat greater opportunity outside the capital for those from manual backgrounds to enter this stream, the provincial schools apparently do not provide the same opportunities for further education offered by Budapest schools.[68]

In Budapest 49 percent of the students enter vocational schools; this percentage drops to 37 percent in provincial towns, and 24 percent in the villages.[69] One argument used to explain this discrepancy is that these vocational schools are actually preferred by students of working-class origin, whereas for middle-class children these schools are selected because of poor academic performance. Nonetheless, there seems to be an underrepresentation of working-class students in those vocational schools which offer greater career possibilities.[70]

> The children of the manual workers are in the majority only in the suburban secondary schools training for relatively unskilled office work. . . .
> *Thus, in the final analysis, those vocational secondary schools which offer better chances for further study or higher prestige and opportunities for becoming medium-level specialists are mainly populated by children of the nonmanual strata.* [Emphasis in original]

This pattern suggests that the advantages accruing from the initial burst of mobility during the period of extensive development are now becoming the determining factors in future class divisions. In one sense, there is nothing startling in these results; parallel processes are observable in the United States and

Western Europe. However, the mobility expectations of young people and their parents have not yet been modified (see table 6.8). Perhaps more surprising, these potentially disturbing developments have not yet led to any obvious stirrings of discontent among the young.[71]

Since no direct studies of discontent among young people are available, measures of satisfaction with career chances have to be interpreted from indirect evidence. One suggestive study[72] focuses on the economic perspectives of younger people. Interestingly, the results appear to suggest a general hopefulness on the part of those questioned with respect to the pace of economic progress and increases in the standard of living. Many show an awareness and understanding of the nature of the economic problems that confront Hungary, but the majority feel that these problems are both minor and temporary (see table 6.9). Place of residence and membership in KISZ (Community Youth League) do differentiate among respondents; those from Budapest and nonmembers of KISZ have a somewhat less optimistic attitude toward the future.[73] Students from Budapest and managers with earnings in excess of 3,000 forints a month also had a less positive evaluation of the performance of the economy during the previous two years.[74] These findings imply that a relatively small group, who may be a bit more sophisticated than most, are less sanguine about the economy. Significantly, their more negative views of the economy may be a response to their having reached the limits of mobility, as well as a more protective concern that they not lose any of their benefits. The sulking of this small group, however, has not resulted in any visible festering.

Most studies of youth attitudes avoid contentious social and political issues. Rather, the focus primarily is on leisure and recreational activities, with a few studies centering on foreign relations and general awareness of world tensions.[75]

Studies show that television viewing during the week is greater among youth outside the capital, whereas in Budapest, recreational activities with friends is the most important leisure time activity (see table 6.10).[76] Although the impact of television on younger people is an issue, there are no studies showing either positive or negative influences on viewers.[77]

Another study on interpersonal relations and communication among youth suggests that political issues are not of central concern when young people get together.[78] Most said that music was a major topic of discussion.[79] This study also suggests that parental influences are stronger among those whose parents are in white-collar, rather than blue-collar, occupations. Frequency of television viewing again is related to education and social status.[80] Those lower on both scales watch television more, whereas those with more education and higher status prefer going to the movies and/or listening to the radio.[81]

On the surface, these studies seem to imply that the level of political and ideological awareness is something that can be taken for granted. But do young people have real commitments to the future of socialism, or are they so disenchanted or unconcerned with public life that they withdraw into a focus on

Table 6.8. Occupational Plans of Youth

(percentages)

Occupation	Percent
Manager or professional	43.9
Lower-level manager, technician	19.1
Office worker or services	10.6
Industrial worker	16.1
Agricultural manual	.6
Independent	1.1
Housewife	1.7
Others	6.9
	100

Source: Judith H. Sas, "Way of Life and Family Aspirations," in Miklós Szántó, ed., *Ways of Life* (Budapest: Corvina Press, 1977), p. 274.

Table 6.9. Perspectives on Economic Issues among Youth

(percentages)

Likely Duration of Economic Difficulties	Magnitude of Economic Difficulties		
	Great (N=82)	Middling (N=501)	Minor (N=102)
Permanent	42	18	6
Temporary	55	81	92
Don't know	2	1	1
No answer	1	-	1
	100	100	100

Source: Ilona Dögei, "Gazdasági nézetek a fiatalok körében," *Ifjúsági Lapkiadó Vállalat Közleménye*, no. 3 (1978), p. 7.

Table 6.10. Distribution of Free-time Activities
among Apprentice Skilled Workers
(percentages)

		Location	
Activities		Budapest	Provincial
Daily			
Cultural activities[a]		43	58
Sports		8	3
Diversion, hobbies		3	-
Social activities, recreation		35	29
Rest		11	10
	Total	100	100
	Hours	3.7	3.1
Saturday			
Cultural activities[a]		35	54
Sports		10	3
Diversion, hobbies		1	3
Social activities, recreation		39	33
Rest		15	7
	Total	100	100
	Hours	6.9	6.0
Sunday			
Cultural activities[a]		44	51
Sports		11	6
Diversion, hobbies		-	-
Social activities, recreation		34	32
Rest		11	10
	Total	100	100
	Hours	9.3	7.9

[a]includes watching television

Source: Ferenc Pártos, ed., "Az ipari szakmunkástanulók világa," *Ifjúsági Lapkiadó Vállalat Közleménye*, no. 1 (1978), p. 54.

issues of immediate personal relevance? One recent study directed itself to this issue.[82] The respondents were asked to compare capitalist and socialist systems—both present and future conditions—on three dimensions: foreign, economic and military policy (see table 6.11). A majority felt that the foreign policy initiatives of the socialist camp are now ahead of those of capitalist societies whereas the economic strengths of the capitalist world are superior. The military preparedness of the socialist world was thought to be equal to that of the capitalist world. With respect to the future, a majority believed that socialist societies would strengthen their relative positions on all three dimensions. This response set was consistent across occupational and educational lines. However, there was a small group who felt that in foreign policy and economic terms socialist states would decline in comparison to the capitalist world. This small group consisted mostly of women, those who have less than eight years of education, agricultural or industrial laborers, and those who never listen to radio news and whose general level of information is low.[83]

This study may be interpreted as suggesting that the essence of socialist ideology is well internalized among Hungarian young people. Thus socialization efforts toward the inculcation of perspectives which support government policy and reinforce the general strengths of socialism seem to be contributing to political consensus in Hungary, even if they do not always yield an appropriate level of "socialist consciousness."[84] It is only among a small majority of young people that this consensus is questionable.

At the same time, the gaps in the data demand that only the most hesitant generalizations be put forward. In Hungary, the picture of youth is not without elements of stress, yet there is little intimation that Party goals are threatened. Yet, there is nothing to suggest that Party directives have a particularly high priority among youth. What strikes one most about youth in Hungary is that their most manifest life concerns are much the same as those that characterize young people everywhere—music, friends, recreation, and an eager, if not overflowing, optimism about the future. Open attempts to focus on the contradictions within their society are apparently not on their agenda. The posture adopted by youth appears to focus on maneuvering within the interstices of what exists in order to find a niche within which life can be enjoyed without too great a psychological investment in those things which are beyond attainment.[85]

Work and the Workplace

The Hungarian constitution's emphasis on work reflects the notion that the very basis of social order resides in labor. "The citizens serve the cause of socialist construction through their work, participation in work competition, tightening of labor discipline, and improvement of working methods."[86] This formally

Table 6.11. Opinions on the Balance of Power between the
Two World Systems (N=922)
(percentages)

| | Sphere of Activity | | |
Opinion	Foreign Policy	Economic	Military
There is a balance of strength between the two world systems.	34	42	63
The socialist world system is stronger.	52	32	25
The capitalist world system is stronger.	10	22	6
Don't know/no answer	4	4	6
Total	100	100	100
There *will* be a balance of strength between the two world systems.	24	30	50
The socialist world system *will* be stronger.	67	61	41
The capitalist world system *will* be stronger.	3	4	2
Don't know/no answer	6	5	7
Total	100	100	100

Source: Ágota Horváth and Endre Sik, "Közvélemény-kutatás a fiatalok külpolitikai véleményéről" *Ifjúsági Lapkiadó Vállalat Közleménye*, no. 1 (1977), p. 25.

stated importance of labor aside, there are acknowledged problems in such areas as labor turnover, absenteeism, productivity, and quality control in many factories. Several years ago when an exposé of these conditions was considered for publication, both the author and the editor of the journal considering it were arrested.[87] More recently, however, inquiries into workplace problems have appeared. One such study centered on nine intensive interviews with workers at the Ikarus Bus Factory in Budapest. It was done by two young sociologists, Tamás Földvári and Zoltán Zsille, and was published in a KISZ publication, *Mozgó Világ* (The World in Motion).[88] This article focused on the lifestyles, interests, and motivations of workers, and on the nature of work organization. The authors show that there is considerable dissatisfaction with the planning and organization of work and that workers are not terribly concerned about the quality of their work performance. It is suggested that most workers do no more than the absolute minimum, in order to conserve their energies for more lucrative private sector activities, or for their private household plots where they are able to produce food for themselves or for sale in the many markets in the city. The authors also indicate that there is considerable theft of factory materials which are either sold or used personally. A picture is presented of general ideological and political indifference among workers, who are neither well informed, nor terribly concerned about the state of the economy or the general issues of industrial democracy.

Perhaps this article exaggerates; most striking is the fact that it was published at all. Critical material of this sort is not greeted with the threat of imprisonment, yet neither Földvári nor Zsille still work at the institute which sponsored the research (the Trade Unions' Theoretical Research Institute). Their work was severely criticized in the next issue of the same journal[89] as to form, inaccuracies and ideological shortcomings. Földvári is now employed at the Research Institute for Higher Education; at this writing Zsille has not found another position.

The ill fortune of these writers notwithstanding, the issues they raised are well recognized by persons directly involved in the management of the economy, including Rezső Nyers, one of the prime movers behind the introduction of the New Economic Mechanism in 1968.[90] Nyers acknowledges that there are obvious limits to the money that can be earned in the industrial sector, whereas there are substantial opportunities to supplement wages in the private arena. Indeed, approximately 17 percent of all workers seek a second job to add to their earnings.[91]

Another problem in labor force commitment and discipline is represented by commuting workers, those who continue to reside in villages and commute to jobs either in Budapest or in other industrial centers. Their proportion of the industrial workforce has steadily increased: 32.1 percent in 1949, 37.3 percent in 1960, and 40 percent at present.[92] In a sample of 786 of these workers, 60.7 percent of unskilled laborers, 56.8 percent of the semiskilled, and 50.1 percent of skilled workers had peasant backgrounds. Only 10 percent have severed personal and social ties with their villages; 35 percent continue to maintain strong ties with their villages on the basis of their wives maintaining membership in the local cooperative.[93] Consequently, it is argued, these workers never fully adjust to industrial work demands, since they view their jobs as simply a means (perhaps temporary) by which to make money.

This problematic character of labor's commitment surely is not solely the result of defective worker motivations. Other circumstances, especially the housing shortage, preclude the possibility of many workers moving into the cities, and thus adopting an urban life style. Consequently, the adaptation made by commuters to their circumstances is perhaps all that can be expected.[94]

Important studies on the nature of and commitment to work have been undertaken by Lajos Héthy and Csaba Makó.[95] Their research has received the support of both the Sociology Research Institute and the National Council of Trade Unions. One recent publication reports interviews with 543 workers, 25 trade union functionaries and 30 managers in 15 units of three plants.[96] This study sought worker appraisals of their jobs and work environments, as well as their general perspectives on change. Workers' perceptions of the Party also were investigated. Respondents were asked what they thought important about their work situation (see table 6.12). To the vast majority, wages (98 percent) and job security (96 percent) were of primary importance. Somewhat less important were prospects for promotion. They were then asked to evaluate their own situation against these criteria. Most (78 percent) thought that they had job security but fewer than half (48 percent) said their salary met their expectations. This emphasis on material compensation was of considerable interest, and Héthy and Makó were asked to comment on this aspect of their results by *Népszabadság*.[97]

> . . . it would be incorrect to say that workers are only interested in money; we are saying it is of particular importance, because they want to furnish their homes better, purchase durable consumer items; many often live in inadequate housing and so on . . . .the pressure for higher earnings is moderated when higher earnings are attained . . . . It is especially evident among the young that working conditions and interesting work are considerably more important than money; more and more look for more than earnings.

In this connection, 80 percent of the workers polled think interesting work is important, but 55 percent are not satisfied that their jobs are as interesting as they would wish (see table 6.13). On the other hand, more feel that their jobs are encumbered with more responsibility than they feel necessary. It appears that few workers would readily accept an increase in job responsibility. This might suggest definite limits to the types of decisionmaking for which workers would accept increased involvement. The Héthy and Makó study addressed this issue. Most workers felt that they are able to handle decisions con-

Table 6.12. Evaluations of Working Conditions by Workers
(percentages)

Working Conditions	Proportion of workers who:		
	evaluated this highly	are of the opinion that their jobs are characterized by this condition	difference
High wages	98	50	48
Job security	96	78	18
The possibilities of developing more skills	63	41	22
The possibilities of developing greater general education	45	40	5
The possibilities of promotion and getting ahead	18	18	-

Source: Lajos Héthy and Csaba Makó, *Az Automatizáció és a Munkástudat* (Budapest: Research Institute of Sociology, Scientific Research Institute for Labor Safety, 1975), p. 79.

Table 6.13. Evaluations of Work Characteristics by Workers
(percentages)

Characteristics of Work	Proportion of those workers who:		
	view this as important	are of the opinion that their jobs are characterized by this condition	difference
Intensity	80	55	25
Independence	73	60	13
The possibilities of making further use of what is learned	73	48	25
Responsibility	72	79	-7
Variety	67	46	21
Improving one's skills	66	37	29
Necessity to learn new things	58	34	24
Possibilities to develop new work techniques	47	17	30

Source: Lajos Héthy and Csaba Makó, *Az Automatizáció és a Munkástudat* (Budapest: Research Institute of Sociology, Scientific Research Institute for Labor Safety, 1975), p. 81.

cerning changes in the organization of their work, or methods of improving their own training (see table 6.14). However, they perceive more limited possibilities for involvement in major decisions concerning the introduction of machinery, manpower planning and employment, and especially production slowdowns and potential plant closings.

These attitudes surely would have implications for the introduction of any form of worker self-management. There appears to be no overwhelming concern on the part of the Hungarian workers studied for an increase in job responsibility. On the contrary, these workers appear to accept their dependence on the decision making of others. This is highlighted by their attitudes toward the Party's representation of their interests (see table 6.15). An overwhelming proportion (89 percent) feel that the Party pays sufficient attention to their general concerns. In some areas, such as job security, grievance procedures, better working conditions, and recreational possibilities, the Party actually is perceived as paying more attention than would be justified by workers' feelings about the importance of the issues. Where workers felt that the Party did not pay sufficient attention to some issues, the respondents also seemed to feel these issues lay in the sphere of responsibility of the trade unions.

Thus these data suggest a perception of a consensual alignment of the interests of the workers and of the Party. As with students, there is no significant dissatisfaction with the ideological posture of the Party, or with the functioning of the Party on their behalf.

If any area exists in which workers appear uniformly dissatisfied, it is with their immediate work surroundings. A large proportion define health, safety and physical qualities of the work environment as important, but not characteristic of their situations. The level of dissatisfaction appears to be less in the areas of work time (shifts) and the physical and mental demands of the job.

There are some other studies which support, albeit indirectly, this general view of workers as having interests narrowly focused on salary and working conditions. In one survey of 700 workers[98] from Budapest and three other industrial centers, only 38 percent appeared to take an active interest in the affairs of their workplace. Fifty-eight percent were moderately interested, and 4 percent not interested at all. Those indicating higher interest levels were primarily those who had worked in that factory longer, who were Party members, and who were engineers or managers.[99] Another study[100] asked about the topics that workers discuss on the job. The one theme which involved both white- and blue-collar workers was job-related problems. Television programs and sports followed, with politics far behind (see table 6.16).

These last two studies, although not of the same magnitude as the Héthy and Makó work, nor as forcefully presented as Földvári and Zsille's analysis, do support the view that Hungarian workers have a rather limited perspective on what is of interest and importance to them.

What appears to be of significance to Hungarian workers is not the potential intrinsic satisfaction of the job, but its financial rewards. Organizational

Table 6.14. Workers' Perceptions of Their Potential Involvement
in Decision Making
(percentages)

	Possibilities for Involvement		
Types of Decision	yes	no	don't know
Changing the organization and surroundings of work	72	24	4
Workers'choice of courses for further training	64	28	8
Distribution of one's time	61	36	3
Determination of premiums and other incentives	57	40	3
The ranking and categorization of workers	49	48	3
The promotion of workers	48	45	7
The determination of the basis on which wages are paid for job	46	52	2
Dismissal of workers and layoffs	45	45	10
Disciplinary arrangements	44	48	8
The possibility of changing work places	42	51	7
The development of production plans	30	59	11
The introduction of new machines and equipment	24	65	11
Manpower planning (planning for future manpower needs)	13	76	11
Employment of workers	11	82	7
Restrictions on production and the closing of the plant	6	53	41

Source: Lajos Héthy and Csaba Makó, *Az Automatizáció és a Munkástudat* (Budapest: Research Institute of Sociology, Scientific Research Institute for Labor Safety, 1975), pp. 96-97.

Table 6.15. Evaluation by Workers of Party Involvement in Specific Activities
(percentages)

| | Proportion of workers according to whom the activity is: | | |
Type of Activity	very important	paid sufficient attention to by the Party	not paid sufficient attention to by the Party
The determination of workers' interests in the general social, economic and political conditions	90	89	4
The awakening of strong political attitudes and self-consciousness among workers	87	76	12
The improvement of workers' material situation, standard of living	85	80	15
Complete job security	84	88	4
The raising of workers' educational development	73	86	6
The management of workers' grievance procedures	72	75	18
The securing and improving of working conditions	69	79	9
The securing for workers of sufficient rest and recreational possibilities	55	77	16

Source: Lajos Héthy and Csaba Makó, *Az Automatizáció és a Munkástudat* (Budapest: Research Institute of Sociology, Scientific Research Institute for Labor Safety, 1975), p. 113.

Table 6.16. Occurrence of Conversational Themes within
Circles of Blue-collar and White-collar Workers
(percentages)

	Worker Group	
Theme	blue-collar workers	white-collar workers
	(N=213)	(N=136)
Work-related problems	90	96
Politics	50	68
Television programs	84	74
Sports	70	50

Source: László Kulcsár, "Témak és szerepek a köznapi kommunikáció egyik jelentős
szinterén—a munkahelyen," *Rádió és Televizió Szemle*, nos. 2-3 (1975), p. 68.

advancement and increased workplace responsibility are not widely sought. There is an accompanying sense of partisan dependence in which major issues are left to the Party, which will defend their interests. Where there is more personal concern is in things more relevant to personal and familial affairs, wages, and better and healthier working conditions.

These results may be a disappointment to those who would have hoped that socialism would alter the essentials of human character and that industrious, responsible workers would emerge. Although this has not happened, neither is there great opposition on the part of the workers toward the ideological tenets or political forms of socialism. No doubt, more enthusiasm for work would be shown if the wage structure provided appropriate incentives. Thus it is in the relatively open area of the private sector that workers are searching for and finding their opportunities.

Leisure Time

There are two significant areas of research dealing with leisure time in Hungary. The first of these focuses on time budgets and is associated with the international time-budget project in which Alexander Szalai has played a major role.[101] The second area of research has a more normative applied character. It is concerned largely with generating means by which the general cultural level of the population may be raised.

Both research directions seek to measure whether there have been quantitative and/or qualitative changes in the uses of leisure time, and whether there is visible development of a socialist lifestyle.[102]

The use of leisure time is affected in part by personal access to technological means of diversion. Thus the purchase of consumer items such as television sets and tape recorders has shown considerable growth. On the other hand, more traditional means of cultural transmission such as movies, theatrical performances, and book buying, have either increased at a slower pace or have declined. This shift is contrary to that expected under socialist transformation, but it mirrors comparable changes in Western Europe.[103]

Some interesting shifts in the amount of time spent on work and leisure activities have been documented in two surveys. The first, sponsored by the Central Statistical Office, involved interviews with a randomly selected national sample (N = 12,156). In 1972 a somewhat smaller national sample (8,821) was studied by the Mass Communications Research Center (see table 6.17). There appears at first glance to be a visible decline in the amount of time spent on work. However, on closer inspection the decline in number of working hours is explained by the reduced amounts of time spent in traveling to and from work, working around the house, and looking after children. There actually was an increase in the amount of time spent on paid employment. This trend is sub-

Table 6.17. Structure of Activities of the Adult Population in 1963 and 1972
(in hours)

Activity		Year	
		1963	1972
		(N=12,156)	(N=8,821)
I.	Total recreation	10.8	10.1
	Sleep	8.3	8.0
	Personal provisions	2.5	2.1
II.	Work in total	10.2	9.8
	Paid employment	5.2	5.6
	Transport	0.7	0.5
	Work in and around the house	3.5	3.0
	Looking after children	0.5	0.4
	Other	0.3	0.3
III.	Leisure time	3.0	4.0
	Reading, studying	0.7	0.4
	Social relations	0.8	0.8
	Watching television	0.4	1.2
	Listening to radio	0.4	0.2
	Sporting or cultural performances	0.1	0.0
	Active sports, walking, excursions	0.1	0.2
	Other amusements	0.2	0.2
	Resting	0.3	1.0
IV.	No data	-	0.1
	Total	24.0	24.0

Source: Tamás Szecskő, "Ways of Life and Mass Communications," in Miklós Szántó, ed., *Ways of Life* (Budapest: Corvina Press, 1977), p. 328.

stantiated by survey material on the importance of work, which shows that individuals seek out additional work opportunities to supplement their incomes.

The other pursuits showing substantial increases in time allocated are television viewing and passive relaxation. The amount of time spent reading and studying has declined. Given the stress placed on reading and studying, this result must be perturbing to those responsible for upgrading the cultural level of the population. It might be mentioned that listening to the radio is an activity which can be enjoyed while doing other things, whereas television is less likely to serve as a background for other activities. This factor implies that radio listening might not have declined, or television viewing increased, as much as has been suggested.[104]

Miklós Szántó focuses more specifically on free time by examining opinions toward the "Free Saturday" available every other week to workers.[105] Respondents could assess the significance of this free time in any of three ways. The first choice defines the "Free Saturday" as simply another day, but one in which the normal chores of housework do not have to be attacked as strenuously. This view is more characteristic of women than of men, particularly among unskilled workers. In the second choice, "Free Saturday" makes it possible to define Sunday as a day of total rest. This view is especially characteristic of female white collar and intellectual workers. The third choice defines "Free Saturday" as part of a longer weekend, and is more common among male white collar and intellectual workers. Szántó notes that married males between the ages of 20 and 50 years, especially those in service occupations, use much of this extra time to supplement their incomes with parttime work.[106]

Additional data on the general uses of leisure time are presented in a paper by Iván Vitányi, who examined survey material collected by the Mass Communications Research Center in 1972.[107] Vitányi provides general summary statements of the uses of free time across sex, age, class and place of residence; these data indicate the complex character of leisure time use.[108]

Sex

There appears to be a relatively clear sexual differentiation in leisure time activity. Men tend to involve themselves with home repairs, going to restaurants, and taverns, fishing and going to the horse races. Women were more involved in activities such as handicrafts, growing plants, going to church and reading. However, there are some activities in which the sexes show approximately the same level of involvement. Examples are gardening, visiting, walking and cultural activities such as learning languages, and movie and concert attendance. One of Vitányi's conclusions is that involvement in cultural life has been one of the important results of the general emancipation of women.

Age

Young people under the age of 30 are more involved in activities away from home with friends. These activities consist largely of going to movies, concerts and cultural and recreational activities in community cultural centers. They also read more, and spend more time studying languages than do those who are over 30. Vitányi notes that the same activity plays a different role, depending on the age group involved. Two examples are walking and playing cards. Among young people walking is usually considered recreational, whereas among older persons it represents attention to health. Card playing is defined as a game for the young, but as a social occasion for their parents.

Residence

There are some general leisure activities, such as going to the theater, museums or concerts, which may be limited by proximity of residence. Other activities seemingly not spatially restricted, such as reading, listening to the tape recorder, and collecting stamps, are nevertheless more frequently found among urbanites. Gardening, which city dwellers can enjoy only on weekends, is more available to rural residents. Frequenting the local tavern and church attendance are likewise more typical outside of Budapest.

Social strata

Major leisure activities among white-collar workers involve outings via automobile, going to their cottages, taking care of pets, visiting friends and relatives, reading material relevant to their jobs and learning languages. Among those activities in which working class people are more active than the national average are swimming, physical exercise in general, card playing, chess, going to the movies and visiting community cultural centers.

The Hungarian regime continues to be concerned about how to increase reading as a means of cultural enrichment. Vitányi quotes figures suggesting that 22.6 percent of the adult Hungarians spend some time each day reading books. By contrast the figure for the USSR is 36.6 percent and for the United States only 7.1 percent.[109] Comparatively, then, Hungary fares well. Nevertheless a greater amount of more serious reading is being encouraged.[110]

This emphasis on cultural improvement is examined in a study of 392 respondents from four Budapest factories which attempts to measure the cultural involvement of individuals.[111] Of this sample, 68 percent were skilled workers, 36 percent had completed eight years of school, and 10 percent had a secondary education. The educational background of this sample was somewhat above the national average for workers.[112] The results showed that 74 to

80 percent had no particular interest in the fine arts, and 53 percent of those interviewed had no paintings in their homes.[113]

The quality of information derived from these studies is often very simple, and on some levels approaches the banal. The measurement of financial expenditures and activities does show that there has been an increase in leisure time and that the more traditional forms of recreation are in competition with television. Perhaps the most meaningful commentary is provided by the regime's concern for upgrading the standards of cultural taste, involvement and interest of the average Hungarian.

In Hungary the traditional forms of class distinction have been obscured to some extent by the entry of the children of peasants and workers into positions of responsibility. In a small way this change may threaten some intellectuals, who with few exceptions do not take a critical oppositional posture toward the regime. One balm for the discomforts of this accepting stance may be to show that the cultural standards of the masses are of such a base nature that they are incompetent to run their own affairs without the guiding hand of those who are endowed with the requisite skills. This then establishes a reward structure in which intellectuals who might otherwise pose a threat to the social order obtain compensations for their acceptance of the system by faulting those in whose name it has been established.[114]

Moral and Ethical Preferences and Life Aspirations

An orthodox Marxist response defines all ideas and values as rooted in the economic bases of society. In a society in which capitalist economic relations dominate, the definitions of good and evil, right and wrong, reflect the interests of those who control the economy. In a socialist state, since the exploitative character of capitalism no longer exists, a different moral order ought to be in evidence.[115]

In line with these expectations of a new socialist morality, Miklós Szántó, one of the researchers principally concerned with the impact of socialism on cultural and leisure time pursuits, defines the socialist way of life in terms of the values of self-realization, equal opportunity, community cohesion, and identification with the goals of society.[116]

One of the problems in attempting to define this new moral order is that the values mentioned do not appear to be strikingly different from those usually defined as core concerns in nonsocialist contexts.[117]

But these definitional problems aside, there have been significant changes in the structure of Hungarian society from its quasi-feudal pre-World War II character. There are two studies which graphically reflect the impact of socialism on the moral fiber of the country. The first is an analysis of religious involvement, the second is a study of the quality of life which seeks, among other things, to probe the moral perspectives of Hungarians. Although these studies did not explicitly seek to uncover "socialist values," they do show a trend away from traditional sources of moral and ethical direction.

The latest available survey dealing with the impact of religion is an analysis by Miklós Tomka, who aggregates data collected in seven surveys from the period 1972-1975, all of which were based on national random samples.[118] Religious commitment is defined by one's response to the question, "Are you a religious person?" While there are analytic difficulties with this very generally phrased question, Tomka argues that its very ambiguity allows for a self-defined religious quality to be made evident.

In every survey there is an approximately even division between religious and nonreligious respondents (see table 6.18). But there are differences along the dimensions of age, education, participation in the labor force, and place of residence.[119] Those defining themselves as religious tend to be older (61.5 percent are 50 years of age or older), less educated (61.5 percent have eight or fewer years of schooling), inactive workers (65 percent are housewives or pensioners), and resident in rural areas (55.7 percent). Tomka's data show that one in four of those 20 to 24 years of age define themselves as religious, as compared with two out of three of those 50 years of age or older. Of the older respondents, 47.3 percent of factory workers and 70.7 percent of agricultural laborers define themselves as religious. With regard to education, 9.4 percent of those between the ages of 20 and 49 years with university education are religious, as compared with 69.2 percent of those 60 years of age or older with eight years of education.[120]

These results clearly support the generalization that those younger, better educated and more involved in the society express a lower level of religious identification. This might imply that the regime's antireligious efforts have had a significant impact among the most maleable segments of the population. More generally however, we may simply be witnessing the emergence of a more secular, rationally oriented moral order developing, in which individuals have fewer ideological normative guidelines on which to base crucial life decisions.

The other study which focuses on values is the Hungarian Quality of Life project, whose director Elemér Hankiss is a senior researcher at the Institute for Literary Studies. The study is being jointly funded by five institutes: the National Committee for Technical Development, the Institute for Culture, the Mass Communications Research Center, the Sociology Research Institute, and the Institute for Literary Studies. In addition UNESCO is providing support for the publication of the final report in 1980, and for computer time and links with Western universities. The collaborators on this project, Róbert Manchin, a sociologist, and László Füstös, a mathematician, provide an interdisciplinary approach which has been advocated as a means to overcome traditional research barriers and rivalries.[121]

The Quality of Life research program began in 1972 with a pilot study involving 120 interviews with industrial workers and engineers.[122] Conceptual

Table 6.18. Religious Identification of the Adult Population in 1972, 1974, and 1975, in Seven Independent Samples
(percentages)

| Are you a religious person? | 1972 | | | | | | 1974 | 1975 |
	Sample 1	Sample 2	Sample 3	Sample 4	Sample 5	Total		
	(N=1,773)	(N=1,763)	(N=1,827)	(N=1,661)	(N=1,805)	(N=8,829)	(N=1,186)	(N=5,972)
Yes	44.0	45.3	44.9	47.3	48.7	46.0	47.2	44.8
No	47.1	46.1	46.8	46.6	46.0	46.6	50.6	53.2
Don't know	6.7	7.4	6.0	5.1	3.9	5.8	1.3	1.3
No answer	2.2	1.2	2.3	1.0	1.4	1.6	0.9	0.7
Total	100	100	100	100	100	100	100	100

Source: Miklós Tomka, "A vallási önbesorolás és a társadalmi rétegződés," *Szociológia*, no. 4 (1977), p. 523.

and measurement refinements have been made consistently. In late 1977, 1,500 respondents selected from a national sample were interviewed by means of the final, detailed questionnaire. The study is focused on quality of life values, by which is meant "all those use values that are necessary to human and social existence and are conveyed to the people by various goods, services, environmental factors, social institutions and everday human interaction."[123] So far only tentative and incomplete results are available in a working paper prepared for UNESCO.

The research distinguishes moral attitudes among three occupational groups: engineers, skilled and unskilled workers. Skilled and unskilled workers rank utilitarian happiness, family life and social progress highly. Skilled workers place less emphasis on duty, principle, and religion, and unskilled workers place the demands of conscience, religion and a relativistic view of morality at the bottom of their list. Engineers define as most important the general notion of responsibility, family and issues of conscience, while giving less emphasis to the issues of utilitarian happiness, duty and religion (see table 6.19). All three groups place religion at or near the bottom rank of moral obligations. Thus in this study the decline of moral precepts based on religion cuts across both educational and occupational distinctions.

Respondents also were asked to choose the ten most attractive and ten least attractive human qualities.[124] They were then asked to identify the qualities most characteristic of people as they actually are. The human characteristics thought to be most in evidence are those which the authors classify as "petty bourgeois" and "enterprising." On virtually every dimension, especially those which are defined as moral, the preferred qualities were not the ones perceived (see table 6.20). It is inferred that Hungarians exhibit behavior concerned by and large with immediately salient aspects of life. Similarly, there is some doubt as to whether the fundamental values of Hungarians have been significantly altered by their sociopolitical environment.

The limited evidence available suggests that Hungarians are concerned with material advantages and family, and that they perceive what are termed "petty bourgeois" characteristics in their neighbors, in spite of their preference for higher moral qualities than those in evidence.

None of these data contradict the notion which suggests that money, appropriate leisure, and a recognition of the critical importance of education co-exist with a bland acceptance of the existing political order. This is hardly an exciting profile of "socialist man," yet it does indicate the posture of a population whose moral and ethical choices are defined and limited by the circumstances of their lives rather than by an adhesion to any formulas derived from the abstract theoretical formulations of socialist theory.

Table 6.19. Moral Attitudes and Preferences according to Occupation
(percentages)

	Occupation and Rank					
	Engineers		Skilled Workers		Unskilled Workers	
Attitudes and Preferences	Proportion	Rank	Proportion	Rank	Proportion	Rank
1. Responsibility	41	1	24	4	31	4
2. Family	35	2	39	2	50	1
3. Conscience	33	3	22	6	11	7
4. Principles	30	4	15	8	20	6
5. Relativistic open	27	5	23	5	7	8.5
6. Social progress	22	6	36	3	32	3
7. Utilitarian happiness	20	7	46	1	42	2
8. Duties	17	8	19	7	29	5
9. Religion	11	9	0	9	7	8.5

Source: Elemér Hankiss et al., *Quality of Life Models: Hungarian Experiences in Quality of Life Research* (Budapest: Institute for Culture and Hungarian Academy of Sciences, 1976), table 43.

Table 6.20. Human Qualities: Preferred and Perceived

(percentages)

	Preferences and Perceptions			
			Among Hungarians this quality is:	
Qualities	preferred by	perceived by	lacking	in surplus
Pragmatic				
strong minded, resolute	25	18	7	
versatile	20	15	5	
enterprising	15	25		10
Intellectual				
intelligent	21	14	7	
educated	23	9	14	
original thinker	25	15	10	
Petty bourgeois				
family minded	51	48	3	
thrifty	24	28		4
diligent, hard worker	35	45		10
law-abiding, tractable	18	40		22
patient	10	20		10
Moral				
reliable	35	25	10	
well meaning, honest	30	25	5	
modest, not conceited	45	20	25	
trustworthy, truthful	50	25	25	
frank, natural	30	15	15	
fair minded, just	50	30	20	
strong character, mature personality	30	8	22	
Psycho-physical				
jovial, good sense of humor	33	24	9	
clean, trim	25	35		10
settled, cool-headed	21	16	5	

Source: Elemér Hankiss et al., *Quality of Life Models: Hungarian Experiences in Quality of Life Research* (Budapest: Institute for Culture and Hungarian Academy of Sciences, 1976), table 45.

Social Problems and Social Policy

The broad range of social problems and social policy issues requires that we narrow our focus considerably in this section. We shall concentrate on a few areas which illuminate some of the dilemmas and contradictions involved in planning and coordinating a modern society. Three topics will be highlighted: 1) the issues felt by workers to be significant questions of public interest, 2) the incidence of suicide, and 3) problems in establishing equal access to social benefits and services.

What are the social issues which the average man on the street defines as important? The research mentioned earlier by Lajos Héthy and Csaba Makó on factory workers sheds some light on this question.[125] The most important issues were the prevention of war and the housing problem (see table 6.21). If we collapse the two columns headed "very interesting" and "interesting" the problems of war and peace remain foremost, followed by a concern with science and technical developments, and health problems. The issues in which the respondents were less interested were problems in cultural life, the educational system, crime, pollution and the nation's economy.[126] The overall generally low level of "very interesting" responses suggests that the questions did not tap the issues thought to be important by this sample of workers.

Whatever the most critical problems faced by Hungarians, for an increasing number each year these problems become unmanageable. There surely is no reason to believe that Hungarians are genetically more predisposed to killing themselves than any other national group. But the extraordinarily high suicide rate in the country testifies to the severity of the strains imposed on the lives of many. Although suicide in Hungary is not a new problem, one of the first intensive studies of this phenomenon was published in 1976 by the Demographic Research Institute. The study dealt with the 853 suicides which were committed in Budapest in 1972.[127]

The research procedures were rather more detailed than those of most survey studies. First, intensive interviews were held with relatives of the suicide victim. These focused not only on personal background characteristics, but also on situational antecedents such as family circumstances and specific personal conflicts which preceded the suicide. Second, an autopsy was performed on each victim, which sought to discover any organic disease or malfunction.

Suicide in Hungary is higher among males than among females, and increases directly with age (see table 6.22). The frequency is lower for those living within family settings. A sizable proportion of those who ended their lives had problems with alcohol and/or drugs; 24 percent were, on the basis of the post-mortem, defined as alcoholics, and 43 percent were taking drugs of some kind.[128] More than 80 percent had some kind of chronic health disorder; heart disease was evident in 69.6 percent of the individuals, 52.4 percent showed evidence of arteriosclerosis, 82.3 percent had vascular disorders, and in 4.8 per-

Table 6.21. Workers' Evaluation of Importance of Social Issues
(percentages)

Social Issue	Workers to whom this question is:		
	very interesting	interesting	slightly interesting
Prevention of war and the problem of assuring peace	36	40	22
Housing problems	24	22	27
Problems of youth	22	38	20
Health problems	19	44	30
Science and technical developments	14	53	30
Environmental pollution	14	43	33
The nation's economic problems	14	40	39
Problems of crime	11	33	35
Educational problems	8	27	43
Problems of cultural life	6	38	46

Source: Lajos Héthy and Csaba Makó, *Az Automatizáció és a Munkástudat* (Budapest: Research Institute of Sociology, Scientific Research Institute for Labor Safety, 1975).

Table 6.22. Suicides according to Age and Sex

Age Group	Sex					
	Males		Females		Total	
	number	per 100,000[a] inhabitants	number	per 100,000[a] inhabitants	number	per 100,000[b] inhabitants
10 - 19	11	8.1	7	5.3	18	6.7
20 - 29	40	25.7	32	19.8	72	22.7
30 - 39	56	47.0	31	23.3	87	34.5
40 - 49	95	68.8	67	40.9	162	53.6
50 - 59	85	73.3	81	59.3	166	65.7
60 - 69	76	80.1	77	59.9	153	68.5
70 or older	78	150.8	116	114.1	194	126.5
Unknown			1			
Total	441	48.9[b]	412	39.5[b]	853	43.9

[a] 1970 census figures

[b] rate based on total population (including those less than 10 years of age)

Source: *A Budapesti Öngyilkosok vizsgálata, 1972* (Budapest: A Népességtudományi Kutató Intézet Közleménye, no. 44, 1976), p. 45.

cent of the cases there was evidence of a malignancy.[129]

Perhaps the most surprising result was that there is a higher incidence of suicide among male manual workers living outside the capital than among those living in Budapest. This finding contradicts other suicide studies, in which urban regions uniformly exhibit higher rates than do rural areas.[130] This suggests that rural areas in Hungary, especially for those with limited occupational skills, may be highly stressful environments. It may be significant that religious belief is more common among rural women than men; religion may tend to restrain the impulse toward suicide. The urbanization and industrialization of Hungarian society may be placing additional burdens on those least able to cope with changes in their environment.

It is fascinating that policy initiatives designed to deter suicides are nowhere in evidence. There are no crisis centers, nor any special medical or psychiatric facilities designed to help alleviate the sorts of acute distress which may culminate in suicide. At the same time, there also are no special organizations concerned with handicapped children, the mentally retarded or victims of debilitating diseases such as multiple sclerosis. The paucity of specialized institutional arrangements for individuals affected by these problems apparently results from social policy coordination and planning being directed to more general welfare issues. Undoubtedly it also results from limited resources. Further, no special interest groups—even where the concerns center around such apolitical topics as health—are allowed to organize outside the established framework of health care delivery. An unarticulated but genuine fear of the concept of citizen-based special interest groups seems apparent. Rather than risk the rise of such groups, the main thrust of Hungarian social policy involves "the allocation of part of the social product for the sake of integrating the community and assuring its members of the right to live."[131] On this level there is some pride taken in the increasing proportion of national income that has been devoted to providing such general benefits.[132] But there are important allocational problems involved, even with general social benefits, and the issue of whether those most in need are in fact receiving their fair share remains open.

Even those generally supportive of this policy posture raise questions about its effectiveness. For example, Zsuzsa Ferge argues that although the general effects of redistribution, both in terms of cash benefits and services, appear to be successful, there remain problems in establishing equity. It seems clear that the more socially prominent and politically powerful are able to obtain a variety of "hidden benefits" through their personal and professional contacts.[133] These important, informal social networks significantly affect the allotment of available resources.

In the critical and sensitive area of housing, for example, Ferge shows that a higher-than-expected proportion of relatively well-off individuals were able to obtain high-quality government subsidized apartments at lower-than-average rents.[134] Significantly, however, once these facts surfaced, the subsidies were removed. Yet the fact that these inequities occurred illustrates an important problem in a society in which resources are distinctly limited and informal influence is unevenly distributed.

Inequalities in access to medical services represent another important social problem. These services are in principle available to everyone at minimum cost through a comprehensive program of health insurance. However, approximately 17 percent of the population does not utilize their right to these services because they live at some distance from medical facilities.[135] Further, even where there is relatively easy access to physicians and hospitals, custom requires that patients offer gratuities to health care personnel to ensure considerate attention. This practice is well entrenched culturally. It goes without saying that it is more difficult for those at the lower end of the income scale to afford this practice.

Housing and health care are issues which affect every individual at some point. The inequities associated with the distribution of these services may suggest that, rather than integrating the community, the very rationality of the plans to ensure equal access become divisive elements when coupled with differential information and influence.

The failure of policy to diminish differences in attitudes between groups and strata in Hungary is demonstrated by a study on attitudes toward income differences by Róbert Angelusz and Judit Pataki.[136] The research was conducted at three different time periods (1969, 1973, and 1974). The sample size is not mentioned for the 1969 study; 1,307 persons were interviewed in 1973, and 590 in 1974. These were national random samples.

There was some increase between 1973 and 1974 in the proportion of individuals who thought income differences should become smaller (see table 6.23). However, this attitude is very much influenced by education (see table 6.24). The greater the amount of education, the greater the support for larger income differences. Only three groups—housewives, pensioners, and agricultural laborers—were consistently less enthusiastic about increasing income differences and more supportive of minimizing them.[137]

It appears as if any zeal which remains in Hungary for achieving greater equality of rewards is limited to those whose age, education or lack of occupational skills makes it difficult for them to grapple with the complexities of a modernizing social order. The essentially conservative character of these widespread attitudes casts some doubt on the likely effectiveness of attempts to minimize socioeconomic differences.

The problem of perceived economic differences also is examined in a study by Márta Nagy, in which a national random sample of 1,500 respondents was asked about their images of wealth and poverty in the country.[138] Only 22 percent of those questioned said that there were no rich people in Hungary, whereas one-third denied the existence of poverty.[139] Significantly, this denial of the extremes of wealth and poverty came disproportionately from persons with lower educational and occupational qualifications. Judgments of wealth were made more frequently on the basis of consumption patterns,

Table 6.23. Perspectives on Income Differences in 1973[a] and 1974
(percentages)

Income differences should:	Year	
	1973	1974
	(N=1,307)	(N=590)
Be greater than they are at present	22	12
Remain as they are now	13	14
Be smaller than they are now	45	58
Don't know	18	14
No answer	2	2
Total	100	100

[a]In 1973, the question referred to the previous four to five years.

Source: Róbert Angelusz and Judit Pataki, "A jövedelemkülönbségek alakulásának tükröződése a közvéleményben," *Rádió és Televizió Szemle*, no. 4 (1975), p. 125.

Table 6.24. Perspectives on Income Differences according to Amount of Education
(percentages)

Income differences should be:	Amount of Education			
	fewer than 8 years	8 years	high school	university
greater than at present,	18	13	80	82
the same as at present,	63	16	14	9
less than at present.	19	71	6	9
Total	100	100	100	100

Source: Róbert Angelusz and Judit Pataki, "A jövedelemkülönbségek alakulásának tükröződése a közvéleményben," *Rádió és Televízió Szemle*, no. 4 (1975), p. 126.

rather than occupational achievement. Thus the owning of a car, a house or apartment, and a cottage on Lake Balaton were crucial symbols in defining wealth for 37 percent of the respondents. There were some differences between occupational groups on what was thought to constitute the symbols of wealth. Thus 39 percent of the skilled workers, but only 29 percent of intellectual workers, defined wealth in terms of occupation.[140] For intellectual workers and administrators, the automobile was the most frequently mentioned measure of wealth. For agricultural laborers and pensioners, having a house or apartment was the primary focus.

The only occupational category generally agreed to have greater possibilities for amassing wealth was the *Maszekok* or those who earn their livelihood in the private sector as shopkeepers, repairmen, or tradesmen.[141] This linking of private entrepreneurship and potential wealth was particularly characteristic of Party members, and the more educated segments of the sample.[142] For Party members, the existence of the private sector is a direct ideological challenge, whereas for those with greater educational qualifications, the lack of high-level training among the *Maszekok* coupled with perceived wealth may well be a source of resentment.

To this time in Hungary, efforts directed to control or eliminate class differences have not evidenced much success. Nor has the quest for the "good life" been replaced by a heightened sense of collective interest. While some few deny the existence of the extremes of wealth and poverty, most seem well aware of these distinctions. This awareness has not resulted in a desire for levelling all differences, except perhaps among those who are disadvantaged by reason of age and skill to compete effectively.

With all of the scrambling within the interstices of social policy for advantage, one area that appears neglected is that dealing with complex personal problems. Social planning and policy in Hungary have been directed primarily toward the most obvious economically defined needs.

Politics and Ideology

There have been official expressions of concern about the lack of ideological zeal in Hungary.[143] Yet the high level of indifference to ideological questions may not presage opposition or apostasy, but may simply indicate that there are no perceived alternatives to afford a challenge to—or to stimulate interest in—orthodox beliefs.

On this basis there is no reason to raise serious questions about the support afforded the regime in Hungary. The evidence presented in this chapter suggests that most Hungarians do not see their form of government as transient, nor do they find socialism to be fragile, unable to offer competitive solutions to world problems. Indeed, there is a sedate optimism about the role of socialism—

perhaps especially the role of the USSR—on the international scene. This finding emerged in a study by Ildikó Szabó on knowledge about the relations among the USSR, the United States, and China, and their role in world affairs.[144] This survey was based on a randomly selected national sample of 830 persons between the ages of 14 and 30 years. The vast majority of these younger people felt that the USSR's international importance is increasing (see table 6.25). Fewer saw the stature of the United States or China growing, and 20 percent saw their importance decreasing.

The survey also sought to elicit general knowledge about these aspects of international relations. The respondents showed an understanding that the ties between China and the USSR are not without difficulty; overall, Soviet-Chinese relations were viewed as less positive than either Soviet-United States or Chinese-United States relations. The nature of the relationship between the United States and China was unknown to 6 percent of those questioned, more than twice the proportion of those who did not comment on the nature of USSR-China ties. China's role in international affairs, although seen as more influential than that of France or England, is still thought to be of much less significance than those of the USSR and the United States (see table 6.26). The respondents unequivocally saw relations among the three countries improving. This view held even for Chinese-Soviet relations, although the level of optimism was somewhat lower than for the links between the United States and the USSR. Few feel that relations among these countries will deteriorate (see table 6.27).

What little politically relevant survey data we have suggests that there is widespread acceptance and perhaps respect—if not enthusiasm—for prevailing political and ideological tenets in Hungary. Equally important is the apparently low salience of these issues for most Hungarians. The Kádár regime has worked diligently to minimize the contentious threat of ideological devisiveness. More important, this regime has been the most effective in the nation's history in raising the standard of living and in offering a range of economic and educational opportunities to its citizens. Under such conditions, ideological disaffection seems unlikely.

Ethnicity and Foreign Cultures

Hungary is ethnically relatively uniform if not homogeneous. Although many of the country's citizens can trace their origins to places outside the current boundaries of the nation, few indeed retain non-Hungarian self-identities. There are small groups of Romanians, Serbs, Slovaks and Germans who are afforded the opportunity to send their children to primary schools in which these non-Hungarian languages are the medium of instruction; however, the numbers who avail themselves of this are few. The only ethnic group which presents problems in cultural integration is the approximately 300,000 Gypsies.[145] The once fester-

Table 6.25. Perceived Trends in the International Influence of the USSR, the United States, and China[a]

(percentages)

Trend	Country		
	USSR	United States	China
Grew	83	32	38
Stayed the same	11	44	34
Declined	3	20	19
Don't know	3	4	9
Total	100	100	100
N =	830	830	830
Weighted average[b]	2.83	2.12	2.21
N =	800	791	755

[a]Question: "During the last few years, what has been the trend of the international influence of the USSR, the United States, and China?"

[b]The values of the weighted average range from 1 - 3. The closer the values approach 3, the greater the perceived international influence of the respective country (1 = decline; 2 = stayed the same; 3 = grew).

Source: Ildikó Szabó, "Ismeretek és Vélemények a Szovjetúnióról, az Egyesült Államokról és Kínáról," *Ifjúsági Lapkiadó Vállalat Közleménye*, no. 4 (1977), p. 14.

Table 6.26. Perceived Role Played by Five Nations in World Affairs
(weighted average[a], by educational level)
N = 792

Country	Educational Level				
	8 or fewer years of schooling	trade school	secondary school	college or university	total
USSR	4.47	4.74	4.84	4.95	4.79
United States	4.45	4.56	4.69	4.91	4.58
China	3.39	3.38	3.51	3.60	3.44
France	3.39	3.22	3.26	3.39	3.31
England	3.32	3.29	3.13	3.23	3.25

[a]The values of the weighted average range from 1 to 5. The closer the average is to 5, the greater the role played by the country, and the closer the average is to 1, the lesser the role played.

Source: Ildikó Szabó, "Ismeretek és Vélemények a Szovjetúnióról, az Egyesült Államokról és Kináról," *Ifjúsági Lapkiadó Vállalat Közleménye*, no. 4 (1977), p. 10.

Table 6.27. Perceptions concerning Future Development of Relations among the Three Countries: USSR, China, and the United States
(percentages)
N=830

Countries and Sphere Relations	will improve	will remain the same	will worsen	don't know	total	weighted average[a]
			Development			
USSR - United States						
economic	74	19	2	5	100	2.76
scientific	80	14	1	5	100	2.82
political	62	29	3	6	100	2.63
USSR - China						
economic	49	39	4	8	100	2.49
scientific	39	49	3	9	100	2.39
political	50	34	7	9	100	2.48
United States - China						
economic	46	39	4	11	100	2.46
scientific	39	46	3	12	100	2.40
political	41	40	8	11	100	2.37

[a]The values of the weighted average range from 1 to 3. The closer the average is to 3, the greater the expectation of improving relations; while the closer to 1, the greater the expectation that relations will worsen.

Source: Ildikó Szabó, "Ismeretek és Vélemények a Szovjetunióról, az Egyesült Államokról és Kínáról," *Ifjúsági Lapkiadó Vállalat Közleménye*, no. 4 (1977), p. 20.

ing antisemitism which excluded Jews from higher education and professional careers is no more. But then the Jewish population of Hungary which at one time numbered 800,000 has been reduced to an estimated 50,000 to 80,000 as a result of the Holocaust and emigration.[146]

The only ethnic issue that generates significant concern in Hungary is not one internal to that country, but rather focuses on the large Hungarian minority in Romania. The tensions this problem has generated suggest that the tolerance inherent in socialist internationalism has not been able to transcend traditional enmities between the nations of Eastern Europe.[147]

Two surveys have attempted to measure the nature of national sentiments and to obtain evaluations by Hungarians of their neighbors. The first sought to uncover the cultural and historical circumstances which generate pride and shame among Hungarians.[148] The authors of this survey, György Hunyadi, Endre Hann, and Katalin Pörzse, drew their sample from four groups: workers 25 years of age and under (N=1,286); workers between the ages of 26 and 60 (N=126); university students (N=136); and intellectual workers (N=128). The sampling procedures are not detailed.

Two closed-ended questions were asked: 1) What do you think is most characteristic of Hungary's history? and 2) What, in your opinion, aided the country most in its historical development? For each question, three response choices were provided: 1) peaceful periods in which work was the primary involvement of the country's inhabitants; 2) the country's struggles for independence; and 3) the repressed revolutionary struggles.

More than half of the intellectuals defined the independence struggles as most characteristic of the past. Among the workers, by contrast, none of the three choices was selected by any significant proportion. Only among older workers and those with less education did "peaceful periods" constitute the primary selection. No specific percentages are given; this makes the findings difficult to evaluate. The authors urge that those with less education were prone to choose the most general answer, since many did not feel competent to think carefully about an answer to this question.[149]

One difficulty that some of the respondents may have had is that no definitions were given to clarify the differences between struggles for independence and repressed revolutionary struggles. It can only be assumed that independence struggles refer to the events in 1848 and 1867, which eventually gave Hungary a more prominent place in the dual monarchy. "Repressed revolutionary struggles" may well refer to the same events, or as seems more likely, to the 1919 Council's Republic and its repression by the Horthy regime.

On the second question, however, conceptual difficulties were not apparent. All four groups felt that the repressed revolutionary struggles were most instrumental in defining the future progress of the country.[150]

The respondents were asked whether they felt proud to be Hungarian. Their answers were overwhelmingly positive: 93 percent of the younger workers, 94 percent of the older workers, 76 percent of the university students, and 82 percent of the intellectuals responded positively.[151] The reasons given for their pride varied among the groups. Among intellectual workers and older workers, historical struggles were most often named. For university students, Hungarian literature was a source of pride. For many of the older workers, the traditions of the worker's movement was a source of pride as it was for a sizable proportion of the intellectuals. The majority of younger workers singled out agriculture. Few took exceptional pride in industrial developments or in the army.

On the other side of the issue, 32 percent of the younger workers, 38 percent of the older workers, 62 percent of the university students, and 85 percent of the intellectuals indicated that there also was something to be ashamed of.[152] The lowest percentages of positive responses to this question were from workers with fewer than eight years of education and from non-Party members. The highest proportions of acknowledgement of reasons for shame were among men, older persons, and members of the KISZ.[153]

Most frequently mentioned as something Hungarians ought to be ashamed of was the role played by the Horthy regime and fascism, which was mentioned by 51 percent of the younger workers, 56 percent of the older workers, 67 percent of the university students and 80 percent of the intellectuals. Only 10 percent of the total sample referred to events in 1956 and fewer still—mostly university students—mentioned the period of the 1950s in general. Only 34 individuals in the entire sample mentioned such current issues as worker morale, the incidence of defection, and the gypsy problem.[154]

The second study, by György Csepeli, was designed to discover the opinions of a national random sample of Hungarians as to how closely they felt they resembled their neighbors on four dimensions: culture, historical destiny, temperament, and standard of living.[155] At this writing this study only is available as a working paper; the data analysis is not fully reported.

In an overall summary table in which all opinions were averaged on a scale of one to seven, with seven awarded to the country which in the opinion of the respondent most closely resembled Hungary, the following scores are presented:[156]

USSR	27
Czechoslovakia	21
Poland	21
East Germany	17
Yugoslavia	11
Austria	7
Romania	7

Thus overall the USSR is placed closest to Hungary. However, there were some differences among the four dimensions (see table 6.28). In the areas of culture, temperament, and standard of living, the responses suggested similarity between the USSR and Hungary. However, concerning historical destiny, Poland was more frequently selected as being most similar to Hungary. On all four dimensions Yugoslavia, Austria and Romania are placed at the bottom of the list.

Table 6.28. Perceptions of the Closeness of Neighboring Countries on Four Dimensions
(percentages)

Country	Dimension			
	culture	historical destiny	temperament	standard of living
	(N=364)	(N=354)	(N=309)	(N=366)
USSR	73	53	73	61
East Germany	59	25	34	56
Czechoslovakia	51	55	42	51
Poland	42	64	70	31
Yugoslavia	24	24	27	29
Austria	24	21	18	22
Romania	9	30	10	10

Source: György Csepeli, "Kísérlet a szomszéd népek iránti attitudok közvéleménykutatási eszközökkel való megragadására," (Budapest: Mass Communications Research Center, Mühely series) 9, no. 24 (November 10, 1978), p. 14.

373

Education of the respondents has a strong distinguishing effect. On the category of culture, only those with the most modest educational qualifications saw the USSR as the country most similar to Hungary. Those with more education place the German Democratic Republic first, with the USSR second, and Czechoslovakia a close third. This better educated group also gave a higher score to Austria than did the two groups with less education.

On the dimension of historical destiny, those with less than eight years of education placed the USSR first. Those having completed eight years defined Poland as more similar. The proportions shift significantly for the most educated group, with Poland selected most frequently, followed by Czechoslovakia, and the USSR.

On the issue of temperament, those with lower educational qualifications again defined the USSR as most similar, but those with high school or university education named Poland. Regarding standard of living, the most educated segment of the sample selected East Germany as being closest to Hungary; those with less education chose either the USSR or Czechoslovakia.

The author recognizes that the ability to make distinctions on these four dimensions may be problematic for those with little formal education. But the common element to all educational groups on all dimensions was their low ranking of the similarity between Hungary and Romania.[157]

While there is no clamour for a return of territory, the perceived ill treatment of the Hungarian minority in Romania has apparent consequences for how close Hungarians feel toward that country. And although education may be a factor in the ability to discern differences and similarities, the relatively high similarity perceived between Hungary and the USSR on all dimensions, by all educational groups, does suggest a significant degree of emotional support and sympathy for the dominant nation in the Eastern European socialist family.

Market Research

The difference between survey work oriented to the market place as opposed to ideological concerns is directly evidenced by the publications and surveys within the area of market research. Surveys on leisure time activities are laden with a concern for the development of "appropriate" activities. By contrast, market research surveys seek to understand leisure and consumption patterns without having to struggle with normative burdens.

The two major centers which are involved in market surveys are the Institute for Market Research and the Department of Market Research at Karl Marx University. The institute has a staff of approximately 150. In 1978 they completed 46 studies ranging from the use of cosmetics, plans for washing machine purchases, and general shopping practices to Christmas shopping plans.[158] Unfortunately all of these studies are restricted and access is limited to persons who have the specific permission of the contracting firm. The Department of Market Research has a staff of seven and is the training ground for researchers who either will be employed directly by various firms, or who will join the institute staff. Texts and case study materials used in classes rely heavily on Western European and American methods.[159]

Three journals are available in which some general surveys, publicity and information on industrial and commercial possibilities are presented. *Marketing-Piackutatás* (Marketing-Marketing Research) is the publication of the Market Research Institute. *Marketing in Hungary* and the *Hungarian Importer* are published in English by the Hungarian Chamber of Commerce. Some of the subjects presented in recent issues deal with the practical applications of market research for Hungarian firms wishing to penetrate foreign markets,[160] an examination of marketing in the United States,[161] and how the images of commercial enterprises may have an impact on sales.[162]

One article written by László Szabó, director of the Market Research Institute, reports summary results of a survey of 4,500 households which constitute the national apparel panel.[163] The purpose was to study clothing purchase patterns and to discover the methods that firms could adopt to increase their sales. The reason for this kind of study is suggested by the level of what are termed the "hidden imports" of clothing on the part of Hungarian tourists going to the West. Particularly among women, one of the corollaries of Western travel is shopping for clothes. Szabó states that 5 to 6 percent of women's dresses and coats, 12 to 13 percent of pullover sweaters, and as much as 23 percent of the knitted wear worn by Hungarian women is bought abroad.[164] It also appears that small shopkeepers have a considerable share of the clothing market; approximately one-third of all clothing purchased in Hungary is tailor-made.[165] With this high level of imported and made-to-measure clothing it is apparent that Hungarian clothing manufacturers are losing a considerable portion of the national market because of their lack of response to what the consuming public wants. The results of this survey suggest that age and occupation are crucial facts in fashion consciousness, whereas place of residence and income levels are less significant. Young people, intellectual workers, and students follow and frequently buy their garments on the basis of fashion trends. Given the well-known popularity of jeans among young people, it comes as no surprise that about a year after this article was published, a licensing arrangement with Levi Strauss was completed.[166]

Although much of the research done is contract work directed to specific marketing problems, Magdaléna Hoffman recently published a general survey on household management practices among 1,650 families in Budapest.[167] This study was done over a three-year period, 1972 to 1974. Two of the study's topics, financial management and decision making within the family, are of particular interest here.

The results show that 81 percent consider their system of money management to be good, because they have no debts (see table 6.29). However, there

Table 6.29. Quality of Household Management according to Per Capita Income, in Forints
(percentages)

Household Management	Per Capita Income									
	less than 800	801-1,000	1,001-1,200	1,201-1,400	1,401-1,600	1,601-1,800	1,801-2,000	2,001-2,200	2,201 or more	average
No debts	50.7	50.8	49.4	30.1	37.4	33.3	29.3	31.7	35.8	41.3
Does not spend unnecessarily	13.4	11.4	11.9	19.0	12.2	14.2	17.2	25.0	9.4	13.9
The material situation is good	6.6	3.8	8.8	14.4	16.3	14.2	18.2	13.3	16.4	11.2
Life circumstances are improving	3.1	5.9	6.9	3.3	7.3	6.6	7.1	5.0	6.9	5.5
Well organized	7.9	9.2	13.1	12.5	8.9	7.5	9.1	13.3	5.7	9.4
Total of good quality management	81.7	81.1	90.1	79.3	82.1	75.5	80.9	88.3	74.2	81.3
The material situation is bad	7.9	10.3	2.5	4.6	2.4	1.9	4.0	3.3	5.7	5.5
Manages poorly	4.2	1.6	4.3	5.7	12.3	13.2	8.0	3.4	17.0	7.2
Badly organized	.3	1.6	.6	1.3	.8	-	1.0	-	.6	.7
Total of poor quality management	12.4	13.5	7.4	11.6	15.5	15.1	13.0	6.7	23.2	13.4
No answer	5.9	5.4	2.5	9.2	2.4	9.4	6.1	5.0	2.8	5.3

Source: Magdaléna Hoffman, *A Magyar Háztartások Gazdálkodási modellje* (Budapest: Közgazdasági és Jogi Könyvkiadó, 1977), p. 136.

appears to be a threshhold income beyond which control over debt declines. Thus one-half of the families with per capita monthly incomes of less than 800 forints had no debts, whereas only 29.3 percent of those with per capita monthly incomes between 1,801 and 2,000 forints reported being debt free. Of those families earning 1,601-1,800 forints, 13.2 percent admitted to managing their money badly, but this was the case for only 1.6 percent of those in the 800-1,000 forint category.

Most respondents said that the management of family income is done jointly by husband and wife (see table 6.30). This pattern is somewhat more characteristic of intellectual workers than of the peasantry. Hoffman argues that, in reality, the wife-mother is usually the person who plans and organizes major family purchases.[168] This is a traditional female responsibility which predates socialism and the increasing work involvement of women in Hungary. The fact that women have assumed new professional roles in addition to being encumbered by customary demands is indicative both of the demands on, and the considerable influence wielded by, women.

The general value of Hoffman's work is that it provides a view of what Hungarians themselves think of their personal financial situations. It is apparent that a major segment of the population manages well, is debt free, and has enough confidence in the future to consider purchasing a variety of goods. This does not imply that the consumption drives of Hungarians are motivated by what has been called "acquisitive dissent" in which the energies directed toward consumerism are a means by which the populace shows its distaste for other aspects of their lives which are controlled by ideological directives.[169] Money is important and, when available, it is spent on items which provide convenience and comfort, such as washing machines, refrigerators, summer cottages, and automobiles. This can well be seen as natural, and not as motivated by any sense of political opposition.

The public material on market research can only examine the tip of the iceberg. There may be more surveys in this area than on any other subject covered in this study.[170] That this type of research is conducted so freely offers further evidence of the pragmatism of the consumer market place in Hungary, as well as the economic importance of stimulating consistent and optimistic buying patterns.

CONCLUSION

The material available in the social surveys undertaken and published during the last several years does not offer a picture of a population dedicated to achieving great change in the social order. It is clear that many see the relative laxity in political, economic and cultural spheres as a means by which they can "do their own thing." This does not involve a search for metaphysical bliss, as

Table 6.30. The Distribution of Family Financial Decisions by Location and Occupation
(percentages)

| | Decision is first determined by: | | | |
	husband	wife	together	other
Location				
Budapest	13.3	19.5	42.2	25.0
Cities	9.5	12.1	65.5	12.9
Villages	5.3	9.9	63.3	21.5
Occupation of Head of Household				
Intellectual	2.3	15.9	75.0	6.8
White collar	5.4	14.9	68.9	10.8
Worker	10.9	15.4	58.2	15.5
Peasant	8.5	2.8	69.0	9.7
Average	8.2	12.0	59.2	20.6

Source: Magdaléna Hoffman, *A Magyar Háztartások Gazdálkodási modellje* (Budapest: Közgazdasági és Jogi Könyvkiadó, 1977), p. 173.

it does among some in the West, but rather provides an opportunity to make the best of a less-than-perfect situation.

Socialist consciousness, a priority concept guiding much of the social research work, does not appear to have surfaced much beyond the typescript in which it is set. However, this does not portend opposition, but rather defines that whatever is now, is preferable to what might be. The adaptability of Hungarians has not created a revolutionary proletariat, but rather an accepting, somewhat conservative people who have structured their ambitions to blend with the reality which is within reach. This is most striking among the young, where one might expect to find some signs of rebellion. For the moment there are no indications, even among those who have been brought up to expect more, that they will react with hostility to receiving less.

Among those who are older, with limited skills and education, and who had their formative experiences prior to World War II, are many who do not show much interest in anything beyond their most immediate concerns. They have been cast into the dustbin of history, and rather than whimper about their marginality to the life around them, have found a niche in which to survive.

One curiosity in the findings is that one of the most vilified images in contemporary Hungarian life is one that is actually encouraged. There is nothing that is castigated more than the "petty bourgeois" life style; yet this is enhanced by the determination of the nation's leadership to raise the standard of living. Most Hungarians do not place negative moral connotations on wealth. If anything, money is a prime concern and its adept management is something in which considerable pride is taken.

Nationalism, which has often been a festering sore in central Europe has not been dissipated, nor has it been encouraged. However, socialist internationalism has not penetrated deeply into the cultural matrix. The problem of the large Hungarian minority in Romania is the one issue around which national sentiments crystallize. Aside from this, traditional enmities are under control along with appreciation of the strength of the USSR and socialism as effective alternatives to Western power.

The simple picture which emerges is that most Hungarians are seeing better days, and they want them to get better still. Although the guiding premises within the institutional structure concern enhancing equality, this has by no means been achieved, and there are still visible, distinct elements of social class differentiation. However, no one appears overly threatened by this contrast between social goals and reality. The acceptance of contradiction is perhaps the best measure of the confidence placed in the leadership of the country, which has since 1956 worked to create this awkward, confused, but viable system.

The differences that do exist between Hungary and the West may well be reflected in the version of the game of Monopoly that is currently popular in Hungary. In the Western game, there is usually one winner, and his good fortune is to some extent based on the bad luck of his competitors. There is a great deal of activity, buying, selling, renting and mortgaging properties, and inflation and bankruptcy are very much part of the game. In the Hungarian version, very little happens. The players take their turns, and go around the board, obtaining a car, an apartment, and a cottage on Lake Balaton. There is little tension and everyone wins. While this is surely an oversimplification, the emphasis on everyone winning something is evident in Hungary today, both in the economic and political arenas. It is not easy to construct a real life game on this basis, but the effort certainly is there.

NOTES

1. Tibor Huszár, Kálmán Kulcsár, and Sándor Szalai, eds., *Hungarian Society and Marxist Sociology in the Nineteen-Seventies* (Budapest: Corvina Press, 1978), p. 14.
2. Béla Köpeczi, "Ideologies, Attitudes and Ways of Life in Socialist Society," in *Ways of Life: Hungarian Sociological Studies*, ed. Miklós Szántó (Budapest: Corvina Press, 1977), pp. 48-49.
3. L. Szántó, "Social Science Policy in the Hungarian People's Republic," *Social Science Organization and Policy* (The Hague: Mouton, 1974), pp. 235-38, 239-50.
4. "A szociológia helyzetéről és feladatairöl," *Szociológia*, no. 1 (1977), pp. 1-10; "A szociológia-oktatás és szociológus-képzés helyzetéröl és továbbfejlesztésének feladatairól," *Szociológia*, no. 2 (1977), pp. 234-39.
5. Tibor Ritter, "A gazadasági tudatformálás hatásjelenségei," *Magyar Hirlap*, 2 July 1978, p. 5.
6. Ibid.
7. Tibor Huszár et al., eds., *Hungarian Society and Marxist Sociology;* Miklós Szántó, ed., *Ways of Life.*
8. *Rádió és Televizió Szemle: Recent Studies 1976-1977* (Budapest: Mass Communications Research Center, 1978); *An Overview of Sociological Research in Hungary* (Budapest: Akadémia Kiadó, 1978).
9. One complex and detailed study which is at the moment unfinished is: Elemér Hankiss et al., *Quality of Life Models: Hungarian Experiences in Quality of Life Research* (Budapest: Institute for Culture and Hungarian Academy of Sciences, 1976).
10. György Józsa and Péter Radi, "Ideológia feladatok a XI Kongresszus után," *Társadalmi Szemle*, no. 8-9 (1975), pp. 30-34.
11. George Schöpflin, "Hungary's Intellectuals Turn Away from Marx," *Times* (London), 3 February 1978, p. 7.
12. One American journal has published material that is not publishable in Hungary; see *Telos*, no. 37 (Fall 1978), p. 4.
13. György Aczél, "Continuation and Regeneration," *Népszabadság*, May 1,

1977, p. 5, in Joint Publications Research Service, no. 69, 130, pp. 60-62.

14. József Lick, "A tudományos viták helyzete a szociológiában," *Szociológia*, no. 1 (1976), pp. 80-85.

15. Personal communication from László I. Váradi, Head of Mass Communications Department, Mass Communications Research Center.

16. Personal communication from Edit Molnár, vice-director, Mass Communications Research Center.

17. Róbert Angelusz, G. L. Nagy, and R. Tardos, "A téves és a "nem tudom" válaszok alakulása ismeretkérdéseknél," *Módszertan* 7, no. 16 (October 20, 1976).

18. In 1978, a new publication, *Tanulmányok, Beszámolók, Jelentések*, was issued by the Mass Communications Research Center in which all material previously prepared for the *Tanulmányok* and *Rádió és Televizió Szemle* and other occasional papers will be published.

19. There are a great many people who kindly took time from their busy schedules to speak to me about the organization and substance of their work. I should like to thank László Váradi, Róbert Manchin, Elemér Hankiss, Tamás Rozgonyi, Róbert Angelusz, Erika Bácskai, László Kulcsár, Ferenc Békés, and the secretaries and library staff at the Mass Communications Research Center. I was also kindly received by Kálmán Kulcsár, Director of the Research Institute of Sociology; Tamás Szecskő, Director of the Mass Communications Research Center; Dr. László Molnár, Chairman, and Dr. Magdaléna Hoffman, Department of Market Research, Karl Marx University. Dr. András Blahó, Department of World Economics, Karl Marx University, also helped me to make arrangements and appointments with several researchers.

20. Tamás Szecskő, "Ways of Life and Mass Communications," in *Ways of Life*, ed. Miklós Szántó, p. 337; József Lick, "A propaganda kutatásának néhány eredménye," *Szociológia*, no. 3 (1977), pp. 282-90.

21. László Váradi, "Kinek nincs rádiója?" *Rádió és Televizió Szemle*, nos. 2-3 (1975), pp. 55-60. This study was conducted on a national representative sample of 4,500 by Hungarian Radio and Television. The number actually interviewed was 4,441. In the published tables, only percentages are given.

22. Ibid., p. 60.

23. Ibid.

24. Emőke Valkó, "A Rádió 1975 októberi müsorreformjának közönségfogadtatása," *Tanulmányok* 8, no. 8 (1976). This study was conducted by mail. Three thousand adults were randomly selected from a nationwide sample. The data were collected between November 24-30, 1975; 1,198 questionnaires were returned, a return rate of 40 percent.

25. Ibid., p. 80.

26. Ibid., p. 87.

27. Katalin Farkas, "Vélemények alakulása a televizio-és rádió-müsorokról, valamint a tájékoztatásról, 1978 elején," *Közlemények* 10, no. 17 (July 3, 1978).

28. Ibid., p. 19.
29. Ibid., pp. 16-19.
30. András Szekfű, "A Magyar sajtó olvasói," *Tanulmányok* 8, no. 2 (1976). The 1972 survey was based on a planned sample of 10,000; the actual sample size was 8,829. The 1974 study covered 4,500 individuals drawn from a national random sample. Both studies excluded those under 20 years of age.
31. Ibid., pp. 218-19.
32. Ibid., p. 218.
33. Ferenc Békés, "Adalékok az ismeretek méréséhez, struktúrájához és tipológiájához," (Candidate's dissertation, Budapest, 1977).
34. Ibid., pp. 149-54.
35. Ferenc Békés, "Hol a határ a felesleges és a hasznos tudás között?" *Rádió és Televizió Szemle*, no. 1 (1976), p. 116.
36. Pál Löcsei, "A házasságbomlás problémái Magyarországon," *Szociológia*, no. 2 (1977), p. 168.
37. László Cseh-Szombathy, "The Main Characteristics of the Contemporary Hungarian Family," in Huszár et al., *Hungarian Society and Marxist Sociology*, p. 227.
38. Ibid., p. 226. The percentage differences are accounted for by the number of widows.
39. Ibid., p. 231. These figures are attributed to Vilmos Szilágyi, *Pszichoszexuális fejlődés-Párválasztási szocializáció* (Budapest: Tankönyvkiadó, 1976).
40. Ibid., p. 229.
41. Michael Kaser, *Health Care in the Soviet Union and Eastern Europe* (Boulder, Colorado: Westview Press, 1976), p. 168.
42. Ibid., p. 184.
43. Cseh-Szombathy, "The Main Characteristics of the Contemporary Hungarian Family," p. 233.
44. Kaser, *Health Care*, p. 168; Ivan and Nancy Volgyes, *The Liberated Female: Life, Work and Sex in Socialist Hungary* (Boulder, Colorado: Westview Press, 1977), p. 153.
45. Volgyes and Volgyes, *The Liberated Female*, p. 157.
46. Kaser, *Health Care*, p. 184.
47. Two articles in which results are discussed are: Marietta Pongrácz and Edit Molnár, "A népesedési kérdésekkel kapcsolatos közvéleménykutatás néhány elözetes eredménye," *Demográfia* 18, no. 4 (1975): 435-61; Edit Molnár, "A családonként ideálisnak tartott gyermekszám interpretálásának néhány problémája," *Demográfia* 19, nos. 2-3 (1976): 212-27. The study on which the above two papers report was conducted on a randomly selected sample of 2,000 households.
48. Pongrácz and Molnár, "A népesedési kérdésekkel," p. 446.
49. Cseh-Szombathy, "The Main Characteristics of the Contemporary Hungarian Family," p. 233.
50. Pongrácz and Molnár, "A népesedési kérdésekkel," p. 452.

51. Molnár, "A családonként ideálisnak," p. 224.
52. Volgyes, *The Liberated Female*, pp. 131-36.
53. Molnár, "A családonként ideálisnak," p. 224.
54. Volgyes, *The Liberated Female*, pp. 53-57. The Volgyes' argue that women work primarily as a means of self-expression. Other available data question this conclusion. One study conducted, albeit in a predominantly agricultural area, suggests that financial concerns are the main reason for working, see Judith H. Sas, "Way of Life and Family Aspirations," in Miklós Szántó, *Ways of Life*, p. 289. In yet another study which focused on the possibilities of increasing the proportion of women in the labor force the results support Sas' contention that most women in Hungary are motivated to work so as to help meet the demands of expenses at home. Only 10-15 percent of women had other than financial reasons for working. The general conclusion drawn was that it was not really possible to expect a greater proportion of women to work. The only potential source of female labor to be activated were younger women, who were either single or with small families. Older women with families to look after and with fewer skills were less likely to be a source of labor; see Ildikó Hrubos, "A női munkaerötartalék aktivizálásának lehetösegei és korlátai," *Szociológia*, no. 2 (1976), pp. 224-25. The difference in interpretation is more likely the consequence of social class factors, where women who occupy higher-level positions would respond that their jobs are fulfilling, while women in lower-level positions may work primarily for the money. Since most working women in Hungary do occupy these lower positions, surveys would tend to reinforce this result. The Volgyes' however did not select their sample randomly and their interviews show a more intimate if somewhat different picture.
55. Pongrácz and Molnár, "A népesedési kérdésekkel," p. 447.
56. Volgyes, *The Liberated Female*, pp. 21-22.
57. Ibid., p. 35.
58. Ibid., pp. 33-51.
59. Ibid., pp. 125-30.
60. Sas, "Ways of Life," p. 292.
61. Ibid., pp. 294-95.
62. Gábor L. Hajnal, "Young Women Doctors in Search of a Husband," *New Hungarian Quarterly* 21, no. 69 (1977): 129-37. The medical profession is one of the areas in which women have at least attained proportionate and numerical equality. In fact among younger age groups there are more women physicians than men. However, they are only in the majority, in pediatrics, and in laboratory work; see *Magyar statisztikai zsebkönyv* (Budapest: Statistiztikai Kiadó Vállalat, 1978), pp. 172-73; Tibor Huszár, "White-Collar Workers, Intellectuals, Graduates in Hungary," in *Hungarian Society and Marxist Sociology*, ed. Tibor Huszár et al., p. 166.
63. János Timár, *Planning the Labor Force in Hungary* (White Plains, New York: International Arts and Science Press, 1966), p. 35.
64. Ralph Turner, "Sponsored and Contest Mobility and the School System,"

American Sociological Review 25, no. 6 (December 1960): 855-67.

65. Walter D. Connor, "Social Change in Eastern Europe," *Problems of Communism* 26 (November-December 1977): 16-32.

66. József Kepecs and András Klinger, "A felsöfokú végzettségüek demográfia adatai," *Szociológia*, no. 4 (1975), pp. 611-23; there are six times the number of economists and engineers, and five times the number of teachers, and four times the number of agricultural specialists in 1975 than there were in 1941. The number of health care specialists and lawyers declined marginally during this time period; see also "Abandoned Diplomas," statement by Dr. Ferenc Marta, secretary general of the Hungarian Academy of Sciences, to József Fahidy, *Magyar Hirlap*, 11 March 1976, Joint Publications Research Service, no. 67, 190, pp. 25-27.

67. Ferenc Gazsó, "Social Mobility and the School," in *Hungarian Society and Marxist Sociology*, ed. Tibor Huszár et al., p. 253.

68. Ibid., p. 254.

69. Ibid., p. 257.

70. Ibid., pp. 258-59.

71. Sas, "Ways of Life," pp. 273-75.

72. Ilona Dögei, "Gazdasági nézetek a fiatalok körében," *Ifjusági Lapkiadó Vállalat Közleménye*, no. 3 (1978).

73. Ibid., p. 8.

74. Ibid.

75. The public opinion series published by Ifjúsági Lapkiadó Vállalat has been in existence since 1973. Several studies on magazine readership, youth's involvement in sports, and the informal associations in KISZ have been published but not reported on in this study. One study on knowledge and opinions of youth on the USSR, the United States, and China is discussed below in the section on politics and ideology.

76. Ferenc Pártos, ed., "Az ipari szakmunkástanulok világa," *Ifjúsági Lapkiadó Vállalat Közleménye*, no. 1 (1978).

77. Judit Karsai, "Két profonnál többet ér: gyermekek tévéhasználat televizió és nevelés," *Rádió és Televizió Szemle*, no. 2 (1978), pp. 72-78; Katalin Hanák, "A tömegkommunikácio életmódalakitó szerepe," *Rádió és Televizió Szemle*, no. 4 (1977), pp. 84-93.

78. Róbert Tardos, "Társas kapcsolatok, kommunikáció a fiatalok körében," *Rádió és Televizió Szemle*, no. 1 (1977), pp. 66-75, no. 2 (1977), pp. 57-64.

79. Several sources suggest that involvement with music is a measure of Hungarian youth's protest against the staid and conservative character of the social order; see Tardos, "Társas kapcsolatok," no. 2, p. 74; Ágnes Losonczi, *Zene, ifjuság, mozgalom* (Budapest: Zeneműkiadó, 1974); Erika Bácskai et al., *Beat* (Budapest: Zeneműkiadó, 1969).

80. Tardos, "Társas kapcsolatok," no. 1 (1977), pp. 73-74.

81. Tardos, "Társas kapcsolatok," no. 2 (1977), pp. 61-64.

82. Ágota Horváth and Endre Sik, "Közvélemény-kutatás a fiatalok külpolitikai

véleményéről," *Ifjúsági Lapkiadó Vállalat Közleménye*, no. 1 (1977). This study was conducted in March 1976, on a random sample of 922 individuals aged 29 or younger.

83. Ibid., p. 24.

84. Ivan Volgyes, "The Goals of Citizenship Training: A Hungarian Perspective," *Studies in Comparative Communism* 10, no. 3 (Autumn 1977): 298-308.

85. There are indications that many younger people, when faced with the prospect of not finding positions within their area of training, seek out positions where the prestige may be lower, but the financial gains higher; see "Abandoned Diplomas," Joint Publications Research Service, no. 67, 190, pp. 25-27.

86. *The Constitution of the Hungarian People's Republic*, 1972, article 14, paragraph 3.

87. Miklós Haraszti, *A Worker in a Worker's State* (Harmondsworth: Penguin Books, 1977). An account of the trial appears on pp. 159-75.

88. Tamás Földvári and Zoltán Zsille, "Hát maguk nem tudták ezt?" *Mozgó Világ*, no. 2 (April 1978), pp. 52-75.

89. Mrs. György Kerekes, "Hozzászólás Földvári Tamás és Zsille Zoltán 'Hát maguk nem tudták ezt?' ....cimű irásához," *Mozgó Világ*, no. 4 (August 1978), pp. 109-112.

90. "A tizéves új gazdásági mechanizmusról, Nyers Rezsö beszélget Föld S. Péterrel," *Látóhatár* (June 1978), p. 159.

91. Béla Köpeczi, "Ideologies, Attitudes and Ways of Life in Socialist Society," in *Ways of Life*, ed. Miklós Szántó, p. 39.

92. János Ladányi, "Községben élo munkások," *Szociológia*, no. 1 (1977), p. 28.

93. Ibid., p. 37.

94. Ibid., pp. 38-39.

95. Lajos Héthy and Csaba Makó, *Az automatizáció és a munkástudat* (Budapest: Research Institute of Sociology, Scientific Research Institute for Labor Safety, 1975).

96. Ibid., p. 371.

97. *Népszabadság*, 13 February 1976, p. 6, in Joint Publications Research Service, no. 66, 985, p. 19.

98. Sándor Erdösi, "A dolgozók érdeklödése és a vállalati tájékoztatás," *Rádió és Televizió Szemle*, no. 4 (1975), pp. 31-44.

99. Ibid., pp. 33-34.

100. László Kulcsár, "Témák és szerepek a köznapi kommunikáció egyik jelentős szinterén–a munkahelyen," *Rádió és Televizió Szemle*, nos. 2-3 (1975), pp. 68-73.

101. Alexander Szalai et al., eds., *The Use of Time: Daily Activities of Urban and Suburban Populations in Twelve Countries* (The Hague: Mouton, 1972).

102. Miklós Szántó, "Thoughts on the Socialist Way of Life," *Ways of Life*, ed. M. Szántó, pp. 352-88; especially 363-71.

103. Magdaléna Hoffman, "Household Budgets," *New Hungarian Quarterly* 18, no. 67: 141, 143.

104. Tamás Szecskő, "Ways of Life and Mass Communications," in *Ways of Life*, ed. M. Szántó, p. 327.

105. Milós Szántó, "Szabadidő és életmód," *A szabadidő szociológiája* (Budapest: Gondolat, 1976), pp. 281-91.

106. Ibid., p. 286.

107. Iván Vitányi, "A Szabadidő-tevékenységek megoszlása és szerkezete," *A szabadidő szociológiája* (Budapest: Gondolat, 1976), pp. 131-70.

108. Ibid., pp. 143-46.

109. Ibid., pp. 165-66.

110. Ibid.

111. Iván Vitányi, "An Investigation into Artistic Taste Among Workers," in *Hungarian Society and Marxist Sociology*, ed. Tibor Huszár et al., pp. 267-80.

112. Ibid., p. 268.

113. Ibid., p. 278.

114. This perspective is assumed in György Konrád and Iván Szelényi, *Az értelmiség útja az osztályhatalomhoz* (Paris: Európai Protestáns Szabadegyetem, 1978).

115. Lewis S. Feuer, "American Travellers to the Soviet Union 1917-32: The Formation of a Component of New Deal Ideology," *Marx and the Intellectuals* (Garden City: Doubleday and Company, 1969), pp. 100-40.

116. Miklós Szántó, "Thoughts on the Socialist Way of Life," in *Ways of Life*, ed. M. Szántó, p. 385.

117. Talcott Parsons, "Some Principal Characteristics of Industrial Societies," *Structure and Process in Modern Societies* (Glencoe: The Free Press, 1960), pp. 132-68.

118. Miklós Tomka, "A vallási önbesorolás és a társadalmi rétegzödés," *Szociológia*, no. 4 (1977), pp. 522-36.

119. Ibid., p. 524.

120. Ibid., p. 525.

121. "A szociológia helyzéteről és feladatairól," *Szociológia*, no. 1 (1977), p. 6.

122. Elemér Hankiss, *Quality of Life Models: Hungarian Experiences in QOL Research* (Budapest: Institute for Culture and Hungarian Academy of Sciences, 1976), p. 1.

123. *QOL Newsletter*, 2 May 1978, p. 3.

124. Ibid.

125. Lajos Héthy and Csaba Makó, *Az automatizáció és a munkástudat*.

126. Ibid., pp. 116-17.

127. *A Budapesti öngyilkosok vizsgálata, 1972* (Budapest: A Népességtudományi Kutató Intézet Közleményei, no. 44, 1976).

128. Ibid., p. 40.

129. Ibid., p. 42.

130. Jack P. Gibbs and Walter T. Martin, "Status Integration and Suicide; a sociological study," (Eugene, Oregon: University of Oregon, 1964).

131. Zsuzsa Ferge, "Societal Policy and Types of Centralized Redistribution," in *Hungarian Society and Marxist Sociology*, ed. T. Huszár et al., p. 59.

132. Ibid., p. 62. The ratio of benefits to total income grew from 18 percent in 1960, to 22.8 percent in 1970, to 24.4 percent in 1972.

133. Ibid., p. 67.

134. Ibid.

135. Michael Kaser, *Health Care in the Soviet Union and Eastern Europe*, p. 180.

136. Róbert Angelusz and Judit Pataki, "A jövedelemkülönbségek alakulásának tükröződése a közvéleményben," *Rádió és Televizió Szemle*, no. 4 (1975), pp. 124-35.

137. Ibid., p. 135.

138. Márta Nagy, "Ki a gazdag? Ki a szegény?" *Rádió és Televizió Szemle*, no. 4 (1975), pp. 136-45.

139. Ibid., p. 141.

140. Ibid., p. 138.

141. Ibid., p. 139.

142. Ibid.

143. *New York Times*, 1 August 1978, p. 115.

144. Ildikó Szabó, "Ismeretek és vélemények a Szovjetúnióról az Egyesült Államokról és Kináról," *Ifjusági Lapkiadó Vállalat Közleménye*, no. 4 (1977).

145. One indication of the problem involved in the integration of Gypsies in Hungary is given by the fact that in 1971, 15 percent of Gypsy children between the ages of 6 and 15 were officially allowed not to attend school; *An account of the researches carried out in 1971 relating to the Life Conditions of Hungarian Gypsies* (Budapest: The Sociological Research Institute, 1976), p. 41, noted in Kálmán Kulcsár, "Social Factors in the Effectiveness of the Law," in *Hungarian Society and Marxist Sociology*, ed. Tibor Huszár et al., pp. 118-19.

146. Paul Lendvai, *Anti-Semitism without Jews* (New York: Doubleday and Co., 1971), pp. 301-25.

147. "Roumanie: des Hongrois en Colère," *L'Express*, 21-28 October 1978, pp. 130-32.

148. György Hunyadi, Endre Hann, and Katalin Pörzse, "Hazafiság és internacionalizmus," *Rádió és Televizió Szemle*, no. 4 (1975), pp. 21-30.

149. Ibid., p. 21.

150. Ibid., p. 23.

151. Ibid., p. 22.

152. Ibid., p. 28.

153. Ibid.

154. Ibid., pp. 29-30.

155. György Csepeli, "Kisérlet a szomszéd népek iránti attitudok kőzvélleménykutatási eszközökkel való megragadására," (Budapest: Mass Communications Research Center, Mühely series), 9, no. 24 (November 10, 1978).

156. Ibid., p. 15.

157. Ibid., p. 19.

158. *Az országos piackutató intézet 1978 évi kutatásai* (Budapest: Országos Piackutató Intézet, 1978). This booklet, part of a methodological report series [Módszertani Közlemények] lists the studies undertaken, but no detailed results are published.

159. The two textbooks used are: Magdaléna Hoffman, *Esettanulmányok, példák és irodalmi szemelvények a piacszervezés köréből* (Budapest: Tankönyvkiadó, 1978). Magdaléna Hoffman and László Molnár, *Piacszervezés: marketing alapismeretek* (Budapest: Tankönyvkiadó, 1978).

160. András Liptay-Wagner, "A Kollektiv exportösztönzés elvei és gyakorlata," *Marketing- Piackutatás*, no. 1 (1977), pp. 19-22.

161. Gábor Hoványi, "Amerikai piac-Amerikai marketing," *Marketing-Piackutatás*, no. 1 (1977), pp. 37-42.

162. György Sibelka, "Kereskedelmi vállalati Imázs," *Marketing-Piackutatás*, no. 2 (1977), pp. 265-69.

163. László Szabó, "Trends in the Hungarian Apparel Commodity Turnover," *Marketing in Hungary*, no. 3 (1977), pp. 28-32.

164. Ibid., p. 29.

165. Ibid., p. 31.

166. Judit Gömöri, "True to Levi's Recipe," *Hungarian Importer* 28, no. 12 (December 1978): 9.

167. Magdaléna Hoffman, *A Magyar háztartások gazdálkodási modellje* (Budapest: Közgazdasági és Jogi Könyvkiadó, 1977).

168. Ibid., p. 178.

169. Philip Hanson, *Advertising and Socialism* (London: Macmillan Press Ltd., 1974), p. 101.

170. Hanson estimates that the Market Research Institute completed 75-100 studies per year, which is considerably more than the number listed for 1978. The difference may be accounted for by the fact that Hanson did not have this listing available, as no documentation was available until 1976. Since his book was published, many firms now have their own market research staff and no longer need to arrange for studies with the Market Research Institute.

7 Poland
Barclay Ward

AN OVERVIEW OF SURVEY RESEARCH IN POLAND

As is the case in other socialist systems, empirical research, including public opinion surveys, cannot be regarded as existing apart from sociology and ideology. Institutionally, sociology has existed in Poland since 1921, when the Polish Institute of Sociology was established in Poznan. Jerzy Wiatr argues that the emergence of sociology in Poland and other Eastern European countries was associated with the rise of Marxism, that it was Marxists who originally introduced sociology as a discipline to the area.[1] During the Stalinist period, however, neither sociology as a discipline nor empirical research as an approach within a discipline prospered. After Stalinism began to fade in the mid-1950s, sociology and empirical research re-emerged. Several research institutions that today are extensively engaged in public opinion surveys were established in this early post-Stalin period. Universities and the Polish Academy of Sciences also began to undertake extensive and sometimes large-scale empirical research, including surveys. In the 1960s the Institute of Philosophy and Sociology of the

Academy of Sciences carried out a major survey of local leaders. This survey was part of the International Studies of Values in Politics, a cross-national survey of local leaders in the United States, Yugoslavia, India, and Poland.[2]

Institutionally, empirical research is at least as well developed in Poland as in any other socialist system. For example, there are 11 centers for media research in Poland, more than in any other Eastern European system. Of course, not all engage in extensive survey work, and some are concerned only with media in specific geographical areas (the Silesian Institute in Opole, for example). Two media research centers are of particular importance, the Center for Public Opinion and Broadcasting Research of the Radio and Television Committee of Polish Radio and Television ("Center for Public Opinion Studies" will do) located in Warsaw, and the Press Research Center of the Worker's Publishing Cooperative Prasa-Ksiazka-Ruch (Press Research Center), located in Krakow.

The Center for Public Opinion Studies, which was established in 1958, undertakes principally audience surveys of radio and television, but it also does survey research on contract for other organizations. Since mid-1975 the center has published a quarterly journal, *Przekazy i Opinie*. Unfortunately, *Przekazy i Opinie* publishes results from the center's public opinion surveys somewhat sparingly, but the little that is published is usually well presented and well analyzed.

The Press Research Center in Krakow, established in 1956, concentrates on the readership of Polish, and sometimes foreign, presses. Since 1958, the Press Research Center has published its quarterly journal, *Zeszyty Prasoznawcze*. *Zeszyty Prasoznawcze* tends to publish survey results more frequently than does *Przekazy i Opinie*, but its reports tend to be less extensive than those of *Przekazy i Opinie*.

The two centers function principally as organizations intended to meet an immediate and concrete objective of improving the quality of broadcasting and press journalism.

Research institutes of various universities and of the Polish Academy of Sciences, in particular the Institute of Philosophy and Sociology, also are engaged in survey studies. Their studies are not conducted periodically as are the audience and readership surveys of the two research centers, but are related to special research projects, of which an opinion survey may only be one part. A current example of this kind of research is an interesting and important project being carried out by the Institute of Sociology at Warsaw University. This study, which is directed by Dr. Jacek Tarkowski, examines the extent to which local political systems are satisfying citizen needs. This project includes opinion surveys of citizens and local governmental and Party leaders, as well as interviews with important leaders in the central government. The project is still in progress, and none of the findings have been published. Moreover, because of the sensitivity of the issues being surveyed, it is quite possible that many of the findings may not be published.

Some other studies currently underway are: attitudes of secondary school students and their parents (Stefan Nowak, Institute of Sociology, Warsaw University); youth attitudes (Władysław Kwaśniewicz, Institute of Sociology, Jagiellonian University in Krakow); attitudes toward education (Wiesław Wiśniewski, Institute of Sociology, Warsaw University); and family attitudes (Danuta Markowska, Center for Research on the Family, Warsaw University).

In Poland, survey research tends to be not only dispersed in terms of the number and variety of institutes engaged in surveys but also decentralized in terms of responsibility for planning. Each institute is largely responsible for planning and carrying out its own surveys and other empirical research. There is no centralized governmental decision making or coordination of survey research projects. This system—or lack of system—gives Polish research in general a kind of variety and vitality, which might otherwise be stifled by centrally established priorities. It also means that there is a good deal of overlap of types of research carried on by the various research centers. Youth attitudes, for example, are explored by several institutes—the Institutes of Sociology at Warsaw University and Jagiellonian University and the institutes that concentrate on media habits. Even the two major media research centers overlap to some extent; for example, some surveys by the Press Research Center include radio and television audience. Also, as already noted, some institutes, such as the Center for Public Opinion Studies, undertake contract surveys for other organizations.

Both the Center for Public Opinion Studies and the Press Research Center make extensive use of young, volunteer interviewers. In the case of the Press Research Center, surveys are organized into 17 survey districts. Bundles of questionnaires are delivered to the head of each survey district. The center in Krakow completes the first portion of each questionnaire stipulating the age, sex, and type of residence (urban or rural) of each prospective respondent. The interviewers then simply find respondents who meet the specified characteristics. Random sampling is used less frequently. Sample sizes are usually about 1,000, but occasionally they may be as large as 10,000. When paid interviewers are used, the sample size is usually smaller than 1,000; interviewers are paid 200 zloties (roughly the price of a dinner at a good restaurant or about three phonograph records). One survey may include two or three research projects.

Conversations with researchers at the Center for Public Opinion Studies indicate that the process just described is similar there. This center utilizes several teams of interviewers. One team of 1,500 unpaid volunteer interviewers does surveys on radio and television reception. Another team of volunteers does surveys on social problems. A third team of about 100 paid interviewers does weekly surveys of opinions on particular radio and television programs. University-based research institutes may use different sampling and interviewing techniques; in the case of the project studying satisfaction of local needs, for example, university students are the interviewers.

From the standpoint of scholars outside each institute, a major problem— already alluded to—is that many of the survey research results are not openly published. Researchers at the Press Research Center estimate that less than one-fifth of the results of their survey results are published openly. Both centers apparently circulate report findings internally ("*tylko do użytku wewnetrznego*").

The number of internal reports varies from year to year, of course. For example, since 1975, these reports of the Center for Public Opinion Studies have averaged about five or six, but in some previous years the numbers were higher; for example, nine in 1972, 14 in 1970.

Why are all studies not published? Some are, no doubt, of substandard quality. A more politically significant reason is that since 1976, when Poland experienced considerable labor unrest, there seems to have been a more cautious approach to publication, especially on politically sensitive issues. The volume of research continues, but the volume of publishing has noticeably diminished. The numbers of studies published for each year and used in this chapter testify to the sharp drop in publishing. In 1975, nine studies were published; in 1976, 11 studies. But in 1977, the number dropped sharply to four; in 1978, five studies were published.

A good deal of attention is given in the professional journals to methodological problems, especially problems dealing with interviewing techniques and construction of questionnaires.[3] Some attention is also given to interpreting the results of surveys. An example of one such study, cited in a later section of this chapter, analyzes the differences between actual and declared readership and finds that the differences are, in fact, substantial. Perhaps because of the attention to methodological problems, the studies appear generally to be of good quality.

Where the reports of the studies tend to be deficient is in the lack of analysis. Findings are usually reported in the form of simple one-way frequency tables. Seldom does one encounter even a bivariate cross-tabulation, much less a more elaborate and sophisticated correlational analysis. Controls are used sparingly. For example, in one table readership may be broken down by place of residence (urban or rural), while in a separate table that break-down may be by educational level; but the two characteristics, residence and education, do not appear together. Because of the lack of correlational analysis and lack of controls, interpretation of the survey results is generally a speculative exercise.

This chapter concentrates on Polish surveys that have been publicly reported from 1975 through 1978. The emphasis is on nationwide surveys undertaken by academic research and professional survey institutions. With only a few exceptions, small, local surveys and readership polls by newspapers are not included in the review.

The substantive topics included in the review are: media habits; family and women; education and youth; work; moral and ethical preferences and life aspirations; social problems and social policy; and politics and ideology. Not included in the review are: leisure time; ethnicity and foreign cultures; and market research. A couple of the omitted topics deserve at least brief comment.

By implication, leisure time is subsumed within several other topics. For example, when respondents in surveys indicate a desire for cultural entertainment, trips abroad, and liberation from excessive work, they are clearly expressing an interest in having leisure time and what they might like to do with their leisure time. A good deal of the sociological research on leisure time is behavioral rather than attitudinal—for example, how much free time an average worker has in a typical day. This kind of behavioral research is not reviewed here.

Attitudes on ethnic differences within Poland is clearly a topic of relatively low priority for published research. Outside of Silesia, the country is ethnically homogeneous, and attitudes on ethnic differences may seem rather unimportant. Inside Silesia, with its German minority, the topic may be somewhat sensitive for publication, if it is researched at all.

SURVEYS OF PUBLIC ATTITUDES AND BEHAVIOR IN POLAND

Media Habits

Probably no activity in Poland is as constantly monitored by surveys as is the public's use of the media. The Center for Public Opinion Studies in Warsaw and the Press Research Center in Krakow undertake frequent and usually large-scale surveys on media habits.

In general, the surveys reveal few surprises. Newspaper readership is large as is the radio audience, and the television audience is growing. Use of the media tends to be noticeably higher in urban than rural areas. Overall usage by men and women is about the same, although there are some interesting differences between the sexes in the types of press that are most read. As is generally the case in every country, education is the strongest determinant of media usage, especially of the press. In brief, except where education and residence (urban or rural) are considered, most of the differences among subgroups in the population are limited to the specific kinds of media utilized and the kinds of themes and approaches to presentation which are preferred.

Polish press readership

In one of the most interesting of the readership surveys, Zbigniew Bajka examines the people who do *not* read.[4] Declared nonreadership is small. In his national sample of about 10,000 respondents, nonreadership is only 7.2 percent and is heavily concentrated in largely rural provinces.[5] For example, nonreadership in Białystok, a largely rural province, is more than 15 percent, whereas in the heavily urban province of Katowice, nonreadership is about 4 percent.

The question, of course, is whether low readership in rural areas is due principally to inherent characteristics of rural life or to some other factor that simply happens to be associated with both rural population and nonreadership. Bajka examines both possibilities.

One characteristic of rural life is that both population and various facilities are dispersed rather than concentrated. One facility of importance here is the proximity of news kiosks, for papers are ordinarily not delivered to homes through subscriptions. The relationship appears to be a strong one, as table 7.1 shows.

Bajka reports further that 53 percent of the group of nonreaders live more than 15 minutes from a news kiosk and that 42 percent do not even have the possibility of passing near a kiosk on their way to work. Clearly, in this respect urban dwellers are greatly advantaged over their rural counterparts.

One factor not necessarily related to rural life but often associated with it is a lower level of education. The evident strength of the relationship between levels of education and nonreadership reported in table 7.2 suggests that although some factors inherent in rural life may, of course, affect readership, education is probably the strongest determinant. Unfortunately, as is characteristic of many of the Polish reports of survey studies, no control is reported for type of residence and for education. Consequently, the relative effects of the two factors cannot be compared.[6]

According to Bajka's study, only about 7 percent of the population is self-declared as nonreaders. This is not to say that roughly 93 percent of the population can be regarded as regular newspaper readers. In another study by Bajka on newspaper readership among workers, he reports that about 60 percent of the workers regularly read newspapers, which is approximately the same percentage for the population as a whole.[7] The principal difference is that the workers are regular readers of fewer titles.[8]

As is so often the case, nationally aggregated figures tend to obscure much that is interesting and important. For example, Bajka's study on workers' readership shows that although workers are slightly behind the population as a whole in reading the national papers, including *Trybuna Ludu*, they tend to be ahead of the population as a whole in reading the local press, the Party press and afternoon papers in particular (see table 7.3).

By looking not at readership as a whole but at the readership of specific newspapers and weekly periodicals, some other differences among subgroups of the population become clearer. For example, if we look at the readership of two major urban daily papers (*Trybuna Ludu* and *Życie Warszawy*) and two major rural daily newspapers (*Chłopska Droga* and *Dziennik Ludowy*), we find that men tend to read the daily papers more than do women, although the situation is mixed, as data from a study by Andrzej Rusinek indicate[9] (see table 7.4).

In sharp contrast with the balance of readership of daily newspapers, the readership of weekly periodicals appears heavily female. In a review of the read-

Table 7.1. Nonreadership by Availability of News Kiosks

Time from Home to News Kiosk	Percent Nonreaders
Up to 5 minutes	3.0
Up to 10 minutes	5.7
Up to 15 minutes	8.2
Over 15 minutes	13.8

Source: Zbigniew Bajka, "Kto Nie Czyta Prasy? " *Zeszyty Prasoznawcze*, no. 1 (1975): 32.

Table 7.2. Nonreadership by Level of Formal Education

Level of Education	Percent Nonreaders
Incomplete primary	61.5
Complete primary	24.5
Trade school	5.3
Incomplete secondary	2.8
Secondary	2.6
Post-secondary	0.7
Incomplete higher	0.6
Higher	0.4

Source: Zbigniew Bajka, "Kto Nie Czyta Prasy? " *Zeszyty Prasoznawcze*, no. 1 (1975): 33.

Table 7.3. Local Newspaper Readership by Locale of Residence
(percentages)

	Local Newspaper					
	Party Papers[a]		Morning Papers		Afternoon Papers	
Locale of Residence	all groups	workers	all groups	workers	all groups	workers
Provincial capital	52	56	27	30	41	54
Other (smaller) city	76	80	21	16	19	19
Village	70	76	11	12	11	14

[a]Papers of the Polish United Workers' Party

Source: Zbigniew Bajka, "Czytelnictwo Prasy Wśród Robotników," *Zeszyty Prasoznawcze*, no. 2 (1976): 45.

ership of 29 weekly publications, Bajka reports that only four have a decidedly male readership (*Polityka, Forum, Motor,* and *Sportowiec*), whereas 11 periodicals have a substantially female readership.[10] Excluding periodicals that seem to be explicitly directed to one sex or the other (such as *Kobieta i Życie* for women and *Sportowiec* for men), we find that female readership is still often greater than is male readership. Table 7.5 provides figures on the readership of major periodicals from Rusinek's report cited above.

One might infer from the figures in table 7.5 that women tend to prefer periodicals that are less politically oriented than *Polityka* and *Forum*, yet *Kultura* and *Prawo i Życie* by no means ignore politically related features.

As in all socialist countries, newspapers—particularly Party papers—are important channels of political communication. When one looks at the readership of the various major daily papers, Party and non-Party, one can see distinctly different patterns of readership in terms of political membership and occupation of readers.

Not surprisingly, Rusinek's report shows that *Życie Warszawy*, which is probably the paper with the best writing in Poland, appeals to the most educated, most highly paid, and next to *Słowo Powszechne*, the least political of readers. Also not surprisingly, *Trybuna Ludu*, the daily paper of the Central Committee of the Polish United Workers' Party (PUWP), appeals to the most political readers, although scarcely more than a third of its readers are members of the Party and fewer than 15 percent of its readers are workers. The figures in table 7.6 compare the readership of *Trybuna Ludu* and *Życie Warszawy* in terms of political affiliation, occupation, education, and income. What the figures in table 7.6 seem to indicate is that *Trybuna Ludu* and *Życie Warszawy* function principally as channels of communication to relatively elite publics. This is not to say, of course, that the Party does not adequately reach the workers, the class whose interests it seeks most to represent. Rather it probably does so not through *Trybuna Ludu* but through the local Party papers, for it will be recalled from figures cited earlier that workers tend to read the local Party papers more than do other segments of Polish society.

All of the observations above are based upon self-declared habits of reading—or not reading—the press. How accurately do the respondents report their habits? Zbigniew Nęcki and Zbigniew Sobiecki studied this problem. They asked a relatively small number of respondents, 112, how frequently they read daily newspapers and how much of the papers they read. They then asked specific questions about the papers to check whether in fact the respondents had actually read what they claimed to have read.[11] What Nęcki and Sobiecki found was that considerable discrepancies exist between actual and declared readership. More than 96 percent of the respondents indicated that they read daily newspapers, whereas in fact less than one-third had read a paper in the two previous days.[12] From their study, Nęcki and Sobiecki suggest applying probability coefficients to declared readership in order to get a more accurate picture. The coefficient for self-declared daily readership is 0.65; for "a few

Table 7.4. Readership of Major Urban and Rural Daily Newspapers by Sex
(percentages)

Newspaper	Sex	
	Women	Men
Urban		
Trybuna Ludu	33.8	66.2
Życie Warszawy	48.3	51.7
Rural		
Chłopska Droga	32.5	67.5
Dziennik Ludowy	58.0	42.0

Source: Andrzej Rusinek, "Zasięg i Struktura Publiczności Wybrannych Dzienników i Czasopism," *Zeszyty Prasoznawcze*, no. 1 (1978): 87-88.

Table 7.5. Readership of Weekly Press by Sex
(percentages)

Weekly Publication	Sex	
	Women	Men
Polityka	41.5	58.5
Forum	41.1	58.9
Kultura	52.7	47.3
Literatura	57.4	42.6
Życie Literackie	54.2	45.8
Prawo i Życie	53.8	46.2
Szpilki	49.7	50.3

Source: Andrzej Rusinek, "Zasięg i Struktura Publiczności Wybrannych Dzienników i Czasopism," *Zeszyty Prasoznawcze*, no. 1 (1978): 88.

times a week," 0.31; for "once a week or seldom," about .0.

Western press readership

Relatively little attention is given in reported Polish research to readership of Western press, but a study by Teresa Turlik-Marecka examined readers in several centers of the International Press and Book Club.[13] Unfortunately, we do not know what controls were applied for availability of papers and periodicals. American daily papers are conspicuous in their omission from the report.

The most popular daily paper is *The Times* of London, which, not surprisingly, tends to be more popular among the better educated readers, those with secondary education or higher. Its popularity is fairly even across age groups but is greatest among younger readers. The next most generally read popular paper is *Le Monde*. What is particularly striking about the *Le Monde* readership is that it is decidedly skewed to older readers (over 60) and the most educated, those with higher education; its popularity is much lower among younger readers and those with less than higher education. The *Frankfurter Allgemeine* also draws its heaviest readership from older readers.

The weekly magazines with the highest general popularity are *Jours de France, Paris-Match,* and *Der Spiegel. Time, Newsweek,* and *Epoca* (the Italian magazine) are all noticeably less popular.

The principal motivation for reading the foreign press in general is to deepen the readers' familiarity with foreign languages; this is especially true for the readers with higher education. Other reasons of particular importance for the sample as a whole included a desire to broaden one's knowledge of world events, general interest, or entertainment.[14] If one compares the readers with higher education with the sample as a whole, one can see noticeably different motivations, as the figures in table 7.7 indicate.

In general, the educated readers are the more serious readers, looking less for general entertainment than for knowledge of world events, knowledge of people in other countries, and information not reported by the Polish press.

Radio and television reception

Although the Center for Public Opinion Studies of the Polish Radio and Television undertakes frequent surveys of radio and television audiences, relatively few of the survey results are published. One can, however, get at least a general idea of television and radio audiences.

In a 1975 survey, the Center for Public Opinion Studies found that about three-quarters of their respondents preferred to watch television, whereas only one-quarter preferred listening to the radio or going to movies.[15] Actual television and radio audiences are, of course, determined not only by the desire to

Table 7.6. Selected Characteristics of *Trybuna Ludu* and
Życie Warszawy Readership
(percentages)

	Characteristic						
	Political Affiliation		Occupation		Education		Monthly Income
Newspaper	PUWP	none	worker	white collar	secondary	higher	over 3,000 zlotys
Trybuna Ludu	34.1	27.5	14.5	45.5	58.8	19.6	16.2
Życie Warszawy	19.4	48.6	9.5	50.5	51.4	48.0	21.6

Source: Andrzej Rusinek, "Zasięg i Struktura Publiczności Wybrannych Dzienników i Czasopism," *Zeszyty Prasoznawcze*, no. 1 (1978): 88.

Table 7.7. Motives for Reading Foreign Press by Level of Formal Education
(percentages)

		Level of Education		
Motive	Total Sample	less than secondary	secondary	higher
Deepen familiarity with foreign languages	54.8	40.1	55.5	66.5
Broaden knowledge of world events	54.6	36.8	55.2	64.2
General interest, entertainment	53.4	63.1	52.1	50.0
Find out what people in other countries are saying, thinking	52.6	43.4	52.7	59.7
Possibility of finding information not in Polish press	48.8	32.8	47.8	62.5

Source: Teresa Turlik-Marecka, "Czytelnictwo Prasy Zachodniej w Klubach MPik," *Zeszyty Prasoznawcze*, no. 1 (1977): 83.

watch or listen but also by the availability of receiving sets and by the availability of programs. Income and place of residence are important considerations. A modest size television set is not inexpensive for most Poles, and whereas television programs are available in most urban areas, their reception in many rural areas is less certain. The figures in table 7.8 indicate the influence of income and place of residence on ownership of radio and television.

Unfortunately, figures on ownership by levels of education are not given, but because we know that there is a strong relationship between levels of education and both occupation and—to a somewhat lesser extent—place of residence, it is reasonable to assume that education is positively related to ownership of radios and television sets. It might be reasonable to assume, therefore, that television and radio audiences also would be defined in part by levels of education: the more educated groups should listen and watch more than do the less educated. In the case of television, this expectation is unfulfilled, and in the case of radio, survey results appear inconclusive.

Piekarski reports that nonviewers of television characteristically have an educational level of secondary school or higher; also, characteristically, they are women, young people between 16 and 24, farmers, and other rural residents.[16]

The Center for Public Opinion Studies takes annual soundings on radio listening. Unfortunately, not all are published. Michał Strzeszewski reports the results of a 1974 survey[17] in which two results stand out. First, definite patterned differences among groups with different levels of education simply do not emerge. Second, the time spent listening to radio has been steadily declining over time, which can be seen when the 1974 survey results are compared with those of 1973 and 1971.

Table 7.9 indicates the percentages of respondents who listen to Program I (popular music, news, and general interest programs of a rather unsophisticated nature) and those who listen both to Program I and to Program II (news, more serious public affairs, classical music, and jazz). The time spent listening to radio is declining over the years, although relatively few people have given up listening to radio altogether.[18]

As in the United States, some attention has been given to perceptions of the quality of television programs, not only for adults but also for children. In Poland, the general perception of Polish television is positive. In the study reported by Piekarski, 68 percent of the respondents found on balance that the programs they watched were more worthwhile than not. Another 25 percent regarded the programs as equally good and bad, while only 7 percent believed that the programs were not good.[19] It is hard to interpret these figures, especially as a general vote of confidence in television, because viewers presumably watch what they find worthwhile.

According to the respondents in the study reported by Piekarski, the major motives for watching television are to fulfill cultural interests (film and theater especially): 61 percent; to keep up with world events: 55 percent; to develop social and political interests: 46 percent; and to compensate for various

Table 7.8. Ownership of Radio and Television Sets by Occupation and
Place of Residence
(percentages)

Occupation, Residence	Receivers	
	radio sets	television sets
Occupation		
Private farmers	80	58
Unskilled workers	83	77
Skilled workers	89	90
White-collar workers	95	93
Place of Residence		
Rural	83	69
Cities under 20,000	87	87
Cities 20,000 to 100,000	90	91
Cities over 100,000	92	93

Source: Michał Strzeszewski, "Z Badań nad Audytorium Radiowym w Polsce," *Przekazy i Opinie*, no. 4 (October-December 1975): 87.

Table 7.9. Radio Program Listening Practices by Educational Level
(percentages)

Educational Level	Listening Practices		
	Program I only	Program II only	Programs I and II
Primary education only	34	4	33
Secondary education and trade school	22	5	29
Higher education	19	9	33

Source: Michał Strzeszewski, "Z Badań nad Audytorium Radiowym w Polsce," *Przekazy i Opinie*, no. 4 (October-December 1975): 93.

deficiencies of everyday life: 45 percent.[20] According to a study reported by Stefania Dzięciołowska, film and theater are, indeed, the most popular types of television programs, with 50 percent of the respondents in her 1975 study indicating that they watch films and 42 percent indicating that they watch theater.[21]

In the case of children's television habits, a question familiar to many American families has been addressed: how much television is good for children? Although children's television is also regarded more positively than negatively, it is interesting to compare the views of parents on children's television with their views of programs for adults. One can detect a greater degree of skepticism about children's programs than about their own. Aleksander Nocun provides data from a 1976 survey undertaken by the Center for Public Opinion Studies;[22] these are reported in table 7.10.

The additional fact that in this survey only 1 percent of the respondents felt that television for children had no value, whereas 15 percent felt that children's television had only harmful effects, reinforces the impression that Polish parents tend to be critical (not necessarily negative) and skeptical judges of the television their children watch.[23] They seem to distinguish both good and bad characteristics. On the other hand, their view of adult television is noticeably more positive.

Some of the media research moves in a quite different direction from that which has been discussed to this point. Two studies of the Center for Public Opinion Studies, one by Teresa Konwicka and one by Irena Tomaszewska, examine the way media messages are received by media users.[24] An interesting aspect of these two studies is that they touch on some theoretical concepts of communications and at the same time seek to directly serve one of the practical objectives of media research noted in the introductory section to this chapter, improving the effectiveness of the media.

Konwicka's study looks at viewers' understanding of political terminology and quantitative reports. Respondents were asked to select from several choices the correct definition of frequently used political terms such as "crises," "exploitation," "neutrality," and "nonproliferation." They were then asked to select from several choices the correct explanation of the same terms when used in the context of a statement. It is not surprising that most terms are well understood by themselves and tend to be understood even more frequently when they are used in context. A few terms ("integration," "extremism," and "nonproliferation") were understood by fewer than half of the respondents when used alone; even in context "integration" and "nonproliferation" fared poorly.[25]

The respondents were also given five pieces of quantitatively reported information, such as rate of construction or amount of production. They were asked to attribute to these quantities terms such as "fast," "slow," or "big." On the average, only about half of the respondents could express an opinion on each quantitative item of information. About one-quarter were unable to interpret any of the five quantities. It is surprising that controls for levels of education explain little, if any, of the differences in the ability to interpret quantitatively presented information. For example, only 21 percent of those respondents with trade school or uncompleted secondary education could express an opinion on all five pieces of information, but no more than 20 percent of those with at least some higher education could do so. Even more striking, a higher percentage of respondents with higher education (28 percent) than those with primary education (26 percent) were unable to interpret any of the five terms.[26]

What the results of Konwicka's study seem to show is that "television language" (her term) may not always communicate much useful information to viewers, especially if the information is quantitatively presented. Her study raises an important question: How can the media most effectively communicate information? Are the most effective media reports those which are objective and factual, or those which are biased and emotional?

Tomaszewska's study explores this question and seeks to explain why some people prefer rational argumentation and why others prefer emotional argumentation. In her study, respondents were given 11 statements of various problems and asked to indicate their preference for one of four possible responses. Two of the possible responses favored one side, two the other; one response on each side was stated in a rational manner, one in an emotional manner. What were considered to be rational statements were constructed to be objective, balanced, logical, and based on concrete facts. Emotional statements, on the other hand, were biased, not concrete, and used sweeping, categorical terms such as "everyone," "never," or "always."

The results of her study demonstrate that, as a rule, individuals are not always rational or always emotional, but tend to be a bit of both. For each respondent, eight of eleven answers in one direction or the other were regarded as indicating a characteristic preference for either rationality or emotionalism. On that basis, three-quarters of the respondents were ambivalent in their answers. On the other hand, if one looks at the relatively small number of respondents whose answers do indicate a definite direction, it is possible to detect an apparent relationship between levels of education and preferences. Of those who have at most a primary education, almost twice as many prefer emotional arguments than prefer rational arguments. Of those with secondary or higher education, four times as many prefer rational arguments than prefer emotional arguments.[27]

Tomaszewska examines the possible effects of three personal characteristics: activeness in seeking information, the tendency of domination or dependence in interpersonal relations, and tolerance towards others. In brief, the findings suggest that active information seekers, dominant personalities, and those who are tolerant generally prefer rational argumentation.[28] Unfortunately, one cannot see distinctly different patterns of responses for the inactive information seekers, the dependent personalities, and the intolerant, for their preferences are about equally divided between rational and emotional argumentation.

Neither Konwicka's study nor Tomaszewska's study establishes any really firm conclusions, but they are important because they deal with the most fundamental problem of media communication: the relative effectiveness of various types of media messages. In any political system, this would be important research, but in an Eastern European socialist system, which necessarily stresses the transmission of political information and values by a state-controlled media, the research has special value.

Summary

The general impression one derives from reviewing reported surveys on media habits is that there are many different patterns of using the media, an impression which perhaps reflects greater diversity of the media themselves than appears quickly and superficially to a Western observer. The most striking association, the one emphasized in this report, is between various aspects of usage of the media (which papers are read, for which motives, which television or radio programs seen or listened to), and the respondents' levels of education.

Family and Women

Examination of the reported results of various surveys dealing with life aspirations and values suggests that the value most strongly held is the desire for a happy family. Moreover, although values tend to change somewhat as people grow older, this value not only remains stable in terms of a rank-ordering of values but actually increases in importance in terms of the proportion of population holding the value. Figures from a 1974 study by the Press Research Center reported in table 7.11 illustrate the point.[29] Of the dozen possible values the top three for each group are given.

When one looks at more specific values of marriage and family—what qualities are most desirable in a spouse, what their family roles should be, and whether wives should work outside the home—noticeable differences between subgroups of the population are evident, especially differences between men and women and among age groups.

Franciszek Adamski reviewed a number of studies on marriage in a 1976 issue of *The Polish Sociological Bulletin*. Although some of the studies had been undertaken several years earlier, there is probably no reason to believe that the findings are less valid now than when the surveys were taken.[30] Two of the surveys covered in Adamski's article illustrate differences of opinion between men and women and among age groups. One of these studies, the results of a press survey of *Sztandar Młodych*, reported in table 7.12, show that men and women have a different ordering of priorities in their models of ideal husbands

Table 7.10. Evaluation of Television Programs
(percentages)

Type of Program	Evaluation		
	entirely good or more good than bad	about evenly good and bad	more bad than good
Programs for children under 8 years	56	30	7
Programs for children, 8 to 14 years	54	36	5
Programs for youth, 15 to 18 years	59	32	4
Programs for adults	73	22	2

Source: Aleksander Nocun, "Kontakty Dzieci i Młodzieży z Programem Telewizyjnym w Opinii Rodziców," *Przekazy i Opinie*, no. 1 (January-March 1978): 66.

Table 7.11. Importance of Family and Other Values by Age Group
(percentages)

Value	Age Group
	Ages 14-25 Years
1. Happy (successful) family	51.1
2. Obtaining education	42.5
3. A certain, continuing position	29.7
	Ages 26 Years and Older
1. Happy (successful) family	64.8
2. Contented and quiet life	46.7
3. A clean conscience	32.3

Source: Andrzej Rusinek, "Wartości Preferowane przez Młodzież," *Zeszyty Prasoznawcze*, no. 1 (1975): 80.

and wives.

Differences between adolescents and young adults in expectations of one's spouse suggest that even over a relatively brief period the process of maturation causes young Polish people to alter their views of what they wish to expect from their marriage partner. One earlier study (1965) of boys and girls in the last year of secondary school and early years of higher schools in Krakow tended to emphasize the importance of emotional values—mutual help, love, satisfaction of emotional needs, understanding, and support.[31] Another survey the same year of somewhat older women at higher schools in Lublin indicated that the expected values were more practical, less emotional (love, for example, was not included as a major condition of marriage). As Adamski notes, "There is more calculation, common sense and prudence about this group of youth."[32]

Over 40 percent of the Polish work force in the socialized sector are women, many of whom are working wives.[33] Clearly, the duality of their role as workers and homemakers challenges the traditional and more simple role of home-bound wives and mothers. In 1974, the Center for Public Opinion Studies conducted a national survey on the question of what role is desirable for women.[34]

A substantial majority of the respondents (61 percent) favor women working. But when questions were raised concerning working wives and how family responsibilities should be carried out, the consensus collapsed. Thirty-six percent prefer that wives not work but be limited to the traditional roles of wives and mothers. Forty-one percent favor wives working, with household chores equally divided between husband and wife. Twenty percent favor women working outside the home but also favor women bearing full responsibility for running the household.[35]

As with other aspects of marriage, marginal but nevertheless noticeable differences between men and women are evident. There are also differences between men and women in families with working wives and those in families where wives do not work, as the information presented in table 7.13 demonstrates.

Not surprisingly, men appear to be generally more traditional in their views of the role of married women. This traditional view is also carried over into perceptions of women in the workplace. These views are reviewed in the section of this chapter devoted to Work and the Workplace.

Education and Youth

Problems of education and youth are naturally related, but at the same time they are quite distinct. Although education has the greatest direct effect on younger people, its importance continues through adulthood. The general problem of youth includes not only education but also generational differences,

Table 7.12. Ideal Spouse Models by Sex
(rank orders)

	Sex	
Model, Ranking	men	women
Ideal Husband Model		
1	Intelligent	Faithful
2	Ingenious in life	Ingenious in life
3	Faithful	Intelligent
4	Laborious	Sense of humor
5	Educated	
Ideal Wife Model		
1	Faithful	Thrifty
2	Intelligent	Faithful
3	Ingenious in life	Intelligent
4	Thrifty	Ingenious in life
5		Sense of humor

Source: Franciszek Adamski, "Model Concepts of Marriage in Poland," *The Polish Sociological Bulletin*, no. 3 (1976): 53.

Table 7.13. Belief That Wives Should Not Work Outside the Home
by Category of Respondent
(percentages)

Category of Respondent	Percent Agreeing
Men whose wives work	45
Men whose wives do not work	53
Working wives	35
Nonworking wives	47

Source: Magdalena Sokołowska, "The Woman Image in the Awareness of Contemporary Polish Society," *The Polish Sociological Bulletin*, no. 3 (1976): 42.

personal relationships (some aspects of which have been reviewed in the previous section), and aspirations for the future (to be reviewed in a later section).

Education

There is little question that education is highly valued by young people in Poland. It was noted earlier that obtaining an education is the second-most frequently chosen life goal (after a happy and successful family) for young people between 14 and 25 years of age.[36] Understandably, this value declines sharply with age. The same 1974 survey by the Press Research Center shows that for respondents over 26 years of age the value of obtaining more education drops to eighth place, with scarcely 13 percent indicating that this is an important value for them (compared with over 42 percent of the respondents under 26 years of age).[37] Presumably, most older people have already received all the formal education that they expect.

We would, of course, be surprised if education were not highly valued among young people, but it is not belaboring the obvious to wonder in more specific terms what kind of value is placed in education. Education may be a means to an end, an instrumentality, for it is a major determinant of one's occupation, a problem young people everywhere confront directly. At the same time, education may be regarded as an end in itself, or relatedly it may bestow more personalized benefits upon those who receive it—status and prestige, for example.

A recent survey research study of Professor Wiesław Wiśniewski of the Institute of Sociology at Warsaw University examines several of these aspects of education.[38] Taken as a whole, Wiśniewski's findings present a somewhat perplexing picture of what education really means to individuals.

Respondents were asked, "If you were, at present, to plan your most important ambitions for life, what would you be more concerned with?" The responses are shown in table 7.14. As we might expect, there are noticeable differences between men and women (see table 7.15).

What is striking is that although the hierarchy of values is the same for men and women, for the latter attaining higher education comes very close to a tie for first place, along with obtaining material security. Of course, attaining higher education may simply be an instrumentality for obtaining material security.

Wiśniewski's study looked at the question of education as an instrumentality from two angles. Respondents were asked, "What do you think decides that people achieve what they want in life?" Then they were asked a more personal, less abstract question, "Which of the reasons quoted in question one had a positive influence on the realization of your personal ambitions?" From a comparison of the first six items of the two sets of responses using only six of fifteen possible responses, it is obvious that education as an abstraction is

Table 7.14. Ambitions of Youth
(percentages)

Ambition	Percent
To obtain material security that would assure an abundant, wealthy life	44
To attain a higher education	39
To gain position which would enable you to decide the future of others	7
Other	4

Source: Wiesław Wiśniewski, "The Place of Education in the System of Values in Polish Society," (Paper presented at the Ninth World Congress of Sociology, Uppsala, Sweden, August 1978), p. 20.

Table 7.15. Ambitions of Youth by Sex
(percentages)

Ambition	Sex	
	men	women
To obtain material security	46	42
To attain higher education	37	41
To gain position to decide future of others	8	7

Source: Wiesław Wiśniewski, "The Place of Education in the System of Values in Polish Society," (Paper presented at the Ninth World Congress of Sociology, Uppsala, Sweden, August 1978), p. 20.

viewed differently from education as an element of one's personal experience. The order of priorities for education changes, but even more striking are the changes in percentages. The values which as abstractions are perceived to be quite important are clearly perceived to be much less important when they are related more concretely to the individuals' experiences. The results of Wiśniewski's study are reported in table 7.16. The figures leave open the question of how valued education is as an instrumentality—a means to an end.

It may well be that higher education is valued less for what it can do for one's career and life goals than for what it can do in a more personal way for individuals. Respondents in Wiśniewski's survey were asked, "What do you think would most influence the rise of your prestige in the eyes of your friends and fellow workers?" The results are found in table 7.17.

Youth

Three categories of values held by youth are reviewed here: general goals and values in life, interpersonal relations, and generational differences.

A 1971 survey reported in 1976 by Bronisław Gołębiowski indicates that urban and rural youth hold generally similar views on what factors contribute most to a happy life and what are the most important material needs[39] (see table 7.18). The slightly more conservative tendencies among the rural youth demonstrated in table 7.18 are also seen in responses found in table 7.19 regarding a hierarchy of material values.

Because respondents were permitted to choose more than one value, it is difficult to interpret the significance of the apparent differences. Nevertheless, some differences are noticeable, especially on items of family, self-indulgence, and consumerism, but considering the contextual differences of urban and rural life (in particular, the greater availability of material pleasures, higher income, and so forth), it is rather surprising that the differences are not greater. One item not included in table 7.19, the importance of having an automobile, actually draws a slightly stronger response (25.8 percent) from the rural youth than from the urban youth (23.4 percent).

How do young people regard each other and others in society? One survey by the Center for Public Opinion Studies reported in 1976 by Krzysztof Kicinski and Jacek Kurczewski suggests that young people are somewhat wary, perhaps a bit distrustful.[40] These results are illustrated in table 7.20. A substantial majority of respondents (81 percent) felt that other people publicly speak differently from the way they think. Betrayal of confidence (74 percent) and stealing state property (70 percent) are other forms of behavior fairly or very frequently experienced.

It would be surprising if inter-generational differences did not exist in Poland. A 1974 study by the Center for Public Opinion Studies reported by Janina Kobel finds that inter-generational differences in values do indeed exist,

Table 7.16. Perceived Importance of Education and Other Factors
in the Realization of Ambitions
(percentages)

| | Type of Factor | | | |
| | factors influencing whether people achieve what they want | | positive influences on realization of personal ambitions | |
Specific Factor	percent	rank	percent	rank
Diligence, sense of duty	75	1	56	1
Knowledge, skill	66	2	25	5
Resourcefulness	65	3	38	2
Education	61	4	18	6
Ambition	60	5	33	3
Ability to get along with people	56	6	30	4

Source: Wiesław Wiśniewski, "The Place of Education in the System of Values in Polish Society," (Paper presented at the Ninth World Congress of Sociology, Uppsala, Sweden, August 1978), p. 20.

Table 7.17. Factors Contributing to Prestige
(percentages)

Factor	Percent
Attainment of a certain level of education	62
Winning a large sum of money	37
Promotion at work	31
Marriage	27
Professional achievement	24

Source: Wiesław Wiśniewski, "The Place of Education in the System of Values in Polish Society," (Paper presented at the Ninth World Congress of Sociology, Uppsala, Sweden, August 1978), p. 13.

Table 7.18. Youth Perceptions of Decisive Values for a Happy Life
by Place of Residence
(percentages)

| | Place of Residence | |
Value	urban	rural
Family life	51.7	52.8
Income	41.8	39.3
Quiet life without surprises	29.1	32.7
Great, mutual love	27.1	28.2
Interesting work	26.7	27.9

Source: Bronisław Gołębiowski, "Aspiracje i Orientacje Życiowe Młodzieży," *Przekazy i Opinie*, no. 1 (January-March 1976): 9.

Table 7.19. Youth Rankings of Material Desires by Place of Residence
(percentages)

| | Place of Residence | |
Material Desire	urban	rural
Housing	57.6	55.5
Bank savings (PKO)	30.9	38.6
Acquiring consumer goods	38.2	30.5
Family help	29.1	34.0
Pleasure (trips abroad, cultural entertainment . . .)	35.4	19.7

Source: Bronisław Gołębiowski, "Aspiracje i Orientacje Życiowe Młodzieży," *Przekazy i Opinie*, no. 1 (January-March 1976): 11.

at least, in the perception of the respondents.[41]

In her survey, all age groups indicated by substantial majorities that they believed a generation gap exists. No more than 13 percent of any one of the three age groups did not believe that a conflict exists. Over 60 percent of the respondents in the middle-aged group (40-59 years) perceived a generational conflict. The youngest respondents (ages 16-29) and the oldest (over 60) were even more likely to see a conflict—over 80 percent of the youngest respondents and about 70 percent of the oldest respondents.[42] When one looks at the agreement on specific values, however, the situation is less clear.

Compared to the two older groups, the group of youngest respondents tends to be more supportive of such norms as sincerity, lack of hypocrisy, and unselfishness (on the other hand, they are somewhat less supportive of honesty) (see table 7.21). The youngest respondents are much less supportive of religiosity. The surprisingly low acceptance of sincerity is interesting when one recalls the finding of Kicinski and Kurczewski that young people believe that other people frequently speak differently from the way they think.

Most norms included in the study, however, are about evenly supported by the three age groups—patriotism, reliability at work, caring for one's family, and self-sacrifice. What patterns there are to inter-generational differences in accepted norms are pale indeed. Certainly, the young people are more secular and less religious, but beyond that the results are too mixed to suggest patterns. It may well be the case that the norms examined by Kobel do not truly tap the intergenerational differences, which in general the respondents feel exist.

Work and the Workplace

A large number of studies are carried out in Poland, as in the other socialist countries, on a wide range of aspects of work and employment. Many, perhaps most, of these studies are behavioral in the sense that they study what workers actually do—what their time schedule is for a typical workday, use of day-care centers for children of working mothers, and so forth. Other studies, some of which are reviewed here, survey attitudes. Five areas of inquiry are included in this section: occupational prestige, interpretations of "good" work, views of one's own work, career ambitions, and working women.

Most of the studies on occupational prestige have been fairly small in scope, usually limited to a particular area, type of area, social or economic group. A national rural survey in 1975 attempted to replicate an earlier study (1958) in Warsaw.[43] Almost 30 occupations were included in the 1975 study. The responses were converted into a scale, such that 1.0 would be a very high rating, whereas 5.0 would be very low. The twelve occupations with the highest prestige in order of their rank in the survey are shown in table 7.22.[44] As can be seen, the rankings are fairly stable over time. "Minister of national govern-

Table 7.20. Frequency of Experienced Forms of Behavior of Others
(percentages)

Form of Behavior	Frequency	
	very frequently	fairly frequently
People say one thing in meetings but really believe differently.	53	28
Betrayal of confidential trust	38	36
Stealing state property when unchecked	36	34
Not standing by marital promises of help and support	18	38
People in difficulty cannot count on help from others.	23	33

Source: Krzysztof Kicinski and Jacek Kurczewski, "Wartości Uznawane przez Młodzież," *Przekazy i Opinie*, no. 1 (January-March 1976): 29.

Table 7.21. Accepted Norms by Age Groups
(percentages)

Norm	Age Group		
	16 to 29 years	40 to 59 years	60 years and older
Sincerity, lack of hypocrisy	22	13	15
Unselfishness	10	3	5
Honesty	53	61	59
Religiosity	14	29	48

Source: Janina Kobel, "Czy Konflikt Pokoleń? " *Przekazy i Opinie*, no. 1 (January-March 1976): 48.

ment" is a notable exception, jumping from eighth place in 1958 (still not a good year for government leaders, perhaps) to second in 1975.

The least prestigious occupations, which include policeman, office clerk, typist, sales clerk, unskilled construction worker, cleaning woman, and unskilled farm worker, are also quite stable over time.

A 1976 study of workers' reading habits conducted by the Press Research Center reported by Bajka asked respondents what they regarded as good work characteristics.[45] The characteristics most valued are conscientiousness (23 percent chose this characteristic), discipline (15 percent), laboriousness (14 percent), comraderie, honesty, and reliability (13 percent), and exactitude (12 percent). The least favored characteristics are efficiency, punctuality, effectiveness, giving help to others, initiative, expertise, and qualifications (all about 5 percent).[46]

Unfortunately, the report of the study does not provide categorical data that would suggest why workers make their choices. We might, however, infer some worker characteristics from the data concerning newspaper readership.

The major deviations from the rank order and percentages cited come from readers of a rural paper (*Gromady-Rolnika Polskiego*) and the major youth paper (*Sztandar Młodych*). For example, readers of the rural paper emphasize much more than the whole sample (and readers of the two major urban papers, *Trybuna Ludu* and *Życie Warszawy*) the importance of laboriousness; indeed, these readers rate laboriousness the most important work norm (24 percent), but emphasize much less discipline and comraderie (6 percent and 8 percent, respectively). These two differences alone raise intriguing—and for now unanswerable—questions regarding the growth in the number of peasant workers—workers who work in industry but continue to live on the farms in a peasant culture.

Readers of the youth paper emphasize much less than the whole sample the characteristics of laboriousness and honesty (both 9 percent), and emphasize much more strongly comraderie (18 percent).

How do workers regard their own work? Gołębiowski's study on youth cited earlier explored this question. In table 7.23, the figures, which show marginal urban-rural differences, indicate in general that work is a means to some other end—to earn money. But some youth see their work in a somewhat different perspective—a calling, a means of satisfaction.[47]

In general, the major difference seems to be that rural youth find less monetary incentive, get less satisfaction, but at the same time see their work much more as a calling than do their urban counterparts. The differences may be chiefly due to differences of the actual work than to place of residence. Presumably many, possibly most, of the rural youth are working on family farms, work that implies a certain kind of family responsibility and a distinct way of life and is therefore much different from other "jobs."

Unless occupations—or at least types of occupations—are distinguished, it is difficult to interpret the results of the broadly constructed surveys. One

Table 7.22. Occupational Prestige

| | Prestige | |
Occupation	rank in 1958 survey	scale score
1. University professor	1	1.26
2. Minister of national government	8	1.47
3. Physician	2	1.49
4. Lawyer	6	1.71
5. Airline pilot	5	1.78
6. Teacher	3	1.91
7. Mechanical engineer	4	1.93
8. Journalist	9	1.98
9. Agronomist	7	1.99
10. Priest	12	2.16
11. Skilled steel worker	10	2.48
12. Lathe tuner	11	2.66

Source: Michał Pohoski, Kazimierz Słomczynski, and Włodzimierz Wesołowski, "Occupational Prestige in Poland, 1958-1975," *The Polish Sociological Bulletin*, no. 4 (1976): 70.

Table 7.23. Youth Views of Own Work by Place of Residence
(percentages)

| | Place of Residence | |
View of Work	urban	rural
A means of earning money	32.4	29.2
Gives satisfaction	33.5	26.7
A necessity	23.2	24.3
A calling	5.5	10.6
An unpleasant burden	2.8	3.1

Source: Bronisław Gołębiowski, "Aspiracje i Orientacje Życiowe Młodzieży," *Przekazy i Opinie*, no. 1 (January-March 1976): 10.

attempt to do this by focusing on the concept of "career" (as contrasted with a job) is the study by the Center for Public Opinion Studies in 1976, reported by Halina Zaleska.[48]

Respondents were asked which characteristics are most frequently assoc-iated with careers in Poland. The distribution of their responses fall into two groups. The first group contains the two strongest responses: high position (27 percent) and education (23 percent); and a second contains characteristics with markedly less support: honor (16 percent), wealth (15 percent), and pro-fessional accomplishment (13 percent).[49]

Not surprisingly, the younger the respondent, the more optimistic are the respondents about actually having a career, and their expectation for a career is quite widespread; 76 percent of the respondents aged 16-24 see themselves as having a career, but the percentage drops sharply to 54 percent for respondents in the next-highest age group (25-39 years).[50]

The status of working women was explored in a study reviewed by Magda-lena Sokołowska, cited earlier.[51] According to Sokołowska's report, men are more inclined to believe that women are paid the same as men for equal work than are women (60 percent for men, 51 percent for women). Men also tend more to believe that a feminine disinclination to undertake responsibility is the principal reason women are not as likely as men to occupy managerial positions. Men are also more likely than women to regard women as less qualified than men to occupy managerial positions.[52]

It is difficult, if not impossible, to compare the surveys on working, for they tend to lack the kinds of specifics that would make comparisons meaning-ful. Lack of controls on the respondents, such as the jobs they currently hold and their educational levels, make it difficult to interpret the findings of the surveys.

Moral and Ethical Preferences and Life Aspirations

Ethical preferences can be summarized here by grouping them into three broad categories: moral values, instrumental values, and expectations of others.

The category of moral values includes those values which an individual considers "right," and which have little or no tangible benefit to the individual. As reported earlier, the values in the category most strongly supported by re-spondents are sincerity, honesty, unselfishness, faithfulness of spouses, reli-gion.[53] To this list we add patriotism—a value fairly evenly supported by all of the age groups in Kobel's study of inter-generational conflict. In fact, patriotism ranks second only to honesty in support from respondents (41 percent for respondents below 60 years of age, but, curiously, markedly lower—34 percent—for respondents over 60 years of age).[54]

It seems reasonable to assume that moral values should be interrelated in such a way as to constitute a kind of set of values. Religious values, for example, may affect other values. The surveys on marriage and premarital relations reviewed by Franciszek Adamski illustrate such a relationship.[55] In a 1971 study of secondary students in Krakow, it was found that almost half of the students (47 percent) believed that premarital sexual relations in the betrothal period should be accepted. No substantial differences between men and women were reported by Adamski. The study also reveals that for practicing Roman Catholics the acceptance of premarital sexual relations is much lower, about 25 percent.[56] If the acceptance of religion as a norm is much lower among young people than among older people, as is reported in Kobel's study, we should not be surprised to find that other values related to religion change as well.

Instrumental values include those values directly related to achieving goals: conscientiousness, discipline, sense of duty, the ability to get along with other people, and reliability. Such values are reported to be well-accepted norms.[57]

It seems perplexing that so many of these strongly held values are violated, as the study reported by Kicinski and Kurczewski shows.[58] It will be recalled that almost three-quarters of the respondents in that study felt that betrayal of confidential trust is experienced fairly frequently or very frequently. More than 80 percent believed that people do not say what they mean at meetings. Seventy percent believed that people will steal state property if they are not checked.

Life aspirations may be grouped into two broad categories: emotional aspirations and material aspirations. By emotional aspirations we mean those aspirations which pertain to the personal feelings of individuals, such as a happy family life or a clean conscience. Briefly, it will be recalled that the balance of these two categories of aspirations seems to shift toward greater emphasis on emotional aspirations as people grow older; not only is a successful family life greatly desired among respondents over 26—as it is among the younger respondents—but the other leading aspirations, a contented and quiet life and a clean conscience, also satisfy emotional rather than material needs.[59]

Three studies cited earlier, by Gołębiowski, Wiśniewski, and Rusinek (1975), deal with both emotional and material aspirations in a way that facilitates comparisons across the studies.[60] The two categories of aspirations will be considered separately. Perfect comparisons are, of course, not possible because the lists of choices for the respondents is seldom exactly the same.

It has already been noted that family values (founding a family, a successful family life, providing for one's family) are the most frequently supported values in surveys. In the study reported by Gołębiowski we find that family is valued slightly more by rural youth than urban youth.[61] Wiśniewski finds a greater difference between men and women in his study, with 60 percent of the women respondents supporting the value of family compared with 53 percent of the men supporting this value.[62] The greatest difference among population sub-groups is seen between younger and older respondents in a study by the Press Research Center, as reported in 1975 by Rusinek. About 51 percent of the respondents under 26 years of age support this value, compared to almost 65 percent of the respondents over 26.

A second emotional aspiration which is strongly supported—although well below the level of family—is a quiet life. The differences between population subgroups is greater for this aspiration than for family. The Gołębiowski study shows that rural youth aspire more to a quiet life (32.7 percent) than do urban youth (29.1 percent).[63] Again, however, age appears to make the greatest difference, as seen in Rusinek's study. Twenty percent of the respondents under 26 years supported this aspiration, but almost 47 percent of the older respondents indicated that they aspire to a quiet life.

Comparing material aspirations is considerably more difficult than comparing emotional values. The values included in the studies are much more specifically defined, whereas material aspirations often have vague definitions, and tend to vary from one study to another. Two material aspirations which are sufficiently similar to allow sensible comparison are acquiring housing and pleasure and entertainment.

The importance of acquiring housing is interesting in two respects. First, of the specific material aspirations included in the studies under review, it is the one most desired (57.4 percent of the respondents in the Gołębiowski study, 43 percent in the Wiśniewski study).[64] Second, it is a material aspiration heavily dependent upon public policy. It was noted earlier that Gołębiowski's study shows that urban youth are slightly more concerned with this aspiration (57.4 percent) than their rural counterparts (55.5 percent).[65] Wiśniewski's survey also turned up an even greater difference between men and women. Forty-six percent of the women respondents selected housing as an aspiration, whereas 41 percent of the men did so.[66]

Pleasure, including entertainment, is a less well defined aspiration than housing, for the term is applied somewhat differently in the surveys. For example, in Gołębiowski's study it includes some specific activities—trips abroad, cultural entertainment, and so forth, whereas in Rusinek's study it is simply defined as time for entertainment. Notwithstanding these differences of definition, pleasure appears to be regarded similarly in the two surveys. It is not surprising that in Rusinek's study the younger respondents regard pleasure and entertainment more highly than older respondents (25.4 percent and 20.7 percent, respectively).[67] The greater difference between population subgroups is that between urban youth and rural youth, found in the Gołębiowski study. Over 35 percent of the urban youth desire this characteristic, but less than 20 percent of the rural youth do.[68]

Two things might be said of the findings on aspirations. First, in terms of the methodology of the surveys and their reports, it is difficult to evaluate the significance of the differences among population subgroups. Often respondents may select more than one response; moreover, the reports of findings often do not indicate how many responses are permitted or whether respondents are compelled to select a certain number of responses. Nevertheless, the direction of differences is interesting and suggestive.

Second, what the findings suggest in general is that Poles are quite realistic in their aspirations. It is well known that the shortage of housing in Poland has become an increasingly serious problem. It is not surprising, therefore, to find that housing is decisively perceived as the principal material need and that it is a slightly more strongly held aspiration among urban youth, for it is in the urban areas where the housing problem is greatest. Nor is it surprising that consumerism is stronger in urban areas, where consumer goods are more available, and that a desire for bank savings is stronger in rural areas, where fewer goods are available on which to spend money.

Social Problems and Social Policy

A number of the findings reviewed in previous sections have touched on the area of social problems and policy. The importance, especially to young people, in obtaining an education, the perceived importance of education as a contributing factor to achieving one's life goals, and the importance of housing as an aspiration deal directly with public policies. Unfortunately, surveys on the effectiveness or desirability of specific public policies either have not been undertaken or have not been reported. Some of Gołębiowski's findings on youth attitudes deal in a general way with social and economic policies and are therefore pertinent to this section.[69]

The respondents in Gołębiowski's study were asked to indicate which three governmental tasks they believed are most important. In table 7.24 we are interested in a few of the tasks given most support. Overwhelmingly, the respondents (more than 78 percent) indicated that the most important task is a significant improvement in the lives of citizens. The second most important task is the modernization of agriculture (almost 50 percent); and, third, the modernization of industry (about 41 percent). This particular order of priorities is surprising when one considers the relatively heavy emphasis the Polish Government places on industrialization. The fourth most frequently cited task is to raise the level and increase the availability of various social services, including day-care centers, preschools, health care, and old age support (about 35 percent for this general area). As is often the case, urban-rural differences are noticeable, but as also noted in previous sections, the significance of these differences may be questionable. Our principal interest, therefore, is in the direction of differences.

We would expect to find that people in an urban environment are more aware of the need and importance of industrialization than are those in a rural environment, as we would expect to find that rural people are more concerned than urban people with the importance of agricultural development. It is interesting to note, though, that urban youth recognize the need for agricultural development more strongly than rural youth recognize the need for industrial development, and that the recognition by urban youth for industrial development is much less than the recognition by rural youth for agricultural development. The direction of differences suggests that the salience of agriculture as a policy area is certainly not limited to rural areas.

The difference between the two groups in emphasis on the level and distribution of social services is intriguing; it suggests, broadly, that rural people might be quite aware of and perhaps displeased with the relative lack of social services in the rural areas. To make a more refined interpretation is difficult, however, because we do not know with which specific social services the respondents are most concerned.

Respondents were also asked which three factors they thought were most responsible for impeding progress in the country. The six factors in the survey which stand out above others are given in table 7.25. They are waste and lack of respect for social property (mentioned by 47 percent of all respondents); bureaucracy, by which is meant unnecessary red tape, (35.5 percent); mutual backscratching and cliquishness (30.5 percent); drunkenness (26.3 percent); suppression of criticism (23.4 percent); and lack of initiative, passivity, and indifference (21.7 percent).[70] Except for drunkenness, suppression of criticism, and lack of initiative, urban-rural differences are marginal.

It should be noted that these particular unwelcome characteristics are not necessarily attributed to the political leadership. Bureaucracy clearly is, of course, but other characteristics are probably believed to be shared between political actors and members of society.

What would help more than anything else to pull these various findings together into a single summary statement would be an elaboration of what is meant by improvement in the life of citizens. In particular, it would be helpful to know whether in the mind of the respondent this concept includes industrial and agricultural development and more effective social services or whether some additional specific tasks are implied. Unfortunately, such elaboration is lacking in Gołębiowski's report.

Politics and Ideology

Building socialism implies changes in society more basic than the effective implementation of social services. In an article cited earlier, Magdalena Sokołowska speaks of the stress Marxist doctrine places on the role of women as full participants in the social economy.[71] This would, of course, be equally true of men. Participation, therefore, is an essential element in the construction of socialism.

Several studies have been made of participatory attitudes. One such study, made by Helena Datner-Śpiewak for the Center for Public Opinion Studies in 1974,[72] uses a rather small sample of about 600 secondary school students in Warsaw. The findings are interesting, and they suggest that participation—social

Table 7.24. Youth Perceptions of Most Important Tasks of Government
by Place of Residence
(percentages)

| | Place of Residence | |
Task	urban	rural
Improve life of citizens	82.3	75.4
Agricultural development and modernization	36.0	66.9
Industrial development and modernization	45.3	33.6
Higher level and greater distribution of social policies	33.3	37.0

Source: Bronisław Gołębiowski, "Aspiracje i Orientacje Życiowe Młodzieży," *Przekazy i Opinie*, no. 1 (January-March 1976): 13.

Table 7.25. Youth Perceptions of Factors Impeding National Development
by Place of Residence
(percentages)

| | Place of Residence | |
Factor	urban	rural
Waste	46.7	49.6
Bureaucracy (unnecessary red tape)	33.3	37.0
Cliquishness	30.1	30.2
Drunkenness	19.8	33.3
Suppression of criticism	26.7	16.9
Lack of initiative	26.5	16.7

Source: Bronisław Gołębiowski, "Aspiracje i Orientacje Życiowe Młodzieży," *Przekazy i Opinie*, no. 1 (January-March 1976): 14.

commitment or social action, as it is called—is accepted as a norm and that its acceptance is probably related to a sense of political efficacy; people who believe that citizens have influence in state affairs are also more likely to accept the norm of social commitment.

Respondents in Datner-Śpiewak's survey were asked whether the average citizen should act on his own affairs and simultaneously on affairs of a more general social concern, or whether he should simply tend to his own business. They strongly supported the first alternative (76 percent); only 13 percent indicated that the average citizen should only tend to his own business.[73]

The respondents were slightly more cautious when asked how individuals were likely to be affected by social commitment. Forty-one percent believed that social commitment sometimes brings with it no difficulty, whereas at other times it brings difficulties. Thirty-three percent believed that social commitment brought troubles, either frequently or sometimes. Only 20 percent indicated that citizens could expect to participate without difficulties.[74]

In a somewhat more abstract perspective, respondents were asked whether they felt the necessity for social commitment. In general, they do, as table 7.26 shows.

The percentage of "don't know's" seems surprisingly high. Although exactly half of the respondents answered yes, with or without qualification, it is interesting to note that the majority gave an ambivalent answer—"probably yes" or "probably no."

Datner-Śpiewak's report is one of the few which attempts any kind of relational analysis. She cross-tabulates (but without statistically testing the strength of relationships) the perceived necessity for social commitment with responses to a question concerning the influence of citizens in state affairs (see table 7.27).

Two points are noteworthy. First, there does appear to be a relationship between the perception of citizen influence and the necessity for social action, although it is possible that by collapsing categories the image is less sharp than it otherwise would be. What this seems to suggest is that social action is seen not as a function of regime mobilization, but as a citizen input and something to be taken seriously, a point Western scholars may too frequently overlook when studying socialist systems.

Second, only slightly more than 30 percent of the respondents perceive any significant citizen influence (no doubt it is the very small number in this group which necessitates the collapsing categories). This raises the question of what amount of influence citizens should have in political decision making, a question which has not found a clear answer, either in Western democratic systems or in socialist systems.

In Gołębiowski's study, almost a third of the respondents indicated that one of the most important tasks is to give citizens a greater share in decision making.[75] Extrapolating from the two studies, we might expect that were Polish citizens to be given a greater share of decision making, their views of

Table 7.26. Perceived Necessity for Social Commitment
(percentages)

Perceived Need for Commitment	Percent
Definitely yes	12
Probably	38
Probably not	27
Definitely no	4
Hard to say	18

Source: Helena Datner-Śpiewak, "Marzący Realiści," *Przekazy i Opinie*, no. 1 (January-March 1976): 38.

Table 7.27. Perceived Necessity for Social Commitment and Citizen Influence
(percentages)

Perceived Necessity for Social Commitment	Perceived Influence of Citizens in State Affairs	
	little	some or much
	(N=419)	(N=111)
Definitely yes or probably	46	65
Definitely no or probably not	35	20
Hard to say	19	15

Source: Helena Datner-Śpiewak, "Marzący Realiści," *Przekazy i Opinie* no. 1 (January-March 1976): 39.

social action and participation would become more positive.

Although we do not have published studies of Polish public opinion on domestic political issues, a small survey in 1976 by the Press Research Center reported by Jerzy Pomorski explores views of Warsaw residents on international issues and war.[76]

Respondents were asked which events were contributing to international tension. Two events or processes drew the strongest responses: Israeli-Arab relations (62 percent) and Maoism in China (60.2 percent). Other problems identified were fighting in Lebanon (38.8 percent), the oil crisis (35.3 percent), the visit of Franz Josef Strauss to China (26.9 percent), Northern Ireland (24.6 percent), and the international monetary crisis (22.2 percent).[77]

One event stands well above others, in the respondents' opinions, as contributing to a reduction of international tension: the Helsinki Agreement (74 percent). Other events they believed contributed to reducing tension were the Polish-West German agreement (59.8 percent), peace in Vietnam (52.9 percent), the Sojuz-Apollo flight (41.9 percent), the agreement on banning underground nuclear tests (31.2 percent), the 25th Congress of the Soviet Communist Party (23.3 percent), and the Vatican Council (19.6 percent).[78]

One gets two impressions from looking at these findings. First, recent events appear more important than earlier events: The Helsinki accords of 1975 appears more important than Poland's 1970 agreement with West Germany. All other things being equal (time, for instance), we might expect the reverse to be true, for the West German agreement certainly affects Poland quite directly and concretely. Second, it would appear that the media do a good job of getting their points across to the people. That Strauss's visit to China (which took place over a year before the survey) could be remembered at all by very many respondents seems remarkable.

According to this survey, Poles appear to be becoming more optimistic about the future. Over three-quarters (78 percent) of the respondents said that they thought less about war than previously or thought about war not at all. Only about 8 percent indicated that they thought about war more frequently.[79]

Unfortunately, no controls are applied. We do not know the ages or levels of education of the respondents. Age, for example, might well explain why even as many as 8 percent think more frequently about war; adolescents are more likely to think about war and other catastrophic events than they had earlier.

CONCLUSION

At the beginning of this chapter, it was argued that empirical research, sociology, and politics are interrelated in Poland, as they are in the other socialist countries. More is involved in this relationship than philosophy. Wiatr explains:[80]

The rapid development of empirical research reflects both the growing demands of the socialist society, for which such research is particularly important, and the "data explosion" which took place in world sociology in the first two decades after World War II . . .. The process of creating a new type of society gives to sociologists a unique opportunity to study the greatest experiment in directed social change, to analyze the new organization of the society *in statu nascendi.*

We cannot evaluate change in this review. Even if there were a sufficient number of studies comparable across time and published at regular intervals—and none of these three conditions is present—the four-year time span of this project would be too short to observe the kinds of fundamental changes Wiatr clearly has in mind. We have, of course, been able to look at inter-generational differences, but it is not possible with the information at hand to ascertain whether these differences are due to a normal process of maturation of individuals or to distinctly different influences operating at particularly important periods when people acquire certain basic values. If the latter case were true we could legitimately infer change. If, for example, members of one generation hold strong religious beliefs because certain socializing agents (such as the church) predominated during their formative years, whereas members of a later generation do not hold such strong beliefs because the same socializing agents were weak during their formative years, we may be reasonably confident that we are observing a change of values over time. Unfortunately, none of the data reviewed here enable us to make this observation.

What we can do is to see in general how the values observed in the surveys reviewed here measure up to what we might expect of a society which for over a quarter of a century has undergone "directed social change." To facilitate such an evaluation we can group the attitudes and values observed in this chapter into three broad categories: personal values, social values, and political values.

Personal values are those values which pertain principally to individuals—career ambitions, material desires, norms accepted as the basis for one's own behavior, religious beliefs, and so forth. In this area the outlook in terms of a socialist society appears positive. By and large, people value such characteristics as honesty, reliability at work, fidelity to one's spouse, and they hold realistic material desires. More importantly, the leaders of tomorrow, members of the younger generation, are noticeably less religious than the older generations.

Social values are those values which pertain to the individual's relationship with others in society and those values which people accept as being good for society as a whole. Views on working women and interpersonal relationships fall within this category. Here the survey results indicate the presence of some attitudes and expectations which are either themselves disfunctional for a socialist system or which are suggestive of a society which has not yet acquired values and habits useful to the advancement of socialism. Because of the collectivist element of socialism, mutual trust and respect would seem to be important and necessary characteristics of society. The surveys, though, reveal a noticeable lack of mutual trust and respect. For themselves, individuals value honesty highly, but they also regard the theft of state property as not unusual. Sincerity is highly valued, but people expect that others will speak differently from the way they feel at meetings. The expectation is that one cannot always count on the help of others when one experiences serious difficulties in life. The role of women in society is another, possibly more profound, example. In Poland, women have been increasingly liberated—either by opportunity or by hard economic necessity—from their traditional role as homemakers. Yet, as Sokołowska reports, traditional (nonsocialist) attitudes toward working women linger, especially among men; there appears to be a lag between structural conditions (women working outside the home) and attitudes.

Political values are those values and attitudes which pertain to the relationships between individuals and the political system. We might organize these values into two areas of political relationships, political inputs (especially participatory attitudes) and political outputs (attitudes regarding outputs of the political system such as housing and social services).

In the area of political inputs, the outlook for a socialist system appears to be quite positive, from the relatively little information we have from the surveys. To put this evaluation into an Eastonian framework, we do not have much hard information on the degree to which Polish people express diffuse support (that is, general support) of the political system or the current political leadership. We do, however, have enough information to make at least a tentative assessment of how the Polish people perceive their relationship to the political system in terms of participation; or in an Eastonian sense, the extent to which they are interested in making demands on the system. In this area in particular that evidence suggests a willingness on the part of the people to participate in political life. The general concept of social commitment is quite strongly supported. Many people feel that citizens should play a greater role in political decision making and that more criticism should be permitted. Indeed, the fact that the responses imply a degree of dissatisfaction (citizens' role should be *greater*, suppression of criticism *impedes* development) indicates that in this area the political values of the people may be somewhat ahead of the actual functioning of the system.

We find, as we might expect to find in a socialist system, that the people are aware of and concerned with outputs of the political system. They expect that their standard of living should be improved, that the country should be agriculturally and industrially developed, and that both the level and distribution of social services should be improved. Two other outputs, housing and education, are strongly desired. We do not have sufficient information from the surveys to ascertain how satisfied or dissatisfied the people are with the outputs, although in the case of social services the expectations of the people have evidently not been met fully. Tarkowski's study on the satisfaction of citizens' needs by local political systems, noted in the introductory section, is currently exploring this important area.

   The critical link between the political system and society is the functioning of the media, which alone would justify the heavy emphasis given to surveys
on media habits. Ithiel De Sola Pool observes that, "Communists think of using
mass media to produce characterological change. Also they are aware of the
possibility of using the mass media as organizational devices, for in Communist
theory the media are just an adjunct to political organization, not an independent base for political power."[81] For the reasons stated earlier, we cannot in
this review assess the success of the Polish media in actually producing change.
We also are not in a position to assess the media's success as an organizational
device. But we can state with confidence that the media are successful in reaching the people. Readership of the press is high (perhaps, as Nęcki and Sobiecki
caution, not quite as high as respondents declare). Radio and television are used
widely. On some specific foreign policy issues the views of the people appear to
be in accordance with those of the political leadership, and the media must
surely be given much of the credit for this situation. In the area of more diffuse
personal, social, and political values, which are affected also by other socializing
agents, the success of the media is less certain.

NOTES

1. Jerzy J. Wiatr, "Status and Prospects of Sociology in Eastern Europe," in *The State of Sociology in Eastern Europe Today*, ed. Jerzy J. Wiatr (Carbondale and Edwardsville, Ill.: Southern Illinois University Press, 1971), p. 4. Sociology, according to Wiatr, "emerged in all Eastern European countries as social protest rather than purely academic discipline." Wiatr explains that the relationship between Marxism, specifically historical materialism, overlaps with sociology in the sense that, "it absorbs empirically established findings of sociology; historical materialism, however, is more general than sociology" (p. 8). Sociology is therefore an autonomous sphere of inquiry within the general framework of Marxist theory. What distinguishes Marxist sociology, according to Wiatr, is that Marxist sociology views political behavior (and by implication, attitudes) within the context of all behavior within society, giving special attention to the class situation. See Jerzy J. Wiatr, *Sociologia Stosunków Politycznych* (Warsaw: Państwowe Wydawnictwo Naukowe, 1978), pp. 494-95.

2. This project spawned a number of articles and two important books. *Values and the Active Community: A Cross-National Study of the Influence of Local Leadership* (New York: The Free Press, 1979) reports the major findings of the project. Adam Przeworski and Henry Teune, *The Logic of Comparative Social Inquiry* (New York: Wiley-Interscience, 1970) analyzes the methodology of comparative research; this book has had a major impact on comparative research.

3. Examples of methodological articles are Zbigniew Bokszanski and Andrzej Piotrowski, "Socjolingwistyczne Aspekty Stosowunia Wywiadu Kwestionariuszowego," *Studia Socjologiczne*, no. 1 (1977): 81-116; Zygmunt Gostkowski and Andrzej P. Wejland, "Poziom Poprawności Metodologicznej Polskich Publikacji Socjologicznych Opartych na Badaniach Surveyowych w Latch 1965-1975," *Studia Socjologiczne*, no. 4 (1977): 33-46; and Paweł Kuczynski, "Metoda Ankietowa w Badaniu Zachowań," *Studia Socjologiczne*, no. 1 (1977): 117-38.

4. Zbigniew Bajka, "Kto Nie Czyta Prasy?" *Zeszyty Prasoznawcze*, no. 1 (1975): 29-42.

5. Ibid., p. 31.

6. Zbigniew Bajka, "Czytelnictwo Prasy Wśród Robotników," *Zeszyty Prasoznawcze*, no. 2 (1976): 39-56. This report is based on a national survey by the Press Research Center of 9,898 respondents over the age of 14. Of the total, 1,840 respondents are workers. About 40 percent of the workers live in villages.

7. Ibid., p. 43.

8. Andrzej Rusinek, "Zasięg i Struktura Publiczności Wybrannych Dzienników i Czasopism," *Zeszyty Prasoznawcze*, no. 1 (1978): 87-88. This study was undertaken by the Press Research Center in 1977. The center interviewed 6,462 respondents over the age of 13 throughout Poland.

9. Zbigniew Bajka, "Czytelnictwo Prasy O Zasięgu Ogólnopolskim," *Zeszyty Prasoznawcze*, no. 3 (1975):85-92. This study by the Press Research Center

included about 10,000 respondents throughout Poland over the age of 14. 10. Zbigniew Nęcki and Zbigniew Sobiecki, "Deklarowane i Rzeczywiśte Czytelnictwo Dzienników," *Zeszyty Prasoznawcze*, no. 3 (1976): 5-14. The small number of respondents (112) in this study was probably due to the experimental nature of the project.

11. Ibid., p. 13.

12. Ibid.

13. Teresa Turlik-Marecka, "Czytelnictwo Prasy Zachodniej w Klubach MPiK," *Zeszyty Prasoznawcze*, no. 1 (1977): 81-83. The Press Research Center administered questionnaires to 635 readers in various centers of the International Press and Book Club (Klub Międzynarodowej Prasy i Książki).

14. Ibid., p. 83.

15. Włodzimierz Piekarski, "Dostępnosc i Wykorzystanie Telewizji w Społeczenstwie Polskim," *Przekazy i Opinie*, no. 2 (April-June 1977):88.

16. Ibid., p. 92.

17. Michał Strzeszewski, "Z Badań nad Audytorium Radiowym w Polsce," *Przekazy i Opinie*, no. 2 (October-December 1975): 85-98. This survey of the Center for Public Opinion Studies included over 800 respondents over the age of 15 throughout Poland whose homes were equipped with a radio.

18. Ibid.

19. Piekarski, "Dostępnosc i Wykorzystanie Telewizji," p. 89.

20. Ibid.

21. Stefania Dzięciołowska, "Popularność Programów Telewizyjnych," *Przekazy i Opinie*, no. 2 (October-December 1975): 78. These figures were from weekly audience surveys carried out by the Center for Public Opinion Studies. The sample is approximately 1,000 persons over 15 years.

22. Aleksander W. Nocun, "Kontakty Dzieci i Młodzieży z Programem Telewizyjnym w Opinii Rodziców," *Przekazy i Opinie*, no. 1 (January-March 1978): 66. This survey of the Center for Public Opinion Studies included an unspecified number of respondents over 16 years of age throughout Poland.

23. Ibid., p. 69.

24. Teresa Konwicka, "Z Badań nad Przystępnością Telewizyjnych Programów Publicystycznych," *Przekazy i Opinie*, no. 4 (October-December 1976): 73-80; Irena Tomaszewska, "Argumentacja Racjonalna czy Emocjonalna? Preferencje Odbiorców Przekazu Propagandowego," *Przekazy i Opinie*, no. 2 (April-June 1978):82-94. Konwicka's study uses a representative sample of "several hundred" Warsaw residents over the age of 15. Tomaszewska's study employs a national sample of 900.

25. Konwicka, p. 76.

26. Ibid., p. 79.

27. Tomaszewaka, p. 89.

28. Ibid., pp. 91-93.

29. Andrzej Rusinek, "Wartości Preferowane Przez Młodzież," *Zeszyty Prasoznawcsze*, no. 1 (1975): 80.

30. Franciszek Adamski, "Model Concepts of Marriage in Poland," *The Polish Sociological Bulletin*, no. 3 (1976): 51-60.

31. Ibid., p. 53.

32. Ibid.

33. Calculated from *Rocznik Statystyczny 1977* (Warsaw: Główny Urząd Statystyczny, 1978), pp. 44 and 46.

34. Magdalena Sokołowska, "The Woman Image in the Awareness of Contemporary Polish Society," *The Polish Sociological Bulletin*, no. 3 (1976): 41-50.

35. Ibid., p. 41.

36. Andrzej Rusinek, "Wartości Preferowane Przez Młodzież," *Zeszyty Prasoznawcze*, no. 1 (1975): 80.

37. Ibid.

38. Wiesław Wiśniewski, "The Place of Education in the System of Values in Polish Society" (Paper presented at the Ninth World Congress of Sociology, Uppsala, Sweden, August 1978). A Polish version of this paper, published in Warsaw in 1978 by the Institute of Sociology, is entitled "Wykształcenie w Aspiracjach Społeczenstwa Polskiego." The study is based on responses to a questionnaire given to a representative national sample of 5,594 respondents between 15 and 45 years of age.

39. Bronisław Gołębiowski, "Aspiracje i Orientacje Życiowe Młodzieży," *Przekazy i Opinie*, no. 1 (January-March 1976): 7-18. This survey of the Center for Public Opinion Studies is based on a representative sample of 1,948 respondents of Polish youth 16 to 29 years.

40. Krzysztof Kicinski and Jacek Kurczewski, "Wartości Uznawane Przez Młodzież," *Przekazy i Opinie*, no. 1 (January-March 1976): 19-32. This study was undertaken by the Center for Public Opinion Studies in late 1973, using a representative national sample of 1,951 respondents from 16-29 years of age.

41. Janina Kobel, "Czy Konflikt Pokoleń? " *Przekazy i Opinie*, no. 1 (January-March 1976): 42-48. This is a rather small survey by the Center for Public Opinion Studies of 614 respondents over the age of 15 throughout Poland.

42. Ibid., p. 44.

43. Michał Pohoski, Kazimierz Słomczynski, and Włodzimierz Wesołowski, "Occupational Prestige in Poland, 1958-1975," *The Polish Sociological Bulletin*, no. 4 (1976): 63-77.

44. Ibid., p. 70.

45. Zbigniew Bajka, "Dobra Robota w Opinii Czytelników Wybranych Gazet i Czasopism," *Zeszyty Prasoznawcze*, no. 2 (1977): 88-90. This study by the Press Research Center is based on a representative national sample of 3,843 respondents over the age of 14.

46. Ibid., p. 90.

47. Gołębiowski, "Aspiracje i Orientacje," p. 10.

48. Halina Zaleska, "Pojęcie Kariery w Wyobrażeniach Odczuciach Społecznych," *Przekazy i Opinie*, no. 1 (January-March 1978): 91-102. This study by the Center for Public Opinion Studies is based on a national stratified-random

sample of 1,000 respondents over the age of 15.
49. Ibid., p. 96.
50. Ibid., p. 97.
51. Sokołowska, "The Woman Image," pp. 41-50.
52. Ibid., p. 42.
53. Adamski, "Model Concepts of Marriage," pp. 51-60; Kobel, "Czy Konflikt Pokoleń?" pp. 42-48.
54. Kobel, "Czy Konflikt Pokoleń?" p. 48.
55. Adamski, "Model Concepts of Marriage," p. 54.
56. Ibid., pp. 54-55.
57. Wiśniewski, "The Place of Education"; Gołębiowski, "Aspiracje i Orientacje," pp. 7-18.
58. Kicinski and Kurczewski, "Wartości Uznawane Przez Młodzież," pp. 19-32.
59. Rusinek, "Wartości Preferowane Przez Młodzież," pp. 79-82.
60. Gołębiowski, "Aspiracje i Orientacje," pp. 7-18; Wiśniewski, "The Place of Education"; Rusinek, "Wartości Preferowane Przez Młodzież," pp. 79-82.
61. Gołębiowski, "Aspiracje i Orientacje," p. 9.
62. Wiśniewski, "The Place of Education," p. 16.
63. Gołębiowski, "Aspiracje i Orientacje," p. 9.
64. Ibid., p. 11; Wiśniewski, "The Place of Education," p. 15.
65. Gołębiowski, "Aspiracje i Orientacje," p. 11.
66. Wiśniewski, "The Place of Education," p. 16.
67. Rusinek, "Wartości Preferowane Przez Młodzież," p. 80.
68. Gołębiowski, "Aspiracje i Orientacje," p. 11.
69. Ibid., pp. 7-18.
70. Ibid., p. 14.
71. Sokołowska, "The Woman Image," p. 45.
72. Helena Datner-Śpiewak, "Marzący Realiści," *Przekazy i Opinie*, no. 1 (January-March 1976): 33-41.
73. Ibid., p. 34.
74. Ibid.
75. Gołębiowski, "Aspiracje i Orientacje," p. 13.
76. Jerzy Pomorski, "Opinie O Międzynarodowym Odprzeżeniu," *Zeszyty Prasoznawcze*, no. 3 (1977): 69-72. This 1976 study by the Press Research Center is based on a sample of 682 Warsaw respondents. Sampling procedures are not described, but the sample evidently is largely made up of respondents with secondary or higher educations.
77. Ibid., p. 71.
78. Ibid.
79. Ibid.
80. Wiatr, "Status and Prospects," p. 12.
81. Ithiel De Sola Pool, "The Mass Media and Politics in the Modernization Process," in *Communications and Political Development*, ed. Lucian W. Pye (Princeton, N.J.: Princeton University Press, 1963), p. 239.

BIBLIOGRAPHY

Adamski, Franciszek. "Model Concepts of Marriage in Poland." *The Polish Sociological Bulletin*, no. 3 (1976): 51-60.

Bajka, Zbigniew. "Kto Nie Czyta Prasy?" *Zeszyty Prasoznawcze* 16, no. 1 (1975): 29-42.

_____. "Czytelnictwo Prasy O Zasięgu Ogólnopolskim." *Zeszyty Prasoznawcze* 16, no. 3 (1975): 85-92.

_____. "Czytelnictwo Prasy Wśród Robotników." *Zeszyty Prasoznawcze* 17, no. 2 (1976): 39-56.

_____. "Dobra Robota w Opinii Czytelników Wybrannych Gazet i Czasopism." *Zeszyty Prasoznawcze* 18, no. 2 (1977): 88-89.

Bartoszewicz, Witold. "Odbiór Serialii Telewizyjnych—Kryteria i Oceny." *Przekazy i Opinie*, no. 2 (April-June 1976): 71-80.

Bokszanski, Zbigniew, and Piotrowski, Andrzej. "Socjolingwistyczne Aspekty Stosowania Wywiadu Kwestionariuszowego." *Studia Socjologiczne*, no. 1 (1977): 81-116.

Connor, Walter D., and Gitelman, Zvi Y., with Huszczo, Adaline, and Blumstock, Robert. *Public Opinion in European Socialist Systems*. New York: Praeger, 1977.

Czajka, Stanisław. *Nauki Społeczne po XVI Plenum KC PZPR*. Warsaw: Książka i Wiedza, 1976.

Datner-Śpiewak, Helena. "Marzący Realiści." *Przekazy i Opinie*, no. 1 (January-March 1976): 33-44.

Dzięciołowska, Stefania. "Popularność Programów Telewizyjnych w Polsce." *Przekazy i Opinie*, no. 4 (October-December 1975): 74-84.

Goban-Klas, Tomasz. "Oddziaływanie Środkow Komunikowania Masowego: Problemy Teorie, Kierunki, Hipotezy." *Przekazy i Opinie*, no. 2 (April-June 1978): 5-35.

_____. "Praktyczna Uzyteczność Badań Prasoznawczych." *Zeszyty Prasoznawcze* 17, no. 2 (1976): 7-24.

_____. "Przekazy Masowe a Wartości Społeczne." *Zeszyty Prasoznawcze* 19, no. 1 (1978): 5-22.

Gołębiowski, Bronisław. "Aspiracje i Orientacje Życiowe Młodzieży." *Przekazy i Opinie*, no. 1 (January-March 1976): 7-18.

Gostkowski, Zygmunt, and Wejland, Andrzej P. "Poziom Poprawności Metodologicznej Polskich Publikacji Socjologicznych Opartych na Badaniach Surveyowych w Latach 1965-1975." *Studia Socjologiczne*, no. 4 (1977): 33-46.

International Studies of Values in Politics. *Values and the Active Community: A Cross-National Study of the Influence of Local Leadership*. New York: The Free Press, 1971.

Jerzak, Josef. "Z Badań nad Typami Postaw Ideowo-Politycznych Młodzieży

Studiujacej." *Studia Socjologiczne*, no. 3 (1975): 217-31.

Kicinski, Krzysztof, and Kurczewski, Jacek. "Wartości Uznawane Przez Młodzież." *Przekazy i Opinie*, no. 1 (January-March 1976): 19-32.

Kobel, Janina. "Czy Konflikt Pokoleń?" *Przekazy i Opinie*, no. 1 (January-March 1976): 42-48.

Konwicka, Teresa. "Z Badań nad Przystepnością Telewizyjnych Programów Publistycznych." *Przekazy i Opinie*, no. 4 (October-December 1976): 73-80.

Kuczynski, Paweł. "Metoda Ankietowa w Badaniu Zachowań." *Studia Socjologiczne*, no. 1 (1977): 117-38.

Nęcki, Zbigniew, and Sobiecki, Zbigniew. "Deklarowane i Rzeczywiste Czytelnictwo Dzienników." *Zeszyty Prasoznawcze* 17, no. 3 (1976): 5-14.

Nocun, Aleksander W. "Kontakty Dzieci i Młodzieży z Programem Telewizyjnym w Opinii Rodziców." *Przekazy i Opinie*, no. 1 (January-March 1978): 65-73.

Nowicki, Stanisław. "Problematyka Krytyki Prasowej w Opiniach Czytelników." *Zeszyty Prasoznawcze* 17, no. 3 (1977): 5-18.

Nowy, Marian. "Stopień Zaspokojenia Zainteresowan Młodego Czytelnika Prasy Krakowskiej." *Zeszyty Prasoznawcze* 19, no. 1 (1978): 89-92.

Penc, Jozef. "Czas Wolny Ludzi Pracy a Jakość Zycia." *Kultura i Społeczenstwo* 21, no. 3 (1977): 111-24.

Piekarski, Włodzimierz. "Dostępnosc i Wykorzystanie Telewizji w Społeczenstwie Polskim." *Przekazy i Opinie*, no. 2 (April-June 1977): 86-94.

Pohoski, Michał; Słomczynski, Kazimierz M.; and Wesołowski, Włodzimierz. "Occupational Prestige in Poland, 1958-1975." *The Polish Sociological Bulletin*, no. 4 (1976): 63-77.

Pomorski, Jerzy. "Badania nad Odbiorca Prasy w Polsce." *Zeszyty Prasoznawcze* 16, no. 3 (1975): 5-20.

_____. "Opinie O Międzynarodowym Odprzezeniu." *Zeszyty Prasoznawcze* 18, no. 3 (1977): 69-72.

Przeworski, Adam, and Teune, Henry. *The Logic of Comparative Social Inquiry*. New York: Wiley-Interscience, 1970.

Pye, Lucian W. *Communications and Political Development*. Princeton, N.J.: Princeton University Press, 1963.

Rusinek, Andrzej. "Wartości Preferowane Przez Młodzież." *Zeszyty Prasoznawcze* 16, no. 1 (1975): 79-82.

_____. "Zasięg i Struktura Publiczności Wybrannych Dzienników i Czasopism." *Zeszyty Prasoznawcze* 19, no. 1 (1978): 87-88.

Siwek, Henryk. "Jakie Materiały Prasowe Są Szczególnie Atrakcyjne Dla Czytelnika?" *Zeszyty Prasoznawcze* 16, no. 4 (1975): 77-82.

_____. "Wartość Poznawcza Wskazników Zasięgu Czytelnictwa Prasy." *Zeszyty Prasoznawcze* 14, no. 2 (1973): 5-22.

Sokołowska, Magdalena. "The Woman Image in the Awareness of Contemporary Polish Society." *The Polish Sociological Bulletin*, no. 3 (1976): 41-50.

Sopuch, Kazimierz. "Uczestnictwo w Kulturze Mieszkancöw Ziemi Koscierskiej." *Kultura i Spoƚeczenstwo* 21, no. 4 (1977): 191-204.

Strzeszewski, Michaƚ. "Z Badań nad Audytorium Radiowym w Polsce." *Przekazy i Opinie*, no. 4 (October-December 1975): 85-98.

Szecskö, Tamas. "Kommunikowanie Masowe: Uwagi O Strategiach Badawczych Spoƚeczenstw Socjalistycznych." *Zeszyty Prasoznawcze* 17, no. 2 (1977): 23-28.

Szostkiewicz, Stefan. "Radio i Telewizja Jako Przedmiot Badań Empirycznych (Kierunki i Zakresy)." *Przekazy i Opinie*, no. 1 (July-September 1975): 73-81.

Tomaszewska, Irena. "Argumentacja Racjonalna Czy Emocjonalna? Preferencje Odbiorców Przekazu Propagandowego." *Przekazy i Opinie*, no. 2 (April-June 1978): 82-94.

Turlik-Marecka, Teresa. "Czytelnictwo Prasy Zachodniej w Klubach MPiK." *Zeszyty Prasoznawcze* 18, no. 1 (1977): 81-83.

Tyszka, Andrzej. "Wartości Dobrego Życia: Poglady i Opinie." *Przekazy i Opinie*, no. 1 (January-March 1978): 74-90.

Wasiak, Kazimierz. "Czytelnictwo Prasy w Środowisku Szczecińskiej Mƚodzieży Robotniczej." *Zeszyty Prasoznawcze* 16, no. 2 (1975): 37-50.

Wiatr, Jerzy J. *Socjologia Stosunków Politycznych*. Warsaw: Państwowe Wydawnictwo Naukowe, 1978.

_____, ed. *The State of Sociology in Eastern Europe Today*. Carbondale and Edwardsville, Ill.: Southern Illinois University Press, 1971.

Wiśniewski, Wiesƚaw. "The Place of Education in the System of Values in Polish Society." Paper presented at Research Committee 4, Sociology of Education, Ninth World Congress of Sociology, August 1978, at Uppsala, Sweden.

_____. *Wyksztaƚcenie w Aspiracjach Spoƚeczenstwa Polskiego*. no. 5. Warsaw: Instytut Socjologii Uniwersytetu Warszawskiego, 1978.

Zaleska, Halina. "Pojęcie Kariery w Wyobrażeniach i Odczuciach Spoƚecznych." *Przekazy i Opinie*, no. 1 (January-March 1978): 91-102.

8 Romania

Daniel N. Nelson

AN OVERVIEW OF SURVEY RESEARCH IN ROMANIA

Survey research in Romania is not, as of the late 1970s, an advanced art. That such a data-gathering technique is neither widely employed nor used with precision in most cases suggests some of the problems faced by social scientists in authoritarian polities. Although the principal users of survey research in Romania have been empirical sociologists, the role surveys play in collecting data becomes vital to all social science. Thus, we shall consider data derived from a particular technique characteristic of empirical sociology, often reflecting on the wider state of social science in Romania.[1]

An empirical emphasis in social science came to Romania somewhat later than to other parts of communist Europe, but was nevertheless identifiable by the early 1960s. Although concern for having empirical data to test hypotheses about human behavior was not unknown among Romanian scholars in the early communist period,[2] the prevailing orthodoxy of East European social science, even after the passing of Stalin, was of muted attention to the rigorous testing of hypotheses through field research. But there was commitment bordering on excitement among a handful of younger (i.e., in their thirties and forties) Romanian scholars during the first years of the 1960s. Discussion groups became working groups, and these led to the founding of several noteworthy institutions for sociological work that often involved survey research.

First to see the necessity of supporting "interpretations of contemporary social phenomena" with "empirical data, systematically collected by direct investigation . . . " were researchers at the Institute of Philosophy of the Academy of Social and Political Sciences, who began sociological field work in 1961.[3] For five years, this Department of Social Theory of the Institute of Philosophy carried on a lonely, and often—because of the political implications of its research—precarious venture into empirical sociology, especially through survey research. Its chief moving force during these years and into the early 1970s was a young scholar named Mihail Cernea. Cernea formed a small but effective group of researchers around him, including Maria Larionescu, Stefana Steriade, Maria Popescu, and Gheorghe Chepeş. The output of this small unit over the span of less than a decade was prodigious, reaching a peak in the early 1970s as research in progress over several years reached fruition. Early emphases on industrial sociology and mass media were, because of political redirection, later exchanged for work on villages, families, urbanization, and social organizations. The Department of Social Theory was a "trend setter" for Romanian sociology in the use of survey instruments and, more broadly, the application of empirical social science techniques, in part because its work was attentive to scientific criteria (sampling techniques, tests of statistical significance and the like). The trend set by Cernea and his colleagues was transient, however, and the setting for empirical sociology in Romania began to cloud in 1973, a topic to which we return below.

Given impetus by Cernea's group, and a mixture of Party tolerance and encouragement, the Sociological Laboratory of the University of Bucharest was founded in November, 1965, as a "working group," and reorganized as an "institutional unit" in 1969 by Ministry of Education Order Number 739. Its relationship with the Department of Sociology at the University of Bucharest, which was created in 1966, was close—there was overlapping membership of researchers and their projects—although the Laboratory was seen as a broader endeavor, bringing in people with many specialties. Although early discussions were attended by fewer than a dozen individuals, such as H. H. Stahl, N. S. Dumitru and others, the official tolerance and even approval of social science in the late 1960s soon brought older, more recognized scholars into association, most notably Miron Constantinescu (member of the Romanian Academy and President of the Academy of Social and Political Sciences) and Roman Moldovan (corresponding member of the Academy and Vice-President of ASPS). The productivity of the Sociological Laboratory's associates was considerable, including major volumes summarizing Romanian sociological investigations through the 1960s.[4]

Late in 1966, a Center for Sociological Research of the ASPS also was established to concentrate on problems of social change in Romania. Constantin Ionescu, Secretary General of the ASPS, was its director. By 1971, additional institutes that employed survey techniques were established, including 1) the Laboratory of Urban Sociological Research of Bucharest Municipality, founded in 1970 within the Bucharest Design Institute (a part of the municipal government) and headed by Gheorghe Chepeş; 2) the Research Center for Youth Problems, begun in 1968 with Ovidiu Bădina as director and Fred Mahler as deputy director; and 3) an Institute of Political Science and Study on National Problems, established in 1971 and first headed by Constantin Vlad. The foci of research by the first two of these institutions is self-evident, whereas the Institute of Political Science had much broader goals, including the role of state organs, mass participation, political implications of socioeconomic development, social homogenization, Romanian foreign policy, international organizations, and many more. While these activities did not often employ survey techniques in field research, some younger members of the Institute, such as Mircea Preda and Ioan Vida, did conduct surveys and publish articles using survey data. At the Research Office of Romanian Radio and Television, Dr. Pavel Câmpeanu undertook some of the most ambitious and fruitful survey research of the 1960s and early 1970s, heading a research team that produced many reports on Romanian media habits, viewing preferences, and related topics.

The three other universities in Romania (many former technical institutes are now called universities), at Cluj, Iaşi, and Timişoara likewise inaugurated empirical sociology with some vigor in the mid-1960s, reaching a peak of activity and productivity in 1970-72. Ion Aluaş and Achim Mihu were, and continue to be, members of the Philosophy and Sociology Department of Babeş-Bolyai University in Cluj where they directed a large number of research efforts, data from which appeared in limited amounts in works published early in the 1970s.[5] At Timişoara, the University's Laboratory of Sociology was established in 1968 under the aegis of the Economics Faculty as a small nucleus for work involving survey techniques. Francisc Albert, a sociologist, and two staff members operated the Laboratory, coordinating the implementation of research contracts by many of the University's faculty members. Albert himself established a reputation in studies of leisure-time activities.[6] Iosif Natansohn was primarily responsible for the development of empirical sociology at Iaşi, although Corneliu Dimitriu and Alexandru Bărbat and several younger researchers contributed significantly to the output from the "Alexandru Ioan Cuza" University's Department of Sociology and Psychology. Indeed, their survey techniques were among the most advanced in Romania. As with other sociological centers gathering data through surveys, Iaşi researchers received contracts with local Party organs, mass organizations (e.g., the Young Communist League), and economic enterprises to focus on workers' satisfaction, youth problems, rural transformation and village life, and similar topics with political overtones.[7] Funds were made available through planned research budgets of contracting organizations and enterprises.

Although Bucharest's major sociological institutions and the three university centers outside the capital produced more and better studies using survey techniques, the late 1960s and early 1970s saw a proliferation of research groups, departments, and institutes that occasionally conducted surveys (of varying magnitude and quality). The Pedagogical Institute of Bacău established a sociology laboratory that was quite active in the early 1970s; similarly, survey research was from time to time undertaken by the Mining Institute located in Petroşani, the major city in the Jiu Valley. And in many locales, several county or city-level institutions were created that utilized survey research techniques. In *Judeţul* (the county) Cluj, for example, the *Judeţ* Party School (one of which existed for cadres in major centers such as Iaşi, Timişoara, etc.), the Agronomical Institute, the Polytechnic School and the *Judeţ*-level administrative department for labor organization also established sociological sections in which surveys periodically were initiated, often involving university faculty on a contract basis. The ASPS established in the early 1970s "social science centers" around the country, and these also brought survey research into general, if infrequent use. Such centers were efforts to bring together researchers and users of survey research, primarily outside university cities.

The Role and Methods of Survey Research in Romania

One need not speculate long concerning the turn of political events that opened the way for empirical social science and the use of survey instruments. Nicolae Ceauşescu, who succeeded long-time Party leader Gheorghe Gheorghiu-Dej in 1965, was neither secure in his own position nor assured of success in the independent course of development to which the Romanian Party had committed itself in April, 1964. To marshal the academic commuity's support was only one part of a larger effort at mobilization. Moreover, social science potentially offered practical advantages for Ceauşescu's leadership in two respects. First, survey data can assist in identifying socioeconomic problems and acceptable solutions to them. Second, the defeat of political opposition depended on recognizing issues encouraging discontent, and on identifying the groups or locales where political difficulties were, or would soon become, evident. Therefore, the concerns of most sociological studies in Romania were (and continue to be) workers' dissatisfaction, youth problems, media penetration and preferences, value transformation, and matters related to urbanization. From the outset, then, the milieu in which social scientists using survey instruments have worked has been highly politicized, with the goals of research being instrumental for the political needs of the leadership as well as for the rationale of socioeconomic development of Romania. Ceauşescu has said as much on many occasions:

[the Academy of Social and Political Sciences] should be an instrument in
the hands of the Party and State leadership in ideological activity; . . . a
closer link is needed between the theoretical and practical activity . . .
comrades (scholars at the Academy) should be drawn into political,
practical activity . . . social scientists must be in fact Party activists . . . .[8]

In short, then, empirical sociology and the information-gathering technique of survey research gained wider acceptance in Romania in the dozen years
from 1961 through 1973. From hesitant and rudimentary beginnings, surveys
became a common instrument for sociological research after the rapid proliferation of institutions devoted to such endeavors between 1966 and 1971. In the
early 1970s, even county and city political authorities and local economic managers regularly commissioned studies that relied heavily or exclusively on survey
data. Most of these studies were not published for general readership, and if
published at all they often appeared only as mimeographed reports for the Party
or state organ or economic enterprise that had commissioned the research.
Nevertheless, the quantity of books and professional articles in which survey
data was employed rose considerably in the late 1960s and early 1970s (only to
decline later). Perhaps most important, survey research was at work collecting
data to answer a broader range of questions during this brief, but exciting,
period of Romanian sociology.

Because specific comments about the methodology of survey research are
included when discussing each piece of research in this chapter, only the broadest comments will be offered here. Survey research is rudimentary in Romania,
with topical foci the product of Party needs and interests. Sociologists who
conduct surveys do so not because their personal experience suggests testable
hypotheses, but because Party organs (central or local), ministries, economic
units or mass organizations hire them to measure attitudes of interest to their
policy goals. Scientific sampling procedures are not widely understood or
utilized, not because the sociologists are unable, but because their contracts
call for a study of workers in a particular factory or students in a specific locale.
Generalizability, therefore, suffers. In most cases, data are reported in percentages, with few cross-tabulations or statistical tests (the exceptions bring a very
occasional Spearman's rho, t-test, or chi-square, primarily in work by Cernea's
group). At many points in the following report, therefore, the validity of results
will be questioned.

The decline of empirical sociology and survey research was even more
precipitous than their advance. A so-called "mini - cultural revolution" was
brought back to Romania by Nicolae Ceauşescu from a visit to China, and
1971-72 were years of "anti-bourgeois" fervor inaugurated from the top;
Western music, clothing, and hair styles were attacked, entertainment spots
closed, artistic liberty further constrained, and research of social scientists
"redirected" from industrial sociology, mass media, etc. to work on village
life, families, and social organizations. This was accomplished through funding

for desired topics. Whereas other parts of the mini-cultural revolution were soon forgotten, restrictions on social science grew increasingly tight. In part to protest those constraints, Mihail Cernea decided not to return to Romania after attending a World Sociological Conference in September, 1974. The death of Miron Constantinescu, who had lent his name and prestige to survey research, occurred in the same year—a combination of events that seriously weakened the potential of empirical sociology to withstand mounting political pressures.

Precisely why these "political pressures" against empirical sociology were growing after 1972 is difficult to specify. To be sure, Ceauşescu's China visit and the cultural retrenchment in 1971-72 signaled less tolerance of scholarly latitude. But in Romania we are unlikely to find authorities announcing a formal policy to cut back on sociological studies using survey instruments. Instead, a more accurate portrait of the process involved would focus on the changing "mood" of the national elite in the direction of being irritated or annoyed by the few intellectuals who were complicating things with facts when the leadership had not asked for them. A few words expressed by Ceauşescu in such a vein probably sufficed as "policy making," to then be implemented by The Romanian Academy, Ministry of Education, and sub-national Party organs which plan, fund, and commission research endeavors. While survey research and inquiries into topics that lent themselves to such information-gathering techniques were sought by new leadership in the mid-1960s, seven or eight years later the researchers had begun to reach beyond the limits of what had utility for the Party. They discovered, by inference, such things as the rejection by peasants of collectivization when given a choice to sign contracts as a family unit, worker dissatisfaction with participatory outlets designed for them by the Party, and similar findings. Moreover, the Party had already gained information that it required through the work of sociologists in publications from 1965 to 1973, and could set stricter limits of inquiry without reducing, in the short run, benefit to the central apparatus. While we may question the wisdom of assumptions regarding the continuity of mass opinion over time, it seems clear that fundamental social data from a decade of research were regarded as sufficient by the mid-1970s to reduce basic research, constrain topics to those with immediate policy application, and reduce publication opportunities.

It seems safe to say that from the Party's perspective the *raison d'etre* for survey research had faded, that the mood of leaders (perhaps Ceauşescu himself) had changed regarding the product of empirical sociology, and that major proponents of such endeavors were no longer present in Romania after 1974. In an environment of that nature, it becomes less surprising that many of the institutions which had been established over a decade were cut back or abolished between 1973 and 1977. Cernea's Department of Social Theory of the Institute of Philosophy was dismantled in 1975, with some of its principal researchers being "retired" or shifted to other duties. The Department of Sociology at the University of Bucharest has essentially ceased to function in that there are no longer (since 1977) degrees granted in sociology. The Laboratory of Sociology at the university was eliminated as well. The Office of Research of Romanian Radio and Television has also been cut back in staff and budget since 1973. Gheorghe Chepeş' Laboratory of Urban Sociological Research of Bucharest Municipality operates, but under such strict political control that little of empirical worth can be produced, and the Research Center for Youth Problems also had died out. Constantin Vlad's Institute for Political Science has been "integrated" with the Ştefan Gheorghiu Academy in the Party higher school's palatial new building, a move which seems to have brought its research under more watchful eyes. In four years, then, survey research and the empirical study of society were seriously impaired.

THE ORIENTATION OF THIS STUDY

The remainder of this chapter deals with Romanian survey research, particularly that which measures opinion and attitudes in the public, during a period (mid to late 1970s) in which the quantity of survey data reported in published sources decreased. Paradoxically, however, the *idea* of empirical research seems to have conquered. No longer will one read that surveys are "bourgeois" or that the focus of legitimate sociology should be the criticism of Western research. Instead, the Party uses the rhetoric of empirical social science in calling on social scientists to study phenomena characteristic of Romania's stage of development, to make their contribution toward generalizing the experience of building socialism, and to approach new problems facing the evolution of human society.[9] Concern for applying "advanced methods" in social sciences to "enhance their contribution to solving problems" such as labor productivity, material wastefulness, and inefficient management often is part of the Party elite's rhetoric.[10]

In such an atmosphere, surveys of utility to the Party are emphasized. Research for this chapter, which covered many major journals such as *Viitorul Social* (The Social Future) and *Viaţa Economică* (Economic Life), lesser-known periodicals such as *Forum* (a journal of higher education), monographs, and institutional reports, did not reveal survey data in published form on topics of an ideological, ethnic or market-analysis nature (as do other chapters in this volume). This paucity is, no doubt, a direct reflection of recent politically imposed restraints on this type of research.

Many studies of public opinion in Romania that hold considerable interest for Western scholars are mimeographed for "internal use only"— i.e. duplicated but not "published." This report does not include such materials, although some are available to Western social scientists through personal contacts. The topics of "internal" studies are more sensitive, but the methodology is no more sophisticated. In lieu of broad survey research in some areas, this report includes what might be termed "limited surveys." These include non-random samples of individuals, e.g. all apprentice locksmiths at a particular Bucharest trade school from whom attitudinal data are gained with a questionnaire. In addition, nonquantified information has been cited from a research effort that included hundreds of in-depth interviews without a standardized questionnaire. These research endeavors are reported insofar as they measure opinions within the Romanian public and do so using data-gathering techniques that approximate a survey.

SURVEYS OF PUBLIC ATTITUDES AND BEHAVIOR IN ROMANIA

Media Habits

Among the most sophisticated survey research teams to have worked in Romania, and the only one to establish a representative national sample is the Office of Research of Romanian Radio and Television (*Oficiul de Studii şi Sondaje al Radioteleviziunii Române*). As early as 1972, the director of this office, Dr. Pavel Câmpeanu, had published works of impressive breadth and insight. Revealing statistics, still regarded as the most authoritative about Romanian media habits, came out of a survey of 6,300 subjects in 19 Romanian counties (*judeţe*). Câmpeanu found that television, even at that early stage of broadcast media development in Romania, produced a much more intense memory and recall about national events,[11] had the greatest impact on young adults in terms of reducing their attention to printed media,[12] was strongly related to a preference for "easy" (i.e., Western style) music vis-a-vis Romanian folk music[13] and was relied upon over other media for both knowledge and distraction[14] (see tables 8.1 and 8.2).

The vast majority of Câmpeanu's research efforts are never published in professional journals but are, instead, for the internal consumption of Party organs concerned with propaganda and the management of radio and television. Although the usefulness of such research for the Party cannot be disputed, cutbacks in 1973 nevertheless affected the Office of Research of Romanian Radio and Television, reducing Câmpeanu's staff.

Since the research of this group was seen as "nonproductive" (i.e., having no physical "product"), it was among those programs to come under budgetary constraints. Nevertheless, Câmpeanu's team has an advantage over many sociological institutions—it occupies a central position from which to observe national policy and, although no one in the team occupies a position of high authority in radio and television, their salaries make them somewhat more independent of contract work. This does not mean, of course, that the researchers earn high

Table 8.1. Sources of Public Knowledge about 1970 Floods

Source	Percent of Respondents
Acquaintances	8.5
Catastrophe in their vicinity	7.0
Radio	12.0
Printed media	16.0
Television	50.0

Source: Pavel Câmpeanu, *Radio Televiziune Public* (Bucharest: Editura Ştiinţifică, 1972), p. 134.

Table 8.2. Reading after Television Introduced in Home

(percentages)

	Amount of Reading	
Group	more than before	less than before
15-19 years	17.5	19
20-24 years	12.5	15
25-29 years	7.0	25
30-39 years	4.0	31
40-49 years	3.0	28
50-59 years	0.8	31
60 years and older	3.0	2

Source: Pavel Câmpeanu, *Radio Televiziune Public* (Bucharest: Editura Ştiinţifică, 1972), p. 146.

salaries or that their positions are absolutely secure. Instead, being salaried means that income does not depend on signing contracts with Party organs or enterprises; the research office, as an institution, and its members therefore depend less for their continuance on doing applied research for some client. Simply put, they know what is going on and have some autonomy with which to test hypotheses of their choosing.

Perhaps the greatest advance made by this research organization is the achievement of a national sample. In the late 1960s, Câmpeanu and his colleagues established a network of 2,000 unpaid assistants in villages and city neighborhoods throughout Romania. The Office of Research contacts these 2,000 assistants, not through local Party or state organs, but directly via letter, hence bypassing these other authorities. The local assistants perform their functions without pay, if for no other reason than the fact that their contact with radio and television in Bucharest is a status symbol.

Topics covered by the Office of Research of Romanian Radio and Television in 1977-78, as yet unpublished and unavailable, have included such widely differing subjects as information about the 1977 earthquake (measuring the variable impact of different media in different locales), and public attitudes towards a series of Western films from the United States shown on Romanian television in the spring and summer 1978—especially, the values the public inferred from such productions. Media research occasionally appears in professional journals, although the decision to publish such information is certainly contingent on the author's assessment of what is acceptable politically as well as the self-censorship of journal editors.

A good example of media research by Câmpeanu's team that was published in a professional journal is his 1978 article, "Evaluation of Current Events Information" in *Viitorul Social*, the major sociological journal.[15] He uses a 1977 sample of 1,600 people obtained in 452 urban and rural localities, including Bucharest. Both sites and respondents were randomly selected. Câmpeanu compares attitudinal data from these respondents with views expressed by thirty "media specialists."[16] Câmpeanu hypothesizes that, although the public sample and specialists might have different criteria by which they judge current events to be important or not important, utilitarian or not utilitarian, most events will be evaluated in analogous ways by the two sets of respondents. Ten current events items were selected for January, 1977, and ten for April, 1977. Both the public and specialist samples were asked to state which of the ten listed events they regarded as important. The number of events seen as important by each respondent was not limited (i.e., a subject could regard all ten as important). Percentages in table 8.3, therefore, are the proportion of the sample mentioning a particular event as important to them. For example, *all* of the specialists thought the April, 1977, legalization of the Spanish Communist Party was important. The results seem inconclusive; further, raw data are not provided, and no significance tests are reported in the article. Yet there are some enlightening similarities and differences within and between elites and mass public in specific substantive areas.

Media elites in Romania seem more concerned about political than non-political events, and they rate external political events as more important than does the mass citizenry. The public sample attached greater importance to internal political events and to nonpolitical occurrences. Câmpeanu did discover considerable variation between months; for instance, the public's rating of non-political events in April, 1977, went up considerably from January, 1977, no doubt because the specific topics of a nonpolitical nature that were "in the news" in April seemed more germane to more people. Such news items as the North Sea oil spill and the Romanian soccer team's victory over Spain measured in April brought public attention to the nonpolitical sphere (as denoted by Câmpeanu's classification), whereas a congress of agricultural leaders and the commemoration of the 1907 peasant uprising led in the political classification for the citizenry in the same month (see table 8.3).

Such findings suggest the Romanian public is, not surprisingly, parochial in its concerns, attributing importance to current events outside the political realm (sports, environment or taking a new census) and to those which concern domestic politics (decrees by President Ceauşescu, national meetings in Bucharest, or national celebrations). The importance of external political events, with some exceptions, is given a lower evaluation. One obvious exception was the inauguration of a new American president in January, 1977, which was rated above most other nonpolitical or domestic political events at that time. Media elites, by contrast, are consistently more conscious of the importance of external political occurrences—for example, January events such as the first meeting between the government and opposition in Spain and Carter's inaugura-tion (which received an even higher rating among elites than in the public sample), or the April events which included troubles in Zaire, Cyrus Vance's first Moscow visit, and the legalization of the Communist Party of Spain. The propaganda specialists also exhibited greater variation over time in their evalua-tion of the importance of domestic political events, seeing them as more im-portant than other topics in January, but considerably less than external events in April; the pattern was reversed for the public sample.

As intriguing as such media research is from a Western perspective, one must nevertheless note the gaps that remain. Câmpeanu could ask only for ratings of current events that had been reported in Romanian newspapers or on radio and television. Thus there were no reports in the Romanian media of President Ceauşescu's admission at a news conference after the March 4, 1977, earthquake that Romanian oil reserves were approaching depletion;[17] of the troublesome period in Romanian-American trade;[18] or of Jiu Valley miners' complaints that were being aired many months before the August, 1977, walk-outs. Such topics, usually not reported by media in communist states, were understandably missing from the study. But Câmpeanu also did not ask for evaluations pertaining to the March 4, 1977, earthquake—for example, the rescue efforts, mobilization efficiency, and related matters—which did receive

Table 8.3. Importance of Current Events in Media to Public and Specialists
(percentages)

Event[a]	Those Considering Event Important (January 1977)		Event[a]	Those Considering Event Important (April 1977)	
	specialists	public		specialists	public
Competition	56.7	48.0	Congress	90.0	80.6
Decree	63.3	55.1	May First	13.3	34.9
Winter	10.0	52.0	Unemployment	40.0	44.0
Carter	93.3	61.0	Humanity	50.0	58.3
Egypt	20.0	24.6	Zaire	40.0	29.1
Spain	53.3	34.6	1907	46.7	68.9
Locusts	20.0	31.6	Vance	46.7	28.5
Fatherland	43.3	39.8	Soccer	66.7	59.5
Census	76.7	79.8	P. C. Spain	100.0	46.3
Basketball	23.3	35.1	Explosion	16.7	53.4

[a]Event key:

Competition: Announcement of competition to exceed the 1977 Plan
Decree: Presidential decree regarding dismissals and appointments
Winter: Difficult winter in the West
Carter: Carter inauguration as U. S. President
Egypt: Events in Egypt
Spain: First meeting between government and opposition in Spain
Locusts: Locust invasion in the Middle East
Fatherland: Establishment of Falcons of the Fatherland Organization
Census: New national census in Romania
Basketball: Victory of a Bucharest team in national competition
Congress: National congress of managers of socialist agricultural units
May First: Increasing production before May
Unemployment: Rising unemployment in capitalist states
Humanity: New statements on the humanity and solidarity of the Romanian government
Zaire: Armed struggle in Zaire
1907: Memorials to the 70th anniversary of the 1907 peasant uprising
Vance: Vance's visit to Moscow
Soccer: Romanian team's victory over Spain
P. C. Spain: Legalization of the Spanish Communist Party
Explosion: North Sea oil fire

Source: Pavel Câmpeanu, "Evaluarea Informaţiei de Actualitate," *Viitorul Social* 7, no. 1 (1978):97-99.

media attention during March and April, 1977. Stories of heroism were mixed with many articles and reports critical of inefficiency and lack of preparedness. But perhaps these, too, are among the "non-issues" of Romanian politics. The regime will sometimes cite failures and use criticism in the media as a tool for socialization, but apparently is unwilling to give the public a view of its own collective disenchantment.

The impact of broadcast media on daily activities (particularly leisure time) of citizens has also been the subject of Romanian survey research. We return to the topic of leisure time research below. But a study by Argentina Firuţa, "Changes in the Mode of Life of the Working Class," is worth mentioning here.[19] A large 1976 sample (2,742) of workers employed in twelve enterprises in Braşov, Argeş, and Iaşi counties (counties selected because of their different levels of industry and urbanization) indicated that their preference for leisure-time activity was television. Firuţa was able to differentiate preferences of mature (more than 30 years of age) workers from those of youthful workers (30 and under). Asked to rank various kinds of activities (television, lectures, film, radio, visiting friends, museum, sports, walking, etc.) in terms of their first, second and third choices for spending free time, the most frequently mentioned first and second choices for older workers was television, with visiting friends and taking walks virtually tied for third choice. Younger workers also regarded television as an attractive way to spend their free time, mentioning it second only to lectures as a first choice and citing it most often as a second choice.

The Western observer may doubt the excitement potential of "lectures," but there can be no such doubts concerning the important place television occupies in the free time of both young and mature working-class people in Romania. For political leaders, television clearly is the way to reach urban workers. It not only is becoming the most pervasive mass medium in Romania, but the preferences of workers indicate that it already has the greatest penetration into their use of time. But were we to conduct a survey of rural Romanians, who comprise nearly 50 percent of the population, the findings would differ dramatically. Even into the 1980s, most Romanian villagers will not possess radio or television, and printed media will remain for several more years the most pervasive communications medium among Romanian peasants, whereas television is present to the same degree as radio only in the most urban and highly developed locales. When several counties are compared regarding possession of radios and televisions, urban (and usually more well-to-do) populations have a higher ratio of televisions to radios, suggesting that certain media will have to be "targeted" at certain parts of a country if the central regime is to maximize the effect of propaganda (see table 8.4). In a country where even the most advanced counties, such as Huneadoara, Constanţa and Braşov, have only one television per seven or eight people, however, radio remains the broadcast medium of greatest penetration, with printed media reaching more households than either radio or television. (This is, of course, most true in less-developed

Table 8.4. Television and Radio Penetration in Selected
Romanian Counties, 1974

County	Media Penetration		
	television sets per capita	radios per capita	ratio or television sets to radios
Braşov	.146	.146	1.00
Cluj	.103	.137	.75
Constanţa	.139	.132	1.05
Hunedoara	.113	.115	.98
Timiş	.137	.177	.77
Covasna	.077	.154	.50
Harghiţa	.058	.131	.44
Iaşi	.067	.090	.74
Vrancea	.058	.070	.83
Vilcea	.051	.078	.66

Source: Author's calculations from Ion Iordan, Petre Gaştescu and D. I. Oancea, *Indicatorul Localităţilor Din România* (Bucharest: Editura Academiei Republicii Socialiste România, 1974), pp. 7-38.

counties such as Iaşi, Vrancea, Vilcea and others where there is a television for only one of 16-18 citizens, and radios are not much more evident.)

Family and Women

Sociological research employing surveys have used the family as a level of analysis primarily when the aim of the research was to identify components of values and beliefs among youths, workers, and other social groups. The family is viewed not in the anthropological sense of being more "natural" or "fundamental" level of human organization, but is instead examined for the socialization functions it performs and its efficiency as a unit for organizing work. Members of the former Department of Social Theory in the Institute of Philosophy at the Academy of Social and Political Sciences have been responsible for most of the publications in recent years based on surveys of the family.

Mihail Cernea's investigations into the impact of economic organization on family life were undertaken in the 1960s, and as early as 1971 resulted in a study on changes in peasant families which followed the imposition of cooperative farms.[20] Some of his later work about peasant families found outlets in Western journals; it focused on "the extent of influence that the family system is able to exert upon the formal organization" (i.e., cooperative farms and, by implication, the Party's ability to control rural social change).[21] Perhaps the most politically significant finding of Cernea's family research is that the peasants prefer the family to other artificial units for the organization of agricultural labor (the team or brigade). This is evident in Cernea's data regarding results of a 1971 shift away from the team/brigade model to a system by which peasants in cooperatives (94 percent of all peasant families in Romania) chose if they wanted to sign contracts with the cooperative as 1) part of a team of 25 to 30 members, 2) a family unit, 3) part of a group of families to carry out joint work, or 4) as individual members of the cooperative. The degree to which cooperative members preferred contracts as a family unit was impressive, with both team and individual contracts less valued (see table 8.5). For almost three decades, the Party's intention clearly had been to "do away with familism" among peasants through the creation of the cooperative farms.[22] The work unit of the family group or kinship system was to be replaced by what Cernea calls the new matrix of *echipa* and *brigada* (team and brigade). Cernea and his colleagues strongly imply that this effort had failed; they demonstrate clearly that the family retained its strong influence on the functioning of socioeconomic organizations created by the Party. Also unstated, but clearly implied, is that peasants' apathy (or antipathy) toward the units meant to replace the family groups as a work organization matrix had had a negative impact on the productivity of cooperative farms. Thus Cernea refers to the "reduced capacity [of teams and brigade] as economic inducement for the cooperative farm

Table 8.5. Types of Agricultural Work Units and Their Membership in 1971 and 1972

	Year 1971 Work Units number	percent	Members number	percent	1972 Work Units number	percent	Members number	percent	1972 compared with 1971 distribution of additional individuals in 1972 over various types percent	number of members in each type compared with 1971=100
Type of Work Unit										
Single families	16,001	17.4	24,996	18.4	30,193	21.4	47,268	23.0	31.7	189.1
Groups of families	1,201	1.3	6,348	7.7	2,114	1.5	11,844	5.8	7.8	186.6
Teams	1,198	1.3	30,845	22.7	1,382	1.0	39,537	19.2	12.4	128.2
Individuals	73,476	80.5	73,476	54.2	107,298	76.1	107,298	52.1	48.1	146.0
Total	91,876	100.0	135,665	100.0	140,987	100.0	205,947	100.1	100.0	151.8

Source: Mihail Cernea, "The Large-Scale Formal Organization and the Family Primary Group," *Journal of Marriage and the Family* (November 1975), p. 931.

451

members."[23]

In her article, "The Family and the Genesis of Socialist Consciousness in the Young Generation," Ecaterina Springer (who writes under the pseudonym of Timişan), deals with parental notions of the kinds of values their male and female children, respectively, should hold.[24] Springer, who was a doctoral candidate under Cernea prior to the disbanding of the Department of Social Theory, writes on the basis of her survey research, although almost no data nor the nature of questionnaire items (i.e., force-choice or open-ended) are reported in the article being cited here.[25] In a survey of Agricultural Cooperative presidents (sampled because of contract responsibilities), Springer found that these officials wanted their male and female children to hold similar values. She concludes that because there is a strong correlation (rho = .955) between the hierarchy of values these parents seek for male as opposed to female children, that older prejudices against females have changed.[26]

Although Springer does not discuss this, it is worth noting the apparent lack of parental concern for the sorts of politically relevant values that the Party leadership might prefer (e.g., patriotism, selflessness, collective consciousness). A distinctly different set of values received the greatest attention from Springer's respondents. Industry (*hărnicie*), intelligence, and sincerity top the lists for both boys and girls, with being cultured, attentive and having a spirit of initiative not far behind for both sexes. Ambition, abstinence from smoking and drinking, and compassion (*milă*) are lowest in the value hierarchy for both boys and girls.

A sociologist of Cernea's group who used the technique of in-depth interviews, but who conducted so many over several years that she obtained the equivalent of a survey of Romanian families, is Stefana Steriade. Her research, only a small portion of which has been published, uses an approach perhaps most accurately labeled as anthropological. Steriade has carefully recorded interviews of a randomly sampled panel of 104 subjects (each individual from a different family) over time, and thus has amassed a huge body of longitudinal data. Unfortunately, articles based on her data have been severely edited, and Steriade's original notes are far more credible and revealing. No compilation of quantified data from these notes has been made, however, such that interesting relationships between and among demographic characteristics and attitudes or behaviors can be gauged solely from Steriade's intuitive assessments.

Although Steriade's data are not presented systematically, the findings nevertheless seem impressively documented by the many case studies. Steriade emphasizes that the family often plays a paramount role in the achievement of personal aims; the family implants values, and it either helps or restrains a family member in the fulfillment of life goals. One senses from these interviews that the family remains vital in the future perspectives of Romanians. Not only does the family critically affect goal definition and goal achievement, but the sustenance of the family itself becomes a goal. As Steriade points out, were Romanians to choose between "the continuation of studies, promotions at work, and establishing a family, one can identify the priority accorded to the last alternative."[27]

Further, "The family is present as a scheme of values in the parent-child relationship; the childrens' futures are given a fundamental value. This character is seen in the fact that aspirations of the parents are transferred to the children and, moreover, from the fact that personal self-aspirations have a secondary value (aspirations for objects such as furniture, clothing, car, etc.)."[28]

The family, then, remains as the centerpiece of social organization in Romania, despite earlier efforts to supplant it as an economic production unit in agriculture and to displace the family as the principal locus of socialization. One might have expected research such as Steriade's to discover some effect of collectivist socialization or organizational efforts to minimize familial influence on goal orientations. Values and their achievement are still strongly related to the nuclear family and, in peasant Romania, the extended family as well.

Education and Youth

Educational processes and matters related to young people are pervasive in social science literature in Romania, including reports of empirical sociological research. The major concerns in educational research have to do with the socializing impact of the educational system and its relationship to other sources of values, especially the family. Research on youth often is directed at "generational gaps" in values, and the integration of youths into the work force. During the first years of the 1970s, the Research Center for Youth Problems produced a number of studies (many of them authored and/or directed by Fred Mahler) including "Improving the Political Education of the Young Communist League," "The Genesis and Dynamics of Adolescent Ideals," "The Adolescent and Moral Options," and "Reciprocal Views of Parents and Children in the Family Context."[29] As such titles imply, the Research Center had the primary task of investigating the values, ideals, and beliefs of young people. The Party leadership is understandably concerned about the emerging political culture in generations born under communist rule. Survey research is an important tool in describing the ideals of young people, explaining the sources of the values they hold, and predicting the course of future value change.

Between 1975 and 1977, the best research on youth problems continued to be associated with Fred Mahler. In "Aspects of Relations Between Generations and Values in the Process of Developing Socialist Consciousness," Mahler uses data from an earlier survey, jointly conducted with Cătălin Mamali, to portray the coincidence of values between parents and offspring.[30] The study is based on a random sample of 100 Bucharest families that included children between the ages of 16 and 21 years. Thirty-five statements were presented, individually, to parents and children in the sampled families. The subjects were to identify their position on a five-point scale from "complete agreement" to "complete disagreement"; answers of "complete agreement" were scored as +10, "agreement" as +5, "disagreement" as -5 and "complete disagreement" as -10. Mahler is able to calculate a mean degree for all statements for both parents and children. For example, one questionnaire item is: "At present, differences between social and moral values of youths and preceding generations are greater than in the past." The weighted mean on this item is 3.40 for parental opinion and 4.58 for the youths[31] (see table 8.6).

The findings of Mahler's research may seem surprising to the Western observer. He concludes that there exists in general a relatively high degree of similarity between the values of parents and adolescents and that the trend is towards a greater homogeneity of values between generations.[32] At the same time, there is some heterogeneity of values, especially on certain issues of family relationships and religion. On the statement, "The family reproduces a type of authoritarian relationship," the parents moderately agreed (3.60), while offspring were ambivalent (.95). The six value statements about which differences between parents and children were greatest are listed below. Ranked on an "agreement scale" from 1-35, with "1" indicating total accord and "35" indicating least agreement, the generation gap can be substantively identified. The importance of money, for example, is a value statement with which youths agree much more than parents.

> It is important to have money (youths, 6th; parents, 12th).
> A lasting relationship between male and female must be based on marriage (parents, 10th; youths, 16th).
> The family reproduces a type of authoritarian relationship (parents, 22nd; youths, 28th).
> The family is an institution which restrains individual liberties (parents, 25th; youths, 21st).
> The current type of family is fully satisfactory (parents, 15th; youths, 20th).
> The role of religion in society should be reduced (youths, 24th; parents, 29th).

For the most part, however, Mahler concludes that there is little if any "generation gap" in Romania. This finding may be in part a function of his sample, taken entirely from municipal Bucharest, where media socialization efforts are more numerous and consistent. Moreover, Bucharest parents are perhaps more likely than those in any other locale in Romania to have had education and professional training equal to those of their children. Thus, Mahler's findings may be skewed towards homogeneity of values primarily because his sample includes more young people who have been thoroughly socialized, as well as more parents who share educational experiences with their children, than is the case elsewhere in the country. We also are unable to gauge the statistical significance of his findings since no raw data are reported or significance tests cited.

Prior to 1975, numerous studies addressed socializational and youth values. Among these were Mahler and Cinca, " Improving the Political Education of the Communist League," and Cinca's own "Political Knowledge of Youths from Dolj and Vaslui Counties" (both using a survey of about 3,000 young workers, peasants and students to focus on levels of political information); "The Genesis and Dynamics of Adolescent Ideals" by Bazac, Dumitrescu, Mahler and Radulian using 6,000 subjects to identify social, political and work ideals; and Vasile Popescu's "The Meaning of Lives: A Research Problem in Moral Sociology."[33] The focus of all these studies is on the degree to which the values held by young people mirror what one might characterize as the Party's image of how youths should value work, equality, and collective goals, and on the role of educational institutions in producing or reinforcing such beliefs.

In collaboration with Radu Enache, Mahler also has written on the socialist consciousness and socialist education of youth.[34] In their view, given that the future of society depends in part on the moral-political profile, the spirit and comportment, the ideals, values and attitudes of citizens, it follows that educational processes are critical to the building of a socialist society. Citing recent Party decrees, decisions, and pronouncements to the same effect, Mahler and Enache turn to many of the surveys, cited above, which were conducted earlier in the 1970s.

Again, what the investigators do not deduce from their data sometimes appears more interesting than the findings they do elaborate. Mahler's own 1972 data, first reported in an article, "The Adolescent and Moral Options," show that in a sample of 2,733 adolescents ages 16 to 21, 48.8 percent regarded "personal ideals" as primary, 37.7 percent rated "general ideals" of highest priority, while 7.4 percent said "pragmatic ideals" came first in their minds. (There was a nonresponse rate of 8.5 percent.) "General ideals" are such things as sacrifice for common cause, or setting aside personal interests for the general good; these are seen by Mahler as being those most coincident with the Party's social goals. Both "personal ideals" (friendships, worthwhile profession, good family relations) and "pragmatic ideals" (advancement, material benefits) are substantially less consistent with the socialist conscience ostensibly desired for youths by Party leaders. Paradoxically, Mahler views the results as showing that more than 85 percent of youth values are consistent with socialism. Presumably one could as easily infer that more than half of these young people have been less than fully receptive to the priorities defined by the political leadership.

Similarly, the work Mahler did with Mamali and Ene in 1973, to which Enache and Mahler refer in their 1977 article, is open to differing interpretations. The earlier investigation, "Reciprocal Views of Parents and Children in the Family Context,"[35] documented the existence of a value "hierarchy" among adolescents (16 to 21 years old) which suggested priorities of a personal, not social, nature. The highest-ranking value, for instance, was "to be happy in love," and "to succeed in personal life" was a close second (see table 8.7). Mahler and Enache, looking back on these data, suggest that they represent

Table 8.6. Social and Moral Values of Youth and Prior Generations
(percentages)

	Extent of Agreement[a]					
Generation	agree completely	agree	disagree	disagree completely	don't know	wieghted mean[b]
Parents	26.60	37.23	14.36	8.51	12.77	3.40
N	(50)	(70)	(27)	(16)	(24)	
Youth	30.08	41.46	11.38	4.88	12.20	4.58
N	(37)	(51)	(14)	(6)	(15)	

[a]Proposition: Do youth place greater importance on social and moral values than did prior generations?

[b]See explanation of weighting procedure used by Mahler accompanying Table 8.7.

Source: Fred Mahler, "Aspecte ale Relaţei Diferenţiale a Generaţiilor cu Valorile în Procesul Dezvoltării Conştiinţei Socialiste," in *Coordonate Valorice ale Civilizaţie Socialiste*, ed. Alexandru Tănăse and Liubomira Miroş (Bucharest: Editura Academiei, 1976), p. 200.

Table 8.7. Ranking of Values among Romanian Youth

Value	Index of Agreement[a]
To be happy in love	8.46
To be successful in personal life	8.33
To take part in a group with a strong collectivist spirit	7.82
To defend one's ideals	7.69
To do nothing in life to bring discredit	7.48
To give greater attention to others	5.91

[a]Index of Agreement is on a +10 to -10 scale. In a sample of youth from 100 Bucharest families, those who responded in "complete agreement" with a value statement were coded "10," in "agreement" as 5, "disagreement" as -5 and "complete disagreement" as -10. From the frequency of responses falling into each coded category, a weighted mean response for all youth was obtained which Mahler and Enache list as the "index of agreement."

Source: Radu Enache and Fred Mahler, "Educarea Tineretului în Spiritul Valorilor Conştiinţei Socialiste," in *Conştiinţa Socialistă si Participare Socială*, ed. Constantin Potîngă and Vasile Popescu (Bucharest: Editura Academiei Republicii Socialiste România, 1977), p. 83.

overall a "positive moral" orientation, since the general and personal priorities again far outweigh the "pragmatic" concerns of youths. The authors do, however, recognize that the subordination of personal interests to general societal aims is lacking in Romania, and that young people "insufficiently understand that their individual happiness depends on the collective. . . ." Such attitudes are said to result from conceptions more commonly held before young people are integrated into the work force, and before they are involved in production. This posture is therefore a "parasitism," an indicator of the nonintegration of many young people.[36] The assumption is that political consciousness will dawn once an economic role is assumed, and thus that surveys which discover attitudinal problems among youths reflect merely a lack of political maturity among adolescents. Heavy reliance is placed, then, on the socializing effect of the workplace. The authors do not consider an alternative interpretation such as that the educational system is not fully successful in inculcating the appropriate values for new socialist citizens.

In view of the perceived importance of work for youth attitudes, it is not surprising that surveys are being done of the attitudes of young workers. The next section of this chapter deals with attitudes toward work and the workplace. Here we can limit our attention to one important research collection, "Industrial Youth: The Dynamic of Socio-professional Integration," edited by Ovidiu Bădina and Cătălin Mamali.[37] Although this work was published in 1973, and based on research conducted in 1972, it represents an unsurpassed effort in terms of breadth and, for Romanian sociology, sophistication. The studies were carried out by the Research Center for Youth Problems in cooperation with Bucharest University's Faculty of Philosophy's Psychology Section (Zissu Weintraub was coordinator for the student researchers involved).

The project involved careful and systematic questionnaire construction, sampling, and data collection. The breadth of coverage also was impressive; the random sample of 6,251 workers from 14 to 30 years of age was taken from 21 counties and three kinds of industrial enterprises—machine making, chemical refining, and textile manufacturing. The number of workers selected from each county was proportional to the number of young workers employed in that county. The sample also was representative in terms of a number of other demographic characteristics.[38]

Distilling the findings of such a massive project is bound to do some injustice to the work. But some of the findings are sufficiently interesting to demand attention. Work satisfaction among youths was of overriding concern, especially since it reflects in part their acceptance of socialist values. Roman Cresin's contribution, "Aspects Concerning Professional Mobility and Fluctuation among Youth," begins by citing the project's findings about the desires of young workers to change their place of work, or the type of job they perform. About half wanted a change in place of work, and approximately 40 percent wanted a different kind of job. Between 18.7 percent and 24.7 percent, depending on the category of industry, had already changed their job slightly since beginning full-time employment.

Cresin also reports the responses to a more specific question in which control was added for a worker's appreciation of his profession. Asked, "Do you want to change your profession?" (i.e., not just place of work of the specific task assigned, but the entire focus of one's work), only about 10 percent of the workers who found satisfaction in their work wanted to change professions; however, one-fifth to one-sixth of those who expressed an indecisiveness about their work satisfaction also wanted to change their entire career orientation. As one would expect, the correlation between work satisfaction and career satisfaction is high (see table 8.8).

A strong correlation also exists between a desire for job change and whether or not a worker performs tasks for which he or she was trained. Interestingly, however, even among the 79 percent of workers who have jobs relevant to their training, more than five out of seven also would like to change careers. These respondents represent about 58 percent of the full sample.

Other articles in the Bădina-Mamali collection are equally revealing concerning the attitudes of young Romanian workers. Asked how to increase workers' productivity, the method most often cited, regardless of industry, was "improvement of the co-interest system," by which workers refer to a need for greater connection between their pay and their productivity.[39] Also interesting are the data which indicate that 10 percent of the young workers suffer from nervous disorders, and that fewer than two-thirds said they suffered no noticeable medical problems of any kind.[40]

From the Party leadership's perspective, then, survey research aimed at youth paints an ambiguous picture of what the generation born in the late 1940s through 1960 thinks about or believes in. On the one hand, "pragmatic" goals that emphasize career and money are not at the top of adolescents' priorities. On the other hand, Romanian sociologists have not disguised the fact that youths have failed to adopt "collective/socialist" values to a sufficient extent. Further, there are identifiable problems of attitude and work and career satisfaction among workers. At the same time, the apparent ambiguity of these findings may result as much from the imprecision of survey techniques and the reticence of investigators and editors to convey all reasonable interpretations of the data as from the realities being described.

Work and the Workplace

The arenas in which survey research has been put to most frequent use in Romania are those of workers' attitudes and participatory behavior in the workplace. Attitudes of workers toward their workplace, management, pay and benefits, fellow employees, and related topics have undeniable ideological import. Romanian political leaders are bound to be concerned for the willingness of workers to involve themselves in factory and community-level structures, e.g., workers' councils, citizen committees, and people's councils. The productivity of industrial labor assumes great importance for the socioeconomic goals of the Party as well. Thus, from ideological, political, and socioeconomic standpoints, the leadership attaches importance to the current state of opinion within the working class. Worker participation in Romania is described and analyzed in terms of the demographic characteristics of workers, e.g., the proportion of males vs. females, young vs. old, or Party vs. non-Party, who involved themselves in workers' councils and related structures. The relationships between measures of work satisfaction and participation, however, are rarely examined.

Research undertaken at the Institute of Political Science and Study on National Problems in the early 1970s, continuing into 1975-76, exhibits some of this inability—or unwillingness— to ask the most interesting questions. Mariana Sîrbu, who has published extensively on the subject of social integration,[41] found a high degree of dissatisfaction regarding pay among a sample of 610 workers randomly selected from all industrial units in the city of Tirgoviste. About 40 percent of all workers regarded their pay as unsatisfactory, with 58 percent of the 40-49 age group being dissatisfied. A majority of workers who had completed secondary or higher education were unhappy about pay, although almost half of those with fourth-grade education and less were also dissatisfied. (Workers with only primary education most often thought their pay was acceptable.)[42] Unfortunately, Sîrbu does not deal with the workplace effects of unhappiness with compensation.

The Sîrbu data are supported by Zissu Weintraub's findings that, even among young workers, pay tops the list of items contributing to dissatisfaction. More than one-fourth of machine construction and chemical refining employees cite salary as their biggest complaint, and textile industry workers mention inadequate pay about 20 percent of the time.[43] Overall, Weintraub discovers a level of job dissatisfaction of 14.4 percent in the textile industry and 18.4 percent among chemical workers. Those who were generally "satisfied" with their job constituted a bare majority of young workers in all three industrial sectors.

Workers' Councils (*Consiliilor Oamenilor Muncii*) and participation in them have been the subjects of survey research for several years. In some cases, these investigations have employed such techniques as participant observation to ascertain the nature of participation in council debates. Studies tend to focus on questions such as, "Of members differentiated in terms of Party status and occupation, who talks the most in council meetings?" It is not surprising that these studies show that the same people who are important in local Party and state organs also dominate workers' councils.[44] Further, many workers seem largely uninformed about council members and activities. On the average (there is some variation among industrial branches), 25 to 33 percent of workers cannot identify any of their elected council representatives by name. It should be noted that, until 1978, on a typical Workers Council only 8 of 19 members were elected.[45] If workers' councils played significant roles on behalf of industrial labor in Romania, it seems reasonable that one-third of those interviewed would not have found it impossible to identify even one of their rather small number of elected representatives. Two-thirds to three-fourths of machine and chemical workers in a 1976 sample knew either none or only a few of their elected council members.

Similarly, there are few positive inferences to be drawn from data about the participation of young workers (under 30 years of age) in factory-production meetings. Production meetings occur prior to general assemblies of a factory or enterprise. At production meetings, workers air grievances and make suggestions about working conditions, quality control, and pay as these problems related to their shift, department, or section within the enterprise. At this lower organizational level, one might expect workers to be more, not less, participatory. Generally, however, young workers do not make any proposals at production meetings[46] (see table 8.9). Of the one-third of young workers in a nationwide sample who indicated that they *did* make proposals at production meetings, a sizeable proportion (about 40 percent) thought their proposals would have *no effect* (see table 8.10). Another way of looking at the same data is that only 60 percent of the 33 percent who make proposals (this amounts to about 20 percent of the young workers sampled) participate with a sense that their participation makes any difference.

Some of the reasons that workers do not sense efficacy are revealed by the distribution of responsibilities among employees for preparation of the general assemblies of the enterprise, which follow production meetings. Survey research indicates that only those employees whose "highest" political identity is with the Party (as opposed merely to Young Communist League members or trade union members) "prepare for the session," while others perform functions with no hint of initiative such as "filling a role," "accomplishing some task," or simply attending[47] (see table 8.11). Because the Party will set general assembly agendas as well as assign roles and tasks to others, the motivation for those other than Party activists to propose, suggest, or complain at production meetings is likely to be diminished. Similarly, survey data also indicate that Party members among industrial laborers are between four and five times more likely to initiate activities within the enterprise's channels for participation as are workers whose "highest" political identity is the *sindicat* (trade union). Asked when they might take "initiative," non-Party workers overwhelmingly gave answers implying that they would only do so when they were given a task to accomplish or a role to fill via a direct request or obligation—responses which are, of course, in fundamental contradiction with the common usage of "initiative." Significantly, 27.8 percent of non-Party workers in the same 1975 sample declined to respond to this question.

Occupationally, Romania is still an agricultural country. In 1974, 40 percent of all people employed were in various areas of agriculture, and 37.7 percent were in industry and construction.[48] Survey research about "work and the workplace" has therefore included a focus on peasants' productivity and partici-

Table 8.8. Career Satisfaction and Desire To Change Jobs
among Young Workers, by Industry

	Industry					
	machine construction		chemical		textile	
	Desire to change jobs?					
Satisfied with career?	no	yes	no	yes	no	yes
Yes	41.5	11.9	42.5	9.4	43.2	9.7
Ambivalent	12.0	16.3	12.2	17.4	13.4	19.3
No	3.5	14.8	4.4	14.1	2.6	11.8
Total	57.0	43.0	59.1	40.9	59.2	40.8

Source: Roman Cresin, "Aspecte Privind Mobilitatea şi Fluctuaţia Profesională a Tinerilor,"
in *Tineret Industrial*, ed. Ovidiu Bădina and Cătălin Mamali (Bucharest: Editura Academiei,
1973), p. 37.

Table 8.9. Participation in Production Meetings by Young Workers according
to Factory Type
(percentages)

| | Factory Type | | |
Worker Participation	machine building	chemical refining	textile manufacturing
Make proposals	39	32.7	35.2
Do not make proposals	61	67.3	64.8
N	(3,160)	(1,561)	(1,515)

Source: Ovidiu Bădina, "Participarea Tinerilor la Procesul de Realizare a Unor Invenţii,
Inovaţii şi Raţionalizari," in *Tineret Industrial*, ed. Ovidiu Bădina and Cătălin Mamali
(Bucharest: Editura Academiei, 1973), p. 23.

Table 8.10. Perceived Effect of Workers' Proposals according to Factory Type
(percentages)

	Factory Type		
Perceived Effect	machine building	chemical refining	textile manufacturing
Proposals have an effect.	59.8	60.3	66.1
Proposals have no effect.	43.2	39.7	33.9
N	(1,232)	(509)	(534)

Source: Ovidiu Bădina, "Participarea Tinerilor la Procesul de Realizare a Unor Invenţii şi Raţionalizari," in *Tineret Industrial*, ed. Ovidiu Bădina and Cătălin Mamali (Bucharest: Editura Academiei, 1973), p. 123.

Table 8.11. Participation in General Assemblies of the Enterprise
by Organizational Identity
(percentages)

	Organizational Identity		
Extent of Participation	PCR[a]	UTC[a]	Sindicat[a]
I prepared for the session.	18.9	9.2	4.4
I filled a role.	28.1	31.8	21.4
I accomplished some task.	46.4	30.8	26.6
I was only present.	6.6	28.2	47.6

[a]Key: *PCR = Partidul Comunist Roman*
  UTC = Uniunea Tineretului Comunist (Young Communist League)
  Sindicat = trade union organization

Source: Mariana Sîrbu, "Integrarea în Munca şi Participarea Publică în Procesul Dezvoltarii Conştiintei Socialiste," in *Conştiinţă Socialistă şi Participare Socială*, ed. Constantin Potîngă and Vasile Popescu (Bucharest: Editura Academiei, 1977), p. 42.

pation in cooperatives. (As was mentioned above, considerable attention also has been devoted to the peasant family and its transformation.) For example, a 1974 survey was based on a random sample of six of the 112 cooperative farms in Iaşi County. Two hundred eighty cooperative members were interviewed (2.83 percent of the total population in these cooperatives), using a forced-choice questionnaire of 24 items. The emphases in the questions were on the attitude of peasants towards participatory behavior and their degree of concern about the cooperative in relation to personal or material goals.

The author, Despina Strugariu, notes large variations among cooperatives in terms of interest and participation in cooperative affairs with the percentage of peasants saying they were "always interested" varying from 35.6 percent to 53 percent and those "never interested" ranging from 18 percent to only 8.7 percent.[49] There is little analysis of reasons for the varied interest and participation, however, again suggesting the sensitivity of such issues. Data from this research show that about as many cooperative peasants have as primary concerns *preocupări* (better pay), conditions of life, and noncooperative matters such as focus on "the future consolidation and development of the cooperative economy."[50] We suspect that the distribution might be skewed towards the latter response because of peasants' perceptions of what "ought" to be said. And since some peasants regard conditions of life as their chief concern but equate that with the general betterment of the cooperative, the proportion of peasants who stated "noncollectivist" concerns (more than 42 percent) seems noteworthy.

From these and a number of other studies,[51] Romanian workers and peasants can be portrayed as moderately dissatisfied with conditions of life and work, and as relatively uninterested in political matters. Pay tends to be the biggest workplace complaint, but issues contributing to unhappiness are broader. Educated middle-aged workers exhibit high levels of dissatisfaction, and some disenchantment among the poorly-educated or youngest workers also is evident. The potential political relevance of these concerns is not being ignored by the Romanian Party leadership. At the same time, these evidences of dissatisfaction and political apathy may not be particularly unusual when viewed in a comparative cross-national context.

Leisure Time

For many years, the authoritative work on leisure time in Romania was being done by Francisc Albert at the University of Timişoara. His book, *Dialogue with Leisure Time* (1970), set standards for subsequent research in this area.[52] From 1970 to 1972, Albert continued to publish articles based on his survey data on leisure-time usage.[53] There were a few other works published at about the same time that touched on free-time activities, e.g., Câmpeanu's work focusing on preferences for television in relation to other media.[54]

The 1976 survey upon which Argentina Firuţa bases his article in *Viitorul Social* offers a recent view of how workers in Romania prefer to distribute their free time.[55] Moreover, his data are stratified by location such that we can distinguish among leisure-time preferences in urban, suburban, and village locales (see table 8.12). The sample includes more than 2,700 respondents from three counties.

As table 8.13 shows, television, without question, has become the preferred way for workers to spend their free time, whereas radio now plays a very minor role. This is consistent regardless of locale; 36.3 percent of city workers listed television as their first choice, 34.3 percent of workers living in suburban locales did so, and 44 percent of village workers regarded television as their first choice. The sample may be of somewhat limited generalizability, since it consists primarily of urban workers (only 470 of 2,742 in the sample were from villages). However, the research was conducted in counties of varying socioeconomic levels (Braşov, for example, was 65.3 percent urban in 1975, whereas Argeş and Iaşi counties were both less than 40 percent urban),[56] and therefore likely taps differential media penetration. Nevertheless, data from workers probably incorporate a bias away from artistic-intellectual activities (e.g., visiting museums, or artisan shops) and toward visual media.

Although "lectures" were the second most frequently mentioned first choice, their dramatically smaller popularity as a second or third choice seems to imply that the preference is shallow—perhaps a function of what the respondents assumed were appropriate responses. More consistent and apparently more credible are responses listing films as the preferred second choice and walking as the preferred third choice. When Romanian workers cannot watch television, they most often would prefer to see a film. If that, too, is unavailable, they will take a walk. A scenario in which citizens, lacking television, would go to a lecture seems less persuasive.

Moral and Ethical Preferences and Life Aspirations

As noted above, research on Romania's youth has focused on similarities and differences between their values, beliefs, and aspirations, and those of older generations. Workers, too, have been a focus of survey research of this genre. We can develop further our picture of the moral and ethical aspects of Romanian citizens' life aspirations by examining Pavel Câmpeanu's survey work on value symmetry.

Published in 1975, Câmpeanu's "Valoare şi Simetrie" is an intriguing attempt to ascertain empirically the degree of an individual's value symmetry, both over time (one year) and on an affective (positive-to-negative) dimension.[57] First, Câmpeanu sought to discover whether the hierarchy of

Table 8.12. Leisure-time Preferences of Workers

	Locale								
	town (N = 675)			suburban (N = 1,543)			village (N = 470)		
				Preference					
Activity	first[a]	second[a]	third[a]	first	second	third	first	second	third
Television	36.3	22.1	10.7	34.3	21.9	8.0	44.0	20.9	10.2
Lectures	32.2	11.1	5.2	29.6	8.2	5.5	15.1	7.3	7.2
Film/theatre	9.5	28.4	14.1	15.3	26.0	11.5	11.3	20.6	9.8
Radio	1.6	9.0	9.5	2.4	10.6	9.4	1.7	16.2	11.5
Visit friends	3.2	7.4	15.7	2.3	11.1	17.0	4.3	11.1	18.7
Museum	0.7	1.9	2.0	0.3	2.1	3.5	0.8	1.1	1.7
Crafts	1.9	1.8	3.4	2.0	2.2	3.2	2.3	1.9	1.9
Sports	8.7	8.0	11.0	7.9	7.6	10.6	9.4	9.8	10.0
Walking	4.3	9.5	21.2	4.0	9.3	24.7	2.6	8.1	14.5
Other	1.3	0.7	7.4	1.9	1.0	6.6	8.5	3.0	14.5

[a]"First," "Second," and "Third" refer to a subject's preferences. For example, 36.3 percent of workers from towns indicated that television constituted for them a "first preference." If they could not pursue their first choice, the largest percentage of town workers (28.4 percent) then prefers films.

Source: Argentina Firuța, "Schimbări în Modul de Viața al Clasei Muncitoare," *Viitorul Social* 7, no. 1 (January-March, 1978): 77.

Table 8.13. Leisure-time Preferences
(percentages)

Preference	Activity									
	television	lectures	film	sports	walking	visit friends	radio	crafts	museum	other	no response
First choice	36.4	27.8	13.1	8.3	3.9	2.9	2.1	2.1	0.5	2.9	0.0
Second choice	21.8	8.9	25.6	8.2	9.1	10.0	11.3	2.0	1.8	1.3	0.0
Third choice	9.0	3.7	11.9	10.7	21.9	16.8	9.8	3.2	2.8	8.2	0.2

Source: Argentina Firuța, "Schimbări în Modul de Viața al Clasei Muncitoare," *Viitorul Social* 7, no. 1 (January-March, 1978): 77.

values remained similar over time in an "experimental" group of 87 apprentice locksmiths at a Bucharest trade school. The group was "experimental" in that it was all male, 90 percent of whom had recently arrived from rural areas, and all were 16 or 17 years of age. The author also examines symmetry of affect; that is, whether high regard or commendation for a positive value (e.g., modesty) is mirrored by equally strong disregard for its inverse (e.g., immodesty). If to be honorable (*cinstea*) is highly valued, is being dishonorable (*necinstea*) viewed negatively with the same intensity? While Câmpeanu's sample was neither large nor of high generalizability, he nevertheless moves away from simply unidimensional survey techniques. His is one of the few Romanian efforts at looking at value intensity.

Each respondent was given a list of twelve "positive" values and their opposites and asked in a questionnaire to identify which of these listed values he felt was most important, i.e., about which value did he feel most strongly? Over a year, values remained quite consistent, but other findings were less expected. Although predictable items such as honor, courage, intelligence, and modesty headed the list of positive values, none was mentioned by more than 20.5 percent of the respondents (see table 8.14). ("Honor" was most frequently mentioned.) The data seem to describe substantial value heterogeneity despite the essential homogeneity of the respondent group.

Câmpeanu also creates a threefold classification of value types. Five values are labeled "moral," four are considered "intellectual-spiritual," and three are "physical." There is a slight trend over time toward "physical" values, which include beauty, force, and skill (*iscusința*); the mean proportion of responses for these three values rises from 4.3 percent to 5.6 percent. At the same time, values classified as "moral" slipped from a mean percentage of 11.4 percent to 10.7 percent and "intellectual-spiritual" values from 7.5 percent to 7.3 percent.[58] Looking at the negative values, the inverses of modesty, courage, devotion, honor and dignity (Câmpeanu's "moral" values) declined in the intensity with which they were viewed, from a mean of -16.3 percent to -14.9 percent.[59] The inference must be highly tentative, but the data suggest that young Romanians may be moving slightly away from "moral" values and toward "physical" values. Because the data reflect changes in a short span of time within a homogeneous group, such findings suggest a worthwhile direction for further investigation. Unfortunately, no replication of this research has been attempted on a larger scale. Câmpeanu's own conclusions extend beyond what his data warrant. Nevertheless, he suggests intriguing thoughts such as:

One possible implication of these specifics [is that] there is a tendency toward disequilibrium between individual needs and the dominant realities of social relations. . . . with the advance of urbanization, this distance [between individual moral needs and the moral ambiance of society] will lead to a loss of [individual] energy. . . .[60]

Table 8.14. Ranking of Values in Câmpeanu Sample

Value Category	Percent of Responses	Rank
Honor	20.5	1
Courage	15.0	2
Intelligence	12.5	3
Modesty	12.0	4
Beauty	11.0	5
Talent	10.5	6
Devotion	5.0	7
Dignity	4.5	8
Cheerfulness	4.0	9
Culture	3.0	10
Skill	2.0	11
Force	0.0	12

Source: Pavel Câmpeanu, "Valoare şi Simitrie," in *Civilizaţia Socialistă şi Valorile Ei*, ed. Alexandru Tănăse (Bucharest: Editura Ştiinţifică şi Enciclopedică, 1975), p. 213.

The life aspirations of youth, and the relationships between such aspirations and family and school, were analyzed by Mihail Cernea and Ecaterina Springer in "Family, School and Professional Orientations of Youth."[61] Combining data from 15 previous studies, Cernea and Springer ask whether there is agreement among the various research efforts regarding the influence of family, school, and "other agents" in the distribution of professional orientations. The 15 studies cumulatively surveyed 6,817 respondents.

The surveys are found to be in essential agreement, and their findings generally to be statistically significant. Broadly, the data suggest that the family remains by far the most influential agent in orienting an adolescent towards a career path; this was true for 57 percent of the respondents. School was cited as primarily responsible for the professional inclinations of youths by fewer than 10 percent of the combined sample, and various other agents were named by another 10 percent. Approximately 13 percent of the respondents suggested that their own decisions accounted for their professional orientation (and 676 gave no response).[62]

Cernea and Springer also cite research by Achim Mihu and Voicu Lascuş (sociologists in Cluj) regarding the lack of commitment to an agricultural life among offspring of peasants. Only 4.4 percent of a sample of 940 rural youths (grades 7-10) thought that they wanted to adopt the same agricultural occupation as their father, and only 8.6 percent thought agriculture was an acceptable profession.[63] Mihu and Lascuş suggest this survey finding has identified "anamolies in the existing structure of youths' consciences regarding their occupational desires or possibilities in life."[64] Although this would appear to offer evidence contradicting Cernea and Springer's argument about the impact of family, one should keep in mind the likelihood that most peasant families urge their children to leave the fields for more education and a better life.

Social Problems and Social Policy

It is clear that social problems of increasing range and complexity have been produced by the acceleration of modernization processes in Romania in the 1960s. Transforming peasants to industrial workers, and their residences from village homes to high-rise apartment blocs necessarily has been socially disruptive. Survey research into matters that touch upon these sensitive arenas of social tension and conflict, or on policy-relevant public opinion, are done under contract between the Party and research institution. The findings are communicated in but a few copies, and generally are not made public. Moreover, crime statistics, as Westerners understand that term, are not made public. Hence we have only limited survey-produced data to report.

Existing studies are, nevertheless, important and merit attention. Mircea Preda and Ioan Vida, of the Institute for Political Science and National

Problems, conducted a study in late 1974 (published in 1975) regarding "Ethical, Political and Juridical Interferences at the Level of Individual Conscience."[65] Interestingly, this research was completed prior to the integration of the Institute into Ştefan Gheorgiu Academy. Further, Preda is no longer involved in survey research. Using a sample of 1,712 taken from the Jiu Valley—the site of a miner's strike and violence in 1977 that necessitated military intervention and a Ceauşescu visit—Preda and Vida probe public attitudes toward antisocial behavior.

"Hooliganism" is the term commonly used by Romanian and other Eastern European writers to describe antisocial behavior in a manner acceptable to the Party. Use of this term implies that a small minority of social outcasts perpetrates the behavior which is harmful to citizens. But although the terminology may be artificial or limiting, the questions asked in such surveys are potentially of considerable import; they appear to tap dimensions of citizen commitment to existing social and political institutions. For example, are citizens' commitments to the current system strong enough that they would intervene when witnessing antisocial behavior? Preda and Vida decline to draw a general conclusion to this question, although they do state that a "passive attitude" toward hooliganism is widespread.[66] Indeed, almost half of those interviewed suggested that either witnessing hooliganism would prompt *no* response from them or—for a small percentage—that they had never witnessed a case of such negative behavior.

Correlates of noninterventionist (passive) attitudes toward nonsocial behavior are found to include education and age. Older and more "prepared" citizens (those with more education, more political indoctrination, and more professional training) say with greater frequency that they will intervene. If younger and less "prepared" people are most passive toward antisocial behavior, then one can presume that young workers are among the least inclined to act in accord with the values prescribed by existing institutions. Preda and Vida do not make such an inference, but the congruence of the data and the 1977 worker unrest in the Jiu Valley seem too suggestive to be merely coincidental.

Domestic, noncriminal conflicts are the subject of another interesting research effort. This study did not use survey instruments, but did involve interviews in the course of reviewing the activities of "adjudication commissions" (*comisiile de judecata*) for a sample of huge new living quarters (a *cartier*) on the outskirts of Bucharest, with the intent of gauging the relationship between such living conditions and interpersonal conflicts.[67] These commissions, established in 1968,[68] are composed of neighborhood residents who deal with civil disputes on a prelitigation basis, imposing small fines occasionally, but usually resolving conflicts by applying the pressure of community opinion through their decisions. The authors of this study, Liviu Damian and E. Dobrescu of the Sociological Laboratory of Municipal Bucharest, categorized the disputes adjudicated by the commissions, and reported that conflicts between spouses represent a higher proportion of cases in newer residential quarters than in older, established units of similar type. The vast new complex called "Drumul Taberei," with scores of huge prefabricated apartment buildings, registered 68.6 percent husband-wife disputes as opposed to "Vechiul Militari," the older district, where 53.3 percent of disputes were between spouses. Conversely, disputes outside the nuclear family accounted for 46.7 percent in the oldest district, and 31.2 percent in the newest.[69]

The generalizability of these may be limited. But they do provide some support for the authors' hypothesis that this form of "bloc" living—presumably, an accompaniment of urbanization—provokes increased conflicts in interpersonal relations. However, especially since the article does not report on conflict rates (per capita, per family, or changes in these measures over time) inferences from these data remain speculative.

Politics, Ideology, and Other Matters

There has been little survey research on the bases of Party rule in Romania, on the public acceptance of Marxist-Leninist ideology, on ethnicity and problems of cultural diversity, or in the area of market research. What has been done rarely is publicly available. My intention here, therefore, is to comment briefly on inferences that might be drawn from the very limited attitudinal data, and from nonsurvey data, that have been published.

Some measurement of citizen opinion about people's councils, local Party organs, and other subnational institutions has been done in Romania. In the early 1970s, work was undertaken for the Party and the joint Party-State administrative organ overseeing local government (the Committee for Problems of People's Councils—*Comitetul Pentru Problemele Consiliilor Populare*, or C. P. C. P.) that involved a massive survey of the Romanian population regarding council activities and their relations with the mass citizenry. A simultaneous study was undertaken surveying people's council deputies. Reliable sources have indicated to me that the sample size for citizen responses was "tens of thousands," and the deputy sample was of several thousand. Data from these surveys have never been published or made generally available within the Romanian scholarly community. This is, of course, only one example of the limits imposed on empirical sociology, as well as of its *raison d'etre* from the Party's viewpoint.

Records from local authorities have been used by Ioan Vida to write about the extent of citizen proposals (for public projects, new laws, etc.) during electoral campaigns as compared with nonelection periods.[70] Although not based on surveys, these data can be used to draw inferences about citizens' political attitudes. Pursuant to decrees in 1972 and 1973,[71] citizens without any Party or state position may propose, suggest, or complain 1) during electoral campaigns, 2) in people's councils and public meetings, and 3) through personal contacts such as telephone calls, letters, or the traditional form of petitioning leadership, the "audience."

Of these various forms of citizen expression, individual proposals—those *not* made at a public forum but instead through letter, phone call or audience— were resolved or acted upon at a much higher rate by local authorities (94.4 percent within the year) than were proposals made through other mechanisms.[72] This suggests that the informal ties such as *relaţii, pile* (connections or pull) or *bakshish* (bribing via money or other means) continue to have relevance in communist Romania. That such techniques are more effective seems likely to reinforce doubt or antipathy towards public forums and organizational channels which are formally designated for expressing complaints, suggestions, and otherwise communicating with government. Vida also notes that citizen proposals and complaints are more often about housing than any other topic. This is consistent with a finding from my own limited survey of Romanian people's council deputies in which "quality of life" problem areas were most often cited by deputies as the paramount issue needing attention—more so, for example, than economic or education-related matters.[73]

On the other topics around which this volume is organized, no published survey research can be reported for Romania. On the subject of ideology, for example, one can sometimes make inferences from values held by youths or workers about their acceptance of Marxist-Leninist ideology. These data have been discussed in previous sections of this chapter. But surveys dealing directly with citizen views on ideological issues are unknown. Ethnic divisions in Romania still are politically sensitive. Official statistics indicate that Hungarians account for 8.4 percent of the population, Germans 2 percent, and other ethnic groups 1.8 percent—although it seems likely that more people could identify themselves as Hungarian if they thought it would be helpful. Unfortunately, no published attitudinal data touch on perceptions of ethnicity, the treatment of ethnic groups, evaluations of educational or employment opportunities for persons of different ethnic backgrounds, etc. Market research (product preferences, or assessments of an item's market potential) is known in Romania. One can encounter university students in commerce who have been involved in small, local surveys of "consumers"—e.g., of tram and trolley riders, of residents in new housing developments where the adequacy of provisioning has been criticized by some, or of shoppers in stores regarding their product preferences. Published output from these projects, however, does not appear in major Romanian journals, although it seems apparent that in-house distribution of findings to ministries, specific enterprises or local authorities who contract for such research, does occur.

SUMMARY

Romanian empirical sociology has been forced to undergo greater restrictions in the mid- and late 1970s than in the previous decade. Survey research continues to be done, perhaps more frequently by more people, but with increased constraint on the topics selected. There is now a noticeably lower output of quantitative findings in published form. In-house contract research dominates survey research. Moreover, sampling techniques often leave much to be desired, and findings are almost always reduced to percentages, with no raw data or statistical tests of significance presented upon which to base one's assessments of the findings.

Despite these problems, we can determine a good deal about public opinion in Romania from looking at recently published findings—albeit sometimes by inferring from what is *not* treated or discussed. As reported here, survey research indicates that:

1. Romanian media habits are increasingly dominated by attention to television.
2. Media elites and the public differ regarding their perception of news events, with the public being more parochial and nonpolitical.
3. The family retains its central role and importance in Romanian life, being preferred as a unit of economic organization over collective alternatives; values and the achievement of them are still strongly related to the family; youth's values do not differ dramatically from those of their parents.
4. Parents appear not to differentiate significantly between female and male children in terms of the hierarchy of values they seek for them.
5. "Pragmatic" goals are not at the forefront of youths' priorities; but a lack of "collective" values does exist, reflecting on the inability of Romanian education to create a new socialist youth.
6. Workers are somewhat dissatisfied, particularly about pay. Their dissatisfaction is coincident with lack of enthusiasm for participatory channels at the work place.
7. Peasants also are not uniformly oriented toward socialist values or participation in local economic or political structures.
8. Leisure-time preferences emphasize television, films, and walking.
9. Moral and ethical preferences and life aspirations are changing, but not in a magnitude that can be readily seen over a short span of time. The direction of this change might be away from "moral judgments" and towards valuing skills, power, beauty, and other physical aspects of life.
10. Life aspirations are strongly influenced by the family; however, rural youths tend to reject agricultural occupations.
11. Social problems (e.g., hooliganism and domestic conflict) appear to be on the rise. Many citizens are unwilling to involve themselves if they witness hooliganism. Familial disputes occur with greater frequency in new housing projects.

12. Political attitudes have been measured, but this information is not published. Related data tend to indicate citizens' preferences for nonorganizational, nonpublic contact with their local government, and an emphasis on housing problems as their chief concern.

NOTES

1. The preparation of this chapter was facilitated by grants from the International Communication Agency and the University of Kentucky Research Foundation. The author also wishes to thank Dr. Mihail Cernea and many sociologists in Romania for their cooperation and comments as I prepared this chapter.
2. There was, for example, an attempt in 1956-57 to revive Dimitrie Gusti's empirical study of village life in Romania by members of the Institute of Economic Research. This endeavor, however, met with sharp rebuke from the Party in *Lupta de Clasă*, where such studies were branded as bourgeois.
3. This is Cernea's own description of his goals as he reflected on them in 1974 in *Viitorul Social* (Special Issue for the 8th World Congress of Sociology in Toronto, Canada, August, 1974), p. 119.
4. For example, *Cercetări Sociologice Contemporane* in 1966, *Sociologie Generala* in 1968 and *Integrarea Socială a Tineretului* in 1969, all of which were published in Bucharest by Editura Academiei under the editorship of Miron Constantinescu.
5. See Ion Aluaş, *Probleme Sociologice ale Tineretului* (Cluj, 1973); Achim Mihu, *ABC-ul Investigaţiei Sociologice* (Cluj, 1973); and Mihu, *Studentul şi Opinia Publică* (Cluj, 1973).
6. Francisc Albert, *Dialog Cu Timpul Liber* (Bucharest: Editura Politica, 1970); Albert, "Antinomii ale Timpului Liber," in *Contribuţii la Sociologia Culturii de Masă*, ed. Mihail Cernea (Bucharest: Editura Academiei, 1970); Albert, "Tendinţe Actuale în Sociologia Timpului Liber," in *Cultura-Umanism*, ed. Francisc Albert (Timişoara, 1972).
7. Iosif Natansohn, *Sociologia în Acţiune*, vol. 1 (1972), vol. 2 (1973) (Iaşi: Editura Junimea); Alexandru Bărbat, "Cercetare Sociologica Zonala," *Viitorul Social* 1, no. 1 (1972): Bărbat, "Ce Devine Ruralul," *Viitorul Social* 2, no. 4 (1973); Corneliu Dimitriu, *Constelaţia Familiala şi Deformarile Ei* (Bucharest: Editura Didactică şi Pedagogică, 1973).
8. Nicolae Ceauşescu, "Speech at the Working Meeting of the Party Active from the Sphere of Ideology and Political and Cultural-Educational Activity," (July 9, 1971), Supplement to *Romania Today* no. 8/201 (1971), pp. 11-12, 14.
9. See, for example, *Congresul al X-lea al Partidului Comunist Român* (Bucharest: Editura Politica, 1969), p. 72.
10. *Directives of the Eleventh Congress of the Romanian Communist Party*

Concerning the 1976-1980 Five-Year Plan (Bucharest: Meridiane Publishing House, 1975), p. 50.

11. Pavel Câmpeanu, *Radio Televiziune Public* (Bucharest: Editura Ştiinţifică, 1972), p. 134.

12. Ibid., p. 146.

13. Ibid., p. 155.

14. Ibid.

15. Pavel Câmpeanu, "Evaluarea Informaţiei de Actualitate," *Viitorul Social* 7, no. 1 (1978): 95-101.

16. Ibid., p. 96.

17. "Rumania Admits Its Oilfields Approach Depletion," *New York Times*, 19 March 1977.

18. "Rumanian Trade—Troubled Growth," *New York Times*, 27 February 1977.

19. Argentina Firuţa, "Schimbări în Modul de Viaţa al Clasei Muncitoare," *Viitorul Social* 7, no. 1 (1978): 75-81. Also relevant is Maria Moldoveanu and George Patrescu, "Aspiraţii Culturale Specifice în Noile Cartiere Urbane," *Viitorul Social* 7, no. 1 (1978): 88-94. They note that 94 percent of a July 1976 survey of 252 people from 48 apartment buildings distributed among all occupational categories in Braila had televisions, while only 68 percent possessed radios, 48 percent had book shelves, 25 percent had record players, 7 percent had cameras and 5 percent had tape recorders. Overall, 80.93 percent preferred broadcast media to books or other endeavors in their free time according to Moldoveanu and Patrescu, "Aspiraţii Culturale Specifice," p. 90.

20. Mihail Cernea, "Changing Society and Family Change: The Impact of the Cooperative Farm on the Peasant Family," mimeographed (Stanford: Center for Advanced Study in the Behavioral Sciences, 1971).

21. Mihail Cernea, "The Large-Scale Formal Organization and the Family Primary Group," *Journal of Marriage and the Family* (November 1975), p. 927.

22. Ibid., pp. 928-29.

23. Ibid., p. 929.

24. Ecaterina Timişan (Springer), "Familia şi Geneza Conştiinţei Socialiste a Tinerei Generaţii," in *Conştiinţă Socialistă şi Participare Socială*, ed. Constantin Potîngă and Vasile Popescu (Bucharest: Editura Academiei Republicii Socialiste România, 1977), pp. 89-106.

25. It should be added that Ms. Springer did not write the conclusion to the article identified in the previous footnote. Writing under a pseudonym, unable to cite relevant "data," and being constrained to accept additions from an editor pertaining to one's conclusions are some of the factors inhibiting empirical sociology in Romania for those who wish to communicate their findings.

26. Timişan (Springer), "Familia şi Geneza Conştiinţei Socialiste," pp. 101-102.

27. Stefana Steriade, "Incercări de Detectare Sociologică a Valorilor: Indivizii şi Valorile," in *Civilizaţia Socialistă şi Valorile Ei*, ed. Alexandru Tănăse (Bucharest: Editura Ştiinţifică şi Enciclopedică, 1975), p. 205.

28. Ibid.

29. E. Cinca and Fred Mahler, *Perfecţionarea Învăţămîntului Politica U. T. C.*, in the series *Raport de Cercetare* (Bucharest: Centrul de Cercetari Pentru Problemele Tineretului, 1973); D. Bazac et al., *Geneze şi Dinamica Idealului În Adolescenţă* (Craiova: Editura Scrisul Românesc, 1974); Fred Mahler, Cătălin Mamali, and G. Ene, *Imaginea Reciprocă a Părintilor şi Copiilor în Cadrul Familiei* (Bucharest: Centrul de Cercetări Pentru Problemele Tineretului, 1973).

30. Fred Mahler, "Aspecte ale Relaţiei Diferenţiale a Generaţiilor Cu Valorile în Procesul Dezvoltării Conştiinţei Socialiste," in *Coordonate Valorice ale Civilizaţiei Socialiste*, ed. Alexandru Tănăse and Liubomira Miroş (Bucharest: Editura Academiei Republicii Socialiste România, 1976).

31. Ibid., pp. 197-201.

32. Ibid., pp. 197 and 200.

33. Cinca and Mahler, *Perfecţionarea Învăţămîntului*; E. Cinca, *Cunoştinţe Politice ale Tinerilor din Judeţele Dolj şi Vaslui*, in the series *Raport de Cercetare* (Bucharest: Centrul de Cercetări Pentru Problemele Tineretului, 1974); D. Bazac et al., *Geneza şi Dinamica Idealului*; Vasile Popescu, *Sensul Vieţii—Problemă de Cercetare în Sociologia Moralei* (Bucharest: Editura Ştiinţifică, 1971).

34. Radu Enache and Fred Mahler, "Educarea Tineretului în Spiritul Valorilor Conştiinţei Socialiste," in *Conştiinţă Socialistă şi Participare Socială*, ed. Constantin Potîngă and Vasile Popescu (Bucharest: Editura Academiei Republicii Socialiste România, 1977).

35. Mahler, Mamali, and Ene, *Imaginea Reciprocă*.

36. Radu Enache and Fred Mahler, "Educarea Tineretului în Spiritul Valorilor Conştiinţei Socialiste," in *Conştiinţă Socialistă*, ed. Potîngă and Popescu, p. 84.

37. Ovidiu Bădina and Cătălin Mamali, eds., *Tineret Industrial: Dinamica Integrării Socioprofesionale* (Bucharest: Editura Academiei Republicii Socialiste România, 1973).

38. Ovidiu Bădina, "Preliminarii La o Cercetare," in *Tineret Industrial*, ed. Bădina and Mamali, pp. 9-16.

39. Ovidiu Bădina and Cătălin Mamali, "Indicatori Tehnici şi Umani ai Integrării Tinerilor în Muncă," in *Tineret Industrial*, ed. Bădina and Mamali, p. 66.

40. Ibid., p. 69.

41. Mariana Sîrbu, "Integrarea Socială Urbană şi Interese Profesionale," in *Integrare în Muncă şi Dezvoltarea Conştiinţei Socialiste* (Tirgovişte, 1974); Sîrbu, "Integrarea Tinerilor în Noile Intreprinderi Industriale," *Viitorul Social* 4, no. 1 (1975).

42. Mariana Sîrbu, "Integrarea în Muncă şi Participarea Politica în Procesul Dezvoltarii Conştiinţei Socialiste," in *Conştiinţă Socialistă şi Participare Socială*, ed. Potîngă and Popescu, pp. 104-105.

43. Zissu Weintraub, "Indicatori Motivaţionali ai Integrarii Profesionale," in *Tineret Industrial*, ed. Bădina and Mamali, pp. 37-38.

44. Florian Popa-Micşan, " 'Informaţie-Participare' şi 'Responsabilitate-Decizie' in Activitatea Consiliilor Oamenilor Muncii," *Viitorul Social* 6, no. 3 (1977): 451.

45. Ion Petrescu, *Psihosociologia Conducerii Colective a Întreprinderii Industriale* (Craiova: Scrisul Românesc, 1977), p. 53.

46. Ovidiu Bădina, "Participarea Tinerilor la Procesul de Realizare a Unor Invenții, Inovații și Rationalizari," in *Tineret Industrial*, ed. Bădina and Mamali, p. 123.

47. Mariana Sîrbu, "Integrarea în Muncă și Participarea Politică în Procesul Dezvoltarii Conștiinței Socialiste," in *Conștiință Socialistă și Participare Socială*, ed. Potîngă and Popescu.

48. Ion Șandru, *România: Geografie Economică* (Bucharest: Editura Didactică și Pedagogică, 1975), p. 66.

49. Despina Strugariu, "Participarea Cooperatorilor la Activitatea de Conducere," *Viitorul Social* 3, no. 4 (1974): 749-58.

50. Ibid., p. 757.

51. See, for example, Elisabeta Traistaru, "Factorii Economici și Psihosociali ai Stabilității Forței de Muncă în Întreprinderile Industriale," *Viitorul Social* 3, no. 2 (1974); Ion Petrescu, *Psihosociologia Conducerii Colective a Întreprinderii Industriale* (Craiova: Scrisul Românesc, 1977); Maria Popescu, *Conducere, Participare, Conștiință* (Bucharest: Editura Academiei, 1973); Nicolae Radu-Rădulescu, *Forța de Muncă Stabilitate-Mobilitate* (Bucharest: Editura Științifică si Enciclopedică, 1977).

52. Albert, *Dialog Cu Timpul Liber*.

53. For example, Francisc Albert, "Antinomii ale Timpului Liber," in *Contribuții la Sociologia Culturii de Masa*, ed. Cernea; Albert, "Tendințe Actuale in Sociologia Timpului Liber," in *Cultura-Umanism*, ed. Albert.

54. Câmpeanu, *Radio Televiziune Public*.

55. Argentina Firuța, "Schimbări in Modul de Viața al Clasei Munciteare," p. 77.

56. Vasile Cucu, *Geographie și Urbanizare* (Iași: Editura Junimea, 1976), p. 80; his chapter 4 gives a useful comparison in statistical terms between and among *județe*.

57. Pavel Câmpeanu, "Valoare și Simetrie," in *Civilizația Socialistă și Valorile Ei*, ed. Tănăse, pp. 208-239.

58. Ibid., p. 213.

59. Ibid., p. 218.

60. Ibid., p. 239.

61. Mihail Cernea and Ecaterina Timișan (Springer), "Familia, Școala și Orientarea Profesionala a Tinerilor," *Forum* 16, no. 10 (October 1974): 37-47.

62. Ibid., p. 42.

63. Achim Mihu and Voicu Lascuș, "Pentru Care Profesiuni Opteaza Tineretul Școlar?" *Era Socialista*, no. 7 (1973), p. 38.

64. Ibid.

65. Mircea Preda and Ioan Vida, "Interferențe ale Eticului, Politicului și Juridicului la Nivelul Conștiinței Individuale," *Viitorul Social* 4, no. 2 (1975): 322-30.

66. Ibid., p. 327.

67. Liviu Damian and E. Dobrescu, "Noile Ansambluri de Locuieşi Ameliorarea Relaţiilor Umane," *Viitorul Social* 3, no. 2 (1974): 394-404.
68. "Legea Nr. 59/1968 Privind Comisiile de Judecata," *Buletinul Oficial*, no. 27 (9 Marţie 1973).
69. Damian and Dobrescu, "Noile Ansambluri," p. 399.
70. Ioan Vida, "Participarea Maselor la Adoptarea Planului şi Bugetului: Expresie a Autonomiei Locale," mimeographed (Bucharest: Academia Ştefan Gheorghiu, 1977).
71. Ibid., p. 21.
72. Ibid., p. 28.
73. Daniel N. Nelson, "Issues in Local Communist Politics: The Romanian Case," *Western Political Quarterly* 30, no. 3 (September 1977): 391.

BIBLIOGRAPHY

Books, Monographs, Articles

Albert, Francisc. *Dialog cu Timpul Liber*. Bucharest: Editura Politica, 1970.
_____. "Antinomii ale Timpului Liber." In *Contribuţii la Sociologia Culturii de Masa*, edited by Mihail Cernea. Bucharest: Editura Academiei, 1970.
_____. "Tendinţe Actuale în Sociologia Timpului Liber." In *Cultura-Umanism*, edited by Francisc Albert. Timişoara, 1972.
Aluaş, Ion. *Probleme Sociologice ale Tineretului*. Cluj, 1973.
Bădina, Ovidiu. "Preliminarii la o Cercetare." In *Tineret Industrial: Dinamica Integrarii Socioprofesionale*, edited by Ovidiu Bădina and Cătălin Mamali. Bucharest: Editura Academiei, 1973.
_____. "Participarea Tinerilor la Procesul de Realizare a Unor Invenţii, Inovaţii şi Raţionalizari." In *Tineret Industrial: Dinamica Integrarii Socioprofesionale*, edited by Ovidiu Bădina and Cătălin Mamali. Bucharest: Editura Academiei, 1973.
_____, and Mamali, Cătălin, eds. *Tineret Industrial: Dinamica Integrării Socioprofesionale*. Bucharest: Editura Academiei, 1973.
_____. "Indicatori Tehnici şi Umani ai Integrării Tinerilor în Muncă." In *Tineret Industrial: Dinamica Integrării Socioprofesionale*, edited by Ovidiu Bădina and Cătălin Mamali. Bucharest: Editura Academiei, 1973.
Bărbat, Alexandru. "Cercetare Sociologica Zonala." *Viitorul Social* 1, no. 1 (1972).
_____. "Ce Devine Ruralul." *Viitorul Social* 2, no. 4 (1973).
Bazac, D.; Dumitrescu, I.; Mahler, Fred; and Raduluian, V. *Geneza şi Dinamica Idealului În Adolescenţă*. Craiova: Scrisul Românesc, 1974.
Ceauşescu, Nicolae. "Speech at the Working Meeting of the Party Active from

the Sphere of Ideology and Political and Cultural-Educational Activity." *Romania Today*, no. 8/201 (1971).

Cernea, Mihail. "Changing Society and Family Change: The Impact of the Cooperative Farm on the Peasant Family." Mimeographed. Stanford: Center for Advanced Study in the Behavioral Sciences, 1971.

_____. "The Large Scale Formal Organization and the Family Primary Group." *Journal of Marriage and the Family* (November 1975).

_____, ed. *Contribuţii la Sociologia Culturii de Masa*. Bucharest: Editura Academiei, 1970.

_____, and Timişan (Springer), Ecaterina. "Familia, Şcoala şi Orientarea Profesionala a Tinerilor." *Forum* 16, no. 10 (Octombrie 1974).

Câmpeanu, Pavel. *Radio Televiziune Public*. Bucharest: Editura Ştiinţifică, 1972.

_____. "Evaluarea Informaţiei de Actualitate." *Viitorul Social* 7, no. 1 (1978).

Cincă, E. *Cunoştiinte Politice ale Tinerilor din Judeţele Dolj şi Vaslui*. Bucharest: Centrul de Cercetări Pentru Problemele Tineretului, 1974.

_____, and Mahler, Fred. *Perfecţionarea Învăţămîntului Politica U. T. C.* Bucharest: Centrul de Cercetări Pentru Problemele Tineretului, 1973.

Constantinescu, Miron, ed. *Cercetări Sociologice Contemporane*. Bucharest: Editura Academiei, 1966.

_____. *Sociologie Generala*. Bucharest: Editura Academiei, 1968.

_____. *Integrarea Socială a Tineretului*. Bucharest: Editura Academiei, 1969.

_____, et al. *Sociological Thought in Romania*. Bucharest: Meridiane Publishing House, 1974.

Cucu, Vasile. *Geografie şi Urbanizare*. Iaşi: Editura Junimea, 1976.

Damian, Liviu, and Dobrescu, E. "Noile Ansambluri de Locuieşi Ameliorarea Relaţiilor Umane." *Viitorul Social* 3, no. 2 (1974).

Dimitriu, Corneliu. *Constelaţia Familiala şi Deformarile Ei*. Bucharest: Editura Didactică şi Pedagogică, 1973.

Enache, Radu, and Mahler, Fred. "Educarea Tineretului în Spiritul Valorilor Conştiinţei Socialiste." In *Conştiinţa Socialista şi Participare Sociala*, edited by Constantin Potîngă and Vasile Popescu. Bucharest: Editura Academiei, 1977.

Firuţa, Argentina. "Schimbări în Modul de Viaţa al Clasei Muncitoare." *Viitorul Social* 7, no. 1 (1978).

Golianu, Alexandru, and Radovan, Paul, eds. *Cercetări Sociologice în Activitatea de Partid*. Bucharest: Editată de Revista *Munca de Partid*, 1971.

Iordan, Ion et al. *Indicatorul Localităţilor din România*. Bucharest: Editura Academiei, 1974.

Mahler, Fred. "Aspecte ale Relaţiei Diferenţiale a Generaţiilor Cu Valorile în Procesul Dezvoltarii Conştiinţei Socialiste." In *Coordonate Valorice ale Civilizaţiei Socialiste*, edited by Alexandru Tănăse and Liubomira Miroş. Bucharest: Editura Academiei, 1976.

_____; Mamali, C.; and Ene, G. *Imaginea Reciprocă a Părinţilor şi Copiilor* în Cadrul Familiei. Bucharest: Centrul de Cercetări Pentru Problemele Tineretului, 1973.

Mihu, Achim. ABC-ul Investigaţiei Sociologice. Cluj, 1973.

_____. Studentul şi Opinia Publică. Cluj, 1973.

_____, and Lascuş, Voicu. "Pentru Care Profesiuni Opteaza Tineretul Şcolar?" Era Socialista, no. 7 (1973).

Moldoveanu, Maria, and Patrescu, George. "Aspiraţii Culturale Specifice în Noile Cartiere Urbane." Viitorul Social 7, no. 1 (1978).

Natansohn, Iosif. Sociologia în Acţiune. vol. 1 (1972) and vol. 2 (1973). Iaşi: Editura Junimea.

Nelson, Daniel N. "Issues in Local Communist Politics: The Romanian Case." Western Political Quarterly 30, no. 3 (September 1977).

New York Times. "Rumania Admits Its Oilfields Approach Depletion." (March 18, 1977).

_____. "Rumanian Trade-Troubled Growth." (February 27, 1977).

Petrescu, Ion. Psihosociologia Conducerii Colective a Întreprinderii Industriale. Craiova: Scrisul Românesc, 1977.

Popa-Micşan, Florian. " 'Informaţie-Participare' şi 'Responsabilitate-Decizie' în Activitatea Consiliilor Oamenilor Muncii." Viitorul Social 6, no. 3 (1977).

Popescu, Maria. Conducere, Participare, Conştiinţă. Bucharest: Editura Academiei, 1973.

Popescu, Vasile. Sensul Vieţii-Problema de Cercetare în Sociologia Moralei. Bucharest: Editura Ştiinţifică, 1971.

Potîngă, Constantin, and Popescu, Vasile, eds. Conştiinţă Socialistă şi Participare Socială. Bucharest: Editura Academiei, 1977.

Preda, Mircea, and Vida, Ioan. "Interferenţe ale Eticului, Politicului şi Juridicului la Nivelul Conştiinţei Individuale." Viitorul Social 4, no. 2 (1975).

Radovan, Paul, and Golianu, Alexandru, eds. Cercetări Sociologice în Activitatea de Partid. Bucharest: Editată de Revista Munca de Partid, 1971.

Radu-Rădulescu, Nicolae. Forţa de Muncă Stabilitate-Mobilitate. Bucharest: Editura Ştiinţifică şi Enciclopedică, 1977.

Romanian Communist Party. Congresul al X-lea al Partidului Comunist Român. Bucharest: Editura Politică, 1969.

_____. Directives of the Eleventh Congress of the Romanian Communist Party Concerning the 1976-1980 Five-Year Plan. Bucharest: Meridiane.

Şandru, Ion. România: Geografie Economică. Bucharest: Editura Didactică şi Pedagogică, 1975.

Sîrbu, Mariana. "Integrarea Tinerilor în Noile Întreprinderi Industriale." Viitorul Social 4, no. 1 (1975).

_____. "Integrarea în Muncă şi Participarea Politică in Procesul Dezvoltarii Conştiinţei Socialiste." In Conştiinţă Socialistă şi Participare Socială, edited by Constantin Potîngă and Vasile Popescu. Bucharest: Editura Academiei, 1977.

————. "Integrarea Socială Urbana și Interese Profesionale." In *Integrare în Muncă și Dezvoltarea Conștiinței Socialiste*, Tirgoviște, 1974.

Steriade, Ștefana. "Incercări de Detectare Sociologică a Valorilor: Indivizii și Valorile." In *Civilizația Socialistă și Valorile Ei*, edited by Alexandru Tănăse. Bucharest: Editura Științifică și Enciclopedică, 1975.

Strugariu, Despina. "Participarea Cooperatorilor la Activitatea de Conducere." *Viitorul Social* 3, no. 4 (1974).

Tănăse, Alexandru, ed. *Civilizația Socialistă și Valorile Ei.* Bucharest: Editura Științifică și Enciclopedică, 1975.

————, and Miroș, Liubomira, eds. *Coordonate Valorice ale Civilizației Socialiste.* Bucharest: Editura Academiei, 1976.

Timișan (Springer), Ecaterina. "Familia și Geneza Conștiinței Socialiste a Tinerei Generații." In *Conștiință Socialistă și Participare Socială*, edited by Constantin Potîngă and Vasile Popescu. Bucharest: Editura Academiei, 1977.

Trasnea, Ovidiu, and Voiculescu, Marin, eds. *Studii de Știința Politică.* Bucharest: Editura Politică, 1973.

Vida, Ioan. "Participarea Maselor la Adoptarea Planului și Bugetului: Expresie a Autonomiei Locale." Mimeographed. Bucharest: Academia Ștefan Gheorghiu, 1977.

Weintraub, Zissu. "Indicatori Motivaționali ai Integrarii Profesionale." In *Tineret Industrial: Dinamica Integrarii Socioprofesionale*, edited by Ovidiu Bădina and Cătălin Mamali. Bucharest: Editura Academiei, 1973.

Periodicals Consulted

Analele Universitatii Bucuresti: Științe Politice și Economice (1972-1977)
Forum (1973-1977)
Era Socialista (1974-1977)
Revista Româna de Drept (1974-1977)
Romania Today (1971-1977)
Viața Economica (1974-1977)
Viitorul Social (January 1972-May 1978)

Other References

Buletinul Oficial
Anuarul Statistica

9 Summary and Conclusions

William A. Welsh

There have been some differences, both in topical emphasis and in results, among the socialist systems of Eastern Europe and the Soviet Union in the conduct of survey research. Generally, however, similarity has been the rule. Surely some of the similarity is due to diffusion. Both academic and Party researchers in the Soviet Union and throughout Eastern Europe meet frequently to discuss what they are doing and the problems they are encountering. At the same time, there is relatively little formal cross-national coordination of survey research. Relatedly, the variations in emphasis lead us to assume that the broad similarities are due to the fact that many of the problems to which survey research is addressed are common throughout Eastern Europe. The commonality of these problems presumably stems in part from the similar socioeconomic and political superstructures. Some of the differences derive from historical and cultural factors, as well as from the different levels and rates of socioeconomic development represented by these countries. From this perspective, it would be surprising to find that survey researchers in countries as different as the German Democratic Republic, Yugoslavia, the Soviet Union, and Bulgaria were asking the same questions. On the other hand, cultural and technological diffusion have resulted in a remarkable degree of similarity in the major problems faced by advanced industrializing and industrialized societies.

Our strategy in this chapter will be to review the major findings of this study under each of nine topical headings. In so doing, we will attempt to highlight two important cross-cutting themes: 1) the nature of the factors which distinguish among population subgroups, and thus define the social stratification system in Eastern Europe; and 2) the extent to which survey evidence permits conclusions about the nature and degree of citizen support for these socialist systems.

MEDIA HABITS

Research on media habits in Eastern Europe and the Soviet Union has focused on four topics: 1) the socioeconomic characteristics of various media audiences; 2) the relationships among attention to the respective media; 3) the impact of mass media attention on the use of other information sources, especially books; and 4) the effectiveness of the media in providing information, in encouraging social activism, and in helping to address citizen concerns.

Generally, media attention is high throughout Eastern Europe and the Soviet Union. However, there are inter-nation differences in the proportion of the population which appears to be outside the mass media system, i.e., does not regularly have access to radio, television, or newspapers. This group represents only about 2 or 3 percent of the population in the German Democratic Republic, perhaps 10 to 12 percent in Bulgaria, nearly 25 percent in Hungary and as much as one-third of the population in rural areas of Yugoslavia. In every East European country except Czechoslovakia (where no such research is reported), socioeconomic status distinguishes levels of attention to the mass media. However, the possession of radios and television sets is sometimes the same for different socioeconomic groups, as was found to be the case in one town in the Soviet Union. But in Eastern Europe, it is likely to be urban residents with secondary or higher education who are sure to have television sets and radios, and are likely to read newspapers regularly. Access and actual use are not the same, however. Proportionately, the group most likely to use the electronic media (especially television) is composed of younger, less-educated urban workers. Bulgaria is a slight exception; there, residence alone is the strongest predictor of television and radio attention. Education is positively correlated with use of the electronic media, but its effect is largely indirect; rural residence and a lower level of formal education are closely related.

Generally, television has overtaken radio for both informational and entertainment purposes, except for certain rural areas and during weekend hours in the less developed countries, such as Bulgaria. Radio also has remained stronger in the GDR, perhaps partly because East Germans have access to a variety of radio broadcasts from several Western countries. Television and radio have cut substantially into both the entertainment and informational functions of newspapers. However, this has meant an actual decline in newspaper circulations only in Yugoslavia. The impact of the electronic media on newspaper reading has been least in Hungary, where a plurality of the population still relies primarily on newspapers as regular sources of information. There may be some distinction in this regard between national and regional newspapers. Research in Bulgaria shows that many readers feel that regional newspapers are the only useful sources of local news. Unfortunately, nearly all of the East European research on media habits deals with national publications.

Although socioeconomic status broadly defined predicts the use of television and radio, newspaper reading is more specifically related to amount of formal education. This is especially true in Poland, Hungary, Yugoslavia, and Bulgaria. Education and age also were found to be the predictors of attention to the Western press in Poland.

There is official concern, especially in Bulgaria and Hungary, that increased attention to television may reduce the amount of time spent reading literature or other more intellectually stimulating materials. The published evidence on this question, however, is inconclusive. As a leisure-time activity, books are said to be preferred to television in Czechoslovakia. Students in one Sofia high school reported that they would still rather read a good book than watch television or go to a movie. On the other hand, a few more systematic studies suggest that reading may be declining, especially among workers.

Some studies of the effectiveness of the media have been done, especially in Romania and Bulgaria. The Romanian studies uniformly show that television is the most effective mass medium: it generates better recall of events, and is generally preferred for informational as well as entertainment purposes. There is specific evidence in Romania that increased television watching has reduced the interest of young people in printed media. The Bulgarian studies have not attempted to compare the effectiveness of the several media, but rather have concentrated on the impact of one or the other, most often newspapers. These studies suggest skepticism about the effectiveness of the press, along several dimensions. Although there is a correlation between exposure to politically relevant newspapers and social activism among young people, it was concluded that the actual effects of the press could not be fully documented. There is considerable doubt about the ability of Bulgarian newspapers, with the exception of *Rabotnichesko Delo*, to assist in correcting social ills. Newspapers are felt to do an inadequate job of contributing to the preparation of young people for family life. In terms of effectiveness of information dissemination, the two studies arrived at distinctly different conclusions.

Studies have been done of public preferences among several types of information presented in the media. In the Soviet Union, information on foreign affairs is consumed more readily than is information on local or national affairs.

In Romania, preferences vary between the mass citizenry and societal elites; the public seems to be more interested in domestic politics and nonpolitical subjects, whereas a sample of media elites preferred news about foreign politics, and was generally higher on political interest than was the mass sample. Finally, Bulgarian studies have shown a substantial amount of selectivity in newspaper reading; the amount of selectivity varies with formal education. Generally, the lower the education, the more selective and fragmentary is the reading of the newspaper.

FAMILY AND WOMEN

Two major emphases in recent survey research in Eastern Europe and the Soviet Union have been the changing occupational and familial roles of women, and the impact that these role changes have had on the family. These changes take place against a backdrop of continued belief that the family is important. Although Yugoslav research, for example, shows that there is increased individualism and independence on the part of members of rural families, the family unit generally is highly valued throughout Eastern Europe. Nearly all East German youth, for example, hope to marry, and 90 percent want to have children. The importance of the family also has been affirmed in Romanian research, in which it was discovered that family considerations take precedence over possible work promotions, or opportunities for further study.

But if the family continues to be valued as a social unit, it clearly is presented with the need for substantial adjustment as urbanization and industrialization bring about changes in the roles of women. Indeed, the most important familial conflicts are related in one way or another to the dual roles of worker and housewife that approximately half of the women in Eastern Europe and the Soviet Union (nearly 80 percent in the GDR) now have assumed. The motivations for seeking employment outside the home are both economic and psychological for East European women. In Yugoslavia, nearly half of the working women say they would prefer not to work, but in Bulgaria nearly three-fourths say they would work even if they didn't have to. The principal difficulties created by this duality of role have to do with having and taking care of children, and meeting the housework demands. The heavy household burden of women is a source of concern in every country studied. Generally, between one-half and three-fourths of all working women in Eastern Europe and the Soviet Union do most or all of the housework. It appears as if this is not a preferred state of affairs anywhere but in Yugoslavia and rural Hungary. In Bulgaria, the number of women who willingly accept this situation is about one-third of those who are confronted with it. But in Hungary and Yugoslavia, the majority of women, especially in rural areas, do not want to change the traditionally defined familial division of labor between men and women. It is also worth noting that the proportion of men who believe that their wives should work outside the home is uniformly 10 to 15 percent below the proportion of women who say they should be free to do so.

Two of the problems affecting the changing nature of the family in Eastern Europe and the Soviet Union are shortages of appropriate housing, and the unavailability or unacceptability of public day-care facilities. Surveys in Bulgaria have shown that housing problems constitute a source of conflict within young families and affect preferences for family size. In Hungary, the difficulty of access to appropriate housing for young families not only affects their attitudes toward having children, but also seems to be a factor in the high divorce rate. In the Soviet Union, the fact that many young couples must live with parents for some time adversely affects some marriages and is generally a source of concern.

In four of the countries studied—Yugoslavia, Hungary, Bulgaria, and the German Democratic Republic—women commented on problems in day-care facilities. It is significant that, in Yugoslavia and in Hungary, working women see better day-care facilities as the principal answer to the problem of overwork. That is, they do not desire to change the traditional division of labor within the family, but rather expect that the state should make available child-care facilities that would ease their burdens. In East Germany, working women said that the lack of appropriate day-care facilities would be the major factor which might force them to give up their jobs. In Bulgaria, only 40 percent of working women in one city have entrusted their children to day-care centers, and 14 percent of those indicate that, because of their uneasiness about these facilities, they would leave their jobs to care for their children if economic circumstances permitted.

In East Germany and Yugoslavia, surveys have attempted to determine some social effects of the increasing number of working women. East German researchers discovered that the employment of the mother had no significant effect on the school performance of the child. In Yugoslavia, the focus has been on the effect of professional employment of women on their participation in sociopolitical activities. It was discovered that the employment of women does not seem to have had a positive or a negative effect on their participation in political or self-management activities. Women are still much less active than men, and there seems to be little difference between women who work outside the home and those who do not. Rural women in Yugoslavia have much less free time, and consequently are much less organizationally involved than are urban women. One Yugoslav study also determined that the employment of the women outside the home actually improved the quality of the marriage, and of intra-family relationships generally.

In Romania and Czechoslovakia, researchers have been interested in the impact of the family on the transmission of values to children. Czechoslovak research shows the family tends to be a relatively democratic structure. Girls and boys are treated essentially the same, although there are some differences between fathers and mothers in the familial roles and values they prefer for their male and female offspring, respectively. In Romania, it was similarly discovered that parents in a sample of higher-status rural families generally desired the same values for boys and girls. The emphasis clearly was on nonpolitical personal values, such as intelligence and sincerity; values such as patriotism, selflessness, or collective consciousness were not highly rated.

One of the distinct differences among the countries studied has to do with the degree of attention paid to disintegrative forces at work within the family. Thus in the Soviet Union, Bulgaria, Hungary and Czechoslovakia, studies looking at the causes of divorce are prominent. By contrast, in the German Democratic Republic there is little research published on disintegrative forces, notwithstanding the high divorce rate. During the period 1975-77, no studies on this subject were found for Poland, Romania, or Yugoslavia, as well. In the Soviet Union, divorce proceedings are usually initiated by the wife, with the main reason given being the alcoholism of the husband. Soviet men were judged to be responsible for the breakup of the marriage more than half of the time. In Bulgaria, men were held responsible in more than 80 percent of the cases; the principal cause was unfaithfulness. The relevant Czechoslovak study focused on factors which keep marriages together. These were discovered to be children, love, dedication, and sexual harmony, in that order. However, it was noted that in marriages where children were the most important consolidating factor, the marriage partners were the least happy.

EDUCATION AND YOUTH

There is little doubt there has been more recent survey research in Eastern Europe and the Soviet Union on young people than on any other subject. Concerns about the values of young people, especially their commitment to socialism as an ideology and as an operating social order, are serious in almost every country. Both academic sociologists and researchers attached to Party organs have spent a great deal of time looking into these issues.

Broadly, East European and Soviet young people can be characterized as socially conscious, but their level of socialist consciousness is modest—far too modest to suit the regimes. The sensitivity of these young people to the importance of personal relationships is great; in the Soviet Union, for example, youth are found to value personal relationships more than preparation for their future careers. Young people throughout Eastern Europe routinely value a happy marriage and appropriate occupational opportunities far more highly than more specifically material values. Materialism may be somewhat more characteristic of young people in Hungary than elsewhere, based on the research we have examined. Other modest qualifications are necessary, as well. In Romania, research shows that children tend to be somewhat more materialistic than their parents. In Bulgaria, young people identified material shortages as representing a major societal problem. Overall, however, materialism is not a dominant value. In Bulgaria, even among Komsomol members, personal qualities such as helpfulness and a good educational background are valued far more than appropriate ideological and political postures, or active involvement in the Komsomol itself.

The proportion of young people who have personally oriented (as opposed to societally oriented) goals is a matter of some official concern. For example, in Romania a plurality of young people was identified as having personal ideals rather than general ones. In Bulgaria, more than 40 percent of the young people surveyed had personally oriented goals; this was barely fewer than the number who had what were considered to be appropriately concrete societally oriented life plans.

In at least four countries—Yugoslavia, Hungary, Bulgaria, and the Soviet Union—research has identified political passivity, or political activity with inadequate ideological motivation. In Yugoslavia, political activism is at least as low among young people as among their parents. Those who are active tend to be involved in the partisan political arena, rather than in instruments of self-management. The most politically active tend to be highly skilled young workers; university students, rural youth, and unskilled and semiskilled laborers are much less active. A fascinating relationship was discovered between socioeconomic status and participation. Among working youth, the greater the income, the greater the participation. But among university students, the lower the income, the greater the participation. It was concluded that this represents a "classical left-oriented articulation of the social dissatisfaction of the underprivileged." Among Yugoslav young people, orientations toward socialism and toward self-management are held by a surprisingly small proportion. The results vary by study; between 33 percent and 60 percent have a self-management orientation, whereas between 37 and 50 percent are "followers of socialism."

In Hungary, it has been discovered that, although students generally exhibit confidence about the future of socialism, they definitely are not inclined toward political activism. One study showed that young people do not discuss politics with their friends, nor is politics an important topic of conversation in the home. Similarly, in the Soviet Union politics is discussed even less in the home than at work, and people spend relatively little of their spare time on political activities.

Fascinating research has been published in Bulgaria on the motivation of Komsomol members to undertake public work. Motives having to do with the intrinsic nature of the Komsomol as a political organization declined with age, whereas motives which refer to social or personal instrumentalities increased dramatically in significance. We also recall that Komsomol members do not attach much importance to a Marxist-Leninist orientation or active Komsomol involvement in naming ideal qualities for their colleagues and friends. Taken together, these findings suggest that, even within the Komsomol, pragmatic personal and social factors rapidly become the most important motives for social activism. This kind of pragmatism also is implied by Polish studies which identify attitudes of skepticism and wariness in young people.

Probably the most positive systemic orientations among the youth studied were found in Hungary. There is considerable optimism toward the future, although students from Budapest and nonmembers of the Communist Youth League were somewhat less optimistic. Even concrete assessments of recent economic performance were basically positive, although again students in Budapest, especially those from managerial families, were somewhat less positive. Hungarian students acknowledge the greater economic accomplishments of capitalism, but exhibit confidence about the future of socialism, and optimism about the nature of Hungarian ties with the Soviet Union.

This picture of the values of youth is rendered more complex by the absence of evidence of any significant generation gap in Eastern Europe or the Soviet Union. Many parents of present-day secondary and university students in Eastern Europe were socialized in pre-communist times. If a new socialist mentality is being imparted, we could reasonably expect some substantial intergenerational value differences. Romanian researchers find differences between young people and their parents to be small, although young people are more concerned about employment income, and are somewhat less supportive of the institution of marriage than are their parents. This definitely is not true in the German Democratic Republic, where there is strong support for the institution of marriage, and where a high proportion of young people say they are opposed to cohabitation. Generational differences in values are said to be modest, at best, in Poland. The most obvious one is the fact that young people are substantially more secular than their parents. This is not surprising, given the relatively high level of overt religious affiliation of Polish adults. East German research shows that young people's ideas about the family and the appropriate nature of marriage relationships are still strongly influenced by those of their parents, although "adherence in part" (rather than "in full") was characteristic of more than half of the young people studied.

Research has been done in the Soviet Union, Bulgaria, and Hungary concerning the factors which influence occupational preference and choice by young people. In the Soviet Union, young people tend to select a career because of its occupational status rather than the nature of the work. Generally, children from SES-homogeneous families want to raise their social status, whereas children from SES-heterogeneous families seem to prefer an occupational status somewhere between that of the mother and the father. In the Soviet Union, occupational rankings do not vary significantly between students from regular schools and students from technological high schools, or young workers. The most highly valued occupations are in the creative intelligentsia. (Enrollments are up in humanistic courses in the universities, and down in engineering and other technical areas.) By contrast, in Bulgaria, there are distinct differences between students in regular high schools and those in technical schools. The differences are predictable; those in technical schools are much more oriented toward engineering and related careers. Laboring occupations are not valued highly in either country. In Hungary, social backgrounds are critical determinants of occupational choice, although this is somewhat less true outside Budapest. Yet both young people and their parents in Hungary have significant mobility aspirations for the young people, often independent of the family's social circumstances.

Research in Poland, Yugoslavia, and Bulgaria has addressed differences in value systems between urban and rural young people. In Poland and Yugoslavia, the differences between urban and rural youth are very small; they have similar values concerning family life, marriage, and personal happiness. In Bulgaria, some differences were noted, particularly with regard to the concern shown by young people for certain modern "vices," such as drinking and smoking, and casual attitudes toward premarital sex. Young people in the rural areas exhibited far more concern about these problems than did students in the cities.

Level and nature of education are the most important predictors of the values of young people. Most studies focus on students; thus, relatively high homogeneity of values can be expected. In the few studies which contrast educated young people and less-educated young workers, distinct differences emerge. In Bulgaria, for example, young workers are less concerned about crime in general, and significantly less concerned about the rapidly increasing incidence of crimes against socialist property. In some cases, although education is the major predictor of youth values, researchers discover that social background, especially including the level of education and the nature of the occupation of the parents, is an important antecedent factor. This is especially the case in Hungary and the Soviet Union.

WORK AND THE WORKPLACE

Recent surveys in Eastern Europe and the Soviet Union suggest that there are identifiable problems in the areas of attitudes toward work, job satisfaction and resulting labor turnover, and management participation in the workplace by workers. These problems do not seem demonstrably different from those in nonsocialist societies experiencing similar economic changes. Nevertheless, there is great official concern about these problems.

One of the most serious difficulties seems to be an inadequately developed sense of collective responsibility among factory workers. There is evidence of relative indifference toward the theft of socialist property and toward the quality of one's own work. Surveys in Hungary, for example, have pinpointed the seriousness of these two matters. In Bulgaria, fewer than 50 percent of the workers polled could identify a sense of collective responsibility in their workplace. And although the misuse of socialist property is thought by general population samples in Bulgaria to be a major problem, workers themselves seem less concerned about it, and are disinclined to report co-workers who are guilty of such behavior. In Poland, workers feel that conscientiousness toward the performance of one's own job is the most important workplace virtue, but place much less emphasis on efficiency or the concept of helping co-workers. Broadly, the attitudes of workers in Eastern Europe and the Soviet Union toward their jobs seem to be instrumental, which is typical of most industrial nations. However, in Poland there is a distinct contrast between urban and rural workers in this regard; young rural workers are substantially less instrumental, and much more likely to see their job as an end in itself. Yet these rural youth perceive themselves to be less well-compensated and report lower job satisfaction than is the case for urban workers.

Labor turnover has been high in several industries in these countries, perhaps somewhat higher than we might expect in societies that have relatively structured employment circumstances. At the same time, a majority of workers in most of these countries indicate that their jobs are acceptable or good. In Czechoslovakia, an especially high proportion say that their work provides good or comparatively good economic circumstances for their families. Job dissatisfaction is highest among the youngest and least-educated workers, and among middle-aged (40 to 50 years), better-educated workers. The turnover naturally is greater among the first category; this has been documented in surveys done in the Soviet Union, Romania, and Bulgaria. In Romania, half of young workers would like to change jobs and fully 40 percent of them would like to change professions. Naturally the level of dissatisfaction varies among industries, and even among specific plants, as research in the German Democratic Republic has shown. The predictors of job satisfaction seem to be reasonably consistent: especially important is duration of employment in a given location, which varies inversely with job dissatisfaction. For example, a Czechoslovak study noted that employment stability and the proper use of one's qualifications in one's job were the major predictors of workplace satisfaction. The thrust of research in the Soviet Union is similar, where workers' perceptions of the appropriateness of the work they are doing to their own qualifications are a major factor in job satisfaction.

Although Czechoslovak workers apparently are not as concerned about their level of compensation, concern with wages and the incentive structure is widespread elsewhere in Eastern Europe and the Soviet Union. The practice of workers acquiring second jobs is especially widespread in Hungary, where fewer than half of industrial workers indicate satisfaction with their wages. In Romania, young workers are found to feel strongly that pay and productivity are not adequately correlated. In Bulgaria, there is noticeable skepticism about the evaluation of socialist competition in the workplace, and the incentive structure is frequently criticized. A plurality of Bulgarian workers prefer a combination of material and nonmaterial incentives, but if asked to choose one or the other, the overwhelming choice is improved material compensation.

Automation has been a major factor in increasing job dissatisfaction in these countries. However, the specific effects of automation may vary between locations. In the Soviet Union, automation has increased the number of young workers who believe that they are inadequately prepared for their work. By contrast, in Bulgaria, young workers seem to be attracted to plants that use more highly automated production processes, whereas older workers are more likely to feel threatened. Further, in the Soviet Union, the coming of automation has shifted the focus of perceived workplace problems from specific job activities to more general concerns about working conditions in the plant. By contrast, in Bulgaria, "objective" job terminations—those associated with specific concerns about one's own work activity—have increased significantly, whereas "subjective" (nonspecific) motivations for job terminations have been declining since the beginning of the 1970s.

It is noteworthy that in the Soviet Union and Bulgaria relationships between workers and managers in industrial enterprises constitute an increasingly important problem. Whether this is a result of the increasing introduction of production and management automation is unclear. In the Soviet Union, trade unions are perceived by workers to have become more important because of the implications of automation. In Bulgaria, the proportion of job terminations attributed by workers to problems in these relationships increased from slightly more than 1 percent of all job terminations at the beginning of the 1970s to approximately 10 percent by 1975. Bulgarian research also shows that there has been a good deal of confusion surrounding the introduction of automated procedures, and that the general reaction has been one of indifference, especially among rank-and-file workers. The same Bulgarian study showed that 20 percent of the managers and leadership cadres in the plant were actively opposed to the introduction of automation.

The other important area of workplace research has concerned the sociopolitical participation of workers. Generally, surveys discover that the level of political and ideological disinterest among workers is high; this has been shown especially in Hungary, Romania, Yugoslavia, and Bulgaria. With respect to the workplace, there seems little desire on the part of workers to become more involved in management and decision making. In some cases, as many as half of the workers interviewed indicate interest in these activities, but their actual level of involvement remains low. The continued dominance of workplace decision structures by managers and Party activists is clear.

Even in Yugoslavia, where the self-management ideology is reasonably well-entrenched, several studies have revealed the dominance of managers. Workers are little informed and basically uninterested. The principal predictors of workers' information levels about self-management activities are education, level of job, and duration of employment. Relatedly, the more favorable one's position in the social-occupational hierarchy, the stronger his or her commitment to self-management principles. Membership in the League of Communists is shown to be relevant, but less important. Yugoslav workers do not seem especially interested in sharing in more enterprise responsibility; for example, they are collectively disinclined to share the risks of entrepreneurial activity that might be undertaken by their firm.

The situation is similar in Romania. Many workers are uninformed about the workers' councils and management activities within their plants. Persons who are active in Party and government activities outside the plant also dominate within. Most young workers in Romania do not make proposals at production meetings, and nearly half of the one-third of all workers who do make such proposals felt that the proposals had no effect. Romanian research finds that only Party members actively prepare for participation in workplace meetings and activities. Similarly, non-Party workers show little initiative toward greater involvement in workplace activities, and little desire for increased responsibility on the job. Interestingly, there appears to be a higher level of interest in affairs of the work collective among agricultural workers in Romania. However, there is a good deal of unexplained variation among the collectives studied. Thus, the proportion of those who state that they are "always interested" in affairs of the collective varies from 35 to 53 percent.

The situation in Hungary seems little different. For example, many Hungarian workers feel that their jobs are less interesting than desired, but few would want more creative and interesting jobs if it also meant more responsibility. They are not inclined to be involved in plant decision making involving anything beyond their own specific work situations. Those who are more interested are persons who have been on the job longer, Party members, and engineers and managers. Again, the continuing dominance of a workplace elite seems well documented. Significantly, 89 percent of the workers polled in one Hungarian study said they felt that the Party organization within the factory took care of their basic concerns well. And in those cases where the Party organization was perceived to be less effective, the workers felt that those tasks were the responsibilities of the trade unions in any case. Thus, although job dissatisfaction is present in some industries in Eastern Europe and the Soviet Union, workers do not seem to be sufficiently concerned about whatever problems exist to seek more involvement in choice taking affecting their working situation.

LEISURE TIME

Because of the increasing amount of leisure time available to many East European and Soviet citizens, especially workers, as a result of shortened work weeks—and also because of the unencouraging past record of leisure-time usage, especially on the part of workers—the regimes in these countries show great concern about the implications of unproductive use of leisure time. The use of leisure time in Eastern Europe is "unproductive" in two senses: first, it is increasingly used in passive ways; and second, leisure-time activities rarely include political or ideological work, or efforts at continuing education or professional betterment.

Passive leisure-time activities, principally involving watching television, listening to the radio, or talking with family and friends, has been shown to constitute between 70 and 87 percent of the leisure time of East European citizens, with the exception of the German Democratic Republic, where the proportion of passive leisure time is 40 percent. The rapid increase in the use of television has been a major factor in this development. Television has now surpassed radio as an entertainment medium in every country in which such studies have been done, and is more important for informational purposes in most. Television even has cut into movie attendance, notably in Bulgaria. The highest proportion of time spent on political and ideological activities by any group of workers studied was 5 percent; in some studies, the percentage involved in these activities was so small that it was not even mentioned in the results. Similarly, there is indifference toward continuing education programs, except among certain categories of professionals.

Also of concern are the major differences among social strata, both in the amount of leisure time available and in the ways in which leisure time is used. Thus researchers in Yugoslavia conclude that distinctly different lifestyles, based in considerable part on the nature of the use of free time, are developing, and that this tends to concretize and exacerbate differences among social classes. Typical is the situation in Czechoslovakia, where housewives and cooperative farmers are shown to have substantially less free time than other groups. Interestingly, in Czechoslovakia there is essentially no difference in the time for leisure available to white-collar and to blue-collar workers, but there are very substantial differences in how the time is used. Such interstratum differences are noticeable in Hungary, the German Democratic Republic and the Soviet Union. Such differences may be declining somewhat in Yugoslavia, especially in terms of distinctions by sex: male-female differences in the use of leisure time definitely are declining there. Similarly, studies done both in the Soviet Union and in Hungary have shown that women have substantially more leisure time now than was the case a few years ago, and that this has resulted, among other things, in a greater involvement in cultural activities on the part of women. Soviet studies also show that men now spend more time with the children on Saturdays than do women, and that there has been a substantial increase in the amount of time available for joint family leisure on weekends. Still, men have more free time than do women—in East Germany, the difference ranges from six to ten hours per week.

Not surprisingly, reading represents one of the principal differences among social groups in the use of leisure time. In Czechoslovakia, 60 percent of white-collar workers count reading as an important leisure-time activity, but this is the case only for 30 percent of blue-collar workers, and 23 percent of agricultural workers. Reading is low among industrial workers in Bulgaria, a problem which has prompted specific programs designed to increase the consumption of books by these workers. In Hungary, book buying is decreasing, and there is a corresponding decrease in the amount of time spent reading.

Studies in Bulgaria have suggested that movie attendance and reading are positively correlated, and it is thus inferred that young people's attendance at movies has not diminished their interest in reading. However, third factors which could be related to both movie attendance and frequency of reading were not examined in these studies.

MORAL AND ETHICAL PREFERENCES AND LIFE ASPIRATIONS

Several findings which help define the moral and ethical postures and life aspirations of East European and Soviet citizens already have been dealt with in this chapter. These concerned such things as workers' attitudes toward socialist property, rankings by young people of different kinds of occupations, the personal qualities that young people value in their friends and colleagues, and the extent of development of a generalized socialist consciousness. We shall not repeat those findings here. Certain other lines of inquiry have not yet been discussed, especially the extent of materialism in citizen values, the relative importance of personal and family goals vis-a-vis professional ones, the extent of support for religious values, the perceived congruence of valued ideals and actual behavior of members of society, and the lines of value cleavage which most clearly distinguish groups of citizens.

Broadly, the research we have examined suggests that citizens—especially youth—in these socialist societies are not materialistic, and that they value a happy family life and successful marriage substantially more than material or occupational success. This was true in Bulgaria, for example; at the same time we discovered that fewer than half of Bulgarian students are found to have well-formulated societally oriented life plans, and nearly as many had personally oriented plans. Polish respondents name characteristics such as sincerity and honesty (but also, especially among young people, patriotism) as important moral values, and designate conscientiousness and discipline as important personal/instrumental values. Hungarian workers indicate personal happiness and successful family life to be their most important ideals. It may be that materialistic values are most entrenched in East Germany and Hungary. In East Germany, owning a car and having a private home are critically important aspirations to many. In Hungary, researchers have labeled the values most in evidence among the population as "petty bourgeois" and "enterprising"; we noted that a substantial number of Hungarian workers take second jobs to supplement their incomes. Financial upward mobility also is characteristic of many Yugoslav respondents. Generally, however, a happy family life seems to be the most valued ideal; this has been shown especially in studies done in Poland, Bulgaria, and the Soviet Union.

The significance of religious values varies among the states of Eastern

Europe. The typical case is described by research done in Hungary and Poland, which shows that religious values are much more important for respondents who are older, less educated, and living in rural areas. Some regional differences are observable in Yugoslavia; the influences of religious values is evident among Slovenian and Croatian respondents. However, only 12 percent of the respondents in one poll in Serbia claimed religious identification. Only 4 percent of Croatian students are highly religious; approximately 21 percent have some religious leanings. However, surprising support was shown for religious education in a poll conducted in rural Czechoslovakia. More than 50 percent of the villagers said they were religious. Perhaps more surprising, approximately two-thirds of those not professing religion agreed with the proposition that religious instruction strengthened morality in young people. This point of view was held especially by rural women; there was less support for religion or religious in-struction among those with secondary or higher educations. In East Germany, more than half of the population apparently claims religious identification, but few are active churchgoers.

Interesting studies have been done in Hungary and Poland of the perceived congruence between valued ideals and the actual behavior of members of society. In Poland, although sincerity and honesty are highly valued characteris-tics, three-fourths of those polled feel that the betrayal of confidential trust is common. Seventy percent of the Polish respondents believe that people will steal state property if they are not watched, and 80 percent say that people do not mean what they say at meetings. In Hungary, sharp distinctions were noted between the qualities most highly valued and those thought to be in evidence. As noted, the evidenced values are labeled bourgeois and enterprising (i.e., materialistic), whereas the most valued qualities again have to do with honesty and respect in personal relationships.

Only in Yugoslavia has there been research attempting to define the principal lines of value cleavage in society. One study suggests that two such distinctions divide Yugoslavs. The first has to do with how income should be distributed. Here, there are differences between lower- and upper-status indi-viduals as to how important educational attainment and the complexity of one's work should be in determining appropriate compensation. Second, Yugoslavs differ significantly in their attitudes toward the value and handling of private property.

A slightly different approach to the nature of moral and ethical prefer-ences has been taken in Romanian research. Here the emphasis has been on the constancy or change in values over relatively short periods of time; the results suggest that values tend to remain constant. However, there is substantial hetero-geneity of values even within socially homogeneous groups of respondents. Substantively, this research suggests a slight trend away from "moral" in the direction of what are characterized as "physical" values.

SOCIAL PROBLEMS AND SOCIAL POLICY

Previous sections of this chapter have discussed some of the problems thought to be most significant by East Europeans, especially the disintegrative forces affecting the family. We also have commented on some aspects of attitudes toward crime, a subject which provides a suitable point of departure for this section.

There is considerable concern about what are thought to be inappropriate citizen values regarding crime, especially the theft of socialist property, and hooliganism. Surveys done in Bulgaria, Poland, and Czechoslovakia suggest that workers, in particular, are less concerned than they should be about the confiscation of public property for private use. In Romania, research shows that passive attitudes toward hooliganism are widespread. And in Bulgaria, citizen knowledge of the criminal code as well as of the activities of preventive and law enforcement organs is very low. The proportion of East European citizens who say they feel it their responsibility to contact authorities if they observe the commission of crime is generally high; the Bulgarian figure of 78 percent is typical. On the other hand, when respondents are asked to characterize their own and others' behavior, a different picture emerges. In Poland and Czechoslovakia, research suggests that this citizen passivity is a principal source of crime. The Bulgarian research delved somewhat deeper, discovering that inadequacies in government organs (including the "negative examples of some prominent persons") were thought by more than half of the respondents to be a major factor encouraging crime. Alcoholism and material shortages also were emphasized. Another factor was the problematic equality of enforcement of the law; 40 percent of the Bulgarian respondents felt that the principal of equality before the law was not always upheld.

Concern about crime varies substantially among social strata. In Bulgaria, those least concerned about crime were non-Party members, persons of lower education and lower-status occupations, and included a disproportionate number of minority ethnics. Similarly, in Romania it was discovered that older and better-educated persons are much more likely to intervene if they see a crime being committed.

Other significant societal problems have been identified in surveys done in Eastern Europe during the past three years; these include alcoholism, insincerity and deviousness in interpersonal relationships, income and wealth differentials, inadequate access to appropriate housing, material shortages, suicide (in Hungary) and problems of environmental deterioration (in Czechoslovakia). Again, this assemblage of problems does not seem collectively atypical of rapidly modernizing societies. It is noteworthy that Bulgarian research has shown dramatic differences between mass and leadership samples in perceptions of the most serious negative influences in society. The mass samples have emphasized problems of private morality and deteriorating interpersonal relationships, whereas the leadership samples emphasized problems of public morality and factors affecting the efficiency of government. These differences are not surprising, but they do bespeak a problem in the development of consensus on a policy agenda.

Alcoholism is thought to be a serious problem in Bulgaria, the Soviet Union, and Poland, and is found to be a significant correlate of suicides in Hungary. In Bulgaria, alcoholism was the second most remarked factor encouraging crime, and was the factor thought by young men and women to be the most undesirable characteristic in members of the opposite sex. More than one-quarter of the Poles sampled felt that drunkenness was a significant factor impeding social progress there; rural respondents were more concerned about drunkenness than were urban respondents. This parallels a distinction found in Bulgarian research, in which the mass sample showed great concern about excessive drinking, whereas the elite sample attributes little significance to this problem. In Hungary, alcoholism was shown to be the single most prevalent physical disability among suicide victims.

The socially destabilizing effects of persisting income and wealth differentials have been observed in surveys done in Hungary and Yugoslavia. In Yugoslavia, these differences have led to the emergence of demonstrably different lifestyles on the part of the intelligentsia, urban workers, and agricultural workers. In the cities, these differences have produced strong tendencies toward social and residential segregation, such that the variations among the neighborhoods in the quality of life in major Yugoslav cities are great. In Hungary, although income differentials are seen as a social problem, there are relatively few persons consistently in favor of reducing such differentials: these categories include housewives, pensioners, and agricultural laborers. In general, there is a direct relationship between income and support for income differentials, as we might expect: the higher the income, the greater the support for differentials. It is interesting that in Hungary between one-fourth and one-third of the respondents deny the existence of any extremes of wealth—i.e., they argue that there are no rich and no poor. Those who do assert the existence of extremes are primarily persons of lower education and occupational status, some of whom apparently feel themselves to be part of that lower extreme.

Constrained access to appropriate housing already has been noted as a factor influencing the fertility of East European women, and affecting the nature of familial relationships, especially among the married young, many of whom must live for some time with parents. Surveys identifying housing as a significant problem have appeared in the German Democratic Republic, Romania, and Hungary. In Romania, one study suggested that residence in high-rise living blocks tends to promote interpersonal conflicts. And in Hungary, the housing problem is seen in the context of the system of informal pay offs and influence, which results in inequities in access to basic human services and goods, such as housing and medical care.

Two additional, related aspects of the problem of income and wealth differentials are a) the persistence of material shortages, which in some countries exacerbate other problem areas, such as crime, and b) the impact on living standards of inadequately developed social infrastructure. In the past three years, surveys suggesting the importance of material shortages have appeared in Bulgaria, for example. Young people in one poll suggested that material shortages constituted a major impediment to the ability of Bulgarians to adequately defend their socialist system to foreigners. More than 20 percent of Bulgarian respondents in another study indicated that material shortages were a major contributing factor to crime. In Yugoslavia, fewer than half of the respondents in one study indicated satisfaction with any element of their living standards, except for the availability and quality of food. Inadequate investment in social infrastructure is thought to be a major contributing factor.

Most of the problems mentioned so far appear to be present to one degree or another throughout Eastern Europe and the Soviet Union; certain other difficulties seem to be peculiar to specific locations. Thus the problem of an unusually high suicide rate continues to plague Hungary. It should be emphasized that this is an historical phenomenon that significantly predates the socialist period. Suicide in Hungary is higher among males, and increases directly with age. Autopsies performed on suicide victims in Budapest revealed that a substantial number were alcoholics, drug dependent, and had chronic health problems. Significantly, Hungarian statistics show that suicide is higher among male manual workers living outside Budapest than among any other social category. This reversal of the usual preponderance of urban residents among suicides suggests to Hungarian researchers that the processes of urbanization and industrialization have been at least as hard on persons living outside the major urban locations. In this connection, Hungarian researchers also have been looking carefully at the myriad difficulties of commuting workers, those who work in the city but live in the countryside at considerable distance from their place of work.

Finally, one Czechoslovak survey showed widespread citizen concern about environmental deterioration. More than half of the respondents expected this deterioration to continue, and saw the need for increased government action, for example, in the protection of cultural monuments.

It is unfortunate that few surveys have been done of citizen perceptions of the adequacy of social service programs. We noted above that women in several East European countries are concerned about the availability of appropriate day-care facilities, and that this has affected the attitudes of many toward their work. There is some evidence of wider concern with social services. For example, in Poland respondents indicated that among the most important tasks confronting government are those involving improved human service programs. The need for better social services in the countryside was especially emphasized. Yugoslav respondents say that there are important social policy needs in such areas as the improvement of health facilities in rural communes, better roads, better educational facilities, and economic support to provide more jobs. Hungarian respondents identify unequal access to medical care as a problem, and note that the system of informal influence and payoffs has resulted in substantial inequities in de facto citizen access to medical care. Urban-rural distinctions in the availability of medical care also are great in Hungary. East German respondents similarly emphasized the importance of continuing to improve social service programs. At the same time, although these calls for improved social services imply (with the possible exception of Yugoslavia) that the role of government in the everyday lives of citizens should be expanded, it is nevertheless the case that excessive bureaucratization has been noted as a significant social problem by approximately one-third of the respondents in polls taken in Bulgaria and Poland.

If citizens are increasingly aware of social problems of this kind, and increasingly willing to express their concerns, they nevertheless remain poorly informed about how they might become involved in finding solutions. One Yugoslav survey documented the unfamiliarity of citizens with how they personally might become involved. And where there is concern, one of the factors apparently inhibiting citizen action is the fear of the implications of social criticism. Thus 23 percent of one Polish sample indicated that the suppression of criticism was a major factor impeding social progress; urban respondents were more concerned about this than were rural respondents.

POLITICS AND IDEOLOGY

A very considerable part of the survey research done on political and ideological subjects is not published. All survey research is potentially policy sensitive; research dealing directly with political and ideological matters is all the more so. We have some sense of the kinds of research being carried out by sociologists attached to Party organs in the Soviet Union and Eastern Europe. This research often emphasizes the effectiveness of political propaganda and political education, the effectiveness of the work of leadership cadres in the workplace, and the efficiency of local Party secretaries and committees. Further, as we noted earlier, a great deal of research is being done on political awareness and commitment among young people, particularly in the Party youth organizations. Unfortunately, only a very small percentage of the many studies on these subjects is ever published or made generally available.

Overtly, the value of social commitment (social activism) is widely accepted. For example, surveys in Poland have demonstrated this, although showing that the acceptance of social activism as a value is closely related to one's personal sense of political efficacy (i.e., one's sense that he or she can have some influence on the political process). In the Soviet Union, attendance at political lectures, especially among young people, is reasonably high; political awareness is found to be significantly higher among those who do attend lectures than among those who do not. However, the acceptance of this value in the abstract does not always manifest itself in behavior. Thus in Poland there is widespread evidence of political and ideological indifference; only 30 percent of those persons who accept in principle the importance of social commitment felt that there was any significant citizen influence on the political process. In the Soviet Union, attraction to sociopolitical work is limited to a relatively small proportion of those studied. One study suggested that certain personality characteristics were the principal predictors of involvement in sociopolitical work; the most important were the need to acquire authority, the desire for social interaction, a high achievement orientation, and a desire for status, prestige, knowledge, and the opportunity for creative activity. Sociopolitical activity needs were found to be higher among single people, and especially among women. Among workers, the higher motivations toward sociopolitical work were found among Party members; among intellectuals, surprisingly, sociopolitical motivation was higher among non-Party members.

We have already remarked on the relatively high level of disinterest in political and ideological matters, especially among workers. We discover that East European and Soviet citizens generally do not spend leisure time on political-ideological work or education. Workers do not discuss politics on the job, and youth do not discuss politics with their friends. Families do not discuss politics among themselves. Young people—especially Komsomol members—value personal qualities (friendliness, helpfulness, a good education) far more highly than they value a Marxist-Leninist world view, or a record of social activism. Indeed, fewer than 10 percent of a Bulgarian sample of Komsomol members attached central importance to these ideological and political elements. Workers are shown not to participate actively in self-management organs in Yugoslavia, Hungary, and Romania, where this opportunity is greatest, and they generally do not seem to seek more responsibility in the workplace. In the Soviet Union, the percentage of time spent by workers on political work is small. Nearly half of those surveyed indicate that they fail to condemn those who deviate from the norms of communist morality. Czechoslovak citizens are said to show a poor appreciation of the expanded opportunities for participation in public life.

Even within the Party, political attentiveness and motivation is not what it might be. Soviet Party members are not well informed about meetings, and one-third of them never speak at Party meetings. Many Party members feel that discussions in these meetings have little result, and only 40 percent of one sample reported doing Party work "with pleasure." In Bulgaria, more than half of the Party rank and file apparently is not certain that Party political education is successful.

One fascinating study was done in Bulgaria of the attitudes of Party first secretaries toward their work. It was discovered that only 6 percent of the local first secretaries preferred ideological work; the others preferred organizational, local contact, or other activities. Thirty percent do not have a preference among Party tasks. A total of 34 percent say they perform their work in part unwillingly, mainly because of overwork. It was discovered that many Party first secretaries delegate work poorly, and that most were pressured into taking their jobs by the Party organization, rather than seeking the position on the basis of their own motivations. Bulgarian Party secretaries, when asked what qualities are most important for the performance of their job, most often name characteristics such as will and firmness, and being demanding and exacting. Many fewer said "openness" or "self-initiative"; these findings suggest an essentially hierarchical view of their tasks.

In Yugoslavia, several studies have been done of the relationship between partisan political activity and involvement in self-management organs. The relationship is found to be substantial. A plurality of the persons active in self-management organs also are members of the League of Communists; they are male, and tend to be skilled workers or managers. Unskilled workers and, to a lesser extent, technical specialists are somewhat underrepresented in self-management structures. Yugoslav respondents consistently remark about problems in the flow of information from top to bottom in these structures. The level of political and organizational information held by workers is low.

Thus it seems reasonable to characterize public postures toward ideology and politics in Eastern Europe and the Soviet Union in terms such as passivity, withdrawal, and uncertainty. As Hungarian research suggests, the modal posture is "unenthusiastic but accepting." At the same time, there is ample evidence that both population and leadership groups in these countries are at least mildly positive in their orientation toward socialism as a mode of socioeconomic organization. (It must be stressed that there are no published studies which deal directly with the appraisal by either mass or leadership groups of the performance of given communist parties as ruling administrations.) In Czechoslovakia, one poll suggested that socialism was overwhelmingly preferred to capitalism; more than 95 percent of the respondents so indicated on almost every dimension. The only problem area seemed to be the comparison between socialism and capitalism in terms of utilizing ideas, thinking, and education. Here "only" 82.6 percent of the respondents felt that socialism performed better. In Hungary, there is a sedate optimism about the future of socialism, and about the nature of the ties between Hungary and the Soviet Union. Similarly, Polish respondents are optimistic about the prospects that major war can be avoided. This appears to be related in part to their optimism about the future of socialism as a system. Perhaps significantly, where the accomplishments of socialism are lauded, respondents seem to have in mind accomplishments that deal directly with the improvement of the human condition, or with the provision of means for social advancement. Thus a study done in Czechoslovak villages revealed that respondents felt the most important accomplishments of socialism were improvement in health services, and an expansion of educational opportunities. (The abolition of classes was a possible response, but was chosen by a very small number of those surveyed.)

Finally, more specific inquiries in Yugoslavia and Romania have generated some fascinating hypotheses about citizen postures toward governmental units in socialist systems. Yugoslav research shows that the closer the social unit is to the respondent, the more critically it is likely to be evaluated. Thus the local commune is the principal focus of critical feelings on the part of Yugoslavs interested in politics. In Romania, research has been done on the kinds of concerns on which sufficient initiative was shown by citizens to bring them to the attention of local authorities. The principal findings from this research were: 1) that individual proposals through informal contacts were acted upon at a much higher rate by local authorities than were proposals that were made through formal channels—e.g., at meetings of people's councils or other public meetings; and 2) the majority of complaints to public bodies concern housing or other material issues having to do with the quality of life.

ETHNICITY AND FOREIGN CULTURES

Notwithstanding the historical—and in a few cases, contemporary—significance of ethnic problems in the Soviet Union and Eastern Europe, there has been precious little recent survey research on these subjects. What has been done tends not to deal with the most politically sensitive issues. One Yugoslav study did discover that younger Croatians are substantially less nationalist than are those of older ages. Soviet research has attempted to determine the extent of awareness of ethnic differences among various groups in that country; the research concluded that notions of what constituted ethnicity, and how important it was, varied according to education and socioeconomic status. Relatedly, the higher the level of the respondent's education, the less likely that the respondent observed ethnic or other subcultural practices.

National pride was shown to be high among Hungarian respondents; it was lowest among university students (of whom 76 percent said they were proud to be Hungarian). Significantly, few took pride in the industrial development of the country during the past thirty years, but social development and the restructuring of the class system was applauded. Few persons of non-Hungarian background now living in Hungary who could send their children to schools which offer instruction in their native languages do so, presumably some indication of the extent to which they have discarded identification with their ethnic origins. At the same time, of course, this preference could simply indicate a concern for the social mobility of their children.

A Hungarian sample was asked to identify the country most similar to Hungary. Apparently, both Western and Eastern European countries were legitimate responses. Broadly, the Soviet Union was thought to be most similar to Hungary, except along the dimension of "historical destiny"; here, Poland was thought most similar. It is especially noteworthy that it was primarily among persons with lower education that the Soviet Union was frequently named; the more educated tended to name Poland or, with regard to the standard of living, the German Democratic Republic. The author of this study notes that the ability to make distinctions along several dimensions of similarity might have been problematic for those with less formal education. In a similar vein, Bulgarian respondents were asked to name the country which was the greatest supporter of peace and socialism; the overwhelming response was the Soviet Union. Manual workers were the least likely to name the Soviet Union; 26 percent of the workers who responded did not choose the USSR. Yugoslav respondents were found to be equally informed about and oriented toward both East and West. We infer from available studies that this is not characteristic of any other East European country.

In concluding and trying to assess these findings, it would be well for us to recall the focus of this project. We are dealing only with research conducted or published during the period 1975 to 1978, and we have limited ourselves almost entirely to data gathered through surveys. Consequently, the comments in this or preceding chapters do not purport to address in a comprehensive way any of the topics around which the work is organized. Nor can we always be confident that the results we report are typical or representative of the research—survey or other—that may have been done on these subjects. We know that a very considerable amount of survey research, especially on the subjects of politics, ideology and youth, is carried out but neither published nor given wide distribution. Finally, we have not considered it our responsibility to comment in detail on the probable validity of these findings. The introductory chapter to this volume tries to set the problem of assessing validity in context, but it can do so only speculatively, since the establishment of validity rests in part on access to the original data collections, which in nearly every case we do not have.

The bounded tentativeness which characterizes this enterprise should not, however, be interpreted as rendering the enterprise meaningless. On the contrary, there is strong reason to believe that these surveys have told us a good deal that is illuminating and useful about the changing character of the socialist systems of the Soviet Union and Eastern Europe. We may wonder aloud whether nearly 90 percent of Bulgarians really believe that the Soviet Union is the greatest supporter of peace and socialism (doubtless the percentage would have been lower had the question not linked those two concepts), or whether more than 90 percent of Czechoslovak citizens really overwhelmingly prefer socialism to capitalism. But where the findings are of dubious validity as indicators of behavioral predispositions, they are nevertheless important indicators of the regimes' felt needs to plump their own legitimacy. Further, we suspect that most readers will have little difficulty imagining the contexts in which challenges to validity should be entered.

We have said before, but it bears repeating in conclusion, that one of the most important findings emerging from this project has been the documentation of the growing magnitude and significance of survey research throughout the socialist countries of Eastern Europe and the Soviet Union. More surveys are being done, and they are being done significantly better. Many of them address critically important issues in the social, economic, and political evolution of these societies. The use of surveys has grown in large part because effective governance seems to demand it. In small part, the growth seems to have come at the cautious initiative of social researchers who feel, as do their colleagues in nonsocialist systems, that the pursuit of concrete, reliable evidence is a critical part of scientific inquiry. We can deeply hope—and we can do everything in our power to encourage—that the results of this research will increasingly be made available, not only within Eastern European societies but to researchers every-where. Perhaps even more important, we must share the hope that both political practitioners and scholars in Eastern Europe and the Soviet Union themselves share, namely, that the generation of this kind of solid evidence about the actual evolution of socialist systems ultimately will result in significant improvements in the conditions of life for the human beings who live in them.

Index of Names

Aczél, György, 380
Adamski, F., 404, 406, 407, 418, 431, 432, 433
Aganbegian, A. G., 300
Ahtik, M., 131
Alan, Josef, 217, 239, 240
Albert, Francisc, 438, 463, 474, 477, 478
Alekseev, B. K., 49, 51, 53, 54, 72, 77
Alekseeva, V. G., 26, 67, 68, 69, 75
Aluaş, Ion, 438, 474, 478
Anderson, Oskar, 251
Angelusz, Róbert, 363, 364, 365, 381, 387
Antonenko, V. G., 70, 76

Antonov, A. I., 25, 67
Ardenski, Vladimir, 193, 202
Arutiunian, Iu. V., 49, 72, 78
Arzenšek, Vladimir, 104, 127, 128, 313
Assmann, Georg, 297
Aver'ianov, L. Ia., 75
Avguštin-Rihtman, D., 128
Avramov, Velko, 202

Babin, B. A., 46, 71, 77
Babović, Dušan, 131
Bačević, Ljiljana, 125, 126, 130, 132
Bácskai, Erika, 381, 384
Bădina, Ovidiu, 438, 457, 458, 461,

462, 476, 477, 478, 481
Bahtijarević, S., 111, 112, 129, 131
Baikova, V. G., 47, 50, 71, 72, 77
Bajka, Zbigniew, 393, 394, 395, 415, 429, 431, 433
Balagushkin, E. G., 46, 71, 77
Bărbat, Alexandru, 438, 474, 478
Bartoszewicz, W., 433
Bathke, G., 302
Baučić, Ivo, 129
Bauer, Rolf-W., 307
Baum, G., 284, 312
Bazac, D., 455, 476, 478
Becker, Jürgen, 315
Békés, Ferenc, 325, 329, 381, 382
Belova, V. A., 68, 74
Beluhan, A., 131
Benc, Milan, 131
Bender, Peter, 317
Berg, Helene, 243
Bernard, G., 310
Bischoff, M., 318
Bisky, Lothar, 284, 285, 300, 313, 314
Blahó, András, 381
Blumstock, Robert, 6
Bogišić, B., 124
Boh, Katja, 124
Böhme, Ulrich, 298
Bokszanski, Z., 429, 433
Bolčić, Silvano, 104, 105, 109, 127, 128, 133
Bolgov, V. I., 70, 77
Bollinger, Klaus, 317
Bondarskaia, G. A., 74
Bonev, Hristo, 143, 145, 146, 199, 202
Borrmann, Rolf, 267, 303, 308
Brandt, Willy, 289
Braungart, Joachim, 312
Brezhnev, L., 14, 65, 73, 121
Bročić, Ljubinka, 128, 131
Brudnyi, V. I., 34, 40, 68, 70, 75, 76

Bruk, S. I., 56, 57, 58, 73, 78
Bulgakov, Nikolai, 21
Bumazheva, E. Iu., 79
Büttner, Werner, 306

Čaldarović, Ljerka, 125
Čaldarović, Ognjen, 129
Čalić, Dušan, 96, 127, 131
Câmpeanu, Pavel, 438, 443, 444, 445, 446, 447, 463, 464, 467, 468, 475, 477, 479
Carter, Jimmy, 446, 447
Caserman, Andrej, 125
Ceauşescu, Nicolae, 7, 439, 440, 441, 446, 470, 474, 478
Cernea, Mihail, 437, 440, 441, 450, 451, 452, 469, 474, 475, 477, 478, 479
Chakalov, Boris, 139, 198
Charisius, A., 317
Chepeş, Gheorghe, 437, 438, 442
Christfreund, W., 298, 299
Chuiko, L. V., 67, 68, 74
Chuprov, V. I., 65, 73
Cifrić, Ivan, 113, 129, 130, 131
Cinca, E., 455, 476, 479
Connor, Walter D., 12, 238, 384, 433
Constantinescu, M., 437, 441, 474, 479
Cooper, Bruce, 65
Cresin, Roman, 457, 458, 461
Cseh-Szombathy, L., 382
Csepeli, György, 372, 373, 387
Cucu, Vasile, 477, 479
Czajka, Stanisław, 433

Dalichow, K., 307, 313, 314, 318
Damian, Liviu, 470, 478, 479
Damjanović, Mijat, 95
Danchev, Nikolai, 188, 201
Danov, Vasil, 167, 169, 200
Datner-Śpiewak, H., 421, 423, 424, 432, 433

Davtian, S. A., 67, 74
De Sola Pool, I., 428, 432
Demidova, A. I., 19, 66, 73
Denitch, Bogdan, 318
Dienelt, Otto, 302, 303
Dietrich, Hans, 315
Dilić, Edhem, 125, 127, 131
Dimitriu, Corneliu, 438, 474, 479
Dimitrov, Lyuben, 157, 162, 168, 200
Dineva, Mariya, 198
Djordjević, Toma, 131
Dobierzin, Olaf, 318
Dobrescu, E., 470, 478, 479
Dögei, Ilona, 337, 384
Dolzhanskaia, A., 67
Dubček, Alexander, 205, 227, 234
Ducke, Kurt, 309
Dumitrescu, I., 455, 478
Dumitru, N. S., 437
Dunskus, Petra, 298
Dzięciołowska, S., 402, 430, 433
Džinić, Firdus, 85, 125, 126, 130, 132

Ehrlich, Werner, 308
Eliseeva, I. I., 67, 75
Elsner, Eva-Maria, 304, 305
Enache, Radu, 455, 456, 477, 479
Enders, Ursula, 311
Ene, G., 455, 476, 479
Engels, Friedrich, 303
Erdösi, Sándor, 385

Fabiunke, H., 301
Fabry, Viliam, 240
Fahidy, József, 384
Farkas, Katalin, 381
Ferge, Zsuzsa, 362, 387
Ferligoj, Anuška, 127
Feshbach, Murray, 65
Feuer, Lewis S., 386
Fidanov, Dimitur, 183, 184, 201
Filippov, F. R., 30, 31, 34, 68, 75

Filiukova, L. F., 75
Firsov, B. M., 67, 74
First-Dilić, Ruža, 125, 126, 132, 134
Firuţa, Argentina, 448, 464, 465, 466, 475, 477, 479
Fischer, Herbert, 312, 317, 318
Fisher, Dan, 67
Földvári, Tamás, 341, 345, 385
Förschner, G., 298, 299
Forst, W., 306
Förster, Heinz, 317
Förster, P., 311
Förster, Peter, 300
Freitag, Joachim, 301
Fricke, Karl W., 316
Friedrich, Horst, 312
Friedrich, Walter, 244, 246, 250, 251, 266, 268, 269, 297, 298, 299, 300, 301, 306, 307, 309, 313
Fritsche, Ute, 306
Fröhlich, Ruth, 308
Fuchs, Renate, 298
Füstös, László, 323, 354

Ganchev, Dimitur, 186, 192, 201, 202
Gaştescu, Petre, 449
Gazsó, Ferenc, 384
Geidel, W., 284, 312, 313
Geiger, Theodor, 295
Geissenhöhner, G., 302
Gentvainite, V., 30, 33, 68, 75
Gerasimova, I. A., 75
Gerold, Dieter, 315
Gerth, Werner, 307
Gheorghiu-Dej, G., 439
Gibbs, Jack P., 386
Gitelman, Zvi Y., 2, 3, 12, 238, 433
Glavanakov, Krasi, 198
Glavanakov, Lyuben, 198
Goati, Vladimir, 93, 94, 95, 96, 99, 125, 127, 130, 132

Goban-Klas, Tomasz, 433
Göhler, Helma, 313
Gołębiowski, B., 410, 412, 415,
    416, 418, 419, 420, 421, 422,
    423,431,432,433
Golianu, Alexandru, 479, 480
Golovatiuk, V. M., 65, 73
Gömöri, Judit, 388
Gordon, L. A., 43, 44, 45, 70, 77
Goriunov, S. P., 71, 72, 77
Gostkowski, Z., 429, 433
Gottwald, Klement, 233
Gras, F.-W., 307
Gritchin, V. N., 22, 67
Grundmann, S., 310
Grunert-Bronnen, B., 315
Guboglo, M. N., 56, 57, 58, 73, 78
Günther, Walter, 305
Gusti, Dimitrie, 474

Hahn, Joachim, 313
Hajnal, Gábor L., 383
Halpern, Joel, 132
Hammel, E. A., 126, 132
Hanák, Katalin, 384
Hankiss, Elemér, 323, 354, 357,
    358, 380, 381, 386
Hann, Endre, 371, 387
Hanson, Philip, 388
Haraszti, Miklós, 385
Harke, Erdmann, 311
Hauser, K., 306
Havemann, Robert, 290
Heidmann, Eberhard, 317
Hellfeldt, G., 312
Hennig, Werner, 244, 246, 250,
    251, 297, 298, 299, 300, 301,
    308
Hepner, Vladimír, 211, 220, 222,
    238, 239, 241
Herter, D., 310
Héthy, Lajos, 323, 342, 343, 344,
    345, 346, 347, 359, 360, 385,
    386

Hilbig, Klaus, 303
Hilgenberg, D., 317, 318
Hille, Barbara, 306, 307, 309
Hinze, Liselotte, 261, 306
Hinze, P., 310, 311
Hoffman, Magdaléna, 375, 376,
    377, 378, 381, 385, 388
Hölzler, Ingrid, 261, 304, 309
Honecker, Erich, 254, 296, 302
Horn, Rüdiger, 317
Horthy, Miklos, 371, 372
Horvat, Branko, 125, 126, 132
Horváth, Ágota, 340, 384
Hoványi, Gábor, 388
Hrubos, Ildikó, 383
Hübner, Christoph, 317
Hundt, Rudolf, 300
Hunyadi, György, 371, 387
Husák, Gustáv, 234
Huszár, Tibor, 380, 382, 383, 384,
    386, 387
Huszczo, Adaline, 433
Hüttner, H., 306

Iadov, V. A., 40, 69, 70, 76
Iankova, Z. A., 67, 68, 75
Inderbiev, M. T., 75
Ionescu, C., 438
Iordan, Ion, 449, 479
Ivanov, Iu. K., 37, 39, 69, 76
Ivanova, N. V., 36, 69, 76

Jacob, Philip, 115
Jaide, Walter, 306, 307, 309
Janićijević, M., 133
Janišová, Helena, 210, 239, 240
Jenkis, Helmut W., 315
Jerzak, Josef, 433
Jilek, Miroslav, 128, 132
Joffe, Josef, 297
John, Erhard, 284, 312
Józsa, György, 380
Jugel, Martina, 272, 301, 306, 309
Jurovský, Anton, 218, 240

Kabo, E. A., 48
Kádár, Janos, 367
Kadibur, T. S., 67, 75
Kaffenberger, H., 302
Kaganov, A. B., 34, 68, 75
Kaiser, Gerd, 302
Kalaitan, N. E., 74
Kapitanski, Iordan, 200
Kardelj, Edvard, 125
Karsai, Judit, 384
Kaser, Michael, 382, 387
Katriak, Martin, 240, 241
Kayser, Marianne, 304
Kellerer, Hans, 251
Kepecs, József, 384
Kerekes, Mrs. G., 385
Kessel, Wolfgang, 308
Khalatbari, Parviz, 301, 304
Kharchev, A. G., 24, 67
Kicinski, K., 410, 413, 414, 418, 431, 432, 434
Kirillova, M. V., 72
Kirinčić, Miroslav, 132
Klauzer, Jagoda, 127
Klement'ev, E. I., 60, 61, 72, 73, 78
Klemm, W., 316
Klinger, András, 384
Klopov, E. V., 43, 44, 45, 70, 77
Knauer, Klaus, 308
Kobel, Janina, 410, 413, 414, 417, 418, 431, 432, 434
Koch, Herbert, 245
Kogan, L. N., 24, 26, 67, 74
Koitla, Kh., 74
Kolarić, Vesna, 132
Kolokol'nikov, V., 29, 67, 68, 75
Kononiuk, B. Z., 69, 76
Konrád, György, 386
Konwicka, Teresa, 402, 403, 404, 430, 434
Köpeczi, Béla, 320, 380, 385
Koppisch, V., 306
Kornhauser, A., 132

Korobeinikov, V., 66, 74
Kotliar, A. E., 36, 38, 76
Koudelková, Anna, 239
Kovalev, A. G., 70, 76
Kovaleva, M. M., 46, 71, 77
Kozhuharova, Veska, 156, 175, 201
Koziolek, Helmut, 244, 314
Krambach, Kurt, 273, 299, 310, 314
Krecker, Margot, 305
Krevnevich, V. V., 37, 69, 76
Krieger, Henning, 318
Krivoruchko, A. N., 25, 67
Křížová, Eva, 219, 240
Ksenofontova, V., 15, 34, 66, 68, 75
Kuczynski, Paweł, 429, 434
Kugelmann, Ludwig, 303
Kuhrig, Herta, 244, 261, 304, 305, 306
Kulcsár, Kálmán, 380, 381, 387
Kuppe, Johannes, 302
Kurczewski, Jacek, 410, 413, 414, 418, 431, 432, 434
Kutev, Angel, 201
Kwaśniewicz, W., 391

Ladányi, János, 385
Ladensack, Klaus, 309
Laidmiae, V. I., 23, 67, 74
Lanc, Ante, 113, 114, 129, 134
Langguth, Dieter, 314
Larionescu, Maria, 437
Lascuş, Voicu, 469, 477, 480
Lauterbach, G., 298
Lay, Vladimir, 129, 132
Lazarova, Erika, 201
Lazarsfeld, P., 250
Lazić, Slobodan, 125
Leenen, W.-R., 315, 316
Lendvai, Paul, 387
Lešnik, Rudi, 128, 133
Lesokhina, L. N., 15, 66, 76
Letić, Franjo, 133

Levykin, I. T., 46, 71, 77
Lick, József, 381
Lindner, Werner, 245
Linhart, Jiří, 240
Lippold, Gerhard, 311
Liptay-Wagner, A., 388
Litvintsev, Iu., 72, 77
Livada, Svetozar, 129
Lobanova, L. I., 37, 69, 76
Löcsei, Pál, 382
Losonczi, Ágnes, 384
Lötsch, Manfred, 301, 310
Lubrano, Linda L., 6, 8
Ludwig, Rolf, 300, 301
Ludz, Peter C., 302, 306, 318
Lukanov, Dimitur, 167, 169, 200
Lundberg, G., 250
Lünser, Horst, 315

Macháček, Ladislav, 216, 223, 225, 226, 229, 230, 231, 240
Machonin, Pavel, 207, 238
Mader, Julius, 317
Magdalenić, Ivan, 108, 128, 133
Magyas, Emil, 301
Mahler, Fred, 438, 453, 454, 455, 456, 476, 478, 479
Makó, Csaba, 323, 342, 343, 344, 345, 346, 347, 359, 360, 385, 386
Mamali, Cătălin, 453, 455, 457, 458, 461, 462, 476, 477, 478, 479, 481
Manchin, Róbert, 323, 354, 381
Mannheim, Karl, 295
Manolov, Valentin, 198
Mansurov, N. S., 74
Marangunić, Davor, 133
Maříková, Iva, 211, 220, 221, 238, 239
Markowska, Danuta, 391
Maršić, Ivan, 133
Marta, Ferenc, 384
Martin, Walter T., 386

Marx, Karl, 258, 276, 295, 303
Matějů, Petr, 239
Matulenis, A., 33, 68, 75
Melzer, Manfred, 315
Mesić, Milan, 104, 127, 133
Mettke, Jörg R., 289, 316
Metzner, Bernhard, 304
Meyer, Hansgünter, 301
Mežnarić, Silva, 88, 125, 127
Mihailovic, Srćko, 93
Mihovilović, M., 91, 106, 114, 126, 127, 128, 133
Mihu, Achim, 438, 469, 474, 477, 480
Milovanović, D., 133
Minaeva, I., 69, 76
Minkov, Minko, 199
Mirčev, Dimitar, 124
Miroş, Liubomira, 456, 476, 479, 481
Mitov, Cvetan, 133
Model, Horst, 318
Moldovan, Roman, 437
Moldoveanu, Maria, 475, 480
Molnár, Edit, 333, 381, 382, 383
Molnár, László, 381, 388
Mordkovich, V. G., 48
Muchnik, I. V., 66
Müller, Jörg, 273, 310
Müller, Uta, 318
Muzdybaev, K., 67, 74

Nagy, G. L., 381
Nagy, Márta, 363, 387
Natansohn, Iosif, 438, 474, 480
Naumann, M., 316
Naumann, Michael, 297
Naumann, W., 311
Nawrocki, Joachim, 297
Nęcki, Zbigniew, 396, 428, 430, 434
Nelson, Daniel N., 7, 478, 480
Nenashev, M. F., 46, 71
Nesterova, S. L., 73, 78

Netsenko, A. V., 70, 77
Niebsch, Gerda, 305
Nietz, Horst, 310
Nikolov, Elit, 199
Nochevnik, M. N., 40, 41, 70, 76
Nocun, A., 402, 405, 430, 434
Nolepa, Gerda, 271, 275, 276, 301, 310
Novosel, Pavao, 85, 102, 103, 118, 119, 125, 126, 127, 130, 133
Novotný, Antonín, 234
Nowak, Stefan, 391
Nowicki, Stanisław, 434
Nowy, Marian, 434
Nyers, Rezső, 341, 385

Oancea, D. I., 449
Obradović, Josip, 101, 102, 105, 127, 133
Ohlenburg, Harro, 309
Ollík, Teodor, 240
Onikov, L. A., 43, 44, 70, 77
Onken, Dieter, 318
Orlov, Iu. M., 46, 71, 77
Oshavkov, Zhivko, 137, 198, 200
Osipov, G. V., 66, 73
Ostojić, Neda, 125
Otto, Elmar D., 317

Pälicke, Waltraud, 315
Panev, Baicho, 182, 201, 202
Paniukov, V. S., 65, 73
Panova, Elena, 193, 195, 202
Pantić, Dragomir, 99, 109, 127, 128, 133
Parsons, Talcott, 386
Pártos, Ferenc, 338, 384
Pataki, Judit, 363, 364, 365, 387
Patrescu, George, 475, 480
Patrushev, V. D., 37, 39, 69, 76
Pätz, Helga, 311, 312
Pelikán, Jiří, 316
Penc, Jozef, 434
Perfil'ev, M. N., 49, 51, 53, 54, 72, 77
Peschke, M., 305
Pešić, Vesna, 110, 128, 133
Petak, Antun, 97, 124, 125, 126, 127, 133
Petev, Todor, 201
Petković, Stanko, 129, 133
Petrescu, Ion, 477, 480
Petrov, Hristo, 178, 182, 201
Philipp, H., 313
Picaper, Jean-Paul, 303
Piekalkiewicz, J., 238
Piekarski, W., 400, 430, 434
Pietrzynski, Gerd, 299, 309, 311
Pinther, Arnold, 268, 308
Piotrowski, A., 429, 433
Pisca, Ladislav, 239
Pittmann, John, 317
Podunavac, Milan, 133
Pohoski, Michał, 416, 431, 434
Pomorski, Jerzy, 425, 432, 434
Pongrácz, Marietta, 333, 382, 383
Popa-Micşan, F., 476, 480
Popescu, Maria, 437, 477, 480
Popescu, Vasile, 455, 456, 462, 475, 476, 477, 479, 480, 481
Popović, M., 109, 128, 129, 133
Popovski, Vlado, 124
Pörzse, Katalin, 371, 387
Potîngă, C., 456, 462, 475, 476, 477, 479, 480, 481
Pozdniakov, P. V., 46, 50, 71, 77
Preda, Mircea, 438, 469, 470, 477, 480
Prokopec, Jiří, 239
Proll, Rotraud, 313
Protasova, P. A., 68
Prusák, P., 240, 241
Przeworski, Adam, 429, 434
Puljiz, Vlado, 134
Pusić, Eugen, 115, 129, 134
Pusić, Vesna, 101
Pye, Lucian W., 432, 434

Quaas, M., 311

Rabe, Ulrich, 298
Radi, Péter, 380
Radić, A., 124
Radovan, Paul, 479, 480
Radu-Rădulescu, N., 477, 480
Raduluian, V., 478
Raikov, Zdravko, 144, 199
Rak, Vladimír, 240
Randlíková, Anna, 211, 220, 221, 238
Ranft, Gudrun, 301
Rauer, Annemarie, 306
Remnek, Richard, 65
Rentzsch, Siglinde, 308
Riabushkin, T. V., 65
Riazhiskikh, I. A., 76
Riedel, Heide, 257, 259, 302
Ritter, Tibor, 380
Rittershaus, J., 299, 300
Rodzinskaia, I., 67
Rozgonyi, Tamás, 381
Rozhin, V. P., 69
Ruble, Blair, 65
Rus, Veljko, 101
Rusinek, Andrzej, 394, 396, 397, 399, 405, 418, 419, 429, 430, 431, 432, 434
Rutkevich, M. N., 68
Rutkovskii, B. A., 70, 76
Ruzhzhe, V. L., 67, 75

Safarov, P. A., 77
Saksida, Stane, 125, 129, 130
Sälzler, A., 261, 263, 305, 306
Samodelov, A., 72, 77
Şandru, Ion, 477, 480
Sas, Judith H., 337, 383, 384
Sauer, Brigitte, 318
Savov, Sasho, 201
Scharnhorst, Erna, 303
Schille, Joachim, 267, 308
Schmelzer, Georg, 273, 310

Schmidt-Kolmer, E., 263, 301, 305
Schmunk, Günter, 279, 315
Schmutzler, Olaf, 317, 318
Schneider, Gernot, 301, 316, 318
Schoder, L., 305
Scholz, H., 305
Schöpflin, George, 380
Schreiber, Dieter, 301
Schröder, F.-H., 300
Schröder, Harry, 308
Schulz, H., 315
Schütze, Otmar, 308
Schwarz, G., 273
Schwarzenbach, R., 298
Sdobnov, V. M., 74
Seferagić, Dušica, 125, 129, 134
Sekulić, Duško, 134
Selivanova, V. A., 71
Serdar, Vladimir, 134
Šetinc, Marjan, 130, 134
Shalin, Dmitri, 65, 74
Shapiro, V. D., 67, 75
Shchenev, V. P., 65, 73
Shliapentokh, V., 65, 74
Shubkin, V., 66, 74
Shubkin, W. N., 300
Sibelka, György, 388
Šiber, Ivan, 96, 102, 116, 117, 125, 127, 130, 134
Sielaff, Wolfgang, 300, 313
Sik, Endre, 340, 384
Sikorskii, V., 72, 78
Šimek, M., 239
Simmel, Georg, 295
Singer, Rudolf, 256, 303
Sipovský, Stefan, 240
Sîrbu, Mariana, 459, 462, 476, 477, 480, 481
Siwek, Henryk, 434
Słomczynski, K., 416, 431, 434
Sobiecki, Zbigniew, 396, 428, 430, 434
Sokhan', L. V., 48, 72
Sokolov, V. M., 48, 72, 78

Sokołowska, M., 407, 417, 421, 427, 431, 432, 434
Solomon, Peter, 65
Solov'ev, N. Ia., 75
Sommer, Dietrich, 300, 313
Sommer, Erika, 267, 268, 308
Sopuch, Kazimierz, 435
Spangenberg, B., 272, 301
Spasovska, L., 151, 199
Spitak, Vlasta, 83, 121, 125, 127, 129, 130, 135
Springer, E., 452, 469, 475, 477, 479, 481
Stahl, H. H., 437
Staikov, Zahari, 137, 170, 198, 200
Stalin, Josip, 15, 389, 436
Štambuk, Maja, 124, 134
Štampar, Dubravka, 131
Starke, Kurt, 300
Starovoitova, G., 55, 72, 78
Staufenbiel, Fred, 284, 312
Stefanov, Ivan, 173, 201
Stefanov, Nano, 139, 171, 198, 201
Steitz, Lilo, 271, 275, 276, 301, 310
Steriade, Stefana, 437, 452, 453, 475, 481
Stöckmann, Peter, 312
Stojić, Ljuba, 125
Stollberg, Rudhard, 270, 272, 299, 301, 304, 309, 311
Stompler, Wolfgang, 312, 314
Strassburger, J., 310
Strauss, Franz-Jozef, 425
Strugariu, Despina, 463, 477, 481
Strützel, D., 284, 312
Strzeszewski, M., 400, 401, 430, 435
Sudau, Renate, 306
Sukhochev, I., 66
Supek, Rudi, 124, 125, 132, 134
Svensson, Roswitha, 307
Sviridov, N. A., 37, 39, 69, 77
Szabó, Ildikó, 367, 368, 369, 370, 387
Szabó, László, 375, 388
Szalai, Alexander, 280, 281, 283, 303, 311, 349, 385
Szalai, Sándor, 380
Szántó, L., 380
Szántó, Miklós, 337, 350, 351, 353, 380, 381, 383, 385, 386
Szecskő, Tamás, 350, 381, 386, 435
Szekfű, András, 326, 327, 328, 382
Szelényi, Iván, 386
Szilágyi, Vilmos, 382
Szostkiewicz, S., 435

Tal' iunaite, M., 33, 68, 75
Talalai, M. I., 36, 38, 69, 76
Tănăse, Alexandru, 456, 468, 475, 476, 477, 479, 481
Tanić, Živan, 134
Tannenbaum, Arnold, 101
Tarasenko, A. A., 48, 71, 78
Tardos, Róbert, 381, 384
Tarkowski, Jacek, 390, 427
Tauermann, Klaus, 314
Terent'ev, A. A., 48, 71, 78
Teune, Henry, 429, 434
Tietze, Gerhard, 279, 315
Tihomir, Borzan, 113, 114, 129, 134
Tikhonovich, V. A., 72
Timár, János, 383
Timişan (E. Springer), 452, 469, 475, 477, 479, 481
Titma, M. Kh., 15, 34, 35, 66, 69, 75
Tomanović, Velimir, 94, 96, 100, 127, 134
Tomaszewska, Irena, 402, 403, 404, 430, 435
Tomić, Stojan, 134
Tomka, Miklós, 354, 355, 386
Tönnies, F., 295
Topalov, M. N., 64, 66

Toš, Niko, 124, 125, 129
Traistaru, E., 477
Trasnea, Ovidiu, 481
Trenc, Pavle, 131
Tsanov, Misho, 137, 170, 198
Tsonev, St., 201
Turlik-Marecka, T., 398, 399, 430, 435
Turner, Ralph, 383
Tyszka, Andrzej, 435

Uesseler, Manfred, 317
Ulč, Otto, 227, 241
Ule, Mirjana, 88, 127, 135
Ullmann, Arndt, 301
Usenin, V. I., 40, 41, 70, 76
Usmankhodzhaev, I., 73, 78

Valentei, D. C., 79
Valkó, Emőke, 381
Vance, Cyrus, 446, 447
Vaněk, A., 212
Váradi, László, 381
Vasilev, Kiril, 159, 200
Večerník, Jiří, 213, 215, 239
Vershlovskii, S., 15, 66, 76
Vida, Ioan, 438, 469, 470, 471, 477, 478, 480, 481
Vidaković, Sunca, 133
Vitányi, Iván, 351, 352, 386
Vítek, Karel, 239
Vítková, Věra, 239
Vlad, Constantin, 438, 442
Voge, Sonja, 310
Voiculescu, Marin, 481
Voigt, Dieter, 307
Voigt, Otto, 309
Volgyes, Ivan, 241, 382, 383, 385
Volgyes, Nancy, 382, 383
Vortmann, Heinz, 304, 309, 316
Voss, Evelin, 317
Voženílek, Jiří, 240
Vozmitel', A. A., 66
Vrcan, Srdjan, 135
Vujević, Miroslav, 102, 118, 125, 135

Vybornov, L., 66

Walter, Kurt, 245
Walther, Rosemarie, 264, 306
Wasiak, Kazimierz, 435
Weber, Max, 295
Weckesser, E., 310, 311
Weidig, Rudi, 244, 246, 297, 299, 300, 309, 310
Weintraub, Zissu, 457, 459, 476, 481
Wejland, A., 429, 433
Welskopf, Rudolf, 300
Wennrich, Walter, 302
Wesołowski, W., 416, 431, 434
Weymar, Thomas, 314
Wiatr, Jerzy J., 389, 425, 426, 429, 432, 435
Wiedemann, Dieter, 300, 313
Wild, Käthe, 298
Wilke, Manfred, 316
Williams, Tennessee, 59
Wilsdorf, S., 300, 301
Winkler, Gunnar, 279, 298, 315
Wippold, Gerda, 315
Wiśniewski, W., 391, 408, 409, 410, 411, 418, 419, 431, 432, 435
Wunsch, Regina, 311

Zajc, Drago, 124, 125
Zaleska, Halina, 417, 431, 435
Zdravomyslov, A., 69
Zeidler, Ingeburg, 300
Zhabskii, M. I., 67, 74
Zhavoronkov, A. V., 66
Zhivkov, Todor, 155, 161
Ziegler, B., 283, 303
Zobel, Martin, 304
Zsille, Zoltán, 341, 345, 385
Zupančić, Milan, 124, 134
Županov, Josip, 116, 118, 125, 128, 130
Zvonarević, Mladen, 83, 85, 121, 125, 127, 129, 130, 135
Zwiener, K., 261, 305

Subject Index

Abortion
  as a source of family conflicts in Bulgaria, 153
  effects of on family life and roles of women in Hungary, 330

Absenteeism
  as focus of research on work and workplace in Hungary, 341

Academy of Sciences
  Bulgarian Academy of Sciences (BAN)
    role of in survey research, 136, 138, 139, 140, 141, 171, 193

Czechoslovak Academy of Sciences
  role of in survey research, 206, 213, 219

German Democratic Republic (Akademie der Wissenschaften der DDR)
  role of in survey research, 444, 461

Hungarian Academy of Sciences (MTA)
  role of in survey research, 320, 322, 323, 342, 354

Polish Academy of Sciences
  role of in survey research, 389-390

Romanian Academy of Sciences
role of in survey research,
437, 441
USSR Academy of Sciences
role of in survey research, 13,
14, 16, 49, 59

Academy of Social and Political
Sciences (ASPS)
role of in survey research in
Romania, 437, 438, 440,
441, 450

Academy of Social Science and
Social Administration (Sofia)
sociological research units
attached to, Bulgaria, 139,
187

Activism, Political (See also
Consciousness, Political)
effectiveness of in transportation industry in Bulgaria, 187

Activism, Social (See also
Consciousness, Socialist)
acceptance of value of, cross-
national summary, 500-501
among youth as induced by
media in Bulgaria, 145
and reading among youth in
Bulgaria, 187
antecedents of, 4
factors affecting in USSR, 48-49
levels of, cross-national summary, 501

Activism, Sociopolitical
modes of among Serbian youth
in Yugoslavia, 92-94

Agitation (See also Propaganda)
effectiveness of Party in USSR,
43, 46, 48

Agricultural Collectivization
attitudes toward in Czechoslovakia, 219

Akademie für Gesellschaftswissenschaften (AfG) (Berlin-Ost)
role of in social research in
German Democratic
Republic, 244, 250, 270, 273

Akademie, Medizinische
(Magdeburg)
role of in survey research in
German Democratic
Republic, 263

Albanians
living conditions of in Yugoslavia, 120
use of mass media by Albanian
minority in Serbia, Yugo-
slavia, 86

Alcoholism (See also Crime; Social
Problems)
as social problem
Bulgaria, 185, 188
cross-national summary, 498

Anketomanija (Survey-mania)
in Yugoslavia, 80

Antisocial Behavior
public attitudes toward in Romania, 470

Art
level of citizen information
about, USSR, 21, 23

Attitudes
and beliefs, 2
and public opinion, 3
and self-reported behavior, 3
and values, 2
defined, 2

Audience Research (See also Media
Habits)
in Bulgaria, 142-143
in Kosovo, Yugoslavia, 86
in Serbia, Yugoslavia, 86

Authority
political, 1
youth and other attitudes toward, Bulgaria, 158

Automation
impact of on work in USSR, 37,
40
survey research on effects of on
worker social consciousness
in Hungary, 323
types of labor disputes related to
introduction of, USSR, 41
worker attitudes toward
Bulgaria, 167, 169
cross-national summary, 491-
492
USSR, 37, 40-41

Beliefs
defined, 2

Bilingualism
origins and consequences of,
USSR, 56-59

Birth Control
attitudes of working women toward, German Democratic
Republic, 263

Birthrate (See also Births; Fertility)
effects of housework burdens
on, Bulgaria, 150
effects of on
educational system in Czechoslovakia, 217
family life and roles of
women in Hungary, 330-
331, 332-333

Births
increase in rate of among unmarried women in German
Democratic Republic, 264,
265

Books (See also Literature; Media
Habits)

citizen attitudes toward and
preferences concerning,
Czechoslovakia, 208

Bosnia
as a major source of social
science research in Yugoslavia, 82

Bulgaria
abortion
as source of family conflicts, 153
Academy of Sciences (BAN)
Institute of Philosophy of,
136
Institute of Sociology of,
136, 138, 139, 140, 141,
171, 193
Academy of Social Science and
Social Administration (Sofia)
sociological research units attached to, 139, 187
activism, political
effectiveness of in transportation industry, 187
activism, social
among youth, 145, 187
alcoholism
elite and citizen attitudes toward, 185, 188
audience research
foci of, 142-143
authority
youth and other attitudes
toward, 158
automation
worker attitudes toward, 167,
169
birthrate
effects of housework burdens
on, 150
Bulgarian Sociological Association
roles of in survey research,
140

Center for Journalism Research
(Sofia)
surveys of newspaper readership by, 146
Center for the Scientific Study
of Youth (Sofia)
role of in survey research,
136, 139-140, 172, 177
(State) Cinematography Enterprise
research by Sociological Research Center of, 139, 172
child care
effects of on family conflicts
and on employment of
women, 152-153
Communist Party
Party secretaries' bases for
accepting their positions,
189, 190
Party secretaries' perceptions
of their most important
functions, 189, 191
Party secretaries' relationships with rank-and-file,
189, 191
qualities perceived by Party
secretaries as most important for their jobs, 189,
190
research conducted by sociologists attached to district
committees of, 180
crime
alcoholism as factor influencing, 179-180, 183
attitudes of convicted criminals toward categories of,
183-184
citizen attitudes toward, 180-
184
citizen inclination to call
authorities to report, 181

Bulgaria (continued)
differences in citizen attitudes toward categories of,
183
factors influencing levels of
citizen awareness of, 181
factors inhibiting citizen involvement in, 181, 182
reasons for citizen concerns
about, 180-181
social and occupational factors influencing activism
against, 183
criminal code
citizen knowledge of, 181
divorce
elite and citizen attitudes
toward, 184-185
reasons for, 153-154
education
differences among occupa-
tional and age groups in
formal, 155, 156
reasons for specialization in,
160
significance of in delineating
socioeconomic and politi-
cal development, 196-197
student perceptions of
adequacy of ideological
training in, 160-161
factors critical to success
in school, 160
education and youth, 154-162
foci of research on, 155
equality
citizen perceptions of in
application of law, 183
ethnicity
problems of minority ethnic
groups, 193
ethnicity and foreign cultures,
193-195

family and women, 149-154
effects of housing conditions
on preferred family size,
153
foci of research on, 149
press treatment of family life,
146, 148
social changes affecting, 152-
154
summary of findings concerning, 197
fertility
effects of education on attitudes toward, 153
foreign countries
attitudes toward, 193-195
Higher Institute of National
Economy (Varna)
Sociological Laboratory of,
137, 160
job satisfaction
factors affecting, 164-167
job terminations
effects of age and education
on reasons for, 165
subjective vs. objective reasons for, 165
Journalists, Union of Bulgarian
survey research unit attached
to, 139
Komsomol (Communist Youth
League)
age and nature of task motivation in, 161, 162, 168
characteristics of members of,
187
decision making within, 187
effectiveness of in schools,
162
survey research unit attached
to, 139
values and ideological orientations of members of, 157-
158, 159, 162

Bulgaria (continued)
labor turnover
factors affecting, 164-165
law
citizen perceptions of equality in application of, 183
law of 1975 on social research, 7
leisure time, 170-176
activities of industrial workers during, 175
foci of research on, 170
movie attendance and reading
of literature by youth
during, 173
movie attendance in use of,
172-173
Party perceptions of political
and ideological importance
of, 170-171
reading of literature during,
173-176
use of by national sample of
citizens and by workers,
171
life aspirations
factors influencing among
youth, 176-177, 178, 182
market research, 195
media effectiveness, 142, 143-
149
in aesthetic education of
youth, 145-146
in preparing youth for family
life, 146
informational adequacy
among workers as measure
of, 146
media habits, 142-149
effects of educational level on
patterns of newspaper
reading, 143, 144
readership of Komsomol
newspaper, 142

readership of printed media
by Komsomol members,
145
reading of national and regional newspapers, 146-
147, 148
moral and ethical preferences
and life aspirations, 176-179
movies
origins and characteristics of
preferred by youth, 172
political education
perceptions of Party rank-
and-file and leadership of
effectiveness of, 192
politics and ideology, 186-192
foci of research on, 186
unpublished research by
Communist Party dealing
with, 186
prestige, social
youth and other attitudes
toward, 158
propaganda, political and ideological
studies of effectiveness of,
186
public opinion
definition of in recent Bulgarian works, 138
public property
leadership and worker attitudes toward protection
of, 185
regime confidence
and status of survey research,
11-12
Scientific Institute for the
Study of Work (Sofia)
role of in survey research,
149
social problems and social
policy, 5, 179-185

Bulgaria (continued)
different elite and mass perceptions of, 184-185, 497
foci of research on, 179-180
socialization, political
effectiveness of among youth,
162
survey research, 3, 136-203
appropriate context for interpreting results of, 197-
198
functions of, 196
history of, 136-137
institutions engaged in, 139-
140
laws concerning, 7, 140
methodology of, 7-8, 138-
139
policy relevance of, 137
publication practices and constraints concerning, 140-
141
sampling as element of, 138-
139
summary of current circumstances of, 195-196
women
attitudes of toward
employment outside
home, 152
family size, 153
fashion, 150, 152
effects of housework on
employment and leisure
time of, 149, 150
reading and cultural activities among, 151
life aspirations of young, 176
roles of, 149-152
work and workplace, 163-170
attitudes toward jobs among
local Communist Party
secretaries, 187-192

discipline problems in, 166-167, 168

effects of relationships among workers on attitudes toward, 164

foci of research on, 163

incentives in, 163

preferred by local Party secretaries, 187-189

socialist consciousness in work brigades, 179

worker attitudes toward material and nonmaterial incentives, 163, 164

worker evaluations of leadership cadres in industry, 169-170

youth

evaluation of occupations by, 177

life aspirations of, 157

problems in socialization of as motivation for research on, 155

socialist consciousness of, 162, 197

summary of findings of survey research on, 197

values and concerns of, 155, 157-160, 179

Child Care

effects of on family and women in Bulgaria, 152-153

effects of on roles of women cross-national summary, 496

in German Democratic Republic, 260, 262-263

Citizen Needs

extent to which local political systems address in Poland, 390

Citizen Proposals

action on by local authorities in Romania, 472

during electoral and nonelectoral periods in Romania, 471-472

Clothing

consumer preferences for and purchases of, Hungary, 375

Collectivization, see Agricultural Collectivization

Comparative Cross-national Summary (See also Cross-national Summary)

education and youth, 487-490

ethnicity and foreign cultures, 503-504

family and women, 485-487

leisure time, 493-495

media habits, 483-485

moral and ethical preferences and life aspirations, 495-496

social problems and social policy, 497-500

politics and ideology, 500-503

work and workplace, 490-493

Consciousness, Political (See also Activism, Political)

effects of Communist Party membership on, USSR, 48-49

effects of personal characteristics on, USSR, 46, 48

lack of among workers in Hungary, 341

of youth in Czechoslovakia, 237

Consciousness, Socialist (See also Activism, Social)

extent of development of, Hungary, 379

focus of survey research on, Hungary, 320

in work brigades in Bulgaria, 179

of youth

in Bulgaria, 197

in Hungary, 336, 339

in Romania, 452-454, 455
of workers in German Democratic Republic, 273

Consumer Groups
market research on in German
Democratic Republic, 293

Consumer Needs
market research on in German
Democratic Republic, 293

Consumer Opinions and Attitudes
as principal focus of market
research in German Demo-
cratic Republic, 292

Consumer Satisfaction
as measure of social problems
in German Democratic Re-
public, 288

Consumption, Personal
attitudes toward as measures of
perceptions of wealth in Hungary, 363, 365, 366
patterns of among Prague households, Czechoslovakia, 220
patterns of in market research in
German Democratic Repub-
lic, 292

Crime (See also Hooliganism; Social
Problems)
alcoholism as factor influencing
in Bulgaria, 179-180, 183
as social problem in German
Democratic Republic, 288
attitudes of criminals toward
categories of, Bulgaria, 183-
184
citizen attitudes toward, 4
in Bulgaria, 180-184
cross-national summary, 497
citizen inclination to call authorities to report in Bulgaria, 181
social and occupational factors
influencing activism against
in Bulgaria, 183

Criminal Code
citizen knowledge of, Bulgaria,
181

Croatia
statistical techniques in surveys
in, Yugoslavia, 83

Cross-national Summary (See also
Comparative Cross-national
Summary)
alcoholism
as social problem, 498
automation
worker attitudes toward, 491-
492
child care
effects of on roles of women,
496
crime
citizen attitudes toward, 497
family
conflicts in, 485-487
importance of, 485
housing
effects of problems in on
family, 486
income and wealth differentials
as social problem, 498-499
job satisfaction
factors affecting, 491-492
labor turnover
reasons for, 491
leisure time
social status as factor affecting, 494
media
effectiveness, 484
media habits
factors influencing levels of
media attention, 483
political involvement
attitudes toward, 501-502
religious values
significance of, 495-496
social activism
acceptance of value of, 500-
501
levels of, 501
women
roles of, 486

workers
collective responsibility a-
mong, 490-491
relations of with manage-
ment, 492
sociopolitical participation
of, 492-493
youth
education as predictor of
values of, 490
occupational preferences of,
489-490
political activity of, 488-489
urban-rural differences in
values of, 490
values of, 487-490

Cultural Articles
possession of by different social
groups in USSR, 26

Cultural-Evaluative Orientations
differences among age groups in
Karelia related to, USSR, 59,
61

Czechoslovakia
agricultural collectivization
attitudes toward, 219
Association of Socialist Youth
(Bratislava)
role of in social research, 216,
217, 223-224, 229
birthrate
effect of on educational system, 217
books
citizen attitudes toward, 208
Communist Party
Czech-Slovak conflicts within, 234-235
evaluations of and attitudes
toward role of among rural
population, 232-234
consciousness, political
of youth, 237

consumption, personal
patterns of among Prague
households, 220
Czech Scientific Technical Association (Pardubice)
role of in social research, 218
Czechoslovak Academy of Sciences, 206
role of Institute of Philosophy and Sociology of in
social research, 213, 219
Czechoslovak Institute for Labor
Research (Bratislava)
research on sociology of the
workplace by, 218
education and youth, 213, 216-
218
ethnicity and foreign cultures,
234-235
family
living standards of, 213, 214
family and women, 210, 212-
213, 214-215
mate selection in research on,
212-213
fertility rates
survey research on, 210, 212
government structure
Czech National Council in
federal structure, 234
effects of federal structure on
conduct of social research,
234-235
Slovak National Council in
federal structure, 234
housing
patterns of in Prague, 212
income distribution
research on, 213, 215, 219-
220
Institute for Research on Cultural Questions (Prague and
Bratislava)

Czechoslovakia (continued)
  role of in social research, 205,
    208, 210, 216, 227, 237
  leisure time, 220-223
    preferences of youth con-
      cerning, 220, 221-222
    use of by rural population,
      220, 223
  marriage
    factors influencing quality
      of, 212-213
  media habits, 207-210
    absence of research on, 208
    attitudes toward popular
      singers, 208-209
    youth attitudes toward visual
      arts, 209-210
  moral and ethical preferences
    and life aspirations, 223-227
  Opponents' Commission
    role of in review of research
      studies to be published,
      206
  political education
    youth attitudes toward, 229-
      230
  political participation
    factors influencing levels of,
      233-234
  politics and ideology, 229-234
  Prague
    demographic and residential
      characteristics of, 209-210
  regime confidence
    and status of survey research,
      11-12
  religion
    attitudes of rural population
      toward, 224-225, 227
    comparison of science and
      religion by rural Slovaks,
      232
  rural population
    cultural and societal profile
      of, 217-218

scientific workers
  mobility of, 219
social deviance
  prevalence of various forms
    of, 227
social problems and social policy, 227-229
  attitudes toward cultural
    monuments as measure of,
    227, 228-229
  attitudes toward protection
    of natural environment as
    measure of, 227-228
  education as factor influenc-
    ing attitudes toward, 228
  urban-rural differences in atti-
    tudes toward, 228
socialism, achievements of
  perceptions of by rural Slo-
    vaks, 232
survey research, 204-241
  conditions of, 5, 7, 235-236
  effect of political climate on,
    238
  institutions engaged in, 204-
    205
  methodology of, 7-8, 205-
    206
  policy-relevant roles of, 206-
    207
  publication of results of, 204-
    206, 236-238
  quality of, 207
  topics not covered in pub-
    lished, 237
women
  importance of research on,
    210
  work conditions of, 210, 218-
    219
work and workplace, 218-220
  factors influencing job satis-
    faction, 218
  income differentials as mea-
    sure of conditions in, 219-
    220

Czechoslovakia (continued)
    job satisfaction in, 224
    work style preferences in
      Slovakia, 219
    workers
      aesthetic education of, 216
    youth
      attitudes of parents toward
        socialization of, 213
      attitudes of toward
        political education and
          political work, 229-232
        popular singers, 216
      consciousness, political and
        social, of, 237
      cultural life of, 209-210, 216
      education of, 217-218
      evaluations of socialism and
        capitalism among, 224,
        226
      leisure time of, 216
      political knowledge of, 223-
        224, 225
      reading interests among, 210,
        211
      research on socialization of,
        213, 216
      work satisfaction of, 216-217

Delegate System (See also Political
    Participation; Self Management;
    Work and Workplace)
    functioning and implementation
      of, Yugoslavia, 115-116, 118

Deputies to Local Soviets
    attitudes of, USSR, 49
    attitudes toward usefulness of
      their work among, USSR, 54
    effects of social status on job-
      related problems of, USSR,
      52-53
    relationships between Party
      status and work satisfaction
      among, USSR, 51

Divorce (See also Divorce Rate)
    attitudes of youth toward, Ger-
      man Democratic Republic,
      268
    elite and citizen attitudes to-
      ward, Bulgaria, 184-185
    reasons for, Bulgaria, 153-154
    reasons for in rural western
      Belorussia, USSR, 29

Divorce Rate (See also Divorce)
    effects of on family structure in
      German Democratic Repub-
      lic, 264, 265
    reasons for in USSR, 24, 27
    reasons for increase in, Hungary,
      330

Education (See also Education and
    Youth; Education, Political;
    Youth)
    attitudes of youth and parents
      toward, Poland, 390-391
    attitudes toward, Poland, 408-
      410, 411
    effects of on attitudes in USSR,
      62
    evaluations of by youth in Po-
      land, 408, 410, 411
    influence of social status on,
      USSR, 30-34
    occupational and age differences
      in, Bulgaria, 155, 156
    significance of in delineating
      socioeconomic and political
      differences in Bulgaria, 196-
      197
    specialization in, Bulgaria, 160
    student perceptions of adequacy
      of ideological training in,
      Bulgaria, 160-161
    student perceptions of factors
      critical to success in, Bul-
      garia, 160

Education and Youth, 2
    Bulgaria, 154-162
    comparative cross-national sum-
        mary, 487-490
    Czechoslovakia, 213, 216-218
    German Democratic Republic,
        264, 266-269, 272
    Hungary, 334-339, 340
    Poland, 406, 408-413
    Romania, 453-458, 461
    USSR, 27, 30-35
    Yugoslavia, 92-101

    foci of research on, Bulgaria,
        155
    foci of research on, Yugo-
        slavia, 92

Education, Political (See also Polit-
    ical Information; Politics and
    Ideology; Propaganda; Youth)
    audience evaluation of know-
        ledge received through,
        USSR, 47
    perceptions of of Party rank-
        and-file and leadership in
        Bulgaria, 192
    propagandists' evaluation of au-
        dience interest in, USSR, 47
    youth attitudes toward, Czech-
        oslovakia, 229-230

Educational Opportunity
    social class background as deter-
        minant of, Hungary, 335

Employment (See also Work and
    Workplace)
    changing structure of, German
        Democratic Republic, 273

Equality (See also Social Problems)
    citizen perceptions of in appli-
        cation of law in Bulgaria,
        183

Ethnicity (See also Ethnicity and
    Foreign Cultures; Linguistic
    Behavior)

attitudes toward nationalism in
    Croatia, Yugoslavia, 120
determinants of as perceived by
    Tatars in USSR, 55
linguistic characteristics and
    ethnic-cultural orientations
    in USSR, 60

Ethnicity and Foreign Cultures, 2
    Bulgaria, 193-195
    comparative cross-national sum-
        mary, 503-504
    Czechoslovakia, 234-235
    German Democratic Republic,
        290-291
    Hungary, 367, 371-374
    USSR, 49, 55-59
    Yugoslavia, 120-121

    observance of ethnic rituals
        among Tatars in USSR, 55
    problems of minority ethnic
        groups in Bulgaria, 193

Family (See also Family and Wom-
    en; Family Life; Family Size)
    changes in, Yugoslavia, 87-88
    conflicts in, cross-national sum-
        mary, 485-487
    differences between traditional
        and current structures of,
        German Democratic Repub-
        lic, 263-264
    effects of on life aspirations in
        Romania, 452-453
    factors influencing differences in
        attitudes toward, Poland,
        418-419
    impact of on organization of
        agricultural work in Romania,
        450-451
    impact of on youth socialist
        consciousness in Romania,
        452-453
    importance of, cross-national
        summary, 485

influence of on career orientations of youth in Romania, 469

living standards of, Czechoslovakia, 213, 214

official attitudes toward role of, German Democratic Republic, 258

Family and Women
Bulgaria, 149-154
comparative cross-national summary, 485-487
Czechoslovakia, 210, 212-213, 214-215
German Democratic Republic, 258, 260-264, 265
Hungary, 330-334
Poland, 404-406, 407
Romania, 450-453
USSR, 24-29
Yugoslavia, 87-92

changes of roles of in rural Croatia, Yugoslavia, 87-88
foci of research on, Bulgaria, 149
foci of research on, Poland, 404
housekeeping by women in German Democratic Republic, 260
mate selection in research on, Czechoslovakia, 212-213
social changes affecting in Bulgaria, 152-154
summary of survey research concerning in Bulgaria, 197

Family Life (See also Moral and Ethical Preferences and Life Aspirations)
as focus of life aspirations and values in Poland, 404, 405
perceptions of press treatment of, Bulgaria, 146, 148

Family Size
effects of housing conditions on, Bulgaria, 153
factors affecting attitudes toward, Hungary, 331

Fertility (See also Birthrate)
as focus of survey research in Czechoslovakia, 210, 212
effects of education on attitudes toward, Bulgaria, 153
low levels of in European Russia, USSR, 24
Moslem vs. non-Moslem attitudes toward, USSR, 27

Foreign Countries (See also Ethnicity and Foreign Cultures)
citizen perceptions of similarities and closeness of, Hungary, 372-374

Foreign Policy
citizen views of, Poland, 425

Gastarbeiter
presence of, German Democratic Republic, 290

German Democratic Republic
Akademie der Wissenschaften der DDR
role of in social research, 244, 261
Akademie für Gesellschaftswissenschaften (AfG) (Berlin-Ost)
role of in social research, 244, 250, 270
Akademie, Medizinische (Magdeburg)
surveys of working women by, 263
birth control
attitudes of working women toward, 263

births
  increase in rate of among un-
    married women, 264, 265
child care
  effects of on working plans
    of women, 260, 261-263
consciousness, socialist
  among workers, 273
consumer attitudes
  as focus of market research,
    292
consumer groups
  market research on, 293
consumer needs
  market research on, 293
consumer satisfaction
  as measure of social prob-
    lems, 288
crime
  as measure of extent of social
    problems, 288
divorce
  attitudes of youth toward,
    268
divorce rate
  effects of on family structure,
    264, 265
education and youth, 264, 266-
    269, 272
employment
  changing structure of, 273
ethnicity and foreign cultures,
    290-291
family
  official attitudes toward role
    of, 258
  traditional vs. current struc-
    tures of, 263-264
family and women, 258, 260-
    264, 265
  housekeeping by women in
    research on, 260
foreigners and foreign countries
  attitudes toward, 290-291

German Democratic Republic
  (continued)
  Freie Deutsche Jugend (FDJ)
    role of in social research, 246
  Freier Deutscher Gewerkschafts-
    bund (FDGB)
    role of in social research, 246
  Gastarbeiter
    presence of, 290
  Gewerkschaftshochschule "Fritz
    Heckert" (Bernau)
    role of in social research, 244
  Institut für Bedarfsforschung
    (Leipzig)
    role of in survey research,
      277
  Institut für Gesellschaftswissen-
    schaften beim Zentral-
    komittee der SED
    role of in social research, 271,
      284
  Institut für Hygiene des Kindes-
    und Jugendalters
    role of in conduct of survey
      research, 261
  Institut für Marktforschung
    (Leipzig)
    role of in social research, 245,
      277, 285, 292, 293
  Institut für marxistisch-
    leninistische Philosophie der
    AfG (Berlin-Ost)
    role ot in social research,
      270
  Institut für marxistisch-
    leninistische Soziologie der
    AfG (Berlin-Ost)
    role of in survey research,
      243, 270
  Institut für Meinungsforschung
    beim Zentralkomitee der
    SED (Berlin-Ost)
    role of in survey research,
      243, 288, 290

juvenile delinquency
as social problem, 288
labor sociology
foci of research in, 269, 270
labor turnover
sources of data for research
on, 270
legitimacy, regime
as constraint on survey research, 294
leisure time, 276-285
attention to mass media as
element in use of, 256
differences by sex and occupation in availability of,
278, 280-281
foci of research on, 277
implications of Marxist-
Leninist conception of,
276-277
life aspirations
materialistic values as element
of, 287
market research, 292-293
methods of consumer surveying in, 292-293
media, electronic
attention to West German,
254-255
media habits, 254-258, 259
audience research as element
of research on, 255-258
of youth, 285
publication of results of research on, 256
minority groups
absence of problems con-
cerning, 290
moral and ethical preferences
and life aspirations, 286-287
foci of research on, 286
personal consumption
as focus of market research,
292

German Democratic Republic
(continued)
personality
need for authority and structure as dimension of, 287
political information
level of concerning West
Germany, 289
politics and ideology, 288-290
attitudes toward West German politics as measures
of, 289
petitions for emigration as
indicators of citizens'
attitudes toward, 289-290
propaganda, political
impact on citizen images of
foreign countries, 291
regime confidence
and status of survey research,
11-12
religion
church membership as mea-
sure of attitudes toward,
286
research
scientific vs. political criteria
in, 266-267
shift work
attitudes toward and effects
on family life of, 270-271,
272
social problems and social policy, 287-288
housing as example of, 268
socialist personality
religious values and formation
of, 286
*Staatliche Zentralverwaltung für
Statistik (SZS)*
role of in social research, 246-
247, 273

survey research, 3, 5, 7, 242-318
  as area of scholarly inquiry,
    248-249
  factors affecting publication
    of, 295
  foci of, 249-251
  institutions engaged in, 243-
    245
  legal basis of, 246-247
  methodology of, 7-8, 243,
    249, 250-252, 294-295
    296
  overview of, 242-245
  planning and financing of,
    246-247
  policy functions of, 247-248,
    293-294
  political control of, 294
  Praxisverbundenheit as crite-
    rion influencing, 249, 250,
    252, 293, 297
  roles and significance of, 247-
    249, 293-294
  sampling approaches and
    techniques in, 251
  topical and source coverage in
    study of, 252-253
  validity and reliability in, 296
television
  program content of, 258, 259
  social structure of viewers of,
    256, 257, 258
time budgets
  research on, 278-279
*Wissenschaftlicher Beirat "Die
  Frau in der sozialistischen
  Gesellschaft"*
  role of in survey research,
    244, 245, 261
*Wissenschaftliche Räte der
  gesellschaftswissenschaftlichen Forschung*
  role of in social research, 244-
    245, 250

German Democratic Republic
  (continued)
*Wissenschaftlicher Rat für
  Jugendforschung*
  role of in social research, 244
*Wissenschaftlicher Rat für
  Sozialpolitik und Demo-
  graphie*
  role of in social research, 244
*Wissenschaftlicher Rat für
  soziologische Forschung*
  role of in social research, 244,
    245, 250
*Wissenschaftlicher Rat für
  wirtschaftswissenschaftliche
  Forschung*
  role of in social research, 244
women
  day care of children as factor
    affecting work plans of,
    260, 261-263
  physical well-being of
    working, 260, 263
  reasons for emphasis in social
    research on, 258
  research on working, 258,
    260-264
  roles of, 258, 260-261
  work motives of, 260-261
  youth attitudes toward em-
    ployment of, 268
work and workplace, 269-276
  foci of research on, 270,
    276
workers
  attitudes toward work and
    workplace, 271, 274-275
  cultural activities and aspira-
    tions of, 278, 284
youth
  attitudes of toward marriage
    and family, 267-268
  factors influencing societal
    circumstances of, 268-269

foci of research on, 267
importance of research on, 264, 266, 269
influences of family and day care centers on development of, 260, 261, 263
leisure time activities of, 267, 268-269, 284-285
opinions of concerning division of Germany, 288-289
reading habits of, 285
school performance of when mother works, 260, 263
time budgets of, 285

Zentrales Forschungsinstitut des Verkehrswesens der DDR (Dresden)
role of in social research, 245

Zentrales Forschungsinstitut für Arbeit (Dresden)
role of in social research, 245, 270

Zentralinstitut für Jugendforschung (ZfJ) (Leipzig)
role of in social research, 244, 266-267, 268, 269, 284

Germany
opinions of GDR citizens concerning division of, 288-289

Government
tasks of as seen by youth in Poland, 420, 422

Health Care
absence of facilities for persons with special needs in Hungary, 362, 363
factors limiting equal access to, Hungary, 363
variations in availability and use of by social status in Yugoslavia, 113

Hooliganism (See also Crime; Social Problems)

public attitudes toward, Romania, 470

Household Management
characteristics of, Hungary, 375-377, 378

Housing (See also Social Problems and Social Policy)
as material aspiration in Poland, 419, 420
as social problem
in Hungary, 359, 360
in Romania, 472
effects on family life in Hungary, 330, 331
effects on family, cross-national summary, 486
effects on interpersonal conflicts in Romania, 470-471
factors limiting equal access to, Hungary, 362-363
government planning of, USSR, 25
patterns of in Prague, Czechoslovakia, 212
shortage of as factor in commuting in Hungary, 342

Human Needs
variations in satisfaction of as social problem in Yugoslavia, 113, 114

Hungary
abortion
effects of on family life and roles of women, 330
absenteeism
as focus of research on work and workplace, 341
Academy of Sciences *(MTA)*
role of in survey research, 320, 322, 323, 342, 354
automation
effects of on worker social consciousness, 323

birthrate
effects of on family life and
roles of women, 330-331,
332-333
Central Statistical Office
role of in survey research,
320, 323, 330, 349
clothing
consumer preferences re-
garding, 375
Communist Youth League
(KISZ)
role of in survey research,
320, 323, 336, 341, 372
consciousness, political
lack of among workers, 341
consciousness, socialist
extent of development of,
379
focus of survey research on,
320
of youth, 336, 339
Cooperatives Research Institute
role of in survey research,
323
cultural activities
of women during leisure time,
351
Demographic Research Institute
role of in survey research,
359
divorce rate
reasons for increase in, 330
education and youth, 334-339,
340
educational opportunity
social background as determinant of, 335
ethnicity and foreign cultures,
367, 371-374
family and women, 330-334
family size
attitudes toward, 331

Hungary (continued)
foreign countries
citizen perceptions of, 372-
374
health care
absence of facilities for persons with special needs in,
362, 363
factors limiting equal access
to, 363
household management
characteristics of, 375-377,
378
housing
effects on family life, 330,
331
factors limiting equal access
to, 362-363
perceptions of problems in,
359, 360
shortage of as factor in commuting, 342
Hungarian Socialist Workers
Party
role of in survey research,
320
ideology
indifference toward as measure of political attitudes,
366, 367
income differences
attitudes toward, 363, 364-
365
Institute for Culture
role of in survey research,
354
Institute for Literary Studies
role of in survey research,
354
Institute for Market Research
role of in survey research,
320, 374, 375

interest groups
    regime fear of citizen-based, 362
labor turnover
    as focus of research on work and workplace, 341
leisure time, 349-353
    factors affecting differential availability and use of, 351-353
    parttime work as element in allocation of, 351
    passive vs. nonpassive activities in, 349-351
    time budgets as focus of research on, 349-351
life, quality of
    survey research on, 323, 353, 354, 356
market research, 374-377, 378
    foci of, 374, 375
marriage
    attitudes toward, 330
Marxism-Leninism
    influence of on research, 6
Mass Communications Research Center (Budapest)
    role of in survey research, 320, 322, 323, 324, 349, 351, 354
media, electronic
    social structure of audiences of, 324, 325, 326
media habits, 323-329
    audience research in research on, 324-329
    relationships among radio, television, and newspaper use in, 325
minorities
    status of Gypsy and Jewish, 367, 372
moral and ethical preferences and life aspirations, 353-358

Hungary (continued)
    preferred vs. observed human qualities, 356, 358
National Committee for Technical Development
    support of for survey research, 354
national pride
    social and occupation differences in sources of, 371-372
nationalism
    in attitudes toward Hungarian minority in Romania, 371, 374, 379
personal consumption
    as measures of perceived wealth, 363, 365, 366
politics and ideology, 366-367, 368-370
quality control
    as focus of research on work and workplace, 341
regime
    citizen support for, 366, 367
regime confidence
    and status of survey research, 11-12
religion
    factors affecting religious involvement, 353, 354-355, 356, 362
Research Center of the Hungarian Trade Unions
    role of in survey research, 320, 323, 341
Samizdat, 6, 321
sex, premarital
    links of to divorce and marriage, 330
    youth attitudes toward, 330
social mobility
    effects of educational system on, 334, 335-336

social problems and social
  policy, 359-366
  foci of research on, 359
  workers' perceptions of sig-
    nificant issues, 359, 360
social services
  factors limiting equal access
    to, 359, 362-363
socialist lifestyle
  development of in research
    on leisure time, 349, 353
suicide
  causes of, 359, 361, 362
survey research, 3, 5, 6, 319-388
  foci of, 319-320
  institutions engaged in, 320,
    322-323
  methodology of, 7, 8, 320,
    321-322, 323
  policy functions of, 321-322
  publication of results of, 320,
    321
  sampling requirements and
    topic selection in, 322
  training of researchers for,
    320
values and moral obligations
  attitudes of workers toward,
    356, 357
women
  household responsibilities and
    roles of, 331, 334
  work attitudes of, 331, 334
work
  organization of, 341
work and workplace, 339, 341-
  349
  foci of research on, 341
  sex discrimination in remu-
    neration in, 331, 334
  workers' attitudes toward,
    342, 343
  workers' evaluations of, 342,
    344

Hungary (continued)
  worker productivity
    as focus of research on work
      and workplace, 341
  worker self management
    attitudes toward, 342, 345,
      346-347, 349
  workers
    attitudes of toward work-
      place participation, 342,
      345, 346-347, 349
    commitment to work of,
      342
    commuting and workplace
      problems among, 341-342
    lifestyles of, 341
    perceptions held by of Party,
      342
  youth
    attitudes of toward leisure
      time, 336, 338
    discontent among, 336
    evaluations of capitalism and
      socialism by, 339, 340
    occupational plans of, 335-
      336, 337
    perceptions of concerning
      foreign policy, 366-367,
      368-370
    perspectives of on economic
      issues, 337, 339
Ideology (See also Politics and
  Ideology)
  effectiveness of ideological prop-
    aganda in Bulgaria, 186
  indifference toward and politi-
    cal attitudes in Hungary, 366,
    367
  relevance of in interpreting con-
    ditions in Eastern Europe, 5
Income Distribution
  as social problem, cross-national
    summary, 498-499

attitudes toward in
Czechoslovakia, 213, 215,
219-220
Hungary, 363, 364-365
Serbia, Yugoslavia, 109-110
Industrial Sociology
as area of social research in
Yugoslavia, 101
Institutes, Roles of in Survey Re-
search
Cooperatives Research Institute,
Hungary, 323
Czechoslovak Institute for Labor
Research (Bratislava), 218
Demographic Research Institute,
Hungary, 359
Higher Institute of National
Economy (Varna), Bulgaria,
137, 160
Institute for Culture, Hungary,
354
Institute for Literary Studies,
Hungary, 354
Institute for Market Research,
Hungary, 320, 374, 375
Institute for Research on Cul-
tural Questions (Prague),
Czechoslovakia, 205, 208,
210, 216, 227, 237
Institute for Social Research
(Zagreb), Yugoslavia, 109,
121
Institute for Sociology and
Philosophy (Ljubljana),
Yugoslavia, 109
Institute of Political Science and
Study on National Problems,
Romania, 438, 459, 469-470
Institute of Social Sciences
(Belgrade), Yugoslavia, 109
Mining Institute (Petrosani),
Romania, 439
Pedagogical Institute (Bacau),
Romania, 429

Polish Institute of Sociology
(Poznan), 389
Scientific Institute for the Study
of Work (Sofia), Bulgaria,
149
Silesian Institute (Opole),
Poland, 390
Intelligentsia
of Armenia, USSR, 21
Interest Communities, Self-
managing (See also Self Management)
in funding of research in Yugoslavia, 81
Interest Groups
regime fear of citizen-based in
Hungary, 362
Job Satisfaction (See also Labor
Turnover; Work and Workplace)
factors   affecting in Bulgaria,
164-167
factors affecting, cross-national
summary, 491-492
reasons for, USSR, 36-37, 40-42
Job Terminations, see Labor Turnover
Journalism
Center for Journalism Research
(Sofia)
surveys of newspaper readership by, Bulgaria, 146
Union of Bulgarian Journalists
survey research unit of, Bulgaria, 139
Juvenile Delinquency (See also
Crime; Hooliganism; Youth)
as social problem in German
Democratic Republic, 288
Komsomol (Communist Youth
League)
age and nature of task motivation in, Bulgaria, 161, 162,
168

characteristics of members of, Bulgaria, 187

decision making within, Bulgaria, 187

effectiveness of in school functioning as perceived by members in Bulgaria, 162

survey research unit attached to, Bulgaria, 139

values and ideological orientations of members of, Bulgaria, 157-158, 159, 162

Labor, see Work and Workplace

Labor Sociology

foci of research in, German Democratic Republic, 269, 270

Labor Turnover (See also Automation; Job Satisfaction)

as focus of research on work and workplace in Hungary, 341

factors affecting in Bulgaria, 164-165

information sources in research on, German Democratic Republic, 270

on state farms in USSR, 39

reasons for

cross-national summary, 491

USSR, 36

Language Proficiency (See also Ethnicity)

in second language in Moldavia, USSR, 57

Law (See also Criminal Code; Crime; Social Problems)

equality in application of, Bulgaria, 183

Legitimacy, Regime

and survey research in German Democratic Republic, 294

Leisure Time, 2 (See also Media Habits; Moral and Ethical Preferences)

Bulgaria, 170-176

comparative cross-national summary, 493-495

Czechoslovakia, 220-223

German Democratic Republic, 276-285

Hungary, 349-353

Romania, 463-464, 465, 466

USSR, 42-45

Yugoslavia, 106-108

age differentiation in availability and use of, Hungary, 352

allocation of in German Democratic Republic, 278, 282-283, 284

cultural facilities in use of in Croatia, Yugoslavia, 108

differences by sex and occupation in availability of, German Democratic Republic, 278, 280-281

effects of education on use of, USSR, 44

factors affecting availability and use of

Hungary, 351-353

USSR, 42-43

foci of research on

Bulgaria, 170

German Democratic Republic, 277

Marxist-Leninist conception of, German Democratic Republic, 276-277

mass media in use of, German Democratic Republic, 256

movie attendance in use of, Bulgaria, 172-173

of industrial workers, Bulgaria, 175

part-time work as element in allocation of, Hungary, 351

Party perceptions of importance of, Bulgaria, 170-171

passive vs. nonpassive in Hungary, 349-351

preferences of youth concerning, Czechoslovakia, 220, 221-222

reading of literature during, Bulgaria, 173-176

sexual differentiation in availability and use of, Hungary, 351-352

social status as factor affecting, cross-national summary, 494

socioeconomic differentiation in availability and use of, Hungary, 352-353

socioeconomic differentiation in cultural activities in, Yugoslavia, 106

socioeconomic differentiation in cultural needs related to, Yugoslavia, 106

time budgets as focus of research on, Hungary, 349-351

urban-rural differentiation in availability and use of, Hungary, 352

urban-rural differentiation in use of, Yugoslavia, 106-107

use of by rural population in Czechoslovakia, 220, 223

use of by workers and others in Bulgaria, 171

use of by working women in Yugoslavia, 108-114

use of by youth in Croatia, Yugoslavia, 106

Life Aspirations, 2 (See also Moral and Ethical Preferences; Values; Youth)

emotional vs. material in Poland, 418-419

materialistic values in, German Democratic Republic, 287

of eighth grade youth in USSR, 31

of secondary school graduates in Lithuania, USSR, 32-33

of youth in Bulgaria, 176-177, 178, 182

Life, Quality of
survey research on, Hungary, 323, 353, 354, 356

Lifestyles
and attitudes in USSR, 62

social and occupational differentiation in in Yugoslavia, 110-111

socialist lifestyle and leisure time in Hungary, 349, 353

urban in Serbia, Yugoslavia, 107

Linguistic Behavior (See also Ethnicity)
effects of language of school instruction on among rural Tatars in USSR, 58

Literature (See also Books; Media Habits; Leisure Time)
neglect of by mass citizenry, 4

Living Standards
as measure of social development in Yugoslavia, 112

Local Government (See also Politics and Ideology)
values and development in, Yugoslavia, 115

Macedonia
surveys in, Yugoslavia, 81

Market Research, 2
Bulgaria, 195

German Democratic Republic, 292-293
Hungary, 374-377, 378
Yugoslavia, 121-122
Bureau of Market Research
research conducted by in Yugoslavia, 121
consumer surveying in, German Democratic Republic, 292-293
foci of
Hungary, 374-375
Yugoslavia, 121-122
Institute for Market Research
role of in survey research in Hungary, 320, 374, 375

Marriage (See also Family; Family and Women)
age differentiation in attitudes toward, Poland, 406
attitudes toward, Hungary, 330
decisions about, USSR, 24-25, 27
quality of, Czechoslovakia, 212-213
sexual differentiation in attitudes toward, Poland, 404, 406, 407
stability of, USSR, 25

Marxism-Leninism (See also Politics and Ideology)
influence of on research in Hungary, 6

Media Attention
factors influencing levels of, cross-national summary, 483

Media Audiences
socioeconomic differentiation in, Yugoslavia, 85-86

Media Effectiveness
cross-national summary, 484
in aesthetic education of youth in Bulgaria, 145-146
in Bulgaria, 142, 143-149

in preparing youth for family life in Bulgaria, 146
in Romania, 443, 444
information held by workers as measure of, Bulgaria, 146

Media, Electronic
attention to West German in German Democratic Republic, 254-255
characteristics of audiences of, Poland, 390, 398, 400-404, 405
education and attention to, Poland, 400, 401
income differentiation in attention to, Poland, 400
social structure of audiences of, Hungary, 324, 325, 326

Media Habits, 2 (See also Leisure Time)
Bulgaria, 142-149
comparative cross-national summary, 483-485
Czechoslovakia, 207-210
German Democratic Republic, 254-258, 259
Hungary, 323-329
Poland, 393-404, 405, 428
Romania, 443-450
USSR, 17, 20-24, 26
Yugoslavia, 84-87

audience research in studies of German Democratic Republic, 255-258
Hungary, 324-329
Yugoslavia, 86
education and newspaper reading in Bulgaria, 143, 144
effectiveness of media in study of, Poland, 402-404
foci of research on, Yugoslavia, 84
media penetration in study of, Romania, 448-450
of youth in German Democratic Republic, 285

publication of research on, German Democratic Republic, 256

radio, television, and newspaper use in, Hungary, 325

readership as indicator of, Yugoslavia, 86, 87

readership of Komsomol newspaper in research on, Bulgaria, 142

readership of printed media by Komsomol members in Bulgaria, 145

reading of national and regional papers in Bulgaria, 146-147, 148

regional differences in, Yugoslavia, 86-87

social differences in printed media preferences in study of, Hungary, 325, 327-329

television ownership as indicator of, Yugoslavia, 86-87

views on current events in study of, Romania, 445-448

youth attitudes toward visual arts in Czechoslovakia, 209-210

Media, Mass
absence of research on attention to, Czechoslovakia, 208

low use of as source of information in Yugoslav republics, 85-86

socioeconomic differentiation in use of in Serbia, Yugoslavia, 85-86

Media, Printed
attention to Western in Poland, 398,399

characteristics of readership of, Poland, 390, 393-398, 399

television viewing and readership of, Romania, 443-444

Minority Ethnic Groups (See also Ethnicity)
absence of problems concerning, German Democratic Republic, 290

Gypsies and Jews as in Hungary, 367, 372

problems of, Bulgaria, 193

Moral and Ethical Preferences and Life Aspirations, 2 (See also Life Aspirations)
Bulgaria, 176-179

comparative cross-national summary, 495-496

Czechoslovakia, 223-227

German Democratic Republic, 286-287

Hungary, 353-356

Poland, 417-420

Romania, 464, 467-469

Yugoslavia, 108-112

attitudes of workers toward, Hungary, 356, 357, 358

foci of research on
German Democratic Republic, 286
Poland, 417

publication of research on, Czechoslovakia, 223

Morality, Communist
and political and social activism in USSR, 48-49

Movies (See also Leisure Time)
audience preferences concerning, USSR, 20-21

opinions of youth about, USSR, 22

youth preferences concerning, Bulgaria, 172

National Pride (See also Ethnicity and Foreign Cultures; Patriotism)
social and occupation differences in sources of, Hungary, 371-372

Nationalism (See also Ethnicity and Foreign Cultures; Patriotism)
  attitudes toward Hungarian minority in Romania as measure of, Hungary, 371, 374, 379
  attitudes toward in Croatia, Yugoslavia, 120

Newspapers
  circulation of in Serbia, Yugoslavia, 86
  education and readership of, Poland, 394, 395, 396
  evaluation of coverage in, USSR, 20
  sexual differentiation in readership of, Poland, 394, 396, 397
  urban-rural differentiation in readership of, Poland, 393-394, 395

Occupational Choice
  regulation of, USSR, 35
  student attitudes toward, USSR, 34-35

Occupational Prestige
  workers' views of, Poland, 413, 415, 416

Opponents' Commission
  role of in review of research in Czechoslovakia, 206

Patriotism (See also National Pride; Nationalism)
  as moral value in Poland, 417

Peasants (See also Self Management)
  in management of cooperatives in Romania, 463

Personality
  need for authority and structure as dimension of, German Democratic Republic, 287
  religious values and, German Democratic Republic, 286

Poland
  Academy of Sciences (PAN)
    role of in survey research, 389-390
  Center for Public Opinion Studies (Warsaw)
    role of in survey research, 390, 391, 392, 393, 398, 400, 402, 406, 410, 417, 421
  citizen needs
    extent to which local political systems address, 390
  education
    as abstraction and as experience for youth, 410, 411
    attitudes of youth and parents toward, 390-391, 408
    attitudes toward, 408-410, 411
    sexual differentiation in evaluation of by youth, 408, 409
  education and youth, 406, 408-413
  family
    differences in attitudes toward, 418-419
  family and women, 404-406, 407
    foci of research on, 404
  family life
    as focus of life aspirations and values, 404, 405
  foreign policy
    citizen views of events in, 425
  government, tasks of
    as seen by youth, 420, 422
  housing
    as material aspiration, 419, 420
  information seeking
    and rational vs. emotional argumentation, 403

life aspirations
  emotional vs. material, 418-
    419
marriage
  age differentiation in
    attitudes toward, 406
  sexual differentiation in atti-
    tudes toward, 404, 406,
    407
media, electronic
  characteristics of audiences
    of, 390, 398, 400-404,
    405
  educational and attention to,
    400, 401
  income differentiation in
    attention to, 400
media habits, 393-404, 405, 428
media effectiveness in study
    of, 402- 404
media, printed
  characteristics of readership
    of, 390, 393-398, 399
moral and ethical preferences
    and life aspirations, 417-
    420
  foci of research on, 417
newspapers
  education and readership of,
    394, 395, 396
  sexual differentiation in read-
    ership of, 394, 396, 397
  urban-rural differentiation in
    readership of, 393-394,
    395
occupational prestige
  workers' views of, 413, 415,
    416
participation, social
  citizen attitudes toward, 421,
    423, 424
patriotism
  as moral value, 417

Poland (continued)
  policy, public
    importance of as seen by
      youth, 419, 420, 422
  Polish Institute of Sociology
    (Poznan)
    historical role of in social re-
      search, 389
  political efficacy
    effects of on attitudes toward
      social commitment and
      participation, 423
  political information
    readership of Party news-
      papers as measure of, 394,
      395, 396
  political terminology
    understanding of as test of
      media effectiveness, 402
  politics and ideology, 421, 423-
    425, 427
    in attitudes toward citizen
      participation in decision
      making, 423, 425
    political change as element
      of, 427
  Press Research Center (Krakow)
    role of in survey research,
      390, 391, 393, 404, 415,
      418, 425
  regime confidence
    and status of survey re-
      search, 11-12
  religion
    as moral value, 417, 418, 426
    attitudes of youth toward,
      413
  sex, premarital
    religious beliefs and youth
      attitudes toward, 418
  Silesian Institute (Opole)
    role of in survey research,
      390

social change
  as reflected in results of sur-
    vey research, 426-428
social criticism
  suppression of, 2, 421
social problems and social policy, 420-421, 422
  youth perceptions of most
    critical, 421, 422
social services
  availability of as social prob-
    lem, 420, 421
sociology
  emergence of as discipline,
    389
survey research, 3, 5, 6, 389-435
  coverage of topics in study
    of, 391-392
  decentralization of planning
    and execution of, 391
  factors affecting publication
    of results of, 391-392
  institutions engaged in, 390
  labor unrest as factor influ-
    encing publication of re-
    sults of, 392
  methodology of, 7-8, 391,
    392, 419-420
  sampling procedures in, 391
  selection of interviewers for,
    391
television
  quality of programming on,
    400, 402, 405
values
  generational differences in,
    410, 413, 414, 426, 427
Western printed media
  factors affecting reading of,
    398, 399
women
  attitudes toward employment
    of outside the home, 406
  changing roles of 427

Poland (continued)
  sexual differentiation in atti-
    tudes toward roles of, 406
  work
    characterization by youth
      workers of their own, 415,
      416
    newspaper readership and at-
      titudes of workers toward,
      415
    worker definitions of most
      desirable traits for, 415
  work and workplace, 413, 415-
    420
    foci of research on, 413
    sexual differentiation in views
      of treatment of women in,
      417
  youth
    foci of research on values of,
      410
    life ambitions of, 408, 409
    urban-rural differences
      in perceptions of tasks of
        government, 420-421
      in values and aspirations
        of, 410, 412, 418, 419
    values of, 410, 412-413, 414,
      426, 427
    values of concerning inter-
      personal relations, 410,
      412, 414

Policy, Public
  importance of as seen by youth
    in Poland, 419, 420, 422

Political Efficacy
  effects of on attitudes toward
    social commitment and parti-
    cipation in Poland, 423

Political Information (See also
  Politics and Ideology; Propaganda)
  about West Germany in German
    Democratic Republic, 289

readership of Party newspapers as measure of, Poland, 394, 395, 396

sources of among industrial workers, USSR, 50

Political Participation (See also Delegate System; Politics and Ideology; Self Management)

and policy interests in Yugoslavia, 117

and socioeconomic status among Serbian youth in Yugoslavia, 94

antecedents of, 4

attitudes of Yugoslav youth toward, 101

attitudes toward, cross-national summary, 501-502

during electoral and nonelectoral periods in Romania, 471-472

factors influencing levels of, Czechoslovakia, 233-234

in self management and delegate systems in Yugoslavia, 118

urban-rural differences in youth attitudes and behavior toward, Yugoslavia, 97

Political Terminology
understanding of as test of media effectiveness in Poland, 402

Politics and Ideology, 2 (See also Political Participation; Politics, Party)

Bulgaria, 186

comparative cross-national summary, 500-503

Czechoslovakia, 229-234

German Democratic Republic, 288-290

Hungary, 366-367, 368-370

Poland, 421, 423-425, 427

Romania, 471-472

USSR, 43, 46-54

Yugoslavia, 113, 115-120

attitudes toward West German politics as measure of, German Democratic Republic, 289

foci of research on, Bulgaria, 186

in attitudes toward citizen participation in decision making in Poland, 423, 425

petitions for emigration as indicators of citizen attitudes toward, German Democratic Republic, 289-290

political change as element of, Poland, 427

unpublished research by Communist Party dealing with, Bulgaria, 186

Politics, Party
bases for accepting Party secretary position in Bulgaria, 189, 190

Party secretaries' perceptions of their most important functions in Bulgaria, 189, 191

qualities seen by Party secretaries as most important for their position in Bulgaria, 189, 190

relationships between Party secretaries and rank-and-file in Bulgaria, 189, 191

Prague
demographic and residential characteristics of, Czechoslovakia, 209-210

Prestige, Social
youth and other attitudes toward, Bulgaria, 158

Propaganda (See also Political Information)
effectiveness of

in Bulgaria, 186
in German Democratic Re-
public, 291
in USSR, 43, 46, 48

Propagandists
attitudes of toward their work in
USSR, 50

Public Lectures
public reactions to, USSR, 20

Public Opinion (See also Survey Research)
and attitudes, 3
changes in formation of, Yugoslavia, 118
definition of, Bulgaria, 138
monist view of, 3
pluralist view of, 3

Public Property
leadership vs. worker attitudes
toward protection of, Bulgaria, 185

Quality Control
as focus of research on work and
workplace in Hungary, 341

Regime
citizen support for, Hungary,
366, 367

Regime Confidence
and status of survey research,
cross-national comparison,
11-12

Reliability (See also Survey Research, Methodology of)
problems of
in social research in USSR, 15
in survey research, 10-11

Religion (See also Moral and
Ethical Preferences)
as moral value in Poland, 417,
418, 426
attitudes of rural population
toward, Czechoslovakia, 224-
225, 227

attitudes of youth toward,
Poland, 413
attitudes toward, Hungary, 353,
354-355, 356, 362
church membership as measure
of attitudes toward, German
Democratic Republic, 286
claimed belief in
among members of League of
Communists, Yugoslavia,
111
in Slovenia and Croatia,
Yugoslavia, 111-112
comparison of science and by
rural Slovaks in Czechoslovakia, 232
significance of, cross-national
summary, 495-496

Romania
Academy of Sciences
role of in survey research,
437, 441
Academy of Social and Political
Sciences (ASPS)
role of in survey research,
437, 438, 440, 441, 450
antisocial behavior
public attitudes toward, 470
citizen proposals
action on by local authorities,
472
during electoral vs. nonelectoral periods, 471-472
consciousness, socialist
of youth, 453-454, 455
role of family in development
of among youth, 452-453
education and youth, 453-458,
461
family
and career orientations of
youth, 469
and organization of agricultural work, 450-451

and socialist consciousness among youth, 452-453
effects of on life aspirations, 452-453
family and women, 450-453
hooliganism
public attitudes toward, 470
housing
complaints about as social problem, 472
conditions of and interpersonal conflicts, 470-471
Institute of Political Science and Study on National Problems
role of in survey research, 438, 459, 469-470
Laboratory of Urban Sociological Research (Bucharest)
role of in survey research, 438, 442, 470
leisure time, 463-464, 465, 466
media
effectiveness of, 443, 444
media habits, 443-450
media penetration as focus of research on, 448-450
views of current events in study of, 445-448
media, printed
television viewing and readership of, 443-444
Mining Institute (Petrosani)
role of in survey research, 439
moral and ethical preferences and life aspirations, 464, 467-469
Office of Research of Romanian Radio and Television
role of in survey research, 438, 442, 443, 445
peasants
in management of cooperatives, 463

Romania (continued)
Pedagogical Institute (Bacau)
role of in survey research, 439
People's Councils
attitudes toward, 471
political participation
during electoral vs. nonelectoral periods, 471-472
politics and ideology, 471-472
regime confidence
and status of survey research, 11-12
Research Center for Youth Problems
role of in survey research, 438, 453, 457
social problems and social policy, 5, 469-471
survey research, 5-7, 436-481
coverage of sources in study of, 442-443
development of, 436-442
foci of, 439
institutions engaged in, 437-439
methodology of, 7-8, 440-442, 445
policy roles of, 439-440
publication of results of, 440-442
sampling methods in, 445
summary of results of, 473-474
television
and printed media, 443-444
impact of on use of leisure time, 448, 464
values
generational differences in, 453, 454, 455, 456
work and workplace, 458-463
job satisfaction as focus of research on, 459

workers
   age and leisure time prefer-
      ences of, 448
   attitudes of, 464, 465-466
   in management of workplace,
      459-463
   in Worker's Councils, 459-
      460
Young Communist League
   role of in supporting survey
      research, 438, 460
youth
   attitudes of toward work,
      457-458
   career satisfaction of, 458,
      461
   impact of family on socialist
      consciousness of, 453-454
   in workplace management,
      460, 461-462
   life aspirations of, 469
   occupational plans of rural,
      469
   political education of, 455
   values of rural male, 464,
      467-468
   values of vs. values of parents,
      453-457
   work satisfaction of, 457-458

Rural Population
   cultural and societal profile of,
      Czechoslovakia, 217-218

Samizdat
   Hungary, 6, 321

Scientific Workers
   mobility of, Czechoslovakia, 219

Segregation, Social
   as cause and effect of housing
      segregation in Yugoslavia,
      113

Self Management (See also Politics
   and Ideology; Work and Workplace)

acceptance of ideology of, Yugoslavia, 109, 110
and socioeconomic development
   in Yugoslavia, 115
attitudes of workers toward,
   Hungary, 342, 345, 346-347,
   349
attitudes toward among youth
   in Yugoslavia, 94
information held by workers
   about, Yugoslavia, 102
readiness of workers to accept
   risks and responsibilities in,
   Yugoslavia, 104, 105
success of, Yugoslavia, 104

Self-managing Enterprises
   League of Communists domina-
      tion of, Yugoslavia, 101-102
   studies of power, participation,
      and decision making in,
      Yugoslavia, 101-102

Self-managing Interest Communities (SIC)
   in funding of research in Yugo-
      slavia, 81

Serbia
   dependence on urban samples
      in, Yugoslavia, 83
   political sensitivity of surveys
      from, Yugoslavia, 84

Sex, Premarital
   attitudes toward, USSR, 25
   opinions of Moscow students
      concerning, USSR, 26
   related to divorce and mar-
      riage in Hungary, 330
   religion and youth attitudes
      toward, Poland, 418
   youth attitudes toward, Hun-
      gary, 330

Shift Work
   attitudes of workers toward
      and effects on family life

of, German Democratic Republic, 270-271, 272

Slovenia
as a major source of social science research in Yugoslavia, 82
political sensitivity of surveys from, Yugoslavia, 84
surveys using statistical techniques in, Yugoslavia, 83

Social Activism, see Activism, Social

Social Change
as reflected in results of survey research in Poland, 426-428

Social Criticism
suppression of, Poland, 2

Social Development
successes and weaknesses in, Yugoslavia, 112

Social Deviance (See also Crime)
prevalence of various forms of, Czechoslovakia, 227

Social Indicators
survey research in development of, Yugoslavia, 83

Social Mobility
effects of educational system on, Hungary, 334, 335-336

Social Participation (See also Consciousness, Social; Political Participation; Activism, Social)
citizen attitudes toward, Poland, 421, 423, 424

Social Problems, 2, 5
attitudes toward cultural monuments as, Czechoslovakia, 227, 228-229
attitudes toward protection of natural environment as, Czechoslovakia, 227-228

awareness and understanding of methods for solving, Yugoslavia, 113
education as factor influencing attitudes toward, Czechoslovakia, 228
elite vs. mass perceptions of, Bulgaria, 184-185, 497
in Bulgaria, 5
in Romania, 5
urban vs. rural attitudes toward, Czechoslovakia, 228
workers' perceptions of, Hungary, 359, 360
youth perceptions of, Poland, 421, 422

Social Problems and Social Policy (See also Alcoholism; Crime; Divorce; Social Services)
Bulgaria, 179-185
comparative cross-national summary, 497-500
Czechoslovakia, 227-229
German Democratic Republic, 287-288
Hungary, 359-366
Poland, 420-421, 422
Romania, 469-471
Yugoslavia, 112-113, 114

foci c᾽ research on
Bulgaria, 179-180
Hungary, 359
Yugoslavia, 112

Social Segregation
as cause and effect of housing segregation in Yugoslavia, 113

Social Services
availability of as social problem in Poland, 420, 421
factors limiting equal access to, Hungary, 359, 362-363

Social Stratification
  educational achievement related to, USSR, 34

Socialism
  achievements of as seen by rural Slovaks, Czechoslovakia, 232
  youth attitudes toward vitality of socialist countries and of Czechoslovakia, 224, 226
  Hungary, 339, 340, 367-370

Socialist Alliance of Working People (SAWP)
  as sponsor of research on delegate system in Yugoslavia, 115
  contribution of to design of surveys in Yugoslavia, 82
  members of in Worker's Councils in Yugoslavia, 115-116

Socialist Consciousness, see Consciousness, Socialist

Socialist Lifestyle
  development of in research on leisure time in Hungary, 349, 353

Socialist Personality
  and religious values, German Democratic Republic, 286

Socialization (See also Education and Youth)
  attitudes of parents toward, Czechoslovakia, 213
  effectiveness of among youth in Bulgaria, 162

Sociology
  emergence of as discipline in Poland, 389

Sociopolitical Activism, see Activism, Sociopolitical

Sociopolitical Concepts (See also Political Information)
  extent of correct understanding of, Yugoslavia, 119

Soviets, see Deputies

Strikes
  participation in in Slovenia, Yugoslavia, 104

Suicide
  survey research on causes of, Hungary, 359, 361, 362

Survey Research
  Bulgaria, 136-203
  cross-national similarities in, 482-483
  Czechoslovakia, 204-241
  German Democratic Republic, 242-318
  Hungary, 319-388
  Poland, 389-435
  Romania, 436-481
  USSR, 13-79
  Yugoslavia, 80-135

  as area of scholarly inquiry in German Democratic Republic, 248-249
  decentralization of
    Poland, 391
    Yugoslavia, 81
  foci of
    Bulgaria, 196-198
    Czechoslovakia, 236-238
    German Democratic Republic, 249-253
    Hungary, 319-320, 322
    Poland, 391-392
    Romania, 439, 442-443
    USSR, 16
    Yugoslavia, 84
  functions and roles of, 8-9
    Bulgaria, 137, 196
    Czechoslovakia, 206-207
    German Democratic Republic, 247-249, 293-294
    Hungary, 321-322
    Poland, 391-392, 428
    Romania, 439-440
    USSR, 14-15
    Yugoslavia, 81-82, 122-123

institutions engaged in
Bulgaria, 139-140
Czechoslovakia, 204-205
German Democratic Republic, 243-245
Hungary, 320, 322-323
Poland, 390
Romania, 437-439
USSR, 13-14
Yugoslavia, 81, 125n
interpreting results of, 504-505
Bulgaria, 197-198
legal bases of
Bulgaria, 140
German Democratic Republic, 246-247
methodology of, 2, 9-12
Bulgaria, 7-8, 138-139, 195
Czechoslovakia, 7-8, 205-206
German Democratic Republic, 7-8, 243, 249, 250-252, 294-296
Hungary, 7-8, 321-322, 323
Poland, 7-8, 391, 392, 419-420
Romania, 7-8, 440-442
USSR, , 7-8, 15-16
Yugoslavia, 5, 7-8, 83
Praxisverbundenheit as criterion influencing conduct of in German Democratic Republic, 249, 250, 252, 293, 297
publication of results of
Bulgaria, 140-141
Czechoslovakia, 204-206, 236-238
German Democratic Republic, 295
Hungary, 320, 321
Poland, 391-392
Romania, 440-442
USSR, 17
Yugoslavia, 82

Survey Research (continued)
recent developments in and current status of
Bulgaria, 5, 6-7, 136-137, 195-196
Czechoslovakia, 5, 7, 207, 235-236, 238
German Democratic Republic, 5, 7, 242-245, 294
Hungary, 5, 6, 320-322
Poland, 5, 6, 389-393
Romania, 5, 7, 436-442
USSR, 5, 6, 13-15
Yugoslavia, 5-6, 80-84, 115
sampling procedures in
Bulgaria, 139
German Democratic Republic, 251
Hungary, 322
Poland, 391
Romania, 445
USSR, 15
Yugoslavia, 83
summary of results of
Bulgaria, 196-198
Czechoslovakia, 235-238
German Democratic Republic, 293-297
Hungary, 377, 379-380
Poland, 422-428
Romania, 473-474
USSR, 59, 62-63
Yugoslavia, 122-123
training of researchers in
Hungary, 320
Poland, 391
USSR, 16, 18
validity and reliability of results of, 9-11
German Democratic Republic, 296

Television (See also Leisure Time; Media, Electronic)
age structure of viewers of, German Democratic Republic, 256, 257
audience characteristics in USSR, 23-24
in use of leisure time in Romania, 448, 464
program content of, German Democratic Republic, 258, 259
quality of programming on, Poland, 400, 402, 405
social structure of viewers of, German Democratic Republic, 256, 257, 258

Time Budgets
analysis of, USSR, 42-43
and actual daily activities of urban workers in USSR, 45
research on, German Democratic Republic, 278-279

Trade Unions (See also Work and Workplace)
worker attitudes toward roles of, USSR, 37, 40

Traditionalism
as competing ideology with self management in Serbia, Yugoslavia, 109

Urban Planning
in dealing with social, spatial, and workplace segregation in Yugoslavia, 113

USSR
Academy of Sciences
role of in survey research, 13, 14, 16, 49, 59
activism, social
factors affecting, 48-49
art
level of citizen information about, 21, 23

aspirations, career
influence of social status on, 34
of youth, 27, 30
attitudes
developed through vospitanie, 15
automation
and labor disputes, 41
impact of on work, 37, 40
worker attitudes toward, 37, 40-41
bilingualism
origins and consequences of, 56-59
consciousness, political
effects of Communist Party membership on, 48-49
effects of personal characteristics on, 46, 48
cultural articles
possession of by different social groups, 26
cultural-evaluative orientations
age differentiation in Karelia in, 59, 61
deputies to local soviets
attitudes of, 49
attitudes toward usefulness of their work among, 54
effects of social status on job-related problems of, 52-53
Party status and work satisfaction among, 51
divorce rate
reasons for, 24, 27, 29
education
influence of social status on, 30-34
education and youth, 27, 30-35
educational level
and attitudes, 62
ethnic rituals
observance of among Tatars, 53

USSR (continued)
  ethnic-cultural orientations
    effects of linguistic character-
      istics on, 60
  ethnicity and foreign cultures,
    49, 55-59
  ethnicity and nationality
    determinants of as seen by
      Tatars, 55
  family and women, 24-29
  fertility
    low levels of in European
      Russia, 24
    Moslem vs. non-Moslem atti-
      tudes toward, 27
  housing
    government planning of, 25
    needed improvements in, 24
  intelligentsia
    of Armenia, 21
  job satisfaction
    reasons for, 36-37, 40-42
  labor turnover
    on state farms, 39
    reasons for, 36
  language proficiency
    in second language in Molda-
      via, 57
  leisure time, 42-45
    amount of, 42-43
    education and use of, 44
    use of, 42-43
  life plans
    of eighth grade youth, 31
    of secondary school graduates
      in Lithuania, 32-33
  lifestyles
    and attitudes, 62
  linguistic behavior
    effects of language of school
      instruction on, 58
  marriage
    decisions about, 24-25
    stability of, 25, 27

media, cultural
  attitudes of visitors to exhib-
    its in Estonia toward, 23
media habits, 17, 20-24, 26
morality, communist
  and political activism, 48-49
  and social activism, 48-49
movies
  audience preferences concern-
    ing, 20-21
  opinions of youth about, 22
newspapers
  evaluation of coverage in, 20
occupational choice
  regulation of, 35
  student attitudes toward, 34-
    35
political education
  evaluation of knowledge re-
    ceived through, 47
  propagandists' views of audi-
    ence interest in, 47
political information
  held by industrial workers, 50
politics and ideology, 43, 46-54
propaganda and agitation
  effectiveness of Party, 43, 46,
    48
propagandists
  attitudes of toward their
    work, 50
public lectures
  reactions to, 20
regime confidence
  and status of survey research,
    11-12
reliability
  problems of in social re-
    search, 15
research
  centralization of, 13
sex, premarital
  attitudes toward, 25
  opinions of Moscow students
    concerning, 26

USSR (continued)
  social stratification
    educational achievement and
      changes in, 34
  socioeconomic status
    effects on attitudes of, 62
  sociologists
    education and current posi-
      tions of, 18-19
  Soviet Sociological Association
    scientific-research sections of,
      64
  survey research, 3, 5, 6, 13-79
    functions of, 14-15
    methodology of, 7-8, 15-16
    sampling procedures in, 15
    training of researchers in, 16,
      18
  television
    audience characteristics, 23-
      24
  time budgets
    analysis of, 42-43
    and actual daily activities of
      workers, 45
  trade unions
    worker attitudes toward roles
      of, 37, 40
  validity
    problems of in social re-
      search, 15
  vospitanie (upbringing)
    survey research on, 15
  VUZ
    educational goals and achieve-
      ments of students at, 30,
      34-35
  women
    nationality differences in ex-
      pected number of child-
      ren, 28
    roles of, 24
  work
    job selection by fishermen as
      attitudes toward, 39

  work and workplace, 36-42
  workers
    relationships of with mana-
      gers, 40
  youth
    value orientations of, 35
    workplace attitudes of, 38

Validity, see Survey Research,
  Methodology of

Value Orientations
  influence of social stratum on,
    Yugoslavia, 110
  institutes conducting research
    on, Yugoslavia, 108-109

Values (See also Moral and Ethical
  Preferences; Youth)
  defined, 2
  generational differences in
    Poland, 410, 413, 414, 426,
      427
    Romania, 453, 454, 455, 456
  of workers in Hungary, 356, 357

Vospitanie (Upbringing)
  survey research on, USSR, 15

VUZ
  educational goals and achieve-
    ments of students at, USSR,
    30, 34-35

Wissenschaftliche Räte, see under
  German Democratic Republic

Women
  age of marriage of, Yugoslavia,
    89
  attitudes of toward
    family size in Bulgaria, 153
    fashion in Bulgaria, 150, 152
    fertility and contraception in
      Slovenia, Yugoslavia, 89
    future in Yugoslavia, 90-91
    participation in workplace in
      Yugoslavia, 104
    work outside the home in
      German Democratic Re-
      public, 260-261

work outside the home in
Hungary, 331, 334
attitudes toward employment of
outside the home
in Bulgaria, 152
in Poland, 406
day care of children and work
plans of, German Democratic
Republic, 260, 261-263
effects of housework on
employment and leisure time
of, Bulgaria, 149, 150
reading and cultural activities
among, Bulgaria, 151
roles of, Hungary, 331, 334
employment and work of
Czechoslovakia, 210, 218-219
German Democratic Repub-
lic, 258, 260-264
Yugoslavia, 88-89
fertility rates among working,
Yugoslavia, 88-89
importance of research on
Czechoslovakia, 210
German Democratic Repub-
lic, 258
life aspirations of, Bulgaria, 176
nationality differences in expected number of children in
USSR, 28
physical well-being of working,
German Democratic Repub-
lic, 260, 263
roles of, 4
Bulgaria, 149-152
cross-national summary, 486
German Democratic Repub-
lic, 258, 260-261
Hungary, 331, 334
Poland, 427
Yugoslavia, 87, 88, 89, 92
sexual differentiation in attitudes toward roles of, Poland, 406

Women (continued)
sociopolitical activities of, Yugoslavia, 88
youth attitudes toward employment of, German Democratic
Republic, 268
Work
attitudes toward among Party
secretaries in Bulgaria, 187-
192
job selection by fishermen as
attitudes toward, USSR, 39
newspaper readership and
workers' attitudes toward,
Poland, 415
organization of, Hungary, 341
Party secretaries' preferences
concerning, Bulgaria, 187-189
worker definitions of desirable
traits for, Poland, 415
youth workers' characterization
of their own in Poland, 415,
416
Work and Workplace, 2
Bulgaria, 163-170
comparative cross-national summary, 490-493
Czechoslovakia, 218-220
German Democratic Republic,
269-276
Hungary, 339, 341-349
Poland, 413, 415-420
Romania, 458-463
USSR, 36-42
Yugoslavia, 101-106
communication networks in,
Yugoslavia, 102
conditions of, Hungary, 342,
343, 344
foci of research on
Bulgaria, 163
German Democratic Repub-
lic, 270, 276

Hungary, 341
Poland, 413
housing segregation and segregation in, Yugoslavia, 113
income differentials in, Czechoslovakia, 219-220
job satisfaction in
  Czechoslovakia, 218, 224
  Romania, 459
material vs. nonmaterial incentives in, Bulgaria, 163, 164
problems of discipline in, Bulgaria, 166-167, 168
relationships among workers in,
  Bulgaria, 164
sex discrimination in remuneration in, Hungary, 331, 334
sexual differentiation in views of
  treatment of women in, Poland, 417
summary of research concerning,
  Bulgaria, 197
work incentives in, Bulgaria, 163
work style preferences in Slovakia as attitudes toward,
  Czechoslovakia, 219
worker evaluation of leadership
  cadres in industry in Bulgaria, 169-170

Worker Productivity
as focus of research on work and
  workplace in Hungary, 341

Workers
aesthetic education of, Czechoslovakia, 216
age and leisure time preferences
  of, Romania, 448
attitudes of toward workplace
  participation in Hungary,
  342, 345, 346-347, 349
attitudes toward work and workplace, 4
German Democratic Repub-
  lic, 271, 274-275

collective responsibility among,
  cross-national summary, 490-
  491
commitment to work of, Hungary, 342
commuting as source of workplace problems among, Hungary, 341-342
cultural activities among strata
  of, German Democratic Republic, 278, 284
job dissatisfaction among, 5
lifestyles of, Hungary, 341
participation of
  in management of workplace
    in Romania, 459-463
  in Worker's Councils in Ro-
    mania, 459-460
perceptions held by of Party in
  Hungary, 342
relations with management
  cross-national summary, 492
  in USSR, 40
sociopolitical participation of,
  cross-national summary, 492-
  493
survey research on, Romania,
  464, 465-466

Worker's Councils
influence of on democracy in
  self-managing enterprises in
  Yugoslavia, 101-102

Youth (See also Education and
  Youth)
attitudes of toward
  delegate system in Yugoslavia,
    94, 95
  marriage and family in Ger-
    man Democratic Repub-
    lic, 267-268
  political education and politi-
    cal work in Czechoslovakia,
    229-232
  popular singers in Czechoslo-
    vakia, 216

self management in Yugo-
slavia, 96, 98-99
self-managing bodies in Yugoslavia, 101
social and economic equality
in Yugoslavia, 96
use of leisure time in Hungary,
336, 338
work in Romania, 457-458
workplace in USSR, 38
backgrounds of
and educational choice in
Yugoslavia, 96, 100
and occupational choice in
Yugoslavia, 96, 100
career satisfaction of, Romania,
458, 461
consciousness, political and
social, of, Czechoslovakia,
237
consciousness, socialist, of, Bulgaria, 162
cultural life of, Czechoslovakia,
209-210, 216
discontent among, Hungary, 336
education and values of, cross-
national summary, 490
education of, Czechoslovakia,
217-218
evaluations of capitalism and
socialism by
Czechoslovakia, 224, 226
Hungary, 339, 340
factors influencing societal circumstances of, German
Democratic Republic, 268-
269
foci of research on, 4
German Democratic Repub-
lic, 267
Poland, 410
ideological orientations of,
Yugoslavia, 96

Youth (continued)
impact of family on socialist
consciousness of, Romania,
453-454
importance of research on, German Democratic Republic,
264, 266, 269
influence of on social development in Yugoslavia, 92
influences of family and day
care centers on, German
Democratic Republic, 260,
261, 263
leisure time of
Czechoslovakia, 216
German Democratic Repub-
lic, 267, 268-269, 284-285
life aspirations of
Bulgaria, 157
Poland, 408-409
Romania, 469
occupational evaluations by,
Bulgaria, 177
occupational plans of
Hungary, 335-336, 337
Romania, 469
occupational preferences of,
cross-national summary, 489-
490
participation of in workplace
management in Romania,
460, 461-462
political activity of, cross-
national summary, 488-489
political education of, Romania,
455
political knowledge of, Czechoslovakia, 223-224, 225
problems in socialization of as
motivation for research on,
Bulgaria, 155
reading habits of
Czechoslovakia, 210, 211

German Democratic Republic, 285
school performance of when mother works in German Democratic Republic, 260, 263
socialization of
    Bulgaria, 155
    Czechoslovakia, 213, 216
summary of findings of survey research on, Bulgaria, 197
time budgets of, German Democratic Republic, 285
urban-rural differences
    in life aspirations of, Poland, 410, 412, 418, 419
    in perceptions of of tasks of government in Poland, 420-421
    in values of
        Bulgaria, 179
        cross-national summary, 490
values of
    Bulgaria, 155, 157-160
    cross-national summary, 487-490
    Poland, 410, 412-413, 414, 426, 427
    USSR, 35
values of concerning interpersonal relations in Poland, 410, 412, 414
values of rural male in Romania, 464, 467-468
values of vs. those of parents
    cross-national summary, 489
    Romania, 453-457
work satisfaction of
    Czechoslovakia, 216-217
    Romania, 457-458

Yugoslavia
    activism, sociopolitical
        among Serbian youth, 92-94

Albanians
    discrimination and prejudice against, 120
    living conditions of, 120
anketomanija (survey-mania), 80
audience research, 86
Bosnia
    as major source of social research, 82
Bureau of Market Research
    role of in research, 121
Center for Migration Research (Zagreb)
    role of in survey research, 120
communications research
    in sociopolitical organizations, 85
    in workplace, 85
Croatia
    surveys using statistical techniques in, 83
delegate system
    functioning and implementation of, 115-116, 118
education and youth, 92-101
    foci of research on, 92
ethnicity and foreign cultures, 120-121
    foci of research on, 120
family
    changes in, 87-88
family and women, 87-92
    changes of roles of in rural households in Croatia, 87-88
foreign policy
    attitudes of Croatians toward Yugoslav, 121
health care
    availability and use of by social status, 113
human needs
    satisfaction of as social problem, 113, 114

Yugoslavia (continued)
  income distribution
    attitudes toward in Serbia,
      109-110
  industrial sociology
    as area of social research, 101
  Institute for Social Research
    (Zagreb)
    role of in survey research,
      109, 121
  Institute for Sociology and
    Philosophy (Ljubljana)
    role of in survey research,
      109
  Institute of Social Sciences
    (Belgrade)
    role of in survey research,
      109
  League of Communist Youth
    and sociopolitical participa-
      tion of Serbian youth, 92,
      94
  League of Communists
    and design of surveys, 82
    as core of sociopolitical
      activists, 92, 94
    attitudes of toward emanci-
      pation of women, 89
    members of in Worker's
      Councils, 115-116
    survey research on, 115
    use of media sources by in
      Serbia, 86
  leisure time, 106-108
    cultural needs and use of, 108
    socioeconomic differentiation
      in cultural activities dur-
        ing, 106
      in cultural needs related
        to, 106
    use of
      by working women, 108,
        114
      by youth in Croatia, 106
      urban-rural differences in,
        106-107

lifestyles
  and social and occupational
    status, 110-111
  in Serbian cities, 107
living standards
  improvements in as measure
    of social development, 112
local government
  values and development in,
    115
Macedonia
  surveys in, 81, 85
market research, 121-122
media audiences
  socioeconomic differentiation
    in, 85-86
media habits, 84-86
  audience research on, 86
  differences in television
    ownership as indicators of,
      86-87
  foci of research on, 84
  readership as indicators of,
    86, 87
  regional differences in, 85,
    86-87
media, mass
  low use of as source of infor-
    mation in various repub-
      lics, 85
  socioeconomic differentiation
    in use of in Serbia, 85-86
moral and ethical preferences
  and life aspirations, 108-112
nationalism, ethnic
  attitudes toward in Croatia,
    120
newspapers
  circulation of in Serbia, 86
political participation
  and policy interests, 117
  and socioeconomic status
    among Serbian youth, 94
  attitudes of Yugoslav youth
    toward, 94, 97, 101

Yugoslavia (continued)
  opportunities for in self
    management and delegate
    systems, 118
  urban-rural differences in
    youth attitudes and be-
    havior toward, 97
  politics and ideology, 113, 115-
    120
  public opinion
    changes in formation of, 118
  regime confidence
    and status of survey research,
    11-12
  religion
    claimed belief in
      among members of League
        of Communists, 111
      in Slovenia and Croatia,
        111-112
  segregation, social
    and housing segregation, 113
  self management
    acceptance of ideology of,
      109, 110
    and socioeconomic develop-
      ment, 115
    attitudes toward among
      youth, 94
    information held by workers
      about, 102
    readiness of workers to
      accept risks and responsi-
      bilities in, 104, 105
    success of, 104
  self-managing enterprises
    League of Communists and
      elite domination of, 101-
      102
    power, participation, and
      decision making in, 101-
      102
  Self-managing Interest Com-
    munities (SIC)
    in funding of research, 81

Serbia
  dependence on urban samples
    for surveys in, 83
  political sensitivity of surveys
    from, 84
Slovenia
  as major source of social re-
    search, 82
  political sensitivity of surveys
    from, 84
  surveys in, 81
  surveys using statistical tech-
    niques in, 83
social development
  successes and weaknesses in,
    112
social indicators, 83
social problems
  awareness and understanding
    of, 113
social problems and social policy, 112-113, 114
  foci of research on, 112
Socialist Alliance of Working
  People (SAWP)
  and design of surveys, 82
  and research on delegate
    system, 115
  members of in Worker's
    Councils, 115-116
sociological research
  quality of, 82-83
sociopolitical concepts
  understanding of, 119
strikes
  participation in, 104
survey research, 3, 5-6, 80-135
  constraints on, 81, 82, 115
  decentralization of, 81, 115
  factors affecting publication
    of, 82
  methodology of, 5, 7-8, 83
  recent developments in, 80-
    84
  sampling methods in, 83

Yugoslavia (continued)
  validity of rural samples and
    results in, 83
  traditionalism
    as competing ideology with
      self management in Serbia,
      109
  urban planning
    in dealing with social, spatial,
      and workplace segregation,
      113
  value orientations
    influence of social stratum
      on, 110
    institutes conducting research
      on, 108-109
  women
    age of marriage of, 89
    attitudes of toward
      fertility and contraception
        in Slovenia, 89
      future, 90-91
      participation in workplace,
        104
    employment and work of, 88-
      89
    roles of, 87-89, 92
    sociopolitical activities of, 88
  work and workplace, 101-106
  Worker's Councils
    and democracy in self-
      managing enterprises, 101-
      102
    and League of Communists,
      115-116
    and Socialist Alliance of
      Working People, 115-116
  workplace
    communication networks in,
      102
    housing segregation and segre-
      gation in, 113

youth
  attitudes of toward
    delegate system, 94, 95
    self management, 96, 98-
      99
    self-managing bodies, 101
    social and economic
      equality, 96
  backgrounds of
    and educational choice,
      96, 100
    and occupational choice,
      96, 100
  ideological orientations of, 96
  influence of on social
    development, 92
Yugoslav Sociological Association
  role of in social research, 101

About the Contributors

ROBERT BLUMSTOCK (Ph.D., University of Oregon) is Associate Professor of Sociology at McMaster University, Canada. His articles have appeared in *Szociológia*, the *Canadian Review of Sociology and Anthropology* and other journals. He held an appointment as visiting lecturer at Karl Marx University in Budapest. He was a contributing author to *Public Opinion in European Socialist Systems* (1977), and edited *Bekevar: Working Papers on a Canadian Prairie Community* (1979).

WESLEY A. FISHER (Ph.D., Columbia University) is Assistant Professor and Associate Chairman in the Department of Sociology, and member of the Russian Institute, at Columbia. He serves as a project coordinator for the US-USSR Binational Commission in the Social Sciences and Humanities. He is co-editor of *Social Stratification and Mobility in the USSR* (1973) and author of *The Soviet Marriage Market: Marriage Patterns in Russia and the USSR* (1980). He has published several articles on Soviet sociology and on marriage and the family in the Soviet Union.

GEORGE KLEIN (Ph.D., University of Illinois) is Professor of Political Science and Chairman of the European Studies Program at Western Michigan University. He has authored articles and chapters in several research compendia dealing with worker self-management and ethnic nationalism in Yugoslavia and Czechoslovakia.

JAROSLAV KREJČÍ (J.D., Charles University[Prague]) is Senior Lecturer in Comparative Cultural Analysis at the University of Lancaster, England. Between 1940 and 1954 he held both academic appointments and positions in the economic planning apparatus in Prague. After a forced absence of 12 years from scholarly work, he returned to the Institute of Economics in Prague between 1966 and 1968. He has been at Lancaster since 1969. His numerous research publications in Czech, Slovak, German and English deal with both sociological (e.g., *Social Change and Stratification in Postwar Czechoslovakia*, 1972) and economic aspects of East European affairs.

LINDA L. LUBRANO (Ph.D., Indiana University) is Professor in the School of International Service at The American University. She is author of numerous articles and chapters dealing with Soviet science and science policy. She is author of *Soviet Sociology of Science* (1976), and co-author and co-editor of *The Social Context of Soviet Science* (1980). She is currently working on another book on contemporary science in the Soviet Union. Her research on the Soviet Union has been supported by grants from the National Science Foundation and the American Council of Learned Societies, and by four Ford Foundation Foreign Area fellowships.

PETER CHRISTIAN LUDZ (1931-1979) was Professor of Political Science at the University of Munich. He received his Ph.D. from the Free University of Berlin. His numerous contributions to research on the GDR include *The Changing Party Elite in East Germany* (English ed., 1972), *Two Germanys in One World* (1973) and *Mechanismen der Herrschaftssicherung* (1980). He was editor of *Studien und Materialien zur Soziologie der DDR* (2nd ed., 1971) and director of studies for and co-author of *Materialien zum Bericht zur Lage der Nation* (1971, 1972, 1974) and the *DDR Handbuch* (2nd ed., 1979). His professional activities brought him frequently to the United States; he held appointments at Columbia University, the New School for Social Research, and Macalester College.

DANIEL N. NELSON (Ph.D., The Johns Hopkins University) is Associate Professor of Political Science at the University of Kentucky. He is author of *Local Communist Politics* (1978), and editor and co-author of *Subnational Communist Politics: Comparing Participation and Policymaking* (1978). He has written numerous articles and chapters on East European affairs, especially Romanian and Polish politics.

JANET SCHWARTZ (Ph.D., Cornell University) is Research Associate in the Department of Sociology at the University of Maryland. Her articles on occupational and social stratification in the Soviet Union have appeared in *Social Forces* and the *International Review of Modern Sociology*. She is presently co-principal investigator in research on "Civil-Military Relations in the Soviet Union," supported by the National Council for Soviet and East European Research.

KATE TOMLINSON holds the M.A. from the School of Advanced International Studies, The Johns Hopkins University. Since contributing to this book, she has joined the Congressional Research Service as a Research Assistant.

BARCLAY WARD (Ph.D., The University of Iowa) is Assistant Professor of Political Science at The University of the South. Prior to beginning his academic career, he was a U. S. Foreign Service Officer from 1961 to 1975. He is co-investigator (with W. A. Welsh and J. A. Kuhlman) on a Ford-supported study of public policy in Eastern Europe, and has authored several professional papers on Polish politics. He was Visiting Scholar at the Institute for Organization, Management and Control Sciences, Polish Academy of Sciences, Warsaw, in 1976.

WILLIAM A. WELSH (Ph.D., Northwestern University) is Professor of Political Science at the University of Iowa. He is co-author of *Comparative Communist Political Leadership* (1973) and author of *Leaders and Elites* (1979) and numerous articles, chapters, and professional papers on various aspects of communist studies. His research on Eastern Europe has been supported by the Ford, Alexander von Humboldt, and Earhart foundations. He has held visiting appointments at the International Institute for Applied Systems Analysis (Laxenburg, Austria), the University of Munich, the University of Istanbul, and the International Institute of Management (West Berlin). In August, 1981, he will become Professor of Political Science at Arizona State University.

SUSAN L. WOODWARD (Ph.D., Princeton University) is Assistant Professor of Political Science at Williams College. She is the author of several articles and numerous professional papers on Yugoslav politics, and was Visiting Fellow at the Center of International Studies, Princeton University, in 1975-1976. She previously taught at Northwestern University and Mount Holyoke College.